PERSONAL INJURY

Liability, Compensation, and Pr

Second Edition

PERSONAL INJURY LAW

Liability, Compensation, and Procedure

Second Edition

PETER BARRIE MA

Barrister, Recorder

OXFORD

UNIVERSITY PRESS

OXFORD
UNIVERSITY PRESS

Great Clarendon Street, Oxford OX2 6DP

Oxford University Press is a department of the University of Oxford.
It furthers the University's objective of excellence in research, scholarship,
and education by publishing worldwide in

Oxford New York

Auckland Cape Town Dar es Salaam Hong Kong Karachi
Kuala Lumpur Madrid Melbourne Mexico City Nairobi
New Delhi Shanghai Taipei Toronto

With offices in

Argentina Austria Brazil Chile Czech Republic France Greece
Guatemala Hungary Italy Japan South Korea Poland Portugal
Singapore Switzerland Thailand Turkey Ukraine Vietnam

Published in the United States
by Oxford University Press Inc., New York

First published 2002
Second Edition 2005

British Library Cataloguing in Publication Data

Data available

Library of Congress Cataloging in Publication Data
Barrie, Peter, MA.
   Personal injury law: liability, compensation, and procedure / Peter
Barrie.—2nd ed.
      p. cm.
   Rev. ed. of: Compensation for personal injuries. 1st ed. 2002.
   Includes index.
   ISBN 0-19-927571-8 (alk. paper)
   1. Personal injuries—England. 2. Damages—England. I. Barrie,
Peter, MA. Compensation for personal injuries. II. Title.
   KD1954.B37 2005
   346.4203'23—dc22   2004029476

ISBN 0–19–927571–8

978-0-19-927571-7

1 3 5 7 9 10 8 6 4 2

Typeset by RefineCatch Limited, Bungay, Suffolk
Printed in Great Britain
on acid-free paper by
Antony Rowe Ltd, Chippenham

PREFACE

This book has a new title for the Second Edition, but it continues to have the same purpose as before, to set out as much of the law relating to personal injury claims as can conveniently be included in a single volume.

The major change for this edition has been in the treatment of the Civil Procedure Rules, where a narrative discussion has replaced the reproduction of a substantial part of the Rules and practice directions dealing with general matters of civil procedure, since it is thought that practitioners are likely to have ready access to these materials from other sources, such as online services or *Blackstone's Civil Practice*, to which extensive cross-references have been provided. The rules relating to specific topics of particular relevance to personal injury claims have been retained. Other chapters have been updated or rewritten as the pace of change has demanded.

Again I express my thanks to the writers and colleagues who have, without knowing it, contributed to this book and to my brother, Dr Richard Barrie, for his help with the medical information. In particular I am grateful to those who have used the updating website, and those who have commented on the book or sent me news of developments in the world of personal injury claims. The website will now move to a new address within OUP at www.oup.com/uk/law/practitioner/cws. I can still be contacted with suggestions or brickbats at peter.barrie@guildhallchambers.co.uk.

I have tried to state the law as it stands at 31 July 2004.

Peter Barrie
Guildhall Chambers
Bristol

ACKNOWLEDGEMENTS

Sixteen illustrations reproduced from *Oxford Textbook of Functional Anatomy, Volume 1: Musculoskeletal System, Revised Edition* edited by Pamela C.B. MacKinnon and John F. Morris (1994) by permission of Oxford University Press © Pamela C.B. MacKinnon and John F. Morris 1994; Two illustrations reproduced from *Oxford Textbook of Functional Anatomy*, Volume 3: *Head and Neck* edited by Pamela MacKinnon and John Morris (1990) by permission of Oxford University Press © Pamela MacKinnon and John Morris 1990; Two illustrations reprinted from *Cunningham's Manual of Practical Anatomy, Volume 1: Upper and Lower Limbs* edited by G.J. Romanes (Oxford Medical Publications, 15th edn, 1986) by permission of Oxford University Press © Oxford University Press 1966, 1977, 1986; Two illustrations reprinted from *Cunningham's Textbook of Anatomy* edited by G.J. Romanes (Oxford Medical Publications, 12th edn, 1981) by permission of Oxford University Press © Oxford University Press 1964, 1972, 1981; The Judicial Studies Board *Guidelines for the Assessment of General Damages in Personal Injury Cases* (7th edn, 2004) reprinted by permission of Oxford University Press © Judicial Studies Board 2004; *Diagnostic Criteria for Posttraumatic Stress Disorder and Acute Stress Disorder* reproduced with permission from the *Diagnostic and Statistical Manual of Mental Disorders*, 4th edn, Text Revision, © 2000; Crown copyright material reproduced with the permission of the Controller of Her Majesty's Stationery Office; Rehabilitation Code reproduced by permission of the Bodily Injury Claims Management Association (BICMA), © BICMA 2002.

CONTENTS—SUMMARY

Contents—Summary

CONTENTS

TABLE OF CASES

TABLE OF STATUTES

References are to chapter and paragraph number. Those beginning with a, b, c, d, refer to the unnumbered preliminary chapters. Where a paragraph number appears in bold, the relevant section is set out in full.

International legislation

TABLE OF STATUTORY INSTRUMENTS
AND PRACTICE DIRECTIONS (PD)

References are to chapter and paragraph number. Those beginning with a, b, c, d, refer to the unnumbered preliminary chapters. Where a paragraph number appears in bold, the relevant section is set out in full.

TABLE OF NON-STATUTORY SOURCES

References are to chapter and paragraph number. Those beginning with a, b, c, d, refer to the unnumbered preliminary chapters. Where a paragraph number appears in bold, the relevant section is set out in full.

a

LEGAL WORDS AND REFERENCES

A. Introduction

The purpose of this chapter is to assist readers who have no specialist legal **a.01** background to understand some of the language used by litigation lawyers. This includes an explanation of some terms used before the new Civil Procedure Rules (CPR) came into force and which may puzzle young lawyers when they are encountered in old books and reports. There are three sections: a glossary of common legal words, a translation and explanation of a few Latin phrases, and finally an explanation of abbreviations and references to law reports and other textbooks that may be encountered in the course of a personal injury claim. The glossary may also provide a form of quick reference to areas of difficulty.

B. Glossary

Administrator   A person appointed to administer the estate of someone who **a.02** has died intestate, i.e. without leaving a will. A female administrator is called an administratrix. Where there was a will, the equivalent is an executor or executrix. In personal injury cases, a fatal accidents claim is usually brought by the administrator or executor on behalf of the estate of the deceased and the dependants.

Affidavit   Before the CPR, evidence in writing was given by way of a sworn **a.03** statement called an affidavit. Although affidavits have not been abolished they have become very rare and in personal injury claims they have been replaced by witness statements containing a Statement of Truth.

a.04 **Barrister** A lawyer who provides consultancy services, including specialist advice and advocacy at hearings, to the clients of solicitors. Barristers are independent individual practioners but usually work together in groups, in a set of chambers. In personal injury cases the rules of conduct generally prevent clients approaching a barrister direct: a solicitor must give the instructions. This restrictive practice is intended to protect the public because a solicitor will be better placed to know which barristers are competent and suitable for a particular case, and to negotiate fees with the barrister's clerk or business manager.

a.05 **Cause of action** A set of facts which would establish a legal category giving a ground for liability: for example, the occasion when the defendant was negligent (see Chapter 2).

a.06 **Circuit judge** A senior judge of the county court. Circuit judges also sit in the Crown Court for criminal cases. The more serious county court trials will be held before a circuit judge. A circuit judge may also be approved to sit in the High Court (a 'section 9 Judge' under s 9 of the Supreme Court Act 1981). Often, therefore, the transfer of a personal injury case to the High Court will not actually result in a trial by a High Court judge. A circuit judge in the county court is addressed as 'Your Honour'.

a.07 **Common law** The law of England and Wales as it has been defined by the development of decided case law over the years. The common law is increasingly being replaced by statute law but remains important. For example, the law of negligence on which much personal injury litigation is based, has been created by the common law. The common law creates rules of law by the principle of precedent that a judge is bound to follow the previous decision of a higher court on the point in issue.

a.08 **County court** The local courts in England and Wales where civil disputes between citizens are decided. The most serious civil disputes are decided in the High Court but in recent years an ever-increasing jurisdiction has been given to the country courts, and now all except the most complex or high value civil disputes are decided in the county courts.

a.09 **CPR** The Civil Procedure Rules 1998 which came into force on 26 April 1999 and brought radical changes to the conduct of civil claims in England and Wales: familiarly known to lawyers as the Woolf reforms.

a.10 **Damages** An award of money compensation.

a.11 **Deputy district judge** A lawyer in private practice who sits part time as a district judge.

District judge   A judge of the county court. A district judge will deal with   **a.12**
most pre-trial hearings and has a limited jurisdiction to decide final hearings,
which can be enlarged with the consent of the parties. The trend is for district
judges to deal with an ever-increasing proportion of civil hearings. A district
judge is notionally junior to a circuit judge, though in reality the distinction is
more a case of different roles than of seniority. A district judge is addressed as
'Sir' or 'Madam'.

Executor/executrix   The person (male/female) appointed under a will to   **a.13**
administer an estate.

General damages   Losses which cannot be calculated by arithmetic, such as   **a.14**
injury damages for pain and suffering and loss of amenity; contrasted with
special damages.

Hansard   The official record of proceedings in Parliament. Traditionally   **a.15**
judges had to interpret Acts of Parliament, a process described as discovering the
intentions of Parliament, solely from the words used in the Act of Parliament. In
Pepper v Hart [1993] AC 593 the House of Lords said that it would be prepared
to look at the record of debates as an aid to interpretation, although this is in
practice rare.

JSB Guidelines   Published guidance on the level of injury damages compiled   **a.16**
for the Judicial Studies Board which is the training body for judges.

Judgment   The formal record of the decision of the court, which is necessary   **a.17**
in order to invoke the court's powers of enforcement.

Jury   A jury is not employed to decide personal injury claims, which are   **a.18**
decided by a single judge, unless the case is based on allegations of malicious
prosecution or false imprisonment when a jury may be required.

Law Lords   The judges of the highest appeal court, the House of Lords, who   **a.19**
are also members of the legislative House of Lords. The government proposes
in the Constitutional Reform Bill to create a Supreme Court of the United
Kingdom with judges who will no longer have this dual role.

Lords Justices of Appeal   The permanent judges of the Court of Appeal,   **a.20**
described in writing in reports as, for example, 'Smith LJ'. In spite of the name,
they are not peers.

Limitation   The time limit on bringing a claim. The rules of limitation are   **a.21**
complex and the main source is the Limitation Act 1980. In personal injury
claims the basic rule is that a claim must be started within three years from
the date of injury. However, there are complex exceptions where some facts
may not be available until later; there is an overriding discretion to allow a case

started later to carry on when it is fair to do so; and the time limits do not apply to children or incapable adults.

a.22 Master of the Rolls The senior judge of the Court of Appeal Civil Division.

a.23 Neutral citation By *Practice Direction* at [2001] 1 WLR 194 all major decisions of the High Court and Court of Appeal after 11 January 2001 have a neutral reference which should be used in addition to the law report reference, and have paragraph numbers rather than page numbers.

a.24 Nuisance A legal cause of action imposing liability arising out of the defendant's use of property, either affecting other occupiers nearby (private nuisance) or affecting the public in the use of a highway (public nuisance).

a.25 Ogden Tables The Ogden working party led the way to an accurate calculation of future financial loss based on actuarial principles, and gives its name to the Tables which set out the figures on which the courts rely for this exercise: see Chapter 23 on multipliers.

a.26 Pain and suffering and loss of amenity The traditional expression for general damages awarded to compensate for an injury and its consequential disability, a phrase which has surprisingly survived the language revisions of the CPR. In this book the simpler phrase 'injury damages' is preferred.

a.27 Plaintiff The pre-CPR name for a claimant.

a.28 Pleading The pre-CPR name for a statement of case, a formal document in which a litigant sets out his case for the benefit of the court and his opponent indicates what is agreed and what is disputed so as to define the issues.

a.29 Precedent The respect accorded to previous decisions on the same point, also known as the doctrine of *stare decisis*. A judge at a trial (the judge at first instance) is obliged to follow a previous decision of the Court of Appeal or the House of Lords and to give persuasive respect to a previous decision made at the same or higher level at first instance. The Court of Appeal is generally bound by its own previous decisions, though since 1961 the House of Lords may depart from its own previous decisions in certain circumstances.

a.30 Presumption An inference that will be drawn by the court in the absence of any other evidence to contradict or, as lawyers say, to rebut the presumption.

a.31 Privy Council The Judicial Committee of the Privy Council has Law Lords who determine appeals from a dwindling number of Commonwealth jurisdictions. The interest for personal injury cases is that, though not technically binding on courts in England and Wales, the decisions have very strong persuasive authority, as, for example, in *The Wagon Mound* cases on foreseeability in negligence and nuisance.

Queen's Bench   The High Court is organized in three divisions: Family, Chancery and Queen's Bench Divisions. Common law cases including all personal injury claims are dealt with in the Queen's Bench Division. It is curious that this archaic name has survived the recent reforms.   **a.32**

Real evidence   Actual things produced in evidence, as opposed to the testimony, written or spoken, of witnesses.   **a.33**

Solicitor   The lawyer responsible for conducting a case. The broad comparison with the role of a general practitioner in medicine is often made but is misleading. A solicitor is likely to be highly specialized in his area of practice and will take responsibility for managing the whole of the claim, employing the assistance of expert doctors, engineers and barristers as appropriate, but rather than pass responsibility to the hospital specialist as a GP will do, the solicitor maintains control throughout.   **a.34**

Special damages   Losses which can be calculated by arithmetic. Traditionally special damages were limited to past loss, and future loss was counted as general damages even if it was to be assessed on a multiplier/multiplicand calculation. Now the term is used to describe the schedule that a claimant must serve with his claim, setting out all his claims for financial losses both past and future.   **a.35**

Statutory instrument   Subordinate legislation made in the exercise of a power granted by Act of Parliament. A statutory instrument may be challenged if it goes beyond the powers (Latin *ultra vires*) granted by Parliament, or if Parliament's requirements for approval have not been followed. Statutory instruments are numerous: for example, the many Regulations governing safety at work.   **a.36**

Strict liability   Liability arising from the existence of specified facts regardless of fault; sometimes also called absolute liability.   **a.37**

Third party   The pre-CPR name for an additional party brought into the proceedings, now called a Part 20 Defendant. If a defendant brings a claim against a third party, the claimant will not have any claim directly against the third party unless the third party is also made an additional defendant to the original claim.   **a.38**

Tort   The law of torts comprises the rules of law which determine when a person may incur liability to another as a result of what he does or fails to do, without depending on any prior relationship to define their responsibilities to each other such as a contract or a trust. Most personal injury claims are tort claims.   **a.39**

Trespass   In ordinary speech trespass means only going onto someone's land without permission but as a legal wrong it includes trespass to the person by deliberately assaulting or falsely imprisoning someone or trespass to goods.   **a.40**

a.41 **Vicarious liability**   Where a person is liable for an act committed by someone else on his behalf. The commonest situation is employment: an employer is liable for the acts of his employees committed within the scope of their employment. In most injury claims about the acts of an employee, it is the employer who will be named as the defendant (and who will hold the relevant liability insurance policy).

a.42 **Witness**   A person who gives evidence to a court. Witnesses of fact describe what happened, usually in writing in the first place and if necessary, for example if there is a dispute about the facts, by oral evidence under oath at a trial. A witness can state only the facts and not his opinion about the facts, unless he has special knowledge and experience on the topic so that he can be regarded as an expert, in which case his opinion is admissible.

a.43 **Woolf reforms**   The Civil Procedure Rules 1998 followed the recommendations of a committee chaired by Lord Woolf. They came into force on 26 April 1999 with the aim of providing quicker, cheaper and more efficient access to justice for litigants in civil cases.

C. Legal Latin

a.44 *Bona fide*   In good faith.

Causa causans and *causa sine qua non*   An immediate cause and, in contrast, a 'but-for' cause, literally a cause without which there would be nothing.

a.45 *De bene esse*   To assume a proposition to be true for the time being, or to assume that evidence is admissible, for the sake of the argument, while keeping an open mind whether it is true or admissible.

Ejusdem generis   Of the same kind.

a.46 *Ex gratia*   A payment made freely as a gift without legal obligation; an accident victim who receives an ex gratia payment to help him usually does not have to account for it against a claim for compensation.

Ex turpi causa non oritur actio   No action can be brought based on wickedness; a person who is injured in the course of committing a wrong may be prevented from bringing a claim.

a.47 *Mens rea*   A guilty mind: a mental element is necessary in most crimes and most torts but situations of strict or absolute liability, as under some health and safety regulations, are those where no *mens rea* need be proved.

Novus actus interveniens   A new intervening act—some event which breaks the chain of causation between the defendant's wrongful act and the claimant's harm so that the defendant is not liable for the harm.

Per incuriam   A decision that was made in ignorance of a relevant statute or   **a.48** other decision so that it is not a binding authority under the rules of *stare decisis*.

Puisne   A High Court judge.

Prima facie   On the face of it: a *prima facie* case is one which seems sound so   **a.49** far, but might be contradicted by further evidence.

Pro bono   Most lawyers are willing to assist poor people without charge in some cases from time to time and this is called *pro bono* work.

Quantum   How much: the amount of damages.   **a.50**

Quantum meruit   How much is it worth: when the court has to assess a reasonable payment in the absence of prior agreement.

Res ipsa loquitur   A Latin phrase meaning 'the thing speaks for itself: a   **a.51** principle of evidence that sometimes when the cause of an incident cannot be directly proved, the known facts are such that the cause may be inferred as negligent.

Stare decisis   The doctrine of precedent by which a previous decision of a higher court must be allowed to stand and must be followed by a later and less senior court. The Court of Appeal is bound by its own previous decisions and the House of Lords is bound unless it decides to operate the Practice Direction of 1961.

Ultra vires   Beyond the powers given: where statute defines the scope of a   **a.52** body's powers, a purported act which is beyond those powers is a nullity.

Volenti non fit injuria   Voluntary acceptance of risk: there is no wrong done if the injured victim willingly and with full knowledge voluntarily accepted the risk of injury.

D. Abbreviations and References

Law reports   In a legal system which gives binding authority to previous   **a.53** decisions accurate reports are essential. The main series are mentioned below. Under the *Practice Note* [2001] 1 WLR 194 the reports from the Incorporated Council of Law Reporting (AC, QB, Ch, ICR and WLR) should be cited in preference to other series unless the case is only reported elsewhere.

AC   Appeal cases (cited as, for example, [2004] AC 123) are the reports from the Incorporated Council of decisions of the Judicial Committee of the House of Lords and the Privy Council. Square brackets are used when the year is the vital identifier of the volume; round brackets are used when the identifier is a volume number in the series and the year is added only for convenience.

a.54 **All ER**   The All England Law Reports (cited as, for example, [2004] 1 All ER 123). These reports cover a wide range of topics but include the most important decisions for personal injury claims.

APIL   The Association of Personal Injury Lawyers.

a.55 **AvMA**   Action against Medical Accidents. The AvMA can be contacted at 44 High Street, Croydon, Surrey CRO 1YB. Helpline: 0845 123 23 52; email: admin@avma.org.uk.

Blackstone's Civil Practice   A comprehensive guide to all aspects of civil practice.

a.56 *Charlesworth on Negligence*   A standard text on negligence. There is some overlap with *Clerk & Lindsell* and the scope is not confined to the strict limits of the tort of negligence. Part of the authoritative and respected Common Law Library.

Clerk & Lindsell on Torts   A standard text on all aspects of tort law which includes almost all personal injury compensation claims. Part of the authoritative and respected Common Law Library.

a.57 *Current Law*   A comprehensive publication of up-to-date legal developments including brief notes of cases.

Green Book   A civil practice guide, formerly the *County Court Practice* but now covering all civil courts.

a.58 *Halsbury's Laws* and *Halsbury's Statutes*   A mammoth multi-volume work covering all aspects of the law, mentioned here because it is often to be found in good public libraries. The volume on Negligence is the part most likely to be of help.

ICR   The Industrial Cases Reports (cited as, for example, [2004] ICR 123).

a.59 **IRLR**   The Industrial Relations Law Reports (cited as, for example, [1999] IRLR 123), mainly concerned with industrial relations and unfair dismissal but including some reports of accident at work litigation.

Kemp & Kemp   The 'Bible' for the assessment of damages, containing two comprehensive volumes on the law of damages in personal injury cases and two volumes with a huge quantity of case reports (of varying authority) on the assessment of injury damages.

McGregor on Damages An excellent textbook of the law on damages **a.60** including, but not limited to, personal injury cases. Part of the authoritative and respected Common Law Library.

Munkman on Employers' Liability A textbook companion to Redgrave (see below).

PIBA The Personal Injuries Bar Association, a specialist organization for **a.61** barristers who practise in personal injuries cases.

PIQR The Personal Injury and Quantum Reports (cited as, for example [2004] PIQR P123 or [2004] PIQR Q123). A specialist series of reports published since 1992 dealing exclusively with personal injury cases.

QBD The Queen's Bench Division of the High Court. This is the Division in **a.62** which compensation cases will proceed if they are serious enough to be in the High Court.

QB The Queen's Bench Reports (cited as, for example [2004] QB 123) from the Incorporated Council, covering High Court and Court of Appeal cases in common law areas.

Redgrave's Health and Safety A book which contains the text of a large **a.63** number of statutes and regulations relevant to health and safety at work.

RTR The Road Traffic Reports (cited as, for example, [2004] RTR 123).

White Book A civil practice guide, formerly the Supreme Court Practice **a.64** covering the High Court and Court of Appeal but now covering all civil courts.

WLR The Weekly Law Reports (cited as, for example, [2004] 1 WLR 123).

b

MEDICAL TERMS AND MEDICAL DRAWINGS

Every personal injury claim involves the proof of injury by way of a medical **b.01**
report. It is usually reasonably clear what general message is intended from the
doctor by the content of the report, but I suspect that many lawyers skim over
the technical parts without fully understanding the details. This chapter is in the
form of a short encyclopaedia of the medical terms commonly encountered in
personal injury practice. For reasons of space, anatomical names are given in the
diagrams, and the names of medicines have not been given.

Medical notes are often compiled in a form of shorthand. Before coming to the **b.02**
substance of this chapter, a few of the commonest forms are described.

#	fracture
+	more, much
+++	a great deal
↑	increasing
↓	reducing
°	no
Dx or Δ	diagnosis
Hx	history of complaint
2/7	two days
2/52	two weeks
2/12	two months
♀	female
♂	male
c/o	complaining of
ISQ	in status quo, in the same condition as before
NAD	no abnormality detected
O/E	on examination

PERLA   pupils equal reacting to light and association
PMH   previous medical history

A. Medical Terms

b.03 **a-** The absence of something. So pyrexial means having a raised temperature and apyrexial means having a normal temperature.

Abduction Moving in a direction outwards from the midline of the body.

Acupuncture A means of pain relief and therapy by the insertion of needles. As acupuncture becomes more widely accepted by Western conventional medicine, so it has become easier to recover in a claim the costs of private treatment undergone in good faith.

b.04 **Acute** A condition which starts and ends quickly; by contrast a long-lasting condition is chronic.

Adduction Moving in a direction inwards towards the midline of the body.

Aetiology The cause of a disease.

b.05 **Affect** Apparent mood or emotion: a psychiatrist describing a patient's demeanour will often include a comment on his affect.

Ambulant or ambulatory Walking.

Amelioration Becoming better.

b.06 **Aneurysm** A swelling of an artery caused by a weak arterial wall; for example an aneurysm in the brain may rupture causing haemorrhage.

Angiography A method of x-ray examination where a contrast medium is added to the blood so that the blood in its vessels can be shown.

Annular Ring-shaped.

b.07 **Anosmia** Loss of the sense of smell.

Anti- Against or opposite or contrary.

Apgar score A measurement of a new born infant's wellbeing, giving a score of 0, 1, or 2 to each of five signs: heart rate, breathing, muscle tone, reflex irritability and skin colour related to the time from delivery; an ideal score for a healthy baby is 10.

b.08 **Aphasia** A speech disorder resulting from brain damage, either by difficulty of understanding (sensory) or by difficulty of expression (motor).

ARDS Adult Respiratory Distress Syndrome.

Arthrodesis   The fusion of bones in a joint so that movement is impossible, which sometimes relieves persistent pain.

Arthroplasty   An operation to replace a joint.   **b.09**

Arthroscopy   An examination of the inside of a joint by the insertion of a fine endoscope.

Asphyxia   Suffocation by obstruction of or interference with the airway.

Aspiration   Sucking out fluid, for example with a syringe.   **b.10**

Asymptomatic   Free of symptoms.

Audiogram   A measurement of hearing sensitivity, using an audiometer to assess the threshold of hearing at different frequencies.

Auricular   To do with the ear (auricle) or with hearing; also, to do with the   **b.11**
atrium of the heart.

Avascular necrosis   The death of tissue as a result of the loss of blood supply. For example, this can be a late complication of a fracture of the neck of the femur.

Avulsion   separation from the body or tearing away by force. An avulsion fracture occurs when a strong tendon tears away a piece of bone at the point where the tendon is attached.

Axial skeleton   The skull and spine; the **axis** is the central line.   **b.12**

Axilla   Armpit.

Behaviour therapy   A treatment of neurotic disorders by instilling conditioned reflex responses.

Belle indifference   An inappropriate absence of emotional response to being   **b.13**
severely disabled or incapacitated by hysterical or somatic symptoms, also a feature of multiple sclerosis.

Biceps   The muscle of the front of the upper arm; **bicipital** means of the biceps.

Bilateral   Involving both sides or, where there are two of an organ, involving both of them.

Bipolar disorder   A severe psychiatric disorder characterized by extreme   **b.14**
changes from euphoria to depression, hyperactivity to apathy.

Black eye   Would be described by a doctor as a periorbital haematoma.

Black lung   Pneumoconiosis, caused by breathing coal dust.

b.15 **Blood alcohol**   The prescribed limits for a driver under s 11 of the Road Traffic Act 1988 are:

  (a) 35 microgrammes of alcohol in 100 millilitres of breath
  (b) 80 milligrammes of alcohol in 100 millilitres of blood
  (c) 107 milligrammes of alcohol in 100 millilitres of urine.

Blood pressure   Both the peak pressure (systolic) and the running pressure between heartbeats (diastolic) are measured; a typical normal blood pressure would be 120/80: the measurements are millimetres of mercury.

Bolus   Dose of a drug to be injected quickly, or a mouthful of food ready to be swallowed.

b.16 **Bone conduction**   The transmission of sound to the inner ear by the bone of the skull rather than by air and the eardrum.

Brachial   Involving the arm; so the brachial artery supplies the arm and the brachial plexus is a collection of nerves in the area of the armpit.

Brachy-   A prefix meaning short.

b.17 **Brady-**   A prefix meaning slow.

Bronchial   Of the air tubes of the lungs.

Buccal   Of the cheek.

b.18 **Burns**   First degree: mild burns causing redness of the skin affecting only the epidermis or outer layer, from which a full recovery will be achieved. Second degree: more severe, with blistering, oedema and destruction of skin surface affecting both the epidermis and the underlying dermis. Third degree: affecting the full thickness of the skin and underlying tissues. Partial thickness burns will usually recover but full thickness will usually require skin grafting.

Bursa   A fibrous sac in the region of a joint or tendon which secretes a synovial fluid to lubricate and protect where there may be friction; **bursitis** is the inflammation of a bursa and Clergyman's Knee describes inflammation of the bursa in front of the kneecap.

Byssinosis   A respiratory condition caused by the inhalation of dust from cotton, flax or hemp, causing breathlessness, a tight chest, and coughing.

b.19 **Calcaneus**   The heel bone or os calcis.

Calcification   Prolonged inflammation or injury can result in the deposit of calcium salts in body tissues.

Calculus   A stone (the plural is calculi), for example gall stones.

14

Caliper splint   An external support for a weakened limb.   **b.20**

Callus   A collection of partly calcified tissue: if seen on x-ray of a fractured bone the presence of callus is a good sign that healing is taking place.

Carcinoma   A cancer arising in the surface lining of the body, especially in the breast, skin, bowel, lungs or womb—contrast with a sarcoma, a cancer which arises from solid tissues; a **carcinogen** is an agent which produces a cancer.

Cannula   A hollow tube which is used to pass fluid into a blood vessel or other   **b.21**
tissue.

Cardiac   Of the heart.

Caries   Tooth (or bone) decay.

Carpal   Of the wrist (carpus).   **b.22**

Carpal Tunnel syndrome   Swelling in the restricted space of the wrist, a space in which the tendons and median nerve pass, so that this nerve is compressed and there is pain, numbness and tingling in the thumb side of the hand. Injections of steroid may help, or a surgical decompression may be undertaken. The syndrome is a common complaint in middle aged women, and there can be vexed questions of causation in those who blame repetitive work such as typing or industrial processes for the onset of the condition.

Cartilage   Gristle.

Catheter   A flexible drainage tube.   **b.23**

Cauda equina   The collection of spinal nerves below the level of the first lumbar vertebra where the spinal cord ends; if compressed by the protrusion of an intervertebral disc there may be acute back pain, leg pain (sciatica) and bladder problems.

Caudal   Of the tail, that is the coccyx area at the base of the spine.

Causalgia   Severe burning pain caused by damage to the body of a nerve in   **b.24**
injury.

Cephal- or cephalo- or cephalic   Of the head.

Cerebral   Of the brain.

Cervical   Of the neck; so the cervical spine comprises the cervical vertebrae   **b.25**
and the neck of the womb is the cervix.

Chondritis   The inflammation of cartilage, as a result of injury or wear; so chondromalacia patellae is a condition of the cartilage behind the kneecap causing pain and stiffness.

Chronic   Lasting for a long time or permanently; contrast with acute.

b.26   **Cicatrix**   A scar.

Claudication   Pain in the leg muscles on walking caused by an inadequate blood supply: usually, intermittent claudication is defined by a walking distance.

Clavicle   Collar bone.

b.27   **Clinical**   Of the observation, examination, diagnosis, and treatment of patients.

Clonus   Repetitive contraction and relaxation of muscles as a result of damage to the nervous system.

Colles' fracture   A typical wrist fracture commonly caused by falling onto an outstretched hand.

b.28   **Coma**   Deep unconsciousness. For assessment, see Glasgow Coma Score.

Comminuted fracture   Broken in several pieces.

Compartment syndrome   The effect of potentially serious swelling confined within a compartment of the body, for example the lower leg or forearm; this can compress blood vessels and lead to muscle atrophy so an operation to relieve the pressure may be needed.

b.29   **Complicated fracture**   A fracture associated with damage to other organs such as muscles, nerves or arteries.

Compound fracture   A fracture associated with a break in the skin so that (unlike a simple fracture) the fracture has been exposed to the potentially infectious outside atmosphere.

Concussion   The shaking up of the brain from violent movement of the head, resulting in bleeding and damage to nerve tissue and loss of consciousness.

b.30   **Conservative treatment**   An approach to treatment which avoids aggressive intervention and aims to maintain the patient while allowing natural healing to take place.

Contact dermatitis   Skin inflammation (eczema) caused by contact with a substance that provokes an allergic reaction.

Contra-indication   A possible adverse consequence of proposed treatment which makes that treatment undesirable or dangerous.

b.31   **Contre coup**   Damage occurring opposite to the point of impact, so for example a blow to the back of the head may result in a contre coup injury to the frontal lobes.

Contusion   A bruise.

Conversion disorder   A psychological condition which results in physical symptoms and disability: sometimes called hysteria.

Copro-   Of the faeces.   **b.32**

Coronal plane   The imaginary vertical line that divides the front of the body from the back (the **sagittal** divides the right half from the left).

Cortex   The outer distinguishable part; so the cerebral cortex is the outer layer of grey matter in the brain (the inner part is the medulla).

Cosmesis   Of a concern for appearance.   **b.33**

Costa   A rib.

Coxa   A hip or hip joint.

Cranium   The head apart from the jaw bone; so a craniotomy is a surgical   **b.34** opening of the skull.

Crepitus   A grinding caused (among other things) by the ends of a fractured bone or by the damaged surfaces of a joint affected by arthritis.

Cruciate   In the shape of a cross, as in the cruciate ligament of the knee.

Crush syndrome   A severe crushing injury may be followed by this condition   **b.35** where myoglobin is released by the muscles and kidney damage can result.

CT or computerized axial tomography (a CAT Scan)   A system of internal x-ray scanning.

Cutaneous   Of the skin.

Cyanosis   Blueness of the skin as a result of a lack of oxygen.   **b.36**

Cytology   A study of cells of the body.

Dactyl   A digit, either finger or toe.

Debility   Weakness, often as a result of lack of use.   **b.37**

Debridement   The removal of damaged tissue, for example the edges of wounds and muscle tissue that is not viable, to encourage rapid healing.

Deciduous teeth   Milk teeth.

Dehiscence   Opening or splitting, as when an operation wound fails to heal   **b.38** and opens as a result of internal pressure.

Depression   Persistent sadness or unhappiness; this may be a normal reaction to an event such as suffering a catastrophic or disabling injury, or a depressive illness which features hopelessness, fear, lack of concentration, confusion, loss of self-esteem, and risk of suicide.

Derma- Of the skin; so **dermatitis** is an inflammation of the skin.

b.39 **Diagnosis** The identification of the disease which is the cause of particular signs and symptoms; **differential diagnosis** is a reasoning process of identifying a list of diseases which present in a similar way as an aid to reaching a diagnosis.

Diastolic The lower of two readings of blood pressure, taken when the ventricles are resting and filling.

Diathermy A method of burning, cutting and coagulating tissues for fine, bloodless surgery by the use of high frequency current.

b.40 **Dilatation** Widening or stretching.

Disarticulation Separation at a joint.

Discectomy Surgical removal of the central part of an intervertebral disc, for example as a treatment of prolapse.

b.41 **Disimpaction** When the broken ends of a bone have been impacted in poor position, traction is applied to disimpact them.

Dislocation Injury to a joint where there is disarticulation of the bearing surfaces and damage to ligaments and capsule of the joint.

Distal Situated more distantly away from the centre: so the fingers are distal to the palm; the opposite is **proximal**, meaning nearer to the centre.

b.42 **Distention** Expansion or swelling, by the pressing outwards of internal pressure.

Dorsal Of the back.

Drain A tube placed in a wound or in surgery to allow the discharge of fluid.

b.43 **DSM IV** A classification of psychiatric conditions: if a condition can be identified within the classification, it is likely to be accepted as a recognized illness for the purposes of the recovery of damages. A similar classification is the ICD 10.

DVT Deep vein thrombosis.

Dys- Bad, defective, abnormal.

b.44 **Eczema** A skin condition featuring scaly red patches and blisters which is a feature of many kinds of dermatitis.

Effusion Fluid moving to, or collecting in, an abnormal site.

Elective   Treatment which, or the timing of which, is chosen, rather than dictated by urgent necessity.

Embolism   Sudden blockage of a blood vessel by material such as a clot carried in the blood stream.   **b.45**

Emphysema   A lung disease in which gas exchange in respiration is impaired by the breakdown of the small air sacs.

Endogenous   Occurring without an obvious external cause.

Endoscopy   Visual examination of the inside of the body by an endoscope.   **b.46**

Endotracheal tube   A plastic tube that is inserted through the mouth into the airway to enable artificial assisted ventilation to be provided.

Epi-   On, over, near, beside.

Epidural   Outside the dura mater, the covering of the brain and spinal cord.   **b.47**

Epilepsy   Vulnerability to fits which may be a consequence of head injury.

Ergonomics   The study of people in a working environment.

Eversion   Turning outwards.   **b.48**

Evulsion   Tearing away by force.

Excision   Cutting off.

Excoriation   An abrasion or tearing to the body surface.   **b.49**

Expectant   Waiting hopefully; so expectant treatment means wait and see.

Exsanguination   The loss of almost all the blood.

External fixator   A means of fixing a fractured bone by attaching a steel bar alongside, fixed to the bone by pins above and below the fracture.   **b.50**

Extradural haemorrhage   Bleeding between the skull and the outer covering of the brain, the dura mater; it is a very dangerous consequence of skull fracture.

Exudate   Fluid that has seeped out.

Extension   Straightening of a joint—compare flexion.   **b.51**

External rotation   Turning outwards.

Facet joints   The facet is a small flat surface as in the joints between vertebrae.

Facies   Facial expression typical of a particular condition.   **b.52**

Fascia   Layers of tissue under the skin, between muscles or around organs.

Fasciculation   Involuntary quivering or twitching of muscles.

b.53   **Fat necrosis**   Death of fatty tissue.

Febrile   Having a fever.

FEV   Forced expiratory volume: a measure of the greatest volume of air exhaled in one second, to be compared with the **FVC** or forced vital capacity which is the greatest volume of a single breath giving a ratio, normally at least 70%, which is reduced in cases of obstructive airway disease.

b.54   **Fibrosis**   Scarring and thickening with fibrous tissue, a healing process following injury or inflammation.

Fistula   An abnormal channel between two organs or between the inner body and the skin.

Fixation   Holding in a fixed position, particularly of bones to allow healing in a correct alignment.

b.55   **Flaccid**   Limp, soft, floppy, a lack of firmness.

Flail chest   A mobile chest wall resulting from rib fractures.

Flexion   The bending of a joint: contrast extension, the straightening.

b.56   **Fluctuant**   A swelling which contains fluid, for example an abscess, on palpation with the fingers will yield to pressure and be fluctuant.

Foetus   The preferred spelling nowadays is fetus: a baby in the womb from about ten weeks after conception.

Foot drop   The loss of the ability to flex the ankle so as to raise the foot, usually as a result of nerve damage.

b.57   **Fracture**   Break. A bone fracture may be **greenstick**, where the bone of a child bends and breaks on one side only rather than fully, **simple** where the soft tissues are not broken, **comminuted** where bone is broken into several fragments, **complicated** where there is also injury to nearby structures, or **compound** where skin is broken over the fracture and there may be infection. The nature of the break may be transverse, oblique or spiral and a fracture dislocation is a fracture across a joint which affects the joint surfaces.

Frontal lobes   The front part of the brain which is highly developed in man and responsible for many higher cognitive functions.

Frozen shoulder   Painful and persistent stiffness of the shoulder that may result from injury causing inflammation of the capsule of the joint.

Functional overlay   A term used to describe complaints of symptoms which **b.58** cannot be fully explained on medical grounds; the term illness behaviour is now more common.

FVC   See FEV.

Gait   The way a person walks.

Glasgow Coma Scale   An internationally recognized system for the assessment **b.59** of the effects of head injury. The score is the total of three measurements:

Best motor response	Obeys commands	6
	Localizes to pain	5
	Flexes/withdraws to pain	4
	Abnormal flexion	3
	Abnormal extension	2
	None	1
Best verbal response	Oriented	5
	Confused	4
	Inappropriate words	3
	Incomprehensible sounds	2
	None	1
Eye opening	Spontaneously	4
	To speech	3
	To pain	2
	None	1
The results are broadly categorized as Severe		8 or less
	Moderate	9 to 12
	Mild	13 to 15

Glenoid   A smooth, shallow depression, for example the cavity in the shoulder blade in which the end of the upper arm bone the humerus is located.

Golfer's elbow   Inflammation of the medial epicondyle of the tendon at the elbow: **tennis elbow** is inflammation of the lateral epicondyle.

Grand mal   A major epileptic seizure.   **b.60**

Grip strength   A measure of the weakness of the muscles of the hand and fingers.

Guarding   Where underlying inflammation produces a reflex tightening of muscles of the abdomen in response to pressure.

Haemo-   Of blood; so a **haematoma** is an accumulation of blood inside the **b.61** body, partially clotted to form a mass, and a **haemarthrosis** is blood within a joint.

Haemorrhage Abnormal bleeding from a vein or artery. Severe haemorrhage may be fatal; less severely may cause surgical shock. Also a challenge for any spelling test.

Hallux Big toe.

b.62 **Hemi-** Half.

Hetero- Different; whereas **Homeo-**, similar and **homo-**, same.

Histology The study of the microscopic structure of the body; **histo-pathology** is the microscopic study of disease processes.

b.63 **Hyper-** Beyond, over, too much. Contrast **Hypo-**, below, less than, too little.

Hypno- Of sleep.

Iatrogenic A disease or disorder caused by medical treatment.

b.64 **ICD 10** An international classification of diseases by the World Health Organization, used in particular in cases of psychiatric injury to show whether a recognized illness has been diagnosed. The American equivalent DSM IV is also used.

Illness behaviour The development of symptoms resulting from unconscious exaggeration by the patient; this is thought by most doctors to be far more common than deliberate malingering; also known as functional overlay, psychosomatic pain or compensation neurosis, though the last is used for a condition that is expected to resolve after the conclusion of a claim.

Impaction Forcing in, so that impacted ends of a fractured bone have been forced together and immobilized at the fracture site.

b.65 **Inflammation** A response to injury, denoted by the suffix -itis. The cardinal signs are redness, heat, swelling, and pain (in Latin rubor, calor, tumor, dolor).

Inferior Lower down in position in a standing person; also **infra-**.

Inter- Between, among or shared.

b.66 **Intra-** Within, inside.

Intro- Into, inwards.

Ischaemia Tissue which is short of oxygen because of an inadequate flow of blood.

b.67 **Iso-** Equal or equivalent.

Jerk   A tendon reflex, muscle contraction in response to brisk tapping of a tendon.

Juxta-   Near to, alongside.

Keloid   An abnormal response to healing resulting in thick scars which are   **b.68**
difficult to improve because surgery may induce an even greater keloid response.

Kirschner wire   A wire or rod passed through bone and used to apply traction.

Kuntscher nail   A strong steel nail that is inserted into the hollow canal of the
femur or tibia to maintain position after fracture.

Kyphosis   Backwards curvature of the dorsal spine (see Lordosis).   **b.69**

Laceration   A wound made by tearing; irregular, unlike a surgical incision.

Lacuna   A gap, space, emptiness.

Lachman test   A method of examining the knee for anterior cruciate ligament   **b.70**
damage by pulling the upper tibia forward from a flexed knee and assessing the
degree of displacement.

Lalo-   Of speech.

Lamina   A thin layer of tissue, as in the arch of a vertebra.

Laparo-   Of the abdominal cavity.   **b.71**

Lasegue's sign   A limitation of thigh bending on straight leg raising when
lying down, which is a sign of pressure on the nerve roots in the lumbar spine.

Latent   Present but not yet having any effect.

Lateral   To the side of the body; **unilateral** is on one side only, **bilateral** is on   **b.72**
both sides, **medial** is towards the midline.

Lavage   Washing out.

Laxity   Slackness.

Lepto-   Fine, soft, slender, delicate, weak.   **b.73**

Lesion   Any injury, wound or abnormality.

Ligament   Strong, flexible material, mainly found binding and supporting
joints.

Lingual   Of the tongue.   **b.74**

Litho-   Of stone.

Livid   Black or blue-black discolouration of bruises.

b.75 **Locomotor** Of voluntary movement.

Lordosis Forward curvature of the lumbar spine (see Kyphosis).

Lumbar Of the lower back and loin.

b.76 **Lumen** The inside of a tube.

Macerate Soften by long contact with liquid.

Macro- Large.

b.77 **Mal-** Bad, abnormal, defective.

Malaise A vague and unspecific term for feeling unwell.

Malingering The deliberate pretending of symptoms of disease, or exaggerating them, for advantage; most doctors find that deliberate malingering is very rare in patients who suffer accidental injuries, but it is more common to find unconscious overstatement of symptoms when a condition has been persistent and illness behaviour may develop.

b.78 **Manipulation** An operation with the hands, often a procedure under anaesthetic aiming to restore movement to a stiffened joint by moving it beyond the limit imposed on the conscious patient by muscle spasm.

Meatus A passage or opening in the body.

Medial Towards the midline of the body; contrast Lateral.

b.79 **Median** Towards the midline dividing right from left sides of the body.

Medulla The inner part of an organ: the outer is the cortex.

Meso- Middle, connecting, intermediate.

b.80 **Meta-** Changed, after, following, beyond.

Metr- Of the womb.

Mesothelioma A tumour of the lining of the lung caused by asbestos dust inhalation.

b.81 **Micro-** Very small.

Mio- Narrowing, diminution.

Mono- Single, one, alone.

b.82 **Morbidity** Being diseased; so the pre-morbid state is the state before the disease or injury.

MRI or Magnetic Resonance Imaging A detailed form of imaging without using radiation which can detect detailed soft tissue changes.

MRSA Multiply Resistant Staphylococcus Aureus, a bacterium—when it causes infection it is difficult to treat because it is resistant to a wide range of commonly used antibiotics.

Myco- Of fungus.   **b.83**

NAD nothing abnormal/no abnormality detected.

Necro- Of death.

Neo- New.   **b.84**

Nephro- Of the kidneys.

Nerve block anaesthesia A form of anaesthesia where the impulses are blocked from passing along the nerve to the brain.

Neuralgia Pain felt in a sensory nerve, which can be as a result of injury to the   **b.85** nerve.

NSAID Non-steroidal anti-inflammatory drugs.

Occam's Razor A philosophical approach to diagnosis that the simplest and if possible, a single explanation should be sought for a range of symptoms and signs.

Occlusion Closing, blocking, or covering; or the relationship of upper and   **b.86** lower teeth.

Oedema An accumulation of fluid in the tissue of the body.

Olfactory Of the sense of smell; the olfactory nerves are vulnerable to damage in head injury and a loss of the sense of smell, which includes much of the sense of taste, may result.

Omni- All.   **b.87**

Ortho- Straight, upright, normal.

Osteo- Of bone.

Osteoarthritis A persistent degenerative joint disease, the onset of which may   **b.88** be a late consequence of injury damage to the ends of bones involved in a joint.

Oto- Of the ear.

-otomy A surgical incision into.

Overt Obvious.   **b.89**

Palmar Of the palm of the hand; compare **plantar**, of the sole of the foot.

Pan-   Of the whole of, all.

b.90 **Para-**   Alongside, apart from.

Paraesthesia   Numbness, tingling, pins-and-needles.

Paraplegia   Paralysis of the lower trunk and both legs.

b.91 **Paresis**   Weakening of muscles short of paralysis.

Patent   Open, unobstructed.

Pathogenic   Able to cause disease.

b.92 **Pathology**   The science of disease and the causes and effects of disease, and diagnosis by laboratory examination of tissues.

Peak expiratory flow   A measurement of the degree of any airway obstruction using a peak flow meter to assess forced expiration.

Percutaneous   Through the skin.

b.93 **Peri-**   Around, about, surrounding.

Peroneal   Of the outer side of the lower leg or fibula.

Petit mal   Minor, brief epileptic attacks in children and adolescents.

b.94 **Phlebitis**   Inflammation of a vein.

Pneumo-   Of the lung.

Pneumothorax   The presence of air in the pleural cavity, which may lead to a collapsed lung.

b.95 **PO$_2$**   The concentration of oxygen in the blood.

Poly-   Many, much, excessive.

Popliteal   Of the hollow behind the knee.

b.96 **Posterior**   Of the back of the body or a part of the body (contrast anterior).

Post-traumatic stress disorder   A recognized anxiety disorder that can be caused by a reaction to a frightening event.

Potts fracture   A broken ankle with fracture of the fibula and fracture or dislocation of the tibia.

b.97 **Pre-**   Before.

Prognosis   An assessment of the likely future course and outcome of a condition.

Prolapse   Downward movement to an abnormal position.

Prone   Lying on the front, face down (**supine** is lying on the back, face up).   **b.98**

Pronation   Turning to be face down; so, rotating the forearm so that the palm of the hand faces down (**supination** is turning the arm so that the palm of the hand faces up).

Proprioception   The sensory system which gives awareness of the relative position of parts of the body.

Prosthesis   Any artificial replacement body part such as a false leg.   **b.99**

Proto-   First, early, primitive.

Proximal   Nearer to the centre of the body (compare Distal).

Pseudo-   False.   **b.100**

Psychiatry   The medicine of mental illness and emotional and behavioural problems.

Psychology   The study of behaviour and mental processes.

Psychometry   The measurement of psychological functions.   **b.101**

Psychosomatic   Of the effect of a mental and emotional condition on physical disorder.

Pyrexia   Fever.

Quadriplegia   Paralysis of all four limbs and the trunk.   **b.102**

Raynaud's disease   A disorder of the fingers with reduced circulation, an illness which, when induced by the use of vibrating tools at work, is known as Vibration White Finger (VWF).

Referred pain   Pain that is felt in a part of the body away from its cause.

Reflex Sympathetic Dystrophy   An organic condition of persistent pain out of   **b.103** proportion to the injury, occurring when the body fails to return to normal after an injury. Changes in temperature are characteristic.

Resection   Surgical removal.

Retroversion   Turning or tilting backwards.

Rotator Cuff   The capsule and tendons around and supporting the shoulder;   **b.104** degenerative change and vulnerability to tearing come with old age.

RSI or Repetitive Strain Injury   A name often given to any disorder caused by sustained repetition of awkward activity, as with musicians, keyboard operators, and machine operators; however this is not usually regarded as a meaningful diagnosis in a medico-legal context.

Sagittal   The vertical plane that divides the body into left and right halves (the **Coronal** plane divides front from back).

b.105   **Scaphoid bone**   A small bone in the wrist which is easily fractured and shows particular difficulty with healing after fracture.

Sciatica   Pain in the leg felt as a result of irritation of the sciatic nerve in the spine, usually as a result of pressure from an intervertebral disc.

Sclerosis   Hardening of tissues from the presence of fibrous tissue.

b.106   **Scolio-**   Twisted.

Scoliosis   Where the spine is twisted to one side.

Sensitization   An exposure to an allergen which has led to priming of the immune system so that subsequent exposure results in an allergic reaction.

b.107   **Sensorineural**   Deafness caused by a defect in the inner ear mechanism. Contrast conductive deafness. Deafness caused by exposure to excessive noise is **sensorineural**.

Sepsis   The presence of bacterial infection.

Sequelae   Strictly the event which follows afterwards, but generally used to imply a causative link, the consequences.

b.108   **SHO**   Senior House Officer—despite the name, a training grade of fairly junior hospital doctor.

Shock   A consequence of severe blood loss, burns or infection with low blood pressure and reduced circulation.

Sigmoid   S-shaped.

b.109   **Sign**   An objective observable indication of disease: compare **symptom**, which is the subjective report of the patient.

Silicosis   Lung disease caused by the inhalation of dust containing silica.

Soft tissue injury   Damage to skin, muscle, tendon or ligament but not bone.

b.110   **Somatic**   Of the body not the psyche; psychosomatic is of both the body and the mind.

Somatoform disorder   A range of psychiatric conditions where the complaint of symptoms cannot be attributed to a physical cause; often a puzzle both to treating doctors (other than in psychiatry) and to judges.

Spasm   Strong involuntary muscle contraction.

Spirometry   A test for the function of the lungs.   **b.111**

Spondylitis   Inflammation of the vertebral joints.

Spondylolisthesis   A congenital displacement forwards of a vertebra, which may cause backache.

Sprain   Stretching or tearing of ligament (compare strain, of muscle).   **b.112**

Stable   In an unchanging condition.

Stasis   Reduced or prevented flow.

Strain   Stretching or tearing of muscle (compare sprain, of ligament).   **b.113**

Stenosis   A narrowing.

Straight leg raising   A slipped disc causes tightness of the sciatic nerve and restricts the height to which a straight leg can be raised in a supine patient; improved movement may be seen with the patient seated or distracted, and a significant difference in the measurement may indicate non-organic pain, illness behaviour or even malingering.

Striated   Striped, grooved, ridged.   **b.114**

Subclinical   So mild that there are no signs or symptoms of disease.

Subcutaneous   Under the skin.

Subluxation   Partial or incomplete dislocation or strain of a joint.   **b.115**

Superficial   Near the surface.

Superior   Above, higher than.

Supination   Turning to lie face up, or turning the arm so that the palm of the   **b.116** hand faces up (compare pronation).

Suture   A surgical stitch.

Symptoms   A subjective indication of disease reported by the patient: compare **signs** which are objectively observable. Although a lawyer will instinctively regard signs as more reliable because of their objectivity, in medical practice the patient's own account of the history is usually taken to be more important for diagnosis.

Syncope   Fainting.   **b.117**

Syndrome   A combination of signs and symptoms making a clinical condition.

Synovial membrane   A membrane within all moving joints which produces the fluid that lubricates the joint.

b.118   **Tachy-**   Abnormally fast, rapid (compare brady-, slow).

Temporal   Of the temples at the sides of the head.

Tennis elbow   Inflammation of the elbow at the attachment of the tendon.

b.119   **Tenosynovitis**   Inflammation of the tendon sheath, often as a result of overuse.

TENS or Transcutaneous Electrical Nerve Stimulation   A treatment for persistent pain by providing a portable device with electrodes that can apply a current to the nerves.

Thenar eminence   The flesh of the palm at the base of the thumb.

b.120   **Therapy**   Treatment.

Thrombosis   The clotting of blood in an artery or vein.

Tinnitus   A sound heard in the head without external cause, often associated with deafness.

b.121   **Tracheostomy**   A procedure to maintain breathing by opening the wind-pipe at the front of the neck and inserting a tube.

Traction   Maintaining a constant pull so that a fractured bone will set in the correct position.

Trauma   Injury caused by a physical event.

b.122   **Trendelenburg test**   A test to assess the function of hip joint muscles by observing a hip drop when standing on one leg.

Triage   A system of sorting patients, derived from use in emergency for the sorting of wounded into groups of those needing urgent treatment, those who will survive without immediate treatment, and those beyond hope of any benefit from treatment.

Tuberosity   A bony prominence to which tendons attach.

b.123   **Ulcer**   An open sore.

Uni-   Single, one.

Valgus   Displaced away from the midline of the body; **varus** is displaced towards the midline.

b.124   **Ventral**   Of the front of the body; **dorsal** is of the back.

Vertex   The top of the head.

Vital capacity The forced vital capacity is the greatest volume of air that can be exhaled with the greatest effort.

Volar Of the palm of the hand or the sole of the foot.   **b.125**

Waddell signs From research (Waddell and others, 'Nonorganic Physical Signs in Low Back Pain' (1980)) features indicative of illness behaviour or malingering in cases of back pain were put forward as:

(a) *symptoms*: tail bone pain, whole leg pain, whole leg numbness, no pain free spells, intolerance, and lack of response to treatment, emergency admissions; and

(b) *signs*: superficial non-anatomical tenderness; pain in the back on axial loading, pain on rotation by the hips rather than by the back, comparing straight leg raising on formal measurement and when distracted, gross regional weakness with no clinical cause, overreaction to examination.

See **c. 37** and **c. 38** below.

Whiplash injury An extension-flexion soft tissue injury of the neck of a kind frequently caused by a rear-end collision road traffic accident. If the head is turned in a collision, the damage may be more widespread.

B. Medical Drawings

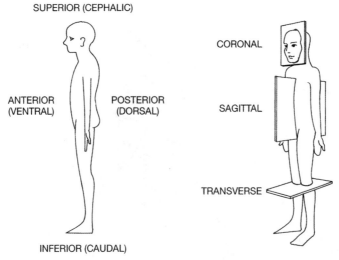

SUPERIOR (CEPHALIC)

CORONAL

ANTERIOR
(VENTRAL)

POSTERIOR
(DORSAL)

SAGITTAL

TRANSVERSE

INFERIOR (CAUDAL)

1. Anatomical terms and planes

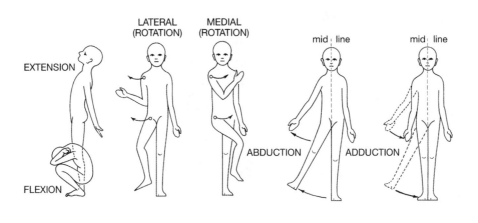

LATERAL
(ROTATION)

MEDIAL
(ROTATION)

mid line

mid line

EXTENSION

FLEXION

ABDUCTION

ADDUCTION

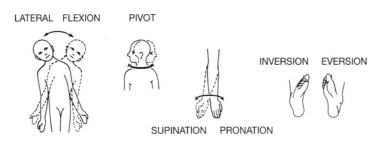

LATERAL FLEXION

PIVOT

INVERSION   EVERSION

SUPINATION   PRONATION

2. Movements in the body

33

Bones

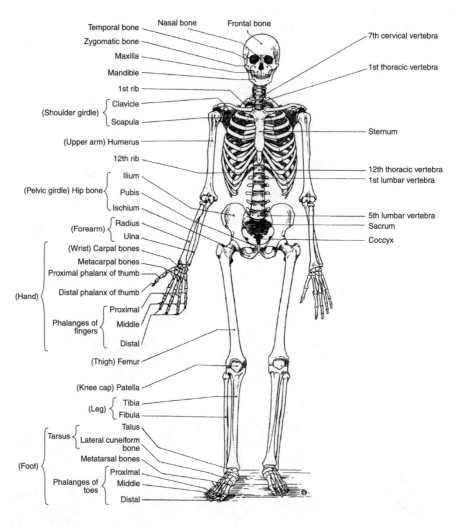

Temporal bone
Nasal bone
Frontal bone
7th cervical vertebra
Zygomatic bone
1st thoracic vertebra
Maxilla
Mandible
1st rib
(Shoulder girdle) { Clavicle
Scapula
Sternum
(Upper arm) Humerus
12th rib
12th thoracic vertebra
1st lumbar vertebra
Ilium
(Pelvic girdle) Hip bone { Pubis
Ischium
5th lumbar vertebra
Sacrum
(Forearm) { Radius
Ulna
Coccyx
(Wrist) Carpal bones
Metacarpal bones
Proximal phalanx of thumb
(Hand) {
Distal phalanx of thumb
Phalanges of fingers { Proximal
Middle
Distal
(Thigh) Femur
(Knee cap) Patella
(Leg) { Tibia
Fibula
Talus
Tarsus { Lateral cuneiform bone
Metatarsal bones
(Foot) {
Phalanges of toes { Proximal
Middle
Distal

3. Skeleton of a man, anterior view

34

Bones

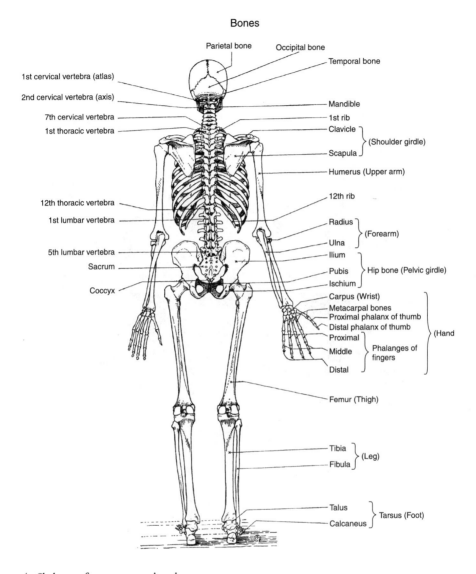

Parietal bone   Occipital bone

Temporal bone

1st cervical vertebra (atlas)

2nd cervical vertebra (axis)

7th cervical vertebra

1st thoracic vertebra

Mandible

1st rib

Clavicle ⎫
          ⎬ (Shoulder girdle)
Scapula ⎭

Humerus (Upper arm)

12th thoracic vertebra

1st lumbar vertebra

12th rib

Radius ⎫
        ⎬ (Forearm)
Ulna ⎭

Ilium ⎫

5th lumbar vertebra

Sacrum

Coccyx

Pubis ⎬ Hip bone (Pelvic girdle)

Ischium ⎭

Carpus (Wrist)
Metacarpal bones
Proximal phalanx of thumb
Distal phalanx of thumb
Proximal ⎫
Middle ⎬ Phalanges of
        fingers
Distal ⎭

(Hand

Femur (Thigh)

Tibia ⎫
       ⎬ (Leg)
Fibula ⎭

Talus ⎫
       ⎬ Tarsus (Foot)
Calcaneus ⎭

4. Skeleton of a man, posterior view

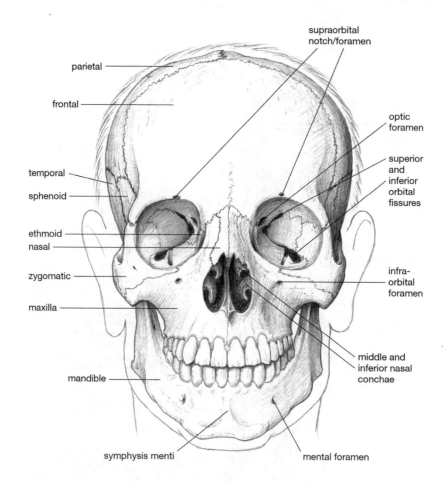

supraorbital
notch/foramen

parietal

frontal

optic
foramen

superior
and
inferior
orbital
fissures

temporal

sphenoid

ethmoid
nasal

zygomatic

maxilla

infra-
orbital
foramen

mandible

middle and
inferior nasal
conchae

symphysis menti

mental foramen

5. **Anterior aspect of skull**

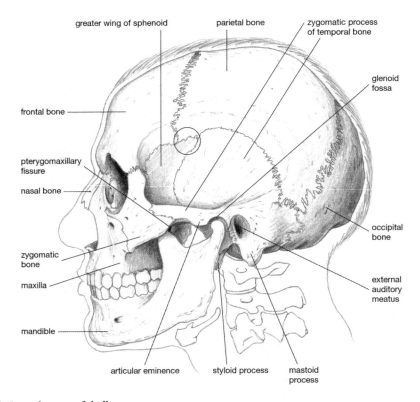

greater wing of sphenoid

parietal bone

zygomatic process
of temporal bone

glenoid
fossa

frontal bone

pterygomaxillary
fissure

nasal bone

zygomatic
bone

maxilla

mandible

occipital
bone

external
auditory
meatus

articular eminence

styloid process

mastoid
process

6. Lateral aspect of skull

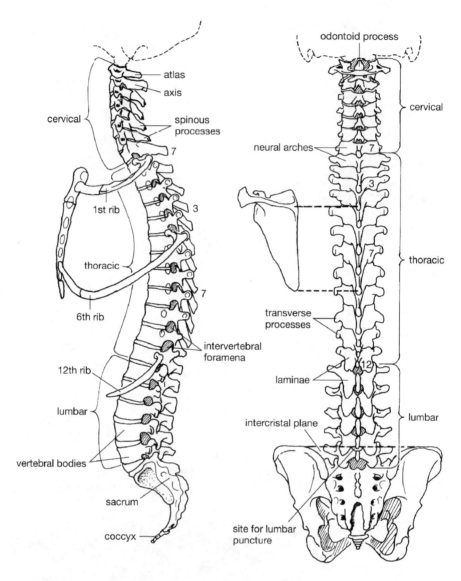

atlas
axis
cervical
spinous processes
1st rib
3
thoracic
6th rib
7
intervertebral foramena
12th rib
lumbar
vertebral bodies
sacrum
coccyx

odontoid process
cervical
neural arches
7
3
7
thoracic
transverse processes
12
laminae
intercristal plane
lumbar
site for lumbar puncture

7. Vertebral column, lateral view

8. Vertebral column, posterior view

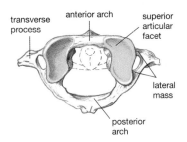

transverse process — anterior arch — superior articular facet — lateral mass — posterior arch

9. Atlas, from above

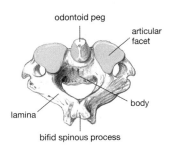

odontoid peg — articular facet — lamina — body — bifid spinous process

10. Axis, from above

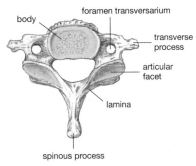

body — foramen transversarium — transverse process — articular facet — lamina — spinous process

11. Cervical vertebra, from above

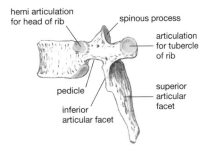

hemi articulation for head of rib — spinous process — articulation for tubercle of rib — pedicle — inferior articular facet — superior articular facet

12. Typical thoracic vertebra, from side

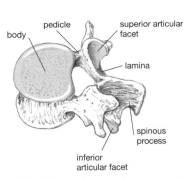

body — pedicle — superior articular facet — lamina — spinous process — inferior articular facet

13. Typical lumbar vertebra, from above and side

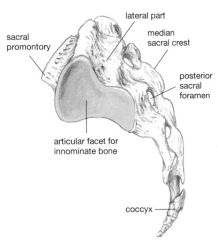

sacral promontory — lateral part — median sacral crest — posterior sacral foramen — articular facet for innominate bone — coccyx

14. Sacrum and coccyx, from side

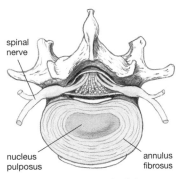

spinal nerve — nucleus pulposus — annulus fibrosus

15. Lumbar intervertebral disc viewed from below

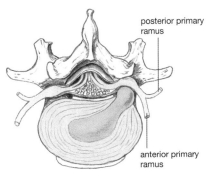

posterior primary ramus — anterior primary ramus

16. Protrusion of nucleus pulposus ('slipped disc')

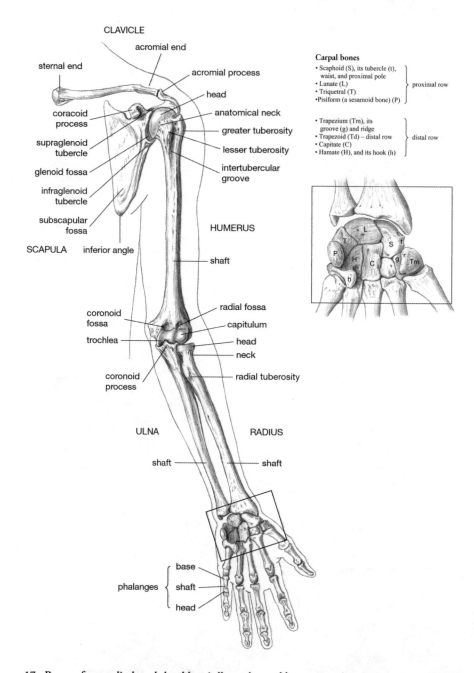

CLAVICLE

acromial end

sternal end

acromial process

head

anatomical neck

coracoid process

greater tuberosity

supraglenoid tubercle

lesser tuberosity

glenoid fossa

intertubercular groove

infraglenoid tubercle

subscapular fossa

HUMERUS

SCAPULA   inferior angle

shaft

coronoid fossa

radial fossa

capitulum

trochlea

head

neck

coronoid process

radial tuberosity

ULNA   RADIUS

shaft   shaft

base

phalanges   shaft

head

Carpal bones

• Scaphoid (S), its tubercle (t), waist, and proximal pole
• Lunate (L)   } proximal row
• Triquetral (T)
• Pisiform (a sesamoid bone) (P)

• Trapezium (Tm), its groove (g) and ridge
• Trapezoid (Td) – distal row   } distal row
• Capitate (C)
• Hamate (H), and its hook (h)

17. Bones of upper limb and shoulder girdle, and carpal bones, anterior view

40

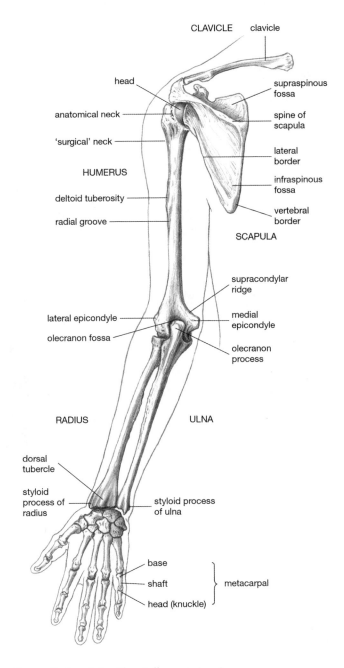

CLAVICLE   clavicle

head

supraspinous fossa

anatomical neck

spine of scapula

'surgical' neck

lateral border

HUMERUS

infraspinous fossa

deltoid tuberosity

radial groove

vertebral border

SCAPULA

supracondylar ridge

lateral epicondyle

medial epicondyle

olecranon fossa

olecranon process

RADIUS

ULNA

dorsal tubercle

styloid process of radius

styloid process of ulna

base

shaft

metacarpal

head (knuckle)

18. Bones of upper limb and shoulder girdle, posterior view

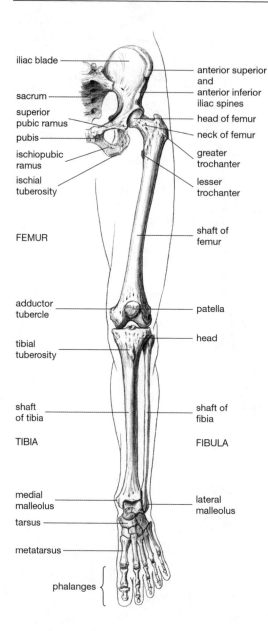

iliac blade

sacrum

superior
pubic ramus

pubis

ischiopubic
ramus

ischial
tuberosity

FEMUR

adductor
tubercle

tibial
tuberosity

shaft
of tibia

TIBIA

medial
malleolus

tarsus

metatarsus

phalanges

anterior superior
and
anterior inferior
iliac spines

head of femur

neck of femur

greater
trochanter

lesser
trochanter

shaft of
femur

patella

head

shaft of
fibula

FIBULA

lateral
malleolus

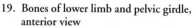

19. Bones of lower limb and pelvic girdle,
    anterior view

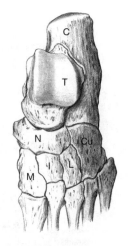

C = calcaneus
T = talus
N = navicular
Cu = cuboid
M = medial cuneiform
I = intermediate cuneiform
L = lateral cuneiform

20. Tarsal bones, dorsal view

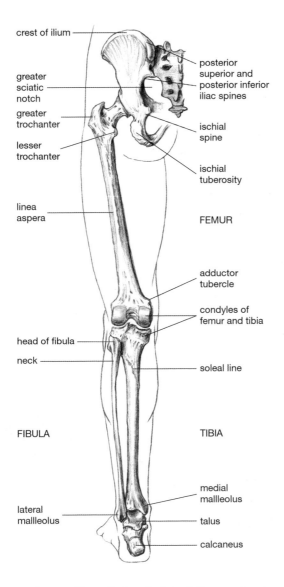

crest of ilium

posterior
superior and
posterior inferior
iliac spines

greater
sciatic
notch

greater
trochanter

ischial
spine

lesser
trochanter

ischial
tuberosity

linea
aspera

FEMUR

adductor
tubercle

condyles of
femur and tibia

head of fibula

neck

soleal line

FIBULA

TIBIA

medial
mallleolus

lateral
mallleolus

talus

calcaneus

21. Bones of lower limb and pelvic girdle, posterior view

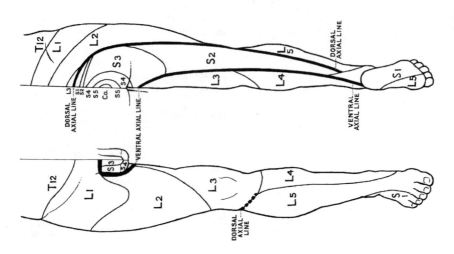

22. Dermatomes showing the distribution of sensory nerves to the upper limbs from the spinal nerves at different levels, anterior and posterior views

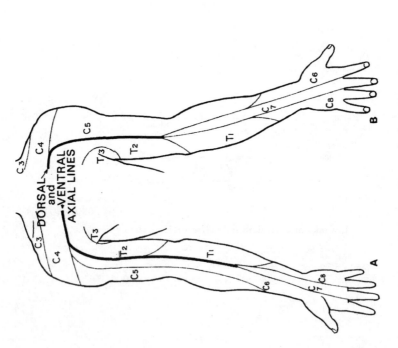

23. Dermatomes showing the distribution of sensory nerves to the lower limbs from the spinal nerves at different levels, anterior and posterior views

C

NOTES ON SOME COMMON INJURIES

This is not a medical textbook. It cannot provide a comprehensive discussion of **c.01** the medical issues that arise in the course of compensation claims. Its purpose is to assist lawyers and others concerned with claims. This chapter, and the discussion of occupational diseases which follows, sets out a superficial explanation of medical aspects of some common types of injury encountered in handling claims sufficient, it is hoped, to help legal practitioners with their understanding of medical reports and of the medical conditions of claimants in these specific areas. Since this makes no claim to be a medically authoritative treatment, the references to research papers have been omitted. The chapter covers: brain injury; whiplash; back injury; post-traumatic stress disorder; illness behaviour.

A. Brain Injury

The brain is rarely injured by direct trauma because it is well protected within **c.02** the skull and any impact severe enough to penetrate this defence is likely to prove fatal. The common cause of injury to the brain is the indirect effect of force on the head from a blow to the skull or rapid deceleration in a car accident or a fall. Within the skull the brain lies within a membrane called the dura (hence 'extradural' or 'subdural' haemorrhage). The dura encloses the brain itself, which is surrounded by cerebrospinal fluid within which the brain has some freedom of movement, and this freedom of movement accounts for the vulnerability of the brain and the contre-coup effect where a blow to one side of the head results in bruising injury to the opposing side. For example, a blow to the back of the head may result in injury to the frontal lobes.

c.03 The internationally recognized scale for assessing the level of consciousness after brain injury, from first assessment by ambulance staff through A & E examination and hospital admission and treatment, is the Glasgow Coma Scale in which the patient is assessed for three types of response: eye opening, voluntary movement and speaking. Full, normal consciousness is a score of 15. Injury is minor at a score of 13 to 15, moderate at a score of 9 to 12, and severe at 8 and below.

Glasgow Coma Scale

Eye opening	Spontaneous	4
	To command	3
	To pain	2
	Nil	1
Best motor response	Obeys commands	6
	Localizes to pain	5
	Normal flexion	4
	Abnormal flexion	3
	Extension	2
	Nil	1
Verbal response	Orientated speech	5
	Disorientated speech	4
	Words only	3
	Sounds only	2
	Nil	1

c.04 Patients who are fully conscious and have no skull fracture are likely to be sent home with careful instructions about observation for signs of complications. Patients at greater risk of haematoma will be admitted or transferred to a specialist neurosurgical unit and given a CT scan.

c.05 Secondary brain damage is likely to be caused by the presence of too much or too little blood. Haemorrhage within the skull (intracranial) resulting in the risk of compression of the brain within the fixed bony box of the skull can occur in the space between the dura and the skull (extradural), in the space between the dura and the arachnoid membrane (subdural) or within the brain itself (intra-cerebral). The brain can compensate to a degree for the presence of additional blood; on a CT scan the free spaces may be obliterated as the brain swells and the cerebrospinal fluid is displaced into the spine. When the limit of this tolerance is reached, however, pressure rises steeply and the brain is squeezed in an inverted cone shape into the only available aperture below the brain stem (coning) with a high risk of severe brain damage or death. The brain is also highly dependent on a good supply of oxygen being maintained, and hence the maintenance of the airway is a vital precaution in the early management of a head injury. The blood flow to the brain depends on a pressure difference between the arterial supply and the brain (perfusion pressure) so that the blood supply is compromised if there is swelling and hence raised pressure within the brain.

Potential complications of head injury are meningitis, hydrocephalus, and **c.06** chronic subdural haematoma. In addition, there is an increased risk of epilepsy, though the risk diminishes the longer the patient survives without a fit. As the patient recovers, the period of amnesia can be assessed and this gives a rough guide to the severity of the injury sustained by the brain. The recovery of a continuous memory of events is not the same as full recovery of consciousness and generally takes longer to achieve.

The consequences of brain injury cover a huge range from full recovery to severe **c.07** impairment and dependence. The cranial nerves are vulnerable to injury and this can affect the senses of smell, taste, sight, and hearing. Speech is often affected. Weakness and loss of co-ordination in limb movements are common. Cognitive deficits include loss of memory and slowness of thought, loss of concentration and loss of initiative, and there are often personality changes such as loss of inhibition, shortness of temper and tactlessness. The assessment of these disabilities is the field of the psychologist or neuropsychologist but it is also important to obtain as much evidence as possible of the pre-accident abilities and personality of the claimant. For a claimant, for example, this will mean taking full evidence of the perceived changes from family and friends and ensuring that the full picture is given to the reporting psychologist. For a defendant, for example, it will mean ensuring that the records of school and work are available and taking care to ask probing questions of the experts instructed.

The progress of a head-injured patient is likely to be slow, with about 70% of **c.08** recovery occurring in the first six months but final recovery often taking two or three years or more to be reached. Even at a fairly late stage when a claim is put forward, there may be considerable scope for a defendant to minimize a claim by actively promoting rehabilitation for the claimant. In severe cases there is likely to be a substantial need for continuing care and support and again it is in the interests of insurers, and preferable for the claimant, to ensure that the immediate family is provided with sufficient practical and financial support to enable family care to continue as far as realistically possible.

The *JSB Guidelines* indicate the features that will be relevant to assessment of **c.09** the seriousness of the individual case. The guidelines for head injuries are:

(A) BRAIN DAMAGE

(a) **Very Severe Brain Damage**   £155,000 to £220,000

In cases at the top of this bracket the injured person will have a degree **c.10** of insight. There may be some ability to follow basic commands, recovery of eye opening and return of sleep and waking patterns and postural reflex movement. There will be little, if any, evidence of meaningful response to environment, little or no language function, double incontinence and the need for full-time nursing care.

The level of award within the bracket will be affected by:

  (i) the degree of insight;
 (ii) life expectancy;
(iii) the extent of physical limitations.

The top of the bracket will be appropriate only where there is a significant effect on the senses and severe physical limitation.

Where there is a persistent vegetative state and/or death occurs very soon after the injuries were suffered and there has been no awareness by the injured person of his or her condition, the award will be solely for loss of amenity and will fall substantially below the above bracket.

(b) Moderately Severe Brain Injury   £120,000 to £155,000

c.11 The injured person will be very seriously disabled. There will be substantial dependence on others and a need for constant care. Disabilities may be physical, for example limb paralysis, or cognitive, with marked impairment of intellect or personality. Cases otherwise within (a) above may fall into this bracket if life expectancy has been greatly reduced.

The level of award within the bracket will be affected by the following considerations:

   (i) the degree of insight;
  (ii) life expectancy;
 (iii) the extent of physical limitations;
  (iv) the degree of dependence on others;
   (v) ability to communicate;
  (vi) behavioural abnormality;
 (vii) epilepsy or a significant risk of epilepsy (unless a provisional damages order provides for this risk).

(c) Moderate Brain Damage

c.12 This category is distinguished from (b) by the fact that the degree of dependence is markedly lower.

   (i) Cases in which there is moderate to severe intellectual deficit, a personality change, an effect on sight, speech and senses with a significant risk of epilepsy and no prospect of employment.   £82,000 to £120,000
  (ii) Cases in which there is a moderate to modest intellectual deficit, the ability to work is greatly reduced if not removed and there is some risk of epilepsy (unless a provisional damages order provides for this risk).   £50,000 to £82,000
 (iii) Cases in which concentration and memory are affected, the ability to work is reduced, where there is a small risk of epilepsy and any dependence on others is very limited.   £23,500 to £50,000

(d) Minor Brain Damage £8,500 to £23,500

c.13

In these cases the injured person will have made a good recovery and will be able to take part in normal social life and to return to work. There may not have been a restoration of all normal functions so there may still be persisting problems such as poor concentration and memory or disinhibition of mood, which may interfere with lifestyle, leisure activities and future work prospects. At the top of this bracket there may be a small risk of epilepsy.

The level of award within the bracket will be affected by:

  (i) the extent and severity of the initial injury;
 (ii) the extent of any continuing, and possibly permanent, disability;
(iii) the extent of any personality change;
 (iv) depression.

(B) MINOR HEAD INJURY £1,250 to £7,000

c.14

In these cases brain damage, if any, will have been minimal.

The level of the award will be affected by the following considerations:

  (i) the severity of the initial injury;
 (ii) the period taken to recover from any severe symptoms;
(iii) the extent of continuing symptoms;
 (iv) the presence or absence of headaches.

The bottom of the bracket will reflect full recovery within a few weeks.

(C) EPILEPSY

(a) Established Grand Mal £55,000 to £82,000   c.15

(b) Established Petit Mal £30,000 to £71,500

The level of award within these brackets will be affected by the following factors:

  (i) whether attacks are successfully controlled by medication and the extent to which the need for medication is likely to persist;
 (ii) the extent to which the appreciation of life is blunted by such medication;
(iii) the effect on working and/or social life;
 (iv) the existence of associated behavioural problems;
  (v) the prognosis.

(c) Other Epileptic Conditions £5,750 to £14,250

c.16–c.17

Cases where there are one or two discrete epileptic episodes, or a temporary resurgence of episodes, but there is no risk of further recurrence beyond that applicable to the population at large. The level of the award within the bracket will be affected by the extent of any consequences of the attacks on, for example, education, sporting activities, working and social life, and their duration.

B. Whiplash

c.18 The heaviness of the head mobile on the neck, combined with the compulsory restraint of the body in a motor car, makes strain injury to the muscles and ligaments of the neck one of the commonest features of relatively low speed road traffic accidents. Ironically, the requirement of seat belts increased the incidence of these injuries at the same time as reducing the incidence of more severe injuries.

c.19 The classic whiplash injury occurs when a car is struck from behind and the body is knocked forward by the seat while the head is forced back into hyper-extension, followed by a snap forward into hyper-flexion. Head restraints fitted to car seats are intended to limit the scope for the head to be forced backwards but in most cases seem to give inadequate protection and fail to prevent the head moving further than the anatomical limit on backwards extension of about 50° to 80°. Front and side impacts and injuries where the neck is rotated can cause similar injuries and can involve more complex structures. The term whiplash has come to be used more generally for acceleration–deceleration injuries of the neck in all directions and in all types of road accident.

c.20 There are seven cervical vertebrae, supporting the head and protecting the spinal cord. The top two, the atlas and the axis, allow the movement of the head and are not usually implicated in whiplash injuries. The lower cervical vertebrae are similar in anatomy to the dorsal and lumbar vertebrae. There are also muscles and ligaments supporting the neck and head. Injuries to the neck can involve damage to the intervertebral discs or to the facet joints of the vertebrae but the great majority of whiplash-type injuries are acute sprains of the soft tissues. The disadvantage of this for legal proof is that there are no physical changes to be observed on x-ray or other imaging techniques and analysis depends on the report of symptoms. These injuries cause principally neck pain, neck stiffness and headache. Shoulder and arm symptoms are common, with numbness and tingling as a result of nerve involvement, and there is often back pain as well. The cervical spine supports the spinal cord leading into the brain stem and in some cases symptoms of brain damage such as vertigo, tinnitus, impaired memory, irritability or depression are seen.

c.21 A delay in onset is common. Many claimants have returned home after an accident believing that no serious injury has been sustained only to find significant neck pain developing over the next 24 hours or so. The absence of immediate hospital treatment or family doctor consultation must not be regarded as an indication that no significant injury was sustained. Most symptoms will have arisen within 48 to 72 hours.

In spite of the disturbing list of possible symptoms of whiplash injuries **c.22** noted above, most injuries are minor and show a full and fast recovery. One third of patients take no time off work; another third return to work within six weeks; nine out of ten return to work within a year. The great majority of neck injuries will completely recover within six to twelve months, and the most rapid recovery will be achieved within a year. There are, however, some cases of persistent symptoms. Further recovery, if there are still symptoms after two or three years from the accident, is unlikely but not impossible.

In spite of the frequency of neck sprain injuries, it seems that the medical **c.23** literature has neither provided a definitive account of the mechanism and cause of injury, nor identified the best treatment regime from a multitude of therapies undertaken for relief of symptoms, nor established a clear basis for deciding the likely prognosis, which remains variable and unpredictable until about two years after injury. Broadly speaking, it seems that well over half of neck-injured patients will have fully recovered within a year from injury and less than 10% have significant symptoms after three years. The facet joints, discs and ligaments are all liable to be implicated in serious injuries. It is better to apply ice than warmth to an injured neck because warmth may encourage internal bleeding. Pain killers and anti-inflammatory drugs are commonly prescribed. The benefits to be gained from a cervical collar are controversial and, as with back injuries, the trend of medical opinion seems to be towards encouraging as much gentle continuing use and movement as can be tolerated, and towards a growing acceptance of the benefits for some from chiropractic treatment.

X-ray of the neck will often show signs of degenerative changes in the cervical **c.24** spine, particularly in older people. These changes are not caused by traumatic injury (the *JSB Guidelines* are perhaps misleading on this) but may become symptomatic as a result of neck trauma. The terminology of osteoarthritis in the cervical spine or cervical spondylosis refers to this degenerative change. These signs are common in the general, symptom-free population. The presence of degenerative change does not mean that the patient was already doomed to suffer major neck pain in the near future. At the same time, neck pain is a common disorder, there is an increased risk of the onset of neck symptoms from whatever cause with increasing age and there is an association between the presence of degenerative change and a poorer prospect of recovery from a whiplash injury. Since the defendant must take the claimant as he finds him, the presence of pre-existing degenerative change may render the defendant liable for the poorer prospect of recovery. Against this, the opinion is often given that a traumatic accident injury has accelerated the onset of symptoms by a given number of years. In a case where the force of the impact was relatively slight it is an understandable view that the neck may have been in a condition where a similar relatively slight event stressing the neck might have resulted in similar symptoms not long afterwards if the accident in question had not done so. Doctors who express opinions on this issue are being forced by the demands of the legal system to guess about an issue which is incidental to medical practice and on which medical literature gives no sound help. A joint meeting under the Civil Procedure Rules almost invariable results in a compromise figure since issues of principle are rarely in dispute.

c.25 Whiplash injuries are sometimes categorized according to the Quebec classification:

0   No complaint about the neck. No physical signs.
I   Neck complaint of pain, stiffness, or tenderness only. No physical signs.
II Neck complaint and musculo-skeletal signs (musculo-skeletal signs include decreased range of motion and point tenderness).
III Neck complaint and neurological signs (neurological signs include decreased or absent deep tendon reflexes, weakness, and sensory deficits)
IV Neck complaint and fracture or dislocation.

c.26 Symptoms and disorders that can be manifested in all grades include deafness, dizziness, tinnitus, headache, memory loss, dysphagia, and temporomandibular joint pain.

c.27 The Quebec Task Force concluded in 1995 that many treatments provided little benefit, and in particular the use of a soft collar and resting tended to prolong symptoms in grade II and III injuries whereas analgesics and anti-inflammatory drugs, mobilization, exercise, and a quick return to work resulted in the best outcomes.

c.28 The *JSB Guidelines* for whiplash type neck injuries are:

(A) NECK INJURIES

c.29 There is a very wide range of neck injuries. Many are found in conjunction with back and shoulder problems.

At the highest level are injuries which shatter life and leave claimants very severely disabled. These may have a value of up to £85,000.

At the lowest level, claimants may suffer a minor strain, may not have time off work, and may suffer symptoms for a few weeks, justifying as little as £750.

(a) Severe

   (i) Neck injury associated with incomplete paraplegia or resulting in permanent spastic quadriparesis or where the injured person, despite wearing a collar 24 hours a day for a period of years, still has little or no movement in the neck and suffers severe headaches which have proved intractable.   **c.30**

        In the region of £82,000

  (ii) Injuries which give rise to disabilities which fall short of those in (a)(i) above but which are of considerable severity; for example, permanent damage to the brachial plexus.   **£36,000 to £71,500**

 (iii) Injuries causing severe damage to soft tissues and/or ruptured tendons. They result in significant disability of a permanent nature. The precise award depends on the length of time during which the most serious symptoms are ameliorated, and on the prognosis.   **In the region of £30,000**

 (iv) Injuries such as fractures or dislocations which cause severe immediate symptoms and which may necessitate spinal fusion. They leave markedly impaired function or vulnerability to further trauma, and some limitation of activities.   **£13,500 to £18,000**

(b) Moderate

   (i) Cases involving whiplash or wrenching-type injury and disc lesion of the more severe type resulting in cervical spondylosis, serious limitation of movement, permanent or recurring pain, stiffness or discomfort and the possible need for further surgery or increased vulnerability to further trauma.   **c.31**

        £7,500 to £13,750

  (ii) Injuries which may have exacerbated or accelerated some pre-existing unrelated condition. There will have been a complete recovery or recovery to 'nuisance' level from the effects of the accident within a few years. This bracket will also apply to moderate whiplash injuries where the period of recovery has been fairly protracted and where there remains an increased vulnerability to further trauma.   **£4,250 to £7,750**

(c) Minor

Minor soft tissue and whiplash injuries and the like where symptoms are moderate: **c.32**

   (i) and a full recovery takes place within about two years;   £2,500 to £4,250

  (ii) with a full recovery between a few weeks and a year.   £750 to £2,500

C. Back Injury

The back comprises the vertebrae of the spine below the neck, with 12 thoracic   **c.33** vertebrae in the relatively stiff structure of the chest where the spine is supported by the rib cage; five lumbar vertebrae with relatively greater freedom of forward and backward movement but relatively less rotation; and the fused vertebrae of the sacrum and coccyx. They are numbered from the top and referred to as T1, L4 and so on. The thoracic and sacral spines curve outwards (kyphosis) and the lumbar spine curves inwards (lordosis). The junctions between these sections at T12/L1 and L5/S1 are particularly susceptible to injury. Each vertebra comprises, at the anterior or front part of the vertebra, a solid vertebral body which bears most of the load, separated from the adjacent vertebrae by an inter-vertebral disc which acts as a shock absorber; transverse processes to each side surrounding a central vertical aperture, the vertebral canal, in which the spinal cord lies; and facet joints to the posterior or back part of the vertebra which control the movement and stability of the joint. The discs comprise a nucleus of an incompressible gel which dries out in old age, surrounded by an annulus of fibres laid rather like a radial car tyre. Bulging of the disc under load is normal and indeed represents the give under load that it is there to provide. A network of ligaments and muscles supports these structures.

c.34 Back pain is not fully explained in the medical literature. It is very common in the general population. When back pain follows after a fall or trip or an episode of heavy lifting it is occasionally possible to identify a clear physical cause such as the prolapse of a disc but far more often the precise cause and origin of pain remains unknown. There are many areas of medical uncertainty. For example, will trauma cause prolapse to a normal disc or will the disc usually have been in a damaged state beforehand? Extremely high loads would be needed to tear the annulus of a healthy disc. Can a disc be said to suffer a prolapse attributable to an episode of trauma if there has been a time delay of weeks or months?

c.35 Back pain is frequently associated with pain in one or both legs. This is a result of pressure on the nerves as they pass from the spinal cord through narrow apertures in the vertebrae, apertures which may be narrowed until the nerve is under pressure as a result of deformation of the joint, swelling of the disc or arthritic narrowing of the joint spaces.

c.36 The following treatment options may be encountered:

    (a) medication with analgesics and non-steroidal anti-inflammatory drugs;
    (b) injections of steroids into the facet joints or near nerve roots;
    (c) epidural injection of anaesthetic and steroid into the spinal canal;
    (d) nerve root block with injection of anaesthetic around a nerve root;
    (e) surgical decompression of the nerve roots in the spine;
    (f) manipulation under anaesthetic;
    (g) fusion of vertebrae together, or stabilisation of an unstable segment;
    (h) fixation with a rod or plate or by bone grafting;
    (i) discectomy for removal of part of a disc which is pressing on a nerve.

The assessment of back pain is particularly dependent on the subjective com- **c.37**
plaint made by the patient or claimant. Even where there are clear clinical signs,
the experience of pain and disability is highly variable. It is therefore a kind of
injury where insurers and, sometimes, judges particularly suspect that there may
be exaggerated complaints made in the context of a claim for compensation. A
large proportion of the cases where insurers resort to covert surveillance filming
is in cases of back injury where there is reason to think that the symptoms
complained of are surprising on the clinical signs, and surveillance provides
the only way of establishing the claimant's level of activity in daily life. To assist
in distinguishing these patients, Waddell, in 1980 and 1984, set out a series of
signs and symptoms which might indicate pain with no organic (physical)
cause. It is important to stress that these are not signs of malingering or
deliberate deception: complaints of pain may well be sincerely and genuinely
made. The seven Waddell symptoms of low back pain are:

(a) tail bone pain;
(b) whole leg pain—nerve root pain will affect only a segment of the leg and
    not the whole circumference;
(c) whole leg numbness;
(d) whole leg giving way;
(e) no pain free spells;
(f) intolerance and no response to any treatment;
(g) emergency admissions with simple backache.

These are complaints which would not be expected in a case where the symptoms are entirely caused by the physical effects of injury to the structures of the
back.

The seven Waddell signs or behavioural responses to examination are: **c.38**

(a) superficial tenderness—skin tender to light pinch over a wide area;
(b) non-anatomical tenderness—with no musculo-skeletal pattern;
(c) simulated test for axial loading—press on the top of the skull and this
    should not cause physical pain in the low back;
(d) simulated rotation—spinal rotation may well cause pain, but if the hands
    are held against the pelvis when the trunk is rotated with the shoulders
    and hips there is no true rotation and should be no physical cause of pain;
(e) distracted tests, comparing the range of movement under formal examin-
    ation with the movement observed at other times such as undressing; or
    in carrying out a test of straight leg raising;
(f) regional weakness—unexpectedly widespread weakness shown by a jerky
    giving way rather than steady resistance to pressure;
(g) regional sensory change—response to light touch over a body area
    inappropriate to the pattern of nerve distribution.

These are observations which are not consistent with what the examiner would expect in a case where the condition is entirely caused by the physical effects of injury to the structures of the back.

c.39 Care is needed in these tests to take account of the genuine impact of pain. For example, if straight leg raising (SLR) is limited on formal examination on the couch but more free on sitting up, part of the reason may be the change of aspect of the pelvis in sitting up and part may be through resistance after experiencing the pain of formal SLR testing on other occasions.

c.40 The *JSB Guidelines* for back injuries are:

c.41 Relatively few back injuries which do not give rise to paralysis command awards above about £25,000. In those that do there are special features.

(a) Severe

c.42
   (i) Cases of the most severe injury which do not involve paralysis but where there may be very serious consequences not normally found in cases of back injury, such as impotence or double incontinence.   **£55,000 to £93,000**

   (ii) Cases which have special features taking them outside any lower bracket applicable to orthopaedic injury to the back. Such features include impaired bladder and bowel function, severe sexual difficulties and unsightly scarring and the possibility of future surgery.   **In the region of £45,000**

   (iii) Cases of disc lesions or fractures of discs or of vertebral bodies where, despite treatment, there remain disabilities such as continuing severe pain and discomfort, impaired agility, impaired sexual function, depression, personality change, alcoholism, unemployability and the risk of arthritis.   **£21,500 to £38,000**

(b) Moderate

c.43
   (i) Cases where any residual disability is of less severity than that in (a)(iii) above. The bracket contains a wide variety of injuries. Examples are a case of a crush fracture of the lumbar vertebrae where there is a substantial risk of osteoarthritis and constant pain and discomfort with impairment of sexual function; that of a traumatic spondylolisthesis with continuous pain and a probability that spinal fusion will be necessary; or that of a prolapsed intervertebral disc with substantial acceleration of back degeneration.   **£15,250 to £21,500**

   (ii) Many frequently encountered injuries to the back such as disturbance of ligaments and muscles giving rise to backache, soft tissue injuries resulting in exacerbation of an existing back condition or prolapsed discs necessitating laminectomy or resulting in repeated relapses. The precise figure depends upon the severity of the original injury and/or whether there is some permanent or chronic disability.   **£6,750 to £15,250**

(c) Minor

Strains, sprains, disc prolapses and soft tissue injuries from which a   **c.44**
full recovery or recovery to 'nuisance' level has been made without
surgery:

    (i) within about five years;   £4,250 to £7,500
    (ii) within about two years.   Up to £4,250

D. Post-traumatic Stress Disorder

Involvement in a serious injury accident brings many causes of distress, anxiety   **c.45**
and upset: the injury itself, worry about money, the inconvenience of treatments, disruption to family life, demands placed on others for help and support
all make the period of recovery stressful and unhappy, and almost always are as a
matter of law excluded from compensation. A small number of victims may be
so badly affected that they suffer recognized psychiatric illness such as depression as a result of these problems. There are many mood disorders and anxiety
disorders which might be relevant to such a claim.

Post-traumatic stress disorder is a specific stress-related anxiety disorder   **c.46**
described in both DSM IV and ICD 10 which is of particular importance to
injury claims, first because it can be a serious consequence of involvement in a
terrifying accident, and secondly because it is a term which is sometimes used
too loosely to describe the non-specific occurrence of a psychological response
to involvement in a shocking event. An acute stress reaction is a short-lived
response to exceptional physical or mental stress which causes symptoms
of daze, depression, anxiety, anger, despair, overactivity, or withdrawal; however these symptoms will resolve, often within hours and certainly within a
few days. An adjustment disorder is a state of emotional distress in response to
a life change such as bereavement, usually suffered by those who have some
pre-existing vulnerability. A post-traumatic stress disorder is a normal response
to extreme trauma which can be long lasting and difficult to treat. It is
characterized by:

    (a) experience of a major traumatic event;
    (b) intrusive recollections, nightmares, or flashbacks of the event;
    (c) avoidance through numbness and emotional blunting;
    (d) increased arousal, startle response, insomnia, and hypervigilance;
    (e) onset within six months of the event, lasting at least one month;
    (f) clinically significant distress and impairment of functioning.

The passages of DSM IV dealing with 309.81 Posttraumatic Stress Disorder and
308.3 Acute Stress Disorder follow.

DSM IV ANXIETY DISORDERS

309.81 Posttraumatic Stress Disorder

Diagnostic Features

c.47 The essential feature of Posttraumatic Stress Disorder is the development of characteristic symptoms following exposure to an extreme traumatic stressor involving direct personal experience of an event that involves actual or threatened death or serious injury, or other threat to one's physical integrity; or witnessing an event that involves death, injury, or a threat to the physical integrity of another person; or learning about unexpected or violent death, serious harm, or threat of death or injury experienced by a family member or other close associate (Criterion A1). The person's response to the event must involve intense fear, helplessness, or horror (or in children, the response must involve disorganized or agitated behavior) (Criterion A2). The characteristic symptoms resulting from the exposure to the extreme trauma include persistent reexperiencing of the traumatic event (Criterion B), persistent avoidance of stimuli associated with the trauma and numbing of general responsiveness (Criterion C), and persistent symptoms of increased arousal (Criterion D). The full symptom picture must be present for more than 1 month (Criterion E), and the disturbance must cause clinically significant distress or impairment in social, occupational, or other important areas of functioning (Criterion F).

c.48 Traumatic events that are experienced directly include, hut are not limited to, military combat, violent personal assault (sexual assault, physical attack, robbery, mugging), being kidnapped, being taken hostage, terrorist attack, torture, incarceration as a prisoner of war or in a concentration camp, natural or manmade disasters, severe automobile accidents, or being diagnosed with a life-threatening illness. For children, sexually traumatic events may include developmentally inappropriate sexual experiences without threatened or actual violence or injury. Witnessed events include, but are not limited to, observing the serious injury or unnatural death of another person due to violent assault, accident, war, or disaster or unexpectedly witnessing a dead body or body parts. Events experienced by others that are learned about include, but are not limited to, violent personal assault, serious accident, or serious injury experienced by a family member or a close friend; learning about the sudden, unexpected death of a family member or a close friend; or learning that one's child has a life-threatening disease. The disorder may be especially severe or long lasting when the stressor is of human design (e.g., torture, rape). The likelihood of developing this disorder may increase as the intensity of and physical proximity to the stressor increase.

c.49 The traumatic event can be reexperienced in various ways. Commonly the person has recurrent and intrusive recollections of the event (Criterion B1) or recurrent distressing dreams during which the event is replayed (Criterion B2). In rare instances, the person experiences dissociative states that last from a few seconds to several hours, or even days, during which components of the event are relived and the person behaves as though experiencing the event at that moment (Criterion B3). Intense psychological distress (Criterion B4) or physiological reactivity (Criterion B5) often occurs when the person is exposed to triggering events that resemble or symbolize an aspect of the traumatic event (e.g., anniversaries of the traumatic event; cold, snowy weather or uniformed guards for survivors of death camps in cold climates; hot, humid weather for combat veterans of the South Pacific; entering any elevator for a woman who was raped in an elevator).

c.50 Stimuli associated with the trauma are persistently avoided. The person commonly makes deliberate efforts to avoid thoughts, feelings, or conversations about the traumatic event (Criterion C1) and to avoid activities, situations, or people who arouse recollections of it (Criterion C2). This avoidance of reminders may include amnesia for an important aspect of the traumatic event (Criterion C3). Diminished responsiveness to the external world, referred to as 'psychic numbing' or 'emotional anaesthesia,' usually begins soon after the traumatic event. The individual may complain of having markedly diminished interest or participation in previously enjoyed activities (Criterion C4), of feeling detached or estranged from other people (Criterion C5), or of having markedly reduced ability to feel emotions (especially those associated with intimacy, tenderness, and sexuality) (Criterion C6). The individual may have a sense of a foreshortened future (e.g., not expecting to have a career, marriage, children, or a normal life span) (Criterion C7).

The individual has persistent symptoms of anxiety or increased arousal that were not present before the trauma. These symptoms may include difficulty falling or staying asleep that may be due to recurrent nightmares during which the traumatic event is relived (Criterion D1), hypervigilance (Criterion D4), and exaggerated startle response (Criterion D5). Some individuals report irritability or outbursts of anger (Criterion D2) or difficulty concentrating or completing tasks (Criterion D3).

Specifiers

The following specifiers may be used to specify onset and duration of the symptoms of **c.51** Posttraumatic Stress Disorder:

Acute.   This specifier should be used when the duration of symptoms is less than 3 months.

Chronic.   This specifier should be used when the symptoms last 3 months or longer.

With Delayed Onset.   This specifier indicates that at least 6 months have passed between the traumatic event and the onset of the symptoms.

Associated Features and Disorders

Associated descriptive features and mental disorders.   Individuals with Posttraumatic Stress   **c.52** Disorder may describe painful guilt feelings about surviving when others did not survive or about the things they had to do to survive. Phobic avoidance of situations or activities that resemble or symbolize the original trauma may interfere with interpersonal relationships and lead to marital conflict, divorce, or loss of job. The following associated constellation of symptoms may occur and are more commonly seen in association with an interpersonal stressor (e.g., childhood sexual or physical abuse, domestic battering, being taken hostage, incarceration as a prisoner of war or in a concentration camp, torture): impaired affect modulation; self-destructive and impulsive behavior; dissociative symptoms; somatic complaints; feelings of ineffectiveness, shame, despair, or hopelessness; feeling permanently damaged; a loss of previously sustained beliefs; hostility; social withdrawal; feeling constantly threatened; impaired relationships with others; or a change from the individual's previous personality characteristics.

There may be increased risk of Panic Disorder, Agoraphobia, Obsessive-Compulsive Disorder, Social Phobia, Specific Phobia, Major Depressive Disorder, Somatization Disorder, and Substance-Related Disorders. It is not known to what extent these disorders precede or follow the onset of Posttraumatic Stress Disorder.

Associated laboratory findings.   Increased arousal may be measured through studies of autonomic functioning (e.g., heart rate, electromyography, sweat gland activity).

Associated physical examination findings and general medical conditions.   General medical conditions may occur as a consequence of the trauma (e.g., head injury, burns).

Specific Culture and Age Features

Individuals who have recently emigrated from areas of considerable social unrest and civil conflict   **c.53** may have elevated rates of Posttraumatic Stress Disorder. Such individuals may be especially reluctant to divulge experiences of torture and trauma due to their vulnerable political immigrant status. Specific assessments of traumatic experiences and concomitant symptoms are needed for such individuals.

In younger children, distressing dreams of the event may, within several weeks, change into generalized nightmares of monsters, of rescuing others, or of threats to self or others. Young children usually do not have the sense that they are reliving the past; rather, the reliving of the trauma may occur through repetitive play (e.g., a child who was involved in a serious automobile accident repeatedly reenacts car crashes with toy cars). Because it may be difficult for children to report diminished interest in significant activities and constriction of affect, these symptoms should be carefully evaluated with reports from parents, teachers, and other observers. In children, the sense of a foreshortened future may be evidenced by the belief that life will be too short to include becoming an adult. There may also be 'omen formation'—that is, belief in an ability to foresee future untoward events. Children may also exhibit various physical symptoms, such as stomachaches and headaches.

Prevalence

c.54 Community-based studies reveal a lifetime prevalence for Posttraumatic Stress Disorder ranging from 1% to 14%, with the variability related to methods of ascertainment and the population sampled. Studies of at-risk individuals (e.g., combat veterans, victims of volcanic eruptions or criminal violence) have yielded prevalence rates ranging from 3% to 58%.

Course

c.55 Posttraumatic Stress Disorder can occur at any age, including childhood. Symptoms usually begin within the first 3 months after the trauma, although there may be a delay of months, or even years, before symptoms appear. Frequently, the disturbance initially meets criteria for Acute Stress Disorder in the immediate aftermath of the trauma. The symptoms of the disorder and the relative predominance of reexperiencing, avoidance, and hyperarousal symptoms may vary over time. Duration of the symptoms varies, with complete recovery occurring within 3 months in approximately half of cases, with many others having persisting symptoms for longer than 12 months after the trauma.

The severity, duration, and proximity of an individual's exposure to the traumatic event are the most important factors affecting the likelihood of developing this disorder. There is some evidence that social supports, family history, childhood experiences, personality variables, and preexisting mental disorders may influence the development of Posttraumatic Stress Disorder. This disorder can develop in individuals without any predisposing conditions, particularly if the stressor is especially extreme.

Differential Diagnosis

c.56 In Posttraumatic Stress Disorder, the stressor must be of an extreme (i.e., life-threatening) nature. In contrast, in **Adjustment Disorder**, the stressor can be of any severity. The diagnosis of Adjustment Disorder is appropriate both for situations in which the response to an extreme stressor does not meet the criteria for Posttraumatic Stress Disorder (or another specific mental disorder) and for situations in which the symptom pattern of Posttraumatic Stress Disorder occurs in response to a stressor that is not extreme (e.g., spouse leaving, being fired).

Not all psychopathology that occurs in individuals exposed to an extreme stressor should necessarily be attributed to Posttraumatic Stress Disorder. **Symptoms of avoidance, numbing, and increased arousal that are present before exposure to the stressor** do not meet criteria for the diagnosis of Posttraumatic Stress Disorder and require consideration of other diagnoses (e.g., a Mood Disorder or another Anxiety Disorder). Moreover, if the symptom response pattern to the extreme stressor meets criteria for **another mental disorder** (e.g., Brief Psychotic Disorder,

Conversion Disorder, Major Depressive Disorder), these diagnoses should be given instead of, or in addition to, Posttraumatic Stress Disorder.

Acute Stress Disorder is distinguished from Posttraumatic Stress Disorder because the symp- **c.57** tom pattern in Acute Stress Disorder must occur within 4 weeks of the traumatic event and resolve within that 4-week period. If the symptoms persist for more than 1 month and meet criteria for Posttraumatic Stress Disorder, the diagnosis is changed from Acute Stress Disorder to Posttraumatic Stress Disorder.

In **Obsessive-Compulsive Disorder**, there are recurrent intrusive thoughts, but these are experienced as inappropriate and are not related to an experienced traumatic event. Flashbacks in Posttraumatic Stress Disorder must be distinguished from illusions, hallucinations, and other perceptual disturbances that may occur in **Schizophrenia, other Psychotic Disorders, Mood Disorder With Psychotic Features,** a **delirium, Substance-Induced Disorders**, and **Psychotic Disorders Due to a General Medical Condition**.

Malingering should be ruled out in those situations in which financial remuneration, benefit **c.58** eligibility, and forensic determinations play a role.

• Diagnostic criteria for 309.81 Posttraumatic Stress Disorder.

A. The person has been exposed to a traumatic event in which both of the following were present:
(1) the person experienced, witnessed, or was confronted with an event or events that involved actual or threatened death or serious injury, or a threat to the physical integrity of self or others
(2) the person's response involved intense fear, helplessness, or horror. **Note:** In children, this may be expressed instead by disorganized or agitated behavior

B. The traumatic event is persistently reexperienced in one (or more) of the following ways:
(1) recurrent and intrusive distressing recollections of the event, including images, thoughts, or perceptions. **Note:** In young children, repetitive play may occur in which themes or aspects of the trauma are expressed.
(2) recurrent distressing dreams of the event. **Note:** In children, there may be frightening dreams without recognizable content.
(3) acting or feeling as if the traumatic event were recurring (includes a sense of reliving the experience, illusions, hallucinations, and dissociative flashback episodes, including those that occur on awakening or when intoxicated). **Note:** In young children, trauma-specific reenactment may occur.
(4) intense psychological distress at exposure to internal or external cues that symbolize or resemble an aspect of the traumatic event
(5) physiological reactivity on exposure to internal or external cues that symbolize or resemble an aspect of the traumatic event

C. Persistent avoidance of stimuli associated with the trauma and numbing of general responsiveness (not present before the trauma), as indicated by three (or more) of the following:
(1) efforts to avoid thoughts, feelings, or conversations associated with the trauma
(2) efforts to avoid activities, places, or people that arouse recollections of the trauma
(3) inability to recall an important aspect of the trauma
(4) markedly diminished interest or participation in significant activities
(5) feeling of detachment or estrangement from others
(6) restricted range of affect (e.g., unable to have loving feelings)
(7) sense of a foreshortened future (e.g., does not expect to have a career, marriage, children, or a normal life span)

c.59   D. Persistent symptoms of increased arousal (not present before the trauma), as indicated by two (or more) of the following:

    (1) difficulty falling or staying asleep

    (2) irritability or outbursts of anger

    (3) difficulty concentrating

    (4) hypervigilance

    (5) exaggerated startle response

E. Duration of the disturbance (symptoms in Criteria B, C, and D) is more than 1 month.

F. The disturbance causes clinically significant distress or impairment in social, occupational, or other important areas of functioning.

Specify if:

Acute: if duration of symptoms is less than 3 months

Chronic: if duration of symptoms is 3 months or more

Specify if:

With Delayed Onset: if onset of symptoms is at least 6 months after the stressor

308.3 Acute Stress Disorder

Diagnostic Features

c.60   The essential feature of Acute Stress Disorder is the development of characteristic anxiety, dissociative, and other symptoms that occurs within 1 month after exposure to an extreme traumatic stressor (Criterion A). For a discussion of the types of stressors involved, see the description of Posttraumatic Stress Disorder. Either while experiencing the traumatic event or after the event, the individual has at least three of the following dissociative symptoms: a subjective sense of numbing, detachment, or absence of emotional responsiveness; a reduction in awareness of his or her surroundings; derealization; depersonalization; or dissociative amnesia (Criterion B). Following the trauma, the traumatic event is persistently reexperienced (Criterion C), and the individual displays marked avoidance of stimuli that may arouse recollections of the trauma (Criterion D) and has marked symptoms of anxiety or increased arousal (Criterion E). The symptoms must cause clinically significant distress, significantly interfere with normal functioning, or impair the individual's ability to pursue necessary tasks (Criterion F). The disturbance lasts for at least 2 days and does not persist beyond 4 weeks after the traumatic event (Criterion G). The symptoms are not due to the direct physiological effects of a substance (i.e., a drug of abuse, a medication) or a general medical condition, are not better accounted for by Brief Psychotic Disorder, and are not merely an exacerbation of a preexisting mental disorder (Criterion H).

c.61   As a response to the traumatic event, the individual develops dissociative symptoms. Individuals with Acute Stress Disorder have a decrease in emotional responsiveness, often finding it difficult or impossible to experience pleasure in previously enjoyable activities, and frequently feel guilty about pursuing usual life tasks. They may experience difficulty concentrating, feel detached from their bodies, experience the world as unreal or dreamlike, or have increasing difficulty recalling specific details of the traumatic event (dissociative amnesia). In addition, at least one symptom from each of the symptom clusters required for Posttraumatic Stress Disorder is present. First, the traumatic event is persistently reexperienced (e.g., recurrent recollections, images, thoughts, dreams, illusions, flashback episodes, a sense of reliving the event, or distress on exposure to reminders of the event). Second, reminders of the trauma (e.g., places, people, activities) are avoided. Finally, hyperarousal in response to stimuli reminiscent of the trauma is present (e.g., difficulty sleeping, irritability, poor concentration, hypervigilance, an exaggerated startle response, and motor restlessness).

Associated Features and Disorders

c.62   **Associated descriptive features and mental disorders.**   Symptoms of despair and hopelessness may be experienced in Acute Stress Disorder and may be sufficiently severe and persistent to meet criteria for a Major Depressive Episode, in which case an additional diagnosis of Major Depressive Disorder may be warranted. If the trauma led to another's death or to serious injury, survivors may feel guilt about having remained intact or about not providing enough help to others. Individuals with this disorder often perceive themselves to have greater responsibility for the consequences of the trauma than is warranted. Problems may result from the individual's neglect of basic health and safety needs associated with the aftermath of the trauma. Individuals with this disorder are at increased risk for the development of Posttraumatic Stress Disorder. Impulsive and risk-taking behavior may occur after the trauma.

Associated physical examination findings and general medical conditions.   General medical **c.63** conditions may occur as a consequence of the trauma (e.g., head injury, burns).

Specific Culture Features

Although some events are likely to be universally experienced as traumatic, the severity and **c.64** pattern of response may be modulated by cultural differences in the implications of loss. There may also be culturally prescribed coping behaviors that are characteristic of particular cultures. For example, dissociative symptoms may be a more prominent part of the acute stress response in cultures in which such behaviors are sanctioned. For further discussion of cultural factors related to traumatic events.

Prevalence

The prevalence of Acute Stress Disorder in a population exposed to a serious traumatic stress **c.65** depends on the severity and persistence of the trauma and the degree of exposure to it.

Course

Symptoms of Acute Stress Disorder are experienced during or immediately after the trauma, last **c.66** for at least 2 days, and either resolve within 4 weeks after the conclusion of the traumatic event or the diagnosis is changed. When symptoms persist beyond 1 month, a diagnosis of Posttraumatic Stress Disorder may be appropriate if the full criteria for Posttraumatic Stress Disorder are met. The severity, duration, and proximity of an individual's exposure to the traumatic event are the most important factors in determining the likelihood of development of Acute Stress Disorder. There is some evidence that social supports, family history, childhood experience, personality variables, and preexisting mental disorders may influence the development of Acute Stress Disorder. This disorder can develop in individuals without any predisposing conditions, particularly if the stressor is especially extreme.

Differential Diagnosis

Some symptomatology following exposure to an extreme stress is ubiquitous and often does not **c.67** require any diagnosis. Acute Stress Disorder should only be considered if the symptoms last at least 2 days and cause clinically significant distress or impairment in social, occupational, or other important areas of functioning or impair the individual's ability to pursue some necessary task (e.g., obtaining necessary assistance or mobilizing personal resources by telling family members about the traumatic experience).

Acute Stress Disorder must be distinguished from a **Mental Disorder Due to a General Medical Condition** (e.g., head trauma) and from a **Substance-Induced Disorder** (e.g., related to Alcohol Intoxication), which may be common consequences of exposure to an extreme stressor. In some individuals, psychotic symptoms may occur following an extreme stressor. In such cases, **Brief Psychotic Disorder** is diagnosed instead of Acute Stress Disorder. If a **Major Depressive Episode** develops after the trauma, a diagnosis of Major Depressive Disorder should be considered in addition to a diagnosis of Acute Stress Disorder. A separate diagnosis of Acute Stress Disorder should not be made if the symptoms are an **exacerbation of a preexisting mental disorder.**

By definition, a diagnosis of Acute Stress Disorder is appropriate only for symptoms that occur within 1 month of the extreme stressor. Because **Posttraumatic Stress Disorder** requires more than 1 month of symptoms, this diagnosis cannot be made during this initial 1-month period. For individuals with the diagnosis of Acute Stress Disorder whose symptoms persist for longer than 1 month, the diagnosis of Posttraumatic Stress Disorder should be considered. For individuals who have an extreme stressor but who develop a symptom pattern that does not meet criteria for Acute Stress Disorder, a diagnosis of **Adjustment Disorder** should be considered.

Malingering must be ruled out in those situations in which financial remuneration, benefit eligibility, or forensic determinations play a role.

c.68 • **Diagnostic criteria for 308.3 Acute Stress Disorder**

A. The person has been exposed to a traumatic event in which both of the following were present:
(1) the person experienced, witnessed, or was confronted with an event or events that involved actual or threatened death or serious injury, or a threat to the physical integrity of self or others
(2) the person's response involved intense fear, helplessness, or horror

B. Either while experiencing or after experiencing the distressing event, the individual has three (or more) of the following dissociative symptoms:
(1) a subjective sense of numbing, detachment, or absence of emotional responsiveness
(2) a reduction in awareness of his or her surroundings (e.g., 'being in a daze')
(3) derealization
(4) depersonalization
(5) dissociative amnesia (i.e., inability to recall an important aspect of the trauma)

C. The traumatic event is persistently reexperienced in at least one of the following ways; recurrent images, thoughts, dreams, illusions, flashback episodes, or a sense of reliving the experience; or distress on exposure to reminders of the traumatic event.

D. Marked avoidance of stimuli that arouse recollection of the trauma (e.g., thoughts, feelings, conversations, activities, places, people).

E. Marked symptoms of anxiety or increased arousal (e.g., difficulty sleeping, irritability, poor concentration, hypervigilance, exaggerated startle response, motor restlessness).

F. The disturbance causes clinically significant distress or impairment in social, occupational, or other important areas of functioning or impairs the individual's ability to pursue some necessary task, such as obtaining necessary assistance or mobilizing personal resources by telling family members about the traumatic experience.

G. The disturbance lasts for a minimum of 2 days and a maximum of 4 weeks and occurs within 4 weeks of the traumatic event.

H. The disturbance is not due to the direct physiological effects of a substance (e.g., a drug of abuse, a medication) or a general medical condition, is not better accounted for by Brief Psychotic Disorder, and is not merely an exacerbation of a preexisting Axis I or Axis II disorder.

c.69 The *JSB Guidelines* for post-traumatic stress disorder are set out below:

c.70 Cases within this category are exclusively those where there is a specific diagnosis of a reactive psychiatric disorder in which characteristic symptoms are displayed following a psychologically distressing event which was outside the range of normal human experience and which would be markedly distressing to almost anyone. The guide-lines below have been compiled by reference to cases which variously reflect the criteria established in the 4th edition of *Diagnostic and Statistical Manual of Mental Disorders* (DSM-IV-TR). The symptoms affect basic functions such as breathing, pulse rate and bowel and/or bladder control. They also involve persistent re-experience of the relevant event, difficulty in controlling temper, in concentrating and sleeping, and exaggerated startle response.

(a) Severe   £34,000 to £55,000

c.71

Such cases will involve permanent effects which prevent the injured person from working at all or at least from functioning at anything approaching the pre-trauma level. All aspects of the life of the injured person will be badly affected.

(b) Moderately Severe   £12,500 to £31,750

c.72

This category is distinct from (a) above because of the better prog-nosis which will be for some recovery with professional help. However, the effects are still likely to cause significant disability for the foreseeable future. While there are awards which support both extremes of this bracket, the majority are between £20,000 and £25,000.

(c) Moderate   £4,500 to £12,500

c.73

In these cases the injured person will have largely recovered and any continuing effects will not be grossly disabling.

(d) Minor   £2,150 to £4,500

c.74

In these cases a virtually full recovery will have been made within one to two years and only minor symptoms will persist over any longer period.

E. Illness Behaviour

The reason for the growth of surveillance video filming is the extreme difficulty **c.75** of establishing the nature of a claimant's condition when the symptoms complained of are not congruent with the clinical signs. It has come to be increasingly accepted that the simple proposition that there is no identified organic basis for symptoms does not mean that the claimant is telling an untruth in complaining of the symptoms, either by deliberately exaggerating or by malingering. On the contrary, the psychological consequences of suffering pain can include the experience of genuinely felt pain and genuinely suffered restrictions and disability without an identifiable physical cause. These symp-toms are felt just as acutely as direct pain with an obvious physical cause, and the claimant is just as much entitled to be compensated for them since, once some injury is foreseeable, the law is clear that the defendant is liable for the full extent of the actual injury sustained, however unforeseeable in extent.

c.76 Anger and distress are common feelings after suffering an accident which was entirely the fault of someone else and finding that the consequence is a persisting painful injury. It is asking a great deal of a claimant, who is examined by a medico-legal specialist on his own behalf under instruction from his lawyer, that he should not omit any significant complaint, that he should steer the exact path of truth, neither doing himself an injustice by omitting or understating any symptom, nor incurring the suspicion of exaggeration by overstatement, and all in explaining a condition that may be quite variable in severity from day to day. When seen by the opposing side's consultant the uncertainty is compounded by a fear of distrust and joint instruction of a single expert, while reducing the number of appointments, places greater significance on this one opportunity and does not remove these human difficulties.

c.77 A good medico-legal specialist will of course be well aware of these concerns and able to take them into account, as will a wise judge. None the less, cases will arise where there is clear evidence of non-organic symptoms. True malingering is thought to be very rare. It is very difficult to establish without evidence of marked inconsistency, either from video evidence or from alternative sources of evidence such as examinations carried out for other purposes or factual evidence of occasions of inconsistent behaviour. Correspondingly, the occurrence of psychological damage as a component in the consequences of an upsetting accident has been more widely recognized. Symptoms may include mood disturbance, flashbacks, nightmares, travel anxiety, panic attacks, and irritability. Intractable pain, loss of employment, and financial hardship can all contribute to the onset of depression. If there is contested litigation of high significance to the prospects for the future, that in itself can be extremely stressful. There has also been an increasing acceptance that it is common for entirely truthful claimants to complain of non-specific symptoms with no obvious physical cause. This is partly because of the variability of reactions to injury between individuals and partly the effects of the range of stress factors identified above.

c.78 Some cases of unexplained persistent pain call for psychiatric examination. There is a range of psychiatric conditions involving complaints of genuinely felt physical symptoms with no ascertainable physical cause. The terminology is variable. The current favoured term is somatoform disorder but this may also be described as a conversion disorder, dissociative disorder or hysteria. These illnesses are too infrequent to be considered here in detail.

c.79 The *JSB Guidelines* for chronic pain follow:

c.80 (a) **Chronic Pain Syndrome**

(i)	Severe	£23,000 to £35,000
(ii)	Moderate	£6,000 to £18,000

(b) **Fibromyalgia**   £19,000 to £35,000

(c) **Chronic Fatigue Syndrome**   In the region of £27,500

(d) **Reflex Sympathetic Dystrophy**   **c.81**
(Also called complex regional pain syndrome)

    (i)   Severe   £28,000 to £55,000
    (ii) Moderate   £14,000 to £21,000

(e) **Somatoform Disorder**   In the region of £25,000

d

NOTES ON SOME OCCUPATIONAL DISEASES

Many personal injury claims arise from a single traumatic event such as a road **d.01** accident or an accident at work. Some claims however arise from circumstances, usually at work, which result in the onset of disease. There are no special principles of law which apply to these cases, and in each case liability will turn on establishing negligence or a breach of regulatory duty; negligence will require proof of a failure to take reasonable care to protect against a foreseeable harm, and causation and damage must be proved. There are particular problems that arise in disease cases. Diseases such as deafness or wrist tenosynovitis occur frequently in the general population and an association with conditions of work cannot simply be inferred from the occurrence of the illness. The time limit for a claim is more likely to be a difficulty since a disease may be developing for some time before it becomes serious enough for a sufferer to contemplate a claim for compensation. This chapter covers: deafness; repetitive strain injury; vibration white finger; dermatitis; occupational asthma; other lung disease; occupational stress.

A. Deafness

The normal range of frequencies heard by a young person is from 20 to 20,000 **d.02** Hz (0.02 to 20 Khz). The measurement of Hertz is of cycles per second. The most sensitive hearing, and the most practically important range of sounds, is from 1 to 5 Khz. The intensity of sound is measured in decibels. The scale reflects a logarithmic increase so that a doubling of the intensity results in a 3 decibel increase. This means that at high levels an apparently modest increase in the number of decibels represents a substantial increase in the intensity of sound. Ordinary conversation will be at a level of about 60dB(A) and the threshold of pain is at about 130dB(A). The reference (A) is to a system of filtering in the machine measurement of noise levels for the sake of accuracy: A-weighted measurements are those generally used in the measurement of noise exposure. Hearing loss is a result not simply of the peak level of noise experienced but also the duration and relentlessness of the noise exposure. Occupational exposure is therefore measured by the exposure averaged over an eight-hour working day.

d.03 The current regime for regulating exposure is the Noise at Work Regulations 1989. The regulations require noise assessments to be undertaken, and recognize two action levels of exposure, a first action level of a daily personal noise exposure of 85dB(A) and a second action level of 90dB(A), and a peak action level of exposure at 200 pascals peak sound pressure. Broadly 85dB(A) is accepted as the level at which sensitive individuals may suffer hearing loss and 90dB(A) is the level at which damage is likely even to robust individuals. At the action levels, personal ear protectors must be provided and ear protection zones must be established. In addition to the specific requirements, there is a general duty under reg 6 to reduce the risk of hearing damage to the lowest level reasonably practicable. It is unrealistic to expect a lawyer to manage the computations of the exposure levels: that this is a matter for experienced expert noise engineers is demonstrated by the Schedule to the 1989 Regulations setting out the formidable calculations of daily and weekly average exposure.

d.04 Old age also causes a gradual hearing loss and it is sometimes the combined effect of occupational exposure and constitutional hearing loss that results in a practical handicap. A history of work in noisy conditions is not itself conclusive of causation and in every case testing by audiometry is essential. A 'notch' of increased hearing loss at around 4 kHz on both sides is strongly characteristic of noise induced hearing loss, but is not decisive. There is no certain medical test that can distinguish noise exposure cases, and attribution depends on establishing a probable causal link from a typical and consistent measured hearing loss and a history of noise exposure. It is therefore essential in every case to consider the life history of the complainant with regard to exposure to noise. Someone who has been exposed to gunfire while serving in the armed forces in his youth, or has frequently attended dances or parties with very loud music, will find it more difficult to attribute hearing loss to a later period of work in a noisy factory. As a working rule, a handicap from hearing loss will arise if the average loss over frequencies 0.5, 1, 2 and 3 kHz is 30dB(HL) or more. There is a British Standard BS 5330 (1976) for the measurement of hearing loss, but current assessments are usually standardized in terms of the *Coles, King, Lutman & Robinson Guidelines* (1992) known as the 'Black Book' or the previous guidance from the British Association of Otorhinolaryngologists (working name ENT·UK [BAO–HNS]) known as the 'Blue Book' (1982).

Hearing loss is frequently associated with tinnitus, a constant noise in the ear. **d.05** Although hearing aids can relieve hearing loss there is no medical remedy for tinnitus except counselling and in severe cases it can be a most distressing affliction.

Many cases arise out of exposure going back before the commencement of the **d.06** 1989 Regulations on 1 January 1990. A particular difficulty is to obtain evidence of the noise levels at the time of the exposure complained of. A date of 1963 is the point at which a reasonably prudent employer should have been aware that noise exposure may result in deafness. This has been taken from the publication in that year of a government booklet 'Noise and the Worker' and 1963 was adopted as the relevant date in the leading case of *Thompson v Smiths Ship Repairers* (see below). However, there have been cases of liability for earlier exposure where disclosure of records has shown that the employer was actually aware of the risk at an earlier date. In addition, a Code of Practice for Reducing the Exposure of Employed Persons to Noise was published in 1972.

A failure by the employee to wear the hearing protection that is provided for **d.07** him may lead to a supplementary allegation of a failure to provide instruction and training required by reg 11, but may also amount to contributory negligence and a breach of the employee's own duty under reg 10(2).

Thompson v Smiths Ship Repairers [1984] 1 All ER 881   This case concerned **d.08** a series of claims for deafness caused by work in shipyards. Mustill J held that 1963 marked the point at which an employer became in breach of duty for failing to provide effective ear protection. The judgment includes a full account of relevant principles about hearing loss.

Ali v Courtaulds Textiles [1999] Lloyd's Rep Med 301   Limitation: as soon as **d.09** it was suggested to the claimant that his deafness might be attributable to his work in the defendant's factory he consulted a solicitor and eight months later received an expert medical opinion supporting attribution. He did not have 'knowledge' for the purpose of s 14 of the Limitation Act 1980 until the medical report was received.

Bragg v Ford Motor Co. [1992] PIQR Q72   In a 47-year-old man, loss of **d.10** hearing and tinnitus sufficient to interfere with normal conversation and disturb sleep; award £11,000, the equivalent of about £13,500 now.

(Numerous claims against Ford Motor Co. in two actions are reported in *Kemp & Kemp* at D3-015 and D3-021.)

d.11 The *JSB Guidelines* for deafness are reproduced below.

d.12 The word 'deafness' is used to embrace total and partial hearing loss. In assessing awards for hearing loss regard must be had to the following:

  (i) whether the injury is one that has an immediate effect, allowing no opportunity to adapt, or whether it occurred over a period of time, as in noise exposure cases;

  (ii) whether the injury or disability is one which the injured person suffered at an early age so that it has had or will have an effect on his or her speech, or is one that is suffered in later life;

  (iii) whether the injury or disability affects balance;

  (iv) in cases of noise-induced hearing loss (NIHL) age is of particular relevance as noted in paragraph (d) below.

(a) Total Deafness and Loss of Speech	£60,000 to £77,000

d.13 Such cases arise, for example, where deafness has occurred at an early age (for example, rubella infection) so as to prevent or seriously to affect the development of normal speech.

(b) Total Deafness	£50,000 to £60,000

d.14 The lower end of the bracket is appropriate for cases where there is no speech deficit or tinnitus. The higher end is appropriate for cases involving both of these.

(c) Total Loss of Hearing in One Ear	£17,500 to £25,000

d.15 Cases will tend towards the higher end of the bracket where there are associated problems, such as tinnitus, dizziness or headaches.

(d) Partial Hearing Loss/Tinnitus

d.16 This category covers the bulk of deafness cases which usually result from exposure to noise over a prolonged period. The disability is not to be judged simply by the degree of hearing loss; there is often a degree of tinnitus present. Age is particularly relevant because impairment of hearing affects most people in the fullness of time and impacts both upon causation and upon valuation.

(i) Severe tinnitus/hearing loss.	£16,000 to £25,000
(ii) Moderate tinnitus/hearing loss.	£8,000 to £16,000
(iii) Mild tinnitus with some hearing loss.	£6,750 to £8,000
(iv) Slight or occasional tinnitus with slight hearing loss.	£4,000 to £6,750

NOISE AT WORK REGULATIONS 1989

1. Citation and commencement

d.17 These Regulations may be cited as the Noise at Work Regulations 1989 and shall come into force on 1st January 1990.

2. Interpretation

d.18 (1) In these Regulations, unless the context otherwise requires—

'daily personal noise exposure' means the level of daily personal noise exposure of an employee ascertained in accordance with Part I of the Schedule to these Regulations, but taking no account of the effect of any personal ear protector used;

'exposed' means exposed whilst at work, and 'exposure' shall be construed accordingly;

'the first action level' means a daily personal noise exposure of 85dB(A);

'the peak action level' means a level of peak sound pressure of 200 pascals;

'the second action level' means a daily personal noise exposure of 90dB(A).

(2) In these Regulations, unless the context otherwise requires, any reference to—

(a) an employer includes a reference to a self-employed person and any duty imposed by these Regulations on an employer in respect of his employees shall extend to a self-employed person in respect of himself;

(b) an employee includes a reference to a self-employed person;

and where any duty is placed by these Regulations on an employer in respect of his employees, that employer shall, so far as is reasonably practicable, be under a like duty in respect of any other person at work who may be affected by the work carried on by him.

4. Assessment of exposure

(1) Every employer shall, when any of his employees is likely to be exposed to the first action level or above or to the peak action level or above, ensure that a competent person makes a noise assessment which is adequate for the purposes— **d.19**

(a) of identifying which of his employees are so exposed; and

(b) of providing him with such information with regard to the noise to which those employees may be exposed as will facilitate compliance with his duties under regulations 7, 8, 9 and 11.

(2) The noise assessment required by paragraph (1) shall be reviewed when—

(a) there is reason to suspect that the assessment is no longer valid; or

(b) there has been a significant change in the work to which the assessment relates;

and, where as a result of the review changes in the assessment are required, those changes shall be made.

5. Assessment records

Following any noise assessment made pursuant to regulation 4(1), the employer shall ensure that an adequate record of that assessment, and of any review thereof carried out pursuant to regulation 4(2), is kept until a further noise assessment is made pursuant to regulation 4(1). **d.20**

6. Reduction of risk of hearing damage

Every employer shall reduce the risk of damage to the hearing of his employees from exposure to noise to the lowest level reasonably practicable. **d.21**

7. Reduction of noise exposure

Every employer shall, when any of his employees is likely to be exposed to the second action level or above or to the peak action level or above, reduce, so far as is reasonably practicable (other than by the provision of personal ear protectors), the exposure to noise of that employee. **d.22**

8. Ear protection

(1) Every employer shall ensure, so far as is practicable, that when any of his employees is likely to be exposed to the first action level or above in circumstances where the daily personal noise exposure of that employee is likely to be less than 90dB(A), that employee is provided, at his request, with suitable and efficient personal ear protectors. **d.23**

(2) Every employer shall ensure, so far as is practicable, that when any of his employees is likely to be exposed to the second action level or above or to the peak action level or above, that employee is provided with suitable personal ear protectors which, when properly worn, can reasonably be expected to keep the risk of damage to that employee's hearing to below that arising from exposure to the second action level or, as the case may be, to the peak action level.

(3) Any personal ear protectors provided by virtue of this regulation shall comply with any enactment (whether in an Act or instrument) which implements in Great Britain any provision on design or manufacture with respect to health or safety in any relevant Community directive listed in Schedule 1 to the Personal Protective Equipment at Work Regulations 1992 which is applicable to those ear protectors.

9. Ear protection zones

d.24   (1) Every employer shall, in respect of any premises under his control, ensure, so far as is reasonably practicable; that—

(a) each ear protection zone is demarcated and identified by means of the sign specified [for the purpose of indicating 'ear protection must be worn' in paragraph 3.3 of Part II of Schedule 1 to the Health and Safety (Safety Signs and Signals) Regulations 1996 (SI 1996/341)] which sign shall include such text as indicates—

(i) that it is an ear protection zone, and

(ii) the need for his employees to wear personal ear protectors whilst in any such zone; and

(b) none of his employees enters any such zone unless that employee is wearing personal ear protectors.

(2) In this regulation, 'ear protection zone' means any part of the premises referred to in paragraph (1) where any employee is likely to be exposed to the second action level or above or to the peak action level or above,

10. Maintenance and use of equipment

d.25   (1) Every employer shall—

(a) ensure, so far as is practicable, that anything provided by him to or for the benefit of an employee in compliance with his duties under these Regulations (other than personal ear protectors provided pursuant to regulation 8(1) is fully and properly used; and

(b) ensure, so far as is practicable, that anything provided by him in compliance with his duties under these Regulations is maintained in an efficient state, in efficient working order and in good repair.

(2) Every employee shall, so far as is practicable, fully and properly use personal ear protectors when they are provided by his employer pursuant to regulation 8(2) and any other protective measures provided by his employer in compliance with his duties under these Regulations; and, if the employee discovers any defect therein, he shall report it forthwith to his employer.

11. Provision of information to employees

d.26   Every employer shall, in respect of any premises under his control, provide each of his employees who is likely to be exposed to the first action level or above or to the peak action level or above with adequate information, instruction and training on—

(a) the risk of damage to that employee's hearing that such exposure may cause;

(b) what steps that employee can take to minimize that risk;

(c) the steps that that employee must take in order to obtain the personal ear protectors referred to in regulation 8(1); and

(d) that employee's obligations under these Regulations.

[12. **Modification of duties of manufacturers etc of articles for use at work and articles of**   **d.27**
fairground equipment**]

[13. **Exemptions**]

[14. **Modifications relating to the Ministry of Defence etc**]

SCHEDULE

PART I

DAILY PERSONAL NOISE EXPOSURE OF EMPLOYEES

[7.4222] The daily personal noise exposure of an employee ($L_{EP,d}$) is expressed in dB(A) and is   **d.28**
ascertained using the formula:

$$L_{EP,d} = 10 \log_{10} \left\{ \frac{1}{T} \int_0^{T_e} \left[\frac{P_A(t)}{P_0} \right]^2 dt \right\}$$

where—

T_e = the duration of the person's personal exposure to sound;

T_0 = 8 hours = 28,800 seconds;

P_0 = 20 µPa; and

$P_A(t)$ = the time-varying value of A—weighted instantaneous sound pressure in pascals in the
undisturbed field in air at atmospheric pressure to which the person is exposed (in the locations
occupied during the day), or the pressure of the disturbed field adjacent to the person's head
adjusted to provide a notional equivalent undisturbed field pressure.

PART II

WEEKLY AVERAGE OF DAILY PERSONAL NOISE EXPOSURE OF EMPLOYEES

[7.4223]–[7.4600]

The weekly average of an employee's daily personal noise exposure (LEP,w) is expressed in dB(A)   **d.29**
and is ascertained using the formula:

$$L_{EP,w} = 10 \log_{10} \left[\frac{1}{5} \sum_{k=1}^{k=m} 10^{0.1(L_{EP,d})k} \right]$$

where—

$(L_{EP,d})k$ = the values of $L_{EP,d}$ for each of the m working days in the week being considered.

B. Repetitive Strain Injury

Cramp of the hand or forearm due to repetitive movement such as typing   **d.30**
has been prescribed disease PDA4 for industrial benefit since 1948. PDA8 is
traumatic inflammation of the tendons and PDA12 is carpal tunnel syndrome.
Thus it has been known for many years that workers undertaking constant
repetitive manual tasks may suffer from inflammatory and disabling conditions
as a result. The medical cause is not fully understood, and it is also true that
such conditions are fairly common in the population at large among those with

no exposure to such activities. The proof of breach of duty and causation in such cases is not straightforward. The difficulties are illustrated by *Pickford v ICI* [1998] ICR 673, where the claimant was a secretary who developed pain in her hands for which no physical cause was found. She claimed that her condition, which had caused her to give up work, was caused by typing for long periods at speed without breaks. The defence was that the cause was not organic but psychogenic. She had the burden of proof and since the judge was not persuaded by her evidence and was uncertain of the cause, her claim failed. The speech of Lord Hope (at 681C) sets out the medical uncertainties of that case and the respectable medical view that the basis of the condition, rare in typists, was in the mind rather than in physical damage. As a psychiatric condition the claimant would find it exceptionally difficult to establish foreseeability since repetitive work would not be expected to cause psychiatric injury to a person of reasonable fortitude in the absence of specific awareness of a most unlikely vulnerability.

d.31 None the less, there are recognized medical conditions which are frequently considered in the context of claims under the banner of RSI or Work Related Upper Limb Disorder (WRULD). The association is convenient for claims but misleading for medicine since these are different conditions. RSI itself may be used as the name of a rather ill-defined medical condition; there are also conditions of:

    (a) tenosynovitis—inflammation of the synovial lining of the tendon sheath in the wrist and forearm;

    (b) De Quervain's syndrome—a common tenosynovitis specifically affecting the extensor tendon of the thumb in the forearm;

    (c) tendonitis crepitans—dry rubbing within the tendon sheath as a result of the lack of fluid; a sign of tenosynovitis;

    (d) Carpal Tunnel Syndrome—compression of the median nerve within the carpal tunnel at the meeting of wrist and hand;

    (e) epicondylitis, or tennis elbow (lateral) and golfer's elbow (medial)—strain or inflammation to the attachment of the tendon to the humerus, a condition which is difficult to associate with work activity since it is a common disease in the general population;

    (f) trigger finger or trigger thumb—a condition in which the finger or thumb locks into position or clicks.

d.32 These medical conditions combine uneasily and no coherent account of the causes of repetitive strain injuries has found general acceptance. The investigation and response to claims may involve orthopaedics, neurology, rheumatology, and psychiatry. The investigation of breach of duty may involve ergonomists or (less satisfactorily) consulting engineers.

If the medical issues of diagnosis and causation have been addressed, claims are **d.33** likely to involve the Provision and Use of Work Equipment Regulations 1998, especially reg 4(3) use only under conditions for which equipment is suitable, and regs 8 and 9 information and training; the Manual Handling Operations Regulations 1992, especially reg 4(1)(a) the obligation to avoid as far as reasonably practicable any operation that involves a risk of injury; and the Health and Safety (Display Screen Equipment) Regulations 1992. The existence of a condition in the arm or wrist proves nothing in legal terms and does not alter the burden of proof. It remains for the claimant to establish duty, breach, and causation of injury in every case.

The date from which a reasonable and prudent employer should have been **d.34** aware of the risks of tenosynovitis and other repetitive injuries is probably a reasonable time after the 1977 publication by the Health and Safety Executive of Guidance Note MS10, though there were earlier Notes for Guidance in 1972 and subsequent guidance in 'Work-related Upper Limb Disorders: A Guide to Prevention' 1990.

Pickford v ICI [1998] ICR 673   The claimant attributed her wrist and arm **d.35** pain to the speed and intensity of typing work, and claimed an association in time between such work and the onset of symptoms. However, her medical evidence could not identify a clear physical cause of her symptoms and the defendant contended that the cause was psychogenic and unforeseeable. Although the Court of Appeal allowed her claim, the House of Lords held that the judge at first instance had been right to conclude that the claimant had not satisfied the burden of proof.

Mughal v Reuters [1993] IRLR 571   A much publicized decision that RSI **d.36** 'does not exist' and that the claimant's specific condition had not been caused by his work as a journalist.

Ball v Post Office [1995] PIQR 5   The claimant proved on medical grounds **d.37** that the condition of trigger finger syndrome had been caused by the duties of his work as a sorter, but the claim was successfully defended on foreseeability because the employer had carried out a sufficient ergonomic survey and the risk of injury had not been identified.

Ping v Esselte Lertrasset [1992] PIQR P74   Several claims tried together, all of **d.38** which were successful chiefly on the ground of a failure to warn of the risks and educate on the means of reducing the risks.

Mountenay v Bernard Matthews [1994] 5 Med LR 293   The employer was **d.39** liable for failure to institute a system of rotation and, in six out of nine claims tried together, medical causation was established.

d.40 *Henderson v Wakefield Shirt Co.* [1997] PIQR P413   Neck and shoulder condition which the claimant attributed to her work as an ironer and presser; successful claim overturned on appeal—it was not the defendant's duty to go so far as to offer a wholly different job and since the claimant was seeing her family doctor and the work pattern was generally safe there was no breach of duty.

d.41 *Alexander v Midland Bank* [2000] ICR 464   Bank workers were engaged in the use of a key pad to enter cheque details and there were breaches of duty in relation to lack of work breaks and inadequate response to initial complaints. The court criticized work practices which resulted in pressure to increase the pace of work such as piecework payment or competition between workers. The claimants complained of fibromyalgia and the court held on the medical evidence, upheld by the Court of Appeal, that causation was established.

d.42 The *JSB Guidelines* for work-related upper limb disorders are provided below.

d.43 This section covers a range of upper limb injury in the form of the following pathological conditions:

(a) Tenosynovitis: inflammation of synovial sheaths of tendons usually resolving with rest over a short period. Sometimes this condition leads to continuing symptoms of loss of grip and dexterity.

(b) De Quervain's tenosynovitis: a form of tenosynovitis, rarely bilateral, involving inflammation of the tendons of the thumb.

(c) Stenosing tenosynovitis: otherwise, trigger finger/thumb: thickening tendons.

(d) Carpal tunnel syndrome: constriction of the median nerve of the wrist or thickening of surrounding tissue. It is often relieved by a decompression operation.

(e) Epicondylitis: inflammation in the elbow joint: medial = golfer's elbow; lateral = tennis elbow.

The brackets below apply to all these conditions but the level of the award is affected by the following considerations regardless of the precise condition:

(i) are the effects bilateral or one sided?

(ii) the level of symptoms, i.e., pain, swelling, tenderness, crepitus;

(iii) the ability to work;

(iv) the capacity to avoid the recurrence of symptoms;

(v) surgery.

(a) Continuing bilateral disability with surgery and loss of employment.	£12,000 to £12,500
(b) Continuing, but fluctuating and unilateral symptoms.	£8,000 to £9,000
(c) Symptoms resolving in the course of two years.	£4,750 to £5,250
(d) Complete recovery within a short period.	£1,250 to £1,900

HEALTH AND SAFETY (DISPLAY SCREEN EQUIPMENT) REGULATIONS 1992

1. Citation, commencement, interpretation and application

. . .

(2) In these Regulations—   **d.44**

(a) 'display screen equipment' means any alphanumeric or graphic display screen, regardless of the display process involved;

(b) 'operator' means a self-employed person who habitually uses display screen equipment as a significant part of his normal work;

(c) 'use' means use for or in connection with work;

(d) 'user' means an employee who habitually uses display screen equipment as a significant part of his normal work; and

(e) 'workstation' means an assembly comprising—

(i) display screen equipment (whether provided with software determining the interface between the equipment and its operator or user, a keyboard or any other input device),

(ii) any optional accessories to the display screen equipment,

(iii) any disk drive, telephone, modem, printer, document holder, work chair, work desk, work surface or other item peripheral to the display screen equipment, and

(iv) the immediate work environment around the display screen equipment.

. . .

(4) Nothing in these Regulations shall apply to or in relation to—

(a) drivers' cabs or control cabs for vehicles or machinery;

(b) display screen equipment on board a means of transport;

(c) display screen equipment mainly intended for public operation;

(d) portable systems not in prolonged use;

(e) calculators, cash registers or any equipment having a small data or measurement display required for direct use of the equipment; or

(f) window typewriters.

2. Analysis of workstations to assess and reduce risks

(1) Every employer shall perform a suitable and sufficient analysis of those workstations **d.45**
which—

(a) (regardless of who has provided them) are used for the purposes of his undertaking by users; or

(b) have been provided by him and are used for the purposes of his undertaking by operators, for the purpose of assessing the health and safety risks to which those persons are exposed in consequence of that use.

(2) Any assessment made by an employer in pursuance of paragraph (1) shall be reviewed by him if—

(a) there is reason to suspect that it is no longer valid; or

(b) there has been a significant change in the matters to which it relates; and where as a result of any such review changes to an assessment are required, the employer concerned shall make them.

(3) The employer shall reduce the risks identified in consequence of an assessment to the lowest extent reasonably practicable.

(4) The reference in paragraph (3) to 'an assessment' is a reference to an assessment made by the employer concerned in pursuance of paragraph (1) and changed by him where necessary in pursuance of paragraph (2).

3. Requirements for workstations

d.46   (1) Every employer shall ensure that any workstation first put into service on or after 1st January 1993 which—

(a) (regardless of who has provided it) may be used for the purposes of his undertaking by users; or

(b) has been provided by him and may be used for the purposes of his undertaking by operators,

meets the requirements laid down in the Schedule to these Regulations to the extent specified in paragraph 1 thereof.

(2) Every employer shall ensure that any workstation first put into service on or before 31st December 1992 which—

(a) (regardless of who provided it) may be used for the purposes of his undertaking by users; or

(b) was provided by him and may be used for the purposes of his undertaking by operators,

meets the requirements laid down in the Schedule to these Regulations to the extent specified in paragraph 1 thereof not later than 31st December 1996.

4. Daily work routine of users

d.47   Every employer shall so plan the activities of users at work in his undertaking that their daily work on display screen equipment is periodically interrupted by such breaks or changes of activity as reduce their workload at that equipment.

5. Eyes and eyesight

d.48   (1) Where a person—

(a) is already a user on the date of coming into force of these Regulations; or

(b) is an employee who does not habitually use display screen equipment as a significant part of his normal work but is to become a user in the undertaking in which he is already employed, his employer shall ensure that he is provided at his request with an appropriate eye and eyesight test, any such test to be carried out by a competent person.

(2) An eye and eyesight test provided in accordance with paragraph (1) shall—

(a) in any case to which sub-paragraph (a) of that paragraph applies, be carried out as soon as practicable after being requested by the user concerned; and

(b) in any case to which sub-paragraph (b) of that paragraph applies, be carried out before the employee concerned becomes a user.

(3) At regular intervals after an employee has been provided with an eye and eyesight test in accordance with paragraphs (1) and (2), his employer shall, subject to paragraph (6), ensure that he is provided with a further eye and eyesight test of an appropriate nature, any such test to be carried out by a competent person.

(4) Where a user experiences visual difficulties which may reasonably be considered to be caused by work on display screen equipment, his employer shall ensure that he is provided at his request with an appropriate eye and eyesight test, any such test to be carried out by a competent person as soon as practicable after being requested as aforesaid.

(5) Every employer shall ensure that each user employed by him is provided with special corrective appliances appropriate for the work being done by the user concerned where—

(a) normal corrective appliances cannot be used; and

(b) the result of an eye and eyesight test which the user has been given in accordance with this regulation shows such provision to be necessary.

(6) Nothing in paragraph (3) shall require an employer to provide any employee with an eye and eyesight test against that employee's will.

6. Provision of training

(1) Where a person—
    (a) is already a user on the date of coming into force of these Regulations; or
    (b) is an employee who does not habitually use display screen equipment as a significant part of his normal work but is to become a user in the undertaking in which he is already employed, his employer shall ensure that he is provided with adequate health and safety training in the use of any workstation upon which he may be required to work.

(2) Every employer shall ensure that each user at work in his undertaking is provided with adequate health and safety training whenever the organization of any workstation in that undertaking upon which he may be required to work is substantially modified.

d.49

7. Provision of information

(1) Every employer shall ensure that operators and users at work in his undertaking are provided with adequate information about—
    (a) all aspects of health and safety relating to their workstations; and
    (b) such measures taken by him in compliance with his duties under regulations 2 and 3 as related to them and their work.

(2) Every employer shall ensure that users at work in his undertaking are provided with adequate information about such measures taken by him in compliance with his duties under regulations 4 and 6(2) as relate to them and their work.

(3) Every employer shall ensure that users employed by him are provided with adequate information about such measures taken by him in compliance with his duties under regulations 5 and 6(1) as relate to them and their work.

d.50

[8. **Exemption certificates**]

[9. **Extension outside Great Britain**]

d.51

SCHEDULE 1

(Which sets out the minimum requirements for workstations which are contained in the Annex to Council Directive 90/270/EEC on the minimum safety and health requirements for work with display screen equipment)

d.52

Extent to which employers must ensure that workstations meet the requirements laid down in this Schedule

1. An employer shall ensure that a workstation meets the requirements laid down in this Schedule to the extent that—
    (a) those requirements relate to a component which is present in the workstation concerned;
    (b) those requirements have effect with a view to securing the health, safety and welfare of persons at work; and
    (c) the inherent characteristics of a given task make compliance with those requirements appropriate as respects the workstation concerned.

d.53

Equipment

2.—(a) *General comment*

The use as such of the equipment must not be a source of risk for operators or users.

d.54

(b) *Display screen*

d.55   The characters on the screen shall be well-defined and clearly formed, of adequate size and with adequate spacing between the characters and lines.

The image on the screen should be stable, with no flickering or other forms of instability.

The brightness and the contrast between the characters and the background shall be easily adjustable by the operator or user, and also be easily adjustable to ambient conditions.

The screen must swivel and tilt easily and freely to suit the needs of the operator or user.

It shall be possible to use a separate base for the screen or an adjustable table.

The screen shall be free of reflective glare and reflections liable to cause discomfort to the operator or user.

(c) *Keyboard*

d.56   The keyboard shall be tiltable and separate from the screen so as to allow the operator or user to find a comfortable working position avoiding fatigue in the arms or hands.

The space in front of the keyboard shall be sufficient to provide support for the hands and arms of the operator or user.

The keyboard shall have a matt surface to avoid reflective glare.

The arrangement of the keyboard and the characteristics of the keys shall be such as to facilitate the use of the keyboard.

The symbols on the keys shall be adequately contrasted and legible from the design working position.

(d) *Work desk or work surface*

d.57   The work desk or work surface shall have a sufficiently large, low-reflectant surface and allow a flexible arrangement of the screen, keyboard, documents and related equipment.

The document holder shall be stable and adjustable and shall be positioned so as to minimize the need for uncomfortable head and eye movements.

There shall be adequate space for operators or users to find a comfortable position.

(e) *Work chair*

d.58   The work chair shall be stable and allow the operator or user easy freedom of movement and a comfortable position.

The seat shall be adjustable in height.

The seat back shall be adjustable in both height and tilt.

A footrest shall be made available to any operator or user who wishes one.

Environment

3.—(a) *Space requirements*

d.59   The workstation shall be dimensioned and designed so as to provide sufficient space for the operator or user to change position and vary movements.

(b) *Lighting*

d.60   Any room lighting or task lighting provided shall ensure satisfactory lighting conditions and an appropriate contrast between the screen and the background environment, taking into account the type of work and the vision requirements of the operator or user.

Possible disturbing glare and reflections on the screen or other equipment shall be prevented by co-ordinating workplace and workstation layout with the positioning and technical characteristics of the artificial light sources.

(c) *Reflections and glare*

Workstations shall be so designed that sources of light, such as windows and other openings, **d.61** transparent or translucid walls, and brightly coloured fixtures or walls cause no direct glare and no distracting reflections on the screen.

Windows shall be fitted with a suitable system of adjustable covering to attenuate the daylight that falls on the workstation.

(d) *Noise*

Noise emitted by equipment belonging to any workstation shall be taken into account when **d.62** a workstation is being equipped, with a view in particular to ensuring that attention is not distracted and speech is not disturbed.

(e) *Heat*

Equipment belonging to any workstation shall not produce excess heat which could cause dis- **d.63** comfort to operators or users.

(f) *Radiation*

All radiation with the exception of the visible part of the electromagnetic spectrum shall be **d.64** reduced to negligible levels from the point of view of the protection of operators' or users' health and safety.

(g) *Humidity*

An adequate level of humidity shall be established and maintained. **d.65**

Interface between computer and operator/user

4. In designing, selecting, commissioning and modifying software, and in designing tasks **d.66** using display screen equipment, the employer shall take into account the following principles:
    (a) software must be suitable for the task;
    (b) software must be easy to use and, where appropriate, adaptable to the level of knowledge or experience of the operator or user; no quantitative or qualitative checking facility may be used without the knowledge of the operators or users;
    (c) systems must provide feedback to operators or users on the performance of those systems;
    (d) systems must display information in a format and at a pace which are adapted to operators or users;
    (e) the principles of software ergonomics must be applied, in particular to human data processing.

C. Vibration White Finger

Vibration transmitted to the hands from tools such as drills, saws or rivetting **d.67** guns can cause a condition of the fingers, mainly to the circulation in the form of blanching and to the nerves resulting in numbness. Muscle strength may also be affected. This condition is generally known as Vibration White Finger or VWF, but may also be called Hand–Arm Vibration Syndrome or HAVS, or Raynaud's phenomenon of occupational origin.

d.68 The characteristic sign of VWF is whitening of all or parts of all or some fingers on exposure to cold. Blueing (cyanosis) may ensue. These are the signs of Raynaud's phenomenon which may be a primary disease or may arise secondary to many causes other than exposure to vibration; but vibration is the commonest secondary cause. Numbness, tingling, and pain are frequently experienced but not necessarily in direct association with blanching. Accordingly the standard objective assessment of VWF, the Stockholm scale, measures blanching and numbness independently.

d.69 The prudent employer minimizes the risk of VWF by a system of work which avoids prolonged use of vibrating tools. The best remedy is to reduce the vibration of the tools used. Work rotation may assist but the benefit from wearing gloves is not clearly established. Education in the risk should include the need to take frequent breaks and report the onset of any symptoms of tingling or numbness—there is a latent period between the experience of vibration and the onset of symptoms, and numbness or tingling in the fingers after the use of vibrating tools is often the first symptom of a developing disease.

VWF cases must be brought in common law negligence. Since 1994 there has been a helpful HSE publication 'Hand–Arm Vibration'. VWF is a prescribed disease for injury benefit and disablement benefit. There are few reported decisions but there is a most useful collection of unreported decisions in *MacDonald and Georges Industrial Diseases Litigation*, paras 5–009 to 5–024, from which it appears that a prudent employer should have been aware of the risk at the latest from 1975 and probably from 1969.

d.70 *Armstrong v British Coal*, 1987, unreported   A guideline case reported only at *Kemp & Kemp*, H6A–008, setting out several awards and a discussion of the condition of VWF.

d.71 *Allen v British Rail Engineering* [2001] PIQR Q101   A case of VWF where only part of the claimant's exposure to injurious vibration amounted to tortious conduct and the judge made a broad apportionment on evidence which was barely sufficient, but which was upheld.

d.72 *Doherty v Rugby Joinery* [2004] EWCA Civ 147   Claimants who contracted VWF while working in the woodworking industry failed to establish that their employer should have known of the risk earlier than 1991–2. After that date, liability for continued use of vibrating tools was established.

d.73 *Brown v Corus* [2004] EWCA Civ 374; [2004] PIQR P30   Successful appeals by claimants with VWF who had used jackhammers intensively. Liability was based on a date of January 1976 when the employer should have known of the risks, but the claims failed at trial because monitoring would have revealed no employees with symptoms and therefore no change of system, and the injuries would have happened anyway. The Court of Appeal held that there was clear evidence of excessive levels of vibration; the judge should not have speculated, when the defendant had failed to justify the continuing working practices; once breaches of duty and causation were established the claimants did not have to prove to what extent a reduction in vibration would have made a difference.

The Taylor-Pelmear Scale (1976)

Stage	Condition	Work and social effect	d.74
0	No blanching of digits	No complaints	
0_T	Intermittent tingling	No interference with activities	
0_N	Intermittent numbness	No interference with activities	
1	Blanching of one or more fingertips with or without tingling and numbness	No interference with activities	
2	Blanching of one or more fingers with numbness usually confined to winter	Slight interference with home and social activities, no interference at work	
3	Extensive blanching. Frequent episodes in summer as well as winter	Definite interference at work, at home and with social activities, restriction of hobbies	
4	Extensive blanching. Most fingers; frequent episodes summer and winter	Occupation changed to avoid vibration exposure because of severity of signs and symptoms.	

Stockholm Workshop Scale (1987)

Vascular changes: **d.75**

Stage	Grade	Description
0		No attacks
1	Mild	Occasional attacks affecting only the tips of one or more fingers
2	Moderate	Occasional attacks affecting distal and middle (rarely also proximal) phalanges of one or more fingers
3	Severe	Frequent attacks affecting all phalanges of most fingers
4	Very severe	As in stage 3, with trophic skin changes in the finger tips

So a record reading '2L(2)/3R(4)' means that the left hand has two fingers at grade 2 while the right hand has four fingers at grade 3.

Sensorineural changes:

Stage	Symptoms
0SN	Exposed to vibration but no symptoms
1SN	Intermittent numbness with or without tingling
2SN	Intermittent or persistent numbness, reduced sensory perception
3SN	Intermittent or persistent numbness, reduced tactile discrimination and/or manipulative dexterity

d.76 The *JSB Guidelines* for vibration white finger follow.

d.77 Vibration White Finger and/or Hand–Arm Vibration Syndrome, caused by exposure to vibration, is a slowly progressive condition, the development and severity of which are affected by the degree of exposure, in particular the magnitude, frequency, duration and transmission of the vibration. The symptoms are similar to those experienced in the constitutional condition of Raynaud's phenomenon.

The Stockholm Workshop Scale is now the accepted table for grading the severity of the condition. The Scale classifies both the vascular and sensorineural components in two complementary tables. Individual assessment is made separately for each hand and for each finger. Any interference with work or social life is disregarded.

Accordingly, depending on individual circumstances, a lower award might be made despite significant disablement where, e.g., employment is unaffected, whilst a higher award might be attracted where there is a lesser disability but a consequential inability to pursue working life.

The vascular component is graded between Stage 0 (no attacks) through mild, moderate and severe to 4V (very severe) where there are frequent attacks affecting all phalanges of most fingers with atrophic changes in the fingertips.

The sensorineural component is graded between Stage 0SN (no symptoms) and 3SN (intermittent or persistent numbness, reduced tactile discrimination and/or manipulative dexterity).

The grade of disorder is indicated by the stage and number of affected fingers on both hands.

The assessment of damages depends upon the extent of the symptoms and their impact upon work and social life.

In a severe case, the injury may be regarded as damaging a hand rather than being confined to the fingers.

The brackets can best be defined and valued as follows:

(i)	Most Serious	£17,500 to £21,000
(ii)	Serious	£9,250 to £17,500
(iii)	Moderate	£4,750 to £9,250
(iv)	Minor	£1,500 to £4,750

D. Dermatitis

Contact dermatitis is sometimes the result of direct contact with an irritant **d.78**
substance, but is more often in occupational cases the result of contact with an
agent which stimulates an allergic reaction by first sensitizing the victim to a
particular substance with the result that a further exposure, sometimes after long
delay, provokes an allergic reaction and the onset of acute symptoms from a level
of exposure that would not otherwise be harmful. Once sensitized the victim
will remain susceptible and will have to avoid even minimal future exposure,
though in most cases removal from the environment of the sensitizer will result
is a great improvement in symptoms. The lesions of dermatitis are often known
as eczema. There is inflammation of the skin with itching, sometimes pain,
redness, and weeping. Crusting may form and in subacute dermatitis itchiness
can be severe.

Patch testing provides a method of establishing the identity of the irritant and **d.79**
once this is known it must be avoided. Common allergens which can be a
source of occupational dermatitis include rubber, chromium, nickel, epoxy
resins, turpentine, glue, and pesticides; common irritants include solvents,
hand cleaning agents, barrier creams, cement, fibreglass, plastics, oils, fertilizer,
and glue.

There are general responsibilities under the Workplace (Health, Safety and Wel- **d.80**
fare) Regulations 1992 for the provision of a safe workplace with effective ventilation (reg 6), sufficient cleanliness (reg 9) and sufficient washing facilities (reg
21), but claims for dermatitis will usually involve consideration of the Control of
Substances Hazardous to Health Regulations 1999. The bones of the 1999
Regulations are reproduced below. These regulations apply from 25 March 1999
and were preceded by the broadly similar 1994 and 1988 Regulations. They set
out the legal basis for liability but the regulations themselves do not list the
maximum exposure limits or occupational exposure standards. For reasons of
space, and because a claim of this character will inevitably require support from
an expert, these limits are not set out. In addition, at common law, these risks are
well understood and an employer is unlikely to be able to contend that dermatitis resulting from exposure to a known irritant or allergen was unforeseeable.

Thus if a claimant is able to establish exposure to an irritant or a sensitising **d.81**
agent coupled with medical evidence of attribution, cases of dermatitis are

difficult to defend. The control of exposure to known irritants or allergens is intended to avoid the risk of such injury. The regulations require such assessment and control of exposure as ought to result in an extremely low risk if these measures are properly and consistently implemented. A defendant would have to prove a very thorough and effective system and in practice would have to provide an alternative explanation for the onset of the illness in order to avoid liability. This difficulty may account for the lack of significant disputed cases in the recent reports.

d.82 *McGhee v National Coal Board* [1973] 1 WLR 1   The claimant contracted dermatitis from work in a brick kiln. On the law as it then stood, he could not complain about his exposure to dust during his work but he alleged that there were inadequate washing facilities and that his exposure continued while he cycled home to wash. This materially increased the risk of injury and was sufficient, and equivalent to making a material contribution to the injury, for liability to be established.

d.83 *Yates v Rockwell Graphic Systems* [1988] ICR 8   An old case under s 29 of the Factories Act 1961 (safe place of work) in which the employer was liable when exposure to contaminated coolant of the claimant's lathe caused dermatitis.

d.84 *Dugmore v Swansea NHS Trust* [2002] EWCA Civ 1689; [2003] PIQR P220   Regulation 7(1) of the Control of Substances Hazardous to Health Regulations 1988 and 1994 creates strict liability to ensure that exposure was prevented or controlled. The claimant, a nurse who developed sensitivity to latex and was unable to continue nursing, succeeded on liability for exposure which sensitized her at a date earlier than the date of a prudent employer's knowledge of the risk. The steps an employer should take did not extend to a duty to sack an employee who wished to continue working with knowledge of the risk in an otherwise safe environment.

CONTROL OF SUBSTANCES HAZARDOUS TO HEALTH REGULATIONS 1999

2. Interpretation

d.85   (1) In these Regulations, unless the context otherwise requires—

          . . .

        'maximum exposure limit' for a substance hazardous to health means the maximum exposure limit approved by the Health and Safety Commission for that substance in relation to the specified reference period when calculated by a method approved by the Health and Safety Commission;
        'occupational exposure standard' for a substance hazardous to health means the standard approved by the Health and Safety Commission for that substance in relation to the specified reference period when calculated by a method approved by the Health and Safety Commission;
        'substance hazardous to health' means any substance (including any preparation) which is—

(a) a substance which is listed in Part 1 of the approved supply list as dangerous for supply within the meaning of the Chemicals (Hazard Information and Packaging for Supply) Regulations 1994 and for which an indication of danger specified for the substance in Part V of that list is very toxic, toxic, harmful, corrosive or irritant;

(b) a substance for which the Health and Safety Commission has approved a maximum exposure limit or an occupational exposure standard;

(c) a biological agent;

(d) dust of any kind, except dust which is a substance within paragraph (a) or (b) above, when present at a concentration in air equal to or greater than—

(i) 10 mg/m3, as a time-weighted average over an 8-hour period, of total inhalable dust, or

(ii) 4 mg/m3, as a time-weighted average over an 8-hour period, of respirable dust;

(e) a substance, not being a substance mentioned in sub-paragraphs (a) to (d) above, which creates a hazard to the health of any person which is comparable with the hazards created by substances mentioned in those sub-paragraphs;

'total inhalable dust' means airborne material which is capable of entering the nose and mouth during breathing and is thereby available for deposition in the respiratory tract.

(2) In these Regulations, any reference to an employee being exposed to a substance hazardous to health is a reference to the exposure of that employee to a substance hazardous to health arising out of or in connection with work which is under the control of his employer.

3. Duties under these Regulations

(1) Where any duty is placed by these Regulations an employer in respect of his employees, he **d.86** shall, so far as is reasonably practicable, be under a like duty in respect of any other person, whether at work or not, who may be affected by the work carried on by the employer except that the duties of the employer—

(a) under regulation 11 (health surveillance) shall not extend to persons who are not his employees; and

(b) under regulations 10 and 12(1) and (2) (which relate respectively to monitoring and information, training etc) shall not extend to persons who are not his employees, unless those persons are on the premises where the work is being carried on.

(2) These Regulations shall apply to a self-employed person as they apply to an employer and an employee and as if that self-employed person were both an employer and employee, except that regulations 10 and 11 shall not apply to a self-employed person.

(3) The duties imposed by these Regulations shall not extend to the master or crew of a sea-going ship or to the employer of such persons in relation to the normal shipboard activities of a ship's crew under the direction of the master.

[4. Prohibitions relating to certain substances]   **d.87**

5. Application of regulations 6 to 12

(1) Regulations 6 to 12 shall have effect with a view to protecting persons against risks to their **d.88** health, whether immediate or delayed, arising from exposure to substances hazardous to health except—

(a) where and to the extent that the following Regulations apply, namely—

(i) the Control of Lead at Work Regulations 1998,

(ii) the Control of Asbestos at Work Regulations 1987;

(b) where the substance is hazardous to health solely by virtue of its radioactive, explosive or flammable properties, or solely because it is at a high or low temperature or a high pressure;

(c) where the risk to health is a risk to the health of a person to whom the substance is administered in the course of his medical treatment;

(d) where the substance hazardous to health is total inhalable dust which is below ground in any mine of coal.

(2) In paragraph (1)(c) 'medical treatment' means medical or dental examination or treatment which is conducted by, or under the direction of, a registered medical practitioner or registered dentist and includes any such examination, treatment or administration of any substance conducted for the purpose of research.

(3) Nothing in these Regulations shall prejudice any requirement imposed by or under any enactment relating to public health or the protection of the environment.

6. Assessment of health risks created by work involving substances hazardous to health

d.89　(1) An employer shall not carry on any work which is liable to expose any employees to any substance hazardous to health unless he has made a suitable and sufficient assessment of the risks created by that work to the health of those employees and of the steps that need to be taken to meet the requirements of these Regulations.

(2) The assessment required by paragraph (1) shall be reviewed regularly and forthwith if—

(a) there is reason to suspect that the assessment is no longer valid; or

(b) there has been a significant change in work to which the assessment relates,

and, where as a result of the review, changes in the assessment are required, those changes shall be made.

7. Prevention or control of exposure to substances hazardous to health

d.90　(1) Every employer shall ensure that the exposure of his employees to substances hazardous to health is either prevented or, where this is not reasonably practicable, adequately controlled.

(2) So far as is reasonably practicable, the prevention or adequate control of exposure of employees to a substance hazardous to health, except to a carcinogen or a biological agent, shall be secured by measures other than the provision of personal protective equipment.

(3) Without prejudice to the generality of paragraph (1), where the assessment made under regulation 6 shows that it is not reasonably practicable to prevent exposure to a carcinogen by using an alternative substance or process, the employer shall apply all the following measures, namely—

(a) the total enclosure of the process and handling systems unless this is not reasonably practicable;

(b) the use of plant, processes and systems of work which minimize the generation of, or suppress and contain, spills, leaks, dust, fumes and vapours of carcinogens;

(c) the limitation of the quantities of a carcinogen at the place of work;

(d) the keeping of the number of persons who might be exposed to a carcinogen to a minimum;

(e) the prohibition of eating, drinking and smoking in areas that may be contaminated by carcinogens;

(f) the provision of hygiene measures including adequate washing facilities and regular cleaning of walls and surfaces;

(g) the designation of those areas and installations which may be contaminated by carcinogens, and the use of suitable and sufficient warning signs; and

(h) the safe storage, handling and disposal of carcinogens and use of closed and clearly labelled containers.

(4) Where the measures taken in accordance with paragraph (2) or (3), as the case may be, do not prevent, or provide adequate control of, exposure to substances hazardous to health to which those paragraphs apply, then, in addition to taking those measures, the employer shall provide those employees with such suitable personal protective equipment as will adequately control their exposure to those substances.

(5) Any personal protective equipment provided by an employer in pursuance of this regulation shall comply with any provision in the Personal Protective Equipment (EC Directive) Regulations 1992 which is applicable to that item of personal protective equipment.

(6) Where there is exposure to a substance for which a maximum exposure limit has been approved, the control of exposure shall, so far as the inhalation of that substance is concerned, only be treated as being adequate if the level of exposure is reduced so far as is reasonably practicable and in any case below the maximum exposure limit.

(7) Without prejudice to the generality of paragraph (1), where there is exposure to a substance for which an occupational exposure standard has been approved, the control of exposure shall, so far as the inhalation of that substance is concerned, be treated as being adequate if—

(a) that occupational exposure standard is not exceeded; or

(b) where that occupational exposure standard is exceeded, the employer identifies the reasons for the standard being exceeded and takes appropriate action to remedy the situation as soon as is reasonably practicable.

(8) Where respiratory protective equipment is provided in pursuance of this regulation, then it shall—

(a) be suitable for the purpose; and

(b) comply with paragraph (5) or, where no requirement is imposed by virtue of that paragraph, be of a type approved or shall conform to a standard approved, in either case, by the Executive.

(9) In the event of the failure of a control measure which might result in the escape of carcinogens into the workplace, the employer shall ensure that—

(a) only those persons who are responsible for the carrying out of repairs and other necessary work are permitted in the affected area and they are provided with suitable respiratory protective equipment and protective clothing; and

(b) employees and other persons who may be affected are informed of the failure forthwith.

(11) In this regulation, 'adequate' means adequate having regard only to the nature of the substance and the nature and degree of exposure to substances hazardous to health and 'adequately' shall be construed accordingly.

8. Use of control measures etc

(1) Every employer who provides any control measure, personal protective equipment or other **d.91** thing or facility pursuant to these Regulations shall take all reasonable steps to ensure that it is properly used or applied as the case may be.

(2) Every employee shall make full and proper use of any control measure, personal protective equipment or other thing or facility provided pursuant to these Regulations and shall take all reasonable steps to ensure it is returned after use to any accommodation provided for it and, if he discovers any defect therein, shall report it forthwith to his employer.

9. Maintenance, examination and test of control measures etc

(1) Every employer who provides any control measure to meet the requirements of regulation **d.92** 7 shall ensure that it is maintained in an efficient state, in efficient working order and in good repair and, in the case of personal protective equipment, in a clean condition.

(2) Where engineering controls are provided to meet the requirements of regulation 7, the employer shall ensure that thorough examinations and tests of those engineering controls are carried out—

(a) in the case of local exhaust ventilation plant, at least once every 14 months, or for local exhaust ventilation plant used in conjunction with a process specified in Column 1 of Schedule 4, at not more than the interval specified in the corresponding entry in Column 2 of that Schedule;

(b) in any other case, at suitable intervals.

(3) Where respiratory protective equipment (other than disposable respiratory protective equipment) is provided to meet the requirements of regulation 7, the employer shall ensure that at suitable intervals thorough examinations and, where appropriate, tests of that equipment are carried out.

(4) Every employer shall keep a suitable record of the examinations and tests carried out in pursuance of paragraphs (2) and (3) and of any repairs carried out as a result of those examinations and tests, and that record or a suitable summary thereof shall be kept available for at least 5 years from the date on which it was made.

10. Monitoring exposure at the workplace

d.93   (1) In any case in which—

(a) it is requisite for ensuring the maintenance of adequate control of the exposure of employees to substances hazardous to health; or

(b) it is otherwise requisite for protecting the health of employees, the employer shall ensure that the exposure of employees to substances hazardous to health is monitored in accordance with a suitable procedure.

(2) Where a substance or process is specified in Column 1 of Schedule 5, monitoring shall be carried out at least at the frequency specified in the corresponding entry in Column 2 of that Schedule.

(3) The employer shall keep a suitable record of any monitoring carried out for the purpose of this regulation and that record or a suitable summary thereof shall be kept available—

(a) where the record is representative of the personal exposures of identifiable employees, for at least 40 years;

(b) in any other case, for at least 5 years.

d.94   [**11. Health surveillance**]

12. Information, instruction and training for persons who may be exposed to substances hazardous to health

d.95   (1) An employer who undertakes work which may expose any of his employees to substances hazardous to health shall provide that employee with such information, instruction and training as is suitable and sufficient for him to know—

(a) the risks to health created by such exposure; and

(b) the precautions which should be taken.

(2) Without prejudice to the generality of paragraph (1), the information provided under that paragraph shall include—

(a) information on the results of any monitoring of exposure at the workplace in accordance with regulation 10 and, in particular, in the case of any substance hazardous to health for which a maximum exposure limit has been approved, the employee or his representatives shall be informed forthwith, if the results of such monitoring show that the maximum exposure limit has been exceeded; and

(b) information on the collective results of any health surveillance undertaken in accordance with regulation 11 in a form calculated to prevent it from being identified as relating to any particular person.

(3) Every employer shall ensure that any person (whether or not his employee) who carries out any work in connection with the employer's duties under these Regulations has the necessary information, instruction and training.

E. Occupational Asthma

Asthma may be described as a variable condition of narrowing of the bronchial airways by inflammation producing airway obstruction and symptoms of wheeze, breathlessness, tight chest, and coughing. In individuals, an exacerbation of the condition may be the result of exposure to an allergen, and sensitivity to a specific allergen may be the consequence of exposure at work. Asthma is a common disease and, although childhood sufferers frequently improve in teen-age years, many continue to suffer symptoms which may be exacerbated by exposure to a range of allergens such as house dust, pollen, or cats. They may also suffer an exacerbation as a result of exposure to a substance at work but this is not what is usually meant by occupational asthma. **d.96**

In general, occupational asthma refers to those who are exposed to the inhalation of a substance which causes sensitization as a result of which further exposure to small and otherwise harmless levels of the same allergen causes acute symptoms which are usually relieved by removal from the exposure. An improvement is therefore usually seen at weekends and holidays. Even if there is complete removal from the exposure, for example by changing to an entirely different work and workplace, in a substantial number of people asthma persists indefinitely but at variable levels of symptoms. The commonest sensitizing agents are di-isocyanates used in paint sprays, foam and plastics manufacture and adhesives, hardening agents, soldering flux, antibiotics, dust, flour, animals and insects, acid anhydrites, platinum, chromium and nickel, and welding fumes; this list is illustrative and by no means complete. **d.97**

In the assessment of asthma, PEFR (peak expiratory flow rate) is measured by blowing as hard as possible into a hand-held meter. The rate achieved can be measured against an expected rate for the sex, height and age of the claimant and a pattern of readings can be examined for the characteristic variability of asthma. Spirometry will test more accurately for FEV_1 which is the volume of air exhaled under force in the first second, and FVC which is the forced vital capacity or the total volume of air in a forced exhalation. **d.98**

Liability in a case of occupational asthma will begin with medical and expert advice on attribution and in identifying the sensitizing agent. The Control of Substances Hazardous to Health Regulations 1999 set out in the previous section in relation to dermatitis, are equally important here in establishing the **d.99** high duty on an employer to assess the risk of exposure and take appropriate protective precautions.

d.100 *Ogden v Airedale HA* [1996] 7 Med LR 153   Agreed damages of £10,000 awarded to a radiographer who suffered occupational asthma as a result of exposure to x-ray chemicals as a result of which he had to change his job.

d.101 The *JSB Guidelines* for asthma are reproduced below.

d.102

(a) Severe and permanent disabling asthma, causing prolonged and regular coughing, disturbance of sleep, severe impairment of physical activity and enjoyment of life and where employment prospects, if any, are grossly restricted.	£23,500 to £36,000
(b) Chronic asthma causing breathing difficulties, the need to use an inhaler from time to time and restriction of employment prospects, with uncertain prognosis.	£14,250 to £23,500
(c) Bronchitis and wheezing, affecting working or social life, with the likelihood of substantial recovery within a few years of the exposure to the cause.	£10,500 to £14,250
(d) Relatively mild asthma-like symptoms often resulting, for instance, from exposure to harmful irritating vapour.	£5,750 to £10,500
(e) Mild asthma, bronchitis, colds and chest problems (usually resulting from unfit housing or similar exposure, particularly in cases of young children) treated by a general practitioner and resolving within a few months.	Up to £2,750

F. Other Lung Diseases

d.103 The medical terminology in this area can be confusing. The following lung diseases commonly arise in relation to claims:

d.104 **Asthma**   Considered in the previous section.

Pulmonary fibrosis   Diffuse scarring and thickening of lung tissue usually arising after inflammation.

Asbestosis   Diffuse non-malignant pulmonary fibrosis caused by the inhalation of asbestos dust fibres. Smoking will not directly cause asbestosis but may substantially increase the chance of contracting it. There is a risk of mesothelioma of about 9 per cent and of lung cancer in a non-smoker of about 5 per cent.

d.105 **Pleural plaques or Hyaline plaques**   Raised areas of fibrous tissue deposited on the lining of the lungs. A precursor of asbestosis, visible on x-ray, usually symptomless but a cause of anxiety and providing good grounds for a provisional award of damages. May be calcified, which takes at least 20 years from exposure.

Pleural thickening   Diffuse pleural thickening is a non-malignant prescribed disease with many causes which may result in a cough and breathing difficulty.

Mesothelioma   Carcinoma (cancer) of the pleura, the lining of the lungs from (sometimes brief) exposure to blue asbestos (crocidolite). The average period from exposure to diagnosis is 30 years. Exposure for months rather than years is sufficient. Smoking does not increase the risk. Mesothelioma is incurable and is invariably fatal, usually within about two years from diagnosis.

Lung cancer   May be associated with asbestosis but also with other causes such as smoking, or none and is not 'occupational' unless associated with asbestosis.   **d.106**

Pneumoconiosis   Lung disease caused by the inhalation of mineral dust. A fibrous reaction may lead to bronchitis and emphysema. Coalworker's pneumoconiosis is caused by carbon deposit and has only minor effect on lung function though in some cases a complication of much greater fibrosis will be severely symptomatic. Silicosis is caused by fine silica particles and is a greater cause of progressive fibrosis, leading to breathlessness and respiratory failure.

Bronchitis   Inflammation of the bronchi, often associated with smoking but sometimes with exposure to dust or irritants: hyper-secretion of mucus leading to obliteration of small airways, inflammation, reduced air flow, and breathlessness.

Emphysema   Often associated with smoking and bronchitis but may also be a consequence of lung damage from dust inhalation: dilatation of the airspaces and obliteration of their walls leads to chronic inflammation of the bronchioles.   **d.107**

Chronic obstructive airway disease   A common disorder which is a consequence of bronchitis or emphysema.

Pneumonia   Inflammation of the alveolae in the lungs resulting from infection.

Substantial exposure to asbestos can result in these extremely serious diseases, which often become apparent many years after the exposure. The average time between exposure and diagnosis is 20 or 30 years.   **d.108**

It is remarkable for how long occupational exposure to asbestos continued to be a part of working life in boilermaking, ships, shipyards, and insulation work after the risks had become very well known. The use of asbestos in industry was first regulated in 1931. It is not difficult for a claimant to prove that occupational exposure to asbestos dust amounts to a employer's (or main contractor's, or building occupier's) duty of care. It is, however, essential to compile as accurate and reliable an occupational history as possible, or if defending a   **d.109** claim, to study the history given to see whether alternative sources of exposure have been excluded. As long as proceedings follow swiftly after diagnosis, limitation is not usually a legal problem but the lapse of time may cause considerable evidential difficulties, not only in identifying relevant exposure but also, quite often, in finding the relevant employers' liability insurer and possibly restoring a defunct company to the register for the purpose of a claim. A useful summary of early regulations and literature showing knowledge of the risk may be found in *Cherry Tree Machine v Dawson* [2001] PIQR P265.

d.110 The discovery of pleural plaques on x-ray will give the claimant knowledge that exposure to asbestos has harmed his lungs even though the condition causes no symptoms; this will start the clock for limitation purposes. Accordingly, proceedings should be started and a provisional award claimed.

d.111 Mesothelioma has caused particular difficulties of causation when contracted by a claimant who has been exposed to asbestos by more than one employer over his working lifetime. The medical evidence was accepted in *Fairchild* (below). However, mesothelioma is triggered by a single fibre so that, although increased exposure to fibres increases the risk, it is impossible to say that one employer or another was, on the balance of probability, more likely to have been responsible for the disease. The House of Lords none the less held any employer responsible for such exposure to be liable, and to be liable in full for the indivisible injury subject only to apportionment between the employers if more than one employer was before the court.

d.112 *Bryce v Swan Hunter* [1987] 2 Lloyd's Rep 426   A Fatal Accidents Act claim for death from mesothelioma where part only of the exposure was a breach of duty but the claimant was able to establish causation following *McGhee v National Coal Board.*

d.113 *Holtby v Brigham & Cowan* [2000] 3 All ER 421   Asbestosis: exposure during a series of employments resulting in successive periods of exposure to asbestos and the judge accepted, and the Court of Appeal upheld, that the effect of exposure was cumulative and discounted the damages against the defendant by 25% on account of the effect of exposure during other employments.

d.114 *Margerson and Hancock v Holland* [1996] PIQR P154 and P358, CA   A successful claim in negligence for mesothelioma contracted as a result of emissions of dust from an asbestos factory into the surrounding area and the exposure of local residents and children who would play in the loading bays.

d.115 *Mulry v Kenyon* [1992] PIQR Q24   A case of pleural plaques in a claimant aged 51 with a high, more than 50%, chance of developing some more serious lung disease; injury damages of £25,000 in 1992 and loss of earnings.

Gabriel v Nuclear Electric [1996] PIQR Q7 An award in a case of meso- **d.116** thelioma of £40,000 injury damages and both lost earnings and DIY capacity for the lost years.

Quinn v Ministry of Defence [1998] PIQR P387 Section 10 of the Crown **d.117** Proceedings Act 1947 prevented a serving sailor in the Royal Navy bringing a claim for asbestos exposure in 1951–2; it applied to any cause of injury. (Section 10 was repealed with effect from 15 May 1987, but not retrospectively, by the Crown Proceedings (Armed Forces) Act 1987.)

Cherry Tree Machine v Dawson [2001] PIQR P265 Successful mesothelioma **d.118** claims based on exposure in the period 1945 to 1961.

Fairchild v Glenhaven Funeral Services [2002] UKHL 22; [2003] 1 AC **d.119** 32 The claimant contracted mesothelioma as a result of his exposure to asbestos dust during his working life, in which he was exposed to asbestos by more than one employer. He could not show that it was more likely that the cause of the illness was an exposure during any particular period of employment but the House of Lords held, following *McGee v NCB*, that exposure which increased the risk was, in the special circumstances of this disease, sufficient to establish liability.

Barker v Saint Gobain Pipelines [2004] EWCA Civ 545 The claimant was **d.120** exposed to asbestos over three periods: employment with two different employ- ers and a period of self-employment. Applying *Fairchild* (above), the claim against one employer succeeded without any apportionment to reflect the period of self-employment because there was one, indivisible injury.

The *JSB Guidelines* on lung disease follow. **d.121**

The level of the appropriate award for lung disease necessarily, and **d.122** often principally, reflects the prognosis for what is frequently a worsening condition and/or the risk of the development of secondary sequelae.

Most of the reported cases are of asbestos-related disease (as to which see (C) below) but, save for asthma (which is also dealt with separately in (D) below), the brackets set out are intended to encompass all other lung disease cases irrespective of causation. In many cases falling under this head provisional awards will be appropriate. At the upper end of the range where serious disabling consequences will already be present and the prognosis is likely to be relatively clear such an award may not be appropriate. Furthermore, in some cases awards may be enhanced where classifiable psychiatric illness is present.

(a) For a young person with serious disability where there is a probability of progressive worsening leading to premature death. £55,000 to £72,500

(b) Lung cancer (typically in an older person) causing severe pain and impairment both of function and of quality of life. The

duration of pain and suffering accounts for variations within this bracket. See also paragraph (C)(b) below.	£42,500 to £55,000
(c) Disease, e.g., emphysema, causing significant and worsening lung function and impairment of breathing, prolonged and frequent coughing, sleep disturbance and restriction of physical activity and employment.	£30,000 to £43,750
(d) Breathing difficulties (short of disabling breathlessness) requiring fairly frequent use of an inhaler; where there is inability to tolerate a smoky environment and an uncertain prognosis but already significant effect on social and working life.	£17,500 to £30,000
(e) Bronchitis and wheezing not causing serious symptoms; little or no serious or permanent effect on working or social life; varying levels of anxiety about the future.	£11,500 to £17,500
(f) Some slight breathlessness with no effect on working life and the likelihood of substantial and permanent recovery within a few years of the exposure to the cause or the aggravation of an existing condition.	£5,750 to £11,500
(g) Provisional awards for cases otherwise falling within (f), or the least serious cases within (e) where the provisional award excludes any risk of malignancy.	£3,000 to £5,750
(h) Temporary aggravation of bronchitis or other chest problems resolving within a very few months.	£1,250 to £3,000

G. Occupational Stress

d.123 There is no special legal regime that applies to claims for the effects of stress and bullying. Cases are decided on ordinary legal principles and these are usually the principles of negligence. To summarize:

(a) The claimant must prove a duty of care, breach of the duty and damage caused by the breach.

(b) An employer owes his employees a duty of care to take reasonable care to protect them from a foreseeable risk of injury.

(c) An employer is vicariously liable for the acts of his employees acting within the scope of their employment and also owes a direct duty to provide a safe place and system of work.

(d) The key points for breach of the duty are the foreseeability of injury and the reasonableness of the defendant's acts or omissions.

(e) To recover damages for psychiatric injury the condition must amount to a recognized psychiatric illness; fear, anxiety, and distress are not enough however keenly felt.

(f) A primary victim is a person directly exposed to the breach of duty and an employee injured as a result of carrying out the duties of his employment is (probably) a primary victim.

(g) A primary victim is not subject to the policy restrictions or control mechanisms that affect secondary victims and need not therefore prove that psychiatric injury was foreseeable to a person of reasonable fortitude.

Guidelines from the Health and Safety Executive published since 1995 should **d.124** have alerted the reasonable and prudent employer to the possibility of ill health being caused by stress at work, and the risk is one which should therefore be included in the risk assessments undertaken in accordance with the Management of Health and Safety at Work Regulations 1999.

The main source of encouragement for claimants in this area is the decision of **d.125** Coleman J in *Walker v Northumberland CC* [1995] 1 All ER 737. The claimant was a primary victim because his illness was caused by the simple act of carrying out the work required of him by his employer. The central feature of the case is that after the first breakdown suffered by the claimant, the employer received and accepted specific advice about the measures that should be taken to protect the claimant from a recurrence, but the employer failed to implement those measures.

Other claims have been less successful. In *Petch v Customs and Excise* [1993] ICR **d.126** 789, the claim failed because the employer had done all that was reasonably required. In *Frost v Chief Constable of South Yorkshire* [1999] 2 AC 455, no liability was established because police officers experiencing a traumatic event in the course of the duties of their employment were secondary victims and could not show the necessary proximity. (See also a number of unreported decisions, collected in an article by Andrew Buchan in [2001] JPIL 5.)

The hurdles a stress claim must surmount if it is to be successful are to prove: **d.127**

(a) A duty of care—not difficult in employment.
(b) Foreseeability of injury—a major problem unless there are specific reasons relating to the individual or the work to put the employer on notice of a real risk of problems.
(c) Breach of duty—this is not proved by the occurrence of illness; an employer's duty is to act reasonably in the circumstances, and not to act as an insurer of the employee's good health.
(d) Causation—illness has usually struck a vulnerable individual when many others doing the same work have coped, and it is not easy to prove that there was a causative breach of duty, rather than merely an employment whose demands provided the opportunity for, or the evidence of, a breakdown.
(e) Damage in the form of a recognized psychiatric illness.

In *Hatton v Sutherland* [2002] EWCA Civ 76; [2002] PIQR P21 the Court of **d.128** Appeal reviewed in four joined cases the principles on which a claim for illness caused by stress at work should be decided, and formulated a set of 16 general principles:

1. There are no special control mechanisms applying to claims for psychiatric (or physical) illness or injury arising from the stress of doing the work the employee is required to do. The ordinary principles of employer's liability apply.
2. The threshold question is whether this kind of harm to this particular employee was reasonably foreseeable: this has two components (a) an injury to health (as distinct from occupational stress) which (b) is attributable to stress at work (as distinct from other factors).
3. Foreseeability depends upon what the employer knows (or ought reasonably to know) about the individual employee. Because of the nature of mental disorder, it is harder to foresee than physical injury, but may be easier to foresee in a known individual than in the population at large. An employer is usually entitled to assume that the employee can withstand the normal pressures of the job unless he knows of some particular problem or vulnerability.
4. The test is the same whatever the employment: there are no occupations which should be regarded as intrinsically dangerous to mental health.
5. Factors likely to be relevant in answering the threshold question include:
    (a) The nature and extent of the work done by the employee. Is the workload much more than is normal for the particular job? Is the work particularly intellectually or emotionally demanding for this employee? Are demands being made of this employee unreasonable when compared with the demands made of others in the same or comparable jobs? Or are there signs that others doing this job are suffering harmful levels of stress? Is there an abnormal level of sickness or absenteeism in the same job or the same department?
    (b) Signs from the employee of impending harm to health. Has he a particular problem or vulnerability? Has he already suffered from illness attributable to stress at work? Have there recently been frequent or prolonged absences which are uncharacteristic of him? Is there reason to think that these are attributable to stress at work, for example because of complaints or warnings from him or others?
6. The employer is generally entitled to take what he is told by his employee at face value, unless he has good reason to think to the contrary. He does not generally have to make searching inquiries of the employee or seek permission to make further inquiries of his medical advisers.

7. To trigger a duty to take steps, the indications of impending harm to health arising from stress at work must be plain enough for any reasonable employer to realize that he should do something about it.

8. The employer is only in breach of duty if he has failed to take the steps which are reasonable in the circumstances, bearing in mind the magnitude of the risk of harm occurring, the gravity of the harm which may occur, the cost and practicability of preventing it, and the justifications for running the risk.

9. The size and scope of the employer's operation, its resources and the demands it faces are relevant in deciding what is reasonable; these include the interests of other employees and the need to treat them fairly, for example, in any redistribution of duties.

10. An employer can only reasonably be expected to take steps which are likely to do some good: the court is likely to need expert evidence on this.

11. An employer who offers a confidential advice service, with referral to appropriate counselling or treatment services, is unlikely to be found in breach of duty.

12. If the only reasonable and effective step would have been to dismiss or demote the employee, the employer will not be in breach of duty in allowing a willing employee to continue in the job.

13. In all cases, therefore, it is necessary to identify the steps which the employer both could and should have taken before finding him in breach of his duty of care.

14. The claimant must show that the breach of duty has caused or materially contributed to the harm suffered. It is not enough to show that occupational stress has caused the harm.

15. Where the harm suffered has more than one cause, the employer should only pay for that proportion of the harm suffered which is attributable to his wrongdoing, unless the harm is truly indivisible. It is for the defendant to raise the question of apportionment.

16. The assessment of damages will take account of any pre-existing disorder or vulnerability and of the chance that the claimant would have succumbed to a stress-related disorder in any event.

One of these cases *Barber v Somerset County Council* was successfully appealed to **d.129** the House of Lords ([2003] UKHL 13; [2004] PIQR P31), where the *Hatton* Guidelines were approved with the warning that they were 'useful practical guidance not having anything like statutory force', and with the observation that the guidance on the good practice of a prudent employer given by Swanick J in *Stokes v GKN (Bolts and Nuts) Ltd* [1968] 1 WLR 1776 remains the best statement of general principle.

d.130   Workplace stress is often associated with overwork and the Working Time Directive may be relevant to the actions of a reasonable and prudent employer.

d.131   *Walker v Northumberland CC* [1995] 1 All ER 737   A social worker suffered a nervous breakdown as a result of the demanding nature of his work and his heavy workload. On his return to work the employer was given medical advice about the measures that ought to be taken to limit the demanding nature of the job in order to protect Mr Walker from the risk of further illness. These measures were not taken and he suffered a second breakdown. He established that the second breakdown resulted from a breach of the employer's duty of care, so that he recovered damages for the consequences of this illness, but he failed to establish a case in respect of the first breakdown.

d.132   *Frost v Chief Constable of South Yorkshire* [1999] 2 AC 455   Police officers on duty at Hillsborough claimed for psychiatric injury sustained as a result of involvement in the tragedy. Claims by those in the immediate area of the fans who died were admitted but claims by those elsewhere failed.

d.133   *Petch v Customs & Excise* [1993] ICR 789   The claimant suffered a breakdown caused by excessive workload but the employer was not negligent because it could not have known this; thereafter the employer had a duty to take reasonable care to prevent recurrence but in this case, unlike in *Walker*, the employer had done so.

d.134   *Hatton v Sutherland* [2002] EWCA Civ 76; [2002] PIQR P241   In four appeals concerning illness induced by stress at work, the Court of Appeal laid down guidelines for the approach to such cases, which are set out above. The broad effect of these guidelines is to restrict the scope for claims of this kind to cases where the employer is presented with clear signs of impending illness and there was a practical and proportionate remedy which should have been provided.

d.135   *Barber v Somerset County Council* [2004] UKHL 13; [2004] PIQR P31   In one of the *Hatton* cases, the decision of the trial judge in favour of the claimant was restored. The guidelines were broadly approved, with the qualification that they should be treated as guidelines rather than as statute, and the decision was based on the facts of the particular case rather than on any question of legal principle.

d.136   In relation to harassment or bullying the direct liability of the employer or school will depend on awareness of the risk, and vicarious liability for the actions of other employees will depend on whether acts were done in the scope of their employment. Note, however, the wide scope of vicarious liability in *Lister v Helsey Hall, The Times*, 10 May 2001 where a boarding school was vicariously liable for acts of sexual abuse by the house warden. All schools should also have a formal policy to deal with bullying. They have a duty to prevent bullying in school but not outside school by school pupils (*B-S v West Sussex CC* (2000) 97 LSG 37). Again, however, the damage must amount to a recognized psychiatric illness if a common law claim is to succeed.

Part A

INTRODUCTION

1

OVERVIEW

A. The Scope of This Book

This book describes the legal rules by which compensation for personal injury **1.01** may be awarded in England and Wales. It is mainly written as a book of first reference for lawyers. It will not have the answers to all the difficult questions, but most cases met in practice are quite straightforward once one has convenient access to the relevant materials; and in the other few difficult cases it will perhaps help at least with finding the questions that the heavy books in the library will answer. I hope the book may also be helpful to others who are involved with compensation claims as advisers or insurers, and to injured people who may wish to present their own claims or to understand what their lawyers are talking about.

The subject has been divided into three sections covering the rules which **1.02** determine liability to pay compensation, the rules which determine the amount of compensation, and the rules for court procedure. As far as space allows, the materials on which the legal rules are based have been provided in full rather than by a description of them. The statutes, regulations and guidance notes often contain within them the answers to the questions which arise in practice, if one takes the trouble to look carefully, while a summary may be misleading or may miss the vital point.

B. The Place of Tort Compensation

1.03 Most of this book is concerned with claims that are made in the law of tort, enforced in the civil courts. The two key characteristics of claims in tort are first, that liability depends on the proof of fault, usually negligence or the breach of some statutory regulation and, secondly, that the amount of compensation awarded should be a sum which puts the injured person, so far as money can do so, into a position as if the injury had not happened, without any arbitrary limit. For a seriously injured claimant who can prove that his injury was caused by the fault of another person who is covered by liability insurance, and who therefore has the means to pay, tort compensation can run into hundreds of thousands, or even millions, of pounds and can make a life-changing difference to the provision of suitable long-term care and support.

1.04 Tort compensation is not available to a person who is injured as a result of a true accident, when it is not possible to prove that the event was the fault of anyone else. This is the case even though reduced tort compensation is available to a person who is injured partly as a result of his own fault, as long as he can prove that it was also partly as a result of the fault of someone else. Lawyers are mainly interested in tort compensation, because of the relatively high level of compensation that may be awarded, and because of the professional skills that are needed to overcome the difficulties of presenting a successful claim to the court on the issues of proving fault and assessing compensation. However, there is also a complex and important system of state benefits which will help an injured person regardless of fault, but in smaller amounts. The benefits which are most likely to be available to an injured person are described in Chapter 27. Even for a claimant who has good grounds for a claim in tort, state benefits may provide much-needed support while the tort claim goes through the court process. In addition there is a special system for compensating victims of crime, which is set out in Chapter 16 and there is a continuing, but as yet inconclusive, debate about the possibility of devising a separate regime of no fault compensation for some victims of clinical mishap in the NHS.

C. The Importance of Insurance

1.05 The system of tort compensation is to a great extent a matter of insurance. Most fault claims arise out of injuries sustained as a result of road accidents or accidents at work, and in both of these areas, liability insurance is compulsory and almost universal. Most business undertakings and public authorities also have public liability cover, and many household insurance policies provide liability cover for the householder and his family. It is rare for a personal injury claim to be brought against a defendant who is not, in one form or another, indemnified by insurance against liability to pay compensation. A claim against an uninsured motorist will be met by the Motor Insurers' Bureau. The involvement of insurers extends also to the cost of litigation. Legal expenses insurance is frequently provided as an addition to motor insurance or household insurance policies, and a conditional fee agreement (CFA) for litigation can only give peace of mind to the claimant when it is accompanied by insurance against the risk of an adverse costs liability if the claim were to fail.

A fault-based system of injury compensation is unfair to people who are injured **1.06** by accident, but one of the justifications for a fault-based system is that the risk of liability will induce people to take care. This disciplinary effect is greatly reduced by the protection given by insurance, but it is worth it to ensure that compensation awards will be paid.

Awards of compensation that are satisfied by insurance companies have to be **1.07** paid for through the premiums of policyholders. The politics of compensation has added to the cost in recent years. Conditional fee agreements increase the costs of claims through the success fee and the litigation insurance premium, as a way of passing to insurers the cost of pursuing unsuccessful claims. The rules for recovering from insurers the cost of state welfare benefits and NHS medical treatment which the state may have provided to the victims of fault accidents have the aim of transferring even more of the cost of injuries from public funds onto insurers and thus to insurance premium payers. Politicians, not lawyers, have been responsible for these increases in the costs to the covered by liability insurance.

The courts recognize these pressures. When, in *Heil v Rankin* [2000] PIQR **1.08** Q187, the Court of Appeal was asked to implement an increase in the level of general damages following a recommendation from the Law Commission, the court expressly took into account representations that had been made by the insurance industry and the NHS about the repercussions of an increase in damages and the effect on insurance premiums: the proposed increases were implemented only in part. But it is for politicians rather than lawyers to decide whether the system of compensation strikes the right balance between the provision of compensation to the victims of fault accidents, and the cost that has to be paid in insurance premiums.

D. A Compensation Culture?

1.09 Lawyers who represent claimants have become used to being abused as ambulance chasers, and to being ridiculed for pursuing unmerited claims. The phrase 'the compensation culture' has become shorthand in the press for deploring a system which is seen to provide compensation for injuries which are simply accidental or for which the victim himself should be held responsible. There are, of course, occasional daft decisions which encourage this view, but lawyers as a class do understand the notion of personal responsibility. An example is the treatment of reckless swimmers in the decision of the House of Lords in *Tomlinson v Congleton BC* [2003] UKHL 47; [2004] PIQR P83, holding that an adult swimmer does not need to be warned about an obvious danger but is to be considered as responsible for his own actions. The reality is that under the CFA regime a sensible lawyer will not pursue a daft claim and a costs insurer will not give protection against the risk of adverse costs. The idea that the country is being swept by a plague of unmeritorious compensation claims is created by a fondness in the media for silly stories, often apocryphal or American, and by the many advertisements in the press and on television for commercial claims management companies. Sometimes the striking story is of a payment that has been agreed by insurers in a settlement. In reality there has been no increase, rather a discernible recent reduction in the number of claims notified to the Compensation Recovery Unit and in the number of claims issued in the courts.

1.10 The increased premiums resulting from financial pressures on insurers have come only in part from an increase in the value of claims and partly from their own investment difficulties. Insurers seem more reluctant than before to fight unmerited claims: many of the ridiculed compensation payments turn out to be settlements that have been agreed by insurers rather than awarded by the courts. It is hard to blame insurers for this, when the political aim of recent changes has been to do away with trials: the burdens of CFA costs and CPR Part 36 penalties falling on an unsuccessful defendant have added greatly to the level of risk run by an insurer which disputes a claim to trial, while a claimant who has an insured CFA runs no personal risk at all.

E. Pocket Calculators

1.11 The invention of the pocket calculator allows for complex and detailed calculations of damages to be undertaken to an accuracy of several decimal places. This approach has been encouraged by the introduction of the Ogden Tables which identify to two decimal places the appropriate multiplier for calculating a future stream of loss. Lawyers and judges have a natural inclination to strive for the award that is right in each case after applying all the complex legal rules. It would be perverse to put the calculator aside in order to reach only a rough estimate of a claim that can easily be got exactly right. All the same it is suggested that for two reasons, lawyers should restrain the inclination to calculate everything precisely. The first reason is that, however complex the mathematics may be, the underlying facts will always be uncertain. It is not always sensible to calculate a multiplier with scientific accuracy to two decimal places when the projection of the claimant's lost prospects of future employment, promotion, state of health and so forth must always be guesswork. Secondly, the lawyers' clients are not often much interested in the way in which their compensation is calculated: they just want to know how much it will be. We must keep in touch with reality when we take out a pocket calculator. It would be a good first step to ignore the pence in every schedule of special damages and counter-schedule.

F. Current Trends

Two recent cases demonstrate the vigour of the House of Lords. In *Rees v Darlington Memorial Hospital NHS Trust* [2003] UKHL 52; [2004] 1 AC 309 the House of Lords created an entirely new cause of action and an entirely new head of damages, a conventional (is this a polite word for arbitrary?) award of £15,000 for the parent's loss of autonomy over the family when a failed sterilization or vasectomy leads to an unwanted pregnancy. Compare this award for the birth of a healthy child with the statutory award of £10,000 for bereavement, an equally arbitrary figure, but one imposed by Parliament and the Lord Chancellor. This astonishing response to the criticism of *McFarlane v Tayside Health Board* [2000] 2 AC 59 shows their lordships as open-minded, imaginative and innovative, looking for a just outcome in a difficult case rather than for certainty and predictability in the development of the law. In *Fairchild v Glenhaven Funeral Services* [2002] UKHL 22; [2003] 1 AC 32, the House of Lords took a bold and innovative approach to the rules of causation, again finding a just outcome in a difficult case. Liability was established not by the causation of the claimant's injury, a fact which the claimant could not prove, but on the causation of a risk of injury, in the special circumstances of prolonged exposure to asbestos at work. **1.12**

In the real world of everyday claims handling, the last five years or so have been a turbulent time, but it seems that the innovations of 1998–9 are beginning to settle down. Lawyers and insurers have had to grapple with the introduction of a new system for the funding of claims by CFAs, and at the same time with the introduction of a reformed system for court proceedings under the CPR. **1.13**

The introduction of CFAs brought, in the name of access to the courts, the profit element of the success fee. At first this was to be paid by the claimant out of his damages, and with hindsight it is not surprising that a number of commercial claims management companies spotted an opportunity for the profitable pursuit of low risk claims. The opportunity has been undermined by the change in the rules which allowed for the success fee to be recoverable from the insurer, because insurers are better equipped to challenge high success fees. The worst excesses of claims handlers have been tamed and the worst difficulties of success fees are being resolved by the introduction of standard staged agreements where the level of success fee depends on the stage in the case at which liability is agreed or established.

1.14 CFAs have however added significantly to the costs that insurers have to meet in an individual case. The risk involved in disputing a claim of moderate value can easily become disproportionate to the value of the claim. The new rules of the CPR and the protocols have been remarkably successful in encouraging the early settlement of valid claims without the need for court proceedings. This trend, coupled with the increased burden of costs, has resulted in a significant reduction in the number of claims issued, and only a tiny fraction of those claims will ultimately be decided by a judicial hearing. This trend seems likely to continue. Alternative dispute resolution has had little impact so far, perhaps because personal injury claims are defended by professional insurers, but there is some scope for greater use of mediation in complex cases. All the same, the central expert task of a lawyer in this field continues to be predicting the likely outcome of the case if there were to be a trial. It is to be hoped that this book will make a small contribution to this art.

Part B

LIABILITY

2

GROUNDS FOR LIABILITY

This chapter considers the grounds on which liability may be established in a **2.01** civil claim for damages. In legal jargon the grounds are known as the causes of action. The chapter is necessary because the law does not simply allow a claim to succeed when the judge thinks that it would be fair to allow it. Instead, a claimant must show that the circumstances of his claim fit in with established categories where claims have been allowed in the past, or which fit in with circumstances established by Parliament.

There are good reasons for the law to be restrictive in this way. Perhaps most **2.02** claims would have the same outcome if it were simply left to the judge to decide what is fair and just on a case by case approach. But established rules about liability will tend towards consistency of outcome. A claimant whose claim failed would feel aggrieved to hear about another claimant whose claim had succeeded in similar circumstances. Where there is consistency, there is predictability. Once the facts are known it will be possible for an experienced lawyer to predict the likely outcome of many cases so that a full trial may not be necessary in order to resolve the claim. A well-established system of rules building on the experience of the past may be more likely to produce a just result in most cases than relying on the whim of a judge on the day, particularly in a field where the defendant is likely to be a commercial insurer whose interests lie in agreeing a well founded claim with the minimum of argument and expense.

Personal injury claims are usually claims in the law of torts. A tort is a civil **2.03** wrong by one person towards another which does not depend on a voluntary pre-existing relationship such as a contract or a trust: everyone has a duty not to commit torts and it is a duty that cannot be escaped. That is not to say that relationships are unimportant: a relationship such as that between an employer and his employee may provide the basis for a duty of care in tort and may also determine the content of the duty.

A. Negligence

2.04 Negligence is an ordinary English word which means carelessness. In law also, the essence of the tort is a failure to take reasonable care. But it is too simple to say that, in law, a lack of care which results in an injury will provide the ground for a claim for compensation. As a matter of public policy there is a limit on the circumstances in which an accidental injury may give rise to an entitlement to compensation. Some injuries are caused by circumstances where there will be no compensation—they are just bad luck. However, the claimant who has suffered personal injury as a result of someone else's fault has a good chance of finding that compensation is available, and it is mainly in the area of pure economic losses that restrictions on tort liability arise.

2.05 The three ingredients of a cause of action in negligence are:

(a) the existence of a duty of care owed to the victim by the defendant;
(b) a breach of that duty, by failing to attain the legal standard of care; and
(c) damage, suffered by the claimant, which was caused by the breach.

(1) A Duty of Care

2.06 There are two points to make about the task of deciding whether a duty of care is owed to the victim of an accident which has caused an injury. The first point is that in the vast majority of such cases this is a question which causes no difficulty at all. In all the situations where injuries are commonly sustained the law is clear. A car driver owes a duty of care to all other road users. An employer owes to his employees a duty of care to provide a safe place and system of work. The first part of this book is concerned with a range of situations where the existence of a duty of care is well settled, and it will be very unusual to find any case of physical injury that is not covered by these categories.

2.07 The second point to make is that, in contrast, beyond these established categories it is possible for new duties of care to be found in new situations. However, the legal tests for deciding whether there should be a duty of care are complex, difficult to apply and the outcome is unpredictable. A brief account is given here of a topic that takes up many pages of theoretical textbooks, and the most interesting recent cases are set out in the case notes, but the likelihood is that these problems will rarely be encountered in day-to-day legal practice.

In the famous case of *Donoghue v Stevenson* [1932] AC 562, which established **2.08**
the liability of a manufacturer in negligence for injury sustained by the ultimate
consumer of a product, Lord Atkin described the scope of negligence in these
words:

> You must take reasonable care to avoid acts or omissions which you can reasonably
> foresee would be likely to injure your neighbour. Who then in law is my neigh-
> bour? The answer seems to be—persons who are so closely and directly affected by
> my act that I ought reasonably to have them in contemplation as being so affected
> when I am directing my mind to the act or omission which are called in question.

This account of the scope of negligence identifies the two key concepts of
reasonableness and foreseeability.

A duty of care is generated by a relationship between one person who owes a **2.09**
duty to be careful to some other person or class of persons who will foreseeably
be affected by the acts or omissions of the first. The test of the kind of relationship that will suffice, set by the House of Lords in *Caparo Industries v Dickman*
[1990] 2 AC 605, is that:

(a) there must be proximity between the defendant and the victim;
(b) it must be fair, just and reasonable that there should be liability; and
(c) there must be no reason of public policy against imposing liability.

Yet the speeches also recognize that this three-part analysis can serve to confuse
what are really different aspects of very similar questions. For example, if it is
fair, just and reasonable to impose liability, this may demonstrate that there is
the necessary proximity. There is also in practice an overlap of these questions
and the question, considered later, whether the damage is too remote from the
wrongful act. The tests are attempts to find a workable way to define the
boundaries of compensation, which is an exercise in public policy. It is not
possible to decide these questions on pure legal theory.

Cases seeking to broaden the scope of duties of care have recently concerned **2.10**
the performance of their responsibilities by public bodies. The case notes summarize the significant recent decisions which should be read by anyone wishing
to resolve a practical problem in this area. Bear in mind, however, in reading
these notes that there is the world of difference between a claim which the
courts refuse to strike out as unarguable, and a case which actually succeeds.

Donoghue v Stevenson [1932] AC 562   The House of Lords held the seller of a **2.11**
defective drink liable to the consumer even though she was not the purchaser.
The case includes a classic statement of the basic rule of negligence liability.

Home Office v Dorset Yacht Co. [1970] AC 1004   Juvenile offenders damaged **2.12**
a yacht while escaping as a result of the carelessness of prison officers and the

Home Office was held liable. The case confirms that there are no technical limits to the fact situations into which a duty of care in negligence may be extended.

2.13 *Kent v Griffiths* [2001] QB 36   The ambulance service was held to owe a duty of care to a patient, when it had failed to respond to an emergency call within a reasonable time.

2.14 *Hill v Chief Constable of West Yorkshire* [1989] AC 53   The estate of a murder victim sought to sue the police for failing to catch the murderer. The claim was struck out because of insufficient proximity between the police and the victim as a member of the public and on grounds of policy.

2.15 *Alexandrou v Oxford* [1993] 4 All ER 328   As a matter of policy the police owe no duty of care to a shop owner to prevent a burglary.

2.16 *Caparo Industries v Dickman* [1990] 2 AC 605   Not a personal injury case but a leading decision on the tests to be applied when it is argued that a duty of care is owed in a novel situation.

2.17 *X (minors) v Bedfordshire County Council* [1995] 2 AC 633   Liability of a public authority for failure to discharge its duty properly, and allegations of failure to protect from sexual abuse; established a distinction (easy to state but difficult to apply) between decisions of policy and operational tasks and left the door open for liability of professional advisers such as psychologists.

2.18 *Barrett v Enfield LBC* [2001] 2 AC 550   In spite of *X* above, the House of Lords refused to strike out a claim that the local authority had failed to make adequate provision for the claimant's upbringing while as a child he was in its care.

2.19 *Phelps v Hillingdon LBC* [2001] 2 AC 619   The House of Lords refused to strike out claims that local authorities had failed to make adequate educational provision for the claimants in relation to diagnosis of dyslexia and appropriate special help.

(2) Breach of the Duty

2.20 The breach of the duty of care is the act or omission giving rise to the claim. Once again, in most common situations where injury is suffered, it is easy to identify the act of negligence: the motorist who drives too fast, or the employer who fails to fit a proper guard onto a dangerous machine.

2.21 The standard of care is the care which should be exercised by a reasonable, ordinarily careful person. This fictional 'reasonable man' is careful to inquire into the existence of possible dangers and acts with prudence to avoid exposing others to the risk of harm. If he is an employer, he takes care to keep up-to-date with current advice on health and safety issues and he implements all those safety precautions which are proportionate to a risk in terms of their cost in money and time. If he is a motorist, he guards carefully against the risk that other road users may not be as careful as he is, and may do foolish things. As a learner driver he still has to drive with the care and skill of a competent driver.

In order to take precautions that are proportionate to the risk, the reasonable **2.22** man will have to foresee the risk. If the risk is so small that injury cannot reasonably be foreseen, the failure to take precautions will not be a breach of the duty of care. In *Bolton v Stone* [1951] AC 850, a pedestrain walking past a cricket ground was hit by a well-struck ball which cleared a seven foot fence. An ordinary careful man does not take precautions against every foreseeable risk and the claim failed. By contrast, in *Paris v Stepney Council* [1951] AC 367, the fact that the claimant had only one eye, so that an injury to his remaining eye would be specially damaging to him, was relevant to the extent of the employer's duty to ensure that he wore protective goggles.

Bolton v Stone [1951] AC 850   Breach of duty: no breach where the risk of a **2.23** cricket ball crossing the fence to strike a pedestrian was so small that a reasonable person would not take additional precautions.

Paris v Stepney Council [1951] AC 367   Standard of care: the claimant injured **2.24** his eye when he was not wearing goggles. He was at risk of graver than usual injury because he had already lost the sight of his other eye. This special high risk was relevant to the standard of care owed to him.

Stokes v GKN [1968] 1 WLR 1776   Where there is a recognized and general **2.25** practice which an employer has followed for a substantial period without mishap the employer is entitled to follow it, though he must also keep abreast of developing knowledge.

Nettleship v Weston [1971] 2 QB 691   The standard of care in driving to be **2.26** applied to a learner driver is the ordinary standard of care, and his inexperience does not provide an excuse for carelessness.

(3) Damage Caused by the Breach

In personal injury claims, the proof of damage is not a difficulty: it is the injury **2.27** for which a claim is made. But it is a legal necessity in the tort of negligence that damage has occurred. We are all careless many times a day, and often towards those to whom we owe a duty of care, but there is no tort of negligence unless the carelessness has caused harm. The position is different in some other causes of action. Trespass, for example, can be committed without proving an actual injury. The time limit for bringing a claim will not start to run until the cause of action is complete, so time does not begin to run for a claim in negligence until the breach of duty has caused damage.

2.28 The damage must have been caused by the breach of the duty of care. In most cases this requirement does not give rise to any difficulty. The breach of duty need not have been the only cause of the injury. It is sufficient if it is a significant, substantial or material cause among others. There must however come a point where a fact is too far removed from an event causing injury—too remote—for it to be sensibly viewed as a cause of the injury.

This topic is discussed in more detail in Chapter 3 on causation and remoteness.

B. Breach of Statutory Duty

2.29 Sometimes it is possible to rely on the fact that the defendant has breached a duty imposed by statute to give a ground for liability to pay damages for an injury caused as a result of the breach. The elements of such liability are:

(a) that the duty laid down by the statute or statutory instrument is of a kind which gives a civil remedy for damages in case of a breach; and

(b) that the duty has not been complied with; and

(c) damage, suffered by the claimant, which was caused by the breach.

It is important to know that only some and not all statutory duties give a civil remedy for breach. Sometimes it is obvious: statutes such as the Occupiers' Liability Act 1957 exist solely to determine the civil liability of the occupiers of land and premises. Sometimes it is obvious because the question is addressed in the statute: the Health and Safety at Work, etc Act 1974 expressly provides in s 47 that breach of its general safety requirements will not create a civil liability. Where a regulatory statute or statutory instrument does not itself say whether there is to be a civil remedy, it is not always easy to decide. The question is interesting academically but fairly unimportant in practice since there is clear law on the matter in relation to all duties likely to be encountered. In particular, the numerous specific provisions which regulate the safety of the workplace usually give a civil remedy while the general regulations, like the 1974 Act, do not. The principle is that a statute of general application will not usually give a civil remedy but a statute which creates duties for the protection of a specific class of people will do so.

2.30 If the statute or regulation is one which gives a remedy, then all that is needed in order to establish liability is a breach of the requirements of the statute or regulation. Negligence is irrelevant. Moral fault is irrelevant. The practicability of compliance is irrelevant unless the terms of the statute or regulation are framed to apply only in limited circumstances such as 'so far as is reasonably practicable'.

In many cases, a breach of statutory duty will be caused by facts which also **2.31** amount to negligence. For the purpose of this book, the commonest situation where this is often the case is with accidents at work, because the common law developed wide duties in tort which are imposed on employers before and alongside the statutory duties imposed under the Factories Acts and the modern framework of regulations. Where both causes of action apply, both may be relied on. The breach of statutory duty will be relied on for two reasons: where there is a breach, fault need not be proved; and where there is a breach, the claimant may be somewhat less vulnerable to allegations of contributory negligence. Negligence will be relied on because the duty of care will always be there in reserve in case there should be some technical problem about the application of the regulations relied on.

Stark v Post Office [2000] PIQR P105   The claimant postman was seriously **2.32** injured when the brake of his bicycle broke and jammed the front wheel. The bicycle had been properly maintained but the employer's obligation under the Provision and Use of Work Equipment Regulations 1992 to provide equipment in efficient working order was absolute and liability was established for the breach where a claim in negligence would have failed.

C. Nuisance

There is only a distant connection between the ordinary meaning of the word **2.33** nuisance and its use in a legal context to describe a particular cause of action. In the law, nuisance refers to a set of rules concerned with land. There are three aspects:

(a) public nuisance, which is where something is done on land which affects the victim in his capacity as an ordinary member of the public, for example as a user of the highway;
(b) private nuisance when something is done on land which affects the victim in his capacity as the occupier or owner of other land; and
(c) the special rule in *Rylands v Fletcher* (1868) LR 3 HL 330 giving strict liability for the consequences of the escape of something harmful that was kept on the defendant's land.

Nuisance as a cause of action is principally concerned with property rights **2.34** rather than personal injuries. The trend has been towards the introduction of foreseeability of damage as a necessary ingredient of private nuisance, with the result that the test for liability, though not the same as negligence, has a family likeness to negligence (see *The Wagon Mound (No. 2)* [1967] 1 AC 517 below) although the exercise of reasonable care or the un-foreseeability of damage cannot excuse a straightforward interference with property rights such as an encroachment.

2.35   In the personal injury context, nuisance most commonly arises as a cause of action in claims for accidents caused by dangers and defects in the highway, created either by users of the highway or by highway authorities. The topic is considered in more detail in Chapter 7. There is some doubt whether damages for personal injuries can be recovered under *Rylands v Fletcher* (see *Hunter v Canary Wharf* [1997] AC 655) though the restriction may apply only to non-occupiers who have to rely on negligence. In practice this restriction is unlikely to affect the outcome of a significant number of cases.

2.36   *Overseas Tankship (UK) Ltd v Miller Steamship Co. Pty (The Wagon Mound (No. 2)* [1967] 1 AC 517   Foreseeability established as the test of remoteness of damage in nuisance. Lord Reid: 'a real risk is one which would occur to the mind of a reasonable man in the position of the defendant and which he would not brush aside as far fetched'.

D. Trespass

2.37   Trespass is a word which has a special use in the law which is not always easily understood. In a study of English legal history trespass is found to be one of the ancient grounds for civil claims but it was overtaken by the action on the case which in turn evolved into negligence.

2.38   Trespass is a deliberate wrong: it may be trespass to land, the type in which the word trespass continues to be used in common speech; it may be trespass to goods, now largely covered by the statutory code of the Torts (Interference with Goods) Act 1977; or it may be trespass to the person which covers all deliberate assaults. One key point is that in all these cases damage is not an essential ingredient. Walking onto someone's land when there is no right to do so amounts to trespass even though no harm is done, and may be the subject of a claim. For example, an injunction might be obtained, even though compensatory damages will not be recovered unless there is some harm to be compensated. Another key point is that all damage flowing from a trespass is actionable whereas in negligence damage must have been of a kind that was a foreseeable result of the breach.

2.39   Trespass to the person covers any violation of the body, including assault, battery and false imprisonment. Battery is the intentional and deliberate use of force on another person. Assault is an act which causes the victim to fear the use of force. In common speech the word assault is used to cover both kinds and to mean a deliberate physical attack. A battery may be so slight that no injury or harm is caused—though bodily contact which has no element of hostility and is just part of the daily round, such as passengers pressed against each other in a crowded train, will not be wrongful. False imprisonment is the term used to describe any wrongful detention or restraint of personal freedom. It need not be false, except in the sense of being unlawful, and it need not be in prison. It is however the tort by which those wrongly held in prison, or in police custody, can seek compensation.

E. Breach of Contract

The common law recognizes certain duties that are imposed on people because **2.40** of their actions or activities and these form the law of torts, but in addition the law recognizes duties and liabilities arising out of legally binding agreements. A contract is simply an agreement that is legally binding. This is not the place to consider the requirements which make a binding agreement. The contents of an agreement are not only those terms which the parties expressly spell out but also terms which the law will imply into the agreement, and these sometimes include a duty to exercise reasonable care. Accordingly there are many contractual relationships which might have a relevance to an injury claim. For example, a bus passenger has made a contract to be carried on the bus and a term will be implied requiring the driver to exercise reasonable care and skill for the safety of passengers. A contract of employment has implied terms requiring the employer to provide a safe system of work, safe premises and equipment, and suitable training and instruction. In most cases however, nothing is to be gained from relying on contracts in these everyday situations. A duty of care is imposed by the law of tort, the content of the duty is identical whether expressed in contract or tort, the quantification of compensation is the same, and in contract there is a greater risk of failing the rules about time limits, since time runs from the breach of the contract rather than from the date of injury.

The common law of contract proved incapable of providing effective protection **2.41** for consumers. The doctrine of privity meant that only a party to the contract could bring a claim for a breach of the contract's obligations, yet only the person who suffered the damage could claim for that loss. In *Donoghue v Stevenson* [1932] AC 562 the law of tort came to the rescue, imposing a duty of care in negligence in respect of personal injury, which was owed not only to the purchaser of the drink but also to the drinker for whom she bought it. The Consumer Protection Act 1987 now imposes strict liability for any injury caused by a defect in a product, a liability imposed not only on the retailer but also on the manufacturer and others concerned in the supply. Also the Contracts (Rights of

Third Parties) Act 1999 has now addressed the worst difficulties of the doctrine of privity.

F. Vicarious Liability

2.42 This is the principle that one person may be liable for a wrongful act done by another. By far the most important situation in which vicarious liability arises is in employment. If an employee doing his job causes injury to someone, the injured person can sue the employer for his employee's wrongdoing. The practical benefit is that the employer will be insured and able to satisfy a judgment. It is also a benefit that the rule removes the need for the claimant to identify precisely by whom a wrongful act was done, if it must have been done within the enterprise by someone for whom the employer must be vicariously liable. In addition, if it is a fellow employee who has been injured, the employer may owe a personal and non-delegable duty to the employee to operate the business safely.

2.43 Not everyone who works for another is an employee, and there is in general no vicarious liability for the acts of independent contractors. This used to cause difficulties when some businesses artificially chose to label their employees as independent sub-contractors, often for tax reasons. The tax benefits have been reduced, and in *Lane v Shire Roofing* [1995] PIQR P147 the Court of Appeal imposed a broad and realistic definition of an employee for these purposes.

2.44 Sometimes an employee is lent by his employer to another business to work for them or at their premises. Here the rule is that vicarious liability for his acts will remain with his usual employer unless there is clear evidence to show such a transfer of responsibility for controlling the manner of his work as to make the temporary employer responsible (*Mersey Docks and Harbour Board v Coggins & Griffith* [1947] AC 1).

2.45 The employer is only vicariously liable for acts done 'in the course of the employment' and not for an act which the employee does 'as a frolic of his own'. The broad principle is that the employer is liable when his employee does his job badly, but is not liable when the employee has departed so far from what he was meant to do that he is no longer doing his job.

2.46 *Mersey Docks and Harbour Board v Coggins & Griffith* [1947] AC 1   Where an employee is lent briefly to another employer and his negligence causes an accident, the general, long-term employer, will be vicariously liable unless it is proved that responsibility to control and direct the employee has been fully transferred to the temporary employer.

McDairmid v Nash Dredging [1987] AC 906   The claimant was employed to **2.47** work as deckhand on a tug and was injured as a result of the negligence of the master of the tug. The House of Lords held that there was no need to consider the question of vicarious liability, as the employer owed a direct and non-delegable duty to the claimant to provide a safe system of work.

Smith v Stages [1989] 1 All ER 833   The first defendant injured the claimant, **2.48** his colleague, while driving them both home from a distant assignment during their employment with the second defendant, without waiting to take reasonable sleep. Although the employer, the second defendant, was not responsible for deciding how and when the men would make the journey, the employer was none the less vicariously liable.

Lane v Shire Roofing [1995] PIQR P147   The claimant, a building worker, **2.49** nominally by contract and for tax purposes self-employed, was injured through a failure to provide proper equipment. Although he was skilled and was working without detailed instructions or control, the defendant was liable as his employer. Control is not decisive and the question was, whose business was it, and who had responsibility for the overall safety of the men doing the work.

Lister v Hesley Hall [2002] AC 215   In a decision which may result in a **2.50** significant broadening of the scope of vicarious liability, a residential school was held vicariously liable for acts of physical abuse carried out by a warden: the abuse was inextricably interwoven with the carrying out of his duties.

Mattis v Pollock (trading as Flamingo's Nightclub) [2003] EWCA Civ 505; **2.51** [2004] PIQR P21   The claimant was involved in a fight in a nightclub which involved a doorman. After the fight the doorman left the club, went home to fetch a knife and returned to the area of the club where he stabbed the claimant causing very serious injuries. He was convicted of causing grievous bodily harm with intent. He was not a licensed doorman and the evidence was that he had been encouraged and expected by the defendant employer to use aggression and violence in the course of his duties. In spite of the element of personal revenge in the stabbing, the Court of Appeal held that the stabbing was directly linked to the events in the club and the employer was vicariously liable for the doorman's actions.

3

CAUSATION AND REMOTENESS

Under this heading we are concerned with two different but related issues. **3.01** First, the requirement that there must be a causal link between the wrongful act of the defendant which provides the ground for liability, and the harm for which the claimant seeks compensation. Secondly, the rule of policy which limits the recovery of compensation to those consequences which are close to the defendant's act, excluding other harm which may have been caused by the defendant's act but which is held to be too remote from it to be compensated.

A. But-for Causes

The first stage in the proof of causation is to show that, but for the defendant's **3.02** act, the claimant would not have suffered the harm. In any incident there will naturally be a very large number of but-for causes, logically going back to the dawn of time. This stage of the inquiry is not concerned to establish legal causation from these facts but only to exclude those claims where a basic relationship of cause and effect cannot be established.

McWilliams v Sir William Arrol & Co. [1962] 1 WLR 295 An experienced **3.03** steel erector fell from a lattice tower and was killed. There was a clear breach of the requirement for a safety harness to be provided. The duty was to provide the harness but not to ensure that it was worn; and it was found, on the basis of his previous practice, that if a harness had been provided the deceased would not have worn it. The widow's claim failed because she had not established a causal connection between the breach and the injury. (Note that the obligations of an employer under modern regulations would be more extensive.)

3.04 *Performance Cars Ltd v Abraham* [1962] 1 QB 33   The defendant collided with the claimant's car and caused damage to the front wing which required a respray. However, the car had been damaged in a previous accident and the repair of that damage also required a respray, which had not been carried out at the date of the second accident. The claimant could not include the cost of the respray in his claim for the second accident because the defendant had damaged a car that was already in need of a respray, so the need did not flow from the defendant's wrongful act.

3.05 *Barnett v Chelsea and Kensington Hospital* [1969] 1 QB 428   The claimant's husband was poisoned with arsenic and attended the hospital, where he was negligently sent away to call his family doctor. Had he been admitted, however, it was proved that the administration of an antidote would have been too late to save his life. Accordingly the claimant failed to establish causation.

3.06 This does not mean that the defendant is liable for all the consequences of his wrongful conduct, but only to those which are attributable to that which made the act wrongful. Lord Hoffmann explained in *Banque Bruxelles v Eagle Star* [1997] AC 191, 213D:

> A mountaineer about to undertake a difficult climb is concerned about the fitness of his knee. He goes to a doctor who negligently makes a superficial examination and pronounces the knee fit. The claimant goes on the expedition, which he would not have undertaken if the doctor had told him the true state of his knee. He suffers an injury which is an entirely foreseeable consequence of mountaineering but has nothing to do with his knee. On [a principle allowing liability for all the consequences] the doctor is responsible for the injury suffered by the mountaineer because it is damage which would not have occurred if he had been given the correct information about his knee. He would not have gone on the expedition and would not have suffered an injury. On . . . the more usual principle, the doctor is not liable. The injury has not been caused by the doctor's bad advice because it would have occurred even if the advice had been correct.

B. A 'Material Contribution' is Sufficient

3.07 If the but-for test is passed, the next stage is to decide which from among the host of but-for causes was of sufficient relevance or closeness to be treated for legal purposes as causative of the act on which the claim is based. We are concerned here with the causes of the event which resulted in harm, and not with the causes of the various kinds of harm that may then have flowed from the event once it had happened. Unfortunately there is no neat phrase which captures the test of sufficient closeness in a way that is useful in practice. Judges will speak of real, effective, or material causes and of the *causa causans* in contrast to the *causa sine qua non*; equally often they will admit that there is no easy way to describe the nature of a sufficient cause except by the application of common sense.

Common sense is straightforward in the case of a single traumatic event but can **3.08** be more difficult in cases of occupational disease. Historically however, the courts have tended to adopt a pragmatic approach to causation where an illness is caused by cumulative episodes of exposure to an injurious substance or event, as shown by the cases of *McGhee* (dermatitis), *Holtby* (asbestosis) and *Allen* (vibration white finger) (below).

Bonnington Castings v Wardlaw [1956] AC 613   The claimant contracted **3.09** pneumoconiosis. During eight years of employment he breathed dust which contained silica particles. Some of this exposure was a breach of statutory duty resulting from the failure of dust extraction equipment but some of the exposure did not involve any breach of duty by the employer. The reason for the disease was the dust from both sources and the issue was whether the claimant could prove that the exposure which was a breach had materially contributed to the disease. Much the greater part of the exposure was from the 'innocent' source but the exposure that was a breach of duty was not negligible. This was sufficient to establish liability.

McGhee v NCB [1973] 1 WLR 1   The claimant's case was that he should have **3.10** been provided with workplace showers to remove dust arising from his work in a brick kiln. He developed dermatitis. The medical evidence was that the cause of the condition was not fully understood but the risk of it was significantly greater if the claimant had to cycle home covered in dust rather than if he could wash the dust off straight away. Materially increasing the risk of injury amounted to making a material contribution and the claim succeeded. The claim was for an indivisible injury. There was no argument in this case that an allowance should be made for a mild dermatitis that the claimant would have suffered even if there had been no breach of duty. That next step was taken in *Holtby*, below.

Wilsher v Essex Area Health Authority [1988] AC 1074   The claimant, a **3.11** newborn baby, needed extra oxygen. A catheter inserted into a blood vessel to measure arterial blood oxygen levels was negligently inserted into a vein resulting in low readings. The claimant developed a condition of the eyes resulting in blindness. This might have been caused by the administration of excess oxygen as a result of the mistake with the catheter, but it might instead have been caused by any of four other identified possible causes, and the excess oxygen was no more likely than the others. Emphasizing that the burden of proving causation lies on the claimant, and limiting *McGhee* to a case where it was known that the presence of the dust caused the dermatitis, the claimant failed because he could not prove that the excess oxygen caused or materially contributed to his condition.

3.12 *Chester v Afshar* [2004] UKHL 41   This case, along with *Fairchild* (at **3.18** below), shows the surprising willingness of the House of Lords to escape from the traditional 'but-for' test of causation in an exceptional case where the result would otherwise be unjust. The claimant had the misfortune to suffer a serious complication of a surgical operation, by pure mischance rather than by negligence in the conduct of the operation. In breach of duty, she had not been warned of the risk. She proved that if she had been warned of it, she would have refused consent to the operation at the time when it was carried out; but it was held that she would probably have agreed to the operation later when exactly the same risk of complication would have arisen. All the same, the House of Lords held on policy grounds that causation was established because of the importance of the duty to warn.

C. Apportionment of Causation

3.13 Where a claimant's condition is the result of cumulative exposure to repeated breaches of duty, causation is simple where a single defendant is responsible for the whole of the exposure and all of it was in breach of duty. With lifetime exposure to harmful work conditions such as excessive noise, it may often be that the exposure was caused by two or more different employers and for some periods of employment neither the employer nor an insurer can be traced. It may be that some of the exposure did not constitute a breach of duty because of changing knowledge and standards of health and safety. In these circumstances the court will make an apportionment so that a defendant is liable for the claimant's disease in proportion to his responsibility for the exposure.

3.14 *Thomson v Smith Ship Repairers* [1984] 1 QB 405   Liability for occupational deafness was apportioned on a time basis according to the length of exposure before and after the date on which the exposure to noise was found to have become tortious.

3.15 *Holtby v Brigham & Cowan* [2000] ICR 1086   Concerned a claim for asbestosis where the claimant had been exposed to asbestos dust for all his working life, only part of which was with the defendant. The claimant proved that this exposure caused or materially contributed to his condition but, since the effects of exposure were cumulative, his damages were reduced by 25% to take account of exposure for which the defendant was not responsible.

Allen v British Rail Engineering [2001] PIQR Q101   A case of VWF where it   **3.16** was clear that only part of the claimant's exposure to injurious vibration by the defendant was tortious conduct by the defendant and there was scant evidence to support an apportionment but the judge made a broad apportionment which was upheld.

D. Mesothelioma

Special problems arise in the causation of mesothelioma, an asbestos-related   **3.17** malignant disease, where there has been more than one employer responsible for wrongful exposure. The expert medical evidence in *Fairchild* (below) showed that the risk of contracting mesothelioma increases with the quantity of dust or fibres inhaled but the condition may be triggered by a single fibre and once caused it is not made worse by additional exposure. The claimant had been wrongfully exposed to asbestos during work for more than one employer and could not show on the balance of probabilities that either employer was more likely than the other to have been responsible for the particular exposure which triggered the disease. The claim therefore failed on the traditional 'but-for' test of causation. The House of Lords held that in these special circumstances, consistent with *McGhee v NCB* (above), proof that each defendant's wrong-doing had materially increased the risk of contracting the disease was sufficient to prove causation. The claimant is entitled to recover in full against either or both of the employer defendants. The question of apportionment was not addressed, except to recognize that if both defendants were before the court, contribution proceedings could determine their respective shares of liability. The decision is notable for the breadth of the discussion of issues of policy and the remedies available under other legal systems, and for the flexibility shown by the House of Lords to seek a just result at the expense of circumventing one of the basic rules of causation.

Fairchild v Glenhaven Funeral Services [2002] UKHL 22; [2003] 1 AC 32   A   **3.18** claimant who has contracted mesothelioma as a result of exposure to asbestos at work can establish causation against both his employers when the following conditions are satisfied:

(1) C was employed at different times and for differing periods by both A and B, and

(2) A and B were both subject to a duty to take reasonable care or to take all practicable measures to prevent C inhaling asbestos dust because of the known risk that asbestos dust (if inhaled) might cause a mesothelioma, and

(3) both A and B were in breach of that duty in relation to C during the periods of C's employment by each of them with the result that during both periods C inhaled excessive quantities of asbestos dust, and

(4) C is found to be suffering from a mesothelioma, and

(5) any cause of C's mesothelioma other than the inhalation of asbestos dust at work can be effectively discounted, but

(6) C cannot (because of the current limits of human science) prove, on the balance of probabilities, that his mesothelioma was the result of his inhaling asbestos dust during his employment by A or during his employment by B or during his employment by A and B taken together.

3.19 *Barker v Saint Gobain Pipelines* [2004] EWCA Civ 545   The claimant was exposed to asbestos over three periods: employment with two different employers, and a period of self-employment. Applying *Fairchild*, the claim against one employer succeeded without any apportionment to reflect the period of self-employment because there was one, indivisible injury.

E. The Test of Foreseeability

3.20 The third stage is to consider how the law limits the scope of those who are entitled to bring a claim. The Privy Council in *The Wagon Mound* [1961] AC 388 (see below) overruled the decision of the Court of Appeal in *Re Polemis* [1923] 3 KB 560 that once some harm was reasonably foreseeable as likely to result from a wrongful act, the wrongdoer was liable for all the consequences directly caused. The Privy Council preferred a rule that the wrongdoer is responsible for all the consequences of a kind that is reasonably foreseeable as a result of the wrongful act, but if a reasonable man would not have foreseen the kind of consequence then it is too remote. The debate should not be given an exaggerated importance. The academic argument about foreseeability as the touchstone of liability probably makes very little difference in practice since:

(a) *The Wagon Mound* has not disturbed the rule that, once damage of a particular kind is foreseeable, liability extends to the full actual consequences within that kind of damage even if the extent of them is unforeseeable; and

(b) the 'kind' of damage has been widely construed.

3.21 *Overseas Tankship (UK) Ltd v Morts Dock and Engineering Co. Ltd (The Wagon Mound)* [1961] AC 388   Fuel oil which was carelessly spilt onto the water of the harbour, spread to the claimant's wharf and, when it later caught fire, damaged the wharf. It was found that it was not reasonably foreseeable that the oil would catch fire. The claim at first succeeded in reliance on the rule that since some harm was foreseeable, all direct damage could be claimed. The Privy Council held that the same test of reasonable foreseeability should apply both to the breach of duty and to the remoteness of damage. The foreseeable damage by fouling was a different kind of damage to damage by fire and since fire damage was of a kind that was not reasonably foreseeable, the claim failed.

F. The Kind of Harm

A generous interpretation of the 'kind' of harm that must be reasonably foresee- **3.22**
able has meant that in personal injury cases the requirement of reasonable foreseeability of damage in *The Wagon Mound* (above) rarely results in a finding that injuries are too remote. This trend is shown by the decisions of *Hughes, Page* and *Jolley* (see below). *Page v Smith* in particular, if it remains good law, makes it difficult to envisage any form of injury that could be regarded as being of a different 'kind' where some injury is foreseeable, so that for personal injury claims the law has for all practical purposes returned to the rule in *Re Polemis* [1923] 3 KB 560. However, lest these cases should seem to sweep away all need to consider the precise nature of the defendant's wrongdoing, there follow the notes of two cases, *Tremain* and *Darby*, curiously both featuring Weil's disease, where the need for an association between risk, precaution and injury was central to the failure of the claims.

Hughes v Lord Advocate [1963] AC 837   The claimant, a child, took a **3.23**
warning lamp and crawled down a manhole which workmen had left unattended. When he stumbled, the lamp caused a violent explosion in which he was badly burned. The injuries differed in degree but not in kind from the injury that was a foreseeable consequence of the negligence, and the fact that the accident was caused in a way which could not have been foreseen was no defence. This case applies a broad view of the 'kind' of damage; it is looking at the cause of the accident rather than the somewhat similar, but logically later issue of full recovery for an injury which proves, as a result of complications, to be of unexpected severity, but the approach is similar on both issues.

Page v Smith [1996] AC 155   A minor road accident might foreseeably have **3.24**
caused physical injury but in fact resulted only in injury caused by shock leading to the recurrence of chronic fatigue. Lord Lloyd said:

> The test in every case ought to be whether the defendant can reasonably foresee that his conduct will expose the [claimant] to risk of personal injury. If so, then he comes under a duty of care to that [claimant] . . . There is no justification for regarding physical and psychiatric injury as different 'kinds' of injury. Once it is established that the defendant is under a duty of care to avoid causing personal injury to the [claimant], it matters not whether the injury in fact sustained is physical, psychiatric or both.

(See further **3.46** below.)

3.25 *Jolley v Sutton LBC* [2000] 1 WLR 1082   The Council should have removed a derelict boat from its land. It was foreseeable that children would play on the boat and might suffer minor injury through rotten wood giving way. In fact, boys aged 13 and 14, jacked up the boat and started to try to repair it, and one of them was severely injured when the boat collapsed on top of him. The Court of Appeal held that the Council was not liable because this 'kind' of accident was not reasonably foreseeable but the House of Lords restored the trial judge's finding for the claimant. The wider risk fell within the Council's duty of care.

3.26 *Wieland v Cyril Lord Carpets* [1969] 3 All ER 1006   The claimant injured her neck is an accident for which the defendant accepted liability. The next day a support collar was fitted, holding her neck in a fixed position. This meant that she could not adjust to her bifocal glasses and as a result she fell and injured her ankle. Treating the relevant 'kind' of damage in *The Wagon Mound* as personal injury, the ankle injury was not too remote, so that the claimant could recover for all her actual injuries.

3.27 *Tremain v Pike* [1969] 1 WLR 1556   The rat population on a farm where the claimant worked became too large. There was a foreseeable risk of injury from a bite or from contaminated food. In fact, the claimant contracted Weil's disease, but the judge held that this was so rare that it was not reasonably foreseeable and the claim (perhaps surprisingly) failed.

3.28 *Darby v National Trust* [2001] PIQR P27   The deceased drowned when swimming in a pool. There was no duty to warn against the risk of drowning but the defendant had been negligent in failing to prohibit swimming because of the risk of Weil's disease. Even if causation could be proved, in that the deceased would have obeyed a notice, still this breach would not result in liability for the different risk of drowning.

G. New Intervening Acts

3.29 Since an event may have many causes, a defendant will sometimes seek to argue that someone else's act has intervened to prevent the operation of cause and effect between his act and the claimant's harm. The conventional metaphor is of breaking the chain of causation, and the shorthand Latin phrase is *novus actus interveniens*. A high test is applied and a defendant will not easily establish that the causative effect of his wrong-doing has been extinguished.

3.30 It may be that the act relied on to break the chain of causation has been an additional cause of the harm. Such an act may be, but need not necessarily be, a further tort against the claimant. In that case the person responsible for the new act may be at risk of becoming an additional defendant, though the claimant will bear in mind that if two wrongdoers are jointly liable for the same damage then the entire claim may be enforced against either of them. If the grounds for a claim against the second wrongdoer are doubtful the claimant may prefer to wait and see whether the first chooses to make the allegation. The second wrongdoer is also at risk of a claim from the existing defendant that he should contribute to the claimant's compensation: the court can decide between them their respective shares. These issues are discussed in more detail in Chapter 40.

Where medical treatment is unexpectedly unsuccessful, the whole actual injury **3.31** will be the basis for compensation on the principle of unexpectedly severe consequences discussed below, but where there is negligence in treatment there is no reason in principle why that should not be capable of breaking the chain of causation. The issue does not normally arise in practice because nothing short of negligence will suffice, and if there is negligence in treatment the hospital will be joined in the action so as to be liable for the consequences of that negligence, if it is proved. It is then no longer necessary or relevant to decide whether, in the absence of the additional defendant, the original wrongdoer would have been liable for the full loss.

Knightly v Johns [1982] 1 WLR 349   The claimant was a police motor cyclist **3.32** who attended a road accident in a tunnel. The inspector at the scene had negligently failed to close the tunnel straight away and ordered the claimant back against the flow of traffic to do this, whereupon he collided with an oncoming car. The trial judge found that the only person liable to the claimant was the motorist responsible for the original accident, but the Court of Appeal held that the motorist's liability to rescuers was limited to the natural and probable consequences, and the negligence of the inspector broke the chain of causation. The inspector alone was liable to the claimant.

Robinson v Post Office [1974] 1 WLR 1176   Negligent treatment: the **3.33** employer argued that the negligence of the treating doctor would have broken the chain of causation and the argument failed on the absence of negligence rather than on any challenge to this principle (see also **3.46** below).

The Liesbosch Dredger v Edison SS [1933] AC 448   This case must be **3.34** included in any discussion of remoteness but its authority is doubtful. *The Edison* sank a dredger, the owners of which had to incur heavy hire charges in fulfilling a dredging contract because they did not have the means simply to buy a substitute dredger. However their loss was capped by the court at the losses they would have incurred up to the point when a replacement could have been obtained, plus the cost of a replacement. The claimant's lack of means made the extra loss too remote to have been caused by the collision. This is not a personal injury case and it is not applicable to a case where the claimant's susceptibility makes the effects of an injury more severe. If the problem had been seen as one of mitigation a different outcome should have resulted, since a lack of means is a valid reason for failing to take steps to mitigate a loss. In *Mattocks v Mann* [1993] RTR 13, the Court of Appeal disregarded *The Liesbosch Dredger* in allowing the cost of car hire until repairs had been completed.

3.35 *Reeves v Metropolitan Police Commissioner* [2000] 1 AC 360   The deceased was a prisoner who was known to be at risk of suicide but the police failed in their duty to protect him from this risk by leaving him unobserved in a cell where suicide was practicable. Because the specific duty of the police was to protect against suicide, that act of the deceased did not break the chain of causation (but it did result in 50% contributory negligence).

3.36 *Webb v Barclays Bank* [2001] EWCA Civ 1141; [2002] PIQR P61   The defendant was responsible for causing the claimant to fall and injure her left knee. The second defendant proposed and undertook an amputation by way of treatment, which was negligent advice and treatment. Although the facts and issues were complex, the Court of Appeal held (at [55]) that the original wrong-doer remained liable to the claimant, because only medical treatment so grossly negligent as to be a completely inappropriate response to the injury inflicted by the defendant should operate to break the chain of causation.

3.37 *Wilson v Coulson* [2002] PIQR P300   The claimant suffered brain damage, but took heroin to relieve his headaches and became addicted, thus worsening the effects of his injury. The injury had not been so severe as to cause him to lose the power to decide not to use heroin, which was therefore a voluntary, deliberate, informed, and unreasonable act which broke the chain of causation and was contrary to public policy so that the effects of taking heroin could not be included in the claim.

H. Mitigation of Loss

3.38 It is unconventional to consider mitigation of loss in the context of causation but it is a topic which follows naturally from considering interruptions to the chain of causation by external events. The rules about mitigation arise out of the possibility of interruption to a chain of causation by the intervening acts or omissions of the claimant himself.

3.39 Law students are taught that the claimant has a 'duty to mitigate his loss' but the reference to duty is misleading. The true rule is that a claimant cannot recover for a loss which could have been prevented by a step which the claimant would have taken if he had been acting reasonably. Conversely, if the claimant acts reasonably in an attempt to reduce or prevent his loss but his attempt fails and the loss is made worse, the whole actual loss and the costs and consequences of the reasonable attempt can be recovered.

There are two aspects of mitigation which are of particular importance in **3.40** personal injury practice: medical treatment and re-employment.

On questions of medical treatment, the courts are generally slow to find that **3.41** a claimant has acted unreasonably in declining to undergo medical treatment that has been offered when the claimant can give an explanation for his decision. It can be reasonable to be apprehensive of the risks of treatment, and to become tired of repeated treatments which seem to provide little benefit. It is most unusual for an injured person to refuse treatment for reasons that are not supportable. Just as medicine has seen a trend towards allowing increasing respect for the views of the patient, so also in the law it is suggested that there is increasing respect for a decision made in good faith against undergoing a risky, invasive, or painful medical procedure.

On questions of employment, the approach of the courts is generally far more **3.42** robust in expecting an injured claimant to look for alternative work, even if the alternatives that the claimant is capable of undertaking are less satisfying and less well paid than the work that the claimant was able to carry out before the injury. Indeed, most of the work of employment consultants is based on identifying alternative work that is within the capabilities of an injured claimant, and it is common for the court to limit the scope of a claim for continuing loss of earnings on the basis of the earnings that the claimant ought to be able to achieve by retraining and making reasonable efforts to find work in an entirely different field.

Richardson v Redpath, Brown [1944] AC 62   The burden of proving a failure **3.43** to mitigate by receiving medical treatment lies on the defendant. (See also *McGregor on Damages*, 17th edn, 7–1019, forcefully doubting the view of the Privy Council that the burden lay on the claimant in *Selvanayagam v University of West Indies* [1983] 1 WLR 585.)

Savage v Wallis [1966] 1 Lloyd's Rep 357   Medical opinion was divided on the **3.44** prospects of success for a possible operation and it was not unreasonable for the claimant to decline to undergo it.

James v Woodall Duckham [1969] 1 WLR 903   The claimant had medical **3.45** advice that his psychosomatic pain would cease once his claim had reached a conclusion. In spite of this he delayed in issuing the writ and in pursuing the claim. He was unable to recover his loss of earnings for this period of avoidable delay.

Geest v Lansiquot [2002] UKPC 48; [2003] 1 All ER 383   The defendant **3.46** argued that the claimant had failed to act reasonably to mitigate her loss because she had refused to undergo surgery to treat her injuries. The Privy Council, rejecting the argument that there had been a failure to mitigate, held that the burden of proof did not lie on the claimant to prove that the refusal was reasonable, but on the defendant to prove that it was not.

I. Unexpectedly Severe Consequences

3.47   A duty of care in negligence requires the defendant to protect against a foreseeable risk of injury. There is a vital distinction between causing unforeseeable injury of a different kind, which *The Wagon Mound* excludes, and causing damage of the same kind but to an unforeseeable extent, which this rule allows. Once the threshold of a breach of duty has been crossed, the rule is that the claimant is entitled to be compensated for the actual extent of his injuries even if the extent of them is severe to a degree that was not reasonably foreseeable. This rule is of far more practical significance for claimants than the debate between *Re Polemis* and *The Wagon Mound* about the test for the beach of duty. In a particularly vivid phrase, the rule is often described as the egg-shell skull or thin skull rule. A defendant must take the victim as he finds him.

3.48   *Smith v Leech Brain & Co* [1962] 2 QB 405   A splash of molten metal burned the deceased's lip. The wound ulcerated and cancer developed, from which three years later he died, because the deceased had had an unknown vulnerability. Once a burn was reasonably foreseeable, the claimant was entitled to recover in full.

3.49   *Robinson v Post Office* [1974] 1 WLR 1176   The claimant slipped on oil and cut his shin, for which his employer was liable. He was given a tetanus injection from which he suffered a rare allergic reaction with severe consequences resulting in brain damage and permanent disability. The employer sought to argue that the doctor who administered the injection was negligent but this failed the but-for test: although the doctor did not follow the proper practice of a test dose, the history of the case showed that the test would not in fact have been positive so the full injection would in any case have been given. The employer therefore had to take the claimant as he was, with his susceptibility, and was liable for all the consequences of the injury.

3.50   *Page v Smith* [1996] AC 155   A minor road accident might foreseeably have caused physical injury but in fact resulted only in injury caused by shock in the recurrence of chronic fatigue. Lord Lloyd said:

> The test in every case ought to be whether the defendant can reasonably foresee that his conduct will expose the [claimant] to risk of personal injury. If so, then he comes under a duty of care to that [claimant] . . . There is no justification for

regarding physical and psychiatric injury as different 'kinds' of injury. Once it is established that the defendant is under a duty of care to avoid causing personal injury to the [claimant], it matters not whether the injury in fact sustained is physical, psychiatric or both.

J. Successive Injuries

In practice the resolution of claims for successive injuries is rarely a practical **3.51** difficulty. The decision of Judge Thompson QC in *Cutler v Egerton* [2000] PIQR Q84 at 93, a case where the claimant sued two drivers who had both caused her neck injuries in successive road accidents, provides a good illustration of a sensible judge considering the impact of different injuries topic by topic and making an apportionment between them.

None the less the decision in *Baker v Willoughby* [1970] AC 467 creates a **3.52** theoretical puzzle. It will be remembered that in *Performance Cars Ltd v Abraham* [1962] 1 QB 33 the cost of a respray could not be claimed because a respray was already needed as a result of an earlier accident: this second wrongdoer had damaged an already damaged car and his act did not cause the need for a respray. The converse situation arose in *Jobling v Associated Dairies* [1982] AC 794. Mr Jobling sued for the consequences of a fall at work, which had impaired his earning capacity. Before trial, he contracted a serious illness that was entirely unrelated to his fall and which prevented him continuing to work at all. Since the court at trial must act on what it knows to be the facts, and it was known that the small chance of supervening illness had now become a fact, Mr Jobling's claim was limited to the earnings lost up to the date when the illness intervened and he would have had to give up work anyway. The accident injury did not cause any loss after this point because even without the accident there would have been no earnings to lose.

In *Baker v Willoughby* [1970] AC 467, the claimant sustained an injured leg. **3.53** The basis of the assessment of damages is not clear but it seems that his earning capacity was impaired. He sued the person responsible for this injury. Before trial, he had the misfortune to be shot in the same leg in the course of an armed robbery and as a result the leg was amputated. He successfully argued that the first wrongdoer should still compensate him in full for the partial loss from the first injury, because if he were to sue the second wrongdoer he would be met with the argument that, as in *Abrahams*, only the added loss flowing from the amputation of a damaged leg could be recovered.

Baker was decided before *Jobling*. If a case similar to Mr Baker's case came to **3.54** trial after *Jobling*, it would be met by the argument that the harm done by the first injury must have come to an end with the supervening event of the second injury which caused a loss which overwhelmed and extinguished the harm from the first accident. This seems to mean that neither the first wrongdoer nor the second would be liable to compensate for the harm attributable to the first accident after the second injury. That is absurd; but the question is, how as a matter of principle is it to be avoided? In *Jobling* the House of Lords appeared to approve the outcome of *Baker*, without giving a coherent reason for treating the situation differently. The best reason seems to lie in the fact that both injuries were caused by tortious acts and the law must therefore compensate for the whole injury by the combination of both potential claims; but it is hard to see why in principle the extent of the first wrongdoer's liability should depend on the character of the subsequent event. I cannot offer any satisfactory answer to the puzzle based on principle but the moral for claimants seems to be that they should try in any such case to bring claims for both accidents to the court at the same time.

3.55 *Baker v Willoughby* [1970] AC 467   The claimant was knocked down and his leg was injured. Subsequently, he was shot in the same leg with the result that the leg was amputated. In a claim to be compensated for the first injury, it was argued that the supervening second injury brought his claim to an end. Pointing out that in a claim for the second injury the assessment only would be for the loss of amenities to a man with an already damaged leg, the House of Lords allowed his claim for the first accident in full.

3.56 *Jobling v Associated Dairies* [1982] AC 794   The claimant injured his back and his earning capacity was impaired. Before his claim for his back injury had been decided, he developed a totally incapacitating illness which he would in any case have suffered. This was held to extinguish any continuing claim for the effects of his accident injury.

3.57 *Cutler v Egerton* [2000] PIQR Q84   An illustration of a case where the judge apportioned each head of damage between the defendants responsible for successive and overlapping injuries.

3.58 *Heil v Rankin* [2001] PIQR Q187   The judge was correct to reduce the claimant's award of future loss on the ground that he would in any case have been unlikely to be able to continue in his job until normal retirement age as a result of the long-term effects of a previous injury.

3.59 *Allen v British Rail Engineering* [2001] EWCA Civ 242; [2001] PIQR Q101   An illustration of apportionment where only part of the claimant's exposure to vibration causing vibration white finger could be the subject of liability: 'the court should not be astute to deny the claimant relief on the basis that he cannot demonstrate with accuracy precisely what proportion of his injury is attributable to the defendant's tortious conduct' (Schiemann LJ at [20], p Q110).

Rahman v Arearose Ltd [2001] QB 351   Negligence in treatment did not **3.60** extinguish the causative effect of the negligence which caused the original injury and the causative effect of each wrong should be apportioned as was just according to causative effect but regardless of moral blameworthiness.

4

PROOF AND UNCERTAINTY

A. Burden and Standard of Proof

In civil proceedings, such as a claim in court for compensation for injury, the **4.01** basic rules of proof are that:

(a) the party who seeks to rely on a fact has the burden of proving it,

(b) a fact is proved to be true if the court finds that it is true on the balance of probabilities, and

(c) the same standard applies to all matters of fact, but the quality of the evidence needed to prove an allegation of serious wrongdoing, such as fraud, will be higher according to the seriousness of the allegation.

One of the functions of the statements of case is to identify the matters of fact **4.02** that are agreed and the matters that are in dispute. If the defence admits a fact asserted by the claimant, the admission can be relied on for proof of the fact. The drafting of a statement of case imposes on the claimant the discipline of setting out, one by one and in a logical order, the facts that have to be proved in order to establish the claim. The drafting of a defence imposes on the defendant the discipline of deciding which matters of fact are agreed, and identifying the area where the true dispute lies.

The defendant must also set out the facts on which he relies, where the defendant **4.03** has the burden of proof. For example, reg 12(3) of the Workplace (Health, Safety and Welfare) Regulations 1992 (the Workplace Regulations) requires that as far as is reasonably practicable the floor in a workplace shall be kept free from any substance which may cause a person to slip. The claimant in a slipping case must prove the presence on the floor of a substance which caused him to slip and must prove that the slip caused him injury. On proof of these facts, if there is no further evidence the claim will succeed. If the defendant wishes to dispute liability on the ground that it had done all that was reasonably practicable, the defendant must assert and prove this, and the same test of proof on the balance of probabilities will apply. In the same way, a defendant who asserts that the claimant has failed to act reasonably to keep his losses to a minimum has the burden of proving it.

4.04 In practice the court receives evidence of the facts by a range of different means. Facts which are admitted in the statements of case are proved by the admission. No further evidence is necessary. Facts which are not admitted may be proved in several ways. The court will take judicial notice of matters which are common knowledge and which are an undisputed part of the background to a case. The documents disclosed to each other by the parties will set out much back-ground material that is often undisputed. Statements of case which have been signed with a statement of truth may be used as evidence of the facts stated in them at all steps of the court proceedings except for the final trial. The Civil Evidence Act 1995 has swept away all the old restrictions on the admission of hearsay evidence in civil proceedings and this means the statements of fact contained in the contemporaneous documents or in witness statements can be put in evidence without restriction and without the need to call the maker of a statement, the penalty being that the weight given to hearsay evidence or documentary evidence will be substantially less than the weight given to a witness who is called at the trial unless there is a good reason for being unable to call the witness. One of the striking characteristics of civil trials is how little dispute there usually is about technical questions of proof outside the limited area in which there is a genuine dispute of fact that goes to the heart of the case.

4.05 Where the evidence of the facts is important, it will usually be proved by the evidence of witnesses. The procedural rules invariably result in a case manage-ment order from the court requiring the parties to exchange in advance of the trial the written statements of the witnesses on whose evidence they propose to rely. If the court is to attach weight to the evidence of a witness, the witness must be called at the trial so that his evidence can be tested in cross-examination.

4.06 There may well be gaps in the evidence that is available. It is not necessary for every fact to be proved by direct evidence. The court will draw inferences from the facts that have been proved by evidence.

4.07 *Howard v Bemrose* [1973] RTR 32   After a road accident in which a motor-cycle and a car collided in the dark, the motorcyclist was dead and the car driver could remember nothing of the accident. The court had to draw inferences from the debris on the road and the final positions of the vehicles. The shortage of direct evidence did not prevent the court doing its best to consider such evidence as there was in order to see what facts could be deduced on the balance of probabilities about the circumstances of the collision.

The willingness of the court to draw inferences from the primary facts that have **4.08** been proved by direct evidence is demonstrated also by the rule of evidence for the proof of negligence that is described by the Latin phrase *res ipsa loquitur* or 'the thing speaks for itself': where something was under the control of the defendant, for example a car that he was driving, and a mishap occurs which would not normally have happened in the absence of negligence, for example the car crosses onto the wrong side of the road, then the court may properly find that there was negligence if there is no other evidence to explain how the mishap came to happen.

B. Past and Future Uncertainty

The rule described above is concerned with the proof of the events that have **4.09** happened. Once a fact is proved on the balance of probabilities, it is taken to have been proved conclusively for all the purposes of the case. There are no half measures. Even if, at the outset, there was some doubt about the proof of a fact, once the court has made its finding on the balance of probabilities, then the certainty of the finding takes the place of the previous doubt. The floor on which the claimant slipped was either wet or dry. The judge cannot escape the responsibility of deciding the facts and resolving any conflict between the evidence of the various witnesses.

In many cases it will be necessary for the court to make findings about the **4.10** future, as well as about the past. Most obviously in personal injury claims, this arises in relation to damages for future loss. Where the effects of an accident injury continue to influence the life of the claimant, the court has to decide what the future will hold for the claimant, and the court has to decide what the future would have held for the claimant if the accident had not happened, in order to measure the difference for the assessment of damages. The uncertainty of these future events is a different kind of uncertainty from the doubt that may exist over the proof of past facts. A court provided with the fullest evidence could make a ruling about events that have happened with something approaching certainty. No amount of evidence can remove the inherent uncertainty about the chances of future events. Therefore, although it would be possible to decide questions of future uncertainty by applying the test of the balance of probabilities, the law takes a more subtle approach and allows the court to make findings which reflect the degree of probability attaching to future uncertainties. A number of important cases illustrate this approach.

4.11 *Davies v Taylor* [1974] AC 207   This was a Fatal Accidents Act claim where the court had to decide whether the claimant widow would have been reconciled with her estranged husband if he had not died. The trial judge was wrong to decide this on the balance of probabilities. Lord Reid stated:

> When the question is whether a certain thing is or is not true—whether a certain event did or did not happen—then the court must decide one way or the other. There is no question of chance or probability. Either it did or did not happen. But the standard of civil proof is a balance of probabilities. If the evidence shows a balance in favour of it having happened, then it is proved that it did in fact happen . . . You can prove that a past event happened, but you cannot prove that a future event will happen and I do not think the law is so foolish as to suppose that you can. All that you can do is to evaluate the chance, sometimes it is virtually 100%, sometimes virtually nil. But often it is somewhere in between, and if it is somewhere in between I do not see much difference between a probability of 51% of the probability of 49%.

4.12 *Jopling v Associated Dairies* [1982] AC 794   The claimant was injured in an accident which made him unfit for work. By the time of the trial the claimant had suffered an illness which also made him unfit for work, and would have done so even if the accident had not happened. The illness had become a known fact rather than a future chance, and must be taken into account accordingly.

4.13 *Hotson v East Berkshire HA* [1987] AC 750   The claimant, a boy aged 13, fell out of a tree and broke the neck of his femur. This injury carries a risk of complications by avascular necrosis when the blood supply fails resulting in permanent disability. When the claimant was treated at hospital there was a negligent failure to diagnose or treat his fracture. He did develop avascular necrosis. It was held that there had been a 75% chance that avascular necrosis would have developed even if the injury had been properly treated. The trial judge awarded the claimant 25% of the full value of his claim for the loss of the chance of avoiding the complication. This was overturned by the House of Lords. The court had to make a finding of fact about the past event, and the finding that there was a 75% probability of avascular necrosis required a finding of fact that this was attributable to the fall from the tree, leaving no room for an award of the value of chance.

4.14 *Gregg v Scott* [2002] EWCA Civ 1471   A negligent delay in the medical diagnosis of a malignant lump reduced the claimant's chances of five-year survival from 42 to 25%. A majority of the Court of Appeal held, following *Hotson*, that the claimant had suffered no loss. There is a powerful dissenting judgment from Simon Brown LJ, the trial judge who was overruled in *Hotson*.

At the time of writing, the decision of the House of Lords is awaited, and the outcome will be discussed in the updating website for this book (see Preface) as soon as possible.

C. Loss of a Chance

In deciding the factual basis on which a future loss is to be assessed, the court **4.15** will not decide the factual issues by deciding whether projections are true or false according to the balance of probabilities, but may make an assessment of the loss that is weighted according to the likelihood that different events may have happened. However, the court should not use this principle to undermine the use of an actuarial multiplier to calculate a future loss. The conventional approach to a straightforward case does not require detailed consideration of the chances, beyond the adjustments for contingencies that are suggested in the fixing of a multiplier in the application of the Ogden Tables. But where prospects are really uncertain, the 'loss of a chance' approach is necessary. For example, if there was a 60% likelihood that the claimant would have achieved a promotion and an increased rate of pay, the court may award 60% of the loss caused by the loss of promotion.

Allied Maples v Simmons and Simmons [1995] 1 WLR 1602   This was not a **4.16** personal injury case, but a commercial claim where the loss depended on proof that the claimant would have been able to renegotiate an unsatisfactory contractual provision if its solicitors had properly considered and advised about the clause that was included in the contract. It was held that the claimant was entitled to succeed the value of the chance, if it could show that there was a real and substantial chance that the third party on the other side of the negotiation would have acted so as to avoid the loss.

Doyle v Wallace [1998] PIQR Q146   The claimant was seriously injured and, **4.17** but for the accident, she had a 50% chance that she would have been successful in training and qualifying as a teacher. The defendant argued that the court must make a finding on the balance of probabilities. The Court of Appeal held that the claimant's loss of the chance of becoming a teacher fell within the *Allied Maples* principle and the claimant was entitled to damages for the loss of the chance assessed at 50% of the loss.

Herring v Ministry of Defence [2003] EWCA Civ 528; [2004] 1 All ER 44   The **4.18** court had to assess a claim that, if he had not been injured, the claimant would have had a successful career in the police force. The trial judge found that there was a strong likelihood that the claimant's application to join the police force would have been successful, but reflected the uncertainty of this career path by reducing the multiplier for future loss by 25%. The Court of Appeal substituted a reduction of approximately 10% (15.54 became 14), holding that the judge had been wrong to treat the assessment of future loss as the valuation of chance rather than a straightforward multiplier/multiplicand assessment. The 'loss of a chance' approach was only appropriate when there was a chance that the career of the claimant would take a particular course leading to significantly higher earnings.

5

CONTRIBUTORY FAULT

A. The 1945 Act

Section 1(1) of the Law Reform (Contributory Negligence) Act 1945 provides **5.01** that:

> Where any person suffers damage as the result partly of his own fault and partly of the fault of any other person or persons, a claim in respect of that damage shall not be defeated by reason of the fault of the person suffering the damage, but the damages recoverable in respect thereof shall be reduced to such extent as the court thinks just and equitable having regard to the claimant's share in the responsibility of the damage.

Before the enactment of this provision, contributory negligence operated as a **5.02** complete defence to a claim; it was correspondingly more difficult to establish. Now that the court can apportion liability under the 1945 Act, allegations of contributory negligence are extremely common.

The statute gives to the court an unrestricted discretion to decide the extent to **5.03** which the claimant's damages should be reduced so as to give a result which is just and equitable. On the face of it, nothing could be fairer, although in his book, *The Damages Lottery*, Professor Atiyah comments that it might increase the sense of injustice felt by the blameless victim of an accident who has no defendant to sue, to compare his position with that of the victim of negligence who may recover large damages even though he was himself significantly at fault.

When there is a finding of contributory negligence by the claimant it is the **5.04** practice of the courts to determine the apportionment of liability in an extremely broad manner. In spite of the many thousands of pounds that may turn on the difference between say a quarter and a third, judges usually make a finding in terms of a broad fraction or percentage and explain the reasons in very general terms. It is surprising that, apart from the specific area of a failure to use a car seat belt or a motorcycle helmet, no guidelines have ever been articulated.

5.05 Section 1(1) of the 1945 Act refers to 'the claimant's share in the responsibility of the damage' and this phrase would appear to suggest that it is necessary for the court to balance the respective responsibilities of the claimant and the defendant. The apportionment against the claimant would vary not only in accordance with the seriousness of his own fault, but also in accordance with the seriousness and moral blameworthiness of the negligence or breach of duty of the defendant. In *Davies v Swan Motor Co.* [1949] 2 KB 291, Lord Denning MR summarized the approach by asking: 'What faults were there which caused the damage? What are the proportions in which the damages should be apportioned having regard to the respective responsibilities of those in fault?' In practice, however, the assessment of contributory negligence will usually focus almost entirely on the conduct of the claimant.

5.06 The fault that needs to be established against a claimant in order to prove contributory negligence is defined by s 4 of the 1945 Act:

> 'Fault' means negligence, breach of statutory duty or other act or omission which gives rise to liability in tort or would, apart from this Act, give rise to the defence of contributory negligence.

However, this does not mean that the claimant needs to have committed an actionable tort against the defendant or against himself. Quite apart from the fact that this fault has caused no damage to the defendant, it is also not necessary—in spite of the statutory language referring to tort causes of action— that the claimant owed a duty of care or a statutory duty to the defendant. The claimant's fault is a failure to take reasonable care for his own safety, viewed as a matter of fact, objective reasonableness and common sense. It is a contribution to the damage, not a contribution to the accident.

5.07 Because the Act presupposes fault on both sides, there cannot logically be 100% contributory negligence (*Pitts v Hunt* [1991] 1 QB 24). In a factual situation where the victim's fault is seen as the only real cause of the injury, the same result might be achieved by a finding that there is no causation of his injuries by any breach of duty by the defendant. However, there have been cases in the context of industrial accidents (for example, *Jayes v IMI (Kynoch)* [1995] ICR 155) where the court has been prepared to find 100% contributory negligence. It may be relevant that the fault of the defendant was in strict liability for a technical breach of regulations.

Although most personal injury claims are tort based, contract sometimes pro- **5.08** vides an additional or alternative cause of action. For example, claims under consumer protection legislation are usually contractual. Employees would have a cause of action in the contract of employment, though it is rarely relied on. Where the contractual duty relied on is a duty to take reasonable care, parallel to a duty of care in negligence, then contributory negligence may be relied on as a defence.

There are dozens, perhaps hundreds, of reported cases in which an assessment **5.09** of contributory negligence has been made. They all depend on their own facts, and are of limited value as authorities. The cases which follow are only the tip of the iceberg.

B. Cases on General Principles

Davies v Swan [1949] 2 KB 291   An early Court of Appeal decision on **5.10** the 1945 Act, confirming that 'fault' does not mean a breach of the duty of care owed in negligence by the victim to the wrongdoer. A man stood on the side of a rubbish lorry and was injured in a collision. Deduction 20%. Lord Denning at 326: 'The amount of the reduction is such an amount as may be found by the court to be "just and equitable", having regard to the claimant's share in the "responsibility" for the damage. This involves a consideration, not only of the causative potency of a particular factor, but also of its blameworthiness.'

Jones v Livox Quarries [1952] 2 QB 608   Another early decision of principle **5.11** on the nature of 'fault' and the requirement of causation. A man stood on the towbar of a dumper truck and was injured when another vehicle collided with it from the rear. Deduction 20%. Lord Denning at 615: 'Although contributory negligence does not depend on a duty of care, it does depend on foreseeability. Just as actionable negligence requires the foreseeability of harm to others, so contributory negligence requires the foreseeability of harm to oneself.'

Pitts v Hunt [1991] 1 QB 24   A pillion passenger urged the rider to drive **5.12** recklessly, knowing he was unqualified and drunk. The claimant failed entirely on the ground of public policy and shared illegal purpose, but the Court of Appeal disapproved of a finding of 100% contributory negligence as being logically inconsistent with the terms of the Act.

Forsikringsaktieselskapet Vesta v Butcher [1989] AC 852   In a contract claim, **5.13** contributory negligence applies where the breach of contract would also have given rise to a breach of duty in tort; therefore the claimant such as an employee or a doctor's patient cannot avoid contributory negligence by choosing to rely on a contractual course of action.

5.14 *Reeves v Metropolitan Police Commissioner* [2000] 1 AC 360   The police took inadequate precautions to prevent Mr Reeves, who was known to have a suicidal tendency, committing suicide while in custody. The police were held liable subject to 50% contributory negligence for the 'fault' of the deceased in taking his own life.

5.15 *Williams v Devon County Council* [2003] EWCA Civ 365; [2003] PIQR Q68   The claimant was the manager of a school kitchen. A gym bench had been left across the doorway from the kitchen to the hall out of her sight and 'in an extremely silly place'. The Court of Appeal set aside a finding of one third contributory negligence. Latham LJ at [7]: 'While it is easy to say that she should have looked where she was going, that ignores the everyday realities of the working environment. In the absence of any reason for her to suspect that something might have been left across her access to the hall, we consider that she was entitled to assume that the hall had been cleared properly. To say that she should have nonetheless looked to see whether or not something might have been left across the doorway was a counsel of perfection which should not have resulted in a finding of contributory negligence.'

C. Cases on Accidents at Work

5.16 *Caswell v Powell Duffryn Associated Collieries* [1940] AC 152   In this pre-1945 case, *per* Lord Wright at 178: the court should give 'due regard to the actual conditions under which men work in a factory or mine, to the long hours and the fatigue, to the slackening of attention which naturally comes from constant repetition of the same operation, to the noise and confusion in which the man works, to his pre-occupation in what he is actually doing at the cost perhaps of some inattention to his own safety'.

5.17 *Staveley Iron and Chemical Co. v Jones* [1956] AC 627   Contributory negligence may arise in a case of breach of statutory duty but not every risky act or momentary inattention amounts to fault for this purpose. Lord Tucker at 648: 'In Factory Act cases the purpose of imposing the absolute obligation is to protect the workman against those very acts of inattention which are sometimes relied upon as constituting contributory negligence so that too strict a standard would defeat the object of the statute.'

Stapley v Gypsum Mines [1953] 2 All ER 478   The deceased was killed when a   **5.18**
mine roof collapsed while he was acting contrary to his instructions. A broad
view on causation from the House of Lords. Deduction 80%.

Jayes v IMI (Kynoch) Ltd [1985] ICR 155   An experienced workman put his   **5.19**
hand into the moving part of a machine that was unguarded for maintenance.
Assuming a breach of the Factories Act 1961, s 14, the accident was entirely
the fault of the claimant: there is no rule of law that there cannot be 100%
contributory negligence (but see *Pitts v Hunt*, **5.12** above).

Mullard v Ben Line Steamers [1970] 1 WLR 1414   The claimant, an   **5.20**
experienced man, walked into a dark compartment on board a ship where he
was working and fell down an open hatch. He should have realized the danger,
but 'what happened was indeed exactly of the nature intended to be guarded
against by the precautions prescribed by the regulations; and when a defendant's
liability stems from such a breach the court must be careful not to emasculate
those regulations by the side wind of apportionment' (Sachs LJ at 1418).
Contributory negligence was assessed at one third.

Boyle v Kodak [1969] 1 WLR 661   Regulations imposed the duty on both the   **5.21**
claimant, an experienced painter, and the defendant, his employer, to ensure
that the top of a ladder used by the claimant was securely lashed. In order to lash
the ladder, the claimant climbed it when there was an alternative safe means
of access available. Neither party was gravely to blame and the claimant's
contributory negligence was assessed at 50%.

Westwood v Post Office [1974] AC 1   The claimant was injured by falling   **5.22**
through a trapdoor after entering a lift motor room through a door with a
notice 'Only the authorised attendant is permitted to enter'. His disobedience
did not amount to contributory negligence in a claim for breach of statutory
duty.

Fitzgerald v Lane [1989] AC 328   The claimant was a pedestrian who crossed   **5.23**
the road where lights were red against him. The lane of traffic nearest to him
was stationary, but he was struck by the first defendant's car moving in the next
lane, and thrown across the road where he was struck by the second defendant's
car. All three were to blame. The House of Lords held that the approach should
be first to assess the claimant's damages, secondly to reduce them to take
account of the claimant's contributory negligence, and thirdly to apportion
liability between the two defendants under the Civil Liability (Contribution)
Act 1978. Contributory negligence should be measured against the totality of
the negligence of all the defendants.

Parker v PFC Flooring [2001] PIQR P115   The claimant, a sales director of   **5.24**
a small family company, was injured when he climbed onto an unsafe roof. Both

153

he and the company were in breach of the Workplace Regulations. Liability was apportioned 50:50.

D. Cases on Road Accidents

5.25 *Baker v Market Harborough Industrial Co-operative Society* [1953] 1 WLR 1472   Where two vehicles collided head on, both drivers died, and there was no evidence to show that either was the more to blame, liability was apportioned 50:50.

5.26 *Baker v Willoughby* [1970] AC 467   The claimant, a pedestrian crossing the road, was struck by a passing car. Each party had a clear view of the other. Lord Reid at 490: 'A pedestrian has to look to both sides as well as forwards. He is going at perhaps three miles per hour and at that speed he is rarely a danger to anyone else. The motorist has not got to look sideways though he may have to observe over a wide angle ahead: and if he is going at considerable speed he must not relax his observation, for the consequences may be disastrous.' The driver of the car was more blameworthy, and the contributory negligence of the pedestrian was 25%.

5.27 *Eagle v Chambers* [2003] EWCA Civ 1107   The claimant wandered into the road and was struck by the defendant's passing car. It was 11.30 pm, the claimant was drunk and emotional, and the trial judge found her 60% to blame. The Court of Appeal substituted 40%. It was rare for a pedestrian to be found more responsible than the driver unless the pedestrian had suddenly moved into the path of an oncoming vehicle. The court had consistently placed a high burden on drivers to reflect the fact that the car was potentially a dangerous weapon. The driver's conduct was more causatively potent.

5.28 *Meah v McCreamer* [1985] 1 All ER 367   Passenger carried by a driver he knew to be drunk. Deduction 25%.

5.29 *Donelan v Donelan* [1993] PIQR P205   A man insisted that a much younger companion should drive when he knew that she was drunk. Deduction 75%.

E. Children

5.30 In the case of the natural rashness of children, the assessment of fault varies with the individual age and character of the claimant. The test of reasonable care on a particular occasion becomes the reasonable care that is to be expected of an ordinary child of the age of the claimant. There is no legal age limit below which a child cannot be found contributorily negligent, but it is difficult to establish a deduction against very young children and the test is whether the child is of an age such that he can be expected to take care of himself in the circumstances. Sometimes there is an attempt to hold against the child his parent's lack of control. The child cannot be fixed with his parent's negligence but the parent may be vulnerable to a CPR Part 20 claim for contribution from the defendant. For example, if a parent failed to fit an infant into a proper child seat in a car, the parent's contribution under the Civil Liability (Contribution) Act 1978 would follow the approach in *Froom v Butcher* (see **5.33** below).

Gough v Thorne [1966] 1 WLR 1387   Whether a child is contributorily neg-   **5.31**
ligent depends on whether in all the circumstances it is reasonable to expect that child to take precautions for his safety. The claimant, aged 13, obeyed a lorry driver's beckoning and crossed the road in front of the lorry only to be struck by a small car which came along the far side of the lorry. A finding of contributory negligence against the child was overturned.

Morales v Ecclestone [1991] RTR 151   An 11-year-old boy ran out onto a busy   **5.32**
road without looking. Deduction 75%.

F. Seat Belts

One specific area where, unusually, the amount of the deduction that should be   **5.33**
made for contributory negligence has been the subject of specific guidance is in a failure to wear a seat belt in a car. In *Froom v Butcher* [1976] QB 286, the Court of Appeal held that there should be a deduction of 25% if the injuries would have been prevented, and 15% if the seat belt would have made a considerable difference and the injuries would have been a good deal less severe. These are not percentages fixed in law: deductions in between may be made where the evidence justifies it, and it is not impossible to imagine a case where specially culpable bad driving by the defendant resulted in a lower deduction from the claimant's damages; equally in a bad case, for example where the lack of a seat belt resulted in the claimant being thrown out of the car, 25% should not be regarded as an absolute ceiling.

Froom v Butcher [1976] QB 286   Guideline case on the failure to wear a seat   **5.34**
belt: the question is not what was the cause of the accident but what was the cause of the injuries. Deduction 25% if the injuries would have been prevented, 15% if the injuries would have been a good deal less severe and the seat belt would have made a considerable difference.

Hitchens v Berkshire CC, 21 June 2000, CA   The trial judge considered that   **5.35**
the claimant, thrown from the vehicle when not wearing a seat belt, would have

been at least 50% contributorily negligent and perhaps 60% to 70% but he was bound by *Froom v Butcher* to find only 15%. An appeal was compromised at 50% and the Court of Appeal approved the compromise on behalf of a child.

5.36 *Owens v Brimmell* [1977] QB 859   The passenger did not wear a seat belt and knew that the driver was drunk. No deduction for the seat belt because it was not proved that the injuries would have been less serious, but for knowingly being driven by a drunk driver, deduction 20%.

5.37 *Patience v Andrews* [1983] RTR 447   Where a seat belt was not worn, the court should apply *Froom v Butcher* to the actual injuries sustained and must not speculate about what alternative injuries might have been sustained with a seat belt worn.

5.38 *Capps v Miller* [1989] 1 WLR 839   The approach of *Froom v Butcher* applied to motorcycle helmets.

G. Law Reform (Contributory Negligence) Act 1945, ss 1 and 4

1. Apportionment of liability in case of contributory negligence

5.39   (1) Where any person suffers damage as the result partly of his own fault and partly of the fault of any other person or persons, a claim in respect of that damage shall not be defeated by reason of the fault of the person suffering the damage, but the damages recoverable in respect thereof shall be reduced to such extent as the court thinks just and equitable having regard to the claimant's share in the responsibility of the damage: Provided that—

(a) this subsection shall not operate to defeat any defence arising under a contract;

(b) where any contract or enactment providing for the limitation of liability is applicable to the claim, the amount of damages recoverable by the claimant by virtue of this subsection shall not exceed the maximum limit so applicable.

(2) Where damages are recoverable by any person by virtue of the foregoing subsection subject to such reduction as is therein mentioned, the court shall find and record the total damages which would have been recoverable if the claimant had not been at fault.

(5) Where, in any case to which subsection (1) of this section applies, one of the persons at fault avoids liability to any other such person or his personal representative by pleading the Limitation Act 1939, or any other enactment limiting the time within which proceedings may be taken, he shall not be entitled to recover any damages from that other person or representative by virtue of the said subsection.

(6) Where any case to which subsection (1) of this section applies is tried with a jury, the jury shall determine the total damages which would have been recoverable if the claimant had not been at fault and the extent to which those damages are to be reduced.

4. Interpretation

5.40 The following expressions have the meanings hereby respectively assigned to them, that is to say—

'court' means, in relation to any claim, the court or arbitrator by or before whom the claim falls to be determined;

'damage' includes loss of life and personal injury;

'fault' means negligence, breach of statutory duty or other act or omission which gives rise to liability in tort or would, apart from this Act, give rise to the defence of contributory negligence.

6

DEFENCES

Most claims which are defended involve dispute about the facts. They may **6.01** be defended on the ground that the necessary facts are not proved, or by persuading the court to accept contradictory evidence adduced by the defendant. It is possible to speak of a 'defence' of accident or 'Act of God' but in substance this amounts to no more than the claimant failing to prove that the accident should be attributed to negligence or other breach of duty on the part of the defendant. Sometimes however the circumstances of the case give rise to specific legal issues on which a defendant can rely, not just to share the blame with the claimant as with an allegation of contributory negligence, but to escape liability to compensate even though the claimant has suffered damage.

A. Willing Acceptance of Risk

This defence is usually known by the Latin phrase *volenti non fit injuria*. In most **6.02** judgments and textbooks it is shortened to '*volenti*'. Thus, a person who understands the danger and willingly consents to take the risk cannot later complain when injured by the happening of the risk.

An illustration is *Morris v Murray* [1991] 2 QB 6 where the claimant was a **6.03** passenger in a light aeroplane which crashed because of the undoubted negligence of the pilot. The claimant had been drinking all afternoon with the pilot before agreeing to make the flight; the risk was so obvious and great that he was taken to have fully accepted the risk of serious injury.

6.04 Where the defence of willing acceptance of risk is available, it operates as a complete defence. It is all or nothing. It is not possible to apportion the consent and say that the claimant agreed to run certain risks but not the risk of this particular injury so that there should be partial recovery for the excess. Therefore, it is only in strong and clear cases that the defence will be established. Merely to prove that the victim knew of the risk is not the same as to prove that he freely and willingly agreed to accept the risk, and proof merely of knowledge is not enough. However the willing acceptance of risk can be, and frequently is, run as a defence alongside contributory negligence which might well operate as a partial defence in a case of knowledge. The application of the rule to motor car passengers is limited by s 149(3) of the Road Traffic Act 1988 (see below) but it is confirmed in relation to animals by s 5(2) of the Animals Act 1971 and in relation to land and buildings by s 2(5) of the Occupiers' Liability Act 1957. The rule of consent is also relevant to explain the lawfulness of medical treatment which would otherwise amount to an assault, and to explain the lawfulness of injury caused by the ordinary risks of properly conducted sports.

6.05 *Bowater v Rowley Regis* [1944] 1 All ER 465   An employee was asked to take out a horse that was known to the employer and the employee to be unruly. He was injured when it threw him from the cart. Although he knew of the risk, he did not agree to run the risk and the defence of *volenti* failed.

6.06 *ICI v Shatwell* [1965] AC 656   It was argued that the defence of willing assumption of risk could not be used to answer a claim for breach of statutory duty. The House of Lords allowed the defence. Lord Reid said 'there is a world of difference between two fellow servants collaborating carelessly, so that the acts of both contribute to cause injury to one of them, and two fellow servants combining to disobey an order deliberately, though they know the risk involved'.

6.07 *Wooldridge v Sumner* [1963] 2 QB 43   A spectator was injured when he was knocked down by a horse at a competitive horse show. The defence of willing acceptance of risk was argued, but the Court of Appeal analysed the issue as the absence of a breach of the duty of care so that the claim failed on that ground: a sportsman is not under a duty to have regard for the safety of a spectator as long as he plays within the rules of the sport and has adequate skill.

6.08 *Dann v Hamilton* [1939] 1 KB 509   An early case where a passenger in a car knew that the driver was drunk: an early statement that the defence of willing assumption of risk is available in principle to a claim in negligence, but on the facts there was not sufficient knowledge and consent so the claim succeeded.

6.09 *Morris v Murray* [1991] 2 QB 6   The claimant and a friend spent the afternoon drinking and then decided to go for a flight in the friend's aeroplane, which crashed. The claim was defeated because the claimant knew the pilot was so drunk that he could not exercise the normal duty of care, and had willingly assumed the risk of injury resulting from his incapacity.

Owens v Brimmell [1977] QB 859   A modern case of a passenger who knew **6.10** that his driver was drunk: no willing assumption of risk but 20% contributory negligence.

Ogwo v Taylor [1988] AC 431   A firefighter was injured attending a fire started **6.11** by the negligence of the defendant householder. A firefighter does not willingly accept the risk of injury and the claim succeeded.

Baker v Hopkins [1959] 1 WLR 966   A rescuer is not to be taken as willingly **6.12** accepting the risk of injury and may bring a claim against the person who caused the need for rescue.

B. The Claimant's Wrongdoing

Again it is traditional to refer to this rule of law by a Latin phrase: *ex turpi causa* **6.13** *non oritur actio*, usually shortened to *ex turpi causa*. The traditional rule is that no one can bring a claim where the cause of action is founded on his own illegal or immoral act. It is fairly unusual for the rule to be relevant to a personal injury claim but the case notes set out some illustrations. Where it applies, the defence operates as a complete defence to any claim.

Not all illegal or immoral conduct will result in the operation of the defence. **6.14** Conduct must be both serious and relevant to the breach of duty which causes injury. Contributory negligence sometimes amounts to a tort but that does not mean that it becomes a complete defence. Most sets of health and safety regulations impose duties on an employer but also impose a duty on the employee to abide by the regulations, but that does not mean that an employee who is himself in breach is barred from bringing any claim. It is not easy to define the point at which conduct becomes sufficient to bar a claim but in *Pitts v Hunt* [1991] 1 QB 24 the Court of Appeal approved an approach derived from Australian cases to say that the test is whether the conduct has the effect of making it impossible for the court to decide what standard of care should fairly be imposed on the defendant. The claimant in *Pitts* was a pillion passenger who encouraged the rider to ride with extreme recklessness and danger. His participation in this joint illegal enterprise was not only so serious as to prevent the court from determining what standard of care should apply between rider and passenger, it was also directly relevant to the manner in which the motorcycle came to be ridden. The defence succeeded and the claim failed entirely.

6.15 *Pitts v Hunt* [1991] 1 QB 24   The claimant was a pillion passenger who encouraged the rider to ride with extreme recklessness and danger. His participation in this joint illegal enterprise was not only so serious as to prevent the court from determining what standard of care should apply between rider and passenger, it was also directly relevant to the manner in which the motorcycle came to be ridden. The defence succeeded and the claim failed entirely.

6.16 *Murphy v Culhane* [1977] QB 94   A fatal accident claim where the defence admitted the act of killing in an assault and had pleaded guilty to manslaughter, but the court refused to strike out a defence which asserted that the killing took place during an affray that began with an attack by the deceased and others on the defendant.

6.17 *Ashton v Turner* [1981] QB 137   A participant in a burglary was injured by the dangerous and drunken driving of another in the course of the getaway but his claim was excluded on grounds of public policy.

6.18 *Revill v Newbery* [1996] QB 567   The defendant slept in his allotment shed to protect his property from vandals and thieves. The claimant attempted to burgle the shed and the defendant negligently fired a shotgun at the door. Although the claimant admitted attempted burglary, the defence that the injury arose from his own wrongful act was rejected and the defendant was liable subject to two-thirds contributory negligence.

6.19 *Clunis v Camden and Islington Health Authority* [1998] QB 978   The claimant suffered from a mental disorder. He was released from hospital but required continuing treatment. He failed to attend for treatment and committed manslaughter for which he was sentenced to imprisonment. He alleged that his detention was caused by the failure of the health authority to provide treatment. His claim was struck out on grounds of public policy since the claim was founded on his own illegal and immoral act.

6.20 *Kirkham v Chief Constable of Greater Manchester* [1990] 2 QB 283   The police failed to tell the prison about a prisoner's suicidal tendencies, so that precautions were not taken and he committed suicide. Because the deceased had been suffering from depression, and because suicide was the very thing the police were under a duty to protect against, the defence that he willingly accepted the risk of his actions did not apply and the claim succeeded.

6.21 *Reeves v Metropolitan Police Commissioner* [2000] 1 AC 360   A prisoner in custody committed suicide: the defence did not seek to argue in the House of Lords that the fact of suicide was a bar to the claim as a willingly accepted risk or as a wrongful act but argued contributory negligence (not raised in *Kirkham*) and 50% was allowed.

Vellino v Chief Constable of Greater Manchester [2001] EWCA Civ 1249; **6.22**
[2002] PIQR P89   The claimant's own wrongdoing was a complete defence
when he injured himself jumping out of the window of his flat in order to avoid
arrest by the police.

Hewison v Meridien Shipping [2003] PIQR P252   As a result of his injuries **6.23**
the claimant could no longer continue to work offshore oil rigs. His claim for
the loss of future earnings was defeated by the discovery that in obtaining this
employment in the first place he had deliberately concealed the fact that he
suffered from epilepsy which was controlled by medication, but which would, if
known, have precluded him from undertaking such work.

C. Accident, Act of God, Involuntary Act

These phrases are different ways of showing that there was no negligence or **6.24**
arguing that negligence should not be inferred because there is an innocent
explanation for the occurrence of an accident. There can, therefore, be rare cases
where an innocent pedestrian is uncompensated because an accident results
from an unforeseeable crisis such as the sudden unexpected death or
unconsciousness of the driver of a vehicle.

D. Necessity

There is an ill-defined but undoubted principle that an act is not wrongful if it is **6.25**
driven by necessity. So acts in defence of person or property may be excused,
and necessary medical treatment to which the patient is incapable of expressing
consent would be lawful.

E. Limitation

The expiry of the limitation period for a claim will operate as a complete **6.26**
defence to any claim brought, but this is a procedural defence so it applies only
when the defendant chooses to rely on it. In personal injury claims based on
negligence, nuisance or breach of duty, limitation is rarely clear cut in view of
the overriding discretion given by s 33 of the Limitation Act 1980. The defence
of limitation is complex and is considered in detail in Chapter 44.

F. Exclusion Clauses

6.27 At common law there are no restrictions on the freedom of contract and consequently the small print of contracts and the conditions incorporated into tickets or warning notices might seek to exclude liability for injuries however negligently caused. In *White v Blackmore* [1972] 2 QB 651, for example, the operators of a jalopy race were able to escape liability to the widow of a man who was injured as a result of the bad layout of the track fence ropes because of the terms of a warning notice which excluded all liability of the organizers. The Unfair Contract Terms Act 1977 (below) now forbids such exclusions in relation to businesses, though a private person can still seek to limit liability in this way.

G. Road Traffic Act 1988, s 149

149. Avoidance of certain agreements as to liability towards passengers

6.28 (1) This section applies where a person uses a motor vehicle in circumstances such that under section 143 of this Act there is required to be in force in relation to his use of it such a policy of insurance or such security in respect of third-party as complies with the requirements of this Part of this Act.

(2) If any other person is carried in or upon the vehicle while the user is so using it, any antecedent agreement or understanding between them (whether intended to be legally binding or not) shall be of no effect so far as it purports or might be held—

(a) to negative or restrict any such liability of the user in respect of persons carried in or upon the vehicle as is required by section 145 of this Act to be covered by a policy of insurance, or

(b) to impose any conditions with respect to the enforcement of any such liability of the user.

(3) The fact that a person so carried has willingly accepted as his the risk of negligence on the part of the user shall not be treated as negativing any such liability of the user.

(4) For the purposes of this section—

(a) reference to a person being carried in or upon a vehicle include references to a person entering or getting on to, or alighting from, the vehicle, and

(b) the reference to an antecedent agreement is to one made at any time before the liability arose.

H. Unfair Contract Terms Act 1977, ss 1, 2, 10, 11, 13, 14

PART I

1. Scope of Part I

6.29 (1) For the purposes of this Part of this Act, 'negligence' means the breach—

164

(a) of any obligation, arising from the express or implied terms of a contract, to take reasonable care or exercise reasonable skill in the performance of the contract;

(b) of any common law duty to take reasonable care or exercise reasonable skill (but not any stricter duty);

(c) of the common duty of care imposed by the Occupiers' Liability Act 1957 or the Occupier's Liability Act (Northern Ireland) 1957.

(2) This Part of this Act is subject to Part III; and in relation to contracts, the operation of sections 2 to 4 and 7 is subject to the exceptions made by Schedule I.

(3) In the case of both contract and tort, sections 2 to 7 apply (except where the contrary is stated in section 6(4) only to business liability, that is liability to breach of obligations or duties arising—

(a) from things done or to be done by a person in the course of a business (whether his own business or another's); or

(b) from the occupation of premises used for business purposes of the occupier; and references to liability are to be read accordingly [but liability of an occupier of premises for breach of an obligation or duty towards a person obtaining access to the premises for recreational or educational purposes, being liability for loss or damage suffered by reason of the dangerous state of the premises, is not a business liability of the occupier unless granting that person such access for the purposes concerned falls within the business purposes of the occupier].

(4) In relation to any breach of duty or obligation, it is immaterial for any purpose of this Part of this Act whether the breach was inadvertent or inadvertent or intentional, or whether liability for it arises directly or vicariously.

2. Negligence liability

(1) A person cannot by reference to any contract term or to a notice given to persons generally or to particular persons exclude or restrict his liability for death or personal injury resulting from negligence. **6.30**

(2) In the case of other loss or damage, a person cannot so exclude or restrict his liability for negligence except in so far as the term or notice satisfies the requirement of reasonableness.

(3) Where a contract term or notice purports to exclude or restrict liability for negligence a person's agreement to or awareness of it is not of itself to be taken as indicating his voluntary acceptance of any risk.

10. Evasion by means of secondary contract

A person is not bound by any contract term prejudicing or taking away rights of his which arise under, or in connection with the performance of, another contract, so far as those rights extend to the enforcement of another's liability which this Part of this Act prevents that other from excluding or restricting. **6.31**

11. The 'reasonableness' test

(1) In relation to a contract term, the requirement of reasonableness for the purposes of this Part of this Act, section 3 of the Misrepresentation Act 1967 and section 3 of the Misrepresentation Act (Northern Ireland) 1967 is that the term shall have been a fair and reasonable one to be included having regard to the circumstances which were, or ought reasonably to have been, known to or in the contemplation of the parties when the contract was made. **6.32**

(3) In relation to a notice (not being a notice having contractual effect), the requirement of reasonableness under this Act is that it should be fair and reasonable to allow reliance on it, having

regard to all the circumstances obtaining when the liability arose or (but for the notice) would have arisen.

(4) Where by reference to a contract term or notice a person seeks to restrict liability to a specified sum of money, and the question arises (under this or any other Act) whether the term or notice satisfies the requirement of reasonableness, regard shall be had in particular (but without prejudice to subsection (2) above in the case of contract terms) to—

(a) the resources which he could expect to be avaialble to him for the purpose of meeting the liability should it arise; and

(b) how far it was open to him to cover himself by insurance.

(5) It is for those claiming that a contract term or notice satisfies the requirement of reasonableness to show that it does.

13. Varieties of exemption clause

6.33   (1) To the extent that this Part of this Act prevents the exclusion or restriction of any liability it also prevents—

(a) making the liability or its enforcement subject to restrictive or onerous conditions;

(b) excluding or restricting any right or remedy in respect of the liability, or subjecting a person to any prejudice in consequence of his pursuing any such right or remedy;

(c) excluding or restricting rules of evidence or procedure; and (to that extent) sections 2 and 5 to 7 also prevent excluding or restricting liability by reference to terms and notices which exclude or restrict the relevant obligation or duty.

(2) But an agreement in writing to submit present or future differences to arbitration is not to be treated under this Part of this Act as excluding or restricting any liability.

14. Interpretation of Part I

6.34   In this Part of the Act—

'business' includes a profession and the activities of any government department or local or public authority;

'negligence' has the meaning given by section 1(1);

'notice' includes an announcement, whether or not in writing, and any other communication or pretended communication; and

'personal injury' includes any disease and any impairment of physical or mental condition.

7

ROAD ACCIDENTS

A. General Principles

Many personal injury claims arise from road traffic accidents. The liability of **7.01** the road user is a liability in the tort of negligence and driving is therefore judged by the standard of reasonable care.

Because liability turns on the failure to exercise reasonable care, there are few **7.02** hard and fast rules. The exercise of reasonable care is not the same as perfect driving. For example, a driver will not be blamed for an emergency swerve in the heat of the moment that turns out to have been the wrong way. On the other hand, liability may sometimes arise for acts of negligence that are a matter of momentary inattention rather than culpable carelessness. A driver must not assume that another driver will be sensible and careful (see *Truscott v McLaren* [1981] RTR 34 where the driver on a major road at 40 mph kept going when he saw another car approach a minor junction; when they collided the driver on the major road who had the right of way was none the less found 20% to blame).

In a clear case there will often have been a charge of driving without due care **7.03** and attention brought in the magistrates' court. A conviction can be relied on as evidence in a civil claim and will be strong evidence of negligence. It is always worthwhile for the innocent victim of bad driving to press the police to prosecute. However, a conviction will be evidence in support of the case rather than conclusive of liability, and it will not exclude the possibility of contributory negligence being found against any other party involved. The Highway Code provides official advice on good practice. A breach of the Highway Code can be relied on as good evidence of negligence but is not automatically proof of negligence.

7.04 Going out of control, leaving the carriageway or crossing to wrong side of the road, colliding with a stationary and visible obstacle are all examples of driving which will give rise to an inference of negligence, what used to be called *res ipsa loquitur*. In the absence of an explanation the court will find that the driver was negligent if the motor vehicle under his control has behaved in such a way. This is no more than common sense and the move is away from treating it as a formal legal or evidential rule. The ingredients for the application of the inference are:

(a) the thing which caused the accident was under the management or control of defendant;
(b) ordinarily the manner in which the vehicle behaved does not happen without negligence;
(c) no reason for the happening has been given which might account for it having occurred without negligence.

The inference can be rebutted. However, the courts, which are alive to the insurance background of all motoring claims, often find liability in some marginal cases. For example, if there is skidding on ice or snow, it may be held that there is a duty to drive so carefully that there is no risk of injuring others; if the driver has been overcome by illness it may be held that he was negligent to carry on driving after the first warning symptoms of his illness had arisen.

7.05 A breach of the law is not necessarily or automatically negligent. Perhaps it would be more accurate to say that a breach of the law, though usually negligent, may not be a cause accident. A speed that is slightly over the speed limit makes no difference to the outcome if another driver has come round a bend on the wrong side of the road.

7.06 The standard of care is the objective standard of the reasonably careful, prudent motorist. In *Nettleship v Weston* [1971] 2 QB 691, an accident was caused by the elementary incompetence of a learner driver and it was held that he was liable (to his instructor) because the standard is an objective one. An incompetent driver cannot rely on his own shortcomings to argue that he was taking all the care he was capable of.

7.07 One area where a strong inference of negligence arises is where one car collides with the rear of the other. Such accidents, as where the leading car has stopped in the road waiting to turn right, are the cause of a great many neck injury claims. The driver behind is usually found liable: the Highway Code advises drivers to leave enough room to be able to stop. The court will rarely blame the leading driver if he had a sensible reason to stop: the duty is on the driver behind to drive within the limit of his visibility.

Under the European Communities (Rights against Insurers) Regulations 2002 **7.08** if a resident of the United Kingdom suffers loss or injury in a motor accident after 18 January 2003, there is a direct action available against the insurer of the tortfeasor.

If the police attend an accident they will compile a report which is available, **7.09** after any criminal proceedings have been concluded, for a fee. It is essential to obtain a copy of the report in every case in which there is one. Similarly, interested parties are entitled to a copy of the evidence taken at an inquest into a fatal accident and a copy should always be obtained.

These are points of principle. It is not practicable to set out in this chapter **7.10** a narrative account of all the many ways in which the conduct of drivers and pedestrians may give rise to liability. Instead, the case notes illustrate the approach taken. There is of course a risk that it is the decisions that are surprising which attract attention and appeals and therefore come to be reported. For additional help consult Bingham and Berryman's *Motor Claims Cases* where a huge volume of case reports has been collected. Be cautious, however, of excessive reliance on authorities (see *Fosket v Mistry* [1984] RTR 1 and *Practice Direction* [2001] 2 All ER 510). Unless there is a specific issue of principle, most road accident liability cases depend on the facts and are held up rather than assisted by detailed references to previous decisions.

In substantial accident claims before April 1999 it was common to find accident **7.11** reconstruction experts engaged to assist the court with evidence about the occurrence of an accident based on an examination of the scene of the accident and the statements contained in the police report. In truth the main benefit of such a report often lies in the provision of good quality photographs of the scene, the value of which is often very great. Precise information about road layout, visibility range, vehicle dimensions and so forth may also be helpful. On the other hand, judges have often distrusted expert opinions on road accidents, because experts would often enter the area of the judge's responsibility by including comment on the likelihood that the accounts given by particular witnesses were accurate, and comment by way of expressing a conclusion on blame for the accident. The Court of Appeal criticized the use of such experts in *Liddell v Middleton* [1996] PIQR P36. Under the CPR there has been a substantial reduction in the use of accident reconstruction experts and an increased practice of giving joint instructions to a single expert to provide good photographs and to establish uncontroversial background matters such as visibility, gradient and speed limits in any case where this would be a real benefit.

7.12 It cannot be stressed too highly that in a disputed road accident case good, clear photographs of the scene of the accident are essential. It is very unlikely that the judge will visit the scene unless the claim is of exceptional seriousness.

B. Inferring Negligence

7.13 *Widdowson v Newgate Meat* [1998] PIQR P138   The claimant was struck by a van, at night on a dual carriageway, where a pedestrian would not be expected but where there was no impediment to the driver seeing and avoiding a pedestrian. The driver gave no evidence to account for striking the claimant and the Court of Appeal held that an inference of negligence was proper.

7.14 *Howard v Bemrose* [1973] RTR 32   A car and a motorcycle collided in the dark. The cyclist was killed and the car driver remembered nothing. The debris and the final positions of the vehicles left the judge unable to say whether or not the car had crossed to the wrong side of the road. An apportionment 50:50 was upheld.

7.15 *Carter v Sheath* [1990] RTR 12   The claimant, a 13-year-old boy, was struck at a pelican crossing that was green for the car. The boy could remember nothing and neither the driver nor her passenger saw the boy so there was no other direct evidence about the circumstances. The judge held the boy and the driver equally to blame but the Court of Appeal set this aside because the boy had not proved that the driver had been negligent.

C. Standard of Care

7.16 *Nettleship v Weston* [1971] 2 QB 691   An accident was caused by the elementary incompetence of a learner driver and it was held that he was liable (to his instructor) because the standard is an objective one. An incompetent driver cannot rely on his own shortcomings to argue that he was taking all the care he was capable of.

7.17 *Waugh v James Allen Ltd* [1964] 2 Lloyd's Rep 1   The driver of a lorry died from a sudden coronary thrombosis and his lorry injured the claimant. The lorry driver had stopped 15 minutes before the accident feeling unwell, but it was found that he reasonably attributed this to a gastric upset. Although there is a high duty not to drive if one's skill may be impaired, there was no evidence of negligence and the claim failed.

7.18 *Mansfield v Weetabix* [1998] 1 WLR 1263   A collision resulting in property damage was caused by a driver who was unaware that he had a medical condition which impaired his ability to drive. The Court of Appeal held (perhaps surprisingly) that he had done nothing wrong and consequently the claim failed.

Quinn v Scott [1965] 1 WLR 1004   A speeding car driver on a clear, wide **7.19** road came upon a falling tree, braked hard, lost control and crashed into an oncoming van that had pulled up beyond the tree. The car driver was not negligent: high speed alone (which did not at that time break a speed limit) is not evidence of negligence.

Griffin v Mersey Regional Ambulance [1998] PIQR P34   The claimant crossed **7.20** a traffic light controlled junction at a safe speed with the lights on green but had failed to hear or see an ambulance on an emergency call crossing against the red lights. The claimant was found 60% to blame.

Baker v Willoughby [1970] AC 467   A pedestrian with good visibility thought **7.21** he had ample time to cross the road. A driver had the pedestrian in view for 200 yards but collided with him, leading the judge to conclude he must either have been going too fast or failing to keep a proper lookout. Though the Court of Appeal had thought both parties equally to blame, the House of Lords restored the judge's apportionment of 25% against the pedestrian and 75% against the driver. Looking at both causation and blameworthiness, the motorist in his car is the more dangerous to others.

Liddell v Middleton [1996] PIQR P36   The claimant crossed a road **7.22** dangerously near to an approaching car which also failed to see him and could have avoided the collision. The Court of Appeal overturned a finding that the pedestrian was only 25% to blame in favour of 50:50.

Jenkins v Holt [1999] RTR 411   The claimant was driving too fast when the **7.23** defendant started to carry out a u-turn in his path. Neither driver saw the other. The judge held the speeding motorist entirely to blame but the Court of Appeal substituted liability 50:50.

Fletcher v United Counties [1998] PIQR P154   A bus driver started at reason- **7.24** able speed before the claimant, a passenger, had sat down, and then had to make an emergency stop in which the claimant was injured. The Court of Appeal set aside a finding that the driver was at fault: he could not be expected to wait for every passenger to sit down, though it might be otherwise if an infirm passenger or child were involved.

D. Highway Authorities

Burnside v Emerson [1968] 1 WLR 1490   The first defendant's car drove into **7.25** a flood of water on the road and swerved colliding with the claimant's car. The highway authority had failed to maintain the drainage. Liability was apportioned two-thirds against the driver and one-third against the highway authority.

7.26 *Stovin v Wise* [1996] AC 923   At a junction where a bank of earth was known to restrict visibility and improvement works were proposed, a motor cyclist on the major road was injured in a collision with a car emerging from the junction. The car driver sought a contribution from the highway authority but the works were a matter of discretion for the authority and no duty of care was owed to road users.

7.27 *Gorringe v Calderdale MBC* [2004] UKHL 15   The claimant alleged that her road accident was caused by the failure of the highway authority to give her proper warning of a danger by a suitable sign. The House of Lords held that providing road signs was not a part of the duty to maintain the highway under s 41 of the Highways Act 1980, and there was no duty of care at common law that included a private duty to provide warning signs owed to an individual road user.

7.28 *Sandhar and Murray v Department of Transport*, unreported, 26 January 2004   The Railways and Transport Safety Act 2003 has reversed the effect of *Goodes v East Sussex* [2000] 1 WLR 1356 and has amended s 41 of the Highways Act 1980 to impose on highway authorities a duty to deal with snow and ice (see below). However, this applies only after 31 October 2003 and there is no common law liability for incidents before this date.

E. Speed, Time, and Distance

7.29   10 mph is equivalent to 4.47 metres per second
10 mph is equivalent to 14.67 feet per second

A pedestrian walking at 3 mph will take 7.46 seconds to walk 10 metres
A pedestrian walking at 3 mph will take 2.27 seconds to walk 10 feet

In one second a car going at 5 mph will travel 2.23 metres
In one second a car going at 10 mph will travel 4.47 metres
In one second a car going at 20 mph will travel 8.94 metres
In one second a car going at 30 mph will travel 13.41 metres
In one second a car going at 40 mph will travel 17.88 metres
In one second a car going at 50 mph will travel 22.35 metres
In one second a car going at 70 mph will travel 31.28 metres

In one second a car going at 5 mph will travel 7.33 feet
In one second a car going at 10 mph will travel 14.67 feet
In one second a car going at 20 mph will travel 29.33 feet
In one second a car going at 30 mph will travel 44.0 feet
In one second a car going at 40 mph will travel 58.67 feet
In one second a car going at 50 mph will travel 73.34 feet
In one second a car going at 70 mph will travel 102.67 feet

A car going at 5 mph will take 44.84 seconds to travel 100 metres
A car going at 10 mph will take 22.37 seconds to travel 100 metres
A car going at 20 mph will take 11.19 seconds to travel 100 metres
A car going at 30 mph will take 7.46 seconds to travel 100 metres
A car going at 40 mph will take 5.59 seconds to travel 100 metres
A car going at 50 mph will take 4.47 seconds to travel 100 metres
A car going at 70 mph will take 3.20 seconds to travel 100 metres

A car going at 5 mph will take 13.64 seconds to travel 100 feet
A car going at 10 mph will take 6.82 seconds to travel 100 feet
A car going at 20 mph will take 3.41 seconds to travel 100 feet
A car going at 30 mph will take 2.27 seconds to travel 100 feet
A car going at 40 mph will take 1.70 seconds to travel 100 feet
A car going at 50 mph will take 1.36 seconds to travel 100 feet
A car going at 70 mph will take 0.97 seconds to travel 100 feet

F. Highway Code Stopping Distances

7.30

GOOD WEATHER, GOOD VISIBILITY, GOOD ROAD

| Speed | Thinking distance | | Braking distance | | Overall distance | | Speed |
mph	Feet	Metres	Feet	Metres	Feet	Metres	mph
70	70	21	245	75	315	96	70
60	60	18	180	55	240	73	60
50	50	15	125	38	175	53	50
40	40	12	80	24	120	36	40
30	30	9	45	14	75	23	30
20	20	6	20	6	40	12	20

G. Road Traffic Act 1988, s 38(7)

38. The Highway Code

7.31

(7) A failure on the part of a person to observe a provision of the Highway Code shall not of itself render that person liable to criminal proceedings of any kind but any such failure may in any proceedings (whether civil or criminal, and including proceedings for an offence under the Traffic Acts, the Public Passenger Vehicles Act 1981 or sections 18 to 23 of the Transport Act 1985) be relied upon by any party to the proceedings as tending to establish or negative any liability which is in question in those proceedings.

H. Highways Act 1980, ss 41 and 58

41. Duty to maintain highways maintainable at public expense

(1) The authority who are for the time being the highway authority for a highway main-   7.32
tainable at the public expense are under a duty, subject to subsections (2) and (4) below, to maintain the highway.

(1A) In particular, a highway authority are under a duty to ensure, so far as is reasonably practicable, that safe passage along a highway is not endangered by snow or ice.

58. Special defence in action against a highway authority for damages for non-repair of highway

7.33   (1) In an action against a highway authority in respect of damage resulting from their failure to maintain a highway maintainable at the public expense it is a defence (without prejudice to any other defence or the application of the law relating to contributory negligence) to prove that the authority had taken such care as in all the circumstances was reasonably required to secure that the part of the highway to which the action relates was not dangerous for traffic.

(2) For the purposes of a defence under subsection (1) above, the court shall in particular have regard to the following matters:—

(a) the character of the highway, and the traffic which was reasonably to be expected to use it;

(b) the standard of maintenance appropriate for a highway of that character and used by such traffic;

(c) the state of repair in which a reasonable person would have expected to find the highway;

(d) whether the highway authority knew, or could reasonably have been expected to know, that the condition of the part of the highway to which the action relates was likely to cause danger to users of the highway;

(e) where the highway authority could not reasonably have been expected to repair that part of the highway before the cause of action arose, what warning notices of its condition had been displayed; but for the purposes of such a defence it is not relevant to prove that the highway authority had arranged for a competent person to carry out or supervise the maintenance of the part of the highway to which the action relates unless it is also proved that the authority had given him proper instructions with regard to the maintenance of the highway and that he had carried out the instructions.

(3) This section binds the Crown.

8

THE MOTOR INSURERS' BUREAU

A. The MIB Agreements

All motorists should be insured against liability to those they may injure by their **8.01** driving. Such insurance is compulsory but sometimes people drive uninsured and those who do so are unfortunately quite likely to be among the most likely to drive dangerously. The risk has led the industry and government to co-operate in devising a system by which the insurers, through the Motor Insurers' Bureau (MIB), agree to compensate the victims of uninsured or untraced drivers, victims who might otherwise not receive the compensation to which they are entitled. The cost, of course, falls on the insurance premiums of those who do pay. The current address of the MIB is:

> Motor Insurers' Bureau
> Linford Wood House, 6–12 Capital Drive
> Linford Wood, Milton Keynes MK14 6XT
> DX 142620 Milton Keynes 10
> tel: 01908 830001; fax: 01908 671681

The website address, from which the agreements and application form can be downloaded is www.mib.org.uk and inquiries can be addressed to Enquiries@MIB.org.uk.

There are two agreements which set out the obligations of the MIB: the Motor **8.02** Insurers' Bureau (Compensation of Victims of Untraced Drivers Agreement) 2003 and the Motor Insurers' Bureau (Uninsured Drivers Agreement) 1999. These are the current successors to a series of agreements that have been in place since the inception of the MIB in 1946. The agreements are set out in full below because they are complex and an attempt to simplify or summarize would risk encouraging an applicant to underestimate the significance of the detail. This is a vital point: the details of the agreements must be taken seriously and the requirements must be followed precisely. The 1999 Agreement, in particular, sets out some very onerous requirements of notification, often with a degree of detail and repetition that seems excessive; but a failure to comply will give the MIB an opportunity to disclaim liability. No practitioner should ever assume that the MIB would not take such a point. If in doubt, read the cautionary tale in *Silverton v Goodall* [1997] PIQR P451 and the point taken in *Begum v Ullah* [1998] CLY 590.

8.03   The two agreements operate in different ways. With the Uninsured Drivers Agreement, unless a claim is settled by consent, the liability of the MIB is to satisfy an otherwise unsatisfied judgment. A claim will proceed against the named driver; if it is not settled by agreement it goes to trial and the victim obtains a judgment against the driver; and the MIB will satisfy the judgment if the requirements of the Agreement have been complied with. The claimant is entitled to the same recovery as if the driver had been covered by insurance. With the Untraced Drivers Agreement, there is no defendant against whom a civil claim can be brought and the MIB itself assesses the compensation to be awarded subject to a right of appeal to an arbitrator. The 2003 Agreement applies to incidents which appear after 14 February 2003. For incidents before that date, the 1996 Agreement applies and this is less generous with regard to property damage, interest and costs: a copy of the Agreement can be obtained from the MIB website.

8.04   If there are two defendant parties alleged to have been responsible for an accident, only one of whom is untraced or uninsured, then if there is liability in however small a proportion found against the party who is insured, that insurer will have to meet the entire claim and the MIB scheme will not come into play.

8.05   With the Uninsured Drivers Agreement, where there are court proceedings, provided proper notice is given in accordance with the Agreement it is not necessary for the claimant to name the MIB as a defendant to a claim. If there is a dispute whether the uninsured driver is liable, the MIB will support the defence of the claim in the same anonymous way as an insurer. Therefore, unless there is an issue about the liability of the MIB under the terms of the scheme, it is proper for the case to proceed on both liability and the assessment of damages between only the two individual parties, the victim and the uninsured driver, though the driver himself may play little or no active part and the defence is in reality run by the MIB. However, it seems increasingly to be sensible for claimants to join the MIB as second defendant from the outset in any uninsured driver case. The court process will then of itself take over many of the notice obligations arising under the Agreement. The added costs should be minimal and should be recoverable as part of the costs of the action. The MIB generally welcomes being joined. The terms of doing so must of course make clear that the MIB is not sued for primary liability, buy only on the basis of the Agreement so that the MIB is liable when a judgment has not been satisfied in full within seven days; the relief claimed against the MIB is a declaration of its contingent liability.

Sometimes, however, the dispute is not about the negligence of the uninsured **8.06** driver but about the entitlement of the injured person to the indemnity provided by the agreement. For example, cl 6(1)(e) of the Uninsured Drivers Agreement excludes a claim by a passenger who knew that the driver was uninsured, and this has been the subject of many disputes. If the facts on which the MIB claims to be entitled to refuse a claim are in dispute, the MIB will often seek to be joined as a defendant in order to counterclaim for an order that there is no liability under the agreement to meet the claim. On the merits of this exclusion the House of Lords in *White v White* [2001] UKHL 9; [2001] PIQR P281, has held that negligence or carelessness as to whether the driver was insured will not be enough to entitle the MIB to refuse a claim because that does not comply with the terms of the Second EEC Motor Insurance Directive 84/5/EEC that a claim should be met unless the passenger knew there was no insurance.

The MIB has introduced a legal expenses scheme to cover claims under the **8.07** Uninsured Drivers Agreement (see at www.firstassist.co.uk/mibles/). A Motor Insurance Database (MID) has also been set up to give solicitors access to information about any record of insurance in relation to a specific vehicle involved in an accident with their client. The Motor Insurers' Information Centre (MIIC) was established by the insurance industry to oversee the development and ongoing management of the MID (for information see www.miic.org.uk/).

White v White [2001] UKHL 9; [2001] PIQR P281   A moderately claimant- **8.08** friendly conclusion on the issue of the exemption in cl 6(1)(e)(ii) of the 1988 Uninsured Drivers Agreement when a passenger knew or ought to have known that the driver was uninsured: the passenger knew the driver had no driving licence but had given no thought to the question of insurance; carelessness or negligence are not enough and the exception to liability of the MIB did not apply.

Evans v Secretary of State [2001] PIQR P3   An award under the Untraced **8.09** Drivers Agreement does not include interest or costs; the correctness of this limitation has been referred to the European Court of Justice.

8.10   *Stinton v Stinton* [1995] RTR 167   The claimant was a passenger in his brother's car which crashed after both had been drinking. The driver was uninsured. For present purposes the interest of the case is that the notice requirements of the Uninsured Drivers Agreement were strictly applied to exclude the right of the claimant to have the MIB satisfy the judgment he obtained.

8.11   *Dray v Docherty* (1998) CL 99/525   The MIB was not able to escape liability by relying on a failure to meet demands for information that were not necessary or reasonable.

8.12   *O'Mahoney v MIB* [1999] PIQR P149   A pillion passenger on a motorcycle was a user of it on the facts of the case, though a passenger would not always be a user.

8.13   *Norman v Aziz* [2000] PIQR P72   This case includes a warning of the importance of complying strictly with the notice requirements of the Uninsured Drivers Agreement.

8.14   *Silverton v Goodall* [1997] PIQR P451   The claimant, through the fault of the Court office and not himself, did not know the date of issue and gave notice to the MIB late: the MIB's refusal to meet the claim was upheld. Compare *Begum v Ullah* [1998] CLY 590 where the claimant was able to prove an estoppel against the MIB.

8.15   *Pickett v MIB* [2004] EWCA Civ 06   The claimant allowed her boyfriend to drive a car in which she was a passenger, knowing that he was uninsured. When he began to make handbrake turns she asked him to stop, but was injured when the car overturned. The MIB relied on cl 6(1)(e) of the 1988 Agreement. The Court of Appeal held that the consent given by the claimant when she entered the vehicle was capable of being withdrawn before the accident which gave rise to her claim, but the withdrawal must amount to an unequivocal repudiation of the common venture to which consent had been given when entering the vehicle. A request to stop the vehicle was not enough, and the claimant had failed to show that her consent had been withdrawn.

B. The Uninsured Drivers Agreement 1999

MOTOR INSURERS' BUREAU (UNINSURED DRIVERS) AGREEMENT 1999

INTERPRETATION

GENERAL DEFINITIONS

8.16   1. In this Agreement, unless the context otherwise requires, the following expressions have the following meanings—

'1988 Act' means the Road Traffic Act 1988;

'1988 Agreement' means the Agreement made on 21 December 1988 between the Secretary of State for Transport and MIB;

'bank holiday' means a day which is, or is to be observed as, a bank holiday under the Banking and Financial Dealings Act 1971;

'claimant' means a person who has commenced or who proposes to commence relevant proceedings and has made an application under this Agreement in respect thereof;

'contract of insurance' means a policy of insurance or a security covering a relevant liability;

'insurer' includes the giver of a security;

'MIB's obligation' means the obligation contained in clause 5;

'property' means any property whether real, heritable or personal;

'relevant liability' means a liability in respect of which a contract of insurance must be in force to comply with Part VI of the 1988 Act;

'relevant proceedings' means proceedings in respect of a relevant liability (and

'commencement', in relation to such proceedings means, in England and Wales, the date on which a Claim Form or other originating process is issued by a Court or, in Scotland, the date on which the originating process is served on the Defender)

'relevant sum' means a sum payable or remaining payable under an unsatisfied judgment, including—

(a) an amount payable or remaining payable in respect of interest on that sum, and

(b) either the whole of the costs (whether taxed or not) awarded by the Court as part of that judgment or, where the judgment includes an award in respect of a liability which is not a relevant liability, such proportion of those costs as the relevant liability bears to the total sum awarded under the judgment;

'specified excess' means £300 or such other sum as may from time to time be agreed in writing between the Secretary of State and MIB;

'unsatisfied judgment' means a judgment or order (by whatever name called) in respect of a relevant liability which has not been satisfied in full within seven days from the date upon which the claimant became entitled to enforce it.

MEANING OF REFERENCES

2.—(1) Save as otherwise herein provided, the Interpretation Act 1978 shall apply for the **8.17** interpretation of this Agreement as it applies for the interpretation of an Act of Parliament.

(2) Where, under this Agreement, something is required to be done—

(a) within a specified period after or from the happening of a particular event, the period begins on the day after the happening of that event;

(b) within or not less than a specified period before a particular event, the period ends on the day immediately before the happening of that event.

(3) Where, apart from this paragraph, the period in question, being a period of seven days or less, would include a Saturday, Sunday or bank holiday or Christmas Day or Good Friday, that day shall be excluded.

(4) Save where expressly otherwise provided, a reference in this Agreement to a numbered clause is a reference to the clause bearing that number in this Agreement and a reference to a numbered paragraph is a reference to a paragraph bearing that number in the clause in which the reference occurs.

(5) In this Agreement—

(a) a reference (however framed) to the doing of any act or thing by or the happening of any event in relation to the claimant includes a reference to the doing of that act or thing by or the happening of that event in relation to a Solicitor or other person acting on his behalf, and

(b) a requirement to give notice to, or to serve documents upon, MIB or an insurer mentioned in clause 9(1)(a) shall be satisfied by the giving of the notice to, or the service of the documents upon, a Solicitor acting on its behalf in the manner provided for.

CLAIMANTS NOT OF FULL AGE OR CAPACITY

8.18   3. Where, under and in accordance with this Agreement—

(a) any act or thing is done to or by a Solicitor or other person acting on behalf of a claimant,

(b) any decision is made by or in respect of a Solicitor or other person acting on behalf of a claimant, or

(c) any sum is paid to a Solicitor or other person acting on behalf of a claimant,

then, whatever may be the age or other circumstances affecting the capacity of the claimant, that act, thing, decision or sum shall be treated as if it had been done to or by, or made in respect of or paid to a claimant of full age and capacity.

PRINCIPAL TERMS

DURATION OF AGREEMENT

8.19   4.—(1) This agreement shall come into force on 1st October 1999 in relation to accidents occurring on or after that date and, save as provided by clause 23, the 1988 Agreement shall cease and determine immediately before that date.

(2) This Agreement may be determined by the Secretary of State or by MIB giving to the other not less than twelve months' notice in writing but without prejudice to its continued operation in respect of accidents occurring before the date of termination.

MIB'S OBLIGATION TO SATISFY COMPENSATION CLAIMS

8.20   5.—(1) Subject to clauses 6 to 17, if a claimant has obtained against any person in a Court in Great Britain a judgment which is an unsatisfied judgment then MIB will pay the relevant sum to, or to the satisfaction of, the claimant or will cause the same to be so paid.

(2) Paragraph (1) applies whether or not the person liable to satisfy the judgment is in fact covered by a contract of insurance and whatever may be the cause of his failure to satisfy the judgment.

EXCEPTIONS TO AGREEMENT

8.21   6.—(1) Clause 5 does not apply in the case of an application made in respect of a claim of any of the following descriptions (and, where part only of a claim satisfies such a description, clause 5 does not apply to that part)—

(a) a claim arising out of a relevant liability incurred by the user of a vehicle owned by or in the possession of the Crown, unless—

(i) responsibility for the existence of a contract of insurance under Part VI of the 1988 Act in relation to that vehicle had been undertaken by some other person (whether or not the person liable was in fact covered by a contract of insurance), or

(ii) the relevant liability was in fact covered by a contract of insurance;

(b) a claim arising out of the use of a vehicle which is not required to be covered by a contract of insurance by virtue of section 144 of the 1988 Act, unless the use is in fact covered by such a contract;

(c) a claim by, or for the benefit of, a person ('the beneficiary') other than the person suffering death, injury or other damage which is made either—

(i) in respect of a cause of action or a judgment which has been assigned to the beneficiary, or

(ii) pursuant to a right of subrogation or contractual or other right belonging to the beneficiary;

(d) a claim in respect of damage to a motor vehicle or losses arising therefrom where, at the time when the damage to it was sustained—

(i) there was not in force in relation to the use of that vehicle such a contract of insurance as is required by Part VI of the 1988 Act, and

(ii) the claimant either knew or ought to have known that that was the case;

(e) a claim which is made in respect of a relevant liability described in paragraph (2) by a claimant who, at the time of the use giving rise to the relevant liability was voluntarily allowing himself to be carried in the vehicle and, either before the commencement of his journey in the vehicle or after such commencement if he could reasonably be expected to have alighted from it, knew or ought to have known that—

(i) the vehicle had been stolen or unlawfully taken,

(ii) the vehicle was being used without there being in force in relation to its use such a contract of insurance as would comply with Part VI of the 1988 Act,

(iii) the vehicle was being used in the course or furtherance of a crime, or

(iv) the vehicle was being used as a means of escape from, or avoidance of, lawful apprehension.

(2) The relevant liability referred to in paragraph (1)(e) is a liability incurred by the owner or registered keeper or a person using the vehicle in which the claimant was being carried.

(3) The burden of proving that the claimant knew or ought to have known of any matter set out in paragraph (1)(e) shall be on MIB but, in the absence of evidence to the contrary, proof by MIB of any of the following matters shall be taken as proof of the claimant's knowledge of the matter set out in paragraph (1)(e)(ii)—

(a) that the claimant was the owner or registered keeper of the vehicle or had caused or permitted its use;

(b) that the claimant knew the vehicle was being used by a person who was below the minimum age at which he could be granted a licence authorising the driving of a vehicle of that class.

(c) that the claimant knew that the person driving the vehicle was disqualified for holding or obtaining a driving licence;

(d) that the claimant knew that the user of the vehicle was neither its owner nor registered keeper nor an employee of the owner or registered keeper nor the owner or registered keeper of any other vehicle.

(4) Knowledge which the claimant has or ought to have for the purposes of paragraph (1)(e) includes knowledge of matters which he could reasonably be expected to have been aware of had he not been under the self-induced influence of drink or drugs.

(5) For the purposes of this clause—

(a) a vehicle which has been unlawfully removed from the possession of the Crown shall be taken to continue in that possession whilst it is kept so removed,

(b) references to a person being carried in a vehicle include references to his being carried upon, entering, getting on to and alighting from the vehicle, and

(c) 'owner', in relation to a vehicle which is the subject of a hiring agreement or a hire-purchase agreement, means the person in possession of the vehicle under that agreement.

CONDITIONS PRECEDENT TO MIB'S OBLIGATION

FORM OF APPLICATION

8.22   7.—(1) MIB shall incur no liability under MIB's obligation unless an application is made to the person specified in clause 9(1)—

(a) in such form

(b) giving such information about the relevant proceedings and other matters relevant to this Agreement, and

(c) accompanied by such documents as MIB may reasonably require.

(2) Where an application is signed by a person who is neither the claimant nor a Solicitor acting on his behalf MIB may refuse to accept the application (and shall incur no liability under MIB's obligation) until it is reasonably satisfied that, having regard to the status of the signatory and his relationship to the claimant, the claimant is fully aware of the contents and effect of the application but subject thereto MIB shall not refuse to accept such an application by reason only that it is signed by a person other than the claimant or his Solicitor.

SERVICE OF NOTICES ETC.

8.23   8. Any notice required to be given or documents to be supplied to MIB pursuant to clauses 9 to 12 of this Agreement shall be sufficiently given or supplied only if sent by facsimile transmission or by Registered or Recorded Delivery post to MIB's registered office for the time being and delivery shall be proved by the production of a facsimile transmission report produced by the sender's facsimile machine or an appropriate postal receipt.

NOTICE OF RELEVANT PROCEEDINGS

8.24   9.—(1) MIB shall incur no liability under MIB's obligation unless proper notice of the bringing of the relevant proceedings has been given by the claimant not later than fourteen days after the commencement of those proceedings—

(a) in the case of proceedings in respect of a relevant liability which is covered by a contract of insurance with an insurer whose identity can be ascertained, to that insurer;

(b) in any other case, to MIB.

(2) In this clause 'proper notice' means, except in so far as any part of such information or any copy document or other thing has already been supplied under clause 7—

(a) notice in writing that proceedings have been commenced by Claim Form, Writ, or other means,

(b) a copy of the sealed Claim Form, Writ or other official document providing evidence of the commencement of the proceedings and, in Scotland, a statement of the means of service,

(c) a copy or details of any insurance policy providing benefits in the case of the death, bodily injury or damage to property to which the proceedings relate where the claimant is the insured party and the benefits are available to him,

(d) copies of all correspondence in the possession of the claimant or (as the case may be) his Solicitor or agent to or from the Defendant or the Defender or (as the case may be) his Solicitor, insurers or agent which is relevant to—

(i) the death, bodily injury or damage for which the Defendant or Defender is alleged to be responsible, or

(ii) any contract of insurance which covers, or which may or has been alleged to cover, liability for such death, injury or damage the benefit of which is, or is claimed to be, available to Defendant or Defender,

(e) subject to paragraph (3), a copy of the Particulars of Claim whether or not indorsed on the Claim Form, Writ or other originating process, and whether or not served (in England and Wales) on any Defendant or (in Scotland) on any Defender, and

(f) a copy of all other documents which are required under the appropriate rules of procedure to be served on a Defendant or Defender with the Claim Form, Writ or other originating process or with the Particulars of Claim,

(g) such other information about the relevant proceedings as MIB may reasonably specify.

(3) If, in the case of proceedings commenced in England or Wales, the Particulars of Claim (including any document required to be served therewith) has not yet been served with the Claim Form or other originating process paragraph (2)(e) shall be sufficiently complied with if a copy thereof is served on MIB not later than seven days after it is served on the Defendant.

NOTICE OF SERVICE OF PROCEEDINGS

10.—(1) This clause applies where the relevant proceedings are commenced in England or Wales.   **8.25**

(2) MIB shall incur no liability under MIB's obligation unless the claimant has, not later than the appropriate date, given notice in writing to the person specified in clause 9(1) of the date of service of the Claim Form or other originating process in the relevant proceedings.

(3) In this clause, 'the appropriate date' means the day falling—
(a) seven days after—
(i) the date when the claimant receives notification from the Court that service of the Claim Form or other originating process has occurred,
(ii) the date when the claimant receives notification from the Defendant that service of the Claim Form or other originating process has occurred, or
(iii) the date of personal service, or
(b) fourteen days after the date when service is deemed to have occurred in accordance with the Civil Procedure Rules,

whichever of those days occurs first.

FURTHER INFORMATION

11.—(1) MIB shall incur no liability under MIB's obligation unless the claimant has, not later   **8.26**
than seven days after the occurrence of any of the following events, namely—
(a) the filing of a defence in the relevant proceedings,
(b) any amendment to the Particulars of Claim or any amendment of or addition to any schedule or other document required to be served therewith, and
(c) either—
(i) the setting down of the case for trial, or
(ii) where the court gives notice to the claimant of the trial date, the date when that notice is received,

given notice in writing of the date of that event to the person specified in clause 9(1) and has, in the case of the filing of a defence or an amendment of the Particulars of Claim or any amendment of or addition to any schedule or other document required to be served therewith, supplied a copy thereof to that person.

(2) MIB shall incur no liability under MIB's obligation unless the claimant furnishes to the person specified in clause 9(1) within a reasonable time after being required to do so such further information and documents in support of his claim as MIB may reasonably require notwithstanding that the claimant may have complied with clause 7(1).

NOTICE OF INTENTION TO APPLY FOR JUDGMENT

12.—(1) MIB shall incur no liability under MIB's obligation unless the claimant has,   **8.27**
after commencement of the relevant proceedings and not less than thirty-five days before the

appropriate date, given notice in writing to the person specified in clause 9(1) of his intention to apply for or to sign judgment in the relevant proceedings.

(2) In this clause, 'the appropriate date' means the date when the application for judgment is made or, as the case may be, the signing of judgment occurs.

SECTION 154 OF THE 1988 ACT

8.28   13. MIB shall incur no liability under MIB's obligation unless the claimant has as soon as reasonably practicable—

(a) demanded the information and, where appropriate, the particulars specified in section 154(1) of the 1988 Act, and

(b) if the person of whom the demand is made fails to comply with the provisions of that subsection—

(i) made a formal complaint to a police officer in respect of such failure, and

(ii) used all reasonable endeavours to obtain the name and address of the registered keeper of the vehicle.

or, if so required by MIB, has authorised MIB to take such steps on his behalf.

PROSECUTION OF PROCEEDINGS

8.29   14. MIB shall incur no liability under MIB's obligation—

(a) unless the claimant has, if so required by MIB and having been granted a full indemnity by MIB as to costs, taken all reasonable steps to obtain judgment against every person who may be liable (including any person who may be vicariously liable) in respect of the injury or death or damage to property, or

(b) if the claimant, upon being requested to do so by MIB, refuses to consent to MIB being joined as a party to the relevant proceedings.

ASSIGNMENT OF JUDGMENT AND UNDERTAKINGS

8.30   15. MIB shall incur no liability under MIB's obligation unless the claimant has—

(a) assigned to MIB or its nominee the unsatisfied judgment, whether or not that judgment includes an amount in respect of a liability other than a relevant liability, and any order for costs made in the relevant proceedings, and

(b) undertaken to repay to MIB any sum paid to him—

(i) by MIB in discharge of MIB's obligation if the judgment is subsequently set aside either as a whole or in respect of the part of the relevant liability to which that sum relates;

(ii) by any other person by way of compensation or benefit for the death, bodily injury or other damage to which the relevant proceedings relate, including a sum which would have been deductible under the provisions of clause 17 if it had been received before MIB was obliged to satisfy MIB's obligation.

LIMITATIONS ON MIB's LIABILITY

COMPENSATION FOR DAMAGE TO PROPERTY

8.31   16.—(1) Where a claim under this Agreement includes a claim in respect of damage to property, MIB's obligation in respect of that part of the relevant sum which is awarded for such damage and any losses arising therefrom (referred to in this clause as 'the property damage compensation') is limited in accordance with the following paragraphs.

(2) Where the property damage compensation does not exceed the specified excess, MIB shall incur no liability.

(3) Where the property damage compensation in respect of any one accident exceeds the specified excess but does not exceed £250,000, MIB shall incur liability only in respect of the property damage compensation less the specified excess.

(4) Where the property damage compensation in respect of any one accident exceeds £250,000, MIB shall incur liability only in respect of the sum of £250,000 less the specified excess.

COMPENSATION RECEIVED FROM OTHER SOURCES

17. Where a claimant has received compensation from— **8.32**
   (a) the Policyholders Protection Board under the Policyholders Protection Act 1975, or
   (b) an insurer under an insurance agreement or arrangement, or
   (c) any other source,

in respect of the death, bodily injury or other damage to which the relevant proceedings relate and such compensation has not been taken into account in the calculation of the relevant sum MIB may deduct from the relevant sum, in addition to any sum deductible under clause 16, an amount equal to that compensation.

MISCELLANEOUS

NOTIFICATIONS OF DECISIONS BY MIB

18. Where a claimant— **8.33**
   (a) has made an application in accordance with clause 7, and
   (b) has given to the person specified in clause 9(1) proper notice of the relevant proceedings in accordance with clause 9(2),

MIB shall—

   (i) give a reasoned reply to any request made by the claimant relating to the payment of compensation in pursuance of MIB's obligation, and
   (ii) as soon as reasonably practicable notify the claimant in writing of its decision regarding the payment of the relevant sum, together with the reasons for that decision.

REFERENCE OF DISPUTES TO THE SECRETARY OF STATE

19.—(1) In the event of any dispute as to the reasonableness of a requirement made by **8.34**
MIB for the supply of information or documentation or for the taking of any step by the claimant, it may be referred by the claimant or MIB to the Secretary of State whose decision shall be final.

(2) Where a dispute is referred to the Secretary of State—
   (a) MIB shall supply the Secretary of State and, if it has not already done so, the claimant with notice in writing of the requirement from which the dispute arises, together with the reasons for that requirement and such further information as MIB considers relevant, and
   (b) where the dispute is referred by the claimant, the claimant shall supply the Secretary of State and, if he has not already done so, MIB with notice in writing of the grounds on which he disputes the reasonableness of the requirement.

RECOVERIES

20. Nothing in this Agreement shall prevent an insurer from providing by conditions in a **8.35**
contract of insurance that all sums paid by the insurer or by MIB by virtue of the Principal Agreement or this Agreement in or towards the discharge of the liability of the insured shall be recoverable by them or by MIB from the insured or from any other person.

APPORTIONMENT OF DAMAGES, ETC.

8.36   21.—(1) Where an unsatisfied judgment which includes an amount in respect of a liability other than a relevant liability has been assigned to MIB or its nominee in pursuance of clause 15 MIB shall—

(a) apportion any sum it receives in satisfaction or partial satisfaction of the judgment according to the proportion which the damages awarded in respect of the relevant liability bear to the damages awarded in respect of the other liability, and

(b) account to the claimant in respect of the moneys received properly apportionable to the other liability.

(2) Where the sum received includes an amount in respect of interest or an amount awarded under an order for costs, the interest or the amount received in pursuance of the order shall be dealt with in the manner provided in paragraph (1).

AGENTS

8.37   22. MIB may perform any of its obligations under this Agreement by agents.

TRANSITIONAL PROVISIONS

8.38   23.—(1) The 1988 Agreement shall continue in force in relation to claims arising out of accidents occurring before 1st October 1999 with the modifications contained in paragraph (2).

(2) In relation to any claim made under the 1988 Agreement after this Agreement has come into force, the 1988 Agreement shall apply as if there were inserted after clause 6 thereof—

'6A. Where any person in whose favour a judgment in respect of a relevant liability has been made has

(a) made a claim under this Agreement, and

(b) satisfied the requirements specified in clause 5 hereof,

MIB shall, if requested to do so, give him a reasoned reply regarding the satisfaction of that claim.'.

C. The Untraced Drivers Agreement 2003

THE UNTRACED DRIVERS AGREEMENT 2003

INTERPRETATION

General interpretation

8.39   1. (1) In this Agreement, unless the context otherwise requires, the following expressions have the following meanings—

'1988 Act' means the Road Traffic Act 1988;

'1996 Agreement' means the Agreement made on 14 June 1996 between the Secretary of State for Transport and MIB providing for the compensation of victims of untraced drivers;

'1999 Agreement' means the Agreement dated 13th August 1999 made between the Secretary of State for the Environment, Transport and the Regions and MIB providing for the compensation of victims of uninsured drivers;

'applicant' means the person who has applied for compensation in respect of a death, bodily injury or damage to property (or the person on whose behalf such an application has been made) and 'application' means an application made by or on behalf of an applicant;

'arbitrator', where the arbitration takes place under Scottish law, includes an arbiter;

'award' means the aggregate of the sums which MIB is obliged to pay under this Agreement;

'bank holiday' means a day which is, or is to be observed as, a bank holiday under the Banking and Financial Dealings Act 1971;

'judgement' means, in relation to a court in Scotland, a court decree;

'property' means any property whether (in England and Wales) real or personal, or (in Scotland) heritable or moveable;

'relevant proceedings' means civil proceedings brought by the applicant (whether or not pursuant to a requirement made under this Agreement) against a person other than the unidentified person in respect of an event described in clause 4(1);

'specified excess' means £300 or such other sum as may from time to time be agreed in writing between the Secretary of State and MIB;

'unidentified person' means a person who is, or appears to be, wholly or partly liable in respect of the death, injury or damage to property to which an application relates and who cannot be identified.

(2) Save as otherwise herein provided, the Interpretation Act 1978 shall apply for the interpretation of this Agreement as it applies for the interpretation of an Act of Parliament.

(3) Where, under this Agreement, something is required to be done within a specified period after a date or the happening of a particular event, the period begins on the day after the happening of that event.

(4) Where, apart from this paragraph, the period in question, being a period of 7 days or less, would include a Saturday, Sunday, bank holiday, Christmas Day or Good Friday, that day shall be excluded.

(5) Save where expressly otherwise provided, a reference in this Agreement to a numbered clause is a reference to the clause bearing that number in this Agreement and a reference to a numbered paragraph is a reference to a paragraph bearing that number in the clause or schedule in which the reference occurs.

(6) In this Agreement—

(a) a reference (however framed) to the doing of any act or thing by or the happening of any event in relation to the applicant includes a reference to the doing of that act or thing by or the happening of that event in relation to a Solicitor or other person acting on his behalf, and

(b) a requirement to give notice or send documents to MIB shall, where MIB has appointed a Solicitor to act on its behalf in relation to the application, be satisfied by the giving of the notice or the sending of the documents, in the manner herein provided for, to that Solicitor.

Applicants' representatives

2. Where, under and in accordance with this Agreement—   **8.40**

(a) any notice or other document is given to or by a Solicitor or other person acting on behalf of an applicant,

(b) any act or thing is done by or in respect of such Solicitor or other person,

(c) any decision is made by or in respect of such Solicitor or other person, or

(d) any payment is made to such Solicitor or other person,

then, whatever may be the age or other circumstances affecting the capacity of the applicant, that act, thing, decision or payment shall be treated as if it had been done to or by, or made to or in respect of an applicant of full age and capacity.

APPLICATION OF AGREEMENT

Duration of Agreement

8.41   3. (1) This Agreement shall come into force on 14 February 2003.

(2) This Agreement may be determined by the Secretary of State or by MIB giving to the other not less than twelve months notice in writing to that effect.

(3) Notwithstanding the giving of notice of determination under paragraph (2) this Agreement shall continue to operate in respect of any application made in respect of death, bodily injury or damage to property arising from an event occurring on or before the date of termination specified in the notice.

Scope of Agreement

8.42   4. (1) Save as provided in clause 5, this Agreement applies where—
(a) the death of, or bodily injury to, a person or damage to any property of a person has been caused by, or arisen out of, the use of a motor vehicle on a road or other public place in Great Britain, and
(b) the event giving rise to the death, bodily injury or damage to property occurred on or after fourteenth day February 2003, and
(c) the death, bodily injury or damage to property occurred in circumstances giving rise to liability of a kind which is required to be covered by a policy of insurance or a security under Part VI of the 1988 Act, and
(d) it is not possible for the applicant—
(i) to identify the person who is, or appears to be, liable in respect of the death, injury or damage, or
(ii) (where more than one person is or appears to be liable) to identify any one or more of those persons,
and
(e) the applicant has made an application in writing to MIB for the payment of an award in respect of such death, bodily injury or damage to property (and in a case where they are applicable the requirements of paragraph (2) are satisfied), and
(f) the conditions specified in paragraph (3), or such of those conditions as are relevant to the application, are satisfied.

(2) Where an application is signed by a person who is neither the applicant nor a Solicitor acting on behalf of the applicant MIB may refuse to accept the application (and shall incur no liability under this Agreement) until it is reasonably satisfied that, having regard to the status of the signatory and his relationship with the applicant, the applicant is fully aware of the content and effect of the application but subject thereto MIB shall not refuse to accept an application by reason only of the fact that it is signed by a person other than the applicant or his Solicitor.

(3) The conditions referred to in paragraph (1)(f) are that—
(a) except in a case to which sub-paragraph (b) applies, the application must have been made not later than—
(i) three years after the date of the event which is the subject of the application in the case of a claim for compensation for death or bodily injury (whether or not damage to property has also arisen from the same event), or
(ii) nine months after the date of that event in the case of a claim for compensation for damage to property (whether or not death or bodily injury has also arisen from the same event);
(b) In a case where the applicant could not reasonably have been expected to have become aware of the existence of bodily injury or damage to property, the application must have been made as soon as practicable after he did become (or ought reasonably to have become) aware of it and in any case not later than—

(i) fifteen years after the date of the event which is the subject of the application in the case of a claim for compensation for death or bodily injury (whether or not damage to property has also arisen from the same event), or

(ii) two years after the date of that event in the case of a claim for compensation for damage to property (whether or not death or bodily injury has also arisen from the same event);

(c) the applicant, or a person acting on the applicant's behalf, must have reported that event to the police—

(i) in the case of an event from which there has arisen a death or bodily injury alone, not later than 14 days after its occurrence, and

(ii) in the case of an event from which there has arisen property damage (whether or not a death or bodily injury has also arisen from it), not later than 5 days after its occurrence,

but where that is not reasonably possible the event must have been reported as soon as reasonably possible;

(d) the applicant must produce satisfactory evidence of having made the report required under sub-paragraph (c) in the form of an acknowledgement from the relevant force showing the crime or incident number under which that force has recorded the matter;

(e) after making, or authorising the making of, a report to the police the applicant must have co-operated with the police in any investigation they have made into the event.

(4) Where both death or bodily injury and damage to property have arisen from a single event nothing contained in this clause shall require an applicant to make an application in respect of the death or bodily injury on the same occasion as an application in respect of the damage to property and where two applications are made in respect of one event the provisions of this Agreement shall apply separately to each of them.

Exclusions from Agreement

5. (1) This Agreement does not apply where an application is made in any of the following **8.43** circumstances (so that where an application is made partly in such circumstances and partly in other circumstances, it applies only to the part made in those other circumstances)—

(a) where the applicant makes no claim for compensation in respect of death or bodily injury and the damage to property in respect of which compensation is claimed has been caused by, or has arisen out of, the use of an unidentified vehicle;

(b) where the death, bodily injury or damage to property in respect of which the application is made has been caused by or has arisen out of the use of a motor vehicle which at the time of the event giving rise to such death, injury or damage was owned by or in the possession of the Crown, unless at that time some other person had undertaken responsibility for bringing into existence a policy of insurance or security satisfying the requirements of the 1988 Act;

(c) where, at the time of the event in respect of which the application is made the person suffering death, injury or damage to property was voluntarily allowing himself to be carried in the responsible vehicle and before the commencement of his journey in the vehicle (or after such commencement if he could reasonably be expected to have alighted from the vehicle) he knew or ought to have known that the vehicle—

(i) had been stolen or unlawfully taken, or

(ii) was being used without there being in force in relation to its use a contract of insurance or security which complied with the 1988 Act; or

(iii) was being used in the course or furtherance of crime; or

(iv) was being used as a means of escape from or avoidance of lawful apprehension;

(d) where the death, bodily injury or damage to property was caused by, or in the course of, an act of terrorism;

(e) where property damaged as a result of the event giving rise to the application is insured against such damage and the applicant has recovered the full amount of his loss from the insurer on or before the date of the application (but without prejudice to the application of the Agreement in the case of any other claim for compensation made in respect of the same event);

(f) where a claim is made for compensation in respect of damage to a motor vehicle (or losses arising therefrom) and, at the time when the damage to it was sustained—

(i) there was not in force in relation to the use of that vehicle such a contract of insurance as is required by Part VI of the 1988 Act, and

(ii) the person suffering damage to property either knew or ought to have known that was the case

(but without prejudice to the application of the Agreement in the case of any other claim for compensation made in respect of the same event);

(g) where the application is made neither by a person suffering injury or property damage nor by the personal representative of such a person nor by a dependant claiming in respect of the death of another person but is made in any of the following circumstances, namely—

(i) where a cause of action or a judgment has been assigned to the applicant, or

(ii) where the applicant is acting pursuant to a right of subrogation or a similar contractual or other right belonging to him.

(2) The burden of proving that the person suffering death, injury or damage to property knew or ought to have known of any matter set out in paragraph (1)(c) shall be on MIB but, in the absence of evidence to the contrary, proof by MIB of any of the following matters shall be taken as proof of his knowledge of the matter set out in paragraph (1)(c)(ii)—

(a) that he was the owner or registered keeper of the vehicle or had caused or permitted its use;

(b) that he knew the vehicle was being used by a person who was below the minimum age at which he could be granted a licence authorising the driving of a vehicle of that class;

(c) that he knew that the person driving the vehicle was disqualified for holding or obtaining a driving licence;

(d) that he knew that the user of the vehicle was neither its owner nor registered keeper nor an employee of the owner or registered keeper nor the owner or registered keeper of any other vehicle.

(3) Where—

(a) the application includes a claim for compensation both in respect of death or bodily injury and also in respect of damage to property, and

(b) the death or injury and the property damage has been caused by, or has arisen out of, the use of an unidentified vehicle,

the Agreement does not apply to the claim for compensation in respect of the damage to property.

(4) For the purposes of paragraphs (1) and (2)—

(a) references to a person being carried in a vehicle include references to his being carried in or upon, or entering or getting on to or alighting from the vehicle;

(b) knowledge which a person has or ought to have for the purposes of subparagraph (c) includes knowledge of matters which he could reasonably be expected to have been aware of had he not been under the self-induced influence of drink or drugs;

(c) 'crime' does not include the commission of an offence under the Traffic Acts, except an offence under section 143 (use of a motor vehicle on a road without there being in force a policy of insurance), and 'Traffic Acts' means the Road Traffic Regulation Act 1984, the Road Traffic Act 1988 and the Road Traffic Offenders Act 1988;

(d) 'responsible vehicle' means the vehicle the use of which caused (or through the use of which there arose) the death, bodily injury or damage to property which is the subject of the application;

(e) 'terrorism' has the meaning given in section 1 of the Terrorism Act 2000;

(f) 'dependant' has the same meaning as in section 1(3) of the Fatal Accidents Act 1976.

Limitation on application of Agreement

6. (1) This clause applies where an applicant receives compensation or other payment in **8.44** respect of the death, bodily injury or damage to property otherwise than in the circumstances described in clause 5(1)(e) from any of the following persons—

(a) an insurer or under an insurance policy (other than a life assurance policy) or arrangement between the applicant or his employer and the insurer, or

(b) a person who has given a security pursuant to the requirements of the 1988 Act under an agreement between the applicant and the security giver, or

(c) any other source other than a person who is an identified person for the purposes of clauses 13 to 15 or an insurer of, or a person who has given a security on behalf of, such a person.

(2) Where the compensation or other payment received is equal to or greater than the amount which MIB would otherwise be liable to pay under the provisions of clauses 8 and 9 MIB shall have no liability under those provisions (to the intent that this Agreement shall immediately cease to apply except to the extent that the applicant is entitled to a contribution to his legal costs under clause 10).

(3) Where the compensation or other payment received is less than the amount which MIB would otherwise be liable to pay under the provisions of clauses 8 and 9 MIB's liability under those provisions shall be reduced by an amount equal to that compensation or payment.

PRINCIPAL TERMS AND CONDITIONS

MIB's obligation to investigate claims and determine amount of award

7. (1) MIB shall, at its own cost, take all reasonable steps to investigate the claim made in the **8.45** application and—

(a) if it is satisfied after conducting a preliminary investigation that the case is not one to which this Agreement applies and the application should be rejected, it shall inform the applicant accordingly and (subject to the following provisions of this Agreement) need take no further action, or

(b) in any other case, it shall conduct a full investigation and shall as soon as reasonably practicable having regard to the availability of evidence make a report on the applicant's claim.

(2) Subject to the following paragraphs of this clause, MIB shall, on the basis of the report and, where applicable, any relevant proceedings—

(a) reach a decision as to whether it must make an award to the applicant in respect of the death, bodily injury or damage to property, and

(b) where it decides to make an award, determine the amount of that award.

(3) Where MIB reaches a decision that the Agreement applies and that it is able to calculate the whole amount of the award the report shall be treated as a full report and the award shall (subject to the following provisions of this Agreement) be treated as a full and final award.

(4) Where MIB reaches a decision that the Agreement applies and that it should make an award but further decides that it is not at that time able to calculate the final amount of the award (or a part thereof), it may designate the report as an interim report and where it does so—

(a) it may, as soon as reasonably practicable, make one or more further interim reports, but

(b) it must, as soon as reasonably practicable having regard to the availability of evidence, make a final report.

(5) Where it makes an interim or final report MIB shall, on the basis of that report and, where applicable, any relevant proceedings—

(a) in the case of an interim report, determine the amount of any interim award it wishes to make, and

(b) in the case of its final report, determine the whole amount of its award which shall (subject to the following provisions of this Agreement) be treated as a full and final award.

(6) MIB shall be under an obligation to make an award only if it is satisfied, on the balance of probabilities, that the death, bodily injury or damage to property was caused in such circumstances that the unidentified person would (had he been identified) have been held liable to pay damages to the applicant in respect of it.

(7) MIB shall determine the amount of its award in accordance with the provisions of clauses 8 to 10 and (in an appropriate case) clauses 12 to 14 but shall not thereby be under a duty to calculate the exact proportion of the award which represents compensation, interest or legal costs.

Compensation

8.46   8. (1) MIB shall include in its award to the applicant, by way of compensation for the death, bodily injury or damage to property, a sum equivalent to the amount which a court—

(a) applying the law of England and Wales, in a case where the event giving rise to the death, injury or damage occurred in England or Wales, or

(b) applying the law of Scotland, in a case where that event occurred in Scotland,

would have awarded to the applicant (where applying English law) as general and special damages or (where applying the law of Scotland) as solatium and patrimonial loss if the applicant had brought successful proceedings to enforce a claim for damages against the unidentified person.

(2) In calculating the sum payable under paragraph (1), MIB shall adopt the same method of calculation as the court would adopt in calculating damages but it shall be under no obligation to include in that calculation an amount in respect of loss of earnings suffered by the applicant to the extent that he has been paid wages or salary (or any sum in lieu of them) whether or not such payments were made subject to an agreement or undertaking on his part to repay the same in the event of his recovering damages for the loss of those earnings.

(3) Where an application includes a claim in respect of damage to property, MIB's liability in respect of that claim shall be limited in accordance with the following rules—

(a) if the loss incurred by an applicant in respect of any one event giving rise to a claim does not exceed the specified excess, MIB shall incur no liability to that applicant in respect of that event;

(b) if the aggregate of all losses incurred by both the applicant and other persons in respect of any one event giving rise to a claim ('the total loss') exceeds the specified excess but does not exceed £250,000—

(i) MIB's liability to an individual applicant shall be the amount of the claim less the specified excess, and

(ii) MIB's total liability to applicants in respect of claims arising from that event shall be the total loss less a sum equal to the specified excess multiplied by the number of applicants who have incurred loss through damage to property;

(c) if the total loss exceeds £250,000—

(i) MIB's liability to an individual applicant shall not exceed the amount of the claim less the specified excess, and

(ii) MIB's total liability to applicants in respect of claims arising from that event shall be £250,000 less a sum equal to the specified excess multiplied by the number of applicants who have incurred loss due to property damage.

(4) MIB shall not be liable to pay compensation to an appropriate authority in respect of any loss incurred by that authority as a result of its failure to recover a charge for the recovery, storage or disposal of an abandoned vehicle under a power contained in the Refuse Disposal (Amenity) Act 1978 or Part VIII of the Road Traffic Regulation Act 1984 (and in this paragraph 'appropriate authority' has the meaning given in the Act under which the power to recover the charge was exercisable).

Interest

9. (1) MIB shall in an appropriate case also include in the award a sum representing interest **8.47** on the compensation payable under clause 8 at a rate equal to that which a court—

(a) applying the law of England and Wales, in a case where the event giving rise to the death, bodily injury or damage to property occurred in England or Wales, or

(b) applying the law of Scotland, in a case where that event occurred in Scotland,

would have awarded to a successful applicant.

(2) MIB is not required by virtue of paragraph (1) to pay a sum representing interest in respect of the period before the date which is one month after the date on which MIB receives the police report (but, where MIB has failed to seek and obtain that report promptly after the date of the application, interest shall run from the date which falls one month after the date on which it would have received it had it acted promptly).

Contribution towards legal costs

10. (1) MIB shall, in a case where it has decided to make a compensation payment under **8.48** clause 8, also include in the award a sum by way of contribution towards the cost of obtaining legal advice from a Solicitor, Barrister or Advocate in respect of—

(a) the making of an application under this Agreement;

(b) the correctness of a decision made by MIB under this Agreement; or

(c) the adequacy of an award (or a part thereof) offered by MIB under this Agreement

that sum to be determined in accordance with the Schedule to this Agreement.

(2) MIB shall not be under a duty to make a payment under paragraph (1) unless it is satisfied that the applicant did obtain legal advice in respect of any one or more of the matters specified in that paragraph.

Conditions precedent to MIB's obligations

11. (1) The applicant must— **8.49**

(a) make his application in such form,

(b) provide in support of the application such statements and other information (whether in writing or orally at interview), and

(c) give such further assistance,

as may reasonably be required by MIB or by any person acting on MIB's behalf to enable an investigation to be carried out under clause 7 of this Agreement.

(2) The applicant must provide MIB with written authority to take all such steps as may be reasonably necessary in order to carry out a proper investigation of the claim.

(3) The applicant must, if MIB reasonably requires him to do so before reaching a decision under clause 7, provide MIB with a statutory declaration, made by him, setting out to the best of his knowledge and belief all the facts and circumstances upon which his application is based or such facts and circumstances in relation to the application as MIB may reasonably specify.

(4) The applicant must, if MIB reasonably requires him to do so before it reaching a decision or determination under clause 7 and subject to the following provisions of this clause—

(a) at MIB's option (and subject to paragraph (5)) either—

(i) bring proceedings against any person or persons who may, in addition or alternatively to the unidentified person, be liable to the applicant in respect of the death, bodily injury or damage to property (by virtue of having caused or contributed to that death, injury or damage, by being vicariously liable in respect of it or having failed to effect third party liability insurance in respect of the vehicle in question) and co-operate with MIB in taking such steps as are reasonably necessary to obtain judgement in those proceedings, or

(ii) authorize MIB to bring such proceedings and take such steps in the applicant's name;

(b) at MIB's expense, provide MIB with a transcript of any official shorthand or recorded note taken in those proceedings of any evidence given or judgement delivered therein;

(c) assign to MIB or to its nominee the benefit of any judgement obtained by him (whether or not obtained in proceedings brought under sub-paragraph (a) above) in respect of the death, bodily injury or damage to property upon such terms as will secure that MIB or its nominee will be accountable to the applicant for any amount by which the aggregate of all sums recovered by MIB or its nominee under the judgement (after deducting all reasonable expenses incurred in effecting recovery) exceeds the award made by MIB under this Agreement in respect of that death, injury or damage;

(d) undertake to assign to MIB the right to any sum which is or may be due from an insurer, security giver or other person by way of compensation for, or benefit in respect of, the death, bodily injury or damage to property and which would (if payment had been made before the date of the award) have excluded or limited MIB's liability under the provisions of clause 6.

(5) If, pursuant to paragraph (4)(a), MIB requires the applicant to bring proceedings or take steps against any person or persons (or to authorise MIB to bring such proceedings or take such steps in his name) MIB shall indemnify the applicant against all costs and expenses reasonably incurred by him in complying with that requirement.

(6) Where the applicant, without having been required to do so by MIB, has commenced proceedings against any person described in paragraph (4)(a)—

(a) the applicant shall as soon as reasonably possible notify MIB of such proceedings and provide MIB with such further information about them as MIB may reasonably require, and

(b) the applicant's obligations in paragraph (4)(a) to (c) shall apply in respect of such proceedings as if they had been brought at MIB's request.

JOINT AND SEVERAL LIABILITY

Joint and several liability: interpretation

8.50   12. In clauses 13 to 15—

'identified person' includes an identified employer or principal of a person who is himself unidentified;

'original judgement' means a judgement obtained against an identified person at first instance in relevant proceedings;

'three month period' means the period of three months specified in clause 13(3); and

'unidentified person's liability' means—

(a) the amount of the contribution which (if not otherwise apparent) would, on the balance of probabilities, have been recoverable from the unidentified person in an action brought—

(i) in England and Wales, under the Civil Liability (Contribution) Act 1978, or

(ii) in Scotland, under the Law Reform (Miscellaneous Provisions) (Scotland) Act 1940,

by an identified person who had been held liable in full in an earlier action brought by the applicant, and

(b) where a court has awarded the applicant interest or costs in addition to damages, an appropriate proportion of that interest or those costs.

MIB's liability where wrongdoer is identified

13. (1) This clause applies where the death, bodily injury or damage to property in respect of **8.51** which the application is made is caused, or appears on the balance of probabilities to have been caused—
(a) partly by an unidentified person and partly by an identified person, or
(b) partly by an unidentified person and partly by another unidentified person whose employer or principal is identified,

in circumstances making (or appearing to make) the identified person liable, or vicariously liable, to the applicant in respect of the death, injury or damage.

(2) Where this clause applies, MIB's liability under this Agreement shall not exceed the unidentified person's liability and the following provisions shall apply to determine MIB's liability in specific cases.

(3) Where the applicant has obtained a judgement in relevant proceedings in respect of the death, injury or damage which has not been satisfied in full by or on behalf of the identified person within the period of three months after the date on which the applicant became entitled to enforce it—
(a) if that judgement is wholly unsatisfied within the three month period MIB shall make an award equal to the unidentified person's liability;
(b) if the judgement is satisfied in part only within the three month period, MIB shall make an award equal to—
(i) the unsatisfied part, if it does not exceed the unidentified person's liability; and
(ii) the unidentified person's liability, if the unsatisfied part exceeds the unidentified person's liability.

(4) A judgement given in any relevant proceedings against an identified person shall be conclusive as to any issue determined in those proceedings which is relevant to the determination of MIB's liability under this Agreement.

(5) Where the applicant has not obtained (or been required by MIB to obtain) a judgement in respect of the death, injury or damage against the identified person but has received an agreed payment from the identified person in respect of the death, bodily injury or damage to property, that payment shall be treated for the purposes of this Agreement as a full settlement of the applicant's claim and MIB shall be under no liability under this Agreement in respect thereof.

(6) Where the applicant has not obtained (or been required by MIB to obtain) a judgement in respect of the death, injury or damage against the identified person nor received any payment by way of compensation in respect thereof from the identified person MIB shall make an award equal to the unidentified person's liability.

Appeals by identified persons

14. (1) This clause applies where an appeal against, or other proceeding to set aside, the **8.52** original judgement is commenced within the three month period.

(2) If, as a result of the appeal or other proceeding—
(a) the applicant ceases to be entitled to receive any payment in respect of the death, bodily injury or damage to property from any identified person, clause 13 shall apply as if he had neither obtained nor been required by MIB to obtain a judgement against that person;

195

(b) the applicant becomes entitled to recover an amount different from that which he was entitled to recover under the original judgement the provisions of clause 13(3) shall apply, but as if for each of the references therein to the original judgement there were substituted a reference to the judgement in that appeal or other proceeding;

(c) the applicant remains entitled to enforce the original judgement the provisions of clause 13(3) shall apply, but as if for each of the references therein to the three month period there were substituted a reference to the period of three months after the date on which the appeal or other proceeding was disposed of.

(3) Where the judgement in the appeal or other proceeding is itself the subject of a further appeal or similar proceeding the provisions of this clause shall apply in relation to that further appeal or proceeding in the same manner as they apply in relation to the first appeal or proceeding.

(4) Nothing in this clause shall oblige MIB to make a payment to the applicant until the appeal or other proceeding has been determined.

Compensation recovered under Uninsured Drivers Agreements

8.53   15. (1) Where, in a case to which clause 13 applies, judgement in the relevant proceedings is given against an identified person in circumstances which render MIB liable to satisfy that judgement under any of the Uninsured Drivers Agreements, MIB shall not be under any liability under this Agreement in respect of the event to which the relevant proceedings relate.

(2) In this clause 'Uninsured Drivers Agreements' means—

(a) the Agreement dated 21st December 1988 made between the Secretary of State for Transport and MIB providing for the compensation of victims of uninsured drivers,

(b) the 1999 Agreement, and

(c) any agreement made between the Secretary of State and MIB (or their respective successors) which supersedes (whether immediately or otherwise) the 1999 Agreement.

NOTIFICATION OF DECISION AND PAYMENT OF AWARD

Notification of decision

8.54   16. MIB shall give the applicant notice of a decision or determination under clause 7 in writing and when so doing shall provide him—

(a) if the application is rejected because a preliminary investigation has disclosed that it is not one made in a case to which this Agreement applies, with a statement to that effect;

(b) if the application has been fully investigated, with a statement setting out—

(i) all the evidence obtained during the investigation, and

(ii) MIB's findings of fact from that evidence which are relevant to the decision;

(c) if it has decided to make an interim award on the basis of an interim report under clause 7(4), with a copy of the report and a statement of the amount of the interim award;

(d) if it has decided to make a full report under clause 7(3) or a final report under clause 7(4)(b), with a copy of the report and a statement of the amount of the full and final award;

(e) in a case to which clause 13 applies, with a statement setting out the way in which the amount of the award has been computed under the provisions of that clause; and

(f) in every case, with a statement of its reasons for making the decision or determination.

Acceptance of decision and payment of award

8.55   17. (1) Subject to the following paragraphs of this clause, if MIB gives notice to the applicant that it has decided to make an award to him, it shall pay him that award—

(a) in the case of an interim award made pursuant to clause 7(5)(a), as soon as reasonably practicable after the making of the interim report to which the award relates;

(b) in the case of a full and final award made pursuant to clause 7(3) or (5)(b)—

(i) where the applicant notifies MIB in writing that he accepts the offer of the award unconditionally, not later than 14 days after the date on which MIB receives that acceptance, or

(ii) where the applicant does not notify MIB of his acceptance in accordance with sub-paragraph (a) but the period during which he may give notice of an appeal under clause 19 has expired without such notice being given, not later than 14 days after the date of expiry of that period,

and that payment shall discharge MIB from all liability under this Agreement in respect of the death, bodily injury or damage to property for which the award is made.

(2) MIB may, upon notifying an applicant of its decision to make an award, offer to pay the award in instalments in accordance with a structure described in the decision letter (the 'structured settlement') and if the applicant notifies MIB in writing of his acceptance of the offer—

(a) the first instalment of the payment under the structured settlement shall be made not later than 14 days after the date on which MIB receives that acceptance, and

(b) subsequent payments shall be made in accordance with the agreed structure.

(3) Where an applicant has suffered bodily injury and believes either that there is a risk that he will develop a disease or condition other than that in respect of which he has made a claim or that a disease or condition in respect of which he has made a claim will deteriorate, he may—

(a) by notice given in his application, or

(b) by notice in writing received by MIB before the date on which MIB issues notification of its full or (as the case may be) final report under clause 16,

state that he wishes MIB to make a provisional award and if he does so paragraphs (4) and (5) shall apply.

(4) The applicant must specify in the notice given under paragraph (3)—

(a) each disease and each type of deterioration which he believes may occur, and

(b) the period during or within which he believes it may occur.

(5) Where MIB receives a notice under paragraph (3) it shall, not later than 14 days after the date of such receipt (or within such longer period as the applicant may agree)—

(a) accept the notice and confirm that any award it makes (other than an interim award made pursuant to clause 7(5)(a)) is to be treated as a provisional award, or

(b) reject the notice and inform the applicant that it is not willing to make a provisional award.

(6) Where MIB has notified the applicant that it accepts the notice, an award which would otherwise be treated as a full or final award under this Agreement shall be treated as a provisional award only and the applicant may make a supplementary application under this Agreement but—

(a) only in respect of a disease or a type of deterioration of his condition specified in his notice, and

(b) not later than the expiration of the period specified in his notice.

(7) Where MIB has notified the applicant that it rejects the notice, subject to any decision to the contrary made by an arbitrator, no award which MIB makes shall be treated as a provisional award.

APPEALS AGAINST MIB's DECISION

Right of appeal

18. Where an applicant is not willing to accept—   **8.56**

(a) a decision or determination made by MIB under clause 7 or a part thereof, or

(b) a proposal for a structured settlement or a rejection of the applicant's request for a provisional award under clause 17,

he may give notice (a 'notice of appeal') that he wishes to submit the matter to arbitration in accordance with the provisions of clauses 19 to 25.

Notice of appeal

8.57   **19.** (1) A notice of appeal shall be given in writing to MIB at any time before the expiration of a period of 6 weeks from—
   (a) the date on which the applicant receives notice of MIB's decision under clause 16;
   (b) where he disputes a notification given under clause 17(5)(b), the date when such notification is given;
   (c) in any other case, the date on which he is given notification of the decision, determination or requirement.

   (2) The notice of appeal—
   (a) shall state the grounds on which the appeal is made,
   (b) shall contain the applicant's observations on MIB's decision,
   (c) may be accompanied by such further evidence in support of the appeal as the applicant thinks fit, and
   (d) shall contain an undertaking that (subject, in the case of an arbitration to be conducted in England and Wales, to his rights under sections 67 and 68 of the Arbitration Act 1996) the applicant will abide by the decision of the arbitrator made under this Agreement.

Procedure following notice of appeal

8.58   **20.** (1) Not later than 7 days after receiving the notice of appeal MIB shall—
   (a) apply to the Secretary of State for the appointment of a single arbitrator, or
   (b) having notified the applicant of its intention to do so, cause an investigation to be made into any further evidence supplied by the applicant and report to the applicant upon that investigation and of any change in its decision which may result from it.

   (2) Where the only ground stated in the notice of appeal is that the award is insufficient (including a ground contesting the degree of contributory negligence attributed to the applicant or, as the case may be, the person in respect of whose death the application is made), MIB may give notice to the applicant of its intention, if the appeal proceeds to arbitration, to ask the arbitrator to decide whether its award exceeds what a court would have awarded or whether the case is one in which it would make an award at all and shall in that notice set out such observations on that matter as MIB considers relevant to the arbitrator's decision.

   (3) Where MIB has made a report under paragraph (1)(b) or given to the applicant notice under paragraph (2), the applicant may, not later than 6 weeks after the date on which the report or (as the case may be) the notice was given to him—
   (a) notify MIB that he wishes to withdraw the appeal, or
   (b) notify MIB that he wishes to continue with the appeal and send with that notification—
      (i) any observations on the report made under paragraph (1)(b) which he wishes to have drawn to the attention of the arbitrator,
      (ii) any observations on the contents of the notice given under paragraph (2), including any further evidence not previously made available to MIB and relevant to the matter, which he wishes to have drawn to the attention of the arbitrator.

   (4) Where the applicant notifies MIB under paragraph (3)(b) of his wish to continue the appeal, or if the applicant fails within the specified period of 6 weeks to give notification of his wish either to withdraw or to continue with the appeal, MIB shall, not later than 7 days after receiving the notification or 7 days after the expiry of the said period (as the case may be)—

(a) apply to the Secretary of State for the appointment of an arbitrator, or

(b) having notified the applicant of its intention to do so, cause a further investigation to be made into the further evidence sent under paragraph (3)(b)(ii).

(5) Where MIB has caused an investigation to be made into any further evidence supplied by the applicant under paragraph (3)(b)(ii), it shall report to the applicant upon that investigation and of any change in a decision or determination made under clause 7 which may result from it and the applicant may, not later than 6 weeks after the date on which he receives the report—

(a) notify MIB that he wishes to withdraw the appeal, or

(b) notify MIB that he wishes to continue with the appeal.

(6) Where the applicant notifies MIB under paragraph (5)(b) of his wish to continue the appeal, or if the applicant fails within the specified period of 6 weeks to give notification of his wish either to withdraw or to continue with the appeal, MIB shall not later than 7 days after receiving the notification or 7 days after the expiry of the said period (as the case may be) apply to the Secretary of State for the appointment of an arbitrator.

(7) When applying to the Secretary of State for the appointment of an arbitrator MIB may send with the application such written observations as it wishes to make upon the applicant's notice of appeal but must at the same time send a copy of those observations to the applicant.

Appointment of arbitrator

21. (1) In the event of MIB neither applying to the Secretary of State for the appointment of **8.59** an arbitrator in accordance with the provisions of clause 20 nor taking such further steps as it may at its discretion take in accordance with that clause, the applicant may apply to the Secretary of State for the appointment of an arbitrator.

(2) For the purposes of the Arbitration Act 1996 (where the arbitration is to be conducted in England and Wales) the arbitral proceedings are to be regarded as commencing on the date of the making of the application by the Secretary of State or the applicant (as the case may be).

(3) The Secretary of State shall, upon the making of an application for the appointment of an arbitrator to hear the appeal, appoint the first available member, by rotation, of a panel of Queen's Counsel appointed for the purpose of determining appeals under this Agreement (where the event giving rise to the death, bodily injury or damage to property occurred in England and Wales) by the Lord Chancellor or (where the event giving rise to the death, bodily injury or damage to property occurred in Scotland) by the Lord Advocate and shall forthwith notify the applicant and MIB of the appointment.

Arbitration procedure

22. (1) Upon receiving notification from the Secretary of State of the appointment of an **8.60** arbitrator, MIB shall send to the arbitrator—

(a) the notice of appeal,

(b) (if appropriate) its request for a decision as to whether its award exceeds what a court would have awarded or whether the case is one in which it would make an award at all,

(c) copies of—

(i) the applicant's application,

(ii) its decision; and

(iii) all statements, declarations, notices, reports, observations and transcripts of evidence made or given under this Agreement by the applicant or MIB.

(2) The arbitrator may, if it appears to him to be necessary or expedient for the purpose of resolving any issue, ask MIB to make a further investigation and to submit a written report of its findings to him for his consideration and in such a case—

(a) MIB shall undertake the investigation and send copies of the report to the arbitrator and the applicant,

(b) the applicant may, not later than 4 weeks after the date on which a copy of the report is received by him, submit written observations on it to the arbitrator and if he does so he shall send a copy of those observations to MIB.

(3) The arbitrator shall, after considering the written submissions referred to in paragraphs (1) and (2), send to the applicant and MIB a preliminary decision letter setting out the decision he proposes to make under clause 23 and his reasons for doing so.

(4) Not later than 28 days after the date of sending of the preliminary decision letter (or such later date as the applicant and MIB may agree) the applicant and MIB may, by written notification given to the arbitrator and copied to the other, either—

(a) accept the preliminary decision, or

(b) submit written observations upon the preliminary decision or the reasons or both, or

(c) request an oral hearing,

and if either of them should within that period fail to do any of those things (including a failure to provide the other person with a copy of his notification) he or it shall be treated as having accepted the decision.

(5) If the applicant submits new evidence with any written observations under paragraph (4) (b) MIB may at its discretion, but within 28 days or such longer period as the arbitrator may allow, do any of the following—

(a) make an investigation into that evidence,

(b) submit its own written observations on that evidence, and

(c) if it has not already done so, request an oral hearing,

and, except where an oral hearing has been requested, the arbitrator shall (in exercise of his powers under section 34 of the Arbitration Act 1996 if the arbitration is being conducted in England and Wales) determine whether, and if so how, such evidence shall be admitted and tested.

(6) If both the applicant and MIB accept the reasoned preliminary decision that decision shall be treated as his final decision for the purposes of clause 23 (so that clause 23(2) shall not then apply) but if either of them submits observations on that decision the arbitrator must take those observations into account before making a final decision.

(7) If the applicant or MIB requests an oral hearing, the arbitrator shall determine the appeal in that manner and in such a case—

(a) the hearing shall be held in public unless the applicant requests that it (or any part of it) be heard in private;

(b) the hearing shall take place at a location—

(i) in England or Wales, where the event giving rise to the death, bodily injury or damage to property occurred in England or Wales and the applicant is resident in England or Wales,

(ii) in Scotland, where the event giving rise to the death, bodily injury or damage to property occurred in Scotland and the applicant is resident in Scotland, or

(iii) in England, Wales or Scotland in any other case,

which in the opinion of the arbitrator (after consultation with each of them) is convenient for both MIB and the applicant as well as for himself;

(c) a party to the hearing may be represented by a lawyer or other person of that party's choosing;

(d) a party to the hearing shall be entitled to address the arbitrator, to call witnesses and to put questions to those witnesses and any other person called as a witness.

Arbitrator's decision

8.61   23. (1) The arbitrator, having regard to the subject matter of the proceedings, may in an appropriate case—

(a) determine whether or not the case is one to which this Agreement applies;

(b) remit the application to MIB for a full investigation and a decision in accordance with the provisions of this Agreement;

(c) determine whether MIB should make an award under this Agreement and if so what that award should be;

(d) determine such other questions as have been referred to him as he thinks fit;

(e) (subject to the provisions of paragraph (4) of this clause and clause 24) order that the costs of the proceedings shall be paid by one party or allocated between the parties in such proportions as he thinks fit;

and where the arbitrator makes a determination under sub-paragraph (a) that the case is one to which this Agreement applies, all the provisions of this Agreement shall apply as if the case were one to which clause 7(1)(b) applies.

(2) The arbitrator shall notify MIB and the applicant of his decision in writing.

(3) MIB shall pay to the applicant any amount which the arbitrator has decided shall be awarded to him, and that payment shall discharge MIB from all liability under this Agreement in respect of the death, bodily injury or damage to property in respect of which that decision is given.

(4) Where an oral hearing has taken place at the request of the applicant and the arbitrator is satisfied that it was unnecessary and that the matter could have been decided on the basis of the written submissions referred to in clause 22(1) and (2) he shall take that into account when making an order under paragraph (1)(e).

Payment of arbitrator's fee and costs of legal representation

24. (1) Subject to paragraph (2), MIB shall upon being notified of the decision of the arbitra-   **8.62**
tor pay the arbitrator a fee approved by the Lord Chancellor or the Lord Advocate, as the case may be, after consultation with MIB.

(2) In a case where it appears to the arbitrator that, having regard to all the surrounding circumstances of the case, there were no reasonable grounds for making the appeal or bringing the question before him, the arbitrator may, in his discretion, order—

(a) the applicant or,

(b) where he considers it appropriate to do so, any Solicitor or other person acting on behalf of the applicant,

to reimburse MIB the fee it has paid to the arbitrator or any part thereof.

(3) Where, pursuant to paragraph (2), the arbitrator orders—

(a) the applicant to reimburse MIB, MIB may deduct an amount equal to the fee from any amount which it pays to the applicant to discharge its liability under this Agreement;

(b) a Solicitor or other person to reimburse MIB, MIB may deduct an amount equal to the fee from any amount which it pays to that Solicitor or other person to discharge its liability to the applicant under this Agreement.

(4) Where there is an oral hearing and the applicant secures an award of compensation greater than that previously offered, then (unless the arbitrator orders otherwise) MIB shall make a contribution of £500 per half day towards the cost incurred by the applicant in respect of representation by a Solicitor, Barrister or Advocate.

Applicants under a disability

25. (1) If in any case it appears to MIB that, by reason of the applicant being a minor or of   **8.63**
any other circumstance affecting his capacity to manage his affairs, it would be in the applicant's interest that all or some part of the award should be administered for him by an appropriate representative, MIB may establish for that purpose a trust of the whole or part of the award (such trust to take effect for such period and under such provisions as appears to MIB to be appropriate

in the circumstances of the case) or, as the case may be, initiate or cause any other person to initiate the proceedings necessary to have the award administered by an appropriate representative and otherwise cause any amount payable under the award to be paid to and administered by the appropriate representative.

(2) In this clause 'appropriate representative' means—

(a) in England and Wales—

(i) the Family Welfare Association, or a similar body or person, as trustee of the trust, or

(ii) the Court of Protection; and

(b) in Scotland—

(i) a Judicial Factor, or

(ii) a guardian under the Adults with Incapacity (Scotland) Act 2000, or

(iii) (where the applicant is a child) the tutor or curator of the child or a person having parental responsibilities under the Children (Scotland) Act 1995.

ACCELERATED PROCEDURE

Instigation of accelerated procedure

8.64   26. (1) In any case where, after making a preliminary investigation under clause 7, MIB has decided that—

(a) the case is one to which this Agreement applies, and

(b) it is not one to which clause 13 applies,

MIB may notify the applicant of that decision and, instead of causing a full investigation and report to be made under clause 7, may make to the applicant an offer to settle his claim by payment of an award specified in the offer representing compensation assessed in accordance with clause 8 together, in an appropriate case, with interest thereon assessed in accordance with clause 9 and a contribution towards the cost of obtaining legal advice in respect of the making of the application.

(2) Where an offer is made under paragraph (1), MIB shall send to the applicant a statement setting out—

(a) the relevant evidence it has collected disclosing the circumstances in which the death, bodily injury or damage to property occurred, and

(b) its reasons for the assessment of the award.

Settlement by accelerated procedure

8.65   27. (1) The applicant shall not later than 6 weeks after he receives an offer under clause 26 notify MIB of his acceptance or rejection thereof.

(2) Where the applicant notifies MIB of his acceptance of the offer—

(a) MIB shall not later than 14 days after receipt of the acceptance pay to the applicant the amount of the award, and

(b) MIB shall be discharged from all liability under this Agreement in respect of the death, bodily injury or damage to property for which that payment is made.

(3) In the event of the applicant failing to accept the offer within the specified period, the application shall be treated as one to which clause 7(1)(b) applies.

MISCELLANEOUS

Referral of disputes to arbitrator

8.66   28. (1) Any dispute between the applicant and MIB concerning a decision, determination or requirement made by MIB under the terms of this Agreement, other than a dispute relating to MIB's decision for which provision is made by clause 18, shall be referred to and determined by an arbitrator.

(2) Where an applicant wishes to refer such a dispute to arbitration, he shall not later than 4 weeks after the decision, determination or requirement is communicated to him, give notice to MIB that he wishes the matter to be so resolved.

(3) For the purposes of the Arbitration Act 1996 (where the arbitration is to be conducted in England and Wales) the arbitral proceedings are to be regarded as commencing on the date of such application.

(4) Upon receipt of the applicant's notice MIB shall apply immediately to the Secretary of State for the appointment of an arbitrator and in the event of MIB failing to do so the applicant may make the application.

(5) The Secretary of State shall, upon receiving the application for the appointment of an arbitrator to hear the appeal, appoint the first available member, by rotation, of a panel of Queen's Counsel appointed for the purpose of determining appeals under this Agreement (where the event giving rise to the death, bodily injury or damage to property occurred in England and Wales) by the Lord Chancellor or (where the event giving rise to the death, bodily injury or damage to property occurred in Scotland) by the Lord Advocate and shall forthwith notify the applicant and MIB of the appointment.

(6) The applicant and MIB shall, not later than 4 weeks after receiving notification of the appointment of the arbitrator, submit to him a written statement of their respective cases with supporting documentary evidence where available.

(7) Subject to paragraphs (8) to (10), the arbitrator shall decide the appeal on the documents submitted to him under paragraph (6) and no further evidence shall be produced to him.

(8) The applicant may, by notice in writing given to the arbitrator and MIB not later than the date on which he submits the statement of his case, ask the arbitrator to determine the appeal by means of an oral hearing and shall submit to the arbitrator and MIB a written statement, with supporting documentary evidence where appropriate, in support of that request.

(9) The arbitrator shall in such a case seek the view of MIB on the need for an oral hearing and MIB may submit to the arbitrator and the applicant a written statement, with supporting documentary evidence where appropriate, in support of its view.

(10) If, after considering those written submissions, the arbitrator decides that an oral hearing is necessary to determine the dispute—

(a) the hearing shall be held in public unless the applicant requests that it (or any part of it) be heard in private;

(b) the hearing shall take place at a location—

(i) in England or Wales, where the event giving rise to the death, bodily injury or damage to property occurred in England or Wales and the applicant is resident in England or Wales,

(ii) in Scotland, where the event giving rise to the death, bodily injury or damage to property occurred in Scotland and the applicant is resident in Scotland, or

(iii) in England, Wales or Scotland in any other case,

which in the opinion of the arbitrator (after consultation with each of them) is convenient for both MIB and the applicant as well as for himself;

(c) a party to the hearing may be represented by a lawyer or other person of that party's choosing;

(d) a party to the hearing shall be entitled to address the arbitrator, to call witnesses and to put questions to those witnesses and any other person called as a witness.

(11) The arbitrator may, having regard to the subject matter of the proceedings and in an appropriate case, order that his fee or the costs of the proceedings (as determined according to clause 10(1)(b) of, and the Schedule to, this Agreement) or both his fee and those costs shall be paid by one party or allocated between the parties in such proportions as he thinks fit.

(12) Unless otherwise agreed, the decision, determination or requirement in respect of which notice is given under paragraph (2) shall stand unless reserved by the arbitrator.

Services of notices, etc, on MIB

8.67   29. Any notice required to be served on or any other notification or document required to be given or sent to MIB under the terms of this Agreement shall be sufficiently served or given if sent by fax or by Registered or Recorded Delivery post to MIB's registered office and delivery shall be proved by the production of a fax report produced by the sender's fax machine or an appropriate postal receipt.

Agents

8.68   30. MIB may perform any of its obligations under this Agreement by agents.

Contracts (Rights of Third Parties) Act 1999

8.69   31. (1) For the purposes of the Contracts (Rights of Third Parties) Act 1999 the following provisions shall apply.

(2) This Agreement may be—
(a) varied or rescinded without the consent of any person other than the parties hereto, and
(b) determined under clause 3(2) without the consent of any such person.

(3) Save for the matters specified in paragraph (4), MIB shall not have available to it against an applicant any matter by way of counterclaim or set-off which would have been available to it if the applicant rather than the Secretary of State had been a party to this Agreement.

(4) The matters referred to in paragraph (3) are any counterclaim or set-off arising by virtue of the provisions of—
(a) this Agreement;
(b) the 1996 Agreement;
(c) the 1999 Agreement;
(d) either of the agreements which were respectively superseded by the 1996 Agreement and the 1999 Agreement.

(5) This agreement, being made for the purposes of Article 1(4) of Council Directive 84/5/EEC of 30th December 1983—
(a) is intended to confer a benefit on an applicant but on no other person, and
(b) to confer such benefit subject to the terms and conditions set out herein.

Enforcement against MIB

8.70   32. If MIB fail to pay compensation in accordance with the provisions of this agreement the applicant is entitled to enforce payment through the courts.

Transitional provisions

8.71   33. The 1996 Agreement shall cease to have effect after the 13 February 2003 but shall continue in force in relation to any claim arising out of an event occurring on or before that date.

. . .

SCHEDULE
MIB's CONTRIBUTION TOWARDS APPLICANT'S LEGAL COSTS

8.72   1. Subject to paragraph 4, MIB shall pay a contribution towards the applicant's costs of obtaining legal advice determined in accordance with paragraph 2,

8.73   2. That amount shall be the aggregate of—

(a) the fee specified in column (2) of the table below in relation to the amount of the award specified in column (1) of that table,

(b) the amount of value added tax charged on that fee,

(c) where the applicant has opted for an oral hearing under clause and

(d) reasonable disbursements.

TABLE

Amount of the award (1)	Specified fee (2)
Not exceeding £150,000	15% of the amount of the award, subject to a minimum of £500 and a maximum of £3000
Exceeding £150,000	2% of the amount of the award

3. For the purposes of paragraph 2— **8.74**

'amount of the award' means the aggregate of the sum awarded by way of compensation and interest under clauses 8 and 9, before deduction of any reimbursement due to be paid to the Secretary of State for Work and Pensions through the Compensation Recovery Unit (CRU) of his Department (or to any successor of that unit), but excluding the amount of any payment due in respect of benefits and hospital charges.

'reasonable disbursements' means reasonable expenditure incurred on the applicant's behalf and agreed between the applicant and MIB before it is incurred (MIB's agreement not having been unreasonably withheld) but includes Counsel's fees only where the applicant is a minor or under a legal disability.

4. The foregoing provisions of this Schedule are without prejudice to MIB's liability under the provisions of this Agreement to pay the costs of arbitration proceedings or an arbitrator's fee.

9

EMPLOYERS' LIABILITY

A. Common Law Duties

9.01 An employer owes a range of common law duties to his employees in the law of negligence. It has been traditional to categorize these duties under four headings, requiring the provision of safe fellow employees, safe equipment, a safe place of work and a safe system of work. All of these duties arise in the law of negligence and they are therefore examples of a duty to take reasonable care to protect against any foreseeable risk of injury.

9.02 *Wilsons and Clyde Coal v English* [1938] AC 57   An employee was injured by the negligence of a fellow employee in devising a safe system of work. Because of the now obsolete defence of common employment it would not have availed the claimant to establish vicarious liability. The House of Lords held that the obligation at common law to provide a safe system of work is personal to the employer. Even if the performance of the obligation is delegated, the employer remains primarily and directly liable for a negligent failure. The duty to provide a safe system of work is non-delegable.

The standard of care required of an employer is the ordinary duty to take reasonable care, but in practice the courts have applied a high standard, perhaps because the risks of injury arise out of the defendant employer's undertaking.

9.03 *General Cleaning Contractors v Christmas* [1952] AC 180   An experienced window cleaner was injured when following an established, but unsafe system of work. It was no answer to say that the claimant was a skilled man who was well aware of the dangers involved and able to take any necessary precautions. Lord Reid at 194:

> Where a practice of ignoring an obvious danger has grown up I do not think that it is reasonable to expect an individual workman to take the initiative in devising and using precautions. It is the duty of the employer to consider the situation, to devise a suitable system, to instruct his men what they must do and to supply any implements that may be required such as, in this case, wedges or objects to be put on the windowsill to prevent the window from closing.

9.04 Because the duty of the employer is a duty to take reasonable care, liability depends on proving knowledge of the risk, knowledge of precautions that would avoid the risk, and that it is reasonable to require that precautions should have been taken when balancing the practicability and effectiveness of the precautions against the cost and inconvenience of implementing them. General practice is relevant, but is not decisive, and it is the responsibility of an employer to keep abreast of developments.

9.05 *Stokes v GKN (Bolt and Nuts) Ltd* [1968] 1 WLR 1776   In a successful claim in negligence for illness caused by exposure to mineral oils at work, it was held that the employer must keep reasonably abreast of developing knowledge and must apply it with reasonable speed; and an employer with greater than average knowledge may be expected to take better than average precautions.

9.06 *Hayes v Pilkington Glass* [1998] PIQR P303   The claimant developed VWF as a result of his exposure to vibration while operating an electric crane. From 1976 it was known that excessive exposure to vibration from hand-operated tools could cause VWF, but there was no evidence to show that at the time of the claimant's employment, a reasonable and prudent employer should have known of a risk of VWF from the level of vibration created by an electric crane. The defendants were following a recognized and general practice. The claim failed.

B. Breach of Statutory Duty

9.07 The common law duties of an employer continue to provide an important backdrop to compensation claims for accidents at work, and a safety net for a claimant who may be faced with a technical difficulty about the application of the health and safety regulations. The scope of the regulations may indeed be indicative of the standard of care to be expected of a reasonable employer. But the common law is not enough, and the history of statutory protection of employees goes back to the Factories Act 1844. Since January 1993, the framework has been in six sets of regulations made in order to comply with European directives, supported by a range of more specific regulations. It is a mark of the success of the new regulatory code in providing clearly and sufficiently for the control of employers' duties that there has been little litigation about the scope and application of the regulations since they came into force.

The benefit of proving a breach of regulation for a claimant is that once the **9.08** factual breach is proved, the liability of the employer for the consequences of the breach is strict (or absolute) and does not require the proof of negligence or moral fault in addition. On the other hand, many duties under the regulations are qualified so that they apply only 'so far as is reasonably practicable' and this can result in a requirement that is in practice very similar to the duty of care in negligence. So far as a trend can be discerned in recent decisions, it is towards the requirement of a real risk of injury before a claimant can succeed, rather than a merely technical breach, as illustrated by the cases of *Horton*, *Searby*, *Palmer* and *Koonjal* noted below.

The four most important regulations of general application are set out first in **9.09** this chapter: the general part of the Provision and Use of Work Equipment Regulations 1998, the Workplace (Health, Safety and Welfare) Regulations 1992, the Manual Handling Operations Regulations 1992 and the Personal Protective Equipment at Work Regulations 1992. The Management of Health and Safety at Work Regulations 1999 have recently been amended to provide that after 27 October 2003 there is a civil remedy for a breach of these regulations available to employees, but not to others. Among the many areas of employment that are governed by specific regulations, the building industry is an area of particular importance, and this chapter includes the relevant parts of the Construction (Health, Safety and Welfare) Regulations 1996 and the Construction (Head Protection) Regulations 1989.

The regulations derive from European directives. They represent a move **9.10** towards regulation of work with a view to preventing injuries, rather than punishing and compensating in the event of breach. This is the reason for the emphasis on risk assessment. The regulations have not been drafted with the primary purpose of defining the grounds for civil liability, as anyone who has tried to formulate a claim for heavy lifting injury under the Manual Handling Regulations will have discovered. All the same it is central to liability for industrial accidents to identify the relevant regulatory provisions.

There are some instances where the regulations arguably do not fully comply **9.11** with the directives that they were intended to implement. The directives themselves are reproduced in more specialist works, such as *Redgrave's Health and Safety* by Michael Ford and Eric Brown (4th edn, 2002). The most important impact of the directives is that in a borderline case they may be consulted as an aid to interpretation; in addition, where the proposed defendant is an 'emanation of the state' the directives are directly applicable and it is possible that a claimant would be able to rely on wider protection than appears under the regulations. Such cases will be rare and there is not space to debate the issues in detail here.

9.12   Some of the regulations are accompanied by interpreting codes, i.e. Approved Codes of Practice (ACOPs) or Guidance Notes. The strict legal significance of these codes is rather vague, but the court would usually be willing to look at them in a compensation claim as an indication of good practice in judging the conduct of an employer, just as the Highway Code is relevant to the standard of care expected of a driver.

9.13   Some statutory duties are qualified in their terms. For example, the employer's duty may apply only 'so far as is reasonably practicable'. Examples are reg 12(3) of the Workplace Regulations and reg 4(1)(a) of the Manual Handling Regulations. 'Reasonably practicable' is not the same as 'physically possible' and an assessment should be made by the employer in which the seriousness of the risk (both its likelihood and the severity of the consequences if it happens) is balanced against the cost involved in the measures necessary for avoiding the risk (whether in money, time or trouble). If the risk is insignificant in relation to the cost, an employer who decides against taking the precaution will not be in breach of his duty. There is an argument that the construction of 'reasonably practicable' should be weighted against employers by the terms of the European directives, so that the scope for an employer reasonably to decide against undertaking a possible precaution against the risk of injury should be severely limited. Where a regulation imposes a requirement only 'so far as is reasonably practicable', a defendant employer who wishes to rely on this proviso to justify an apparent breach of the regulation must specifically set out in the defence the facts that are relied on to show that everything reasonably practicable was done.

9.14   *Galashiels Gas v O'Donnell* [1949] AC 275   A lift failed when the statute required that a lift must be kept in efficient working order. The claimant was able to establish liability for the breach of the statutory requirement, even though no one could account for the failure of the brake mechanism.

9.15   *Stark v Post Office* [2000] PIQR P105   The claimant was seriously injured when his bicycle broke: a part of the brake had jammed the front wheel. He alleged breach of the Work Equipment Regulations. There had been proper maintenance of the bicycle, and the defect could not have been discovered on any reasonable inspection, so there was no negligence or fault. However, reg 5 imposed an absolute duty on the employer to ensure that the bicycle was in efficient working order, and the claim succeeded.

Edwards v National Coal Board [1949] 1 KB 704   The leading case on the **9.16** balancing exercise to be carried out when deciding whether an employer can argue that it was not reasonably practicable to undertake a possible precaution against the risk of injury. Lord Asquith said:

> 'Reasonably practicable' is a narrower term than 'physically possible' and seems to me to imply that a computation must be made by the owner in which the quantum of risk is placed on one scale and the sacrifice involved in the measures necessary for averting the risk (whether in money, time or trouble) is placed on the other, and that, if it be shown that there is a gross disproportion between them— the risk being insignificant in relation to the sacrifice—the defendants discharge the onus on them.

C. The Work Equipment Regulations

The Provision and Use of Work Equipment Regulations 1998 (sometimes **9.17** shortened to 'the Work Equipment Regulations' or 'PUWER') deal with the safety requirements for a wide range of equipment provided for use at work. It is a curiosity of the regulations that, while they provide comprehensive requirements for the safe use of equipment, including requirements that work equipment should be suitable, well maintained, and free from defects, they do not include a general primary duty on an employer to ensure that appropriate work equipment is provided. The former statutory provision of strict liability for defective equipment under the Employers' Liability (Defective Equipment) Act 1969 continues in force, and the text of s 1 of the Act follows the text of the regulations, but in practice the Work Equipment Regulations have made the statute unnecessary. The text of the general part of the 1998 Regulations has been included here in full, but Parts III (mobile work equipment) and IV (power presses) should be consulted in any case which arises out of those in specific risks. There have been slight changes made between the original 1992 Regulations and the 1998 Regulations: the earlier regulations are relevant to events occurring before 5 December 1998.

The requirements of the Work Equipment Regulations are usually expressed in **9.18** absolute terms, although sometimes with the use of words such as 'good' repair which involve a qualitative judgment. Where an accident has occurred in circumstances which can be attributed to a defect in work equipment, the employer cannot put forward a defence on grounds of having taken reasonable care, or on the reasonable practicality of preventing the defect. The strict liability of the employer towards an injured employee does not, of course, prevent the employer from seeking to pass liability on to any other party who may have been responsible for supplying defective equipment or for a failure of inspection or maintenance.

9.19 *Hammond v Commissioner of Police* [2004] EWCA Civ 830   The claimant was employed as a vehicle mechanic and he was undoing a wheel bolt when it sheared off, causing him to fall awkwardly. The Court of Appeal held that the wheel bolt was not work equipment under the regulations. The regulations do not cover things which are provided for the employee to work on, but only the things provided with which to do the work: loosely described, the tools of the trade.

9.20 *Stark v Post Office* [2000] PIQR P105   The claimant was seriously injured when his bicycle broke: a part of the brake had jammed the front wheel. He alleged breach of the Work Equipment Regulations. There had been proper maintenance of the bicycle, and the defect could not have been discovered on any reasonable inspection, so there was no negligence or fault. However, reg 5 imposed an absolute duty on the employer to ensure that the bicycle was in efficient working order, and the claim succeeded.

9.21 *Horton v Caplin Contracts* [2002] EWCA Civ 1604; [2003] PIQR P180   The claimant was injured when a scaffold tower was caused to fall over by the deliberate act of misuse by a fellow employee. The lack of outriggers did not result in a breach of regs 5 and 20 because the duty to provide equipment that was suitable for its purpose was to be measured by reference to hazards which were reasonably foreseeable. The decision is slightly surprising since the purpose of outriggers on scaffolding is to prevent collapsing in all eventualities, and the alternative allegation that the colleague was acting within the scope of his employment, leading to vicarious liability, does not seem to have been pursued.

9.22 *Searby v Yorkshire Traction* [2003] EWCA Civ 1856   The claimant bus driver was assaulted by a passenger and alleged that a screen should have been provided. The Court of Appeal held that in deciding on the suitability of work equipment, the employer was entitled to take into account the measure of risk, the potential disadvantages of screens, and the resistant attitude of the workforce. The regulations did not require complete and absolute protection, but a consideration of the degree of risk, which was very low. The bus was not unsuitable as work equipment, and the claim failed.

PROVISION AND USE OF WORK EQUIPMENT REGULATIONS 1998

2. Interpretation

9.23   (1) In these Regulations, unless the context otherwise requires—
'the 1974 Act' means the Health and Safety at Work etc. Act 1974;
'employer' except in regulation 3(2) and (3) includes a person to whom the requirements imposed by the Regulations apply by virtue of regulation 3(3)(a) and (b);
'thorough examination' in relation to a thorough examination under paragraph (1), (2), (3) or (4) of regulation 32—

   (a) means a thorough examination by a competent person;

   (b) includes testing the nature and extent of which are appropriate for the purpose described in the paragraph;

'use' in relation to work equipment means any activity involving work equipment and includes starting, stopping, programming, setting, transporting, repairing, modifying, maintaining, servicing and cleaning;

'work equipment' means any machinery, appliance, apparatus, tool or installation for use at work (whether exclusively or not);

and related expressions shall be construed accordingly.

[3. Application]   **9.24**

4. Suitability of work equipment

(1) Every employer shall ensure that work equipment is so constructed or adapted as to be suitable for the purpose for which it is used or provided.   **9.25**

(2) In selecting work equipment, every employer shall have regard to the working conditions and to the risks to the health and safety of persons which exist in the premises or undertaking in which that work equipment is to be used and any additional risk posed by the use of that work equipment.

(3) Every employer shall ensure that work equipment is used only for operations for which, and under conditions for which, it is suitable.

(4) In this regulation 'suitable' means suitable in any respect which it is reasonably foreseeable will affect the health and safety of any person.

5. Maintenance

(1) Every employer shall ensure that work equipment is maintained in an efficient state, in efficient working order and in good repair.   **9.26**

(2) Every employer shall ensure that where any machinery has a maintenance log, the log is kept up to date.

6. Inspection

(1) Every employer shall ensure that, where the safety of work equipment depends on the installation conditions, it is inspected—   **9.27**

   (a) after installation and before being put into service of the first time; or

   (b) after assembly at a new site or in a new location,

to ensure that it has been installed correctly and is safe to operate.

(2) Every employer shall ensure that work equipment exposed to conditions causing deterioration which is liable to result in dangerous situations is inspected—

   (a) at suitable intervals; and

   (b) each time that exceptional circumstances which are liable to jeopardise the safety of the work equipment have occurred, to ensure that health and safety conditions are maintained and that any deterioration can be detected and remedied in good time.

(3) Every employer shall ensure that the result of an inspection made under this regulation is recorded and kept until the next inspection under this regulation is recorded.

(4) Every employer shall ensure that no work equipment—

   (a) leaves his undertaking; or

   (b) if obtained from the undertaking of another person, is used in his undertaking, unless it is accompanied by physical evidence that the last inspection required to be carried out under this regulation has been carried out.

7. Specific risks

9.28   (1) Where the use of work equipment is likely to involve a specific risk to health or safety, every employer shall ensure that—

(a) the use of that work equipment is restricted to those persons given the task of using it; and

(b) repairs, modifications, maintenance or servicing of that work equipment is restricted to those persons who have been specifically designated to perform operations of that description (whether or not also authorised to perform other operations).

(2) The employer shall ensure that the persons designated for the purposes of sub-paragraph (b) of paragraph (1) have received adequate training related to any operations in respect of which they have been so designated.

8. Information and instructions

9.29   (1) Every employer shall ensure that all persons who use work equipment have available to them adequate health and safety information and, where appropriate, written instructions pertaining to the use of the work equipment.

(2) Every employer shall ensure that any of his employees who supervises or manages the use of work equipment has available to him adequate health and safety information and, where appropriate, written instructions pertaining to the use of the work equipment.

(3) Without prejudice to the generality of paragraphs (1) or (2), the information and instructions required by either of those paragraphs shall include information and, where appropriate, written instructions on—

(a) the conditions in which and the methods by which the work equipment may be used;

(b) foreseeable abnormal situations and the action to be taken if such a situation were to occur; and

(c) any conclusions to be drawn from experience in using the work equipment.

(4) Information and instructions required by this regulation shall be readily comprehensible to those concerned.

9. Training

9.30   (1) Every employer shall ensure that all persons who use work equipment have received adequate training for purposes of health and safety, including training in the methods which may be adopted when using the work equipment; any risks which such use may entail and precautions to be taken.

(2) Every employer shall ensure that any of his employees who supervises or manages the use of work equipment has received adequate training for purposes of health and safety, including training in the methods which may be adopted when using the work equipment, any risks which such use may entail and precautions to be taken.

10. Conformity with Community requirements

9.31   (1) Every employer shall ensure that an item of work equipment has been designed and constructed in compliance with any essential requirements, that is to say requirements relating to its design or construction in any of the instruments listed in Schedule 1 (being instruments which give effect to Community directives concerning the safety of products).

(2) Where an essential requirement applies to the design or construction of an item of work equipment, the requirements of regulations 11 to 19 and 22 to 29 shall apply in respect of that item only to the extent that the essential requirement did not apply to it.

(3) This regulation applies to items of work equipment provided for use in the premises or undertaking of the employer for the first time after 31 December 1992.

11. Dangerous parts of machinery

(1) Every employer shall ensure that measures are taken in accordance with paragraph (2) which are effective—

9.32

    (a) to prevent access to any dangerous part of machinery or to any rotating stock-bar; or

    (b) to stop the movement of any dangerous part of machinery or rotating stock-bar before any part of a person enters a danger zone.

(2) The measures required by paragraph (1) shall consist of—

    (a) the provision of fixed guards enclosing every dangerous part or rotating stock-bar where and to the extent that it is practicable to do so, but where or to the extent that it is not, then

    (b) the provision of other guards or protection devices where and to the extent that it is practicable to do so, but where or to the extent that it is not, then

    (c) the provision of jigs, holders, push-sticks or similar protection appliances used in conjunction with the machinery where and to the extent that it is practicable to do so, but where or to the extent that it is not, then

    (d) the provision of information, instruction, training and supervision.

(3) All guards and protection devices provided under sub-paragraphs (a) or (b) of paragraphs (2) shall—

    (a) be suitable for the purpose for which they are provided;

    (b) be of good construction, sound material and adequate strength;

    (c) be maintained in an efficient state, in efficient working order and in good repair;

    (d) not give rise to any increased risk to health or safety;

    (e) not be easily bypassed or disabled;

    (f) be situated at sufficient distance from the danger zone;

    (g) not unduly restrict the view of the operating cycle of the machinery, where such a view is necessary;

    (h) be so constructed or adapted that they allow operations necessary to fit or replace parts and for maintenance work, restricting access to that it is allowed only to the area where the work is to be carried out and, if possible, without having to dismantle the guard or protection device.

(4) All protection appliances provided under sub-paragraph (c) of paragraph (2) shall comply with sub-paragraphs (a) to (d) and (g) of paragraph (3).

(5) In this regulation—

    'danger zone' means any zone in or around machinery in which a person is exposed to a risk to health or safety from contact with a dangerous part of machinery or a rotating stock-bar;

  'stock-bar' means any part of a stock-bar which projects beyond the headstock of a lathe.

12. Protection against specified hazards

(1) Every employer shall take measures to ensure that the exposure of a person using work equipment to any risk to his health or safety from any hazard specified in paragraph (3) is either prevented, or, where that is not reasonably practicable, adequately controlled.

9.33

(2) The measures required by paragraph (1) shall—

    (a) be measures other than the provision of personal protective equipment or of information, instruction, training and supervision, so far as is reasonably practicable; and

    (b) include, where appropriate, measures to minimise the effects of the hazard as well as to reduce the likelihood of the hazard occurring.

(3) The hazards referred to in paragraph (1) are—

    (a) any article or substance falling or being ejected from work equipment;

    (b) rupture or disintegration of parts of work equipment;

    (c) work equipment catching fire or overheating;

    (d) the unintended or premature discharge of any article or of any gas, dust, liquid, vapour or other substance which, in each case, is produced, used or stored in the work equipment;

    (e) the unintended or premature explosion of the work equipment or any article or substance produced, used or stored in it.

(4) For the purposes of this regulation 'adequately' means adequately having regard only to the nature of the hazard and the nature and degree of exposure to the risk.

(5) This regulation shall not apply where any of the following Regulations apply in respect of any risk to a person's health or safety for which such Regulations require measures to be taken to prevent or control such risk, namely—

    (a) the Ionising Radiations Regulations 1985;

    (b) the Control of Asbestos at Work Regulations 1987;

    (c) the Control of Substances Hazardous to Health Regulations 1994;

    (d) the Noise at Work Regulations 1989;

    (e) the Construction (Head Protection) Regulations 1989;

    (f) the Control of Lead at Work Regulations 1998.

13. High or very low temperature

9.34 Every employer shall ensure that work equipment, parts of work equipment and any article or substance produced, used or stored in work equipment which, in each case, is at a high or very low temperature shall have protection where appropriate so as to prevent injury to any person by burn, scald or sear.

14. Controls for starting or making a significant change in operating conditions

9.35 (1) Every employer shall ensure that, where appropriate, work equipment is provided with one or more controls for the purposes of—

    (a) starting the work equipment (including re-starting after a stoppage for any reason); or

    (b) controlling any change in the speed, pressure or other operating conditions of the work equipment where such conditions after the change result in risk to health and safety which is greater than or of a different nature from such risks before the change.

(2) Subject to paragraph (3), every employer shall ensure that, where a control is required by paragraph (1), it shall not be possible to perform any operation mentioned in sub-paragraph (a) or (b) of that paragraph except by a deliberate action on such control.

(3) Paragraph (1) shall not apply to re-starting or changing operating conditons as a result of the normal operating cycle of an automatic device.

15. Stop controls

9.36 (1) Every employer shall ensure that, where appropriate, work equipment is provided with one or more readily accessible controls the operation of which will bring the work equipment to a safe condition in a safe manner.

(2) Any control required by paragraph (1) shall bring the work equipment to a complete stop where necessary for reasons of health and safety.

(3) Any control required by paragraph (1) shall, if necessary for reasons of health and safety, switch off all sources of energy after stopping the functioning of the work equipment.

(4) Any control required by paragraph (1) shall operate in priority to any control which starts or changes the operating conditions of the work equipment.

16. Emergency stop controls

(1) Every employer shall ensure that, where appropriate, work equipment is provided with one **9.37** or more readily accessible emergency stop controls unless it is not necessary by reason of the nature of the hazards and the time taken for the work equipment to come to a complete stop as a result of the action of any control provided by virtue of regulation 15(1).

(2) Any control required by paragraph (1) shall operate in priority to any control required by regulation 15(1).

17. Controls

(1) Every employer shall ensure that all controls for work equipment are clearly visible and **9.38** identifiable, including by appropriate marking where necessary.

(2) Except where necessary, the employer shall ensure that no control for work equipment is in a position where any person operating the control is exposed to a risk to his health or safety.

(3) Every employer shall ensure where appropriate—
  (a) that, so far as is reasonably practicable, the operator of any control is able to ensure from the position of that control that no person is in a place where he would be exposed to any risk to his health or safety as a result of the operation of that control, but where or to the extent that it is not reasonably practicable;
  (b) that, so far as is reasonably practicable, systems of work are effective to ensure that, when work equipment is about to start, no person is in a place where he would be exposed to a risk to his health or safety as a result of the work equipment starting, but where neither of these is reasonably practicable;
  (c) that an audible, visible or other suitable warning is given by virtue of regulation 24 whenever work equipment is about to start.

(4) Every employer shall take appropriate measures to ensure that any person who is in a place where he would be exposed to a risk to his health or safety as a result of the starting or stopping of work equipment has sufficient time and suitable means to avoid that risk.

18. Control systems

(1) Every employer shall— **9.39**
  (a) ensure, so far as is reasonably practicable, that all control systems of work equipment are safe; and
  (b) are chosen making due allowance for the failures, faults and constraints to be expected in the planned circumstances of use.

(2) Without prejudice to the generality of paragraph (1), a control system shall not be safe unless—
  (a) its operation does not create any increased risk to health or safety;
  (b) it ensures, so far as is reasonably practicable, that any fault in or damage to any part of the control system or the loss of supply of any source of energy used by the work equipment cannot result in additional or increased risk to health or safety;
  (c) it does not impede the operation of any control required by regulation 15 or 16.

19. Isolation from sources of energy

(1) Every employer shall ensure that where appropriate work equipment is provided with **9.40** suitable means to isolate it from all its sources of energy.

(2) Without prejudice to the generality of paragraph (1), the means mentioned in that paragraph shall not be suitable unless they are clearly identifiable and readily accessible.

(3) Every employer shall take appropriate measures to ensure that re-connection of any energy source to work equipment does not expose any person using the work equipment to any risk to his health or safety.

20. Stability

9.41 Every employer shall ensure that work equipment or any part of work equipment is stabilised by clamping or otherwise where necessary for purposes of health or safety.

21. Lighting

9.42 Every employer shall ensure that suitable and sufficient lighting, which takes account of the operations to be carried out, is provided at any place where a person uses work equipment.

22. Maintenance operations

9.43 Every employer shall take appropriate measures to ensure that work equipment is so constructed or adapted that, so far as is reasonably practicable, maintenance operations which involve a risk to health or safety can be carried out while the work equipment is shut down, or in other cases—

(a) maintenance operations can be carried out without exposing the person carrying them out to a risk to his health or safety; or

(b) appropriate measures can be taken for the protection of any person carrying out maintenance operations which involve a risk to his health or safety.

23. Markings

9.44 Every employer shall ensure that work equipment is marked in a clearly visible manner with any marking appropriate for reasons of health and safety.

24. Warnings

9.45 (1) Every employer shall ensure that work equipment incorporates any warnings or warning devices which are appropriate for reasons of health and safety.

(2) Without prejudice to the generality of paragraph (1), warnings given by warning devices on work equipment shall not be appropriate unless they are unambiguous, easily perceived and easily understood.

EMPLOYERS' LIABILITY (DEFECTIVE EQUIPMENT) ACT 1969

1. Extension of employer's liability for defective equipment

9.46 (1) Where after the commencement of this Act

(a) an employee suffers personal injury in the course of his employment in consequence of a defect in equipment provided by his employer for the purposes of the employer's business; and

(b) the defect is attributable wholly or partly to the fault of a third party (whether identified or not),

the injury shall be deemed to be also attributable to negligence on the part of the employer (whether or not he is liable in respect of the injury apart from this subsection), but without prejudice to the law relating to contributory negligence and to any remedy by way of contribution or in contract or otherwise which is available to the employer in respect of the injury.

(2) In so far as any agreement purports to exclude or limit any liability of an employer arising under subsection (1) of this section, the agreement shall be void.

(3) In this section

'business' includes the activities carried on by any public body;

'employee' means a person who is employed by another person under a contract of service or apprenticeship and is so employed for the purposes of a business carried on by that other person, and 'employer' shall be construed accordingly;

'equipment' includes any plant and machinery, vehicle, aircraft and clothing;

'fault' means negligence, breach of statutory duty or other act or omission which gives rise to liability in tort in England and Wales or which is wrongful and gives rise to liability in damages in Scotland;

'personal injury' includes loss of life, any impairment of a person's physical or mental condition and any disease.

(4) This section binds the Crown, and persons in the service of the Crown shall accordingly be treated for the purposes of this section as employees of the Crown if they would not be so treated apart from this subsection.

D. The Workplace Regulations

9.47 The Workplace (Health, Safety and Welfare) Regulations 1992 (sometimes shortened to 'the Workplace Regulations') are concerned with safe arrangements for places of work.

9.48 Although the regulations are concerned with the workplace, the scope of reg 5 extends to the maintenance of equipment, devices and systems where a fault is liable to result in a failure to comply with any of the regulations and there is a substantial overlap with the Work Equipment Regulations. The most frequently encountered provision in relation to workplace accidents is reg 12 which requires the employer to keep the floors and traffic routes of the workplace in good condition, free from obstructions, and free from slippery substances. With regard to the permanent construction of the workplace, reg 12(1) and (2) is expressed in absolute terms, but with regard to obstructions or spillages reg 12(3) has a proviso of reasonable practicability.

9.49 In most cases turning on the state of the workplace, the alternative cause of action under the common law will be under the Occupiers' Liability Act 1957, where the standard of care is identical to common law negligence. However, the regulations will usually offer better protection to those who can rely on them.

9.50 *Palmer v Marks & Spencer* [2001] EWCA Civ 1528   The claimant tripped on a weather strip across a doorway. The strip protruded about 9 mm from the floor surface in order to prevent water coming in. There was no negligence, there was no history of any previous accident or complaint, and the claimant was aware of the presence of the weather strip. The trial judge held that was a breach of reg 12 but the Court of Appeal set this aside: the suitability of the floor was to be considered by asking whether the state of the floor was such as to expose any person to a risk to his health and safety.

9.51   *McCondichie v Mains Medical Centre* [2004] Rep LR 4, Court of Session (Outer House)   The claimant was a patient visiting a medical practice who was injured in a slipping accident. The Scottish court rejected the argument that people other than employees, such as this claimant, or a shop customer, can rely on breaches of reg 12 to gain the benefit of strict liability.

WORKPLACE (HEALTH, SAFETY AND WELFARE) REGULATIONS 1992

9.52   [1. Citation and commencement]

2. Interpretation

9.53   (1) In these Regulations, unless the context otherwise requires—
'traffic route' means a route for pedestrian traffic, vehicles or both and includes any stairs, staircase, fixed ladder, doorway, gateway, loading bay or ramp;
'workplace' means, subject to paragraphs (2) and (3), any premises or part of premises which are not domestic premises and are made available to any person as a place of work, and includes—
(a) any place within the premises to which such person has access while at work; and
(b) any room, lobby, corridor, staircase, road or other place used as a means of access to or egress from the workplace or where facilities are provided for use in connection with the workplace other than a public road.

(2) A modification, an extension or a conversion shall not be a workplace or form part of a workplace until the modification, extension or conversion is complete.

(3) Any reference in these Regulations to a modification, an extension or a conversion is a reference, as the case may be, to a modification, an extension or a conversion of a workplace started after 31 December 1992.

(4) Any requirement that anything done or provided in pursuance of these Regulations shall be suitable shall be construed to include a requirement that it is suitable for any person in respect of whom such thing is so done or provided.

(5) Any reference in these Regulations to—
(a) a numbered regulation or Schedule is a reference to the regulation or Schedule to these Regulations so numbered; and
(b) a numbered paragraph is a reference to the paragraph so numbered in the regulation in which the reference appears.

3. Application of these Regulations

9.54   (1) These Regulations apply to every workplace but shall not apply to—
(a) a workplace which is or is in or on a ship within the meaning assigned to that word by regulation 2(1) of the Docks Regulations 1988;
(b) a workplace where the only activities being undertaken are building operations or works of engineering construction within, in either case, section 176 of the Factories Act 1961 and activities for the purpose of or in connection with those activities;
(c) a workplace where the only activities being undertaken are the exploration for or extraction of mineral resources; or
(d) a workplace which is situated in the immediate vicinity of another workplace or intended workplace where exploration for or extraction of mineral resources is being or will be undertaken, and where the only activities being undertaken are activities preparatory to, for the

purposes of, or in connection with such exploration for or extraction of mineral resources at that other workplace.

(2) In their application to temporary work sites, any requirement to ensure a workplace complies with any of regulations 20 to 25 shall have effect as a requirement to so ensure so far as is reasonably practicable.

(3) As respects any workplace which is or is in or on an aircraft, locomotive or rolling stock, trailer or semi-trailer used as a means of transport or a vehicle for which a licence is in force under the Vehicles (Excise) Act 1971 or a vehicle exempted from duty under that Act—

(a) regulations 5 to 12 and 14 to 25 shall not apply to any such workplace; and

(b) regulation 13 shall apply to any such workplace only when the aircraft, locomotive or rolling stock, trailer or semi-trailer or vehicle is stationary inside a workplace and, in the case of a vehicle for which a licence is in force under the Vehicles (Excise) Act 1971, is not on a public road.

(4) As respects any workplace which is in fields, woods or other land forming part of an agricultural or forestry undertaking but which is not inside a building and is situated away from the undertaking's main buildings—

(a) regulations 5 to 19 and 23 to 25 shall not apply to any such workplace; and

(b) any requirement to ensure that any such workplace complies with any of regulations 20 to 22 shall have effect as a requirement to so ensure so far as is reasonably practicable.

4. Requirements under these Regulations

(1) Every employer shall ensure that every workplace, modification, extension or conversion **9.55** which is under his control and where any of his employees work complies with any requirement of these Regulations which—

(a) applies to that workplace or, as the case may be, to the workplace which contains that modification, extension or conversion; and

(b) is in force in respect of the workplace, modification, extension or conversion.

(2) Subject to paragraph (4), every person who has, to any extent, control of a workplace, modification, an extension or a conversion shall ensure that such workplace, modification, extension or conversion complies with any requirement of these Regulations which—

(a) applies to that workplace or, as the case may be, to the workplace which contains that modification, extension or conversion;

(b) is in force in respect of the workplace, modification, extension, or conversion; and

(c) relates to matters within that person's control.

(3) Any reference in this regulation to a person having control of any workplace, modification, extension or conversion is a reference to a person having control of the workplace, modification, extension or conversion in connection with the carrying on by him of a trade, business or other undertaking (whether for profit or not).

(4) Paragraph (2) shall not impose any requirement upon a self-employed person in respect of his own work or the work of any partner of his in the undertaking.

(5) Every person who is deemed to be the occupier of a factory by virtue of section 175(5) of the Factories Act 1961 shall ensure that the premises which are so deemed to be a factory comply with these Regulations.

5. Maintenance of workplace, and of equipment, devices and systems

(1) The workplace and the equipment, devices and systems to which this regulation applies **9.56** shall be maintained (including cleaned as appropriate) in an efficient state, in efficient working order and in good repair.

(2) Where appropriate, the equipment, devices and systems to which this regulation applies shall be subject to a suitable system of maintenance.

(3) The equipment, devices and systems to which this regulation applies are—

(a) equipment and devices a fault in which is liable to result in a failure to comply with any of these Regulations; and

(b) mechanical ventilation systems provided pursuant to regulation 6 (whether or not they include equipment or devices within sub-paragraph (a) of this paragraph).

9.57   [6. Ventilation]

[7. Temperature in indoor workplaces]

8. Lighting

9.58   (1) Every workplace shall have suitable and sufficient lighting.

(2) The lighting mentioned in paragraph (1) shall, so far as is reasonably practicable, be by natural light.

(3) Without prejudice to the generality of paragraph (1), suitable and sufficient emergency lighting shall be provided in any room in circumstances in which persons at work are specially exposed to danger in the event of failure of artificial lighting.

9. Cleanliness and waste materials

9.59   (1) Every workplace and the furniture, furnishings and fittings therein shall be kept sufficiently clean.

(2) The surfaces of the floor, wall and ceiling of all workplaces inside buildings shall be capable of being kept sufficiently clean.

(3) So far as is reasonably practicable, waste materials shall not be allowed to accumulate in a workplace except in suitable receptacles.

9.60   [10. **Room dimensions and space**]

11. Workstations and seating

9.61   (1) Every workstation shall be so arranged that it is suitable both for any person at work in the workplace who is likely to work at that workstation and for any work of the undertaking which is likely to be done there.

(2) Without prejudice to the generality of paragraph (1), every workstation outdoors shall be so arranged that—

(a) so far as is reasonably practicable, it provides protection from adverse weather;

(b) it enables any person at the workstation to leave it swiftly or, as appropriate, to be assisted in the event of an emergency; and

(c) it ensures that any person at the workstation is not likely to slip or fall.

(3) A suitable seat shall be provided for each person at work in the workplace whose work includes operations of a kind that the work (or a substantial part of it) can or must be done sitting.

(4) A seat shall not be suitable for the purposes of paragraph (3) unless—

(a) it is suitable for the person for whom it is provided as well as for the operations to be performed; and

(b) a suitable footrest is also provided where necessary.

12. Condition of floors and traffic routes

9.62   (1) Every floor in a workplace and the surface of every traffic route in a workplace shall be of a construction such that the floor or surface of the traffic route is suitable for the purpose for which it is used.

(2) Without prejudice to the generality of paragraph (1), the requirements in that paragraph shall include requirements that—

(a) the floor, or surface of the traffic route, shall have no hole or slope, or be uneven or slippery so as, in each case, to expose any person to a risk to his health or safety;

(b) every such floor shall have effective means of drainage where necessary.

(3) So far as is reasonably practicable, every floor in a workplace and the surface of every traffic route in a workplace shall be kept free from obstructions and from any article or substance which may cause a person to slip, trip or fall;

(4) In considering whether for the purposes of paragraph (2)(a) a hole or slope exposes any person to a risk to his health or safety—

(a) no account shall be taken of a hole where adequate measures have been taken to prevent a person falling;

(b) account shall be taken of any handrail provided in connection with any slope.

(5) Suitable and sufficient handrails and, if appropriate, guards shall be provided on all traffic routes which are staircases except in circumstances in which a handrail can not be provided without obstructing the traffic route.

[*For the Code of Practice guidance on reg 12, see* **10.30** below.]

13. Falls or falling objects

(1) So far as is reasonably practicable, suitable and effective measures shall be taken to prevent any event specified in paragraph (3).   **9.63**

(2) So far as is reasonably practicable, the measures required by paragraph (1) shall be measures other than the provision of personal protective equipment, information, instruction, training or supervision.

(3) The events mentioned in this paragraph are—

(a) any person falling a distance likely to cause personal injury;

(b) any person being struck by a falling object likely to cause personal injury.

(4) Any area where there is a risk to health or safety from any event mentioned in paragraph (3) shall be clearly indicated where appropriate.

(5) So far as is practicable, every tank, pit or structure where there is a risk of a person in the workplace falling into a dangerous substance in the tank, pit or structure, shall be securely covered or fenced.

(6) Every traffic route over, across or in an uncovered tank, pit or structure such as is mentioned in paragraph (5) shall be securely fenced.

(7) In this Regulation, 'dangerous substance' means—

(a) any substance likely to scald or burn;

(b) any poisonous substance;

(c) any corrosive substance;

(d) any fume, gas or vapour likely to overcome a person; or

(e) any granular or free-flowing solid substance, or any viscous substance which, in any case, is of a nature or quantity which is likely to cause danger to any person.

14. Windows, and transparent or translucent doors, gates and walls

(1) Every window or other transparent or translucent surface in a wall or partition and every transparent or translucent surface in a door or gate shall, where necessary for reasons of health or safety—   **9.64**

(a) be of safety material or be protected against breakage of the transparent or translucent material; and

(b) be appropriately marked or incorporate features so as, in either case, to make it apparent.

15. Windows, skylights and ventilators

9.65   (1) No window, skylight or ventilator which is capable of being opened shall be likely to be opened, closed or adjusted in a manner which exposes any person performing such operation to a risk to his health or safety.

(2) No window, skylight or ventilator shall be in a position when open which is likely to expose any person in the workplace to a risk to his health or safety.

16. Ability to clean windows etc safely

9.66   (1) All windows and skylights in a workplace shall be of a design or be so constructed that they may be cleaned safely.

(2) In considering whether a window or skylight is of a design or so constructed as to comply with paragraph (1), account may be taken of equipment used in conjunction with the window or skylight or of devices fitted to the building.

17. Organisation etc of traffic routes

9.67   (1) Every workplace shall be organised in such a way that pedestrians and vehicles can circulate in a safe manner.

(2) Traffic routes in a workplace shall be suitable for the persons or vehicles using them, sufficient in number, in suitable positions and of sufficient size.

(3) Without prejudice to the generality of paragraph (2), traffic routes shall not satisfy the requirements of that paragraph unless suitable measures are taken to ensure that—

(a) pedestrians or, as the case may be, vehicles may use a traffic route without causing danger to the health or safety of persons at work near it; and

(b) there is sufficient separation of any traffic route for vehicles from doors or gates or from traffic routes for pedestrians which lead onto it;

(c) where vehicles and pedestrians use the same traffic route, there is sufficient separation between them.

(4) All traffic routes shall be suitably indicated where necessary for reasons of health or safety.

(5) Paragraph (2) shall apply so far as is reasonably practicable, to a workplace which is not a new workplace, a modification, an extension or a conversion.

18. Doors and gates

9.68   (1) Doors and gates shall be suitably constructed (including being fitted with any necessary safety devices).

(2) Without prejudice to the generality of paragraph (1), doors and gates shall not comply with that paragraph unless—

(a) any sliding door or gate has a device to prevent it coming off its track during use;

(b) any upward opening door or gate has a device to prevent it falling back;

(c) any powered door or gate has suitable and effective features to prevent it causing injury by trapping any person;

(d) where necessary for reasons of health or safety, any powered door or gate can be operated manually unless it opens automatically if the power fails; and

(e) any door or gate which is capable of opening by being pushed from either side is of such a construction as to provide, when closed, a clear view of the space close to both sides.

E. The Manual Handling Regulations

The Manual Handling Operations Regulations 1992 (sometimes shortened to **9.70** 'the Manual Handling Regulations') are concerned above all with the avoidance of injuries from lifting and moving by hand. They are an attempt to end the epidemic of back strain which causes so much ill-health absence from work, by requiring employers to devise systems of work which minimize the risk of injury.

Litigators must therefore bear in mind that the principal purpose of the regula- **9.71** tions is preventative. If an employer faithfully carries out the obligations under the regulations of assessing the work tasks and avoiding any unassisted manual handling that might cause injury, the incidence of injury should be negligible. The price for this approach is that there is no easy measure of a breach of the regulations in the form of a weight limit. The Health and Safety Executive has published Guidance Notes in the form of HSE Guidance Appendix 1, which is included below, and sets out some detailed assessment guidelines including a helpful diagram of guideline figures for different lifting postures for men and women. The diagram creates a tempting legal short cut to the question of breach and liability, but the Guidance should be read in full, taking into account its limited purpose of assisting employers with risk assessment.

Koonjal v Thameslink Healthcare [2000] PIQR P123   This case concerned **9.72** what constitutes a 'risk' of injury. The claimant was a care assistant who injured her back when pulling a bed away from a wall. She had received appropriate manual handling training. It was held that there was not a sufficient risk of injury from this ordinary task to oblige the employer to avoid the need for her to undertake it under reg 4, and her claim failed.

9.73 *King v RCO Support Services* [2001] PIQR P206   The claimant slipped while carrying out his job of gritting an icy yard. The judge rejected a claim under the regulations because the accident was caused by the claimant stepping onto an untreated area and not by anything to do with his manual handling task. The Court of Appeal held that the claimant was carrying out a manual handling operation so that the risk of slipping had to be avoided unless it was not reasonably practicable to avoid it. Since the defendant had not sought to prove that everything reasonably practical had been done (for example, by the provision of grit) liability followed, subject to contributory negligence of 50%. A rare example of a modern case turning on the statements of case. Compare *Fytche v Wincanton Logistics*, a case under the Protective Equipment Regulations (at **9.91** below), where strict liability is limited to a defect that is relevant to the risk that the equipment is intended to protect against.

9.74 *King v Sussex Ambulance NHS Trust* [2002] EWCA Civ 953; [2002] ICR 1413   An ambulance technician used a carry chair to bring a patient down awkward stairs and strained his back. There was a foreseeable risk of such injury, but there was no available equipment that could have been used to reduce the risk. The only alternative was to call the fire brigade and take the patient out through the upstairs window, which would have caused delay and distress. There had not been a failure to take reasonable care, and in spite of the risk of injury, the claim failed.

9.75 *O'Neill v DSG Retail* [2002] EWCA Civ 1139; [2003] ICR 222   The claimant was carrying a box when a colleague called out to him and he turned towards the call, suffering a back injury. The claimant was aware of the principles of safe manual handling. The weight of the box was within the employer's guidelines. The defendant had provided written instructions, but had failed to give the claimant practical training or to show him a video which warned against twisting. The trial judge rejected the claim, holding that the accident was not foreseeable and would not have been prevented by further training but the Court of Appeal held that there was a breach of the regulations and the employer was liable.

9.76 *Bennetts v Ministry of Defence* [2004] EWCA Civ 486   The claimant hurt her back while sorting mail. A mailbag snagged when she attempted to lift it. There had been inadequate risk assessment and training, but there was no causal link between the absence of training and the claimant's injury, so the claim failed.

MANUAL HANDLING OPERATIONS REGULATIONS 1992

9.77 [1. Citation and commencement]

2. Interpretation

9.78 (1) In these Regulations, unless the context otherwise requires—

'injury' does not include injury caused by any toxic or corrosive substance which—

(a) has leaked or spilled from a load;

(b) is present on the surface of a load but has not leaked or spilled from it; or

(c) is a constituent part of a load;

and 'injured' shall be construed accordingly;

'load' includes any person and any animal;

'manual handling operations' means any transporting or supporting of a load (including the lifting, putting down, pushing, pulling, carrying or moving thereof) by hand or by bodily force.

(2) Any duty imposed by these Regulations on an employer in respect of his employees shall also be imposed on a self-employed person in respect of himself.

[3. Disapplication of Regulations: ships] **9.79**

4. Duties of employers

(1) Each employer shall— **9.80**

(a) so far as is reasonably practicable, avoid the need for his employees to undertake any manual handling operations at work which involve a risk of their being injured.

(b) where it is not reasonably practicable to avoid the need for his employees to undertake any manual handling operations at work which involve a risk of their being injured—

(i) make a suitable and sufficient assessment of all such manual handling operations to be undertaken by them, having regard to the factors which are specified in column 1 of Schedule 1 to these Regulations and considering the questions which are specified opposite thereto in column 2 of that Schedule.

(ii) take appropriate steps to reduce the risk of injury to those employees arising out of their undertaking any such manual handling operations to the lowest level reasonably practicable.

(iii) take appropriate steps to provide any of those employees who are undertaking any such manual handling operations with general indications and, where it is reasonably practicable to do so, precise information on—

(aa) the weight of each load, and

(bb) the heaviest side of any load whose centre of gravity is not positioned centrally.

(2) Any assessment such as is referred to in paragraph (1)(b)(i) of this regulation shall be reviewed by the employer who made it if—

(a) there is reason to suspect that it is no longer valid; or

(b) there has been a significant change in the manual handling operations to which it relates;

and where as a result of any such review changes to an assessment are required, the relevant employer shall make them.

5. Duty of employees

Each employee while at work shall make full and proper use of any system of work provided for **9.81** his use by his employer in compliance with regulation 4(1)(b)(ii) of these Regulations.

[6. Exemption certificate—Military] **9.82**

[7. Extension outside Great Britain]

[8. Repeals and revocations]

SCHEDULE 1

Factors to which the employer must have regard and questions he must consider when making an **9.83** assessment of manual handling operations

Regulation 4(1)(b)(i)

Column 1 *Factors*	Column 2 *Questions*

1 The tasks	Do they involve:
	— holding or manipulating loads at distance from trunk?
	— unsatisfactory bodily movement or posture, especially:
	   — twisting the trunk?
	   — stooping?
	   — reaching upwards?
	— excessive movement of loads, especially:
	   — excessive lifting or lowering distances?
	   — excessive carrying distances?
	— excessive pushing or pulling of loads?
	— risk of sudden movement of loads?
	— frequent or prolonged physical effort?
	— insufficient rest or recovery periods?
	— a rate of work imposed by a process?

2 The loads	Are they: — heavy? — bulky or unwieldy? — difficult to grasp? — unstable, or with contents likely to shift? — sharp, hot or otherwise potentially damaging?
3 The working environment	Are there: — space constraints preventing good posture? — uneven, slippery or unstable floors? — variations in level of floors or work surfaces? — extremes of temperature or humidity? — conditions causing ventilation problems or gusts of wind? — poor lighting conditions?
4 Individual capability	Does the job: — require unusual strength, height, etc? — create a hazard to those who might reasonably be considered to be pregnant or to have a health problem? — require special information or training for its safe performance?
5 Other factors	Is movement or posture hindered by personal protective equipment or by clothing?

HSE GUIDANCE APPENDIX 1

MANUAL HANDLING RISK ASSESSMENT DETAILED ASSESSMENT GUIDELINES FILTER

Introduction

9.84 (1) The Manual Handling Regulations set no specific requirements such as weight limits. Instead, they focus on the needs of the individual and set out a hierarchy of measures for safety during manual handling operations:

(a) avoid hazardous manual handling operations so far as is reasonably practicable;

(b) make a suitable and sufficient assessment of any hazardous manual handling operations that cannot be avoided; and

(c) reduce the risk of injury from those operations so far as is reasonably practicable.

Risk assessment filter

(2) Where manual handling operations cannot be avoided, employers have a duty to make a **9.85** suitable and sufficient assessment of the risks to health. This assessment must take into account the range of relevant factors listed in Schedule 1 to the Regulations. A detailed assessment of every manual handling operation, however, could be a major undertaking and might involve wasted effort. Many handling operations, for example lifting a tea cup, will involve negligible handling risk. To help identify situations where a more detailed risk assessment is necessary, HSE has developed a filter to screen out straightforward cases.

(3) The filter is based on a set of numerical guidelines developed from data in published scientific literature and on practical experience of assessing risks from manual handling. They are pragmatic, tried and tested; they are not based on any precise scientific formulae. The intention is to set out an approximate boundary within which the load is unlikely to create a risk of injury sufficient to warrant a detailed assessment.

(4) The application of the guidelines will provide a reasonable level of protection to around 95% of working men and women. However, the guidelines should not be regarded as safe weight limits for lifting. There is no threshold below which manual handling operations may be regarded as 'safe'. Even operations lying within the boundary mapped out by the guidelines should be avoided or made less demanding wherever it is reasonably practicable to do so.

(5) It is important to remember that the purpose of the guidelines is to avoid wasted time and effort. The use of the filter will only be worthwhile, therefore, where the relevance of the guideline figures can be determined quickly, say within 10 minutes. If it is not clear from the outset that this can be done, it is better to opt immediately for the more detailed risk assessment.

Guidelines for lifting and lowering

(6) The guidelines for lifting and lowering operations assume that the load is easy to grasp with **9.86** both hands and that the operation takes place in reasonable working conditions with the handler in a stable body position. They take into consideration the vertical and horizontal position of the hands as they move the load during the handling operation, as well as the height and reach of the individual handler. For example if a load is held at arm's length or the hands pass above shoulder height, the capability to lift or lower is reduced significantly.

(7) The basic guideline figures for identifying when manual lifting and lowering operations may not need a detailed assessment are set out in Figure 1. If the handler's hands enter more than one of the box zones during the operation, the smallest weight figures apply. It is important to remember, however, that the transition from one box zone to another is not abrupt; an intermediate figure may be chosen where the handler's bands are close to a boundary. Where lifting or lowering with the hands beyond the box zones is unavoidable, a more detailed assessment should always be made.

(8) These basic guideline figures for lifting and lowering are for relatively infrequent operations—up to approximately 30 operations per hour. The guideline figures will have to be reduced if the operation is repeated more often. As a rough guide, the figures should be reduce by 30% where the operation is repeated once or twice per minute, by 50% where the operation is repeated around five to eight times per minute and by 80% where the operation is repeated more than about 12 times per minute.

(9) Even if the above conditions are satisfied, a more detailed risk assessment should be made where:

    (a) the worker does not control the pace of work;

    (b) pauses for rest are inadequate or there is no change of activity which provides an opportunity to use different muscles;

    (c) the handler must support the load for any length of time.

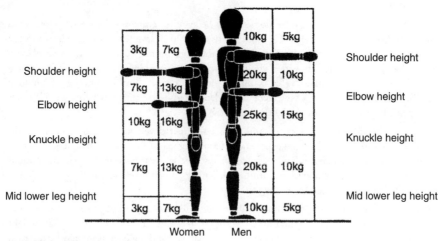

Figure 1. Lifting and lowering

Guidelines for carrying

9.87   (10) Similar guideline figures apply to carrying operations where the load is held against the body and is carried no further than about 10 m without resting. If the load is carried over a longer distance without resting or the hands are below knuckle height then a more detailed risk assessment should be made.

(11) Where the load can be carried securely on the shoulder without first having to be lifted (as for example when unloading sacks from a lorry) the guideline figures can be applied to carrying distances in excess of 10 m.

Guidelines for pushing and pulling

9.88   (12) For pushing and pulling operations (whether the load is slid, rolled or supported on wheels) the guideline figures assume the force is applied with the hands between knuckle and shoulder height. The guideline figure for starting or stopping the load is a force of about 25 kg (i.e. about 250 Newtons) for men and about 16 kg (i.e. about 160 Newtons) for women. The guideline figure for keeping the load in motion is a force of about 10 kg (i.e. about 100 Newtons) for men and about 7 kg (i.e. about 70 Newtons) for women.

(13) There is no specific limit to the distance over which the load is pushed or pulled provided there are adequate opportunities for rest or recovery.

Guidelines for handling while seated

9.89   (14) The basic guideline figure for handling operations carried out while seated, shown in Figure 2, is 5 kg for men and 3 kg for women. These guidelines only apply when the hands are within the box zone indicated. If handling beyond the box zone is unavoidable, a more detailed assessment should be made.

Other considerations: Twisting

9.90   (15) In many cases, manual handling operations will involve some twisting (see Figure 3) and this will increase the risk of injury. Where the handling task involves twisting and turning, therefore, a detailed risk assessment should normally be made. However, if the operation is

230

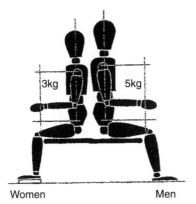

Figure 2. Handling while seated

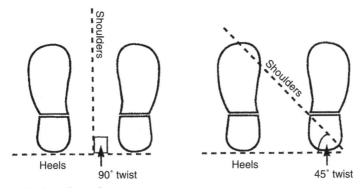

Figure 3. Assessing twist

relatively infrequent (see paragraph 8 of this Appendix) and there are no other posture problems then the filter can be used. In such cases, the basic guideline figures shown above should be reduced if the handler twists to the side during the operation. As a rough guide, the figures should be reduced by about 10% where the handler twists through 45° and by about 20% where the handler twists through 90°.

Remember: The use of these guidelines does not affect the employer's duty to avoid or reduce risk of injury where this is reasonably practicable. The guideline figures, therefore, should not be regarded as weight limits for safe lifting. They are an aid to highlight where detailed risk assessments are most needed. Where doubt remains, a more detailed risk assessment should always be made. Even for a minority of fit, well-trained individuals working under favourable conditions, operations which exceed the guideline figures by more than a factor of about two may represent a serious risk of injury. Such operations should come under very close scrutiny.

F. The Protective Equipment Regulations

The Personal Protective Equipment at Work Regulations 1992 (sometimes **9.91** shortened to 'the Protective Equipment Regulations' or 'PPE') govern the provision and use of protective equipment to ensure the safety of employees. There are lengthy Guidance Notes, which are not included in this book but which may be worth consulting in a difficult or borderline case.

9.92 *Fytche v Wincanton Logistics* [2004] UKHL 31   The claimant was employed as a milk collection driver, so he was exposed to cold weather. He was given protective boots with a steel toecap to protect against anything falling on to his toes. There was a small hole in one boot which did not impair the protection of the toecap, but which allowed water to enter, resulting in frostbite of the toe. The House of Lords upheld the decision that reg 7 created strict liability only in respect of the risks against which the protective equipment was intended to protect the claimant, so that in relation to other risks the claimant had to rely on common law negligence. There had been no negligence in the failure to discover the hole, and the claim failed.

PERSONAL PROTECTIVE EQUIPMENT AT WORK REGULATIONS 1992

9.93   [1. Citation and commencement]

2. Interpretation

9.94   (1) In these Regulations, unless the context otherwise requires, 'personal protective equipment' means all equipment (including clothing affording protection against the weather) which is intended to be worn or held by a person at work and which protects him against one or more risks to his health or safety, and any addition or accessory designed to meet that objective;

(2) Any reference in these Regulations to—

(a) a numbered regulation or Schedule is a reference to the regulation or Schedule in these Regulations so numbered; and

(b) a numbered paragraph is a reference to the paragraph so numbered in the regulation in which the reference appears.

9.95   [3. Disapplication of these Regulations: ships, and when other Regulations apply]

4. Provision of personal protective equipment

9.96   (1) Every employer shall ensure that suitable personal protective equipment is provided to his employees who may be exposed to a risk to their health or safety while at work except where and to the extent that such risk has been adequately controlled by other means which are equally or more effective.

(2) Every self-employed person shall ensure that he is provided with suitable personal protective equipment where he may be exposed to a risk to his health or safety while at work except where and to the extent that such risk has been adequately controlled by other means which are equally or more effective.

(3) Without prejudice to the generality of paragraphs (1) and (2), personal protective equipment shall not be suitable unless—

(a) it is appropriate for the risk or risks involved and the conditions at the place where exposure to the risk may occur;

(b) it takes account of ergonomic requirements and the state of health of the person or persons who may wear it;

(c) it is capable of fitting the wearer correctly, if necessary, after adjustments within the range for which it is designed;

(d) so far as is practicable, it is effective to prevent or adequately control the risk or risks involved without increasing overall risk;

(e) it complies with any enactment (whether in an Act or instrument) which implements in Great Britain any provision on design or manufacture with respect to health or safety in any of the relevant Community directives listed in Schedule 1 which is applicable to that item of personal protective equipment.

5. Compatibility of personal protective equipment

(1) Every employer shall ensure that where the presence of more than one risk to health or safety makes it necessary for his employee to wear or use simultaneously more than one item of personal protective equipment, such equipment is compatible and continues to be effective against the risk or risks in question. **9.97**

(2) Every self-employed person shall ensure that where the presence of more than one risk to health or safety makes it necessary for him to wear or use simultaneously more than one item of personal protective equipment, such equipment is compatible and continues to be effective against the risk or risks in question.

6. Assessment of personal protective equipment

(1) Before choosing any personal protective equipment which by virtue of regulation 4 he is required to ensure is provided, an employer or self-employed person shall ensure that an assessment is made to determine whether the personal protective equipment he intends will be provided is suitable. **9.98**

(2) The assessment required by paragraph (1) shall include—

(a) an assessment of any risk or risks to health or safety which have not been avoided by other means;

(b) the definition of the characteristics which personal protective equipment must have in order to be effective against the risks referred to in sub-paragraph (a) of this paragraph, taking into account any risks which the equipment itself may create;

(c) comparison of the characteristics of the personal protective equipment available with the characteristics referred to in sub-paragraph (b) of this paragraph.

(3) Every employer or self-employed person who is required by paragraph (1) to ensure that any assessment is made shall ensure that any such assessment is reviewed if—

(a) there is reason to suspect that it is no longer valid; or

(b) there has been a significant change in the matters to which it relates, and where as a result of any such review changes in the assessment are required, the relevant employer or self-employed person shall ensure that they are made.

7. Maintenance and replacement of personal protective equipment

(1) Every employer shall ensure that any personal protective equipment provided to his employees is maintained (including replaced or cleaned as appropriate) in an efficient state, in efficient working order and in good repair. **9.99**

(2) Every self-employed person shall ensure that any personal protective equipment provided to him is maintained (including replaced, or cleaned as appropriate) in an efficient state, in efficient working order and in good repair.

[8. Accommodation for personal protective equipment]

9.100

9. Information, instruction and training

9.101   (1) Where an employer is required to ensure that personal protective equipment is provided to an employee, the employer shall also ensure that the employee is provided with such information, instruction and training as is adequate and appropriate to enable the employee to know—

(a) the risk or risks which the personal protective equipment will avoid or limit;

(b) the purpose for which and the manner in which personal protective equipment is to be used; and

(c) any action to be taken by the employee to ensure that the personal protective equipment remains in an efficient state, in efficient working order and in good repair as required by regulation 7(1).

(2) Without prejudice to the generality of paragraph (1), the information and instruction provided by virtue of that paragraph shall not be adequate and appropriate unless it is comprehensible to the persons to whom it is provided.

10. Use of personal protective equipment

9.102   (1) Every employer shall take all reasonable steps to ensure that any personal protective equipment provided to his employees by virtue of regulation 4(1) is properly used.

(2) Every employee shall use any personal protective equipment provided to him by virtue of these Regulations in accordance both with any training in the use of the personal protective equipment concerned which has been received by him and the instructions respecting that use which have been provided to him by virtue of regulation 9.

(3) Every self-employed person shall make full and proper use of any personal protective equipment provided to him by virtue of regulation 4(2).

(4) Every employee and self-employed person who has been provided with personal protective equipment by virtue of regulation 4 shall take all reasonable steps to ensure that it is returned to the accommodation provided for it after use.

9.103   [11. **Reporting loss or defect**]

[12. **Exemption certificates—Military**]

G. The Management Regulations

9.104   The Management of Health and Safety at Work Regulations 1999 (sometimes shortened to 'the Management Regulations') are of general application. When all the new health and safety regulations were introduced in 1992, a distinction was made between the specific regulations we have already considered which give rise to civil liability for a breach, and these general regulations which, like the Health and Safety at Work, etc Act 1974, expressly excluded civil liability. This did not inhibit practitioners from often alleging a negligent failure to carry out risk assessment as the regulations required. Regulation 22 of the 1999 Regulations has now been amended (see below). The amendment is oddly expressed, but the clear intention is that employers may be liable in civil proceedings to employees, although not to others. The amendment applies to causes of action arising after 27 October 2003.

MANAGEMENT OF HEALTH AND SAFETY AT WORK REGULATIONS 1999

1. Citation, commencement and interpretation

(1) These Regulations may be cited as the Management of Health and Safety at Work Regulations 1999 and shall come into force on 29th December 1999. **9.105**

(2) In these Regulations—

'the 1996 Act' means the Employment Rights Act 1996;

'the assessment' means, in the case of an employer or self-employed person, the assessment made or changed by him in accordance with regulation 3;

'child'—

    (a) as respects England and Wales, means a person who is not over compulsory school age, construed in accordance with section 8 of the Education Act 1996; and

    (b) as respects Scotland, means a person who is not over school age, construed in accordance with section 31 of the Education (Scotland) Act 1980;

'employment business' means a business (whether or not carried on with a view to profit and whether or not carried on in conjunction with any other business) which supplies persons (other than seafarers) who are employed in it to work for and under the control of other persons in any capacity;

'fixed-term contract of employment' means a contract of employment for a specific term which is fixed in advance or which can be ascertained in advance by reference to some relevant circumstance;

'given birth' means delivered a living child or, after twenty-four weeks of pregnancy, a stillborn child;

'new or expectant mother' means an employee who is pregnant; who has given birth within the previous six months; or who is breastfeeding;

'the preventive and protective measures' means the measures which have been identified by the employer or by the self-employed person in consequence of the assessment as the measures he needs to take to comply with the requirements and prohibitions imposed upon him by or under the relevant statutory provisions and by Part II of the Fire Precautions (Workplace) Regulations 1997;

'young person' means any person who has not attained the age of eighteen.

(3) Any reference in these Regulations to—

    (a) a numbered regulation or Schedule is a reference to the regulation or Schedule in these Regulations so numbered; or

    (b) a numbered paragraph is a reference to the paragraph so numbered in the regulation in which the reference appears.

2. Disapplication of these Regulations

(1) These Regulations shall not apply to or in relation to the master or crew of a sea-going ship or to the employer of such persons in respect of the normal shipboard activities of a ship's crew under the direction of the master. **9.106**

(2) Regulations 3(4), (5), 10(2) and 19 shall not apply to occasional work or short-term work involving—

    (a) domestic service in a private household; or

    (b) work regulated as not being harmful, damaging or dangerous to young people in a family undertaking.

3. Risk assessment

9.107   (1) Every employer shall make a suitable and sufficient assessment of—

(a) the risks to the health and safety of his employees to which they are exposed whilst they are at work; and

(b) the risks to the health and safety of persons not in his employment arising out of or in connection with the conduct by him of his undertaking,

for the purpose of identifying the measures he needs to take to comply with the requirements and prohibitions imposed upon him by or under the relevant statutory provisions and by Part II of the Fire Precautions (Workplace) Regulations 1997.

(2) Every self-employed person shall make a suitable and sufficient assessment of—

(a) the risks to his own health and safety to which he is exposed whilst he is at work; and

(b) the risks to the health and safety of persons not in his employment arising out of or in connection with the conduct by him of his undertaking,

for the purpose of identifying the measures he needs to take to comply with the requirements and prohibitions imposed upon him by or under the relevant statutory provisions.

(3) Any assessment such as is referred to in paragraph (1) or (2) shall be reviewed by the employer or self-employed person who made it if—

(a) there is reason to suspect that it is no longer valid; or

(b) there has been a significant change in the matters to which it relates; and where as a result of any such review changes to an assessment are required, the employer or self-employed person concerned shall make them.

(4) An employer shall not employ a young person unless he has, in relation to risks to the health and safety of young persons, made or reviewed an assessment in accordance with paragraphs (1) and (5).

(5) In making or reviewing the assessment, an employer who employs or is to employ a young person shall take particular account of—

(a) the inexperience, lack of awareness of risks and immaturity of young persons;

(b) the fitting-out and layout of the workplace and the workstation;

(c) the nature, degree and duration of exposure to physical, biological and chemical agents;

(d) the form, range, and use of work equipment and the way in which it is handled;

(e) the organisation of processes and activities;

(f) the extent of the health and safety training provided or to be provided to young persons; and

(g) risks from agents, processes and work listed in the Annex to Council Directive 94/33/EC on the protection of young people at work.

(6) Where the employer employs five or more employees, he shall record—

(a) the significant findings of the assessment; and

(b) any group of his employees identified by it as being especially at risk.

4. Principles of prevention to be applied

9.108   Where an employer implements any preventive and protective measures he shall do so on the basis of the principles specified in Schedule 1 to these Regulations.

Schedule 1
General Principles of Prevention

. . .

9.109   (a) avoiding risks;

(b) evaluating the risks which cannot be avoided;

(c) combating the risks at source;

(d) adapting the work to the individual, especially as regards the design of workplaces, the choice of work equipment and the choice of working and production methods, with a view, in particular, to alleviating monotonous work and work at a predetermined work-rate and to reducing their effect on health;

(e) adapting to technical progress;

(f) replacing the dangerous by the non-dangerous or the less dangerous;

(g) developing a coherent overall prevention policy which covers technology, organisation of work, working conditions, social relationships and the influence of factors relating to the working environment;

(h) giving collective protective measures priority over individual protective measures; and

(i) giving appropriate instructions to employees.

5. Health and safety arrangements

(1) Every employer shall make and give effect to such arrangements as are appropriate, having **9.110** regard to the nature of his activities and the size of his undertaking, for the effective planning, organisation, control, monitoring and review of the preventive and protective measures.

(2) Where the employer employs five or more employees, he shall record the arrangements referred to in paragraph (1).

6. Health surveillance

Every employer shall ensure that his employees are provided with such health surveillance as is **9.111** appropriate having regard to the risks to their health and safety which are identified by the assessment.

7. Health and safety assistance

(1) Every employer shall, subject to paragraphs (6) and (7), appoint one or more competent **9.112** persons to assist him in undertaking the measures he needs to take to comply with the requirements and prohibitions imposed upon him by or under the relevant statutory provisions and by Part II of the Fire Precautions (Workplace) Regulations 1997.

(2) Where an employer appoints persons in accordance with paragraph (1), he shall make arrangements for ensuring adequate co-operation between them.

(3) The employer shall ensure that the number of persons appointed under paragraph (1), the time available for them to fulfil their functions and the means at their disposal are adequate having regard to the size of his undertaking, the risks to which his employees are exposed and the distribution of those risks throughout the undertaking.

(4) The employer shall ensure that—

(a) any person appointed by him in accordance with paragraph (1) who is not in his employment—

(i) is informed of the factors known by him to affect, or suspected by him of affecting, the health and safety of any other person who may be affected by the conduct of his undertaking, and

(ii) has access to the information referred to in regulation 10; and

(b) any person appointed by him in accordance with paragraph (1) is given such information about any person working in his undertaking who is—

(i) employed by him under a fixed-term contract of employment, or

(ii) employed in an employment business,

as is necessary to enable that person properly to carry out the function specified in that paragraph.

(5) A person shall be regarded as competent for the purposes of paragraphs (1) and (8) where he has sufficient training and experience or knowledge and other qualities to enable him properly to assist in undertaking the measures referred to in paragraph (1).

(6) Paragraph (1) shall not apply to a self-employed employer who is not in partnership with any other person where he has sufficient training and experience or knowledge and other qualities properly to undertake the measures referred to in that paragraph himself.

(7) Paragraph (1) shall not apply to individuals who are employers and who are together carrying on business in partnership where at least one of the individuals concerned has sufficient training and experience or knowledge and other qualities—

(a) properly to undertake the measures he needs to take to comply with the requirements and prohibitions imposed upon him by or under the relevant statutory provisions; and

(b) properly to assist his fellow partners in undertaking the measures they need to take to comply with the requirements and prohibitions imposed upon them by or under the relevant statutory provisions.

(8) Where there is a competent person in the employer's employment, that person shall be appointed for the purposes of paragraph (1) in preference to a competent person not in his employment.

9.113   [8. **Procedures for serious and imminent danger and for danger areas**]

9. Contacts with external services

9.114   Every employer shall ensure that any necessary contacts with external services are arranged, particularly as regards first-aid, emergency medical care and rescue work.

10. Information for employees

9.115   (1) Every employer shall provide his employees with comprehensible and relevant information on—

(a) the risks to their health and safety identified by the assessment;

(b) the preventive and protective measures;

(c) the procedures referred to in regulation 8(1)(a) and the measures referred to in regulation 4(2)(a) of the Fire Precautions (Workplace) Regulation 1997;

(d) the identity of those persons nominated by him in accordance with regulation 8(1)(b) and regulation 4(2)(b) of the Fire Precautions (Workplace) Regulation 1997; and

(e) the risks notified to him in accordance with regulation 11(1)(c).

(2) Every employer shall, before employing a child, provide a parent of the child with comprehensible and relevant information on—

(a) the risks to his health and safety identified by the assessment;

(b) the preventive and protective measures; and

(c) the risks notified to him in accordance with regulation 11(1)(c).

(3) The reference in paragraph (2) to a parent of the child includes—

(a) in England and Wales, a person who has parental responsibility, within the meaning of section 3 of the Children Act 1989, for him; and

(b) in Scotland, a person who has parental rights, within the meaning of section 8 of the Law Reform (Parent and Child) (Scotland) Act 1986 for him.

11. Co-operation and co-ordination

9.116   (1) Where two or more employers share a workplace (whether on a temporary or a permanent basis) each such employer shall—

(a) co-operate with the other employers concerned so far as is necessary to enable them to comply with the requirements and prohibitions imposed upon them by or under the relevant statutory provisions and by Part II of the Fire Precautions (Workplace) Regulations 1997;

(b) (taking into account the nature of his activities) take all reasonable steps to co-ordinate the measures he takes to comply with the requirements and prohibitions imposed upon him by or under the relevant statutory provisions and by Part II of the Fire Precautions (Workplace) Regulations 1997 with the measures the other employers concerned are taking to comply with the requirements and prohibitions imposed upon them by that legislation; and

(c) take all reasonable steps to inform the other employers concerned of the risks to their employees' health and safety arising out of or in connection with the conduct by him of his undertaking.

(2) Paragraph (1) (except in so far as it refers to Part II of the Fire Precautions (Workplace) Regulations 1997) shall apply to employers sharing a workplace with self-employed persons and to self-employed persons sharing a workplace with other self-employed persons as it applies to employers sharing a workplace with other employers; and the references in that paragraph to employers and the reference in the said paragraph to their employees shall be construed accordingly.

12. Persons working in host employers' or self-employed persons' undertakings

(1) Every employer and every self-employed person shall ensure that the employer of any **9.117** employees from an outside undertaking who are working in his undertaking is provided with comprehensible information on—

(a) the risks to those employees' health and safety arising out of or in connection with the conduct by that first-mentioned employer or by that self-employed person of his undertaking; and

(b) the measures taken by that first-mentioned employer or by that self-employed person in compliance with the requirements and prohibitions imposed upon him by or under the relevant statutory provisions and by Part II of the Fire Precautions (Workplace) Regulations 1997 in so far as the said requirements and prohibitions relate to those employees.

(2) Paragraph (1) (except in so far as it refers to Part II of the Fire Precautions (Workplace) Regulations 1997) shall apply to a self-employed person who is working in the undertaking of an employer or a self-employed person as it applies to employees from an outside undertaking who are working therein; and the reference in that paragraph to the employer of any employees from an outside undertaking who are working in the undertaking of an employer or a self-employed person and the references in the said paragraph to employees from an outside undertaking who are working in the undertaking of an employer or a self-employed person shall be construed accordingly.

(3) Every employer shall ensure that any person working in his undertaking who is not his employee and every self-employed person (not being an employer) shall ensure that any person working in his undertaking is provided with appropriate instructions and comprehensible information regarding any risks to that person's health and safety which arise out of the conduct by that employer or self-employed person of his undertaking.

(4) Every employer shall—

(a) ensure that the employer of any employees from an outside undertaking who are working in his undertaking is provided with sufficient information to enable that second-mentioned employer to identify any person nominated by that first mentioned employer in accordance with regulation 8(1)(b) to implement evacuation procedures as far as those employees are concerned; and

(b) take all reasonable steps to ensure that any employees from an outside undertaking who are working in his undertaking receive sufficient information to enable them to identify any person nominated by him in accordance with regulation 8(1)(b) to implement evacuation procedures as far as they are concerned.

(5) Paragraph (4) shall apply to a self-employed person who is working in an employer's undertaking as it applies to employees from an outside undertaking who are working therein; and the reference in that paragraph to the employer of any employees from an outside undertaking who are working in an employer's undertaking and the references in the said paragraph to employees from an outside undertaking who are working in an employer's undertaking shall be construed accordingly.

13. Capabilities and training

9.118　(1) Every employer shall, in entrusting tasks to his employees, take into account their capabilities as regards health and safety.

(2) Every employer shall ensure that his employees are provided with adequate health and safety training—
　　(a) on their being recruited into the employer's undertaking; and
　　(b) on their being exposed to new or increased risks because of—
　　　(i) their being transferred or given a change of responsibilities within the employer's undertaking,
　　　(ii) the introduction of new work equipment into or a change respecting work equipment already in use within the employer's undertaking,
　　　(iii) the introduction of new technology into the employer's undertaking, or
　　　(iv) the introduction of a new system of work into or a change respecting a system of work already in use within the employer's undertaking.
　(3) The training referred to in paragraph (2) shall—
　　(a) be repeated periodically where appropriate;
　　(b) be adapted to take account of any new or changed risks to the health and safety of the employees concerned; and
　　(c) take place during working hours.

14. Employees' duties

9.119　(1) Every employee shall use any machinery, equipment, dangerous substance, transport equipment, means of production or safety device provided to him by his employer in accordance both with any training in the use of the equipment concerned which has been received by him and the instructions respecting that use which have been provided to him by the said employer in compliance with the requirements and prohibitions imposed upon that employer by or under the relevant statutory provisions.

(2) Every employee shall inform his employer or any other employee of that employer with specific responsibility for the health and safety of his fellow employees—
　　(a) of any work situation which a person with the first-mentioned employee's training and instruction would reasonably consider represented a serious and immediate danger to health and safety; and
　　(b) of any matter which a person with the first-mentioned employee's training and instruction would reasonably consider represented a shortcoming in the employer's protection arrangements for health and safety,

in so far as that situation or matter either affects the health and safety of that first mentioned employee or arises out of or in connection with his own activities at work, and has not previously been reported to his employer or to any other employee of that employer in accordance with this paragraph.

[15. Temporary workers]   **9.120**

[16. Risk assessments in respect of new or expectant mothers]

[17. Certificate from registered medical practitioner in respect of new or expectant mothers]

[18. Notification by new or expectant mothers]

[19. Protection of young persons]

[20. Exemption certificates]

[21. Provisions as to (criminal) liability]

22. **Restriction of civil liability for breach of statutory duty**

Breach of a duty imposed on an employer by these Regulations shall not confer a right of action   **9.121**
in any civil proceedings in so far as that duty applies for the protection of persons not in his
employment.

H. Regulation of Construction Work

The construction industry is large, diverse, and dangerous. Although many large   **9.122**
firms have excellent working practices, there is a host of small building firms and
self-employed sub-contractors who fail to take proper care for their own and
others' safety. Those who are cavalier about safe working practices may also be
cavalier about liability insurance, and there is no equivalent of the MIB to
protect the victim of an uninsured small builder.

Ferguson v Welsh [1987] 1 WLR 1553   A demolition contract was awarded to   **9.123**
a small builder and he engaged the claimant, nominally as a sub-contractor. The
claimant was injured when he carried out the work in a dangerous manner. He
succeeded in a claim against the builder who had engaged him, but was unable
to bring a claim home against any party with money or insurance.

Lane v Shire Roofing [1995] PIQR P147   The claimant, a building worker,   **9.124**
engaged nominally as a contractor rather than an employee, and for tax purposes self-employed, was injured through a failure to provide him with proper
equipment. Although he was a skilled man and was working without detailed
instructions, the defendant was held liable as his employer. Control is not
decisive and the question was, whose business was it that he was working in, and
who had responsibility for the overall safety of the men doing the work?

Makepeace v Evans [2001] ICR 241   The claimant, a painter and decorator,   **9.125**
was employed by a firm of sub-contractors. He was injured when a tower
scaffold fell over. The scaffold had been provided by the main contractors. The
Court of Appeal held that a duty of care could be owed by a main contractor if it

provided a piece of equipment that was inherently dangerous and failed to make appropriate health and safety inquiries; but in this case it was an ordinary piece of equipment being lent to an experienced painter and the claim against the main contractor had rightly failed.

9.126   *McCook v Lobo* [2002] EWCA Civ 1760; [2003] ICR 89   The claimant was employed as a labourer by a building contractor and was injured when he fell from a ladder which was not footed or secured. The employer was liable subject to 75% contributory negligence but was uninsured. The claimant tried to establish liability against the owners of the building being converted. Although there had been a breach of the Construction (Design and Management) Regulations 1994 for failing to provide a detailed health and safety plan, this was not causative of the accident and the claims failed.

I. Principal Regulations Applying to Construction Sites

CONSTRUCTION (HEALTH, SAFETY AND WELFARE) REGULATIONS 1996

1. Citation and commencement

9.127   These Regulations may be cited as the Construction (Health, Safety and Welfare) Regulations 1996 and shall come into force on 2nd September 1996.

2. Interpretation

9.128   (1) In these Regulations, unless the context otherwise requires—
'construction site' means any place where the principal work activity being carried out is construction work;
'construction work' means the carrying out of any building, civil engineering or engineering construction work and includes any of the following—
   (a) the construction, alteration, conversion, fitting out, commissioning, renovation, repair, upkeep, redecoration or other maintenance (including cleaning which involves the use of water or an abrasive at high pressure or the use of substances classified as corrosive or toxic for the purposes of regulation 5 of the Carriage of Dangerous Goods by Road and Rail (Classification, Packaging and Labelling Regulations 1994), de-commissioning, demolition or dismantling of a structure,
   (b) the preparation for an intended structure, including site clearance exploration, investigation (but not site survey) and excavation, and laying or installing the foundations of the structure,
   (c) the assembly of prefabricated elements to form a structure or the disassembly of prefabricated elements which, immediately before such disassembly, formed a structure,
   (d) the removal of a structure or part of a structure or of any product or waste resulting from demolition or dismantling of a structure or from disassembly of prefabricated elements which, immediately before such disassembly, formed a structure, and
   (e) the installation, commissioning, maintenance, repair or removal of mechanical, electrical, gas, compressed air, hydraulic, telecommunications, computer or similar services which are normally fixed within or to a structure, but does not include the

exploration for or extraction of mineral resources or activities preparatory thereto carried out at a place where such exploration or extraction is carried out;

'excavation' includes any earthwork, trench, well, shaft, tunnel or underground working;

'fragile material' means any material which would be liable to fail if the weight of any person likely to pass across or work on that material (including the weight of anything for the time being supported or carried by that person) were to be applied to it;

'loading bay' means any facility for loading or unloading equipment or materials for use in construction work;

'personal suspension equipment' means suspended access equipment (other than a working platform) for use by an individual and includes a boatswain's chair and abseiling equipment but it does not include a suspended scaffold or cradle;

'place of work' means any place which is used by any person at work for the purposes of construction work or for the purposes of any activity arising out of or in connection with construction work;

'plant and equipment' includes any machinery, apparatus, appliance or other similar device, or any part thereof, used for the purposes of construction work and any vehicle being used for such purpose;

structure' means—

(a) any building, steel or reinforced concrete structure (not being a building), railway line or siding, tramway line, dock, harbour, inland navigation, tunnel, shaft, bridge, viaduct, waterworks, reservoir, pipe or pipe-line (whatever, in either case, it contains or is intended to contain), cable, aqueduct, sewer, sewage works, gasholder, road, airfield, sea defence works, river works, drainage works, earthworks, lagoon, dam, wall, caisson, mast, tower, pylon, underground tank, earth retaining structure, or structure designed to preserve or alter any natural feature, and any other structure similar to the foregoing or

(b) any formwork, falsework, scaffold or other structure designed or used to provide support or means of access during construction work, or

(c) any fixed plant in respect of work which is installation, commissioning, de-commissioning or dismantling and where any such work involves a risk of a person falling more than 2 metres.

'traffic route' means any route the purpose of which is to permit the access to or egress from any part of a construction site for any pedestrians or vehicles, or both, and includes any doorway, gateway, loading bay or ramp;

'vehicle' includes any mobile plant and locomotive and any vehicle towed by another vehicle;

'working platform' means any platform used as a place of work or as a means of access to or egress from that place and includes any scaffold, suspended scaffold, cradle, mobile platform, trestle, gangway, run, gantry, stairway and crawling ladder.

(2) Unless the context otherwise requires, any reference in these Regulations to—

(a) a numbered regulation or Schedule is a reference to the regulation or Schedule in these Regulations so numbered; and

(b) a numbered paragraph is a reference to the paragraph so numbered in the regulation or Schedule in which the reference appears.

3. Application

(1) Subject to the following paragraphs of this regulation, these Regulations apply to and in relation to construction work carried out by a person at work. **9.129**

(2) These Regulations shall not apply to any workplace on a construction site which is set aside for purposes other than construction work.

(3) Regulations 15, 19, 20, 21, 22 and 26(1) and (2) apply only to and in relation to construction work carried out by a person at work at a construction site.

4. Persons upon whom duties are imposed by these Regulations

9.130 (1) Subject to paragraph (5), it shall be the duty of every employer whose employees are carrying out construction work and every self-employed person carrying out construction work to comply with the provisions of these Regulations insofar as they affect him or any person at work under his control or relate to matters which are within his control.

(2) It shall be the duty of every person (other than a person having a duty under paragraph (1) or (3)) who controls the way in which any construction work is carried out by a person at work to comply with the provisions of these Regulations insofar as they relate to matters which are within his control.

(3) Subject to paragraph (5), it shall be the duty of every employee carrying out construction work to comply with the requirements of these Regulations insofar as they relate to the performance of or the refraining from an act by him.

(4) It shall be the duty of every person at work—

(a) as regards any duty or requirement imposed on any other person under these Regulations, to co-operate with that person so far as is necessary to enable that duty or requirement to be performed or complied with; and

(b) where working under the control of another person, to report to that person any defect which he is aware may endanger the health or safety of himself or another person.

(5) This regulation shall not apply to regulations 22 and 29(2), which expressly say on whom the duties are imposed.

5. Safe places of work

9.131 (1) There shall, so far as is reasonably practicable, be suitable and sufficient safe access to and egress from every place of work and to any other place provided for the use of any person while at work, which access and egress shall be without risks to health and properly maintained.

(2) Every place of work shall, so far as is reasonably practicable, be made and kept safe for, and without risks to health to, any person at work there.

(3) Suitable and sufficient steps shall be taken to ensure, so far as is reasonably practicable, that no person gains access to any place which does not comply with the requirements of paragraphs (1) or (2).

(4) Paragraphs (1) to (3) shall not apply in relation to a person engaged in work for the purpose of making any place safe, provided all practicable steps are taken to ensure the safety of that person whilst engaged in that work.

(5) Every place of work shall, so far as is reasonably practicable and having regard to the nature of the work being carried out there, have sufficient working space and be so arranged that it is suitable for any person who is working or who is likely to work there.

6. Falls

9.132 (1) Suitable and sufficient steps shall be taken to prevent, so far as is reasonably practicable, any person falling.

(2) In any case where the steps referred to in paragraph (1) include the provision of—

(a) any guard-rail, toe-board, barrier or other similar means of protection; or

(b) any working platform, it shall comply with the provisions of Schedule 1 and Schedule 2 respectively.

(3) Without prejudice to the generality of paragraph (1) and subject to paragraph (6), where any person is to carry out work at a place from which he is liable to fall a distance of 2 metres or more or where any person is to use a means of access to or egress from a place of work from which access or egress he is liable to fall a distance of 2 metres or more—

(a) there shall, subject to sub-paragraphs (c) and (d) below and paragraph (9), be provided and used suitable and sufficient guard-rails and toe-boards, barriers or other similar means of protection to prevent, so far as is reasonably practicable, the fall of any person from that place, which guard-rails, toe-boards, barriers and other similar means of protection shall comply with the provisions, of Schedule 1; and

(b) where it is necessary in the interest of the safety of any person that a working platform be provided, there shall, subject to sub-paragraphs (c) and (d) below, be so provided and used a sufficient number of working platforms which shall comply with the provisions of Schedule 2; and

(c) where it is not practicable to comply with all or any of the requirements of sub-paragraphs (a) or (b) above or where due to the nature or the short duration of the work compliance with such requirements is not reasonably practicable, there shall, subject to sub-paragraph (d) below, be provided and used suitable personal suspension equipment which shall comply with the provisions of Schedule 3; and

(d) where it is not practicable to comply with all or any of the requirements of sub-paragraphs (a), (b) or (c) above or where due to the nature or the short duration of the work compliance with such requirements is not reasonably practicable, such requirements of those sub-paragraphs as can be complied with shall be complied with and, in addition, there shall be provided and used suitable and sufficient means for arresting the fall of any person which shall comply with the provisions of Schedule 4.

(4) Means for the prevention of, or for protection from, falls provided pursuant to sub-paragraph (a) and (b) of paragraph (3) may be removed for the time and to the extent necessary for the movement of materials, but shall be replaced as soon as practicable.

(5) A ladder shall not be used as, or as a means of access to or egress from, a place of work unless it is reasonable to do so having regard to—

(a) the nature of the work being carried out and its duration; and

(b) the risks to the safety to any person arising from the use of the ladder.

(6) Where a ladder is used pursuant to paragraph (5)—

(a) it shall comply with the provisions of Schedule 5; and

(b) the provisions of paragraph (3) shall not apply.

(7) Any equipment provided pursuant to this regulation shall be properly maintained.

(8) (a) The installation or erection of any scaffold provided pursuant to paragraph (1) or sub-paragraph (b) of paragraph (3) and any substantial addition or alteration to such scaffold shall be carried out only under the supervision of a competent person.

(b) The installation or erection of any personal suspension equipment or any means of arresting falls provided pursuant to sub-paragraphs (c) or (d) of paragraph (3) shall be carried out only under the supervision of a competent person, and for the purposes of this paragraph installation shall not include the personal attachment of any equipment or means of preventing falls to the person for whose safety such equipment or means is provided.

(9) No toe-boards shall be required in respect of any stairway, or any rest platform forming part of a scaffold, where such stairway or platform is used solely as a means of access to or egress from any place of work, provided that the stairway or platform is not being used for the keeping or storing of any material or substance.

[The provisions detailing the requirements for protecting against falls are contained in the Schedules to the regulations. These are set out immediately below for ease of reference.]

SCHEDULE I
REQUIREMENTS FOR GUARD-RAILS ETC

9.133
1. A guard-rail, toe-board, barrier or other similar means of protection shall—
(a) be suitable and of sufficient strength and rigidity for the purpose or purposes for which it is being used; and
(b) be so placed, secured and used as to ensure, so far as is reasonably practicable, that it does not become accidentally displaced.

2. Any structure or any part of a structure which supports a guard-rail, toe-board, barrier or other similar means of protection or to which a guard-rail, toe-board, barrier or other similar means of protection is attached shall be of sufficient strength and suitable for the purpose of such support or attachment.

3. The main guard-rail or other similar means of protection shall be at least 910 millimetres above the edge from which any person is liable to fall.

9.134
4. There shall not be an unprotected gap exceeding 470 millimetres between any guardrail, toe-board, barrier or other similar means of protection.

5. Toe-boards or other similar means of protection shall not be less than 150 millimetres high.

6. Guard-rails, toe-boards, barriers and other similar means of protection shall be so placed as to prevent, so far as is practicable, the fall of any person, or any material or object, from any place of work.

SCHEDULE 2
REQUIREMENTS FOR WORKING PLATFORMS

Interpretation

9.135
1. In this Schedule, 'supporting structure' means any structure used for the purpose of supporting a working platform and includes any plant and equipment used for that purpose.

Condition of surfaces

9.136
2. Any surface upon which any supporting structure rests shall be stable, of sufficient strength and of suitable composition safely to support the supporting structure, the working platform and any load intended to be placed on the working platform.

Stability of supporting structure

9.137
3. Any supporting structure shall—
(a) be suitable and of sufficient strength and rigidity for the purpose or purposes for which it is being used; and
(b) be so erected and, where necessary, securely attached to another structure as to ensure that it is stable; and
(c) when altered or modified, be so altered or modified as to ensure that it remains stable.

Stability of working platform

4. A working platform shall—
9.138
(a) be suitable and of sufficient strength and rigidity for the purpose or purposes for which it is intended to be used or is being used; and

(b) be so erected and used as to ensure, so far as is reasonably practicable, that it does not become accidentally displaced so as to endanger any person; and

(c) when altered or modified, be so altered or modified as to ensure that it remains stable; and

(d) be dismantled in such a way as to prevent accidental displacement.

Safety on working platforms

5. A working platform shall—

(a) be of sufficient dimensions to permit the free passage of persons and the safe use **9.139** of any equipment or materials required to be used and to provide, so far as is reasonably practicable, a safe working area having regard to the work there being carried out; and

(b) without prejudice to paragraph (a), be not less than 600 millimetres wide; and

(c) be so constructed that the surface of the working platform has no gap giving rise to the risk of injury to any person or, where there is a risk of any person below the platform being struck, through which any material or object could fall; and

(d) be so erected and used, and maintained in such condition, as to prevent, so far as is reasonably practicable—

(i) the risk of slipping or tripping; or

(ii) any person being caught between the working platform and any adjacent structure; and

(e) be provided with such handholds and footholds as are necessary to prevent, so far as is reasonably practicable, any person slipping from or falling from the working platform.

Loading

6. A working platform and any supporting structure shall not be loaded so as to give **9.140** rise to a danger of collapse or to any deformation which could affect its safe use.

SCHEDULE 3

REQUIREMENTS FOR PERSONAL SUSPENSION EQUIPMENT

1. Personal suspension equipment shall be suitable and of sufficient strength for the **9.141** purpose or purposes for which it is being used having regard to the work being carried out and the load, including any person, it is intended to bear.

2. Personal suspension equipment shall be securely attached to a structure or to plant and the structure or plant and the means of attachment thereto shall be suitable and of sufficient strength and stability for the purpose of supporting that equipment and the load, including any person, it is intended to bear.

3. Suitable and sufficient steps shall be taken to prevent any person falling or slipping from personal suspension equipment.

4. Personal suspension equipment shall be installed or attached in such a way as to **9.142** prevent uncontrolled movement of that equipment.

SCHEDULE 4

REQUIREMENTS FOR MEANS OF ARRESTING FALLS

1. In this Schedule, 'equipment' means any equipment provided for the purpose of **9.143** arresting the fall of any person at work and includes any net or harness provided for that purpose.

2. The equipment shall be suitable and of sufficient strength to safely arrest the fall of any person who is liable to fall.

247

3. The equipment shall be securely attached to a structure or to plant and the structure or plant and the means of attachment thereto shall be suitable and of sufficient strength and stability for the purpose of safely supporting the equipment and any person who is liable to fall.

9.144 **4.** Suitable and sufficient steps shall be taken to ensure, so far as practicable, that in the event of a fall by any person the equipment does not itself cause injury to that person.

SCHEDULE 5
REQUIREMENTS FOR LADDERS

9.145 **1.** Any surface upon which a ladder rests shall be stable, level and firm, of sufficient strength and of suitable composition safely to support the ladder and any load, intended to be placed on it.

2. A ladder shall—

(a) be suitable and of sufficient strength for the purpose or purposes for which it is being used;

(b) be so erected as to ensure that it does not become displaced; and

(c) where it is of a length when used of 3 metres or more, be secured to the extent that it is practicable to do so and where it is not practicable to secure the ladder a person shall be positioned at the foot of the ladder to prevent it slipping at all times when it is being used.

3. All ladders used as a means of access between places of work shall be sufficiently secured so as to prevent the ladder slipping or falling.

9.146 **4.** The top of any ladder used as a means of access to another level shall, unless a suitable alternative handhold is provided, extend to a sufficient height above the level to which it gives access so as to provide a safe handhold.

5. Where a ladder or run of ladders rises a vertical distance of 9 metres or more above its base, there shall, where practicable, be provided at suitable intervals sufficient safe landing areas or rest platforms.

7. Fragile material

9.147 (1) Suitable and sufficient steps shall be taken to prevent any person from falling through any fragile material.

(2) Without prejudice to the generality of paragraph (1),

(a) no person shall pass across, or work on or from, fragile material through which he would be liable to fall 2 metres or more unless suitable and sufficient platforms, coverings or other similar means of support are provided and used so that the weight of any person so passing or working is supported by such supports; and

(b) no person shall pass or work near fragile material through which he would be liable to fall 2 metres or more unless there are provided suitable and sufficient guard-rails, coverings or other similar means for preventing, so far as is reasonably practicable, any person so passing or working from falling through that material; and

(c) where any person may pass across or near or work on or near fragile material through which, were it not for the provisions of sub-paragraphs (a) and (b) above he would be liable to fall 2 metres or more, prominent warning notices shall be affixed at the approach to the place where the material is situated.

8. Falling objects

9.148 (1) Where necessary to prevent danger to any person, suitable and sufficient steps shall be taken to prevent, so far as is reasonably practicable, the fall of any material or object.

248

(2) In any case where the steps referred to in paragraph (1) include the provision of—

    (a) any guard-rail, toe-board, barrier or other similar means of protection; or

    (b) any working platform,

it shall comply with the provisions of Schedule 1 and Schedule 2 respectively.

(3) Where it is not reasonably practicable to comply with the requirements of paragraph (1) or where it is otherwise necessary in the interests of safety, suitable and sufficient steps shall be taken to prevent any person from being struck by any falling material or object which is liable to cause injury.

(4) No material or object shall be thrown or tipped from a height in circumstances where it is liable to cause injury to any person.

(5) Materials and equipment shall be stored in such a way as to prevent danger to any person arising from the collapse, overturning or unintentional movement of such materials or equipment.

9. Stability of structures

(1) All practicable steps shall be taken, where necessary to prevent danger to any person, to **9.149** ensure that any new or existing structure or any part of such structure which may become unstable or in a temporary state of weakness or instability due to the carrying out of construction work (including any excavation work) does not collapse accidentally.

(2) No part of a structure shall be so loaded as to render it unsafe to any person.

(3) Any buttress, temporary support or temporary structure used to support a permanent structure pursuant to paragraph (1) shall be erected or dismantled only under the supervision of a competent person.

10. Demolition or dismantling

(1) Suitable and sufficient steps shill be taken to ensure that the demolition or dismantling of **9.150** any structure, or any part of any structure, being demolition or dismantling which gives rise to a risk of danger to any person, is planned and carried out in such a manner as to prevent, so far as is practicable, such danger.

(2) Demolition or dismantling to which paragraph (1) applies shall be planned and carried out only under the supervision of a competent person.

11. Explosives

An explosive charge shall be used or fired only if suitable and sufficient steps have been taken to **9.151** ensure that no person is exposed to risk of injury from the explosion or from projected or flying material caused thereby.

12. Excavations

(1) All practicable steps shall be taken, where necessary to prevent danger to any person, to **9.152** ensure that any new or existing excavation or any part of such excavation which may be in a temporary state of weakness or instability due to the carrying out of construction work (including other excavation work) does not collapse accidentally.

(2) Suitable and sufficient steps shall be taken to prevent, so far as is reasonably practicable, any person from being buried or trapped by a fall or dislodgment of any material.

(3) Without prejudice to the generality of paragraph (2), where it is necessary for the purpose of preventing any danger to any person from a fall or dislodgment of any material from a side or

the roof of or adjacent to any excavation, that excavation shall as early as practicable in the course of the work be sufficiently supported so as to prevent, so far as is reasonably practicable, the fall or dislodgment of such material.

(4) Suitable and sufficient equipment for supporting an excavation shall be provided to ensure that the requirements of paragraphs (1) to (3) may be complied with.

(5) The installation, alteration or dismantling of any support for an excavation pursuant to paragraphs (1), (2) or (3) shall be carried out only under the supervision of a competent person.

(6) Where necessary to prevent danger to any person, suitable and sufficient steps shall be taken to prevent any person, vehicle or plant and equipment, or any accumulation of earth or other material, from falling into any excavation.

(7) Where a collapse of an excavation would endanger any person, no material, vehicle or plant and equipment shall be placed or moved near any excavation where it is likely to cause such collapse.

(8) No excavation work shall be carried out unless suitable and sufficient steps have been taken to identify and, so far as is reasonably practicable, prevent any risk of injury arising from any underground cable or other underground service.

13. Cofferdams and caissons

9.153 (1) Every cofferdam or caisson and every part thereof shall be of suitable design and construction, of suitable and sound material and of sufficient strength and capacity for the purpose for which it is used, and shall be properly maintained.

(2) The construction, installation, alteration or dismantling of a cofferdam or caisson shall take place only under the supervision of a competent person.

Note: These are watertight structures built around a site for construction of an underwater structure, for example building the piers of a bridge.

14. Prevention of drowning

9.154 (1) Where during the course of construction work any person is liable to fall into water or other liquid with a risk of drowning, suitable and sufficient steps shall be taken—
  (a) to prevent, so far as is reasonably practicable, such person from so falling; and
  (b) to minimise the risk of drowning in the event of such a fall; and
  (c) to ensure that suitable rescue equipment is provided, maintained and, when necessary, used so that such person may be promptly rescued in the event of such a fall.

(2) Suitable and sufficient steps shall be taken to ensure the safe transport of any person conveyed by water to or from any place of work.

(3) Any vessel used to convey any person by water to or from a place of work—
  (a) shall be of suitable construction; and
  (b) shall be properly maintained; and
  (c) shall be under the control of a competent person; and
  (d) shall not be overcrowded or overloaded.

15. Traffic routes

9.155 (1) Every construction site shall be organised in such a way that, so far as is reasonably practicable, pedestrians and vehicles can move safely and without risks to health.

(2) Traffic routes shall be suitable for the persons or vehicles using them, sufficient in number, in suitable positions and of sufficient size.

(3) Without prejudice to the generality of paragraph (2), traffic routes shall not satisfy the requirements of that paragraph unless suitable and sufficient steps are taken to ensure that—

(a) pedestrians or, as the case may be, vehicles may use a traffic route without causing danger to the health or safety of persons near it;

(b) any door or gate used or intended to be used by pedestrians and which leads onto a traffic route for vehicles is sufficiently separated from that traffic route to enable pedestrians from a place of safety to see any approaching vehicle or plant;

(c) there is sufficient separation between vehicles and pedestrians to ensure safety or, where this is not reasonably practicable—

(i) there are provided other means for the protection of pedestrians; and

(ii) there are effective arrangements for warning any person liable to be crushed or trapped by any vehicle of the approach of that vehicle;

(d) any loading bay has at least one exit point for the exclusive use of pedestrians; and

(e) where it is unsafe for pedestrians to use any gate intended primarily for vehicles, one or more doors for pedestrians is provided in the immediate vicinity of any such gate, which door shall be clearly marked and kept free from obstruction.

(4) No vehicle shall be driven on a traffic route unless, so far as is reasonably practicable, that traffic route is free from obstruction and permits sufficient clearance.

(5) Where it is not reasonably practicable to comply with all or any of the requirements of paragraph (4), suitable and sufficient steps shall be taken to warn the driver of the vehicle and any other person riding thereon of any approaching obstruction or lack of clearance.

(6) Every traffic route shall be indicated by suitable signs where necessary for reasons of health or safety.

16. Doors and gates

(1) Where necessary to prevent the risk of injury to any person, any door, gate or hatch **9.156** (including a temporary door, gate or hatch) shall incorporate or be fitted with suitable safety devices.

(2) Without prejudice to the generality of paragraph (1), a door, gate or hatch shall not comply with that paragraph unless—

(a) any sliding door, gate or hatch has a device to prevent it coming off its track during use;

(b) any upward opening door, gate or hatch has a device to prevent it falling back;

(c) any powered door, gate or hatch has suitable and effective features to prevent it causing injury by trapping any person;

(d) where necessary for reasons of health or safety, any powered door, gate or hatch can be operated manually unless it opens automatically if the power fails.

(3) This regulation shall not apply to any door, gate or hatch forming part of any mobile plant and equipment.

17. Vehicles

(1) Suitable and sufficient steps shall be taken to prevent or control the unintended movement **9.157** of any vehicle.

(2) Suitable and sufficient steps shall be taken to ensure that, where any person may be endangered by the movement of any vehicle, the person having effective control of the vehicle shall give warning to any person who is liable to be at risk from the movement of the vehicle.

(3) Any vehicle being used for the purposes of construction work shall when being driven, operated or towed—

(a) be driven, operated or towed in such a manner as is safe in the circumstances; and

(b) be loaded in such a way that it can be driven, operated or towed safely.

(4) No person shall ride or be required or permitted to ride on any vehicle being used for the purposes of construction work otherwise than in a safe place thereon provided for that purpose.

(5) No person shall remain or be required or permitted to remain on any vehicle during the loading or unloading of any loose material unless a safe place of work is provided and maintained for such person.

(6) Where any vehicle is used for excavating or handling (including tipping) materials, suitable and sufficient measures shall be taken so as to prevent such vehicle from falling into any excavation or pit, or into water, or overrunning the edge of any embankment or earthwork.

(7) Suitable plant and equipment shall be provided and used for replacing on its track or otherwise safely moving any rail vehicle which may become derailed.

18. Prevention of risk from fire etc

9.158 Suitable and sufficient steps shall be taken to prevent, so far as is reasonably practicable, the risk of injury to any person during the carrying out of construction work arising from—
    (a) fire or explosion;
    (b) flooding; or
    (c) any substance liable to cause asphyxiation.

19. Emergency routes and exits

9.159 (1) Where necessary in the interests of the health and safety of any person on a construction site, a sufficient number of suitable emergency routes and exits shall be provided to enable any person to reach a place of safety quickly in the event of danger.

(2) An emergency route or exit provided pursuant to paragraph (1) shall lead as directly as possible to an identified safe area.

(3) Any emergency route and exit provided in accordance with paragraph (1), and any traffic route or door giving access thereto, shall be kept clear and free from obstruction, and, where necessary, provided with emergency lighting so that such emergency route or exit may be used at any time.

(4) Any provision for emergency routes and exits made under paragraph (1) shall have regard to—
    (a) the type of work for which the construction site is being used;
    (b) the characteristics and size of the construction site and the number and location of places of work on that site;
    (c) the plant and equipment being used;
    (d) the number of persons likely to be present on the site at any one time; and
    (e) the physical and chemical properties of any substances or materials on or likely to be on the site.

(5) All emergency routes or exits shall be indicated by suitable signs.

20. Emergency procedures

9.160 (1) Where necessary in the interests of the health and safety of any person on a construction site, there shall be prepared and, when necessary, implemented suitable and sufficient arrangements for dealing with any foreseeable emergency, which arrangements shall include procedures for any necessary evacuation of the site or any part thereof.

(2) Without prejudice to the generality of paragraph (1), arrangements prepared pursuant to that paragraph shall have regard to those matters set out in paragraph (4) of regulation 19.

(3) Where arrangements are prepared pursuant to paragraph (1), suitable and sufficient steps shall be taken to ensure that—

    (a) every person to whom the arrangements extend is familiar with those arrangements; and

    (b) the arrangements are tested by being put into effect at suitable intervals.

[21. Fire detection and fire-fighting]   **9.161**

[22. Welfare facilities]

[23. Fresh air]

24. Temperature and weather protection

(1) Suitable and sufficient steps shall be taken to ensure, so far as is reasonably practicable, that   **9.162** during working hours the temperature at any indoor place of work to which these Regulations apply is reasonable having regard to the purpose for which that place is used.

(2) Every place of work outdoors shall, where necessary to ensure the health and safety of persons at work there, be so arranged that, so far as is reasonably practicable and having regard to the purpose for which that place is used and any protective clothing or equipment provided for the use of any person at work there, it provides protection from adverse weather.

25. Lighting

(1) There shall be suitable and sufficient lighting in respect of every place of work and   **9.163** approach thereto and every traffic route, which lighting shall, so far as is reasonably practicable, be by natural light.

(2) The colour of any artificial lighting provided shall not adversely affect or change the perception of any sign or signal provided for the purposes of health and safety.

(3) Without prejudice to the generality of paragraph (1), suitable and sufficient secondary lighting shall be provided in any place where there would be risk to the health or safety of any person in the event of failure of primary artificial lighting.

26. Good order

(1) Every part of a construction site shall, so far as is reasonably practicable, be kept in good   **9.164** order and every part of a construction site which is used as a place of work shall be kept in a reasonable state of cleanliness.

(2) Where necessary in the interests of health and safety, the perimeter of a construction site shall, so far as is reasonably practicable, be identified by suitable signs and the site shall be so arranged that its extent is readily identifiable.

(3) No timber or other material with projecting nails shall—

    (a) be used in any work in which the nails may be a source of danger to any person; or

    (b) be allowed to remain in any place where the nails may be a source of danger to any person.

27. Plant and equipment

(1) All plant and equipment used for the purpose of carrying out construction work shall, so   **9.165** far as is reasonably practicable, be safe and without risks to health and shall be of good construction, of suitable and sound materials and of sufficient strength and suitability for the purpose for which it is used or provided.

(2) All plant and equipment used for the purpose of carrying out construction work shall be used in such a manner and be maintained in such condition that, so far as is reasonably practicable, it remains safe and without risks to health at all times when it is being used.

28. Training

9.166   Any person who carries out any activity involving construction work where training, technical knowledge or experience is necessary to reduce the risks of injury to any person shall possess such training, knowledge or experience, or be under such degree of supervision by a person having such training, knowledge or experience, as may be appropriate having regard to the nature of the activity.

29. Inspection

9.167   (1) Subject to paragraph (2), a place of work referred to in column 1 of Schedule 7 shall be used to carry out construction work only if that place has been inspected by a competent person at the times set out in the corresponding entry in column 2 of that Schedule and the person who has carried out the inspection is satisfied that the work can be safely carried out at that place.

(2) Without prejudice to paragraph (1), where the place of work is a part of a scaffold, excavation, cofferdam or caisson, any employer or any other person who controls the way in which construction work is carried out by persons using that part shall ensure that the scaffold, excavation, cofferdam or caisson is stable and of sound construction and that the safeguards required by these Regulations are in place before his employees or persons under his control first use that place of work.

(3) Where the person who has carried out an inspection pursuant to paragraph (1) is not satisfied that construction work can safely be carried out at that place—

(a) where the inspection was carried out on behalf of another person, he shall inform that person of any matters about which he is not satisfied; and

(b) the place of work shall not be used until the matters identified have been satisfactorily remedied.

(4) An inspection of a place of work carried out pursuant to paragraph (1) shall include an inspection of any plant and equipment and any materials which affect the safety of that place of work.

30. Reports

9.168   (1) Subject to paragraphs (5) and (6), where an inspection is required under regulation 29(1), the person who carries out such inspection shall, before the end of the working period within which the inspection is completed, prepare a report which shall include the particulars set out in Schedule 8.

(2) A person who prepares a report under paragraph (1) shall, within 24 hours of completing the inspection to which the report relates, provide the report or a copy there of to the person on whose behalf the inspection was carried out.

(3) The report or a copy thereof prepared for the purposes of paragraph (1) shall be kept at the site of the place of work in respect of which the inspection was carried out and, after that work is completed, shall be retained at an office of the person on whose behalf the inspection was carried out for a period of 3 months from the date of such completion.

(4) A report prepared for the purposes of paragraph (1) shall at all reasonable times be open to inspection by any inspector, and the person keeping such report shall send to any such inspector such extracts therefrom or copies thereof as the inspector may from time to time require for the purpose of the execution of his duties.

(5) No report is required to be prepared under paragraph (1) in respect of any working platform or alternative means of support from no part of which a person is liable to fall more than 2 metres.

(6) Nothing in this regulation shall require—

(a) a report to be prepared in respect of any mobile tower scaffold unless it remains erected in the same place for a period of 7 days or more;

(b) as regards an inspection carried out on a place of work for the purposes of paragraph 1 (ii) of column 2 of Schedule 7, the preparation of more than one report on that place within any period of 24 hours; or

(c) as regards an inspection carried out on a place of work for the purposes of paragraph 2(i) or 3(i) of column 2 of Schedule 7, the preparation of more than one report on that place within any period of 7 days.

[**31. Exemption certificates**]   **9.169**

[**32. Extension outside Great Britain**]

[**33. Enforcement in respect of fire**]

CONSTRUCTION (HEAD PROTECTION) REGULATIONS 1989

1. Citation, commencement and interpretation

(1) These Regulations may be cited as the Construction (Head Protection) Regulations 1989 **9.170** and shall come into force on 30th March 1990.

(2) In these Regulations, unless the context otherwise requires, 'suitable head protection' means head protection which—

(a) is designed to provide protection, so far as is reasonably practicable, against foreseeable risks of injury to the head to which the wearer may be exposed;

(b) after any necessary adjustment, fits the wearer; and

(c) is suitable having regard to the work or activity in which the wearer may be engaged.

2. Application of these Regulations

(1) Subject to paragraph (2) of this regulation, these Regulations shall apply to—   **9.171**

(a) building operations; and

(b) works of engineering construction,

within, in either case, the meaning of the Factories Act 1961.

(2) These Regulations shall not apply to [a diving project within the meaning of regulation 2(1) of the Diving at Work Regulations 1997].

3. Provision, maintenance and replacement of suitable head protection

(1) Every employer shall provide each of his employees who is at work on operations or works **9.172** to which these Regulations apply with suitable head protection and shall maintain it and replace it whenever necessary.

(2) Every self-employed person who is at work on operations or works to which these Regulations apply shall provide himself with suitable bead protection and shall maintain it and replace it whenever necessary.

(3) Any head protection provided by virtue of this regulation shall comply with any enactment (whether in an Act or instrument) which implements any provision on design or manufacture with respect to health or safety in any relevant Community directive listed in Schedule 1 to the

Personal Protective Equipment at Work Regulations 1992 which is applicable to that head protection.

(4) Before choosing head protection, an employer or self-employed person shall make an assessment to determine whether it is suitable.

(5) The assessment required by paragraph (4) of this regulation shall involve—
(a) the definition of the characteristics which head protection must have in order to be suitable;
(b) comparison of the characteristics of the protection available with the characteristics referred to in sub-paragraph (a) of this paragraph.

(6) The assessment required by paragraph (4) shall be reviewed if—
(a) there is reason to suspect that it is no longer valid; or
(b) there has been a significant change in the work to which it relates, and where as a result of the review changes in the assessment are required, the relevant employer or self-employed person shall make them.

(7) Every employer and every self-employed person shall ensure that appropriate accommodation is available for head protection provided by virtue of these Regulations when it is not being used.

4. Ensuring suitable head protection is worn

9.173   (1) Every employer shall ensure so far as is reasonably practicable that each of his employees who is at work on operations or works to which these Regulations apply wears suitable head protection, unless there is no foreseeable risk of injury to his head other than by his falling.

(2) Every employer, self-employed person or employee who has control over any other person who is at work on operations or works to which these Regulations apply shall ensure so far as is reasonably practicable that each such other person wears suitable head protection, unless there is no foreseeable risk of injury to that other person's head other than by his falling.

5. Rules and directions

9.174   (1) The person for the time being having control of a site where operations or works to which these Regulations apply are being carried out may, so far as is necessary to comply with regulation 4 of these Regulations, make rules regulating the wearing of suitable head protection on that site by persons at work on those operations or works.

(2) Rules made in accordance with paragraph (1) of this regulation shall be in writing and shall be brought to the notice of persons who may be affected by them.

(3) An employer may, so far as is necessary to comply with regulation 4(1) of these Regulations, give directions requiring his employees to wear suitable head protection.

(4) An employer, self-employed person or employee who has control over any other self-employed person may, so far as is necessary to comply with regulation 4(2) of these Regulations, give directions requiring each such other self-employed person to wear suitable head protection.

6. Wearing of suitable head protection

9.175   (1) Every employee who has been provided with suitable head protection shall wear that head protection when required to do so by rules made or directions given under regulation 5 of these Regulations.

(2) Every self-employed person shall wear suitable head protection when required to do so by rules made or directions given under regulation 5 of these Regulations.

(3) Every self-employed person who is at work on operations or works to which these Regulations apply, but who is not under the control of another employer or self-employed person or of an employee, shall wear suitable head protection unless there is no foreseeable risk of injury to his head other than by his falling.

(4) Every employee or self-employed person who is required to wear suitable head protection by or under these Regulations shall—

   (a) make full and proper use of it; and

   (b) take all reasonable steps to return it to the accommodation provided for it after use.

7. **Reporting the loss of, or defect in, suitable head protection**

Every employee who has been provided with suitable head protection by his employer shall take **9.176** reasonable care of it and shall forthwith report to his employer any loss of, or obvious defect in, that head protection.

[8. **Extension outside Great Britain**]   **9.177**

[9. **Exemption certificates**]

J. Other Workplace Regulations

Building sites have been singled out for the provision of the text of the principal **9.178** regulations. There are, in addition, other regulatory regimes of limited application which may have to be consulted in an appropriate case, but which it has not been possible to include here for reasons of space. The Noise at Work Regulations 1989, the Health and Safety (Display Screen Equipment) Regulations 1992 and the Control of Substances Hazardous to Health Regulations 1999 have been included in the prelims at **d.17**, **d.44**, and **d.85** above. Other regulations are accessible on the HMSO website for statutory instruments, or in *Redgrave*. Dealing with specific risks they include the Electricity at Work Regulations 1989, the Ionising Radiation Regulations 1999, the Control of Asbestos at Work Regulations 2002, and the Lifts Regulations 1997. Dealing with specific fields of employment there are the Shipbuilding and Ship Repairing Regulations 1960, the Docks Regulations 1988, the Quarries Regulations 1999, and the Diving at Work Regulations 1997. For accidents arising out of the dangerous state of premises the Occupiers' Liability Act 1957 will also be relevant.

10

SLIPPING AND TRIPPING

10.01 Many accidents happen when people fall over. Injuries caused this way are not connected by specific legal principles, but it is convenient to collect in one chapter the legal materials which relate to different types of tripping and slipping accidents. Three topics are considered: falls on pavements or roads, falls in supermarkets and shops, and falls at work, followed by a word on claims handling.

A. Pavements

10.02 Provided the pavement is part of a highway maintainable at public expense—most are—the highways authority has a statutory duty to maintain it under s 41 of the Highways Act 1980. Liability involves these questions:

(a) Is the pavement in a condition which is dangerous to pedestrians?
(b) Is the danger caused by a failure to maintain?
(c) Can the highway authority prove the statutory defence under s 58 of the Act that it has taken all reasonable care by having a proper system of inspection and repair?
(d) Has the danger caused the injury?

Although the 1980 Act does not apply to private paths, the Occupiers' Liability Act 1957 will apply, and it is likely that the cases which explain the standard to be expected on an highway would have persuasive force in deciding whether an occupier had taken such care as was reasonable to ensure that visitors were reasonably safe.

10.03 In addition to the statutory duty under the Highways Act 1980, the highway authority may be liable in public nuisance for a wrongful act or omission on or near the highway whereby the public are prevented from passing freely and safely along the highway. The same facts may also give liability in negligence. However, it will be rare for the common law duties to provide a wider remedy than the 1980 Act. Note also that a privately owned path, over which there is a public right of way, may prove problematic with regard to duties (see *McGeown v N I Housing Executive* [1995] 1 AC 233).

10.04 The vital question is the degree of disrepair to the pavement that will be held to constitute a danger. The fact of tripping does not prove a danger. A series of Liverpool cases in the late 1960s, which are set out below, seemed to establish a rule of thumb that a trip would have to be about an inch high before the courts would regard it as a danger. Thousands of claims were determined on this basis. The modern cases have taken a less formulaic approach, while still emphasizing that there can be many pavement defects that are not serious enough to constitute a danger, even though a pedestrian may have been caused to trip by one of them. In *Mills v Barnsley MBC* [1992] PIQR P291, the corner of a paving brick had broken off leaving a hole ¾" deep with ½" of soft material beneath. A finding that this was a danger was overturned by the Court of Appeal. Steyn LJ said:

> I do not consider that it would be right to say that a depression of less than an inch will never be dangerous but one above will always be dangerous. Such mechanical jurisprudence is not to be encouraged. All that one can say is that the test of dangerousness is one of reasonable foresight of harm to users of the highway . . . In the same way as the public must expect minor obstructions on roads, such as cobblestones, cats eyes and pedestrian crossing studs, and so fourth, the public must expect minor depressions . . . It is important that our tort law should not impose unreasonably high standards.

10.05 In *James v Preseli Pembrokeshire DC* [1993] PIQR P114, two claims based on trips of around ¾ to 1 both failed in the Court of Appeal with similar observations that the court must not set too high a standard of dangerousness. Trips and falls on pavements happen frequently and many are reported to local councils and their insurers: it is perhaps ironic that the Court of Appeal seeks to restrict liability to cases of really serious, dangerous defects by relying on the notion of foreseeability, when their claims experience must have shown to these particular defendants that relatively minor defects can often be implicated in falls causing injury especially to the elderly and infirm.

10.06 In deciding the seriousness of a defect that will amount to a danger, and in deciding whether the highway authority has operated a reasonable system of inspection and repair, the court will take into account the authority's policy and the guidance given in *Delivering Best Value in Highway Maintenance*, a Code of Practice published in 2001 and available at www.dft.gov.uk, Information for Local Authorities link. These will define the frequency with which the road or pavement should be routinely inspected for defects, the description of defects calling for repair, and the response times for effecting a repair. For example, the Code suggests road inspection of trunk roads, major roads, and secondary distributor roads every month, of link roads every three months and of local access roads every twelve months. It suggests inspection of primary walking routes every month, secondary walking routes every three months, link footways every six months, and local access footways every twelve months. Intervention criteria will typically categorize defects as urgent, priority, or routine. Typically a road pothole of 40 mm or more deep and at least 300 mm across in any direction will require prompt repair; similarly on pavements, a pothole or a rocking flagstone creating a trip of 20 mm or more.

For claimants, a defect which is in excess of the authority's own intervention **10.07** criteria will more readily be considered dangerous by the court. Conversely it will be difficult to meet the s 58 defence if the authority acted in accordance with a policy that is consistent with the Code. For defendant authorities, proof that the regime of inspections has been properly carried out may enable the authority to defend liability for serious dangers that have arisen since the last inspection, but documentation that is reliable and complete will be important.

In February 2000, the House of Lords held in *Goodes v East Sussex CC* [2000] **10.08** 1 WLR 1356 that a highway authority's duty to maintain the highway did not extend to keeping it free from ice and snow. This was a departure from previous Court of Appeal decisions. Parliament has (by s 111 of the Railways and Transport Safety Act 2003) reversed this by adding s 41(1A) to the Highways Act 1980: 'In particular, a highway authority are under a duty to ensure, so far as is reasonably practicable, that safe passage along a highway is not endangered by snow or ice' (see **7.32** above). However, this new duty only applies after 31 October 2003. Claims cannot be made for a highway authority's failure to clear ice and snow from a footpath for accidents earlier than this date. It has continued to be the case that on private premises a duty to keep paths cleared or gritted may arise under the Occupiers' Liability Act 1957 or (for employees) under reg 12 of the Workplace (Health, Safety and Welfare) Regulations 1992.

Griffiths v Liverpool Corporation [1967] 1 QB 374   A flagstone projected ½″ **10.09** over the next; there was no appeal against a finding of fact that the pavement was dangerous but this decision was strongly criticized.

Meggs v Liverpool Corporation [1968] 1 WLR 689   Uneven flagstones created **10.10** a trip of ¾″; not dangerous and no liability. Lord Denning MR said:

. . . everyone must take account of the fact that there may be unevenness here and there. There may be a ridge of half an inch or three quarters of an inch occasionally, but that is not the sort of thing that makes it dangerous or not reasonably safe.

10.11 *Littler v Liverpool Corporation* [1968] 2 All ER 343   An uneven flagstone pavement had a trip ½″ high at the edge of a triangular depression. No liability.

10.12 *Mills v Barnsley MBC* [1992] PIQR P291   A missing corner of a paving brick left a hole 1¼″ deep in which the claimant caught her shoe. This was a minor defect of a kind which pedestrians must expect and it was unduly onerous to hold the highway authority liable. No liability. Steyn LJ at P293: 'The plaintiff must prove that the highway was in such a condition that it was dangerous to traffic or pedestrians in the sense that, in the ordinary course of human affairs, danger may reasonably have been anticipated from its continued use by the public.' Dillon LJ at P295: 'The question is whether a reasonable person would regard it as presenting a real source of danger.'

10.13 *James v Preseli Pembrokeshire DC* [1993] PIQR P114   A pavement trip of between ½″ to 1″: no liability. The test of dangerousness is reasonable foresight of harm; at 25 mm highway authorities generally regard a trip as requiring urgent repair but each case turns on its own facts and the courts should not set too high a standard.

10.14 *Staples v West Dorset DC* [1995] PIQR P439   The claimant slipped on algae on the seafront on the Cobb at Lyme Regis. The danger was obvious and the claimant accepted he knew it was slippery, but he claimed that a warning notice should have been put up, encouraged by the fact that such a notice was in fact put up after his accident. The court held that duty under the Occupiers' Liability Act 1957 was only to warn an individual who was unaware of the danger and the claim failed.

B. Supermarkets and Other Premises

10.15 The decisions in this section have arisen out of cases of supermarket customers but the same principles would often apply to falls in comparable circumstances in other types of premises. Liability will arise under the Occupiers' Liability Act 1957, or possibly the Defective Premises Act 1972.

10.16 The leading case is *Ward v Tesco Stores* [1976] 1 All ER 219 where the claimant slipped on some spilled yoghurt in an aisle of a supermarket. Allowing her claim, the Court of Appeal set a very high standard of care for the clearing up of spillages. There must be some reasonably effective system for getting rid of the dangers which may from time to time exist. The court held that in the absence of an explanation from the defendant as to how the accident had happened and to show that it did not result from a lack of care, the judge is entitled to give judgment for the claimant, inferring a breach of the common duty of care because the facts speak for themselves. However, this may be to state too highly the common duty of care. It remains true, however, that a customer who slips on a spillage in a store has a very good prospect of succeeding in a claim.

Ward v Tesco Stores [1976] 1 All ER 219   The claimant slipped on some   **10.17**
spilled yoghurt in an aisle of a supermarket. The Court of Appeal set a very high standard of care for the clearing up of spillages which the occupier has to prove before escaping from an inference of neglect. There must be some reasonably effective system for getting rid of the dangers which may from time to time exist. In the absence of an explanation from the defendant as to how the accident had happened and to show that it did not result from a lack of care, the judge is entitled to infer a breach of the common duty of care.

C. Slipping and Tripping at Work

Regulation 12 of the Workplace (Health, Safety and Welfare) Regulations 1992   **10.18**
applies to places of work. Regulation 12(2)(a) requires that the floor in a workplace or the surface of a traffic route shall have no hole or slope or be uneven or slippery so as, in each case, to expose any person to a risk to his health or safety. Regulation 12(3) states that so far as reasonably practicable, every floor in a workplace and the surface of every traffic route in a workplace shall be kept free from obstructions and from any article which may cause a person to slip, trip or fall. Note that reg 12(2) creates strict liability once slipperiness and causation are proved, with no reasonable practicability defence.

Paragraphs 89 to 98 of ACOP (Approved Code of Practice) amplify the   **10.19**
requirements of the 1992 Regulations, and there are other parts of the 1992 Regulations and the other sets of regulations that may be relevant in a particular case. For example, reg 9 deals with cleanliness. Regulation 9 and the relevant paragraphs of the Code are set out in Chapter 9.

The 1992 Regulations protect everyone present at the workplace, including   **10.20**
employees of other firms and customers, not only the employees of the occupier of the workplace on whom the duty is placed.

Woodward v Renold Ltd [1980] ICR 387   A case before the previous 1992   **10.21**
Regulations where an employer was liable for failing to take any measures to deal with icy conditions in a factory car park.

10.22 *Palmer v Marks & Spencer* [2001] EWCA Civ 1528   The claimant tripped on a weather strip across a doorway. The strip protruded about 9 mm from the floor surface in order to prevent water coming in. There was no negligence, there was no history of any previous accident or complaint, and the claimant was aware of the presence of the weather strip. The trial judge held that was a breach of reg 12, but the Court of Appeal set this aside: the suitability of the floor was to be considered by asking whether the state of the floor was such as to expose any person to a risk to his health and safety.

D. Claims Handling

10.23 It is impossible to overstate the importance of recording a full and accurate description of the cause of the fall at the earliest opportunity. In pavement cases in particular, the defect may be quickly repaired once an accident has drawn attention to it. It is of enormous value to have photographs of the defect and if there is a particular characteristic such as a raised edge which forms a tripping hazard, include a photograph of a ruler against the edge to show how high it is. The exact location of the fall must also be established clearly from the outset. These considerations apply to defendants and insurers seeking to defend a claim just as much as to claimants.

E. Highways Act 1980, ss 41 and 58

41. Duty to maintain highways maintainable at public expense

10.24   (1) The authority who are for the time being the highway authority for a highway maintainable at the public expense are under a duty, subject to subsections (2) and (4) below, to maintain the highway.

58. Special defence in action against a highway authority for damages for non-repair of highway

10.25   (1) In an action against a highway authority in respect of damage resulting from their failure to maintain a highway maintainable at the public expense it is a defence (without prejudice to any other defence or the application of the law relating to contributory negligence) to prove that the authority had taken such care as in all the circumstances was reasonably required to secure that the part of the highway to which the action relates was not dangerous for traffic.

(2) For the purposes of a defence under subsection (1) above, the court shall in particular have regard to the following matters:—

(a) the character of the highway, and the traffic which was reasonably to be expected to use it;

(b) the standard of maintenance appropriate for a highway of that character and used by such traffic;

(c) the state of repair in which a reasonable person would have expected to find the highway;

(d) whether the highway authority knew, or could reasonably have been expected to know, that the condition of the part of the highway to which the action relates was likely to cause danger to users of the highway;

(e) where the highway authority could not reasonably have been expected to repair that part of the highway before the cause of action arose, what warning notices of its condition had been displayed;

but for the purposes of such a defence it is not relevant to prove that the highway authority had arranged for a competent person to carry out or supervise the maintenance of the part of the highway to which the action relates unless it is also proved that the authority had given him proper instructions with regard to the maintenance of the highway and that he had carried out the instructions.

(3) This section binds the Crown.

F. New Roads and Street Works Act 1991, ss 70 and 71

70. Duty of undertaker to reinstate

(1) It shall be the duty of the undertaker by whom street works are executed to reinstate the street. **10.26**

(2) He shall begin the reinstatement as soon as after the completion of any part of the street works as is reasonably practicable and shall carry on and complete the reinstatement with all such dispatch as is reasonably practicable.

71. Materials, workmanship and standard of reinstatement

(1) An undertaker executing street works shall in reinstating the street comply with such requirements as may be prescribed as to the specification of materials to be used and the standards of workmanship to be observed. **10.27**

Note—A Code of Practice entitled *Specification for the Reinstatement of Openings in Highways* issued by the Secretary of State is applied by the Street Works (Reinstatement) Regulations 1992. **10.28**

G. Workplace Regulations, reg 12 and the Approved Code of Practice

12. Condition of floors and traffic routes

(1) Every floor in a workplace and the surface of every traffic route in a workplace shall be of a construction such that the floor or surface of the traffic route is suitable for the purpose for which it is used. **10.29**

(2) Without prejudice to the generality of paragraph (1), the requirements in that paragraph shall include requirements that—

(a) the floor, or surface of the traffic route, shall have no hole or slope, or be uneven or slippery so as, in each case, to expose any person to a risk to his health or safety;

(b) every such floor shall have effective means of drainage where necessary.

(3) So far as is reasonably practicable, every floor in a workplace and the surface of every traffic route in a workplace shall be kept free from obstructions and from any article or substance which may cause a person to slip, trip or fall;

(4) In considering whether for the purposes of paragraph (2)(a) a hole or slope exposes any person to a risk to his health or safety—

(a) no account shall be taken of a hole where adequate measures have been taken to prevent a person falling;

(b) account shall be taken of any handrail provided in connection with any slope.

(5) Suitable and sufficient handrails and, if appropriate, guards shall be provided on all traffic routes which are staircases except in circumstances in which a handrail can not be provided without obstructing the traffic route.

APPROVED CODE OF PRACTICE

Regulation 12 Condition of floors and traffic routes

10.30 (89) Floor and traffic routes should be of sound construction and should have adequate strength and stability taking account of the loads placed on them and the traffic passing over them. Floors should not be overloaded.

(90) The surfaces of floors and traffic routes should be free from any hole, slope, or uneven or slippery surface which is likely to:

(a) cause a person to slip, trip or fall;

(b) cause a person to drop or lose control of anything being lifted or carried; or

(c) cause instability or loss of control of vehicles and/or their loads.

(91) Holes, bumps or uneven areas resulting from damage or wear and tear, which may cause a person to trip or fall, should be made good, Until they can be made good, adequate precautions should be taken against accidents, for example by barriers or conspicuous marking. Temporary holes, for example an area where floor boards have been removed, should be adequately guarded. Account should be taken of people with impaired or no sight. Surfaces with small holes (for example metal gratings) are acceptable provided they are not likely to be a hazard. Deep holes into which people may fall are subject to regulation 13 and the relevant section of this Code.

10.31 (92) Slopes should not be steeper than necessary. Moderate and steep slopes, and ramps used by people with disabilities, should be provided with a secure handrail where necessary.

(93) Surfaces of floors and traffic routes which are likely to get wet or to be subject to spillages should be of a type which does not become unduly slippery. A slip-resistant coating should be applied where necessary. Floors near to machinery which could cause injury if anyone were to fall against it (for example a woodworking or grinding machine) should be slip-resistant and be kept free from slippery substances or loose materials.

(94) Where possible, processes and plant which may discharge or leak liquids should be enclosed (for example by bunding), and leaks from taps or discharge points on pipes, drums and tanks should be caught or drained away. Stop valves should be fitted to filling points on tank filling lines. Where work involves carrying or handling liquids or slippery substances, as in food processing and preparation, the workplace and work surfaces should be arranged in such a way as to minimise the likelihood of spillages.

10.32 (95) Where a leak or spillage occurs and is likely to be a slipping hazard, immediate steps should be taken to fence it off, mop it up, or cover it with absorbent granules.

(96) Arrangements should be made to minimise risks from snow and ice. This may involve gritting, snow clearing and closure of some routes, particularly outside stairs, ladders and walkways on roofs.

(97) Floors and traffic routes should be kept free of obstructions which may present a hazard or impede access. This is particularly important on or near stairs, steps, escalators and moving walkways, on emergency routes, in or near doorways or gangways, and in any place where an obstruction is likely to cause an accident, for example near a corner or junction. Where a temporary obstruction is unavoidable and is likely to be a hazard, access should be prevented or steps should be taken to warn people or the drivers of vehicles of the obstruction by, for example, the use of hazard cones. Where furniture or equipment is being moved within a workplace, it should if possible be moved in a single operation and should not be left in a place where it is likely to be a hazard. Vehicles should not be parked where they are likely to be a hazard. Materials which fall onto traffic routes should be cleared as soon as possible.

(98) Effective drainage should be provided where a floor is liable to get wet to the extent **10.33** that the wet can be drained off. This is likely to be the case in, for example, laundries, textile manufacture (including dyeing, bleaching and finishing), work on hides and skins, potteries and food processing. Drains and channels should be positioned so as to minimise the area of wet floor, and the floor should slope slightly towards the drain. Where necessary to prevent tripping hazards, drains and channels should have covers which should be as near flush as possible with the floor surface.

11

DEFECTIVE PRODUCTS

Where an injury is caused by a defective product there are three potential **11.01** grounds for establishing a right to compensation. First, a defect will probably have been a breach of contract and the purchaser can claim against the seller for this breach. Damages for an injury caused by a breach of contract would be assessed in the same way as a claim in tort. Secondly, there may be a remedy in tort. The classic case of *Donoghue v Stevenson* [1932] AC 562 was a claim in the tort of negligence brought by the person who drank, but did not buy, the ginger beer, against the company which made and bottled it and delivered it in an opaque bottle which prevented inspection of the contents. Thirdly, the Consumer Protection Act 1987 may create strict liability where personal injury or property damage has been caused as a result of a defect in a product. This Act was introduced to comply with a 1985 European directive on product liability, following a path marked out by the United States.

A. Breach of Contract

In the sale of any goods there are terms implied by s 14 of the Sale of Goods Act **11.02** 1979 that the goods should be of satisfactory quality and fit for any particular purpose made known to the seller, and fit for their ordinary use. The test of satisfactory quality is that the goods meet the standard that a reasonable person would regard as satisfactory. In consumer sales there are restrictions on the degree to which these obligations of the seller can be excluded by the small print of a contract, and there are equivalent provisions in relation to hire purchase and consumer credit transactions. A defect in goods which results in personal injury is very likely to constitute a breach of the implied terms of the contract, and if there is a breach, liability is strict and the court is not concerned to inquire how the defect came to be present: it is no defence to a contractual claim that the supplier took all reasonable care.

11.03   If the seller is a retailer or intermediary, his remedy is to rely on the contract by which he himself acquired the goods, and pass liability in turn back along the chain of supply until it reaches the person responsible for the defect.

11.04   At the time of *Donoghue v Stevenson* [1932] AC 562, the rule was that a contract could only be litigated between the parties to the contract and the case extended this in tort at both ends of the transaction, allowing a consumer who did not purchase to bring a claim against a manufacturer who did not sell the goods to the purchaser. At the consumer end, the Contracts (Rights of Third Parties) Act 1999 now enables a third party to benefit from contractual liabilities if the parties to the contract so intend.

11.05   *Vacwell v BDH Chemicals* [1971] 1 QB 88   A claim in negligence and breach of contract where the defendant supplied a chemical but failed to give a warning of the risk of explosion on contact with water. Although there was nothing defective about the chemical, the lack of proper warning was not only negligent but also made the goods not fit for their purpose.

B. Negligence

11.06   The general law of negligence provides a simple remedy in the case of many defective products. There are no technical restrictions on the kind of wrongdoer who may be held liable or the kind of injury-causing fault which may give rise to liability. However, it is not always straightforward to sue in negligence. First, it is necessary to prove that the defendant was at fault. The court will draw a reasonable inference of fault if the nature of the defect is such as would not occur in a carefully undertaken process of manufacture, and the claimant need not then identify the precise point at which a mistake was made. However, it must be shown that it was the defendant who was at fault, either for creating the danger or for failing to observe and remedy the danger, and not someone else in the chain of supply. Secondly, the appropriate defendant must be identified and must be available to be sued and it is common with manufactured products for the chain of supply to be lengthy and often to involve overseas companies, making for practical difficulties. An importer of foreign manufactured goods will often have no reasonable opportunity to examine the goods for safety and may have acted without negligence in relying on the manufacturer to supply safe goods. Thirdly, the manufacturer may escape liability if there was a reasonable probability that the goods would be examined for defects in the course of the chain of supply to the consumer. There was liability for the contents of the ginger beer bottle only because the bottle was sealed and opaque. These complications make it preferable to rely on the statutory liability wherever this is possible.

Donoghue v Stevenson [1932] AC 562   The drinker of ginger beer successfully **11.07** sued the manufacturer claiming that the opaque bottle had contained the remains of a decomposed snail which made her ill.

Carroll v Fearon [1998] PIQR P416   A road accident was caused by the **11.08** disintegration of a tyre. The claim was in negligence because the tyre was manufactured before the commencement of the 1987 Act. The claimant did not need to identify the individual employee or the specific act or omission which led to the defect: if a reputable manufacturer sought to escape liability on the ground that the defect could not have been avoided by taking reasonable care it was in the best position to call evidence about it and in the absence of evidence the court was entitled to conclude that negligence had been established.

Perrett v Collins [1999] PNLR 77   On a preliminary issue it was held that a **11.09** duty of care in negligence was owed by the inspector of a light aircraft who allegedly failed to detect defects which caused the aircraft to crash.

C. Strict Liability under the Consumer Protection Act 1987

Part I of the Consumer Protection Act 1987 provides for strict liability (without **11.10** proof of fault or negligence) where damage is caused wholly or partly by a defect in a product. A product has a defect if the safety of the product is not such as persons generally are entitled to expect. Where there has been a mistake in manufacture the test is fairly easy to apply, but some products are inherently hazardous or are hazardous if incorrectly used, and such a hazard does not of itself make the product less safe than persons are entitled to expect: the presence of appropriate warnings or instructions may be of crucial importance.

The strict liability created by the 1987 Act applies to a wide range of suppliers, **11.11** any or all of whom may be liable to the injured person. These include the manufacturer, both of the goods as purchased and of a defective component incorporated in the goods, the importer of goods from outside the EU, and any supplier in the chain of supply of the goods subject to an escape clause if the supplier is able to identify the producer/importer.

11.12   It is a mark of the effectiveness of the Act that it has generated no significant litigation in relation to the interpretation of its terms, and further discussion will be less useful than a careful reading of the statute itself.

11.13   *Worsley v Tambrands Ltd* [2000] PIQR P95   A claimant who suffered toxic shock syndrome from use of a tampon claimed unsuccessfully that the product was defective because warnings were not sufficiently clear.

11.14   *Richardson v LRC Products* [2000] PIQR P164   A case turning on the facts but which illustrates that the claimant must prove that the defect was caused while the product was in the defendant's control. A condom split, and was found to have ozone damage, but on the evidence the ozone damage happened after the accident and, since condoms do split on occasions for no ascertainable reason, there was no inference of manufacturing defect and the claim failed.

D. Package Holidays

11.15   In view of the popularity of complaints about package holidays, the key part of the Package Travel, Package Holidays and Package Tours Regulations 1992 has been included in this chapter. The regulations create a strict liability of the holiday company when there has been improper performance of the contract.

11.16   *Hone v Going Places Leisure Travel* [2001] EWCA Civ 947   The claimant was injured during an escape from an aircraft after a crash landing. He contended that there was strict liability of the tour operator under reg 15 of the Package Travel, etc Regulations 1992. The Court of Appeal held that liability was not strict but depended on proof of improper performance of the contract. There was no express obligation of safe air carriage so the contractual term was for the use of reasonable care and skill. The claimant could not prove improper performance of this term.

11.17   *Norfolk v My Travel* [2004] 1 Lloyd's Rep 106   A claim under the Package Travel, etc Regulations 1992 for personal injuries sustained on a sea cruise was subject to the absolute limitation period of two years under the Athens Convention.

E. Sale of Goods Act 1979, s 14

11.18   14. **Implied terms about quality or fitness**

(1) Except as provided by this section and section 15 below and subject to any other enactment, there is no implied [term] about the quality or fitness for any particular purpose of goods supplied under a contract of sale.

(2) Where the seller sells goods in the course of a business, there is an implied term that the goods supplied under the contract are of satisfactory quality.

(2A) For the purposes of this Act, goods are of satisfactory quality if they meet the standard that a reasonable person would regard as satisfactory, taking account of any description of the goods, the price (if relevant) and all the other relevant circumstances.

(2B) For the purposes of this Act, the quality of goods includes their state and condition and the following (among others) are in appropriate cases aspects of the quality of goods—
(a) fitness for all the purposes for which goods of the kind in question are commonly supplied,
(b) appearance and finish,
(c) freedom from minor defects,
(d) safety, and
(e) durability.

(2C) The term implied by subsection (2) above does not extend to any matter making the quality of goods unsatisfactory—
(a) which is specifically drawn to the buyer's attention before the contract is made,
(b) where the buyer examines the goods before the contract is made, which that examination ought to reveal, or
(c) in the case of a contract for sale by sample, which would have been apparent on a reasonable examination of the sample.

(2D) If the buyer deals as consumer or, in Scotland, if a contract of sale is a consumer contract, the relevant circumstances mentioned in subsection (2A) above include any public statements on the specific characteristics of the goods made about them by the seller, the producer or his representative, particularly in advertising or on labelling.

(2E) A public statement is not by virtue of subsection (2D) above a relevant circumstance for the purposes of subsection (2A) above in the case of a contract of sale, if the seller shows that—
(a) at the time the contract was made, he was not, and could not reasonably have been, aware of the statement,
(b) before the contract was made, the statement had been withdrawn in public or, to the extent that it contained anything which was incorrect or misleading, it had been corrected in public, or
(c) the decision to buy the goods could not have been influenced by the statement.

(2F) Subsections (2D) and (2E) above do not prevent any public statement from being a relevant circumstance for the purposes of subsection (2A) above (whether or not the buyer deals as consumer or, in Scotland, whether or not the contract of sale is a consumer contract) if the statement would have been such a circumstance apart from those subsections.

(3) Where the seller sells goods in the course of a business and the buyer, expressly or by implication, makes known—
(a) to the seller, or
(b) where the purchase price or part of it is payable by instalments and the goods were previously sold by a credit-broker to the seller, to that credit-broker,

any particular purpose for which the goods are being bought, there is an implied term that the goods supplied under the contract are reasonably fit for that purpose, whether or not that is a purpose for which such goods are commonly supplied, except where the circumstances show that the buyer does not rely, or that it is unreasonable for him to rely, on the skill or judgment of the seller or credit-broker.

(4) An implied [term] about quality or fitness for a particular purpose may be annexed to a contract of sale by usage.

(5) The preceding provisions of this section apply to a sale by a person who in the course of a business is acting as agent for another as they apply to a sale by a principal in the course of a business, except where that other is not selling in the course of a business and either the buyer knows that fact or reasonable steps are taken to bring it to the notice of the buyer before the contract is made.

(6) As regards England and Wales and Northern Ireland, the terms implied by subsections (2) and (3) above are conditions.

(7) Paragraph 5 of Schedule 1 below applies in relation to a contract made on or after 18 May 1973 and before the appointed day, and paragraph 6 in relation to one made before 18 May 1973.

(8) In subsection (7) above and paragraph 5 of Schedule 1 below references to the appointed day are to the day appointed for the purposes of those provisions by an order of the Secretary of State made by statutory instrument.

F. Consumer Protection Act 1987, Part I

PART I
PRODUCT LIABILITY

1. Purpose and construction of Part I

11.19   (1) This Part shall have effect for the purpose of making such provision as is necessary in order to comply with the product liability Directive and shall be construed accordingly.

(2) In this Part, except in so far as the context otherwise requires—
'agricultural produce' means any produce of the soil, of stock-farming or of fisheries;
'dependant' and 'relative' have the same meaning as they have in, respectively, the Fatal Accidents Act 1976 and the Damages (Scotland) Act 1976; 'producer', in relation to a product, means—
   (a) the person who manufactured it;
   (b) in the case of a substance which has not been manufactured but has been won or abstracted, the person who won or abstracted it;
   (c) in the case of a product which has not been manufactured, won or abstracted but essential characteristics of which are attributable to an industrial or other process having been carried out (for example, in relation to agricultural produce), the person who carried out that process;
'product' means any goods or electricity and (subject to subsection (3) below) includes a product which is comprised in another product, whether by virtue of being a component part or raw material or otherwise; and
'the product liability Directive' means the Directive of the Council of the European Communities, dated 25th July 1985, (No.85/374/EEC) on the approximation of the laws, regulations and administrative provisions of the member States concerning liability for defective products.

(3) For the purposes of this Part a person who supplies any product in which products are comprised, whether by virtue of being component parts or raw materials or otherwise, shall not be treated by reason only of his supply of that product as supplying any of the products so comprised.

2. Liability for defective products

(1) Subject to the following provisions of this Part, where any damage is caused wholly or **11.20** partly by a defect in a product, every person to whom subsection (2) below applies shall be liable for the damage.

(2) This subsection applies to—
    (a) the producer of the product;
    (b) any person who, by putting his name on the product or using a trade mark or other distinguishing mark in relation to the product, has held himself out to be the producer of the product;
    (c) any person who has imported the product into a member State from a place outside the member States in order, in the course of any business of his, to supply it to another.

(3) Subject as aforesaid, where any damage is caused wholly or partly by a defect in a product, any person who supplied the product (whether to the person who suffered the damage, to the producer of any product in which the product in question is comprised or to any other person) shall be liable for the damage if—
    (a) the person who suffered the damage requests the supplier to identify one or more of the persons (whether still in existence or not) to whom subsection (2) above applies in relation to the product;
    (b) that request is made within a reasonable period after the damage occurs and at a time when it is not reasonably practicable for the person making the request to identify all those persons; and
    (c) the supplier fails, within a reasonable period after receiving the request, either to comply with the request or to identify the person who supplied the product to him.

(4) Neither subsection (2) nor subsection (3) above shall apply to a person in respect of any defect in any game or agricultural produce if the only supply of the game or produce by that person to another was at a time when it had not undergone an industrial process.

(5) Where two or more persons are liable by virtue of this Part for the same damage, their liability shall be joint and several.

(6) This section shall be without prejudice to any liability arising otherwise than by virtue of this Part.

3. Meaning of 'defect'

(1) Subject to the following provisions of the section, there is a defect in a product for the **11.21** purposes of this Part if the safety of the product is not such as persons generally are entitled to expect; and for those purposes 'safety', in relation to a product, shall include safety with respect to products comprised in that product and safety in the context of risks of damage to property, as well as in the context of risks of death or personal injury.

(2) In determining for the purposes of subsection (1) above what persons generally are entitled to expect in relation to a product all the circumstances shall be taken into account, including—
    (a) the manner in which, and purposes for which, the product has been marketed, its get-up, the use of any mark in relation to the product and any instructions for, or warnings with respect to, doing or refraining from doing anything with or in relation to the product;
    (b) what might reasonably be expected to be done with or in relation to the product; and
    (c) the time when the product was supplied by its producer to another;

and nothing in this section shall require a defect to be inferred from the fact alone that the safety of a product which is supplied after that time is greater than the safety of the product in question.

4. Defences

11.22   (1) In any civil proceedings by virtue of this Part against any person ('the person proceeded against') in respect of a defect in a product it shall be a defence for him to show—

(a) that the defect is attributable to compliance with any requirement imposed by or under any enactment or with any Community obligation; or

(b) that the person proceeded against did not at any time supply the product to another; or

(c) that the following conditions are satisfied, that is to say—

(i) that the only supply of the product to another by the person proceeded against was otherwise than in the course of a business of that person's; and

(ii) that section 2(2) above does not apply to that person or applies to him by virtue only of things done otherwise than with a view to profit; or

(d) that the defect did not exist in the product at the relevant time; or

(e) that the state of scientific and technical knowledge at the relevant time was not such that a producer of products of the same description as the product in question might be expected to have discovered the defect if it had existed in his products while they were under his control; or

(f) that the defect—

(i) constituted a defect in a product ('the subsequent product') in which the product in question had been comprised; and

(ii) was wholly attributable to the design of the subsequent product or to compliance by the producer of the product in question with instructions given by the producer of the subsequent product.

(2) In this section 'the relevant time', in relation to electricity, means the time at which it was generated, being a time before it was transmitted or distributed, and in relation to any other product, means—

(a) if the person proceeded against is a person to whom subsection (2) of section 2 above applies in relation to the product, the time when he supplied the product to another;

(b) if that subsection does not apply to that person in relation to the product, the time when the product was last supplied by a person to whom that subsection does apply in relation to the product.

5. Damage giving rise to liability

11.23   (1) Subject to the following provisions of this section, in this Part 'damage' means death or personal injury or any loss of or damage to any property (including land).

(2) A person shall not be liable under section 2 above in respect of any defect in a product for the loss of or any damage to the product itself or for the loss of or any damage to the whole or any part of any product which has been supplied with the product in question comprised in it.

(3) A person shall not be liable under section 2 above for any loss of or damage to any property which, at the time it is lost or damaged, is not—

(a) of a description of property ordinarily intended for private use, occupation or consumption; and

(b) intended by the person suffering the loss or damage mainly for his own private use, occupation or consumption.

(4) No damages shall be awarded to any person by virtue of this Part in respect of any loss of or damage to any property if the amount which would fall to be so awarded to that person, apart from this subsection and any liability for interest, does not exceed £275.

(5) In determining for the purposes of this Part who has suffered any loss of or damage to property and when any such loss or damage occurred, the loss or damage shall be regarded as having occurred at the earliest time at which a person with an interest in the property had knowledge of the material facts about the loss or damage.

(6) For the purposes of subsection (5) above the material facts about any loss of or damage to any property are such facts about the loss or damage as would lead a reasonable person with an interest in the property to consider the loss or damage sufficiently serious to justify his instituting proceedings for damages against a defendant who did not dispute liability and was able to satisfy a judgment.

(7) For the purposes of subsection (5) above a person's knowledge includes knowledge which he might reasonably have been expected to acquire—

(a) from facts observable or ascertainable by him; or

(b) from facts ascertainable by him with help of appropriate expert advice which it is reasonable for him to seek;

but a person shall not be taken by virtue of this subsection to have knowledge of a fact ascertainable by him only with the help of expert advice unless he has failed to take all reasonable steps to obtain (and, where appropriate, to act on) that advice.

6. Application of certain enactments etc.

(1) Any damage for which a person is liable under section 2 above shall be deemed to have been caused— **11.24**

(a) for the purposes of the Fatal Accidents Act 1976, by that person's wrongful act, neglect or default; . . .

(2) Where—

(a) a person's death is caused wholly or partly by a defect in a product, or a person dies after suffering damage which has been so caused;

(b) a request such as mentioned in paragraph (a) of subsection (3) of section 2 above is made to a supplier of the product by that person's personal representatives or, in the case of a person whose death is caused wholly or partly by the defect, by any dependant or relative of that person; and

(c) the conditions specified in paragraphs (b) and (c) of that subsection are satisfied in relation to that request,

this Part shall have effect for the purposes of the Law Reform (Miscellaneous Provisions) Act 1934, the Fatal Accidents Acts 1976 and the Damages (Scotland) Act 1976 as if liability of the supplier to that person under that subsection did not depend on that person having requested the supplier to identify certain persons or on the said conditions having been satisfied in relation to a request made by that person.

(3) Section 1 of the Congenital Disabilities (Civil Liability) Act 1976 shall have effect for the purposes of this Part as if—

(a) a person were answerable to a child in respect of an occurrence caused wholly or partly by a defect in a product if he is or has been liable under section 2 above in respect of any effect of the occurrence on a parent of the child, or would be so liable if the occurrence caused a parent of the child to suffer damage;

(b) the provisions of this Part relating to liability under section 2 above applied in relation to liability by virtue of paragraph (a) above under the said section 1; and

(c) subsection (6) of the said section 1 (exclusion of liability) were omitted.

(4) Where any damage is caused partly by a defect in a product and partly by the fault of the person suffering the damage, the Law Reform (Contributory Negligence) Act 1945 and section 5 of the Fatal Accidents Act 1976 (contributory negligence) shall have effect as if the defect were the fault of every person liable by virtue of this Part for the damage caused by the defect.

(5) In subsection (4) above 'fault' has the same meaning as in the said Act of 1945.

(6) Schedule 1 to this Act shall have effect for the purpose of amending the Limitation Act 1980 and the Prescription and Limitation (Scotland) Act 1973 in their application in relation to the bringing of actions by virtue of this Part.

(7) It is hereby declared that liability by virtue of this Part is to be treated as liability in tort for the purposes of any enactment conferring jurisdiction on any court with respect to any matter.

(8) Nothing in this Part shall prejudice the operation of section 12 of the Nuclear Installations Act 1965 (rights to compensation for certain breaches of duties confined to rights under that Act).

7. Prohibition on exclusions from liability

11.25 The liability of a person by virtue of this Part to person who has suffered damage caused wholly or partly by a defect in a product, or to a dependant or relative of such a person, shall not be limited or excluded by any contract term, by any notice or by any other provision.

G. Package Travel, Package Holidays and Package Tours Regulations 1992, regs 2, 3, and 15

11.26 1. [Citation and commencement]

11.27 2. Interpretation

(1) In these Regulations—

. . .

'contract' means the agreement linking the consumer to the organizer or to the retailer, or to both, as the case may be;

. . .

'organiser' means the person who, otherwise than occasionally, organises packages and sells or offers them for sale, whether directly or through a retailer;

'the other party to the contract' means the party, other than the consumer, to the contract, that is, the organiser or the retailer, or both, as the case may be;

'package' means the pre-arranged combination of at least two of the following components when sold or offered for sale at an inclusive price and when the service covers a period of more than twenty-four hours or includes overnight accommodation—

    (a) transport;

    (b) accommodation;

    (c) other tourist services not ancillary to transport or accommodation and accounting for a significant proportion of the package,

and

       (i) the submission of separate accounts for different components shall not cause the arrangements to be other than a package;

       (ii) the fact that a combination is arranged at the request of the consumer and in accordance with his specific instructions (whether modified or not) shall not of itself cause it to be treated as other than pre-arranged;

and

'retailer' means the person who sells or offers for sale the package put together by the organiser.

(2) In the definition of 'contract' in paragraph (1) above, 'consumer' means the person who takes or agrees to take the package ('the principal contractor') and elsewhere in these Regulations 'consumer' means, as the context requires, the principal contractor, any person on whose behalf the principal contractor agrees to purchase the package ('the other beneficiaries') or any person to whom the principal contractor or any of the other beneficiaries transfers the package ('the transferee').

3. Application of Regulations

(1) These Regulations apply to packages sold or offered for sale in the territory of the United Kingdom. **11.28**

15. Liability of other party to the contract for proper performance of obligations under contract

(1) The other party to the contract is liable to the consumer for the proper performance of the **11.29**
obligations under the contract, irrespective of whether such obligations are to be performed by
that other party or by other suppliers of services but this shall not affect any remedy or right of
action which that other party may have against those other suppliers of services.

(2) The other party to the contract is liable to the consumer for any damage caused to him by
the failure to perform the contract or the improper performance of the contract unless the failure
or the improper performance is due neither to any fault of that other party nor to that of another
supplier of services, because—

(a) the failures which occur in the performance of the contract are attributable to the
consumer;

(b) such failures are attributable to a third party unconnected with the provision of the
services contracted for, and are unforeseeable or unavoidable; or

(c) such failures are due to—

(i) unusual and unforeseeable circumstances beyond the control of the party by whom
this exception is pleaded, the consequences of which could not have been avoided even if all due
care had been exercised; or

(ii) an event which the other party to the contract or the supplier of services, even with all
due care, could not foresee or forestall.

(3) In the case of damage arising from the non-performance or improper performance of
the services involved in the package, the contract may provide for compensation to be limited in
accordance with the international conventions which govern such services.

(4) In the case of damage other than personal injury resulting from the non-performance or
improper performance of the services involved in the package, the contract may include a term
limiting the amount of compensation which will be paid to the consumer, provided that the
limitation is not unreasonable.

(5) Without prejudice to paragraph (3) and paragraph (4) above, liability under paragraphs
(1) and (2) above cannot be excluded by any contractual term.

(6) The terms set out in paragraphs (7) and (8) below are implied in every contract.

(7) In the circumstances described in paragraph (2)(b) and (c) of this regulation, the other
party to the contract will give prompt assistance to a consumer in difficulty.

(8) If the consumer complains about a defect in the performance of the contract, the other
party to the contract, or his local representative, if there is one, will make prompt efforts to find
appropriate solutions.

(9) The contract must clearly and explicitly oblige the consumer to communicate at the
earliest opportunity, in writing or any other appropriate form, to the supplier of the services
concerned and to the other party to the contract any failure which he perceives at the place where
the services concerned are supplied.

12

THE STATE OF LAND AND BUILDINGS

A. Occupiers' Liability: The 1957 Act

12.01 The Occupiers' Liability Act 1957 begins with a statement that its rules 'shall have effect, in place of the rules of the common law, to regulate the duty which an occupier of premises owes to his visitors in respect of dangers due to the state of the premises or to things done or omitted to be done on them' (s 1(1)). The rules of the common law which were replaced by the 1957 Act comprised a complex and technical range of duties which varied according to the purpose for which a person had come onto another's premises. There were anomalies and inconsistencies which made the law unfair. The purpose of the Act was to bring the law in this area into line with the developing law of negligence. This alignment is found in the common duty of care owed under the Act by the occupier of premises to all visitors on the premises.

12.02 The duty under s 2(2) of the 1957 Act is 'to take such care as in all the circumstances of the case is reasonable to see that the visitor will be reasonably safe in using the premises for the purposes for which he is invited or permitted by the occupier to be there'. This statement of the duty of care is for practical purposes indistinguishable in content from negligence. As with negligence, the same legal duty of reasonable care is owed to all lawful visitors and the question whether the content of the duty should vary in different situations is a question of fact in each case rather than of technical categorisation. In practical terms, the Act creates statutory negligence. Some illustrations of the application of the Act are set out in the case notes below; a lower duty is owed to trespassers (see **12.8** below).

12.03 The 1957 Act applies to 'premises', a word that is widely defined as applying to any premises (land whether or not there is a structure on it) and also to any fixed or moveable structure including any vessel, vehicle or aircraft. The limit on the scope of the definition is that the Act can only apply to things that are capable of having an occupier. The Act also applies to dangers due to things done or omitted to be done on the premises, and this extension to liability for activities and omissions is sometimes overlooked; as a matter of form rather than sub-stance there are probably many claims for acts done on premises which are pursued in negligence without any thought being given to the possibility that liability might more properly arise under the 1957 Act.

B. Common Law

12.04 The words in the opening of the Occupiers' Liability Act 1957 'in place of the rules of the common law' would seem to mean that if the Act applies, the common law does not apply. This must be true in so far as the duty of an occupier used formerly to be regulated by the rules in relation to visitors, invitees and licensees, but it clearly does not mean that there cannot be other legal duties owed in other capacities at the same time as a duty under the Act.

12.05 Section 1(2) refers to 'a person's occupation or control of premises'. It may be technically incorrect to rely on negligence as a simple alternative to liability under the 1957 Act in relation to duties merely of occupation and control, while it is reasonable to rely on the common law in relation to activities or omissions. A parallel duty such as, for example, that which an employer owes under the Workplace (Health, Safety and Welfare) Regulations 1992 can exist alongside liability under the Act and the same facts can be relied on as breaches of each duty.

C. Occupiers and Visitors

12.06 There is no statutory definition of 'occupier' and the common law definition is broad, extending to anyone who has some degree of control of the premises, and allowing the possibility that there may be more than one occupier of the same premises at the same time.

12.07 The common duty of care is owed to 'visitors', a word which again is not defined in the 1957 Act but covers everyone who is on premises by the invitation or permission, express or implied, of the occupier. There is in general an implied permission to walk to the front door of a house and to enter the public parts of business premises, but if a visitor goes into a different part of the premises or if he carries out an unlawful or forbidden purpose, he may turn himself into a trespasser. A trespasser is not owed any duty under the 1957 Act but is owed the more limited duty under the Occupiers' Liability Act 1984 which arises only when the occupier is aware of the danger, when he is or ought to be aware of the presence of the trespasser, and when the risk is such as to call for protection. A person using a public right of way is not a visitor and is owed no duty except, where relevant, the duty under the Highways Act 1980, a rule with surprising results in *McGeown v N I Housing Executive* [1995] 1 AC 233.

D. Trespassers

Liability to trespassers was not part of the 1957 Act because they are not 'visitors' under the pre-1957 common law. Although the duty to trespassers must be less than to lawful visitors, the necessity for the law to provide some limited recourse became clear with the case of *British Railways Board v Herrington* [1972] AC 877 and other cases concerning trespass by children, in that case onto a railway line which was inadequately fenced in the vicinity of a place where children were known to play. These concerns led to the passing of the Occupiers' Liability Act 1984 which puts onto a statutory footing a duty in respect of dangers the occupier knows to exist, owed when he knows that others may come near the danger and it is a danger against which he may reasonably be expected to offer some protection. **12.08**

A number of cases about swimming accidents culminated in the decision of the House of Lords in *Tomlinson v Congleton BC* [2003] UKHL 47; [2004] PIQR P83, which held that an adult of full capacity is responsible for his own actions and the duty owed under the 1984 Act does involve a duty to warn adults about obvious dangers. **12.09**

Tomlinson v Congleton BC [2003] UKHL 47; [2004] PIQR P83   In a public park, a disused quarry formed a lake with beach areas. Prominent signs forbade swimming. The claimant was severely injured when he dived into shallow water and hit his head. The House of Lords held that there was no risk to the claimant arising from the state of the premises or from anything done or omitted to be done (s 1(1)(a) of the 1984 Act), so no duty was owed by the Council under the 1984 Act. Even if there had been no notices forbidding swimming, or warning of the danger, there would have been no breach of duty to the adult claimant, because the danger was obvious. This decision has received much favourable comment as a notable step back from the 'compensation culture'. **12.10**

E. Defences

12.11 Under both the 1957 and 1984 Acts, any warning of a danger is relevant to whether the duty of care has been performed, but is not decisive. If a warning is not enough to absolve the occupier of liability, a warning notice or a contractual term imposed by a business occupier cannot limit liability under the Acts for personal injury or death because of the Unfair Contract Terms Act 1977. The defence of contributory negligence is not expressly mentioned in either Act but has frequently been applied to claims, and the defence of voluntary assumption of risk expressly applies.

F. Liability of Landlords

12.12 Where a building is let on terms that impose a repairing obligation on the landlord, s 4 of the Defective Premises Act 1972 imposes a liability on the landlord in favour of all persons, not only the tenant, in respect of the state of the premises, but the duty only arises on notice of the defect.

12.13 *Wheat v E Lacon & Co* [1966] AC 552   A landlord is no longer the occupier of parts of premises that he has given to the exclusive occupation and control of the tenant (subject to s 4 of the Defective Premises Act 1972); but a landlord remains the occupier of the parts of the premises retained by him such as staircases and passageways.

12.14 *Ogwo v Taylor* [1988] AC 431   The 1957 Act is more concerned with occupation than activities on the premises, and does not oust the common law in such a case. An occupier negligently set fire to his property and a fireman was injured; the successful claim was decided in negligence without reference to the 1957 Act.

12.15 *Jolley v Sutton LBC* [2000] 1 WLR 1082   Liability to children: the local authority was liable where a boat had been abandoned on its land which was in a dangerous condition and was an attraction to children. The land was used for play so the children were not trespassers. The case has attracted more interest on the remoteness of damage since the injuries were of a far more serious kind than was reasonably foreseeable.

12.16 *McGeown v N I Housing Executive* [1995] 1 AC 233   The claimant fell because of a hole in a path across the land of a housing estate. The hole was a danger and had resulted from a failure to maintain the path. Because the public had acquired a right of way over the path, the claimant was no longer a licensee of the owner of the land; she was therefore not a visitor and had no claim.

Gulliksen v Pembrokeshire CC [2002] EWCA Civ 968; [2002] 4 All ER **12.17**
450   A footpath was constructed by the local authority as a part of the provision of a housing estate, and dedicated as a public right of way. The path had been constructed 'by a highway authority' so as to be maintainable at public expense and subject to the s 41 duty to maintain, even though it had been constructed as part of the provision of housing by the Council rather than part of its provision of roads.

Staples v West Dorset DC [1995] PIQR P439   The claimant slipped on algae **12.18**
on the seafront on the Cobb at Lyme Regis. The danger was obvious and the claimant accepted he knew it was slippery, but he claimed that a warning notice should have been put up, encouraged by the fact that such a notice was in fact put up after his accident. The court held that the duty under the 1957 Act was only to warn an individual who was unaware of the danger and the claim failed.

Sykes v Harry [2001] EWCA Civ 167; [2001] QB 1014   The claimant was a **12.19**
tenant who was injured by carbon monoxide emissions from a defective gas fire. There was no evidence that the landlord had knowledge of the defect, but the Court of Appeal held that it was sufficient to establish a breach of duty under s 4(1) of the Defective Premises Act 1972 to show that the injury was caused by a defect of which the landlord ought in all the circumstances to have known, as by taking steps to service or check the fire.

Swain v Natui Ram Puri [1996] PIQR P442   A boy, aged 9, climbed a fence **12.20**
to enter vacant factory premises, and fell through a skylight. He could not prove sufficient knowledge of the defendant that children might come onto the premises: actual knowledge or 'shut-eye' knowledge were required under the 1984 Act. Merely to prove that the occupier ought to have realized that young boys might be tempted to trespass did not amount to reasonable grounds to believe under s 1(3) of the Act.

G. Occupiers' Liability Act 1957, ss 1–3, 5

1. Preliminary

(1) The rules enacted by the two next following sections shall have effect, in place of the rules **12.21**
of the common law, to regulate the duty which an occupier of premises owes to his visitors in respect of dangers due to the state of the premises or to things done or omitted to be done on them.

(2) The rules so enacted shall regulate the nature of the duty imposed by law in consequence of a person's occupation or control of premises and of any invitation or permission he gives (or is to be treated as giving) to another to enter or use the premises, but they shall not alter the rules of the common law as to the persons on whom a duty is so imposed or to whom it is owed; and

accordingly for the purpose of the rules so enacted the persons who are to be treated as an occupier and as his visitors are the same (subject to subsection (4) of this section) as the persons who would at common law be treated as an occupier and as his invitees or licensees.

(3) The rules so enacted in relation to an occupier of premises and his visitors shall also apply, in like manner and to the like extent as the principles applicable at common law to an occupier of premises and his invitees or licensees would apply, to regulate—

(a) the obligations of a person occupying or having control over any fixed or moveable structure, including any vessel, vehicle or aircraft; and

(b) the obligations of a person occupying or having control over any premises or structure in respect of damage to property, including the property of persons who are not themselves his visitors.

(4) A person entering any premises in exercise of rights conferred by virtue of an access agreement or order under the National Parks and Access to the Countryside Act 1949, is not, for the purposes of this Act, a visitor of the occupier of those premises.

2. Extent of occupier's ordinary duty

12.22   (1) An occupier of premises owes the same duty, the 'common duty of care', to all his visitors, except in so far as he is free to and does extend, restrict, modify or exclude his duty to any visitor or visitors by agreement or otherwise.

(2) The common duty of care is a duty to take such care as in all the circumstances of the case is reasonable to see that the visitor will be reasonably safe in using the premises for the purposes for which he is invited or permitted by the occupier to be there.

(3) The circumstances relevant for the present purposes include the degree of care, and of want of care, which would ordinarily be looked for in such a visitor, so that (for example) in proper cases—

(a) an occupier must be prepared for children to be less careful than adults; and

(b) an occupier may expect that a person, in the exercise of his calling, will appreciate and guard against any special risks ordinarily incident to it, so far as the occupier leaves him free to do so.

(4) In determining whether the occupier of premises has discharged the common duty of care to a visitor, regard is to be had to all the circumstances, so that (for example)—

(a) where damage is caused to a visitor by a danger of which he had been warned by the occupier, the warning is not to be treated without more as absolving the occupier from liability, unless in all the circumstances it was enough to enable the visitor to be reasonably safe; and

(b) where damage is caused to a visitor by a danger due to the faulty execution of any work of construction, maintenance or repair by an independent contractor employed by the occupier, the occupier is not to be treated without more as answerable for the danger if in all the circumstances he had acted reasonably in entrusting the work to an independent contractor and had taken such steps (if any) as he reasonably ought in order to satisfy himself that the contractor was competent and that the work had been properly done.

(5) The common duty of care does not impose on an occupier any obligation to a visitor in respect of risks willingly accepted as his by the visitor (the question whether a risk was so accepted to be decided on the same principles as in other cases in which one person owes a duty of care to another).

(6) For the purposes of this section, persons who enter premises for any purpose in the exercise of a right conferred by law are to be treated as permitted by the occupier to be there for that purpose, whether they in fact have his permission or not.

3. Effect of contract on occupier's liability to third party

(1) Where an occupier of premises is bound by contract to permit persons who are strangers to the contract to enter or use the premises, the duty of care which he owes to them as his visitors cannot be restricted or excluded by that contract, but (subject to any provision of the contract to the contrary) shall include the duty to perform his obligations under the contract, whether undertaken for their protection or not, in so far as those obligations go beyond the obligations otherwise involved in that duty.

12.23

(2) A contract shall not by virtue of this section have the effect, unless it expressly so provides, of making an occupier who has taken all reasonable care answerable to strangers to the contract for dangers due to the faulty execution of any work of construction, maintenance or repair or other like operation by persons other than himself, his servants and persons acting under his direction and control.

(3) In this section, 'stranger to the contract' means a person not for the time being entitled to the benefit of the contract as a party to it or as the successor by assignment or otherwise of a party to it, and accordingly includes a party to the contract who has ceased to be so entitled.

(4) Where by the terms or conditions governing any tenancy (including a statutory tenancy which does not in law amount to a tenancy) either the landlord or the tenant is bound, though not by contract, to permit persons to enter or use premises of which he is the occupier, this section shall apply as if the tenancy were a contract between the landlord and the tenant.

(5) This section, in so far as it prevents the common duty of care from being restricted or excluded, applies to contracts entered into and tenancies created before the commencement of this Act, as well as to those entered into or created after its commencement; but, in so far as it enlarges the duty owed by an occupier beyond the common duty of care, it shall have effect only in relation to obligations which are undertaken after the commencement or which are renewed by agreement (whether express or implied) after that commencement.

5. Implied term in contracts

(1) Where persons enter or use, or bring or send goods to, any premises in exercise of a right conferred by contract with a person occupying or having control of the premises, the duty he owes them in respect of dangers due to the state of the premises or to things done or omitted to be done on them, in so far as the duty depends on a term to be implied in the contract by reason of its conferring that right, shall be the common duty of care.

12.24

(2) The foregoing subsection shall apply to fixed and moveable structures as it applies to premises.

(3) This section does not affect the obligations imposed on a person by or by virtue of any contract for the hire of, or for the carriage for reward of persons or goods in, any vehicle, vessel, aircraft or other means of transport, or by or by virtue of any contract of bailment.

(4) This section does not apply to contracts entered into before the commencement of this Act.

H. Defective Premises Act 1972, ss 4–6

4. Landlord's duty of care in virtue of obligation or right to repair premises demised

(1) Where premises are let under a tenancy which puts on the landlord an obligation to the tenant for the maintenance or repair of the premises the landlord owes to all persons who might reasonably be expected to be affected by defects in the state of the premises a duty to take such

12.25

care as is reasonable in all the circumstances to see that they are reasonably safe from personal injury or from damage to their property caused by a relevant defect.

(2) The said duty is owed if the landlord knows (whether as the result of being notified by the tenant or otherwise) or if he ought in all the circumstances to have known of the relevant defect.

(3) In this section 'relevant defect' means a defect in the state of the premises existing at or after the material time and arising from, or continuing because of, an act or omission by the landlord which constituted or would if he had had notice of the defect, have constituted a failure by him to carry out his obligation to the tenant for the maintenance or repair of the premises; and for the purposes of the foregoing provision 'the material time' means—

   (a) where the tenancy commenced before this Act, the commencement of this Act; and
   (b) in all other cases, the earliest following times, that is to say—
      (i) the time when the tenancy commences;
      (ii) the time when the tenancy agreement is entered into;
      (iii) the time when possession is taken of the premises in contemplation of the letting.

(4) Where premises are let under a tenancy which expressly or impliedly gives the landlord the right to enter the premises to carry out any description of maintenance or repair of the premises, then, as from the time when he first is, or by notice or otherwise can put himself, in a position to exercise the right and so long as he is or can put himself in that position, he shall be treated for the purposes of subsections (1) to (3) above (but for no other purpose) as if he were under an obligation to the tenant for that description of maintenance or repair of the premises; but the landlord shall not owe the tenant any duty by virtue of this subsection in respect of any defect in the state of the premises arising from, or continuing because of, a failure to carry out an obligation expressly imposed on the tenant by the tenancy.

(5) For the purposes of this section obligations imposed or rights given by any enactment in virtue of a tenancy shall be treated as imposed or given by the tenancy.

(6) This section applies to a right of occupation given by contract or any enactment and not amounting to a tenancy as if the right were a tenancy, and 'tenancy' and cognate expressions shall be construed accordingly.

5. Application to Crown

12.26 This Act shall bind the Crown, but as regards the Crown's liability in tort shall not bind the Crown further than the Crown is made liable in tort by the Crown Proceedings Act 1947.

6. Supplemental

12.27 (1) In this Act: 'disposal', in relation to premises, includes a letting, and an assignment or surrender of a tenancy, of the premises and the creation by contract of any other right to occupy the premises, and 'dispose' shall be construed accordingly; 'personal injury' includes any disease and any impairment of a person's physical or mental condition.

(2) Any duty imposed by or enforceable by virtue of any provision of this Act is in addition to any duty a person may owe apart from that provision.

(3) Any term of an agreement which purports to exclude or restrict, or has the effect of excluding or restricting, the operation of any of the provisions of this Act, or any liability arising by virtue of any such provision, shall be void.

I. Occupiers' Liability Act 1984, ss 1 and 3

1. Duty of occupier to persons other than his visitors

(1) The rules enacted by this section shall have effect, in place of the rules of the common law, **12.28**
to determine—

(a) whether any duty is owed by a person as occupier of premises to persons other than his
visitors in respect of any risk of their suffering injury on the premises by reason of any danger due
to the state of the premises or to things done or omitted to be done on them; and

(b) if so, what that duty is.

(2) For the purposes of this section, the persons who are to be treated respectively as an
occupier of any premises (which, for those purposes, include any fixed or movable structure) and
as his visitors are—

(a) any person who owes in relation to the premises the duty referred to in section 2 of the
Occupiers' Liability Act 1957 (the common duty of care), and

(b) those who are his visitors for the purposes of that duty.

(3) An occupier of premises owes a duty to another (not being his visitor) in respect of any
such risk as is referred to in subsection (1) above if—

(a) he is aware of the danger or has reasonable grounds to believe that it exists;

(b) he knows or has reasonable grounds to believe that the other is in the vicinity of the
danger concerned or that he may come into the vicinity of the danger (in either case, whether
the other has lawful authority for being in that vicinity or not); and

(c) the risk is one against which, in all the circumstances of the case, he may reasonably be
expected to offer the other some protection.

(4) Where, by virtue of this section, an occupier of premises owes a duty to another in respect
of such a risk, the duty is to take such care as is reasonable in all the circumstances of the case to
see that he does not suffer injury on the premises by reason of the danger concerned.

(5) Any duty owed by virtue of this section in respect of a risk may, in an appropriate case,
be discharged by taking such steps as are reasonable in all the circumstances of the case to give
warning of the danger concerned or to discourage persons from incurring the risk.

(6) No duty is owed by virtue of this section to any person in respect of risks willingly accepted
as his by that person (the question whether a risk was so accepted to be decided on the same
principles as in other cases in which one person owes a duty of care to another).

(7) No duty is owed by virtue of this section to persons using the highway, and this section
does not affect any duty owed to such persons.

(8) Where a person owes a duty by virtue of this section, he does not, by reason of any breach
of the duty, incur any liability in respect of any loss of or damage to property.

(9) In this section—

'highway' means any part of a highway other than a ferry or waterway;

'injury' means anything resulting in death or personal injury, including any disease and any
impairment of physical or mental condition; and

'movable structure' includes any vessel, vehicle or aircraft.

3. Application to Crown

Section 1 of this Act shall bind the Crown, but as regards the Crown's liability in tort shall **12.29**
not bind the Crown further than the Crown is made liable in tort by the Crown Proceedings
Act 1947.

13

ANIMALS

The law concerning liability for injury caused by animals is a compromise **13.01** between two conflicting interests. The behaviour of animals, however tame, cannot always be controlled and may result in injury to others who are blameless. It is reasonable keep an animal, whether as a pet or for agriculture, and yet it is not reasonable to expect that such animals will be kept so closely confined and controlled as to eliminate all risk of injury to others. With the types of animal commonly kept in Britain, whether as pets or for agriculture, people can be expected to know and to cope with the usual and predictable ways that animals behave. The principles of the law reflect this. Broadly, the keeper of an inherently dangerous animal keeps it at his peril and is strictly liable for any injury that the animal may cause. But the keeper of a domesticated animal is not liable for an injury it may cause unless he has been negligent, or there are special reasons for him to believe that the individual animal might be unusually dangerous.

A. Liability under the Animals Act 1971

The Animals Act 1971 contains the rules about liability for injuries caused by **13.02** animals. The statutory rules are in addition to the ordinary principles of the common law. Therefore if, for example, an animal is used as the instrument for a deliberate attack, the perpetrator is liable for the assault in the same way as if the instrument had been a gun. The rules under the statute do not supplant common law liability in negligence but are in addition to it (see the judgment of Roskill LJ in *Draper v Hodder* [1972] 2 QB 556, 578).

13.03 There is strict liability under the 1971 Act for damage (including personal injury) caused by an animal of a dangerous species. A dangerous species is defined under s 6(2) as a species:

    (a) which is not commonly domesticated in the British Islands; and

    (b) whose fully grown animals normally have such characteristics that they are likely, unless restrained, to cause severe damage or that any damage they may cause is likely to be severe.

13.04 The test is *either* that the species is likely unless restrained to cause severe damage, *or* that (however unlikely the occurrence of damage may be) any damage it may cause is likely to be severe. With some animals there is little room for doubt—a lion or an elephant for example. Inclusion in the schedule to the Dangerous Wild Animals Act 1976 would be likely in practice to lead a court to find that a species was dangerous under the 1971 Act, but that list is not decisive. By contrast, in spite of the concerns that led to the enactment of the Dangerous Dogs Act 1991, that Act has no bearing on civil liability, and does not determine whether civil liability would arise for injury caused by a dog that is within the Act. Dogs which fall under the 1991 Act are not of a dangerous species, because under s 6(2)(a) they are commonly domesticated in the British Islands, even though under s 11 of the 1971 Act 'species' includes 'sub-species and variety'.

13.05 For domesticated animals, liability under the 1971 Act turns on the complex provisions of s 2(2). The drafting is very unsatisfactory. Indeed this is by far the most problematic statutory provision that will be encountered in this book. No commentary is an adequate substitute for patiently reading the words of the Act, set out at the end of this chapter. The following account is offered with hesitation.

13.06 The court will look at the three stated requirements in turn. The objective is to make the keeper of a domesticated animal liable for an injury that it has caused only if the damage has been caused by some special characteristic of the animal known to its keeper.

13.07 'Likelihood' does not mean something which is more likely to happen than not, but only something that may happen. 'Severe' is not defined in the Act and this leaves scope under s 2(2)(a) for judicial interpretation. 'Knowledge' means actual knowledge and it is not enough to prove that the keeper ought to have known of the animal's propensity if in fact he did not; of course the more he ought to have known of it, the easier it will be to persuade the court that in fact he probably did know.

13.08 The two situations which most commonly give rise to injury caused by animals are dogs which bite, often biting the children who try to be friendly, and farm livestock straying onto the road. In each case the most difficult question is to decide whether the injury has been caused by a relevant characteristic under s 2(2)(b). If the section is to have some real meaning as a limit on liability, it is inadequate to say that a dog will only bite in the particular circumstances of being irritated by a strange child, or that any horse will only escape in the particular circumstances that the gate of its field has been left open. In practice the section has been given a generous interpretation, so that it is sufficient if a dog is acting in defence of its territory or in defence of its new pups. So in *Curtis v Betts* (below) liability was established when a Bull Mastiff dog in the back of a car attacked a child, on the basis that its territorial instinct was sufficient to amount to a special characteristic. This broad construction of s 2(2) has been definitively adopted by the House of Lords in *Mirvahedy v Henley* (below), so that it may now be quite unusual to find a situation where an animal has caused injury, and the injury cannot be blamed on a characteristic of the animal not normally found except at particular times or in particular circumstances. The behaviour of the animal in particular circumstances does not have to be behaviour that is abnormal for animals of that species. When the characteristics are defined so broadly, it will equally be rare to find that they were not known to the keeper of the animal.

13.09 The person who is liable is the keeper of the animal and this is the person who owns or possesses the animal, or the head of the household of which a person under 16 owns the animal. There can be more than one keeper at the same time. Section 6(3) also prevents a keeper escaping liability by abandoning his animal: he continues to be the keeper until another person becomes a keeper in his place.

13.10 *Curtis v Betts* [1990] 1 WLR 459   A young Bull Mastiff dog injured a child in defence of its territory in the back of a car. The Court of Appeal found the keeper liable: belonging to the Bull Mastiff breed was enough to show for s 2(2)(a) that the damage of a bite was likely to be severe; the territorial instincts of the dog were sufficient to amount to a special characteristic for s 2(2)(b); and it was a characteristic known to the keeper of the dog.

13.11 *Cummings v Grainger* [1977] QB 397   An Alsatian guard dog roamed free in a scrapyard with a sign 'Beware of the Dog' on the gate. The claimant entered as a trespasser and was held to have voluntarily accepted the risk of injury; her claim failed.

13.12 *Gomberg v Smith* [1963] 1 QB 25   Liability for a dog which shot out into the road and caused a road traffic accident (s 27 of the Road Traffic Act 1998 requires a dog on a road to be held on a lead).

13.13 *Draper v Hodder* [1972] 2 QB 556   Liability for Jack Russell puppies which attacked as a pack.

13.14 *Smith v Ainger, The Times,* 5 June 1990   Liability for an Alsatian which knocked over a child, even though the propensity was to attack other dogs: it was rushing to such an attack when it knocked over the claimant.

13.15 *Hunt v Wallis* [1994] PIQR P128   A good illustration of the difficulties of the 1971 Act; a large Border Collie boisterously knocked over the claimant causing a serious injury, but the dog, though lively, had not previously caused concern and he had no propensity or characteristics that was not normally found in a Border Collie. (Note that Pill J compared the dog with the characteristics of others of the same breed.) The claim failed.

13.16 *Gloster v Chief Constable of Greater Manchester* [2000] PIQR P114   A police officer was bitten by a police dog chasing an escaping criminal. The dog had a tendency to bite as a result of its training rather than its character and, there being no negligence, the claim under the 1971 Act failed.

13.17 *Flack v Hudson* [2001] QB 698   A horse, which had a known propensity to be upset by farm machinery, bolted on the approach of a tractor. This was sufficient to establish liability under s 2(2) of the 1971 Act.

13.18 *Mirvahedy v Henley* [2003] UKHL 16; [2003] 2 AC 491   The defendant's horse panicked due to some unknown event and escaped from its field, causing a collision with the claimant's car. The field had been adequately fenced and there was no negligence of the keeper. The behaviour of the horse was not normal behaviour generally for animals of that species, but was normal behaviour for the species in the particular circumstances of being sufficiently alarmed. Applying the approach to s 2(2)(b) of *Cummings v Grainger* and *Curtis v Betts* (above), and inferring on the facts that something must have happened to alarm the horse, these circumstances were sufficient to establish strict liability for the damage caused.

B. Animals Act 1971, ss 1–6

1. New provisions as to strict liability for damage done by animals

13.19   (1) The provisions of sections 2 to 5 of this Act replace—

    (a) the rules of the common law imposing a strict liability in tort for damage done by an animal on the ground that the animal is regarded as ferae naturae or that its vicious or mischievous propensities are known or presumed to be known;

    (b) subsections (1) and (2) of section 1 of the Dogs Act 1906 as amended by the Dogs (Amendment) Act 1928 (injury to cattle or poultry); and

    (c) the rules of the common law imposing a liability for cattle trespass.

    (2) Expressions used in those sections shall be interpreted in accordance with the provisions of section 6 (as well as those of section 11) of this Act.

2. Liability for damage done by dangerous animals

(1) Where any damage is caused by an animal which belongs to a dangerous species, any **13.20** person who is a keeper of the animal is liable for the damage, except as otherwise provided by this Act.

(2) Where damage is caused by an animal which does not belong to a dangerous species, a keeper of the animal is liable for the damage, except as otherwise provided by this Act, if—

(a) the damage is of a kind which the animal, unless restrained, was likely to cause or which, if caused by the animal, was likely to be severe; and

(b) the likelihood of the damage or of its being severe was due to characteristics of the animal which are not normally found in animals of the same species or are not normally so found except at particular times or in particular circumstances; and

(c) those characteristics were known to that keeper or were at any time known to a person who at that time had charge of the animal as that keeper's servant or, where that keeper is the head of a household, were known to another keeper of the animal who is a member of that household and under the age of sixteen.

3. Liability for injury done by dogs to livestock

Where a dog causes damage by killing or injuring livestock, any person who is a keeper of the dog **13.21** is liable for the damage, except as otherwise provided by this Act.

4. Liability for damage and expenses due to trespassing livestock

(1) Where livestock belonging to any person strays on to land in the ownership or occupation **13.22** of another and—

(a) damage is done by the livestock to the land or to any property on it which is in the ownership or possession of the other person; or

(b) any expenses are reasonably incurred by that other person in keeping the livestock while it cannot be restored to the person to whom it belongs or while it is detained in pursuance of section 7 of this Act, or in ascertaining to whom it belongs; the person to whom the livestock belongs is liable for the damage or expenses, except as otherwise provided by this Act.

(2) For the purposes of this section any livestock belongs to the person in whose possession it is.

5. Exceptions from liability under sections 2 to 4

(1) A person is not liable under sections 2 to 4 of this Act for any damage which is due wholly **13.23** to the fault of the person suffering it.

(2) A person is not liable under section 2 of this Act for any damage suffered by a person who has voluntarily accepted the risk thereof.

(3) A person is not liable under section 2 of this Act for any damage caused by an animal kept on any premises or structure to a person trespassing there, if it is proved either—

(a) that the animal was not kept there for the protection of persons or property; or

(b) (if the animal was kept there for the protection of persons or property) that keeping it there for that purpose was not unreasonable.

(4) A person is not liable under section 3 of this Act if the livestock was killed or injured on land on to which it had strayed and either the dog belonged to the occupier or its presence on the land was authorised by the occupier.

(5) A person is not liable under section 4 of this Act where the livestock strayed from a highway and its presence there was a lawful use of the highway.

(6) In determining whether any liability for damage under section 4 of this Act is excluded by subsection (1) of this section the damage shall not be treated as due to the fault of the person suffering it by reason only that he could have prevented it by fencing; but a person is not liable under that section where it is proved that the straying of the livestock on to the land would not have occurred but for a breach by any other person, being a person having an interest in the land, of a duty to fence.

6. Interpretation of certain expressions used in sections 2 to 5

13.24   (1) The following provisions apply to the interpretation of sections 2 to 5 of this Act.

(2) A dangerous species is a species—
(a) which is not commonly domesticated in the British Islands; and
(b) whose fully grown animals normally have such characteristics that they are likely, unless restrained, to cause severe damage or that any damage they may cause is likely to be severe.

(3) Subject to subsection (4) of this section, a person is a keeper of an animal if—
(a) he owns the animal or has it in his possession; or
(b) he is the head of a household of which a member under the age of sixteen owns the animal or has it in his possession;

and if at any time an animal ceases to be owned by or to be in the possession of a person, any person who immediately before that time was a keeper thereof by virtue of the preceding provisions of this subsection continues to be a keeper of the animal until another person becomes a keeper thereof by virtue of those provisions.

(4) Where an animal is taken into and kept in possession for the purpose of preventing it from causing damage or of restoring it to its owner, a person is not a keeper of it by virtue only of that possession.

(5) Where a person employed as a servant by a keeper of an animal incurs a risk incidental to his employment he shall not be treated as accepting it voluntarily.

C. Dangerous Wild Animals Act 1976, Schedule

KINDS OF DANGEROUS WILD ANIMALS

MAMMALS

Common name or names

Marsupials

13.25 The Tasmanian devil

Grey kangaroos, the euro, the wallaroo and the red kangaroo

Primates

13.26 Tamarins

New-world monkeys (including capuchin, howler, saki, spider, squirrel, titi, uakari and woolly monkeys and the night monkey (otherwise known as the douroucouli))

Old-world monkeys (including baboons, the drill, colobus monkeys, the gelada, guenons, langurs, leaf monkeys, macaques, the mandrill, mangabeys, the patas and proboscis monkeys and the talapoin)

Leaping lemurs (including the indri, sifakas and the woolly lemur)

Large lemurs (the broad-nosed gentle lemur and the grey gentle lemur are excepted)

Anthropoid apes (including chimpanzees, gibbons, the gorilla and the orang-utan)

Edentates

Sloths   **13.27**

The giant armadillo

The giant anteater

Rodents

The North American porcupine   **13.28**

The capybara

Crested porcupines

Carnivores

The giant panda and the red panda   **13.29**

Jackals, wild dogs, wolves and the coyote (foxes, the raccoon-dog and the domestic dog are excepted)

The bobcat, caracal, cheetah, jaguar, lion, lynx, ocelot, puma, serval, tiger and all other cats (the domestic cat is excepted)

Hyaenas (except the aardwolf)

Badgers (except the Eurasian badger), otters (except the European otter), and the tayra, wolverine, fisher and ratel (otherwise known as the honey badger)

Cacomistles, raccoons, coatis, olingos, the little coatimundi and the kinkajou

Bears

The African, large-spotted, Malay and large Indian civets, the binturong and the fossa

Pinnipedes

The walrus, eared seals, sealions and earless seals (the common and grey seals are excepted)   **13.30**

Elephants

Elephants   **13.31**

Odd-toed ungulates

Asses, horses and zebras (the donkey, domestic horse and domestic hybrids are excepted)   **13.32**

Rhinoceroses

Tapirs

Hyraxes

Tree and rock hyraxes (otherwise known as dassies)   **13.33**

Aardvark

The aardvark   **13.34**

Even-toed ungulates

The Pronghorn   **13.35**

Antelopes, bison, buffalo, cattle, gazelles, goats and sheep (domestic cattle, goats and sheep are excepted)

Camels, the guanaco and the vicuna (the domestic Ilama and alpaca are excepted)

The moose or elk and the caribou or reindeer (the domestic reindeer is excepted)

The giraffe and the okapi

The hippopotamus and the pygmy hippopotamus

Old-world pigs (including the wild boar and the wart hog) (the domestic pig is excepted)

New-world pigs (otherwise known as peccaries)

Mammalian hybrids with a parent (or parents) of a specified kind

BIRDS

Cassowaries and emu

13.36 Cassowaries

The emu

Ostrich

13.37 The ostrich

REPTILES

Crocodilians

13.38 Alligators and caimans

Crocodiles and the false gharial

The gharial (otherwise known as the gavial)

Lizards and snakes

13.39 Mole vipers and certain rear-fanged venomous snakes (including the moila and montpellier snakes, sand snakes, twig snakes, the mangrove (otherwise known as the yellow-ringed catsnake), the boomslang, the red-necked keelback and the yaniakagashi (otherwise known as the Japanese tiger-snake))

Certain front-fanged venomous snakes (including cobras, coral snakes, the desert black snake, kraits, mambas, sea snakes and all Australian poisonous snakes (including the death adders))

The gila monster and the (Mexican) beaded lizard

Certain front-fanged venomous snakes (including adders, the barba amarilla, the bushmaster, the copperhead, the fer-de-lance, moccasins, rattlesnakes and vipers)

INVERTEBRATES

Spiders

13.40 Wandering spiders

The Sydney funnel-web spider and its close relatives

The Brazilian wold spider

Brown recluse spiders (otherwise known as violin spiders)

The black widow spider (otherwise known as redback spider) and its close relatives

Scorpions

13.41 Buthid scorpions

14

SPORTS INJURIES

Injuries can be caused in sports activities in a variety of ways. This chapter **14.01**
summarizes the legal rules in relation to the following issues:

(a) circumstances where one player may be liable to another player for an
    injury sustained, and the extent to which a willing participant in sport
    accepts the risks of injury that the sport involves;
(b) the liability of referees, umpires and supervisors;
(c) liability to spectators and passers by; and
(d) liability for the state of sports premises and consequential injuries.

There is no special category in law relating to sports. Liability issues are determined by the ordinary law of negligence and assault, and by the application of
the defence of the willing acceptance of risks. The law is found in the cases, and
therefore this chapter takes the form of an extended set of case notes.

A. Liability of Players to Each Other

A player is taken to have consented to the risk of sustaining injury which may **14.02**
occur in the normal and reasonable conduct of the sport by players taking
reasonable care. In deciding whether reasonable care has been taken, players and
spectators must expect that a player will focus his concentration on winning
within the rules. A player or spectator must take the risk of injury by any act
done in the course of the sport, even if it results from an error of judgment or a
lapse of skill, unless there has been a reckless disregard of safety. This is not so
much an application of the defence of willing acceptance of risk, as of defining
the nature of the duty of care. It is not easy to say whether the test of reckless

disregard for safety, derived from Diplock LJ in *Wooldridge v Summer* [1963] 2 QB 43 in relation to spectators, would in practice ever produce a different result from the test of reasonable care in all the circumstances, the circumstances including the context of the sport. A breach of the rules of the game will be relevant but not decisive. Claims for sporting injuries are becoming more common, and clubs and players are wise to ensure that adequate insurance is in place (though a school had no legal duty to insure in *Van Oppen v Bedford Charity* [1990] 1 WLR 235).

14.03 *Condon v Basi* [1985] 1 WLR 866 The claimant's leg was broken as a result of a foul tackle 'in a reckless and dangerous manner' during a game of football. The judge found it to be serious and dangerous foul play which showed a reckless disregard for the claimant's safety. If a player fails to exercise the care appropriate in the circumstances, or acts in a way to which the other player could not be taken to have consented, there may be negligence. The claim succeeded. The standard is objective, but set according to the circumstances. Incompetence is no excuse for the individual (as with the objective standard applied to a learner driver in *Nettleship v Weston* [1971] 2 QB 691) but the standard will be higher in the circumstances of the Premier League than in a local game.

14.04 *Harrison v Vincent* [1982] RTR 8 In a motorcycle and sidecar race the passenger was injured when the rear brake failed and there was a collision with a recovery vehicle poorly parked in an escape lane. The brake failure was a result of negligent maintenance work in the workshop. In a claim against the rider, the standard of care for the poor maintenance was the ordinary standard and not the modified standard of reckless disregard of safety applicable to acts done in the course of violent sport. In the claim against the organizers, since the passenger did not know about the presence of the badly parked recovery vehicle, he could not be said to have willingly accepted the risk.

14.05 *Pearson v Lightening*, *The Times*, 30 April 1998 A golfer played a difficult shot which was deflected to strike the claimant, playing an adjacent hole, in the eye. The Court of Appeal held that a shout of 'Fore' was not sufficient to discharge the duty of care when playing the shot; there was a small but real risk of injury which was sufficient to make the defendant liable.

14.06 *Caldwell v Maguire* [2001] EWCA Civ 1054; [2002] PIQR P45 A race jockey brought a claim against fellow jockeys who had been subject to a finding of careless riding after a stewards' inquiry, but the court held that the threshold of liability was high, an error of judgment or momentary lapse of skill in the course of a competitive race would not be sufficient, and liability was not established.

B. Liability of Referees

Smolden v Whitworth [1997] PIQR P133   A 17-year-old boy playing rugby **14.07**
was seriously injured when a scrum in which he was a hooker collapsed. Rejecting an argument that the referee's duty was only to refrain from deliberately or
recklessly causing injury, the Court of Appeal upheld a finding against the
referee who had failed to implement the laws of the game which were designed
to protect the safety of younger players. The duty of the referee is to apply the
laws of the game, to apply them fairly, to control the match so as to prevent
unnecessary risk of injury and to have particular regard to the young age of the
players.

Van Oppen v Bedford Charity [1990] 1 WLR 235   The claimant was severely **14.08**
injured during a school rugby match, but his claim against the school for
negligence in coaching and supervision failed on the facts. The report concerns
only the claimant's unsuccessful appeal against the failure of his second ground
of claim, that the school had been negligent in failing to have accident insurance
in place to cover him.

Vowles v David Evans and WRU [2003] EWCA Civ 318; [2003] PIQR **14.09**
P29   The defendant was an amateur referee in an amateur rugby match
when the claimant suffered catastrophic injury in a collapse of the scrum. The
Court of Appeal held that it was fair, just and reasonable that a rugby referee
should owe a duty of care to players, and held the referee liable for allowing an
inexperienced player to play in the front row.

C. Liability to Spectators

Wooldridge v Summer [1963] 2 QB 43   A spectator was injured when he was **14.10**
knocked down by a horse at a competitive horse show. The defence of willing
assumption of risk was argued, but the Court of Appeal analysed the issue as the
absence of a breach of the duty of care so that the claim failed on that ground: a
sportsman is not under a duty to have regard to the safety of a spectator as long
as he plays within the rules of the sport and has adequate skill. The spectator's
claim failed.

Wilks v Cheltenham Home Guard Motor Cycle & Light Car Club [1971] **14.11**
1 WLR 668   A spectator at a motorcycle scramble was in a spectator's
enclosure separated from the track by ten feet. The layout was reasonable and in
accordance with the requirements of the sporting body. A rider lost control,
crossed the safe area and injured the spectator. Loss of control is 'just one of the

things that may happen in a motorcycle scramble'. A competitor was held to owe a duty of care to a spectator even though he was trying hard to win the race. But the accident would have to be caused by an incident going beyond mere error of judgment or lapse of skill for liability to arise. The spectator's claim failed.

D. Liability for Grounds and Premises

14.12 *Bolton v Stone* [1951] AC 850   A pedestrian walking outside a fenced cricket ground was hit and injured by a well struck ball. The occupiers of the ground owed a duty of care to users of the footpath, but the accident was so improbable that there was held to be no breach of the duty.

14.13 *Watson v British Boxing Board of Control* [2001] PIQR P16   The claimant sustained serious brain damage in a boxing match and the Board was held liable for failing to ensure that facilities were available to enable the claimant to be resuscitated at the ringside. The decision was based on the special circumstances of the case: the aim in boxing to inflict injury, and the degree of control of boxing assumed by the Board.

14.14 *Morrell v Owen, The Times*, 14 December 1993   The claimant, who was disabled, was at archery practice in a sports hall while discus throwing was held in the same hall. She was struck by a stray discus. The organizers were held to be in breach of their duty of care to her, and the organizers owed her a greater duty than if she had been able bodied.

14.15 *O'Shea v R B Kingston on Thames* [1995] PIQR P208   In an unusually shallow leisure swimming pool, diving was not advisable. The claimant was severely injured when diving because he struck his head against the bottom of the pool. It was held that diving should have been prevented in unsafe areas and signs should have stated that shallow dives only were allowed. The claimant succeeded subject to 50% contributory negligence.

15

DELIBERATELY INTENDED INJURY

The law in relation to deliberately intended injuries has an old-fashioned feel. **15.01** The terminology of assaults is confusing and the cause of action in trespass is less flexible than negligence, with sometimes unexpected consequences for issues such as limitation and the assessment of damages. Assault, battery and false imprisonment are all kinds of trespass to the person.

Damage does not need to be proved in order to establish liability in trespass, **15.02** though compensatory damages will be merely nominal if no harm was done. All harm flowing from a trespass may be the subject of a claim and the requirement in negligence that the kind of harm, if not the extent of it, must be foreseeable does not apply. Aggravated and exemplary damages are much more likely to be awarded in claims of intentional injury than in cases of negligence.

The limitation period for a case of intentional injury is six years rather than **15.03** three, but the discretion under s 33 of the Limitation Act 1980 to extend time does not apply. Since an act must be either trespass or negligence and not both at once, this can be important.

A. Assaults

In practice everybody thinks they know what the word 'assault' means, but **15.04** in legal theory an assault is merely the act of causing someone to be fearful of violence and the infliction of unlawful bodily force is the separate wrong of battery. Consent may be a defence to battery committed in lawful sport or in the course of medical treatment but, at least in the criminal law, consent is no defence if there is no justification for the activity.

15.05 The torts of assault, battery, and false imprisonment are also crimes and a conviction may result in a compensation order made by the criminal court. If such an order is made and paid, the claimant would have to give credit for any sums received in a subsequent civil claim. There may also be compensation from the Criminal Injuries Compensation Authority, as to which see Chapter 16, where it is the Authority's award that is abated by any recovery of damages or compensation.

15.06 *Letang v Cooper* [1965] 1 QB 232   Unintentionally caused injuries may be negligent but cannot be trespass, so a claimant who was accidentally but not intentionally run over by a car could only sue in negligence.

15.07 *Wilson v Pringle* [1987] QB 237   Further consideration of *Letang v Cooper*: it is only the act which has to be intentional in the tort of trespass, there does not have to be an intention that the act should cause injury; also, an act of touching is only a battery if the act is hostile (using that word in a very broad sense).

15.08 *Stubbings v Webb* [1993] AC 498   The complaint was of sexual abuse. The matters occurred during the claimant's childhood but she had a good argument that her date of knowledge was less than three years before issue of proceedings if ss 11(4) and 14 of the Limitation Act 1980 applied. However, those provisions applied only to a case of injury caused by negligence, nuisance or breach of a duty of care and not to a complaint of deliberate assault, for which the limitation period is six years from the date of injury or, in the case of injury to a child, six years from the date of attaining the age of 18. In this kind of case there is no provision for extending time, whether on the grounds of a later date of knowledge under s 14 or under the general discretion of s 33 of the Act.

15.09 *R v Rahman* (1985) 81 Cr App R 349   A parent may lawfully restrain a child's movement as reasonable parental discipline but not where it is unreasonable—as in this case where a father took his daughter forcibly away from foster parents against her will intending to take her to Bangladesh.

15.10 *R v Brown* [1994] 1 AC 212   Consent cannot be a defence to criminal assault, even though the acts caused only minor injuries which were inflicted with the active consent of the victim. The acts were done in the context of sado-masochistic sexual practices and (in contrast with playing sports) there was no good reason for the assault. (A civil claim might fail on grounds of public policy and willing acceptance of risk.)

15.11 *Murphy v Culhane* [1977] QB 94   The defendant who struck the deceased and admitted manslaughter was entitled to defend a claim by alleging that the victim had started the fight as an attack on the defendant.

15.12 *Appleton v Garrett* [1996] PIQR P1   Trespass, and an entitlement to aggravated damages, were established where a dentist carried out large scale and unnecessary treatment to which the claimants would not have consented if they had known the true position.

If an assault is subject to a prosecution in the magistrates' court and any penalty imposed has been paid in full, s 45 of the Offences against the Person Act 1861 rather surprisingly provides a complete defence to any subsequent civil claim. **15.13**

OFFENCES AGAINST THE PERSON ACT 1861

44. If the Justices, upon the hearing of any case of assault or battery upon the merits, where the complaint was preferred by or on behalf of the party aggrieved, shall deem the offence not to be proved, or shall find the assault or battery to have been justified, or so trifling as not to merit any punishment, and shall accordingly dismiss the complaint, they shall forthwith make out a certificate under their hands stating the fact of such dismissal, and shall deliver such certificate to the party against whom the complaint was preferred. **15.14**

45. If any person against whom any such complaint as is mentioned in section 44 of this Act shall have been preferred by or on behalf of the party aggrieved, shall have obtained such certificate, or, having been convicted, shall have paid the whole amount adjudged to be paid, or shall have suffered the imprisonment with hard labour awarded, in every such case he shall be released from all further or other proceedings, civil or criminal, for the same cause. **15.15**

Wong v Parkside NHS Trust [2001] EWCA Civ 1721; [2003] 3 All ER 932   The claimant was subject to repeated acts of harassment by a colleague and was assaulted by her, for which the claimant brought a private prosecution. Upholding a decision to strike out the claim, the Court of Appeal held that the assault must be disregarded in deciding whether there had been an intention to cause harm, because of s 45 of the Offences against the Person Act 1861, and that before the Protection from Harassment Act 1997 came into force there had been no common law tort of harassment falling short of an intention to inflict harm. **15.16**

B. False Imprisonment

False imprisonment is a tort of strict liability and there can be liability even if the person imprisoned is unaware of it and even if the defendant was acting in accordance with the law as it was reasonably thought to be. **15.17**

In cases of assault, compensatory damages will be assessed in exactly the same way as damages in negligence. For false imprisonment, there are guidelines in *Thompson v Metropolitan Police Commissioner* [1998] QB 498. The guidelines should of course be adjusted to take account of inflation and, with higher awards, for the effect of *Heil v Rankin* [2000] PIQR Q187. The RPI adjustment from December 1997 (the date of the award) to September 2004 (about the time of the 7th edition of the *JSB Guidelines*) is 1.175. **15.18**

15.19 Note that the Protection from Harassment Act 1997 creates a specific cause of action which is, like trespass, subject to a six-year limitation period.

15.20 *Murray v Ministry of Defence* [1988] 1 WLR 692   A person may be falsely imprisoned without knowing it. This is the law because of the supreme value attached to the liberty of the individual. Although compensatory damages would be nominal, exemplary damages might be awarded.

15.21 *R v Governor of Brockhill Prison, ex p Evans (No. 2)* [2000] 3 WLR 843   The prison governor calculated a release date in accordance with Home Office guidance but subsequently in a judicial review it was held that the claimant should have been released sooner. She had been falsely imprisoned and was entitled to damages.

C. Protection from Harassment Act 1997, ss 1–3, 6, and 7

1. Prohibition of harassment

15.22 (1) A person must not pursue a course of conduct—
    (a) which amounts to harassment of another, and
    (b) which he knows or ought to know amounts to harassment of the other.

(2) For the purposes of this section, the person whose course of conduct is in question ought to know that it amounts to harassment of another if a reasonable person in possession of the same information would think the course of conduct amounted to harassment of the other.

(3) Subsection (1) does not apply to a course of conduct if the person who pursued it shows—
    (a) that it was pursued for the purpose of preventing or detecting crime,
    (b) that it was pursued under any enactment or rule of law or to comply with any condition or requirement imposed by any person under any enactment, or
    (c) that in the particular circumstances the pursuit of the course of conduct was reasonable.

2. Offence of harassment

15.23 (1) A person who pursues a course of conduct in breach of section 1 is guilty of an offence.

3. Civil remedy

15.24 (1) An actual or apprehended breach of section 1 may be the subject of a claim in civil proceedings by the person who is or maybe the victim of the course of conduct in question.

(2) On such a claim, damages may be awarded for (among other things) any anxiety caused by the harassment and any financial loss resulting from the harassment.

6. Limitation

15.25 In section 11 of the Limitation Act 1980 (special time limit for actions in respect of personal injuries), after subsection (1) there is inserted—
    '(1A) This section does not apply to any action brought for damages under section 3 of the Protection from Harassment Act 1997.'

7. Interpretation of this group of sections

(1) This section applies for the interpretation of sections 1 to 5.

15.26

(2) References to harassing a person include alarming the person or causing the person distress.

(3) A 'course of conduct' must involve conduct on at least two occasions.

(4) 'Conduct' includes speech.

16

CRIMINAL INJURIES COMPENSATION

The idea that public funds should pay compensation to those who have the **16.01** misfortune to be injured as a result of the acts of a criminal dates back to the first compensation scheme of 1964. Initially, a scheme under the royal prerogative made nominally ex gratia payments equivalent to common law damages on the same basis of assessment as in the courts. Although the scheme did not give rise to a formal entitlement, it operated in practice as a fair, formal and efficiently administered scheme. Damages were assessed by the members of the Board who were experienced specialist judges, retired judges and senior practitioners: initially by a single member and on appeal by a panel of three. Their decisions reflected authoritative opinion of the appropriate level of damages and many reports of their decisions are to be found in the volumes of *Kemp & Kemp*.

A. The Statutory Scheme

The current basis for compensation is the statutory scheme established by the **16.02** Criminal Injuries Compensation Act 1995. The main reason for the introduction of the new statutory scheme was to reduce the cost of the scheme by making lower awards. After some political turmoil, the 1996 scheme was introduced, and there have now been slight amendments in the 2001 scheme which applies to applications made after 1 April 2001.

The old common law based scheme may still occasionally be relevant because **16.03** there may be old cases where the possibility of reopening for further application arises, but the occasions for this will be few and this chapter is concerned only with the workings of the 2001 scheme.

16.04   The address of the Criminal Injuries Compensation Authority is:

Criminal Injuries Compensation Authority
Tay House, 300 Bath Street
Glasgow G2 4JR
tel: 0141 331 2726; fax: 0141 331 2287
Freephone: 0800 358 3601 Website: www.cica.gov.uk

16.05   The scheme and tariff are set out in full at the end of this chapter. The following comments are no substitute for reading the text of the scheme.

(a) Time limit: an application should be made as soon as possible after the incident and must be received by the Authority within two years of the incident, though there is power to waive the time limit where an officer considers it is reasonable and in the interests of justice to do so (para 18).

(b) The Authority does not pay legal costs, so an applicant who is legally represented has to pay his own costs.

(c) Compensation is paid to the victim of a crime of violence, trespass on the railway or apprehension of an offender (para 8). It is the nature of the crime rather than its consequences which matters (*R v CICB, ex P Warner* [1987] QB 74). The inclusion of trespass on the railway enables a claim to be made by a train driver shocked by someone jumping onto the track in a suicide attempt.

(d) Injury from the use of a vehicle is not covered except where the vehicle was used deliberately to inflict injury (para 11). In any such case there is often an alternative of a civil claim against an insured driver or a claim under the MIB Uninsured Drivers Agreement giving a common law assessment of damages (but see *R v CICB, ex P Keane* [1998] PIQR P107).

(e) Compensation may be withheld if there is delay, if there is a failure to co-operate with the police after the incident or with the Authority during the claim, if the conduct of the claimant during the incident makes an award inappropriate (when there may be a reduced award), or if the applicant has a bad character (paras 13 to 17). The last two con-siderations have no equivalent in the common law.

(f) The maximum possible award is £500,000.

(g) The minimum possible award is £1,000, and for minor injuries unless they are at least three in number within Note 12, no award will be made.

(h) Basic awards are assessed strictly in accordance with the tariff and there is no discretion for the Authority to pay any different amount. There has been a revision of most awards in the 2001 tariff, though not of the highest and lowest levels. The very highest awards are still much more generous than common law damages, perhaps because originally when the scheme was devised separate claims for care expenses were not going to be allowed.

(i) Multiple injuries are compensated by the formula in para. 27: a full award for the most serious, 30% for the next and 15% for the third most serious, with no award beyond that. The equivalent percentages in the 1996 scheme were 10% and 5% so this is a significant change in favour of claimants.

(j) No award is made for loss of earnings until after 28 weeks' incapacity and then any award is capped at one and a half times the gross average industrial earnings (para 34) and all social security payments and pensions are deducted (paras 31(d) and 32(d)).

(k) Special expenses of care and treatment may be paid but only where there has been incapacity from work for at least 28 weeks; these expenses (but not loss of earnings) may be backdated to the date of injury once this period has elapsed. The cost of private treatment is met only where private treatment is reasonable (para 35).

(l) If civil damages have been received for the same injury, the damages will reduce (and usually extinguish) any criminal injury compensation award; if a civil claim succeeds after a such claim has been paid, the criminal injury compensation award is ignored in the civil claim and must be repaid to the Authority out of the damages recovered (para 48 and *Oldham v Sharples* [1998] PIQR Q82).

16.06 The 2001 scheme contains its own internal appeal procedure. In the first place, before a claims officer of the Authority makes a determination under para 50, where the applicant is represented the officer may have given indicative details of the likely award and invite comments on it. When a determination has been made, para 53 of the scheme allows for the possibility of reconsideration where there is new evidence or a change in circumstances. If there is no new evidence and no change of circumstances, the applicant can ask for a review of the decision under para 58 of the scheme, setting out the reasons for asking for the review and supplying any relevant additional information. A more senior claims officer will then review the decision and again may give an indicative award before reaching a final decision. An applicant must go through the review process before being entitled to bring an appeal against the decision to the Appeal Panel under para 61. The Panel will then decide the appeal, often, but not necessarily, at an oral hearing.

16.07 The decision of the Panel on an appeal exhausts the applicant's entitlement to appeal under the scheme. The Authority is amenable to judicial review under CPR Part 54 (*Blackstone's Civil Practice 2004* 1838). A detailed discussion of the principles of judicial review is beyond the scope of this book. Briefly, the remedy of judicial review allows the court to remedy a legal mistake by the Authority, but does not allow the court to substitute its own view on the merits of the compensation application. The kind of legal mistake that might be addressed by judicial review would generally be a mistake in the interpretation or application of the scheme. There is a limited possibility of attacking a decision for unreasonableness. *Wednesbury* unreasonableness means reaching a decision which is outside the legitimate scope of reasonable disagreement, by failing to take account of relevant considerations, or by allowing irrelevant matters to be taken into account. At the extreme, a decision may be quashed on the ground that it is so unreasonable as to be one which no authority, properly applying its discretion on the facts, could reach without perversity. An application for judicial review must be brought as soon as possible, and in any case within three months of the decision being challenged.

B. Criminal Injuries Compensation Scheme 2001

TABLE OF CONTENTS

16.08

TARIFF OF INJURIES AND STANDARD AMOUNTS OF COMPENSATION

16.09   Levels of compensation.

Descriptions of injury.

Notes to the Tariff.

THE CRIMINAL INJURIES COMPENSATION SCHEME 2001

16.10   (1) This Scheme is made by the Secretary of State under the Criminal Injuries Compensation Act 1995. Applications received on or after 1 April 2001 for the payment of compensation to, or in respect of, persons who have sustained criminal injury will be considered under this Scheme (subject to paragraphs 83–86 below).

Administration of the Scheme

16.11   (2) Claims officers in the Criminal Injuries Compensation Authority ('the Authority') will determine claims for compensation in accordance with this Scheme. Appeals against decisions taken on reviews under this Scheme will be determined by adjudicators. Persons appointed as adjudicators are appointed as members of the Criminal Injuries Compensation Appeals Panel ('the Panel'). The Secretary of State will appoint one of the adjudicators as Chairman of the Panel. The Secretary of State will also appoint persons as staff of the Panel to administer the provisions of this Scheme relating to the appeal system.

(3) Claims officers will be responsible for deciding, in accordance with this Scheme, what awards (if any) should be made in individual cases, and how they should be paid. Their decisions will be open to review and thereafter to appeal to the Panel, in accordance with this Scheme. No decision, whether by a claims officer or the Panel, will be open to appeal to the Secretary of State.

(4) The general working of this Scheme will be kept under review by the Secretary of State. The Accounting Officers for the Authority and the Panel must each, submit reports to the Secretary of State and the Scottish Ministers as soon as possible after the end of each financial year, dealing with the operation of this Scheme and the discharge of functions under it. The Accounting Officers must each keep proper accounts and proper records in relation to those accounts, and must each prepare a statement of accounts in each financial year in a form directed by the Secretary of State. These statements of accounts must be submitted to the Secretary of State and the Scottish Ministers as soon as possible after the end of each financial year.

(5) The Panel will advise, the Secretary of State on matters on which he seeks its advice, as well as on such other matters and at such times as it considers appropriate. Any advice given by the Panel will be referred to by the Accounting Officer for the Panel in his annual report made under the preceding paragraph.

Eligibility to apply for compensation

(6) Compensation may be paid in accordance with this Scheme:　　　　　　　　　　　　**16.12**
    (a) to an applicant who has sustained a criminal injury on or after 1 August 1964;
    (b) where the victim of a criminal injury sustained on or after 1 August 1964 has since died, to an applicant who is a qualifying claimant for the purposes of paragraph 38 (compensation in fatal cases).
For the purposes of this Scheme, 'applicant' means any person for whose benefit an application for compensation is made, even where it is made on his behalf by another person.

(7) No compensation will be paid under this Scheme in the following circumstances:
    (a) where the applicant has previously lodged any claim for compensation in respect of the same criminal injury under this or any other scheme for the compensation of the victims of violent crime in operation in Great Britain; or
    (b) where the criminal injury was sustained before 1 October 1979 and the victim and the assailant were living together at the time as members of the same family.

(8) For the purposes of this Scheme, 'criminal injury' means one or more personal injuries as described in the following paragraph, being an injury sustained in Great Britain (see Note 1) and directly attributable to:
    (a) a crime of violence (including arson, fire-raising or an act of poisoning); or
    (b) an offence of trespass on a railway; or
    (c) the apprehension or attempted apprehension of an offender or a suspected offender, the prevention or attempted prevention of an offence, or the giving, of help to any constable who is engaged in any such activity.

(9) For the purposes of this Scheme, personal injury includes physical injury (including fatal injury), mental injury (that is temporary mental anxiety, medically verified, or a disabling mental illness confirmed by psychiatric diagnosis) and disease (that is a medically recognised illness or condition). Mental injury or disease may either result directly from the physical injury or from a sexual offence or may occur without any physical injury. Compensation will not be payable for mental injury or disease without physical injury, or in respect of a sexual offence unless the applicant:

(a) was put in reasonable fear of immediate physical harm to his own person; or

(b) had a close relationship of love and affection with another person at the time when that person sustained physical and/or mental injury (including fatal injury) directly attributable to conduct within paragraph 8(a), (b) or (c), and

(i) that relationship still subsists (unless the victim has since died), and

(ii) the applicant either witnessed and was present on the occasion when the other person sustained the injury, or was closely involved in its immediate aftermath; or

(c) in a claim arising out of a sexual offence, was the non-consenting victim of that offence, (which does not include a victim who consented in fact but was deemed in law not to have consented); or

(d) being a person employed in the business of a railway, either witnessed and was present on the occasion when another person sustained physical (including fatal) injury directly attributable to an offence of trespass on a railway, or was closely involved in its immediate aftermath. Paragraph 12 below does not apply where mental anxiety or mental illness is sustained as described in this sub-paragraph.

(10) It is not necessary for the assailant to have been convicted of a criminal offence in connection with the injury. Moreover, even where the injury is attributable to conduct within paragraph 8 in respect of which the assailant cannot be convicted of an offence by reason of age, insanity or diplomatic immunity, the conduct may nevertheless be treated as constituting a criminal act.

(11) A personal injury is not a criminal injury for the purposes of this Scheme where the injury is attributable to the use of a vehicle, except where the vehicle was used so as deliberately to inflict, or attempt to inflict, injury on any person.

(12) Where an injury is sustained accidentally by a person who is engaged in:

(a) any of the law-enforcement activities described in paragraph 8(c), or

(b) any other activity directed to containing, limiting or remedying the consequences of a crime,

compensation will not be payable unless the person injured was, at the time he sustained the injury, taking an exceptional risk which was justified in all the circumstances.

Eligibility to receive compensation

16.13   (13) A claims officer may withhold or reduce an award where he considers that:

(a) the applicant failed to take, without delay, all reasonable steps to inform the police, or other body or person considered by the Authority to be appropriate for the purpose, of the circumstances giving rise to the injury; or

(b) the applicant failed to co-operate with the police or other authority in attempting to bring the assailant to justice; or

(c) the applicant has failed to give all reasonable assistance to the Authority or other body or person in connection with the application; or

(d) the conduct of the applicant before, during or after the incident giving rise to the application makes it inappropriate that a full award or any award at all be made; or

(e) the applicant's character as shown by his criminal convictions (excluding convictions spent under the Rehabilitation of Offenders Act 1974 at the date of application or death) or by evidence available to the claims officer makes it inappropriate that a full award or any award at all be made.

(14) In considering the issue of conduct under paragraph 13(d) above, a claims officer may withhold or reduce an award where he considers that excessive consumption of alcohol or use of illicit drugs by the applicant contributed to the circumstances which gave rise to the injury in such a way as to make it inappropriate that a full award, or any award at all, be made.

(15) Where the victim has died since sustaining the injury (whether or not in consequence of it), paragraphs 13 and 14 will apply in relation both to the deceased and to any applicant for compensation under paragraphs 37–44 (fatal awards).

(16) A claims officer will make an award only where he is satisfied:

(a) that there is no likelihood that an assailant would benefit if an award were made; or

(b) where the applicant is under 18 years of age when the application is determined, that it would not be against his interest for an award to be made.

(17) Where a case is not ruled out under paragraph 7(b) (injury sustained before 1 October 1979) but at the time when the injury was sustained, the victim and any assailant (whether or not that assailant actually inflicted the injury) were living in the same household as members of the same family, an award will be withheld unless:

(a) the assailant has been prosecuted in connection with the offence, except where a claims officer considers that there are practical, technical or other good reasons why a prosecution has not been brought; and

(b) in the case of violence between adults in the family, a claims officer is satisfied that the applicant and the assailant stopped living in the same household before the application was made and are unlikely to share the same household again.

For the purposes of this paragraph, a man and woman living together as husband and wife will be treated as members of the same family.

Consideration of applications

(18) An application for compensation under this Scheme in respect of a criminal injury ('injury' hereafter in this Scheme) must be made in writing on a form obtainable from the Authority. It should be made as soon as possible after the incident giving rise to the injury and must be received by the Authority within two years of the date of the incident. A claims officer may waive this time limit where he considers that, by reason of the particular circumstances of the case, it is reasonable and in the interests of justice to do so. **16.14**

(19) It will be for the applicant to make out his case including, where appropriate:

(a) making out his case for a waiver of the time limit in the preceding paragraph; and

(b) satisfying the claims officer dealing with his application (including an officer reviewing a decision under paragraph 60) that an award should not be reconsidered, withheld or reduced under any provision of this Scheme.

Where an applicant is represented, the costs of representation will not be met by the Authority.

(20) A claims officer may make such directions and arrangements for the conduct of an application, including the imposition of conditions, as he considers appropriate in all the circumstances. The standard of proof to be applied by a claims officer in all matters before him will be the balance of probabilities.

(21) Where a claims officer considers that an examination of the injury is required before a decision can be reached, the Authority will make arrangements for such an examination by a duly qualified medical practitioner. Reasonable expenses incurred by the applicant in that connection will be met by the Authority.

(22) A Guide to the operation of this Scheme will be published by the Authority. In addition to explaining the procedures for dealing with applications, the Guide will set out, where appropriate, the criteria by which decisions will normally be reached.

Types and limits of compensation

(23) Subject to the other provisions of this Scheme, the compensation payable under an award will be: **16.15**

(a) a standard amount of compensation determined by reference to the nature of the injury in accordance with paragraphs 26–29;

(b) where the applicant has lost earnings or earning capacity for longer than 28 weeks as a direct consequence of the injury (other than injury leading to his death), an additional amount in respect of such loss of earnings, calculated in accordance with paragraphs 30–34;

(c) where the applicant has lost earnings or earning capacity for longer than 28 weeks as a direct consequence of the injury (other than injury leading to his death) or, if not normally employed, is incapacitated to a similar extent, an additional amount in respect of any special expenses, calculated in accordance with paragraphs 35–36;

(d) where the victim has died in consequence of the injury, the amount or amounts calculated in accordance with paragraphs 37–43;

(e) where the victim has died otherwise than in consequence of the injury, a supplementary amount calculated in accordance with paragraph 44.

(24) The maximum award that may be made (before any reduction under paragraphs 13–15 above) in respect of the same injury will not exceed £500,000. For these purposes, where the victim has died in consequence of the injury, any application made by the victim before his death and any application made by any qualifying claimant or claimants after his death will be regarded as being in respect of the same injury.

(25) The injury, or any exacerbation of a pre-existing condition, must be sufficiently serious to qualify for compensation equal at least to the minimum award under this Scheme in accordance with paragraph 26, but lesser compensation may be paid if an award is reduced under paragraphs 13, 14, or 15 of the Scheme.

Standard amount of compensation

16.16   (26) The standard amount of compensation will be the amount shown in respect of the relevant description of injury in the Tariff, which sets out:

(a) a scale of fixed levels of compensation;

(b) the level and corresponding amount of compensation for each description of injury; and

(c) qualifying notes.

Level 1 represents the minimum award under this Scheme, and Level 25 represents the maximum award for any single description of injury. Where the injury has the effect of accelerating or exacerbating a pre-existing condition, the compensation awarded will reflect only the degree of acceleration or exacerbation.

(27) Minor multiple injuries will be compensated in accordance with Note 12 to the Tariff. The standard amount of compensation for more serious but separate multiple injuries will, unless expressly provided for otherwise in the Tariff, be calculated as:

(a) the Tariff amount for the highest-rated description of injury; plus

(b) 30 per cent of the Tariff amount for the second highest-rated description of injury; plus, where there are three or more injuries.

(c) 15 per cent of the Tariff amount for the third highest-rated description of injury.

(28) Where the Authority considers that any description of injury for which no provision is made in the Tariff is sufficiently serious to qualify for at least the minimum award under this Scheme, it will, following consultation with the Panel, refer the injury to the Secretary of State. In doing so the Authority will recommend to the Secretary of State both the inclusion of that description of injury in the Tariff and also the amount of compensation for which it should qualify. Any such consultation with the Panel or reference to the Secretary of State must not refer to the circumstances of any individual application for compensation under this Scheme other than the relevant medical reports.

(29) Where an application for compensation is made in respect of an injury for which no provision is made in the Tariff and the Authority decides to refer the injury to the Secretary of State under the preceding paragraph, an interim award may be made of up to half the amount of compensation for which it is recommended that such description of injury should qualify if subsequently included in the Tariff. No part of such an interim award will be recoverable if the injury is not subsequently included in the Tariff or, if included, qualifies for less compensation than the interim award paid.

Compensation for loss of earnings

(30) Where the applicant has lost earnings or earnings capacity for longer than 28 weeks as a **16.17** direct consequence of the injury (other than injury leading to his death), no compensation in respect of loss of earnings, or earning capacity will be payable for the first 28 weeks of loss. The period of loss for which compensation may be payable will begin after 28 weeks incapacity for work and continue for such period as a claims officer may determine.

(31) For a period of loss ending before or continuing to the time the claim is assessed, the net loss of earnings or earning capacity will be calculated on the basis of:

(a) the applicant's emoluments (being any profit or gain accruing from an office or employment) at the time of the injury and what those emoluments would have, been during the period of loss; and

(b) any emoluments which have become payable to the applicant in respect of the whole or part of the period of loss, whether or not as a result of the injury; and

(c) any changes in the applicant's pension rights; and

(d) in accordance with paragraphs 45–47 (reductions to take account of other payments), any social security benefits, insurance payments and pension which have become payable to the applicant during the period of loss; and

(e) any other pension which has become payable to the applicant during the period of loss, whether or not as a result of the injury.

(32) Where, at the time the claim is assessed, a claims officer considers that the applicant is likely to suffer continuing loss of earnings and/or earning capacity, an annual rate of net loss (the multiplicand) or, where appropriate, more than one such rate will be calculated on the basis of:

(a) the current rate of net loss, calculated in accordance with the preceding paragraph; and

(b) such future rate or rates of net loss (including changes in the applicant's pension rights) as the claims officer may determine; and

(c) the claims officer's assessment of the applicant's future earning capacity; and

(d) in accordance with paragraphs 45–47 (reductions to take account of other payments), any social security benefits, insurance payments and pension which will become payable to the applicant in future; and

(e) any other pension which will become payable to the applicant in future, whether or not as a result of the injury.

The compensation payable in respect of each period of continuing loss will be a lump sum, which is the product of that multiplicand and an appropriate multiplier. When the loss does not start until a future date, the lump sum will be discounted to provide for the present value of the money. The claims officer will assess an appropriate multiplier, discount factor, or life expectancy by reference to the tables in Note 3, and may make such adjustments as he considers appropriate to take account of any factors and contingencies which appear to him to be relevant. The tables in Note 3 set out the multipliers and (where applicable) discounts and life expectancies to be applied.

(a) Table A is to be applied to various periods of future loss to allow for the accelerated receipt of compensation;

(b) Table B sets out the discount factor, by which the lump sum is to be multiplied, when the loss does not start until various periods in the future;

(c) Table C is a life expectancy table, and in the absence of other factors affecting life expectancy, the table sets out the age to be applied when assessing a multiplier based on pecuniary loss for life.

(33) Where a claims officer considers that the approach in the preceding paragraph is impracticable, the compensation payable in respect of continuing loss of earnings and/or earning capacity will be such other lump sum as he may determine.

(34) Any rate of net loss of earnings or earning capacity (before any reduction in accordance with this Scheme) which is to be taken into account in calculating any compensation payable under paragraphs 30–33 must not exceed one and a half times the gross average industrial earnings at the time of assessment according to the latest figures published by the Office for National Statistics.

Compensation for special expenses

16.18   (35) Where the applicant has lost earnings or earning capacity for longer than 28 weeks as a direct consequence of the injury (other than injury leading to his death), or, if not normally employed, is incapacitated to a similar extent, additional compensation may be payable in respect of any special expenses incurred by the applicant from the date of the injury for:
    (a) loss of or damage to property or equipment belonging to the applicant on which he relied as a physical aid, where the loss or damage was a direct consequence of the injury;
    (b) costs (other than by way of loss of earnings or earning capacity) associated with National Health Service treatment for the injury;
    (c) the cost of private health treatment for the injury, but only where a claims officer considers that, in all the circumstances, both the private treatment and its cost are reasonable;
    (d) the reasonable cost, to the extent that it falls to the applicant, of
        (i) special equipment, and/or
        (ii) adaptations to the applicant's, accommodation, and/or
        (iii) care, whether in a residential establishment or at home, which are not provided or available free of charge from the National Health Service, local authorities or any other agency, provided that a claims officer considers such expense to be necessary as a direct consequence of the injury; and
        (iv) the cost of the Court of Protection or of the curator bonis.

In the case of (d)(iii), the expense of unpaid care provided at home by a relative or friend of the victim will be compensated by having regard to the level of care required, the cost of a carer, assessing the carer's loss of earnings or earning capacity and/or additional personal and living expenses, as calculated on such basis as a claims officer considers appropriate in all the circumstances. Where the foregoing method of assessment is considered by the, claims officer not to be relevant in all the circumstances, the compensation payable will be such sum as he may determine having regard to the level of care provided.

(36) Where, at the time the claim is assessed, a claims officer is satisfied that the need for any of the special expenses mentioned in the preceding paragraph is likely to continue, he will determine the annual cost and select an appropriate multiplier in accordance with paragraph 32 (future loss of earnings), taking account of any other factors and contingencies which appear to him to be relevant.

Compensation in fatal cases

16.19   (37) Where the victim has died in consequence of the injury, no compensation other than funeral expenses will be payable for the benefit of his estate. Such expenses will, subject to the application of paragraphs 13 and 14 in relation to the actions, conduct and character of the deceased, be payable up to an amount considered reasonable by a claims officer, even where the person bearing the cost of the funeral is otherwise ineligible to claim under this Scheme.

(38) Where the victim has died since sustaining the injury, compensation may be payable, subject to paragraphs 13–15 (actions, conduct and character), to any claimant (a 'qualifying claimant') who at the time of the deceased's death was:

(a) the partner of the deceased, being only, for these purposes:

(i) a person who was living together with the deceased as husband and wife or as a same sex partner in the same household immediately before the date of death and who, unless formally married to him, had been so living throughout the two years before that date, or

(ii) a spouse or former spouse of the deceased who was financially supported by him immediately before the date of death; or

(b) a natural parent of the deceased, or a person who was not the natural parent, provided that he was accepted by the deceased as a parent of his family; or

(c) a natural child of the deceased, or a person who was not the natural child, provided that he was accepted by the deceased as a child of his family or was dependent on him.

Where the victim has died in consequence of the injury, compensation may be payable to a qualifying claimant under paragraphs 39–42 (standard amount of compensation, dependency, and loss of parent). Where the victim has died otherwise than in consequence of the injury, and before title to the award has been vested in the victim (see paragraph 50), no standard amount or other compensation will be payable to the estate or to a qualifying claimant other than under paragraph 44 (supplementary compensation).

(39) A person who was criminally responsible for the death of a victim may not be a qualifying claimant. In cases where there is only one qualifying claimant, the standard amount of compensation will be Level 13 of the Tariff, save that where a claims officer is aware of the existence of one or more other persons who would in the event of their making a claim become a qualifying claimant, the standard amount of compensation will be level 10 of the Tariff. Where there is more than one qualifying claimant, the standard amount of compensation for each claimant will be Level 10 of the Tariff. A former spouse of the deceased is not a qualifying claimant for the purposes of this paragraph.

(40) Additional compensation calculated in accordance with the following paragraph may be payable to a qualifying claimant where a claims officer is satisfied that the claimant was financially or physically dependent on the deceased. A financial dependency will not be established where the deceased's only normal income was from:

(a) United Kingdom social security benefits; or

(b) social security benefits or similar payments from the funds of other countries.

(41) The amount of compensation payable in respect of dependency will be calculated on a basis similar to paragraphs 31–34 (loss of earnings) and paragraph 35(d)(iii) (cost of care). The period of loss will begin from the date of the deceased's death and continue for such period as a claims officer may determine, with no account being taken, where the qualifying claimant was formally married to the deceased, of remarriage or prospects of remarriage. In assessing the dependency, the claims officer will take account of the qualifying claimant's income and emoluments (being any profit or gain accruing from an office, or employment), if any. Where the deceased had been living in the same household as the qualifying claimant before his death, the claims officer will, in calculating the multiplicand, make such proportional reduction as he considers appropriate to take account of the deceased's own personal and living expenses.

(42) Where a qualifying claimant was under 18 years of age at the time of the deceased's death and was dependent on him for parental services, the following additional compensation may also be payable:

(a) a payment for loss of that parent's services at an annual rate of Level 5 of the Tariff; and

(b) such other payments as a claims officer considers reasonable to meet other resultant losses.

Each of these payments will be multiplied by an appropriate multiplier selected by a claims officer in accordance with paragraph 32 (future loss of earnings), taking account of the period remaining before the qualifying claimant reaches age 18 and of any other factors and contingencies which appear to the claims officer to be relevant.

(43) Application may be made under paragraphs 37–42 (compensation in fatal cases) even where an award had been made to the victim in respect of the same injury before his death. Any such application will be subject to the conditions set out in paragraphs 56–57 for the re-opening of cases, and any compensation payable to the qualifying claimant or claimants, except payments made under paragraphs 37 and 39 (funeral expenses and standard amount of compensation), will be reduced by the amount paid to the victim. The amounts payable to the victim and the qualifying claimant or claimants will not in total exceed £500,000.

(44) Where a victim who would have qualified for additional compensation under paragraph 23(b) (loss of earnings) and/or paragraph 23(c) (special expenses) has died, otherwise than in consequence of the injury, before such compensation was awarded, supplementary compensation under this paragraph may be payable to a qualifying claimant who was financially dependent on the deceased within the terms of paragraph 40 (dependency), whether or not a relevant application was made by the victim before his death. Payment may be made in accordance with paragraph 31 in respect of the victim's loss of earnings (except for the first 28 weeks of the victim's loss of earnings and/or earning capacity) and in accordance with paragraph 35 in respect of any special expenses incurred by the victim before his death. The amounts payable to the victim and the qualifying claimant or claimants will not in total exceed £500,000.

Effect on awards of other payments

16.20
(45) All awards payable under this Scheme, except those payable under paragraphs 26, 27, 39 and 42(a) (Tariff-based amounts of compensation), will be subject to a reduction to take account of social security benefits (or other state benefits) or insurance payments made by way of compensation for the same contingency. The reduction will be applied to those categories or periods of loss or need for which additional or supplementary compensation is payable, including compensation calculated on the basis of a multiplicand or annual cost. The amount of the reduction will be the full value of any relevant payment which the applicant has received, or to which he has or may have any present or future entitlement, by way of:
   (a) United Kingdom social security benefits (or other state benefits);
   (b) social security benefits or similar payments from the funds of other countries;
   (c) payments under insurance arrangements, including, where a claim is made under paragraphs 35(c) and (d) and 36 (special expenses), insurance personally effected, paid for and maintained by the personal income of the victim or, in the case of a person under 18 years of age, by his parent. Insurance so personally effected will otherwise be disregarded.

In assessing the value of any such benefits and payments, account may be taken of any income tax liability likely to reduce their value.

(46) Where, in the opinion of a claims officer, an applicant may be or may become eligible for any of the benefits and payments mentioned in the preceding paragraph, an award may be withheld until the applicant has taken such steps as the claims officer considers reasonable to claim them.

(47) Where the victim, is alive, any compensation payable under paragraphs 30–34 (loss of earnings) will be reduced to take account of any pension accruing as a result of the injury. Where the victim has died in consequence of the injury, any compensation payable under paragraphs 40–41 (dependency) will similarly be reduced to take account of any pension payable, as a result of the victim's death, for the benefit of the applicant. Where such pensions are taxable, one half of their value will be deducted, but they will otherwise be deducted in full (where, for

example, a lump sum payment not subject to income tax is made). For the purposes of this paragraph, 'pension' means any payment payable as a result of the injury or death in pursuance of pension or any other rights connected with the victim's employment, and includes any gratuity of that kind and similar benefits payable under insurance policies paid for by the victim's employers. Pension rights accruing solely as a result of payments by the victim or a dependant will be disregarded.

(48) An award payable under this Scheme will be reduced by the full value of any payment in respect of the same injury which the applicant has received by way of:

(a) any criminal injury compensation award made under or pursuant to arrangements in force at the relevant time in Northern Ireland;

(b) any compensation award or similar payment from the funds of other countries;

(c) any award where:

(i) a civil court has made an order for the payment of damages;

(ii) a claim for damages and/or compensation has been settled on terms providing for the payment of money;

(iii) payment of compensation has been ordered by a criminal court in respect of personal injuries.

In the case of (a) or (b), the reduction will also include the full value of any payment to which the applicant has any present or future entitlement.

(49) Where a person in whose favour an award under this Scheme is made subsequently receives any other payment in respect of the same injury in any of the circumstances mentioned in the preceding paragraph, but the award made under this Scheme was not reduced accordingly, he will be required to repay the Authority in full up to the amount of the other payment.

Determination of applications, and payment of awards

(50) An application for compensation under this Scheme will be determined by a claims officer, and written notification of the decision will be sent to the applicant or his representative. **16.21** The claims officer may make such directions and arrangements, including the imposition of conditions, in connection with the acceptance, settlement or trust, payment, repayment and/or administration of an award as he considers appropriate in all the circumstances. Any such directions and arrangements, including any settlement or trust may be made having regard to the interests of the applicant (whether or not a minor or a person under an incapacity) as well as to considerations of public policy (including the desirability of providing for the return of any parts of an award which may prove to be surplus to the purposes for which they were awarded) on terms which do not exhaust the beneficial interest in the award and which provide, either expressly or by operation of law, for the balance of any trust fund to revert to the Authority. Subject to any such arrangements, including the special procedures in paragraph 52 (purchase of annuities), and to paragraphs 53–55 (reconsideration of decisions), title to an award offered will be vested in the applicant when the Authority has received notification in writing that he accepts the award.

(51) Compensation will normally be paid as a single lump sum, but one or more interim payments may be made where a claims officer considers this appropriate. Once an award has been paid to an applicant or his representative, the following paragraph does not apply.

(52) Where prior, agreement is reached between the Authority and the applicant or his representative, an award may consist in whole or in part of an annuity or annuities, purchased for the benefit of the applicant or to be held on trust for his benefit. Once that agreement is reached, the Authority will take the instructions of the applicant or his representative as to which annuity or annuities should be purchased. Any expenses incurred will be met from the award.

Reconsideration of decisions

16.22   (53) A decision made by a claims officer (other than a decision made in accordance with a direction by adjudicators on determining an appeal under paragraph 77) may be reconsidered at any time before actual payment of a final award where there is new evidence or a change in circumstances. In particular, the fact that an interim payment has been made does not preclude a claims officer from reconsidering issues of eligibility for an award.

(54) Where an applicant has already been sent written notification of the decision on his application, he will be sent written notice that the decision is to be reconsidered, and any representations which he sends to the Authority within 30 days of the date of such notice will be taken into account in reconsidering the decision. Whether or not any such representations are made, the applicant will be sent written notification of the outcome of the reconsideration, and where the original decision is not confirmed, such notification will include the revised decision.

(55) Where a decision to make an award has been made by a claims officer in accordance with a direction by adjudicators on determining an appeal under paragraph 77, but before the award has been paid the claims officer considers that there is new evidence or a change in circumstances which justifies reconsidering whether the award should be withheld or the amount of compensation reduced, the Authority will refer the case to the Panel for rehearing under paragraph 82.

Re-opening of cases

16.23   (56) A decision made by a claims officer and accepted by the applicant, or a direction by adjudicators, will normally be regarded as final, except where an appeal is reheard under paragraphs 79–82. A claims officer may, however, subsequently re-open a case where there has been such a material change in the victim's medical condition that injustice would occur if the original assessment of compensation were allowed to stand, or where he has since died in consequence of the injury.

(57) A case will not be re-opened more than two years after the date of the final decision unless the claims officer is satisfied, on the basis of evidence presented in support of the application to re-open the case, that the renewed application can be considered without a need for further extensive enquiries.

Review of decisions

16.24   (58) An applicant may seek a review of any decision under this Scheme by a claims officer:
  (a) not to waive the time limit in paragraph 18 (application for compensation) or paragraph 59 (application for review); or
  (b) not to re-open a case under paragraphs 56–57; or
  (c) to withhold an award, including such decision made on reconsideration of an award under paragraphs 53–54; or
  (d) to make an award, including a decision to make a reduced award whether or not on reconsideration of an award under paragraphs 53–54; or
  (e) to seek repayment of an award under paragraph 49.

An applicant may not, however, seek the review of any such decision where the decision was itself made on a review under paragraph 60 and either the applicant did not appeal against it or the appeal was not referred for determination on an oral hearing, or where the decision was made in accordance with a direction by adjudicators on determining an appeal under paragraph 77.

(59) An application for the review of a decision by a claims officer must be made in writing to the Authority and must be supported by reasons together with any relevant additional informa-

tion. It must be received by the Authority within 90 days of the date of the decision to be reviewed, but this time limit may, in exceptional circumstances, be waived where a claims officer more senior than the one who made the original, decision considers that:

(a) any extension requested by the applicant and received within the 90 days is based on good reasons; and

(b) it would be in the interests of justice to do so.

(60) All applications for review will be considered by a claims officer more senior than any claims officer who has previously dealt with the case. The officer conducting the review will reach his decision in accordance with the provisions of this Scheme applying to the original application, and he will not be bound by any earlier decision either as to the eligibility of the applicant for an award or as to the amount of an award. The applicant will be sent written notification of the outcome of the review, giving reasons for the review decision, and the Authority will, unless it receives notice of an appeal, ensure that a determination of the original application is made in accordance with the review decision.

Appeals against review decisions

(61) An applicant who is dissatisfied with a decision taken on a review under paragraph 60   **16.25** may appeal against the decision by giving written notice of appeal to the Panel on a form obtainable from the Authority. Such notice of appeal must be supported by reasons for the appeal together with any relevant additional material which the appellant wishes to submit, and must be received by the Panel within 90 days of the date of the review decision. The Panel will send to the Authority a copy of the notice of appeal and supporting reasons which it receives and of any other material submitted by the appellant. Where the applicant is represented for the purposes of the appeal, the costs of representation will not be met by the Authority or the Panel.

(62) A member of the staff of the Panel may, in exceptional circumstances, waive the time limit in the preceding paragraph where he considers that:

(a) any extension requested by the appellant and received within the 90 days is based on good reasons; and

(b) it would be in the interests of justice to do so.

Where, on considering a request to waive the time limit, a member of the staff of the Panel does not waive it, he will refer the request to the Chairman of the Panel or to another adjudicator nominated by the Chairman to decide requests for waiver, and a decision by the adjudicator concerned not to waive the time limit will be final. Written notification of the outcome of the waiver request will be sent to the appellant and to the Authority, giving reasons for the decision where the time limit is not waived.

(63) Where the Panel receives notice of an appeal against a review decision relating to a decision mentioned in paragraph 58(a) or (b), the appeal will be dealt with in accordance with paragraphs 66–68 (appeals concerning time limits and reopening of cases). Where the Panel receives notice of an appeal against a review decision relating to a decision mentioned in paragraph 58(c), (d) or (e), the appeal will be dealt with in accordance with paragraphs 69–71 (appeals concerning awards) and may under those provisions be referred for an oral hearing in accordance with paragraphs 72–78. The Panel may publish information in connection with individual appeals, but such information must not identify any appellant or other person appearing at an oral hearing or referred to during an appeal, or enable identification to be made of any such person without that person's consent.

(64) The standard of proof to be applied by the Panel in all matters before it will be the balance of probabilities. It will be for the appellant to make out his case including, where appropriate:

(a) making out his case for a waiver of the time limit in paragraph 61 (time limit for appeals); and

(b) satisfying the adjudicator or adjudicators responsible for determining his appeal that an award should not be reconsidered, withheld or reduced under any provision of this Scheme. Subject to paragraph 78 (determination of appeal in appellant's absence), the adjudicator or adjudicators concerned must ensure, before determining an appeal, that the appellant has had an opportunity to submit representations on any evidence or other material submitted by or on behalf of the Authority.

(65) The Panel may make such arrangements for the inspection of the injury as it considers appropriate. Reasonable expenses incurred by the appellant in that connection will be met by the Panel.

Appeals concerning time limits, and re-opening of cases

16.26 (66) The Chairman of the Panel or another adjudicator nominated by him will determine any appeal against a decision taken on a review:

(a) not to waive the time limit in paragraph 18 (application for compensation) or paragraph 59 (application for review); or

(b) not to re-open a case under paragraphs 56–57.

Where the appeal concerns a decision not to re-open a case and the application for re-opening was made more than two years after the date of the final decision, the adjudicator must be satisfied that the renewed application can be considered without a need for further extensive enquiries by the Authority.

(67) In determining an appeal under the preceding paragraph, the adjudicator will allow the appeal where he considers it appropriate to do so. Where he dismisses the appeal, his decision will be final. Written notification of the outcome of the appeal, giving reasons for the decision, will be sent to the appellant and to the Authority.

(68) Where the adjudicator allows an appeal in accordance with the preceding paragraph, he will direct the Authority:

(a) in a case where the appeal was against a decision not to waive the time limit in paragraph 18, to arrange for the application for compensation to be dealt with under this Scheme as if the time limit had been waived by a claims officer;

(b) in a case where the appeal was against a decision not to waive the time limit in paragraph 59, to conduct a review under paragraph 60;

(c) in a case where the appeal was against a decision not to re-open a case, to re-open the case under paragraphs 56–57.

Appeals concerning awards

16.27 (69) A member of the staff of the Panel may refer for an oral hearing in accordance with paragraphs 72–78 any appeal against a decision taken on a review:

(a) to withhold an award, including such decision made on reconsideration of an award under paragraphs 53–54; or

(b) to make an award, including a decision to make a reduced award whether or not on reconsideration of an award under paragraphs 53–54; or

(c) to seek repayment of an award under paragraph 49.

A request for an oral hearing in such cases may also be made by the Authority.

(70) Where a member of the staff of the Panel does not refer an appeal for an oral hearing under the preceding paragraph, he will refer it to an adjudicator. The adjudicator will refer the appeal for determination on an oral hearing in accordance with paragraphs 72–78 where, on the evidence available to him, he considers:

(a) in a case where the review decision was to withhold an award on the ground that the injury was not sufficiently serious to qualify for an award equal to at least the minimum award payable under this Scheme, that an award in accordance with this Scheme could have been made; or

(b) in any other case, that there is a dispute as to the material facts or conclusions upon which the review decision was based and that a different decision in accordance with this Scheme could have been made.

He may also refer the appeal for determination on an oral hearing in accordance with paragraphs 72–78 where he considers that the appeal cannot be determined on the basis of the material before him or that for any other reason an oral hearing would be desirable.

(71) Where an appeal is not referred under paragraphs 69 or 70 for an oral hearing, the adjudicator's dismissal of the appeal will be final and the decision taken on the review will stand. Written notification of the dismissal of the appeal, giving reasons for the decision, will be sent to the appellant and to the Authority.

Oral hearing of appeals

(72) Where an appeal is referred for determination on an oral hearing, the hearing will take **16.28** place before at least two adjudicators. Where the referral was made by an adjudicator under paragraph 70, that adjudicator will not take part in the hearing. On application by the appellant, pending determination, the Chairman or an adjudicator nominated by him may direct that an interim payment be made. Subject to the provisions of this Scheme, the procedure to be followed for any particular appeal will be a matter for the adjudicators hearing the appeal.

(73) Written notice of the date proposed for the oral hearing will normally be sent to the appellant and the Authority at least 21 days beforehand. Any documents to be submitted to the adjudicators for the purposes of the hearing by the appellant, or by or on behalf of the Authority, will be made available at the hearing, if not before, to the Authority or the appellant respectively.

(74) It will be open to the appellant to bring a friend or legal adviser to assist in presenting his case at the hearing, but the costs of representation will not be met by the Authority or the Panel. The adjudicators may, however, direct the Panel to meet reasonable expenses incurred by the appellant and any person who attends to give evidence, at the hearing.

(75) The procedure at hearings will be as informal as is consistent with the proper determination of appeals. The adjudicators will not be bound by any rules of evidence which may prevent a court from admitting any document or other matter or statement in evidence. The appellant, the claims officer presenting the appeal and the adjudicators may call witnesses to give evidence and may cross-examine them.

(76) Hearings will take place in private. The Panel may, however, subject to the consent of the appellant, give permission for the hearing to be attended by observers such as representatives of the press, radio and television. Any such permission will be subject to written undertakings being given:

(a) that the identity of the appellant and of any other persons appearing at the hearing or referred to during the appeal will be kept confidential and will not be disclosed in any account of the proceedings which is broadcast or in any way published without that person's consent; and

(b) that no material will be disclosed or in any other way published from which those identities could be discovered without the consent of the subject.

(77) Where the adjudicators adjourn the hearing, they may direct that an interim payment be made. Where the only issue remaining is the determination of the amount of compensation, the adjudicators may remit the application for final determination by one of themselves in the absence

of the appellant, but subject to the right of the appellant to have a further oral hearing if not satisfied with that determination, in which the adjudicator who made that determination will not take part. On determining the appeal, the adjudicators will, where necessary, make such direction as they think fit as to the decision to be made by a claims officer on the application for compensation, but any such direction must be in accordance with the relevant provisions of this Scheme. Where they are of the opinion that the appeal was frivolous or vexatious, the adjudicators may reduce the amount of compensation to be awarded by such amount as they consider appropriate. The appellant and the Authority will be informed of the adjudicators' determination of the appeal and the reasons for it, normally at the end of the hearing, but otherwise by written notification as soon as is practicable thereafter.

(78) Adjudicators may determine an appeal on the available evidence in the absence of an appellant when they are satisfied that:

(a) he has so requested, or agreed; or

(b) he has failed to attend a hearing and has given no reasonable excuse for his non-attendance; or

(c) he is at the time of the hearing detained in custody or in hospital and is likely to remain so for a period of at least 6 months; or

(d) he is not living in Great Britain and it would not be against the interests of justice to do so.

Rehearing of appeals

16.29   (79) Where an appeal is determined in the appellant's absence, he may apply to the Panel in writing for his appeal to be reheard, giving the reasons for his non-attendance or otherwise why it should be reheard. Any such application must be received by the Panel within 30 days of the date of notification to the appellant of the outcome of the hearing which he did not attend. The Panel will send a copy of the application to the Authority.

(80) A member of the staff of the Panel may waive the time limit in the preceding paragraph where he considers that it would be in the interests of justice to do so. Where he does not waive the time limit, he will refer the application to the Chairman of the Panel or to another adjudicator nominated by the Chairman to decide such applications, and a decision by the adjudicator concerned not to waive the time limit will be final. Written notification of the waiver decision will be sent to the appellant and to the Authority, giving reasons for the decision where the time limit is not waived.

(81) Where a member of the staff of the Panel considers that there are good reasons for an appeal determined in the appellant's absence to be reheard, he will refer it for a rehearing. Where he does not refer it for a rehearing, he will refer the application to the Chairman of the Panel or to another adjudicator nominated by the Chairman to decide such applications, and a decision by the adjudicator concerned not to rehear the appeal will be final. Written notification of the decision on the application for a rehearing will be sent to the appellant and to the Authority, giving reasons for the decision where the application is refused.

(82) Where an appeal is to be reheard, any adjudicator or adjudicators who determined the appeal originally will not take part in the rehearing, and paragraphs 64 (onus on appellant), 65 (inspection of injury), and 72–78 (oral hearings) will apply.

Implementation and transitional provisions

16.30   (83) The provisions of this Scheme come into force on 1 April 2001. All applications for compensation received by the Authority on or after 1 April 2001 will be dealt with under the terms of this Scheme, except that in relation to applications in respect of injuries incurred before that date paragraph 38 of this Scheme shall not apply, but only insofar as it applies to a same sex partner.

(84) Applications for compensation received by the Authority or by the Criminal Injuries Compensation Board ('the Board') before 1 April 2001 will continue to be dealt with according to:

(a) the provisions of the Scheme which came into operation on 1 April 1996 ('the 1996 Scheme'); or

(b) the provisions of the non-statutory Scheme which came into operation on 1 February 1990 ('the old Scheme'). This includes provisions of the earlier non-statutory schemes referred to therein, insofar as they continue to have effect immediately before 1 April 2001 by virtue of the 1996 Scheme or the provisions of any non-statutory Scheme.

The following paragraphs of this Scheme will apply in addition to or in substitution for provisions of the 1996 Scheme as specified below—

(c) Paragraph 35 (d) (iv) will apply additionally to applications otherwise failing to be considered under the 1996 Scheme.

(d) Paragraphs 50, 61–62, 72, 77, and 78–82 of this Scheme will each apply in substitution for the same numbered paragraph of the 1996 Scheme.

(85) From 1 April 2001 applications required by paragraph 84 to be dealt with according to the provisions of the old Scheme will continue to be so dealt with by the Authority, and:

(a) any decision authorised under the old Scheme to be made by a single member of the Board may be made by a single legally qualified member of the Panel appointed for the purposes of this Scheme;

(b) any decision authorised under the old Scheme to be made by at least two members of the Board may be made by at least two legally qualified members of the Panel; and

(c) any decision authorised under the old Scheme to be made by the Chairman of the Board may be made by the Chairman of the Panel or by another legally qualified adjudicator nominated by the Chairman to make such decisions. In this paragraph legally qualified member means a member who is, or has been, qualified to practise as a solicitor, or as a barrister in England and Wales, or as an advocate in Scotland.

(86) Cases which are reopened under paragraph 56 of this Scheme or any corresponding provision of any earlier scheme will be dealt with according to the terms of the scheme under which the initial application was decided.

Notes to the Scheme

(see paragraph 8)

Note 1 Definition of Great Britain   **16.31**

(a) For the purposes of paragraph 8 of this Scheme, an injury is sustained in Great Britain where it is sustained:

(i) on a British aircraft, hovercraft or ship (see Note 2); or

(ii) on, under or above an installation, in a designated area within the meaning of section 1(7) of the Continental Shelf Act 1964 or any waters within 500 metres of such an installation; or

(iii) in a lighthouse off the coast of Great Britain.

(b) For the purposes of paragraph 8 of this Scheme—

(i) an injury is sustained in Great Britain where it is sustained in that part of the Channel Tunnel system incorporated into England under section 10 of the Channel Tunnel Act 1987. However if such an injury is sustained or caused by a non-UK officer acting in the exercise of his functions under the 1993 and 1994 Orders no compensation shall be payable under this Scheme; and

(ii) any injury caused in the following circumstances shall be treated for the purposes of any application for compensation under this Scheme as if the circumstances giving rise to the claim had occurred in Great Britain—

(a) an injury sustained by a UK officer acting, in the exercise of his functions within French or Belgian territory under the provisions of the 1993 and 1994 Orders; or

(b) an injury caused by a UK officer acting in the exercise of those functions within French or Belgian territory, other than an injury to any non-UK officer acting in the exercise of his functions.

In this Note 'the 1993 and 1994 Orders' mean the Channel Tunnel (International Arrangements) Order 1993 (SI 1993/1813) and the Channel Tunnel (Miscellaneous Provisions) Order 1994 (SI 1994/1405) and 'officer' has the same meaning as in those Orders.

16.32   *Note 2 Definition of British craft*

In Note 1 above:

(a) 'British aircraft' means a British controlled aircraft within the meaning of section 92 of the Civil Aviation Act 1982 (application of criminal law to aircraft), or one of Her Majesty's aircraft;

(b) 'British hovercraft' means a British controlled hovercraft within the meaning of that section (as applied in relation to hovercraft by virtue of provision made under the Hovercraft Act 1968), or one of Her Majesty's hovercraft; and

(c) 'British ship' means one of Her Majesty's Ships or any vessel used in navigation which is owned wholly by persons of the following descriptions, namely:

(i) British citizens, or

(ii) bodies corporate incorporated under the law of some part of and having their principal place of business in, the United Kingdom, or

(iii) Scottish partnerships.

The references in this Note to Her Majesty's aircraft, hovercraft or ships are references to aircraft, hovercraft or ships which belong to, or are exclusively used in the service of Her Majesty in right of the government of the United Kingdom.

16.33   *Note 3 Multipliers and Discount Factors for assessing accelerated receipt of compensation, and life expectancy table.*

(See paragraph 32)

16.34   TABLE A

(This converts an annual loss over a period of years into a lump sum payable at the beginning of that period)

Years of loss	Multiplier	Years of loss	Multiplier
5	5	16	11
6	5.5	17	11.5
7	6	18	12
8	7	19	12.5
9	7.5	20	13
10	8	25	15
11	8.5	30	16
12	9	35	17
13	9.5	40	18
14	10	50	20
15	10.5		

TABLE B DISCOUNT FACTORS   **16.35**

Period of Years	Discount in Future	Period of years in Future	Discount
5	.80	17	.48
6	.77	18	.46
7	.74	19	.44
8	.71	20	.42
9	.68	25	.34
10	.65	30	.27
11	.62	35	.22
12	.59	40	.18
13	.57	50	.12
14	.54		
15	.52		
16	.50		

TABLE C LIFE EXPECTANCY TABLE   **16.36**

Age at date of Assessment	Age to which expected to live for purposes of calculation	
	Males	Females
0–25	80 years of age	84 years of age
26–50	81	84
51–60	81	85
61–65	82	85
66–70	83	86
71–73	84	87
74–76	85	87
77–78	86	88
79–80	87	89
81	88	89
82	88	90
83	89	90
84–85	90	91
86	91	92
87–88	92	93
89	93	94
90	94	95

CRIMINAL INJURIES COMPENSATION SCHEME

Levels of compensation   **16.37**

Level 1	£1,000
Level 2	£1,250
Level 3	£1,500
Level 4	£1,750
Level 5	£2,000
Level 6	£2,500
Level 7	£3,300
Level 8	£3,800
Level 9	£4,400
Level 10	£5,500
Level 11	£6,600
Level 12	£8,200
Level 13	£11,000
Level 14	£13,500
Level 15	£16,500

Level 16	£19,000
Level 17	£22,000
Level 18	£27,000
Level 19	£33,000
Level 20	£44,000
Level 21	£55,000
Level 22	£82,000
Level 23	£110,000
Level 24	£175,000
Level 25	£250,000

General Notes to Tariff of Injuries

16.38 *(Notes 1–3 follow paragraph 86 of the Scheme)*

4. Where the tariff compensates for an operation the award includes provision for the normal operation scarring.

5. When compensation is paid for physical injury or for any sexual offence described in the tariff, a separate award for mental injury will not be made (as the tariff award includes an element of compensation for this); save that in the case of an award for physical injury, if the compensation for mental injury is the same as, or higher than, the level of compensation for the physical injury, the applicant will be entitled to awards for the separate injuries calculated in accordance with paragraph 27 of the Scheme (the serious multiple injury formula). When compensation is paid for any sexual offence, a separate award for mental injury will not be made.

TARIFF OF INJURIES

16.39
General	page 332
Head and neck	page 335
Upper limbs	page 339
Torso	page 343
Lower limbs	page 344

Description of Injury	Level	Standard Amount £

GENERAL

16.40
Fatal injury		
One qualifying claimant	13	11,000
Each qualifying claimant if more than one	10	5,500
Burns		
Note 6. For other burn injuries see under individual parts of the body		
Affecting multiple areas of body covering over 25% of skin area, with significant scarring	19	33,000
Infection with HIV/AIDS		
Note 7. Not subject to the multiple injuries formula and may be paid in addition to other awards		
Infection with HIV/AIDS	17	22,000
Loss of foetus	10	5,500
Major paralysis		
Hemiplegia (paralysis of one side of the body)	21	55,000
Paraplegia (paralysis of the lower limbs)	24	175,000
Quadriplegia/tetraplegia (paralysis of all four limbs)	25	250,000
Medically recognised illness/condition—not mental illness		
Moderately disabling disorder where the symptoms and disability persist for more than 6 weeks from the incident/date of onset		

— lasting 6 to 13 weeks	1	1,000
— lasting up to 28 weeks	5	2,000
— lasting over 28 weeks		
— not permanent	7	3,300
— permanent	12	8,200
Seriously disabling disorder where the symptoms and disability persist for more than 6 weeks from the incident/date of onset		
— lasting 6 to 13 weeks	5	2,000
— lasting up to 28 weeks	9	4,400
— lasting over 28 weeks		
— not permanent	12	8,200
— permanent	17	22,000

Mental illness and temporary mental anxiety   **16.41**

Notes:

8. *Mental illness includes conditions attributed to post-traumatic stress disorder, depression and similar generic terms within which there may be:*

(a) *such psychological symptoms as anxiety, tension, insomnia, irritability, loss of confidence, agoraphobia and preoccupation with thoughts of guilt or self-harm; and*

(b) *related physical symptoms such as alopecia, asthma, eczema, enuresis and psoriasis.*

9. *'Medically verified' means that the mental anxiety has been diagnosed by a registered medical practitioner.*

10. *'Psychiatric diagnosis/prognosis' means that the disabling mental illness has been diagnosed or the prognosis made by a psychiatrist or clinical psychologist.*

11. *A mental illness is disabling if it significantly impairs a person's functioning in some important aspect of her/his life e.g. impaired work or school performance or significant adverse effects on social relationships or sexual dysfunction.*

Disabling but temporary mental anxiety lasting more than 6 weeks, medically verified	1	1,000
Disabling mental illness, confirmed by psychiatric diagnosis:		
— lasting up to 28 weeks	6	2,500
— lasting over 28 weeks to 2 years	9	4,400
— lasting 2 years to 5 years	12	8,200
— lasting over 5 years but not permanent	14	13,500
Permanent mental illness, confirmed by psychiatric prognosis:		
— moderately disabling	16	19,000
— seriously disabling	18	27,000

Minor injuries: multiple   **16.42**

Note 12: Minor multiple physical injuries will qualify for compensation only where the applicant has sustained at least 3 separate physical injuries of the type illustrated below, at least one of which must still have had significant residual effects 6 weeks after the incident. The injuries must also have necessitated at least 2 visits to or by a medical practitioner within that 6-week period. Examples of qualifying injuries are:

(a) *grazing, cuts, lacerations (no permanent scarring)*

(b) *severe and widespread bruising*

(c) *severe soft tissue injury (no permanent disability)*

(d) *black eye(s)*

(e) *bloody nose*

(f) *hair pulled from scalp*

(g) *loss of fingernail*

Minor injuries: multiple	1	1,000

Peripheral sensory nerve damage
  — lasting more than 13 weeks

— substantial recovery expected	3	1,500

  — permanent disability

— minor loss	3	1,500
— significant loss (e.g. loss of sensation in large area of leg)	7	3,300
— serious loss (e.g. loss of sensation of hand)	12	8,200

16.43 *Physical abuse of adults*

Note 13: In the case of adult applicants where there has been a series of assaults (sexual and/or physical) over a period of time, it may be that an applicant will qualify for compensation only for the single most recent incident, if in relation to the earlier incidents she/he failed to report them to the police without delay and/or failed to co-operate with the police in bringing the assailant to justice. Where the applicant is entitled to compensation for the series of assaults, she/he will qualify for an award as the victim of a pattern of abuse, rather than for a separate award for each incident.

Serious abuse
  — intermittent physical assaults resulting in an accumulation of healed

wounds, burns or scalds, but with no appreciable disfigurement	5	2,000

Severe abuse

— pattern of repetitive violence resulting in minor disfigurement	10	5,500
Persistent pattern of severe abuse over a period exceeding 3 years	12	8,200

16.44 *Physical abuse of children*
Minor abuse
  — isolated or intermittent assault(s) resulting in weals, hair pulled from

scalp etc.	1	1,000

Serious abuse
  — intermittent physical assaults resulting in an accumulation of healed

wounds, burns or scalds, but with no appreciable disfigurement	5	2,000

Severe abuse
  — persistent pattern of repetitive violence resulting in:
    — moderate multiple injuries (e.g. bruising and minor fractures)

and/or minor disfigurement	10	5,500
— significant multiple injuries	12	8,200
— severe multiple injuries	14	13,500

16.45 *Sexual assault/abuse of victims any age (if not already compensated as a child)*

Note 14: Note 13 (under Physical Abuse of Adults) applies here too.
Indecent assault

— minor—non-penetrative indecent physical act/or acts over clothing	1	1,000
— serious—non-penetrative indecent act/or acts under clothing	5	2,000
— severe—non-penile penetrative and/or oral-genital act or acts	7	3,300

  — pattern of repetitive frequent severe abuse over a period

— up to 3 years	11	6,600
— exceeding 3 years	12	8,200
— resulting in serious internal bodily injuries	17	22,000

Non-consensual vaginal and/or anal intercourse

— by one attacker	13	11,000
— by two or more attackers	14	13,500
— resulting in serious internal bodily injuries	17	22,000

  — resulting in permanently disabling mental illness confirmed by

psychiatric prognosis	18	27,000

  — resulting in serious internal bodily injury with permanent disabling

mental illness confirmed by psychiatric prognosis	19	33,000

— pattern of repeated incidents over a period

— up to 3 years	15	16,500
— exceeding 3 years	17	22,000

Sexual assault/abuse of children (under age of 18 at time or commencement of abuse) and of adults who by reason of mental incapacity are incapable of giving consent **16.46**

Indecent assault

— minor—non penetrative indecent physical act/or acts over clothing	1	1,000
— minor—non penetrative frequent assaults over clothing	3	1,500
— serious—non penetrative indecent act under clothing	5	2,000
— serious—pattern of repetitive indecent acts under clothing	7	3,300

Indecent assault

   — non-penile penetrative and/or oral genital acts

— one incident	7	3,300
— two or more isolated incidents	9	4,400

   — pattern of repetitive, frequent incidents

— over a period up to 3 years	11	6,600
— over a period exceeding 3 years	12	8,200
— resulting in serious internal bodily injuries	17	22,000

Non-consensual vaginal and/or anal intercourse

— one incident	13	11,000
— one incident involving two or more attackers	14	13,500

   — repeated incidents, over a period

— up to 3 years	15	16,500
— exceeding 3 years	17	22,000
— resulting in serious internal bodily injuries	17	22,000
— resulting in permanently disabling mental illness confirmed by psychiatric prognosis	18	27,000
— resulting in serious internal bodily injury with permanent disabling mental illness confirmed by psychiatric prognosis	19	33,000

Sexual assault/abuse—additional awards where the following are directly attributable to sexual assault (whether of an adult or a child)—not subject to the multiple injuries formula & may be paid in addition to other awards **16.47**

Pregnancy	10	5,500

Sexually transmitted disease other than HIV/AIDS

— substantial recovery	10	5,500
— permanent disability	13	11,000
Infection with HIV/AIDS	17	22,000

HEAD & NECK

Burns **16.48**

Head

— minor visible disfigurement	5	2,000
— moderate	9	4,400
— severe	15	16,500

Face

— minor disfigurement	5	2,000
— moderate	10	5,500
— severe	18	27,000

Neck

— minor disfigurement	3	1,500
— moderate	9	4,400
— severe	15	16,500

16.49 *Scarring*

Head

— minor visible disfigurement	3	1,500
— significant disfigurement	7	3,300
— serious disfigurement	10	5,500

Face

— minor disfigurement	3	1,500
— significant disfigurement	9	4,400
— serious disfigurement	13	11,000

Neck

— minor disfigurement	3	1,500
— significant disfigurement	7	3,300
— serious disfigurement	11	6,600

16.49a *Brain*

Balance impaired

— lasting 6 to 28 weeks	3	1,500
— lasting over 28 weeks—recovery expected	7	3,300
— permanent	12	8,200

Brain haemorrhage/stroke

— substantial recovery	9	4,400

Brain damage—impairment of social/intellectual functions

— minor	12	8,200
— moderate	15	16,500
— serious	20	44,000
— very serious	23	110,000
— extremely serious (no effective control of functions)	25	250,000

Concussion

— lasting at least one week	3	1,500

Epilepsy

— post-traumatic epileptic fits—substantial recovery	5	2,000
— fully controlled	12	8,200
— partially controlled	14	13,500
— uncontrolled	20	44,000

Subdural or extradural haematoma

— treated conservatively	9	4,400
— requiring evacuation	12	8,200

16.50 *Ear*

Fractured mastoid	1	1,000

Deafness

— temporary partial deafness		
— lasting 6 to 13 weeks	1	1,000
— lasting more than 13 weeks	3	1,500
— partial deafness (remaining hearing socially useful, with hearing aid if necessary)		
— one ear	8	3,800
— both ears	12	8,200
— total deafness		
— one ear	15	16,500
— both ears	20	44,000

Loss of ear

— partial loss of ear(s)	9	4,400
— loss of ear	13	11,000
— loss of both ears	16	19,000

Perforated ear drum

— one ear	4	1,750
— both ears	6	2,500

Tinnitus (ringing noise in ear(s))

— lasting 6 to 13 weeks	1	1,000
— lasting more than 13 weeks	7	3,300
— permanent		
— other than very severe	12	8,200
— very severe	15	16,500

Vestibular damage (causing giddiness)

— lasting 6 to 28 weeks	3	1,500
— lasting over 28 weeks—recovery expected	7	3,300
— permanent	12	8,200

Eye   **16.51**

Blow out or other fracture of orbital bone cavity containing eyeball

— no operation	7	3,300
— requiring operation	9	4,400

Blurred or double vision

— temporary		
— lasting 6 to 13 weeks	1	1,000
— lasting more than 13 weeks—recovery expected	4	1,750
— permanent		
— slight	9	4,400
— moderate	12	8,200
— serious	14	13,500

Cataracts

— one eye		
— requiring operation	7	3,300
— permanent/inoperable	12	8,200
— both eyes		
— requiring operation	12	8,200
— permanent/inoperable	16	19,000

Corneal abrasions	5	2,000

Degeneration of optic nerve

— one eye	5	2,000
— both eyes	10	5,500

Dislocation of lens

— one eye	10	5,500
— both eyes	14	13,500

Glaucoma	6	2,500

Hyphaema requiring operation

— one eye	3	1,500
— both eyes	6	2,500

Loss of eye

— one eye	18	27,000
— both eyes	23	110,000

Loss of sight

— one eye	17	22,000
— both eyes	23	110,000

Partial loss of vision

— 6/12	11	6,600
— 6/18	12	8,200
— 6/24	14	13,500
— 6/36	15	16,500
— 6/60	16	19,000
substantial loss of vision (both eyes) at least 6/36 in each eye or worse	21	55,000
Residual central floater(s) affecting vision	7	3,300

Retina
  — damage not involving detachment

— one eye	6	2,500
— both eyes	10	5,500

  — detached

— one eye	10	5,500
— both eyes	14	13,500

Significant penetrating injury

— one eye	6	2,500
— both eyes	11	6,600
Traumatic angle recession	6	2,500

16.52 *Face*

Clicking jaw
  — temporary

— lasting 6 to 13 weeks	1	1,000
— lasting more than 13 weeks	3	1,500
— permanent	10	5,500

Dislocated jaw

— substantial recovery	5	2,000
— continuing significant disability	10	5,500

Fractured ethmoid

— no operation	5	2,000
— operation required	9	4,400

Fractured zygoma (malar/cheek bone)
  — no operation

— substantial recovery	5	2,000
— continuing significant disability	9	4,400

  — operation required

— substantial recovery	6	2,500
— continuing significant disability	10	5,500

Fractured mandible and/or maxilla (jaw bones)
  — no operation

— substantial recovery	7	3,300
— continuing significant disability	10	5,500

  — operation required

— substantial recovery	8	3,800
— continuing significant disability	12	8,200
Multiple fractures to face (e.g. Le Fort fractures types 2 & 3)	13	11,000

Numbness/loss of feeling

— temporary lasting more than 13 weeks—recovery expected	3	1,500

  — permanent

— moderate e.g. cheek, forehead	7	3,300
— severe e.g. lip interfering with function	9	4,400

16.53 *Neck*

Fractured hyoid (bone in windpipe)	1	1,000

Strained neck or whiplash injury
  — disabling

— for 6 to 13 weeks	1	1,000
— for more than 13 weeks	6	2,500

  — seriously disabling

— not permanent	10	5,500
— permanent	13	11,000

Nose		**16.54**
Deviated nasal septum		
— no operation	1	1,000
— requiring septoplasty	5	2,000
Fracture of nasal bones		
— undisplaced	1	1,000
— displaced	3	1,500
— requiring manipulation	5	2,000
— requiring rhinoplasty	5	2,000
— requiring turbinectomy	5	2,000
Loss of smell/taste		
— partial loss of smell and/or taste	10	5,500
— total		
— loss of smell or taste	13	11,000
— loss of smell and taste	15	16,500
Partial loss of nose (at least 10%)	9	4,400
Skull		**16.55**
Fracture		
— simple		
— no operation	6	2,500
— depressed		
— no operation	9	4,400
— requiring operation	11	6,600
Teeth		**16.56**
Damage to:		
— tooth/teeth requiring root-canal treatment	2	1,250
— front tooth/teeth requiring crown(s)	3	1,500
Fractured/chipped tooth/teeth requiring treatment	2	1,250
Fractured tooth/teeth requiring apicectomy (surgery to gum to reach root—root resection)	6	2,500
Loss of:		
— crowns	3	1,500
— front tooth/teeth (incisor or canine)		
— one front tooth	4	1,750
— two or three front teeth	6	2,500
— four or more front teeth	8	3,800
— tooth/teeth other than front		
— one tooth	2	1,250
— two or more teeth	4	1,750
Slackening of teeth requiring dental treatment	2	1,250
Tongue		**16.57**
Impaired speech		
— slight	5	2,000
— moderate	10	5,500
— serious	13	11,000
— severe	16	19,000
Loss of speech—permanent	19	33,000
Loss of tongue	20	44,000

UPPER LIMBS

Burns		**16.58**
Minor	3	1,500
Moderate	9	4,400
Severe	13	11,000

16.59 *Scarring*

Minor disfigurement	2	1,250
Significant disfigurement	6	2,500
Serious disfigurement	10	5,500

16.60 *Arm*

Loss of:

— one arm	20	44,000
— both arms	23	110,000

Paralysis of or equivalent loss of function of:

— one arm	19	33,000
— both arms	22	82,000

16.61 *Elbow*

Dislocated/fractured

— one elbow

— substantial recovery	7	3,300
— continuing significant disability	12	8,200

— both elbows

— substantial recovery	12	8,200
— continuing significant disability	13	11,000

16.62 *Finger and Thumb*

Fracture/dislocation of:

— thumb

— one hand

— substantial recovery	5	2,000
— continuing significant disability	9	4,400

— both hands

— substantial recovery	10	5,500
— continuing significant disability	12	8,200

— index finger

— one hand

— substantial recovery	4	1,750
— continuing significant disability	8	3,800

— both hands

— substantial recovery	9	4,400
— continuing significant disability	11	6,600

— one finger other than index finger

— one hand

— substantial recovery	1	1,000
— continuing significant disability	5	2,000

— both hands

— substantial recovery	4	1,750
— continuing significant disability	9	4,400

— two or more fingers other than index finger

— one hand

— substantial recovery	2	1,250
— continuing significant disability	6	2,500

— both hands

— substantial recovery	7	3,300
— continuing significant disability	11	6,600

Loss of:

— finger other than index finger	10	5,500
— two or more fingers	13	11,000
— index finger	12	8,200
— both index fingers	15	16,500

— thumb	15	16,500
— both thumbs	19	33,000
Partial loss of:		
— finger other than thumb or index finger	6	2,500
— two or more fingers other than index finger or thumb	10	5,500
— thumb or index finger	9	4,400
— thumb or index finger—both hands	12	8,200
— thumb and index finger—one hand	12	8,200
— thumb and index finger—both hands	15	16,500

Hand   **16.63**

Fractured hand		
— one hand		
— substantial recovery	5	2,000
— continuing significant disability	10	5,500
— both hands		
— substantial recovery	8	3,800
— continuing significant disability	12	8,200
Loss of, or equivalent loss of function of:		
— one hand	20	44,000
— both hands	23	110,000
Permanently & seriously impaired grip		
— one hand	12	8,200
— both hands	15	16,500

Humerus (upper arm bone)   **16.64**

Fractured		
— one arm		
— substantial recovery	7	3,300
— continuing significant disability	10	5,500
— both arms		
— substantial recovery	12	8,200
— continuing significant disability	13	11,000

Radius (a forearm bone)   **16.65**

Fractured		
— one arm		
— substantial recovery	7	3,300
— continuing significant disability	10	5,500
— both arms		
— substantial recovery	12	8,200
— continuing significant disability	13	11,000

Shoulder   **16.66**

Dislocated		
— one shoulder		
— substantial recovery	4	1,750
— continuing significant disability	10	5,500
— both shoulders		
— substantial recovery	8	3,800
— continuing significant disability	12	8,200
Frozen		
— one shoulder		
— substantial recovery	5	2,000
— continuing significant disability	10	5,500
— both shoulders		

— substantial recovery	7	3,300
— continuing significant disability	12	8,200

16.67 *Tendon & Ligament*
Minor damage
— one arm

— substantial recovery	1	1,000
— continuing significant disability	6	2,500

— both arms

— substantial recovery	5	2,000
— continuing significant disability	9	4,400

Moderate damage
— one arm

— substantial recovery	5	2,000
— continuing significant disability	9	4,400

— both arms

— substantial recovery	9	4,400
— continuing significant disability	12	8,200

Severely damaged
— one arm

— substantial recovery	7	3,300
— continuing significant disability	10	5,500

— both arms

— substantial recovery	11	6,600
— continuing significant disability	13	11,000

16.68 *Ulna (a forearm bone)*
Fractured
— one arm

— substantial recovery	7	3,300
— continuing significant disability	10	5,500

— both arms

— substantial recovery	12	8,200
— continuing significant disability	13	11,000

16.69 *Wrist*
Fractured—colles type
— one wrist

— substantial recovery	9	4,400
— continuing significant disability	12	8,200

— both wrists

— substantial recovery	12	8,200
— continuing significant disability	13	11,000

Fractured/dislocated—including scaphoid fracture
— one wrist

— substantial recovery	7	3,300
— continuing significant disability	11	6,600

— both wrists

— substantial recovery	11	6,600
— continuing significant disability	13	11,000

Sprained
— one wrist

— disabling for 6 to 13 weeks	1	1,000
— disabling for more than 13 weeks	6	2,500

— both wrists

— disabling for 6 to 13 weeks	5	2,000
— disabling for more than 13 weeks	8	3,800

TORSO

Burns			**16.70**
Minor	3	1,500	
Moderate	9	4,400	
Severe	13	11,000	
Scarring			**16.71**
Minor disfigurement	2	1,250	
Significant disfigurement	6	2,500	
Serious disfigurement	10	5,500	
Abdomen			**16.72**
Injury requiring laparotomy	8	3,800	
— including removal or repair of multiple organs	17	22,000	
Back			**16.73**
Fracture of vertebra			
— one vertebra			
— substantial recovery	6	2,500	
— continuing significant disability	10	5,500	
— more than one vertebra			
— substantial recovery	9	4,400	
— continuing significant disability	12	8,200	
Prolapsed invertebral disc(s)			
— seriously disabling			
— not permanent	10	5,500	
— permanent	12	8,200	
Ruptured invertebral disc(s)—requiring surgical removal	13	11,000	
Strained			
— disabling			
— for 6 to 13 weeks	1	1,000	
— for more than 13 weeks	6	2,500	
— seriously disabling			
— not permanent	10	5,500	
— permanent	13	11,000	
Chest			**16.74**
Injury requiring thoracotomy	12	8,200	
Clavicle (collar bone)			**16.75**
Dislocated acromioclavicular joint	5	2,000	
Fractured			
— one clavicle			
— substantial recovery	5	2,000	
— continuing significant disability	9	4,400	
— two clavicles			
— substantial recovery	9	4,400	
— continuing significant disability	11	6,600	
Coccyx (tail bone)			**16.76**
Fractured	6	2,500	
Genitalia			**16.77**
Injury requiring medical treatment			
— no significant permanent damage	4	1,750	
— permanent damage			

	— moderate	10	5,500
	— severe	13	11,000
	Loss of fertility	21	55,000

16.78 *Hernia*

	— hernia	8	3,800
	— hernias	10	5,500

16.79 *Kidney*

	Loss of kidney	17	22,000
	Serious and permanent damage to or loss of both kidneys	21	55,000

16.80 *Lung*

Punctured

	— one lung	7	3,300
	— two lungs	11	6,600

Collapsed

	— one lung	8	3,800
	— two lungs	12	8,200
	Permanent and disabling damage to lungs from smoke or chemical inhalation	10	5,500

16.81 *Pelvis*

Fractured

	— substantial recovery	9	4,400
	— continuing significant disability	13	11,000

16.82 *Rib*

Fractured (or bruised where significant pain lasts more than 6 weeks)

	— one rib	1	1,000
	— two or more	3	1,500

16.83 *Scapula (shoulder blade)*

Fractured

	— one scapula		
	— substantial recovery	6	2,500
	— continuing significant disability	9	4,400
	— two scapulas		
	— substantial recovery	9	4,400
	— continuing significant disability	11	6,600

16.84 *Spleen*

	Loss of spleen	9	4,400

16.85 *Sternum (breast bone)*

Fractured

	— substantial recovery	6	2,500
	— continuing significant disability	10	5,500

LOWER LIMBS

16.86 *Burns*

	Minor	3	1,500
	Moderate	9	4,400
	Severe	13	11,000

16.87 *Scarring*

	Minor disfigurement	2	1,250

Significant disfigurement	6	2,500
Serious disfigurement	10	5,500

Ankle   **16.88**
Fractured or Dislocated
  — one ankle

— substantial recovery	9	4,400
— continuing significant disability	13	11,000

  — both ankles

— substantial recovery	12	8,200
— continuing significant disability	15	16,500

Sprained
  — one ankle

— disabling for at least 6 to 13 weeks	1	1,000
— disabling for more than 13 weeks	6	2,500

  — both ankles

— disabling for at least 6 to 13 weeks	5	2,000
— disabling for more than 13 weeks	8	3,800

Femur (thigh bone)   **16.89**
Fractured
  — one leg

— substantial recovery	8	3,800
— continuing significant disability	11	6,600

  — both legs

— substantial recovery	10	5,500
— continuing significant disability	13	11,000

Fibula (slender bone from knee to ankle)   **16.90**
Fractured
  — one leg

— substantial recovery	6	2,500
— continuing significant disability	8	3,800

  — both legs

— substantial recovery	7	3,300
— continuing significant disability	10	5,500

Foot   **16.91**
Fractured metatarsal bones
  — one foot

— substantial recovery	6	2,500
— continuing significant disability	8	3,800

  — both feet

— substantial recovery	7	3,300
— continuing significant disability	10	5,500

Fractured tarsal bones
  — one foot

— substantial recovery	7	3,300
— continuing significant disability	12	8,200

  — both feet

— substantial recovery	10	5,500
— continuing significant disability	14	13,500

Heel   **16.92**
Fractured heel bone
  — one foot

— substantial recovery	7	3,300
— continuing significant disability	12	8,200

— both feet		
— substantial recovery	10	5,500
— continuing significant disability	14	13,500

16.93   *Hip*
Fractured/Dislocated

— one hip		
— substantial recovery	9	4,400
— continuing significant disability	13	11,000
— both hips		
— substantial recovery	12	8,200
— continuing significant disability	15	16,500

16.94   *Knee*

Arthroscopy (investigative surgery/repair to knee)—no fracture	5	2,000
Patella (knee cap)		
— dislocated		
— one knee		
— substantial recovery	1	1,000
— continuing significant disability	10	5,500
— both knees		
— substantial recovery	6	2,500
— continuing significant disability	12	8,200
— fractured		
— one knee		
— substantial recovery	6	2,500
— continuing significant disability	10	5,500
— both knees		
— substantial recovery	9	4,400
— continuing significant disability	12	8,200
— removal of:		
— one knee	8	3,800
— both knees	10	5,500

16.95   *Leg*
Loss of:

— one leg		
— below knee	19	33,000
— above knee	20	44,000
— both legs	23	110,000
Paralysis of leg	18	27,000

(see also major paralysis (paraplegia))

16.96   *Tendon & Ligament*
Minor damage

— one leg		
— substantial recovery	1	1,000
— continuing significant disability	7	3,300
— both legs		
— substantial recovery	5	2,000
— continuing significant disability	10	5,500
Moderate damage		
— one leg		
— substantial recovery	5	2,000
— continuing significant disability	10	5,500

— both legs		
— substantial recovery	9	4,400
— continuing significant disability	13	11,000
Severe damage		
— one leg		
— substantial recovery	7	3,300
— continuing significant disability	12	8,200
— both legs		
— substantial recovery	11	6,600
— continuing significant disability	15	16,500

Tibia (shin bone)   **16.97**

Fractured		
— one leg		
— substantial recovery	8	3,800
— continuing significant disability	11	6,600
— both legs		
— substantial recovery	10	5,500
— continuing significant disability	13	11,000

Toe   **16.98**

Fractured		
— great toe		
— one foot		
— substantial recovery	6	2,500
— continuing significant disability	12	8,200
— both feet		
— substantial recovery	8	3,800
— continuing significant disability	14	13,500
— two or more toes		
— one foot		
— substantial recovery	1	1,000
— continuing significant disability	6	2,500
— both feet		
— substantial recovery	3	1,500
— continuing significant disability	9	4,400
Loss of:		
— great toe	12	8,200
— both great toes	14	13,500
— one toe (other than great toe)	1	1,000
— two or more toes	9	4,400
Partial loss of:		
— great toe	6	2,500
— both great toes	10	5,500

17

PSYCHIATRIC INJURY

The development of the law on recovery of compensation for psychiatric injury **17.01** has been a gradual increase in the willingness of the courts to overcome a historical suspicion of psychiatry and to recognize and take seriously the merits of such claims. The current state of the law owes much to litigation arising out of the Hillsborough disaster on 15 April 1995 when the police allowed far too many spectators into the football ground resulting in severe crushing of the crowd of supporters—95 people were killed and hundreds more were injured.

A. Recognized Psychiatric Illness

The normal human emotions of grief, distress, anger, and unhappiness lie out- **17.02** side the scope of common law compensation. It is true that an award of damages for pain and suffering and loss of amenity will include an element for the unhappiness of undergoing the consequences of an injury, and it is true that there are some anomalous awards in special situations such as the statutory award for bereavement in a fatal accident claim, and the award for suffering an unintended pregnancy in *Rees v Darlington Hospital* [2003] UKHL 52; [2004] 1 AC 309. But in a claim for psychiatric injury, the claimant must prove the presence of a recognized psychiatric illness in order to be entitled to compensation. The distinction is generally made by assessing whether the claimant has a diagnosis of psychiatric illness according to one of the diagnostic manuals, either DSM IV (the manual of the American Association of Psychiatrists) or ICD 10 (of the World Health Organization). The diagnostic criteria of DSM

IV for post-traumatic stress disorder and acute stress disorder are set out at c.47 above.

17.03 *McLoughlin v O'Brien* [1983] 1 AC 410   The successful claimant was not present at a road accident involving her husband and children, but learned of the accident and visited the hospital two hours later to discover that one child had been killed and the others injured. This was considered sufficiently close, as the aftermath of the accident, to give rise to a claim. Lord Bridge said at 431:

> The common law gives no damages for emotional distress which any normal person experiences when someone he loves is killed or injured. Anxiety and depression are normal human emotions. Yet an anxiety neurosis or a reactive depression may be recognisable psychiatric illnesses, with or without psycho-somatic symptoms. So the first hurdle which a claimant claiming damages of the kind in question must surmount is to establish that he is suffering not merely grief, distress or any other normal emotion, but a positive psychiatric illness.

17.04 *Hicks v Chief Constable of South Yorkshire Police* [1992] 2 All ER 65   The claims were brought by the administrators of the estates of Hillsborough victims who died of traumatic asphyxia which caused loss of consciousness within seconds and death within five minutes. It was held that the victims' fear, however serious, of imminent death and from involvement in the disaster was a normal human emotion for which no damages could be recovered.

B. Primary and Secondary Victims

17.05 The distinction between primary and secondary victims has become an import-ant means by which the courts limit the scope of those who are entitled to bring a claim for pure psychiatric injury. A primary victim is someone who is immedi-ately involved in the wrongful event because he is physically injured, or is within the range of foreseeable physical injury, or reasonably believes that he is at risk. A primary victim can bring a claim for psychiatric injury on ordinary principles of negligence without having to satisfy any special restrictive criteria. A secondary victim is a bystander, someone to whom a duty of care is owed but whose psychiatric injury is suffered as a result of witnessing injury caused to others. For reasons of policy there are significant restrictions on the scope of bystanders who are entitled to bring a claim.

17.06 *Bourhill v Young* [1943] AC 92   The claimant heard the noise of a road accident, which happened about 50 feet away from her, and saw the blood of an injured motorcyclist on the road. She claimed for injury caused by the shock that she suffered as a result of the accident, but her claim failed because she was not within the area of potential physical danger.

Alcock v Chief Constable of South Yorkshire Police [1992] 1 AC 310   In claims   **17.07**
arising out of the Hillsborough disaster, claims for psychiatric injury were
brought by friends and relations of spectators who had been involved, who
witnessed the disaster, or saw it on live television, or heard about it later.
Holding that presence at the stadium was not a sufficient basis of proximity to
give a claim, and that viewing the disaster on television was not equivalent to
being present, the House of Lords held that secondary victims must show not
only that injury was reasonably foreseeable, but also that strict conditions of
closeness (in legal jargon, proximity) are satisfied: closeness of relationship with
a person physically injured in the event, and closeness in time and space to an
accidental event of a character that would distress a person of normal fortitude,
or its immediate aftermath.

C. Claims by Primary Victims

A person who has been directly involved in an incident giving rise to physical   **17.08**
injury, or to the risk of physical injury, is a primary victim who will be entitled
to recover compensation for any psychiatric injury that is caused by the incident. A psychiatric illness may often accompany physical injuries if the claimant
becomes depressed or anxious as a result of the accident. The involvement of the
claimant in a traumatic event may give rise to an adjustment disorder or a posttraumatic stress disorder. There is no legal difficulty about the recovery of full
compensation for such injuries, and there are no technical issues of proximity to
worry about. As *Page v Smith* below shows, it is not necessary for a primary
victim to suffer any physical injury. If he was physically so close to an event such
as a road accident as to be at risk of physical injury, that is sufficient to make
him a primary victim and to support a claim for psychiatric injury.

Page v Smith [1996] AC 105   The claimant might well have been physically   **17.09**
injured in a road accident but in fact escaped without physical injury. The shock
of the accident caused a recurrence of chronic fatigue syndrome. The House of
Lords held that he was a primary victim and could recover even though this
injury was not reasonably foreseeable, because some physical injury had been
foreseeable. Although this was not strictly a case of pure psychiatric injury, it
was a case of injury as a result of shock rather than by direct physical force. This
is an important decision, extending to psychiatric injury the principle that a
wrongdoer is liable for all the actual consequences of his act, however severe, if
some injury is foreseeable.

Attia v British Gas [1988] QB 304   Psychiatric illness followed the destruction   **17.10**
of the claimant's home by fire, without personal injury to anyone, as a result of
the negligence of engineers fitting a central heating system. On a preliminary

issue, the claimant was held to be entitled to claim if she could prove causation and reasonable foreseeability.

17.11 *Cullin v London Fire Authority* [1999] PIQR P314   The claimants were firefighters who attended incidents in which other firefighters died and the claimants were involved in searching for, or attempting to resuscitate them. The Court of Appeal refused to strike out the claims, which could only succeed on the basis that they were primary victims.

17.12 *McLoughlin v Grovers* [2001] EWCA Civ 1743; [2002] PIQR P222   The claimant alleged that he suffered psychiatric injury as a result of the negligence of his solicitors when defending him from a criminal charge. The Court of Appeal held that a contractual cause of action of this kind put the claimant broadly into the position of the primary victim of a tort.

D. Claims by Secondary Victims

17.13 The most interesting and difficult claims for psychiatric injury (often described in the older cases as nervous shock) concern the limits to be drawn as a matter of policy on the range of people who can claim compensation for psychiatric illness suffered as a result of witnessing injury to others. In order to succeed, a claimant who was a secondary victim must prove that:

    (a) he was a witness to the event itself or its immediate aftermath;
    (b) the nature of the event was a single traumatic incident rather than a continuing state of affairs;
    (c) the nature of the event was such that a person of normal fortitude would be likely to be affected by it; and
    (d) he had a close relationship of love and affection with a primary victim whose injuries have been the cause of the claimant's psychiatric illness.

17.14 *Hambrook v Stokes Brothers* [1925] 1 KB 141   The claimant saw an unattended lorry run down the hill towards the place where she had left her children. She was told by a bystander that a child had been injured, and indeed one of her children had suffered serious injury. The shock caused a severe haemorrhage (she was pregnant) and she died some months later. A claim by the estate for her injury was successful.

17.15 *McLoughlin v O'Brien* [1983] 1 AC 410   The successful claimant was not present at a road accident involving her husband and children, but learned of the accident and visited the hospital two hours later to discover that one child had been killed and the others injured. She suffered psychiatric injury as a result.

The involvement was considered to be sufficiently close to the accident, as part of the 'immediate aftermath' of the accident, to give rise to a claim. The Court of Appeal had rejected the claim on policy grounds even though it accepted that the injury was foreseeable.

Walters v North Glamorgan NHS Trust [2002] EWCA Civ 1792; [2003] **17.16** PIQR P232   In a claim for psychiatric injury caused by the death of the claimant's infant child as a result of clinical negligence, so that the claimant was a secondary victim, the legal requirement that injury should have been caused by a single horrifying event, derived from *McLoughlin v O'Brien* (above), was capable of applying to the events which took place over approximately 36 hours, from the onset of serious illness to the death of the child.

Alcock v Chief Constable of South Yorkshire Police [1992] 1 AC 310   In claims **17.17** arising out of the Hillsborough disaster, claims for psychiatric injury were brought by friends and relations of spectators who had been involved, who witnessed the disaster, or saw it on live television, or heard about it later. Holding that presence at the stadium was not a sufficient basis of proximity to give a claim, and that viewing disaster on television was not equivalent to being present, the House of Lords held that secondary victims must show not only that injury was reasonably foreseeable, but also that strict conditions of closeness (in legal jargon, proximity) are satisfied: closeness of relationship with a person physically injured in the event, and closeness to an accidental event, or its immediate aftermath, of a character that would distress a person of normal fortitude.

White v Chief Constable of South Yorkshire [1999] 2 AC 455   Police officers **17.18** on duty claimed for psychiatric injury arising out of the Hillsborough disaster. They were not acting in the immediate area of the deaths (claims for which were admitted) but elsewhere in and around the ground. Their claims as employees were held to be limited by the bystander principles of *Alcock* (above), and as professional rescuers it would not be fair, just or reasonable to put them on a better position than bystanders who could not claim.

E. Stress at Work

There is a detailed discussion of the legal principles which govern claims for **17.19** psychiatric illness suffered as a result of occupational stress at d.123–d.136 above. Briefly, the employer's duty of care to protect his employee from foreseeable risk of injury gives rise to a common law cause of action in negligence where the employee is treated as a primary victim once the difficulties of foreseeability and breach of duty are overcome. The application of ordinary negligence principles was established in *Walker v Northumberland County Council* [1995] 1 All ER 737. The Court of Appeal set out detailed guidelines, which have been considered generally to be rather restrictive of the scope for claims, in *Hatton v Sutherland* [2002] EWCA Civ 76; [2002] PIQR P241 (see **d.128** and **d.134** above). One of these cases, *Barber v Somerset County Council* [2004] UKHL 13; [2004] PIQR P31 was subject to an appeal to the House of Lords, where the decision unusually turned on the findings of fact rather than the legal issues: the general principles set out by the Court of Appeal were approved with the caveat that they are practical guidance without anything like statutory force.

F. Rescuers

17.20 The basic position is that the law has always looked kindly on rescuers, holding that the defendant owes a duty of care not only to those who are injured but also to those who are induced to go to the rescue of the injured. The involvement in the rescue is a sufficient involvement in the accidental event for the rescuer to be regarded as a primary victim.

17.21 *Chadwick v British Railways* [1967] 1 WLR 912   A rescuer at a railway accident who had suffered psychiatric illness succeeded in his claim for damages, even though he was not injured by fear for his own or his children's safety; but foreseeability of injury by shock was necessary in such a claim.

17.22 *McFarlane v E E Caledonia* [1994] PIQR P154   The unsuccessful claimant was on a rescue vessel which attended the Piper Alpha disaster, but he was not personally involved in the rescue work, he was not himself in danger, nor did he fear that he was. Although some of those on the rig were his friends, there was not a sufficient tie of love and affection.

17.23 *White v Chief Constable of South Yorkshire* [1999] 2 AC 455   Police officers on duty in the Hillsborough stadium away from the immediate area in which the victims died claimed to be rescuers, but the House of Lords held that, while approving *Chadwick* (above), it would not be fair, just or reasonable to put them on a better position than bystander spectators.

17.24 *Greatorex v Greatorex* [2000] 1 WLR 1970   An unsuccessful claim for post-traumatic stress disorder by a rescuer: the claimant was a firefighter who attended a road accident where his son had sustained serious injuries as a result of his own negligent driving. However, the rescuer did not expose himself to danger and no duty of care arose regarding his son's self-inflicted injuries.

G. Unfair Dismissal

Difficult issues have arisen with the recovery of compensation for stress-related **17.25** illness resulting from the manner of dismissal from employment. Potential claims are in court proceedings in negligence, and for breach of the implied contractual duty of trust and respect, or in the Employment Tribunal for compensation for unfair dismissal. At common law, *Addis v Gramophone Co.* [1909] AC 488 holds that an employee cannot recover damages in breach of contract for injured feelings, mental distress, or damage to his reputation arising out of the manner of his dismissal. In the regime providing compensation for unfair dismissal under the Employment Rights Act 1996, *Norton Tool Co. v Tewson* [1973] 1 All ER 183 decided that compensation for unfair dismissal is limited to financial losses, and does not include injury to feelings. In *Johnson v Unisys Ltd* [2001] UKHL 13; [2001] ICR 480 the House of Lords held that the statutory regime of compensation for unfair dismissal created a self-contained and exclusive code for resolving claims arising out of unfair dismissal, so that there could not be a claim in negligence at common law for a stress-related illness resulting from the manner of dismissal. However, it is very difficult to draw the line between the dismissal itself, and conduct prior to the dismissal which might be subject to a common law claim. The Court of Appeal refused to strike out a common law claim for stress-related illness arising in *McCabe v Cornwall CC* [2002] EWCA Civ 1887; [2003] IRLR 87.

Two recent decisions of the House of Lords have confirmed that compensation **17.26** for psychiatric injury suffered in circumstances which led to a dismissal should be the subject of a civil claim, rather than an award by the Employment Tribunal. In *Eastwood v Magnox Electric* [2004] UKHL 35; [2004] 3 WLR 322 the House of Lords held that the Employment Tribunal had jurisdiction in relation to the events of a dismissal itself, but if before the dismissal the claimant had acquired a cause of action for a common law claim in relation to the events that led up to a dismissal, either actual or constructive, the fact of the unfair dismissal claim did not extinguish that cause of action, which could be pursued in court. In *Dunnachie v Kingston upon Hull CC* [2004] UKHL 36; [2004] 3 WLR 210, where the Court of Appeal had suggested that the Employment Tribunal could make an award of general damages for injury to feelings caused by the effect of events leading to dismissal, the House of Lords affirmed the traditional view of *Norton Tool* that compensation for unfair dismissal under s 123(1) of the Employment Rights Act 1996 does not extend to non-economic loss such as injury to feelings.

18

CLINICAL NEGLIGENCE

Although it is ever increasing in volume, clinical negligence litigation remains a **18.01** specialist field and therefore a dangerous area for the general legal practitioner. The Law Society maintains a specialist panel of solicitors, and in practice public funding for clinical negligence claims is restricted to those holding a clinical negligence franchise. This chapter does not, therefore, purport to be a sufficient treatment of the law relating to clinical negligence claims for practitioners to use. The leading work is *Clinical Negligence* by Michael J. Powers and Nigel Harris, 3rd edn (Butterworths: London, 2000) and there is a very good practical guide written by Charles Lewis (*Clinical Negligence*, 5th edn (Butterworths: London, 2001)). Here instead is a brief outline of the key principles provided as a matter of general interest.

A. Which Defendant?

NHS treatment gives rise to claims in tort. Private treatment will give rise to an **18.02** additional cause of action in contract but there is no material difference in the grounds for liability. There may, however, be practical procedural differences. For NHS hospital treatment, the NHS Trust responsible for the hospital where treatment is provided will have both vicarious liability for the medical staff of the hospital and a non-delegable primary duty to provide appropriately careful and skilful treatment. It is usual therefore to sue the Trust rather than the individual doctors or nurses whose conduct is in question. The National Health Service Litigation Authority deals with the defence of claims thereafter, but is not the formal defendant. In the case of private treatment however, while the individual practitioner is likely to take personal responsibility for his acts, so that a medical protection society such as the Medical Defence Union will stand behind the defendant of the claim, the institution providing care may still owe a direct duty of care to the patient and vicarious liability for nursing and ancillary staff employed.

B. Proof of Negligence

18.03   Where the cause of injury was an error of technique, no special rules need apply to the question whether a breach of duty has occurred—where an incision is made in the wrong place, or a catheter is inserted into a vein instead of an artery, familiar issues of reasonable care will determine liability. The standard is that of the reasonably competent practitioner in the relevant post or having the relevant qualifications, seniority, and specialist practice.

Such cases however are rare. More often the cause of an unsuccessful outcome is a decision about treatment made by an exercise of clinical judgment. Here the test of breach is the well-known *Bolam* test, from the judgment of McNair J in *Bolam v Friern Hospital Management Committee* [1957] 1 WLR 582:

> The test is the standard of the ordinary skilled man professing to have that special skill . . . A doctor is not guilty of negligence if he has acted in accordance with a practice accepted as proper by a responsible body of medical men skilled in that particular art . . . Putting it the other way around, a doctor is not negligent if he is acting in accordance with such a practice, merely because there is a body of opinion that takes a contrary view.

18.04   This approach was also applied to the issue of causation in *Bolitho v City and Hackney HA* [1993] PIQR P334. In *Bolitho*, there was a negligent failure by a doctor to attend the ward but the trial judge found as a fact that if the doctor had attended she would not have taken the precaution which with hindsight could be seen as the only precaution that would have availed the claimant. As a result, the claimant could not establish causation unless it were also found that the doctor would have been negligent in *Bolam* terms in failing to take the precaution, had she attended.

18.05   It sometimes feels to claimants as though the *Bolam* test must be automatically self-proving in any defended case: if the defence can call a reputable expert to say that the conduct of the defendant was within the range of acceptable practice, that must necessarily demonstrate that there is a responsible body of medical opinion taking that view. The reality is different in two respects. First, a close analysis of the facts of the case is necessary in order to discover precisely whether the defence expert is really seeking to justify the course that was followed.

Disputes may as easily be about the facts as about the scope of proper clinical treatment. Secondly, in *Bolitho*, the House of Lords left open a residual category of case in which the court might inquire whether a particular practice was logically supportable even though a responsible body of doctors might support it. However, the number of cases in which this kind of argument is truly appropriate will be few.

It is no defence that an inexperienced doctor was doing his best. The standard **18.06** of care is objective: it is the standard of the level of expertise applicable to the individual's post, so that a consultant must meet the standard of a reasonably competent consultant and a junior doctor need only meet the standard of a reasonably competent junior doctor. Thus beyond that standard, individual difficulties are no excuse, and might indeed give rise to a separate ground for complaint against the hospital that there was a failure to employ sufficiently competent and experienced staff.

C. Consent

If a surgeon carries out an invasive treatment of a patient, that constitutes a **18.07** trespass to the person if the patient has not given consent. This is the case even if the doctor acts from the highest motives. In the case of an unconscious patient or a patient mentally incapable of giving consent who is in urgent need of treatment, the doctrine of necessity makes treatment lawful: (*F v West Berkshire HA* [1990] 2 AC 1). Outside this narrow category, it is rare for treatment to be provided without consent: there is no legal necessity as far as this question is concerned to follow the invariable practice of obtaining a signature to a written form. Consent might be inferred from willing attendance at the hospital and there need only be consent in broad terms to the treatment proposed. None the less if the surgeon carries out a different treatment from that to which the patient consented, and there is no such pressing need as to amount to necessity, the doctor risks a claim in trespass.

A rather different issue is that of informed consent. Every medical intervention **18.08** carries risks of mishap or complication. The law in England and Wales has made it very difficult for a patient to argue that consent was vitiated by a failure to explain the risks, or to claim compensation on the ground that no prior warning of the risk had been given.

In *Sidaway v Bethlem Royal Hospital* [1985] AC 871, a patient had not been **18.09** warned of the risk of potentially serious complications of surgery to her neck which had materialized. Her claim failed by the application of the *Bolam* test: there was a responsible body of medical opinion that would have warned the claimant of risks exactly in the limited terms used by the doctor. The claimant therefore failed to establish a breach of duty. Even if a breach can be established, in a failure to warn of a risk which should have been explained, it is still difficult for a claim to pass the but-for test of causation unless the claimant can also persuade the court that if the risk had been mentioned as it should have been then consent to the procedure would have been withheld. This is inherently unlikely given that in spite of the risk the claimant has a medical condition for which the doctor recommends the treatment as appropriate and reasonable. A rare case where the argument succeeded was the Australian case of *Rogers v Whittaker* [1992] 3 Med LR 331 where the claimant had lost the use of one eye and her doctor proposed a treatment for it: before the claimant would consent she insisted on detailed advice about complications but was not told that there was a small risk of losing the sight of her other good eye. She was able to establish that if she had known of this risk she would not have undergone the treatment and when the complication did occur she was entitled to be compensated.

18.10 *Chester v Afshar* [2004] UKHL 41   A complaint of clinical negligence for failing to given proper warning of the risks of proposed surgery or other treatment faces a great difficulty in proving that the claimant would not have agreed to the treatment if a proper warning had been given. Usually, the proposed treatment is necessary and appropriate to treat the underlying condition and is recommended by the doctor even though there are risks. In *Chester*, the claimant underwent an operation and negligently she was not warned of a small risk of serious damage. The risk happened through misfortune rather than through negligence in the conduct of the operation. She had been reluctant to undergo the operation. The trial judge found that if she had been warned of the risk, she would have declined the operation at that time, but would probably have had the operation at a later date with exactly the same risk of injury. None the less the House of Lords found that causation was established, refusing to be bound by the traditional 'but-for' test by reasoning that is similar to the decision in *Fairchild* (at **3.18** above). It is likely that this decision will give new impetus to claims relying on a lack of informed consent.

D. Public Funding

18.11 When the Access to Justice Act 1999 removed legal aid from personal injury claims, a restricted scope for public funding of clinical negligence claims was retained. There are good reasons for this. Clinical mishaps can result in catastrophic injuries, but the cost and difficulty of the initial stages of investigating the history and merits of a medical accident can often be so great that it is unreasonable to expect that solicitors or victims of limited means would be able to willing to bear the cost. Public funding will usually cover this initial investigation: if the outcome is to disclose a good case, the normal course will be for the claim to go ahead on a conditional fee agreement like any other personal injury claim, though again there is a mechanism for public funding to continue to give some contributory support in high-cost cases.

Even this limited degree of public funding is sometimes a political football but **18.12** the criticism of the expenditure is unfounded. Where severe injuries have been sustained it would be intolerable to have a system of justice where the victims were effectively precluded from bringing a claim. Where the cause of injury is a road accident or an accident at work, it is a fair assumption that the accident ought not to have happened and if the claimant was not entirely to blame there is a reasonable likelihood that someone else was at fault. Clinical negligence cases are entirely different. Medical mishaps are regrettably inescapable but the fact that there has been an unexpectedly poor outcome does not carry with it any implication at all that negligence by someone will be found to have been the cause. This is why it is essential to be able to investigate fully at the outset with expert advice, and why many claims are investigated but relatively few of them proceed to an award of compensation.

E. Practical Points

Clinical negligence cases are different from personal injury litigation. It is **18.13** unwise for practitioners to take them on without relevant experience and expertise. It is necessary to be familiar with medical notes and language. It is necessary to have access to a range of expert witnesses who are willing to undertake claims of this kind and have a familiarity with the legal approach to liability issues. It is an absolute necessity to obtain the full medical records at the outset before coming to any conclusion, even provisionally, about the history and merits of a potential claim. There is a separate Protocol under the CPR for clinical negligence cases. Finally, the organization AvMA (Action against Medical Accidents) (44 High Street, Croydon, Surrey CRO 1YB, Helpline: 0845 123 23 52) can provide extremely valuable help both to patients and to legal advisers in the consideration of claims and the appointment of suitable experts.

19

INJURIES CAUSING DEATH

There are two different situations to consider. The first is where an injury has **19.01** resulted in a condition which will later result in the death of the claimant, who has not yet died. A common example is a person who has contracted an illness which is likely to result in premature death. The second situation is where death has happened and the survivors of the deceased wish to bring a claim.

A. The Living Claimant's Lost Years

A living claimant has, first, a claim for injury damages. Injury damages can be **19.02** recovered in the usual way, though a shortened expectation of life which shortens the likely period of pain and suffering should in principle be taken into account to reduce the award. In a case where the claimant knows of the likelihood of early death, this awareness is an element that will be added in the assessment of his suffering (Administration of Justice Act 1982, s 1(b)), but no injury damages can be claimed for the fact of a shortened life. Formerly the court might make a specific award for the loss of expectation of life, but this was abolished in 1982 with the introduction of the statutory award for bereavement, which is only available to close family after death and not to a person who knows he will die.

The living claimant can claim for his probable future losses. This includes his **19.03** prospective expenses of treatment and care. If increasing illness will prevent the claimant working, that loss of earnings can be recovered. In addition, a living claimant who faces early death can claim for his net loss of earnings in the 'lost years', the years of his working life when death will prevent him working and earning. The claim is for the net loss in the sense that the claimant must give credit against his loss of 'take home' earnings for the living expenses that he will not have to meet out of that income. The *Harris* formula (see the case note below) of allowing a third of earnings for the personal expenses of the deceased, or a quarter where there are dependent children, was devised for this purpose though it is more commonly encountered in Fatal Accidents Act computations.

B. Claims after Death

19.04 Again there are two different types of claim to be considered. First, by the Law Reform (Miscellaneous Provisions) Act 1934 the cause of action held by a person before his death will pass on death for the benefit of the estate. This includes, for example, a claim for pain and suffering in the period between injury and death if none was brought by the deceased before the death. If the period of suffering is brief, in the course of a virtually instantaneous death, no claim will arise. In *Hicks v Chief Constable of South Yorkshire* [1992] PIQR P433, one of the Hillsborough cases, the deceased were crushed and suffered traumatic asphyxia leading to unconsciousness within seconds and death within minutes; on those facts no claim could be made for the estate, neither could any claim be made for the emotion of fear of impending death. Accordingly no claim can be made for injury damages unless the evidence proves a definite period of physical suffering between injury and death. After death, however, the estate can no longer make any claim for the loss of earnings of the deceased (1934 Act, s 2(b)). Such a claim is replaced by a claim under the Fatal Accidents Act.

19.05 A claim on behalf of the estate is governed by the ordinary rules of limitation, except that where the deceased had not started an action but died before his limitation period had expired, s 11(5) of the Limitation Act 1980 gives a possible extension: his personal representative has a further period of three years from the date of death or the date of knowledge of the personal representative.

19.06 The second type of claim that arises after a death is purely statutory. There is no claim at common law for the death of another person, but the Fatal Accidents Act 1976 gives the dependants of the deceased their own claim for their own loss of the support they would have received if the deceased had not died, based on the wrongful act which caused the death. Sections 1–5 of the 1976 Act are set out in Chapter 29 below. The issues of liability in relation to Fatal Accidents Act claims are exactly those applicable to the injury which caused the death and no separate discussion is needed. A discussion of the assessment of the amount of such claims can be found at **29.32**. The amount of the statutory award for bereavement under the Fatal Accidents Act 1976 was increased to £10,000 from 1 April 2002.

In a claim arising out of foreign or cross-border travel it is important to be aware **19.07** that there are many schemes derived from international treaties or conventions and from European regulations which govern compensation for accidents, often providing for liability without the proof of fault, but fixing a cap on the level of compensation and a shorter time limit for bringing a claim.

Pickett v British Rail Engineering [1980] AC 136   At the age of 51 the claim- **19.08** ant contracted mesothelioma as a result of exposure to asbestos. His expectation of life had been reduced to one year. This is the leading case in which the recovery of damages for his loss of earnings, after deducting his probable living expenses, was allowed.

Harris v Empress Motors [1984] 1 WLR 212   For a 'lost years' claim for loss **19.09** of earnings, in order to assess the amount of income which would be available as the 'surplus' as a rule of thumb or starting point it is reasonable to assume that a married man's own expenses of living will be a third of his net income and for a married man with children the proportion will be a quarter.

Dodds v Dodds [1978] QB 543   The defendant mother was liable for a road **19.10** accident which caused the death of her husband and the claim under the Fatal Accidents Act was brought on behalf of their child. The son had his own individual claim which was not defeated by the negligence of his mother: it amounted to the items for family expenditure benefiting him exclusively and benefiting the whole family, excluding sums spent exclusively for the mother and father. The wife's earnings came into the family pool before the accident and her continuing earnings after the accident must be taken into account.

C. Law Reform (Miscellaneous Provisions) Act 1934, s 1

1. Effect of death on certain causes of action

(1) Subject to the provisions of this section, on the death of any person after the commence- **19.11** ment of this Act all causes of action subsisting against or vested in him shall survive against, or, as the case may be, for the benefit of, his estate. Provided that this subsection shall not apply to causes of action for defamation.

(1A) The right of a person to claim under section 1A of the Fatal Accidents Act 1976 (bereavement) shall not survive for the benefit of his estate on his death.

(2) Where a cause of action survives as aforesaid for the benefit of the estate of a deceased person, the damages recoverable for the benefit of the estate of that person—
    (a) shall not include—
        (i) any exemplary damages;
        (ii) any damages for loss of income in respect of any period after that person's death;

(c) where the death of that person has been caused by the act or omission which gives rise to the cause of action, shall be calculated without reference to any loss or gain to his estate consequent on his death, except that a sum in respect of funeral expenses may be included.

(4) Where damage has been suffered by reason of any act or omission in respect of which a cause of action would have subsisted against any person if that person had not died before or at the same time as the damage was suffered, there shall be deemed, for the purposes of this Act, to have been subsisting against him before his death such cause of action in respect of that act or omission as would have subsisted if he had died after the damage was suffered.

(5) The rights conferred by this Act for the benefit of the estates of deceased persons shall be in addition to and not in derogation of any rights conferred on the dependants of deceased persons by the Fatal Accidents Act 1976 and so much of this Act as relates to causes of action against the estates of deceased persons shall apply in relation to causes of action under the said Act as it applies in relation to other causes of action not expressly excepted from the operation of subsection (1) of this section.

D. Administration of Justice Act 1982, s 1

1. Abolition of right to damages for loss of expectation of life

19.12   (1) In an action under the law of England and Wales or the law of Northern Ireland for damages for personal injuries—

(a) no damages shall be recoverable in respect of any loss of expectation of life caused to the injured person by the injuries; but

(b) if the injured person's expectation of life has been reduced by the injuries, the court, in assessing damages in respect of pain and suffering caused by the injuries, shall take account of any suffering caused or likely to be caused to him by awareness that his expectation of life has been so reduced.

(2) The reference in subsection (1)(a) above to damages in respect of loss of expectation of life does not include damages in respect of loss of income.

20

INQUESTS

After an accident which has resulted in a death, an inquest is likely to be held by **20.01** the coroner, and this provides a useful means of discovering the facts surrounding the accident.

A. The Purpose of Inquests

The coroner has jurisdiction based on the district for which he is appointed and **20.02** has a duty to hold an inquest to inquire into any death where there is reasonable cause to suspect that the deceased has died a violent or unnatural death, or has died a sudden death of which the cause is unknown, or has died in a prison or some other place where an inquest is required. The inquest will usually be held by the coroner sitting alone, but a jury will be involved for deaths in prison or police custody, for many deaths by accident, poisoning or disease, and for a death in circumstances which show a risk to the health and safety of the public. The presence of a jury does not alter the nature and purpose of the inquiry, which is to decide as a matter of fact (a) the identity of the deceased, (b) the place of death, (c) the time of death, and (d) how the deceased came by his death.

Issue (d) is usually the one to which the evidence and the inquiry are chiefly **20.03** directed. However, the inquest is not a general investigation into the reasons for the death, but is limited to ascertaining the means by which the deceased came by his death. The outcome is a conclusion described as a verdict. The choice of verdicts is not formally set out in legislation but the notes to the inquisition in Sch 4 to the Coroner's Rules indicate the following suggested verdicts: death from—

(a) natural causes;

(b) industrial disease;

(c) dependence on drugs or non-dependent abuse of drugs;

(d) want of attention at birth;

(e) suicide;

(f) attempted or self-induced abortion;

(g) accident or misadventure;

(h) sentence of death;

(i) lawful killing;

(j) open verdict;

(k) unlawful killing;

(l) stillbirth.

20.04 The purpose of the inquest is to establish facts, and not to determine (or appear to determine) any question of blame or guilt, or of criminal or civil liability. The possible verdicts relevant to a death for which compensation might be an issue are death by accident or misadventure, death by natural causes, death by unlawful killing or (exceptionally) death for any other reason aggravated by neglect or lack of care or self-neglect. A rider 'aggravated by lack of care' is not concerned with negligence but with a narrow category of failing to provide sustenance, shelter or necessary medical attention (see *R v North Humberside Coroner, ex p Jamieson* [1995] QB 1) and which should be applied only to the first five conclusions in the above list. It is tempting to see a distinction between accident and misadventure, in that an accident is something purely fortuitous while a misadventure is a well-intended plan which miscarried, but in legal terms they mean the same thing and 'accident' is preferred.

B. Procedure

20.05 The work of the coroner is governed by the Coroners Act 1988 and the Coroners Rules 1984. The coroner carries out an inquisitorial procedure, and the coroner is responsible for deciding what evidence should be heard and for calling that evidence before himself or the jury. The coroner sits without robes and is in charge of the procedure adopted. It is his responsibility to ensure that a full and sufficient inquiry is held. Strict rules of evidence do not apply. Witness statements may be read out if no one objects that the witness should be called. Interested parties are entitled to attend and to be represented, and they or their representative will be allowed to ask additional questions of the witnesses, but there is no entitlement to ask questions which seek to go beyond the proper scope of the inquiry. No one may address the coroner or the jury on the facts, but submissions of law can be made, for example on the verdicts that are open on the evidence, or whether the evidence justifies a report under r 43 of the 1984 Rules. The coroner sums up to the jury and gives directions on the law.

Public funding is not generally available for representation at an inquest but the **20.06** Community Legal Service does have a power—very sparingly exercised—to grant funding for representation for an exceptional individual case if there are special reasons to do so.

There is no appeal from the decision of a coroner or a coroner's jury, but the **20.07** coroner is subject to judicial review and there is a limited statutory High Court power to order a new inquest.

The usefulness of an inquest in an injury compensation claim does not lie in the **20.08** verdict that might result but in the early opportunity to discover facts concerning the death. In a fatal accident claim one of the practical problems is that the victim is not able to give his own account of events and it can be difficult to find out what happened. Although an inquest must not apportion blame or decide civil liability, it must discover how the deceased came to die and a coroner may make a report if he believes that action should be taken to prevent a recurrence of fatalities similar to the one under inquiry. In an appropriate case, the Health and Safety Executive may give the coroner a report of its inspector's investigation and conclusions.

The coroner's office will state in advance which witnesses are to be called and is **20.09** usually helpful in the provision of copy statements and exhibits in advance of the inquest. The rules require the coroner to take notes of the evidence and to supply copies after the inquest on request. If the inquest has already been concluded there may still be useful information and cross-examination material to be gained from obtaining copies of the evidence. If the inquest has yet to be held, there are advantages in attending, in spite of the cost of representation: it may be possible to probe witnesses for greater factual detail by questioning, and the presence of the aggrieved family will help to ensure that the circumstances are properly investigated.

Following a fundamental review of coroner services and the Third Report of **20.10** the Shipman Inquiry, the Home Office has published proposals for reform of the coroner and death certification services. Full time legally qualified coroners will be organized in a hierarchy with a Chief Coroner. The purpose of the reforms is to focus on the lessons to be learned and steps to be taken to prevent avoidable deaths, with an increase in the medical scrutiny of deaths: all deaths will be referred to the coroner and a medical team will identify cases needing further investigation. The implementation of the reforms is likely to take some further time and meanwhile details of the proposals can be found at www.homeoffice.gov.uk.

C. Coroners Act 1988, ss 8, 11, and 12

INQUESTS: GENERAL

8. Duty to hold inquest

20.11   (1) Where a coroner is informed that the body of a person ('the deceased') is lying within his district and there is reasonable cause to suspect that the deceased—

(a) has died a violent or an unnatural death;

(b) has died a sudden death of which the cause is unknown; or

(c) has died in prison or in such a place or in such circumstances as to require an inquest under any other Act,

then, whether the cause of death arose within his district or not, the coroner shall as soon as practicable hold an inquest into the death of the deceased either with or, subject to subsection (3) below, without a jury.

(2) In the case of an inquest with a jury—

(a) the coroner shall summon by warrant not less than seven nor more than eleven persons to appear before him at a specified time and place, there to inquire as jurors into the death of the deceased; and

(b) when not less than seven jurors are assembled, they shall be sworn by or before the coroner diligently to inquire into the death of the deceased and to give a true verdict according to the evidence.

(3) If it appears to a coroner, either before he proceeds to hold an inquest or in the courts of an inquest begun without a jury, that there is reason to suspect—

(a) that the death occurred in prison or in such a place or in such circumstances as to require an inquest under any other Act;

(b) that the death occurred while the deceased was in police custody, or resulted from an injury caused by a police officer in the purported execution of his duty;

(c) that the death was caused by an accident, poisoning or disease notice of which is required to be given under any Act to a government department, to any inspector or other officer of a government department or to an inspector appointed under section 19 of the Health and Safety at Work etc. Act 1974; or

(d) that the death occurred in circumstances the continuance or possible recurrence of which is prejudicial to the health or safety of the public or any section of the public,

he shall proceed to summon a jury in the manner required by subsection (2) above.

(4) If it appears to a coroner, [either before he proceeds to hold an inquest, on resuming an inquest begun with a jury after the inquest has been adjourned and the jury discharged] or in the course of an inquest begun without a jury, that there is any reason for summoning a jury, he may proceed to summon a jury in the manner required by subsection (2) above.

(5) In the case of an inquest or any part of an inquest held without a jury, anything done by or before the coroner alone shall be as validly done as if it had been done by or before the coroner and a jury.

(6) Where an inquest is held into the death of a prisoner who dies within a prison, neither a prisoner in the prison nor any person engaged in any sort of trade or dealing with the prison shall serve as a juror at the inquest.

11. Proceedings at inquest

(1) It shall not be obligatory for a coroner holding an inquest into a death to view the body; **20.12**
and the validity of such an inquest shall not be questioned in any court on the grounds that the
coroner did not view the body.

(2) The coroner shall, at the first sitting of the inquest, examine on oath concerning the death
all persons who tender evidence as to the facts on the death and all persons having knowledge of
those facts whom he considers it expedient to examine.

(3) In the case of an inquest held with a jury, the jury shall, after hearing the evidence—

(a) give their verdict and certify it by an inquisition; and

(b) inquire of and find the particulars for the time being required by the Births and Deaths
Registration Act 1953 (in this Act referred to as 'the 1953 Act') to be registered concerning the
death.

(4) In the case of an inquest held without a jury, the coroner shall, after hearing the evidence—

(a) give his verdict and certify it by an inquisition; and

(b) inquire of and find the particulars for the time being required by the 1953 Act to be
registered concerning the death.

(5) An inquisition—

(a) shall be in writing under the hand of the coroner and, in the case of an inquest held with
a jury, under the hands of the jurors who concur in the verdict;

(b) shall set out, so far as such particulars have been proved—

(i) who the deceased was; and

(ii) how, when and where the deceased came by his death; and

(c) shall be in such form as the Lord Chancellor may by rules made by statutory instrument
from time to time prescribe.

12. Failure of jury to agree

(1) This section applies where, in the case of an inquest held with a jury, the jury fails to agree **20.13**
on a verdict.

(2) If the minority consists of not more than two, the coroner may accept the verdict of the
majority, and the majority shall, in that case, certify the verdict under section 11(3) above.

(3) In any other case of disagreement the coroner may discharge the jury and issue a warrant
for summoning another jury and, in that case, the inquest shall proceed in all respects as if the
proceedings which terminated in the disagreement had not taken place.

D. Coroners Rules 1984

POST-MORTEM EXAMINATIONS

5. Delay in making post-mortem to be avoided

Where a coroner directs or requests that a post-mortem examination shall be made, it shall be **20.14**
made as soon after the death of the deceased as is reasonably practicable.

6. Medical practitioner making post-mortem

(1) In considering what legally qualified medical practitioner shall be directed or requested by **20.15**
the coroner to make a post-mortem examination the coroner shall have regard to the following
considerations—

(a) the post-mortem examination should be made, whenever practicable, by a pathologist with suitable qualifications and experience and having access to laboratory facilities;

(b) if the coroner is informed by the chief officer of police that a person may be charged with murder, manslaughter or infanticide of the deceased, the coroner should consult the chief officer of police regarding the legally qualified medical practitioner who is to make the post-mortem examination;

(c) if the deceased died in hospital, the coroner should not direct or request a pathologist on the staff of, or associated with, that hospital to make a post-mortem examination if—

(i) that pathologist does not desire to make the examination, or

(ii) the conduct of any member of the hospital staff is likely to be called in question,

or

(iii) any relative of the deceased asks the coroner that the examination be not made by such a pathologist, unless the obtaining of another pathologist with suitable qualifications and experience would cause the examination to be unduly delayed;

(d) if the death of the deceased may have been caused by any of the diseases or injuries within paragraph (2), the coroner should not direct or request a legally qualified medical practitioner who is a member of a pneumoconiosis medical panel to make the post-mortem examination.

(2) The diseases and injuries within this paragraph are those in connection with which duties are from time to time imposed upon pneumoconiosis medical boards by Part III of the Social Security Act 1975 and any regulations made under that Act.

7. Coroner to notify persons for post-mortem to be made

20.16   (1) Where a coroner directs or requests a legally qualified medical practitioner to make a post-mortem examination, the coroner shall notify the persons and bodies set out in paragraph (2) of the date, hour and place at which the examination will be made, unless it is impracticable to notify any such persons or bodies or to do so would cause the examination to be unduly delayed.

(2) The persons and bodies to be notified by the coroner are as follows—

(a) any relative of the deceased who has notified the coroner of his desire to attend, or be represented at, the post-mortem examination;

(b) the deceased's regular medical attendant;

(c) if the deceased died in a hospital, the hospital;

(d) if the death of the deceased may have been caused by any of the diseases or injuries within Rule 6(2) (other than occupational asthma), the pneumoconiosis medical panel for the area;

(e) if the death of the deceased may have been caused by any accident or disease notice of which is required by or under any enactment to be given—

(i) to an enforcing authority, the appropriate inspector appointed by, or representative of, that authority; or

(ii) to an inspector appointed by an enforcing authority, that inspector;

(f) any government department which has notified the coroner of its desire to be represented at the examination;

(g) if the chief officer of police has notified the coroner of his desire to be represented at the examination, the chief officer of police.

(3) Any person or body mentioned in paragraph (2) shall be entitled to be represented at a post-mortem examination by a legally qualified medical practitioner, or if any such person is a legally qualified medical practitioner he shall be entitled to attend the examination in person; but the chief officer of police may be represented by a member of the police force of which he is chief officer.

(4) Nothing in the foregoing provisions of this Rule shall be deemed to limit the discretion of the coroner to notify any person of the date, hour and place at which a post-mortem examination will be made and to permit him to attend the examination.

8. Persons attending post-mortem not to interfere

A person attending a post-mortem examination by virtue of paragraph (3) or (4) of Rule 7 shall not interfere with the performance of the examination. **20.17**

9. Preservation of material

A person making a post-mortem examination shall make provision, so far as possible, for the preservation of material which in his opinion bears upon the cause of death for such period as the coroner thinks fit. **20.18**

10. Report on post-mortem

(1) The person making a post-mortem examination shall report to the coroner in the form set out in Schedule 2 or in a form to the like effect. **20.19**

(2) Unless authorised by the coroner, the person making a post-mortem examination shall not supply a copy of his report to any person other than the coroner.

11. Premises for post-mortems

(1) No post-mortem examination shall be made in a dwelling house or in licensed premises. **20.20**

(2) Every post-mortem examination shall be made in premises which are adequately equipped for the purpose of the examination.

(3) Where a person dies in hospital possessing premises so equipped, any post-mortem examination of the body of that person shall, with the consent of the hospital authority, be made in those premises unless the coroner otherwise decides.

(4) For the purpose of this Rule no premises shall be deemed to be adequately equipped for the purpose of post-mortem examinations unless they are supplied with running water, proper heating and lighting facilities, and containers for the storing and preservation of material.

INQUESTS

16. Formality

Every inquest shall be opened, adjourned and closed in a formal manner. **20.21**

17. Inquest in public

Every inquest shall be held in public: **20.22**

Provided that the coroner may direct that the public be excluded from an inquest or any part of an inquest if he considers that it would be in the interest of national security so to do.

18. Days on which inquest not to be held

An inquest shall not be held on Christmas Day, Good Friday, or a bank holiday unless the coroner thinks it requisite on grounds of urgency that an inquest should be held on such a day, and no inquest shall be held on a Sunday. **20.23**

19. Coroner to notify persons of inquest arrangements

The coroner shall notify the date, hour and place of an inquest to— **20.24**

(a) the spouse or a near relative or personal representative of the deceased whose name and address are known to the coroner; and

(b) any other person who—

(i) in the opinion of the coroner is within Rule 20(2); and

(ii) has asked the coroner to notify him of the aforesaid particulars of the inquest; and

(iii) has supplied the coroner with a telephone number or address for the purpose of so notifying him.

20. Entitlement to examine witnesses

20.25   (1) Without prejudice to any enactment with regard to the examination of witnesses at an inquest, any person who satisfies the coroner that he is within paragraph (2) shall be entitled to examine any witness at an inquest either in person or by [an authorised advocate as defined in section 119(1) of the Courts and Legal Services Act 1990]:

Provided that—

(a) the chief officer of police, unless interested otherwise than in that capacity, shall only be entitled to examine a witness by [such an advocate];

(b) the coroner shall disallow any question which in his opinion is not relevant or is otherwise not a proper question.

(2) Each of the following persons shall have the rights conferred by paragraph (1)—

(a) a parent, child, spouse and any personal representative of the deceased;

(b) any beneficiary under a policy of insurance issued on the life of the deceased;

(c) the insurer who issued a policy of insurance;

(d) any person whose act or omission or that of his agent or servant may in the opinion of the coroner have caused, or contributed to, the death of the deceased;

(e) any person appointed by a trade union to which the deceased at the time of his death belonged, if the death of the deceased may have been caused by an injury received in the course of his employment or by an industrial disease;

(f) an inspector appointed by, or a representative of, an enforcing authority, or any person appointed by a government department to attend the inquest;

(g) the chief officer of police;

(h) any other person who, in the opinion of the coroner, is a properly interested person.

21. Examination of witnesses

20.26   Unless the coroner otherwise determines, a witness at an inquest shall be examined first by the coroner and, if the witness is represented at the inquest, lastly by his representative.

22. Self-incrimination

20.27   (1) No witness at an inquest shall be obliged to answer any question tending to incriminate himself.

(2) Where it appears to the coroner that a witness has been asked such a question, the coroner shall inform the witness that he may refuse to answer.

23. Adjournment where inspector or representative of enforcing authority etc. is not present

20.28   (1) Where a coroner holds a inquest touching the death of a person which may have been caused by an accident or disease notice of which is required to be given to an enforcing authority, the coroner shall adjourn the inquest unless an inspector appointed by, or a representative of, the enforcing authority is present to watch the proceedings and shall, at least four days before holding the adjourned inquest, give to such inspector or representative notice of the date, hour and place of holding the adjourned inquest.

(2) Where a coroner holds an inquest touching the death of a person which may have been caused by an accident or disease notice of which is required to be given to an inspector appointed by an enforcing authority, the coroner shall adjourn the inquest unless the inspector or a representative of the inspector is present to watch the proceedings and shall, at least four days before holding the adjourned inquest, give to the inspector or representative notice of the date, hour and place of holding the adjourned inquest.

24. Notice to person whose conduct is likely to be called in question

Any person whose conduct is likely in the opinion of the coroner to be called in question at an **20.29** inquest shall, if not duly summoned to give evidence at the inquest, be given reasonable notice of the date, hour and place at which the inquest will be held.

25. Adjournment where person whose conduct is called in question is not present

If the conduct of any person is called in question at an inquest on grounds which the coroner **20.30** thinks substantial and which relate to any matter referred to in Rule 36 and if that person is not present at the inquest and has not been duly summoned to attend or otherwise given notice of the holding of the inquest, the inquest shall be adjourned to enable him to be present, if he so desires.

36. Matters to be ascertained at inquest

(1) The proceedings and evidence at an inquest shall be directed solely to ascertaining the **20.31** following matters, namely—
    (a) who the deceased was;
    (b) how, when and where the deceased came by his death;
    (c) the particulars for the time being required by the Registration Acts to be registered concerning the death.

(2) Neither the coroner nor the jury shall express any opinion on any other matters.

37. Documentary evidence

(1) Subject to the provisions of paragraphs (2) to (4), the coroner may admit at an inquest **20.32** documentary evidence relevant to the purposes of the inquest from any living person which in his opinion is unlikely to be disputed, unless a person who in the opinion of the coroner is within Rule 20(2) objects to the documentary evidence being admitted.

(2) Documentary evidence so objected to may be admitted if in the opinion of the coroner the maker of the document is unable to give oral evidence within a reasonable period.

(3) Subject to paragraph (4), before admitting such documentary evidence the coroner shall at the beginning of the inquest announce publicly—
    (a) that the documentary evidence may be admitted, and
    (b) (i) the full name of the maker of the document to be admitted in evidence, and
        (ii) a brief account of such document, and
    (c) that any person who in the opinion of the coroner is within Rule 20(2) may object to the admission of any such documentary evidence, and
    (d) that any person who in the opinion of the coroner is within Rule 20(2) is entitled to see a copy of any such documentary evidence if he so wishes.

(4) If during the course of an inquest it appears that there is available at the inquest documentary evidence which in the opinion of the coroner is relevant to the purposes of the inquest but the maker of the document is not present and in the opinion of the coroner the content of the documentary evidence is unlikely to be disputed, the coroner shall at the earliest opportunity during the course of the inquest comply with the provisions of paragraph (3).

(5) A coroner may admit as evidence at an inquest any document made by a deceased person if he is of the opinion that the contents of the document are relevant to the purposes of the inquest.

(6) Any documentary evidence admitted under this Rule shall, unless the coroner otherwise directs, be read aloud at the inquest.

38. Exhibits

20.33   All exhibits produced in evidence at an inquest shall be marked with consecutive numbers and each number shall be preceded by the letter 'C'.

39. Notes of evidence

20.34   The coroner shall take notes of the evidence at every inquest.

40. No addresses as to facts

20.35   No person shall be allowed to address the coroner or the jury as to the facts.

41. Summing-up and direction to jury

20.36   Where the coroner sits with a jury, he shall sum up the evidence to the jury and direct them as to the law before they consider their verdict and shall draw their attention to Rules 36(2) and 42.

42. Verdict

20.37   No verdict shall be framed in such a way as to appear to determine any question of—
    (a) criminal liability on the part of a named person, or
    (b) civil liability.

43. Prevention of similar fatalities

20.38   A coroner who believes that action should be taken to prevent the recurrence of fatalities similar to that in respect of which the inquest is being held may announce at the inquest that he is reporting the matter in writing to the person or authority who may have power to take such action and he may report that matter accordingly.

55. Retention and delivery or disposal of exhibits

20.39   Every exhibit at an inquest shall, unless a court otherwise directs, be retained by the coroner until he is satisfied that the exhibit is not likely to be, or will no longer be, required for the purposes of any other legal proceedings, and shall then, if a request for its delivery has been made by a person appearing to the coroner to be entitled to the possession thereof, be delivered to that person, or, if no such request has been made, be destroyed or otherwise disposed of as the coroner thinks fit.

56. Retention and delivery of documents

20.40   Any document (other than an exhibit at an inquest) in the possession of a coroner in connection with an inquest or post-mortem examination shall, unless a court otherwise directs, by retained by the coroner for at least 15 years:

Provided that the coroner may deliver any such document to any person who in the opinion of the coroner is a proper person to have possession of it.

57. Inspection of, or supply of copies of, documents etc.

20.41   (1) A coroner shall, on application and on payment of the prescribed fee (if any), supply to any person who, in the opinion of the coroner, is a properly interested person a copy of any report of a post-mortem examination (including one made under [section 19 of the 1988 Act]) or special examination, or of any notes of evidence, or of any document put in evidence at an inquest.

(2) A coroner may, on application and without charge, permit any person who, in the opinion of the coroner, is a properly interested person to inspect such report, notes of evidence, or document.

SCHEDULE 2

POST-MORTEM EXAMINATION REPORT

THIS REPORT IS CONFIDENTIAL. IT SHOULD NOT BE DISCLOSED TO A THIRD PARTY WITHOUT THE CORONER'S CONSENT   **20.42**

POST-MORTEM EXAMINATION REPORT   Serial No.:
Name of deceased: Coroner:
Address (if known):
Identified by: Place of examination: Date and time of examination:
Observers present at examination:

INTERNAL EXAMINATION

Stated/Estimated date and time of death: Stated/Apparent age:
Nourishment:
Marks of identification (tattoos, old scars, etc.):
Body surface and muscolo-skeletal system, including injuries:

INTERNAL EXAMINATION *

Central nervous system

Cranial cavity
- Skull:
- Brain:
- Meninges:
- Cerebral vessels:

Respiratory system†

- Larynx:
- Trachea:
- Bronchi:
- Pleurae:
- Lung parenchyma:

Thoracic cavity
- *Cardio-vascular system*
- Heart:
  - Weight:
  - Valves:
  - Myocardium:
  - Pericardium:
  - Coronary arteries:
  - Great vessels:

NOTES:

* Description of injuries or of complex pathology may be attached on a separate sheet, provided it   **20.43** is properly identified and signed.

† In cases of suspected pneumoconiosis (or one of the other occupational diseases affecting the lungs) see 'Notes on completing the post-mortem examination report form' obtainable from the coroner.

Alimentary system
Mouth:
Tongue:
Oesophagus:

Abdominal cavity
{
Stomach and contents:
Duodenum:
Intestines:
Liver and gall bladder:
Pancreas:
Peritoneum:

Genito-urinary system
Kidneys and ureters:
Bladder and urine:
Generative organs:
}

Reticulo-endothelial system
Spleen:
Lymph nodes:
Thymus:

Endocrine system
Thyroid:
Pituitary:
Adrenals:

In my opinion the cause of death was:

	I		I
Disease or condition directly leading to death*	(a)	....	
		due to (or as a consequence of)	
Antecedent causes. Morbid conditions, if any, giving rise to the above cause (stating the underlying condition last)	(b)	....	
		due to (or as a consequence of)	
	(c)	....	

II II

Other significant conditions *contributing to the death* but NOT related to the disease or condition causing it†

....

Morbid conditions present but in the pathologist's opinion *NOT contributing to the death.*

Is any further laboratory examination to be made which may affect the cause of death? YES/NO

Comments:

To the best of my knowledge no cardiac pacemaker remains in the body.

Signature and qualifications

Name (in block letters)

NOTES:

* This does not mean the mode of dying, such as (e.g.) heart failure, asphyxia, asthenia, etc. It means the disease, injury or complication which caused death.

† Conditions which did not in the pathologist's opinion contribute materially to the death should NOT be included under this heading, but under 'Morbid conditions present in the pathologist's opinion NOT contributing to the death'.

INQUISITION

An inquisition taken for our Sovereign Lady the Queen at   , in the county (*or as the* **20.44**
case may be) of   on the   day of   19   , [and by
adjournment on the   day of   19   ,] [before and by (^{1})] me A.B., one
of Her Majesty's coroners for the said county (*or as the case may be*), [and the undermentioned
jurors], touching the death of C.D. [a person unknown] [concerning a stillbirth].

The following matters are found—

1. Name of deceased (if known):

2. Injury or disease causing death:(^{2})

3. Time, place and circumstances at or in which injury was sustained:(^{3})

4. Conclusion of the jury/coroner as to the death:(^{4})

5. Particulars for the time being required by the Registration Acts to be registered concerning
the death:

(1) Date and place of death	(2) Name and surname of deceased	(3) Sex	(4) Maiden surname of woman who has married	(5) Date and place of birth	(6) Occupation and usual address

Signature of coroner [and jurors] ....

NOTES

(1) Modify this as necessary according to whether the inquest is held with or without a jury or
partly with and partly without a jury.

(2) In the case of a death from natural causes or from industrial disease, want of attention at
birth, or dependence on, or non-dependent abuse of, drugs insert the immediate cause of death
and the morbid conditions (if any) giving rise to the immediate cause of death.

(3) Omit this if the cause of death is one to which Note 2 applies.

(4) (a) Where the cause of death is one to which Note 2 applies, it is suggested that one of the
following forms be adopted—
    C.D. died from natural causes.
    C.D. died from the industrial disease of
    C.D. died from dependence on drugs/non-dependent abuse of drugs.
    C.D. died from want of attention at birth.

(In any part of the above cases, but in no other, it is suggested that the following words may, where
appropriate, be added: 'and the cause of death was aggravated by lack of care/self-neglect'.)

    (b) In any other case except murder, manslaughter, infanticide or stillbirth, it is suggested
that one of the following forms be adopted—
    C.D. killed himself [whilst the balance of his mind was disturbed].
    C.D. died as a result of an attempted/self-induced abortion.

C.D. died as a result of an accident/misadventure.

Execution of sentence of death.

C.D. was killed lawfully.

Open verdict, namely, the evidence did not fully or further disclose the means whereby the cause of death arose.

(c) In the case of murder, manslaughter or infanticide it is suggested that the following form be adopted—

C.D. was killed unlawfully.

(d) In the case of a stillbirth insert 'stillbirth' and do not complete the remainder of the form.

PART C

QUANTUM

21

COMPENSATION PAYMENTS

This chapter gives a brief overview of the different types of compensation **21.01** payments that may be available to an injured person.

A. Compensatory Damages

The majority of claims are brought in court for common law damages, both for **21.02** the injury sustained and for the consequential financial losses such as a loss of earnings. The theoretical starting point is the standard measure of tort damage that the award should, so far as money can, put the victim back to the position he would have been in if the tort had not occurred. There are two difficulties about the application of this test. The first is that pain and disability cannot be expressed in terms of money, and an award of money will not take them away. The second is that the victim may receive financial benefits arising out of the suffering of the injury which also seek to provide compensation, and the rules for deciding when such payments should be brought into account are complex and inconsistent. The following chapters of this book are concerned with the way in which compensatory damages in tort will be assessed where a claim for personal injury is made.

The only person who can be compensated is the person who was injured. This **21.03** rule holds even where the immediate family of the injured person may have suffered gravely from the effects of his injury. In *Best v Samuel Fox* [1952] AC 716, from the days where a claim could be made for the loss of *consortium*, i.e. the enjoyment of sexual relations, a woman sought to claim damages for her loss due to her husband's injuries and consequent impotence, but it was held that she could not claim. No duty of care was owed to her and the damage that she suffered was too remote. The rule can have a surprising result. For example, if as in *Ward v Newalls Insulation* [1998] PIQR Q41 a partner in a business is injured so that the profits of the partnership are reduced by the loss of his work, the only loss that can be claimed is the injured partner's share of the partnership loss. The other partners have no claim for their share of the loss. There are two established exceptions to this rule which should be noted. If a claimant's injuries result in a need for nursing care which is met by his family or friends, a claim for the value of the care is made in the injured claimant's action, but the damages are recovered on behalf of the carer and it was held in *Hunt v Severs* [1994] 2 AC 350 that they are held in trust for the carer. If a vehicle is damaged while it has been lent by the owner to someone else, the bailment is a sufficient legal basis for the person in possession to bring a claim for the loss or damage of the vehicle as in *O'Sullivan v Williams* [1992] 3 All ER 385, although again any damages recovered are held in trust for the owner.

21.04 Compensatory damages are always assessed at the date of trial rather than the date of injury. Changes in the facts, the law or the value of money up to the date of trial are taken into account. Events which have happened to increase or reduce the effects of the injury will be taken into account, because the court will always prefer to work on the basis of knowledge rather than speculation.

21.05 *Jobling v Associated Dairies* [1982] AC 794   The claim was for injury damages and loss of earnings after a fall at work, but before trial the claimant developed an unrelated illness which incapacitated him so that, even if the injury had not been sustained, he would have been unable to continue working. The defendant was entitled to rely on this fact to extinguish the claim for a continuing loss of earnings.

21.06 Compensatory damages in tort fall into two classes. Where a conventional sum is awarded as reparation for the injury sustained and the consequent pain and disability, this is called general damage, non-pecuniary loss, 'damages for pain and suffering and loss of amenity' or (the name preferred in this book) injury damages. Where a sum is awarded to make good a financial loss, which can be calculated in money by arithmetic, this is special damage, pecuniary loss or (the name preferred in this book) financial loss. Among the financial losses, some will be proved with such particularity that they can be assessed with confidence to the nearest pound, but with others the uncertainties of the future leave the court no alternative but to make a broad estimate.

B. Compensation for Future Loss

The traditional approach of the common law has been to make a single award **21.07**
of lump sum damages in personal injury claims to compensate for both past
and future loss. There have been slight inroads to this principle by the arrangements for provisional awards and structured settlements. The Courts Act 2003,
ss 100 and 101 (when in force) will amend the Damages Act 1996 so as to
enable the court to make an order that damages for future loss should be in
the form of periodical payments, against the wishes of one or both of the
parties and regardless of the size of the award. It appears that there is a political
wish to increase the use of periodical payments. There are, however, considerable practical difficulties with regard to implementing these proposals in a
way that gives adequate security to the claimant. At first glance it might be
thought that a clear benefit of such a regime would be to allow for the rate of
payment to be varied according to changes in the circumstances of the injured
person, but it seems likely that the powers of variation in the level of payments
will be limited to circumstances of a deterioration or improvement in the
claimant's condition. These proposals are discussed in greater detail in Chapter
23 below.

C. Nominal Damages

Nominal damages are awarded when the claimant is able to prove that a wrong **21.08**
has been committed but cannot prove that any quantifiable harm has been
suffered as a result. In ordinary personal injury claims, the possibility of a
nominal award does not generally arise, because damage is a necessary ingredient of a cause of action in negligence. However, a nominal award is a real
possibility in a claim for trespass or false imprisonment.

D. Aggravated Damages

An award of aggravated damages is a compensatory award where an additional **21.09**
amount is awarded to cover the sense of injury caused to the claimant's feelings
or to reflect the fact that such injury was caused by the defendant's bad motive
or deliberate misconduct. These matters would not otherwise count in the
assessment of an award. There are guidelines for cases against the police in
Thompson v Metropolitan Police Commissioner [1998] QB 498 but such cases are
often decided by a civil jury rather than by a judge alone. However, aggravated
damages cannot be awarded in an ordinary personal injury claim based on

negligence or breach of statutory duty, however bad the defendant's conduct may have been.

21.10 *Kralj v McGrath* [1986] 1 All ER 54   In a case of medical negligence where the negligent conduct of an obstetrician had been horrific and excruciatingly painful, the award of damages would take account of the distress suffered but could not include aggravated damages.

21.11 *Appleton v Garrett* [1996] PIQR P1   A dentist carried out grossly negligent and unnecessary treatment for gain, amounting to trespass to the person. Aggravated damages were awarded by an uplift of 15% to the sum awarded for pain, suffering and loss of amenity.

E. Exemplary Damages

21.12 Unlike aggravated damages, which are essentially compensatory on a more generous basis than usual, exemplary damages are not compensatory at all but are awarded to punish the defendant for his bad behaviour. Exemplary damages cannot be awarded in ordinary personal injury claims based on negligence or breach of statutory duty. They can be awarded (a) for oppressive, arbitrary or unconstitutional conduct by servants of the government (including the police), and (b) where the defendant's conduct was calculated to make a profit for himself in excess of the compensation payable to the victim. Exemplary damages are so rarely relevant to personal injury claims that detailed case notes are not appropriate here, but the leading decisions are *Rookes v Barnard* [1964] AC 1129, *Broome v Cassell* [1972] AC 1027 and *AB v South West Water* [1993] QB 507.

F. Wrongful Birth

21.13 Until July 1999, it was considered to be settled law from cases such as *Emeh v Kensington, etc AHA* [1985] QB 1012 that a negligent failure to ensure that sterilization or vasectomy had been effective, resulting in the birth of an unintended child, would give rise to a claim for the cost of the upbringing of the child. However, in *McFarlane v Tayside Health Board* [2000] 2 AC 59 the House of Lords unanimously held that as a matter of legal policy the true claim in such a case was limited to compensating the mother for the experience of pregnancy and childbirth, and no claim could be made for the expenses of bringing up a normal, healthy child born as a result of the negligent treatment. This decision has been much criticized, and in *Parkinson v St James NHS Trust* [2001] EWCA Civ 531; [2002] QB 266, the Court of Appeal qualified the decision in a case where the child had been born with serious disabilities, by allowing a claim for the additional costs resulting from the disabilities. In *Rees v Darlington Memorial Hospital NHS Trust* [2003] UKHL 52; [2003] 4 All ER 987 a court of seven Law Lords was invited to reconsider *McFarlane* in a case where the mother was disabled by being nearly blind, and her anxieties about coping with a child had been her reason for seeking to be sterilized. The House unanimously held that the principle of the *McFarlane* decision was correct. However, in a startling and innovative decision, by a majority, the House created a new 'conventional' award of £15,000 to be paid for the loss of autonomy involved in suffering unwanted pregnancy. The decision in *Parkinson* was questioned, and it is doubtful if the same result would be reached after *Rees*. It would appear that the 'conventional' award of £15,000 is not to be varied according to the particular circumstances of the claimant. The closest comparison is the statutory award for bereavement, currently £10,000 for deaths after 1 April 2002, under s 1A of the Fatal Accidents Act 1976.

G. National Insurance Benefits

The National Insurance system provides a range of financial benefits for those who are injured, some of which arise only for an accident at work and some of which form part of the wider safety net of social security. Chapter 27 below sets out in detail the benefits available and the complex rules governing the inter-relationship between these benefits and the assessment of compensatory damages. **21.14**

H. Private Insurance Benefits

Many private insurance policies provide benefits in the event of injury, from whatever cause, either directly by paying a fixed sum against an identified kind of injury, or indirectly by providing benefits that can cover mortgage payments or other household expenses during a period of incapacity. The benefits received from a policy of this kind for which the victim has paid the premium are generally ignored in the assessment of common law damages so that the claimant receives full compensation from the court as well as the benefits of the insurance. **21.15**

Medical insurance to cover the cost of private treatment may also be relevant to civil claims. Some policies require the policyholder who receives private treatment to include a claim for reimbursement (for the benefit of the insurer) in any civil claim. **21.16**

I. Criminal Injuries Compensation

21.17 The details of the current scheme are set out in Chapter 16 above. Since 1996, the scheme has not provided compensation based on a common law assessment, but its own system of tariff based awards and limited recovery of loss of earnings or other expenses. Where a civil claim is brought, any criminal injuries compensation award must be repaid from the proceeds and no question of double recovery can arise.

22

INJURY DAMAGES

A. Pain and Suffering and Loss of Amenity

To a philosopher it is impossible to use a sum of money to make good a physical **22.01** injury. But the difficulty of assessment does not mean that no damages should be awarded. The law provides that a fair and just award of compensation is one that is consistent with the awards that have been made to other victims for their injuries.

The traditional, if rather cumbersome title for compensation to make reparation **22.02** for non-pecuniary damage sustained in an injury is 'damages for pain and suffering and loss of amenity'. Surprisingly the phrase is retained in the Civil Procedure Rules 1998. It describes two rather than three notional categories of loss. The pain and suffering is the subjective experience of the victim, while the loss of amenity resulting from disability is capable of being objectively assessed. The distinction helps to explain why a substantial award is to be made to a victim in a coma, who is completely unaware of his injuries, for the loss of amenity. Apart from this, it is a distinction which serves little useful purpose and in this book the award of general damages for non-pecuniary loss is usually referred to as injury damages: the award that is made for the injury itself rather than for the consequent financial losses.

Lim Poh Choo v Camden and Islington AHA [1980] AC 174   The claimant **22.03** had no awareness of her injured state. She was not entitled to damages for pain and suffering but she was entitled to an award for loss of amenities.

22.04 The range of awards that has developed in this way runs from damages of a few hundred pounds for minor injuries that quickly recover, up to a maximum of around £200,000 for the most severely injured.

22.05 In *Heil v Rankin* [2000] PIQR Q187, a five judge Court of Appeal responded to the Law Commission's 1999 report, which had recommended substantial increases in the levels of all but the smallest awards of injury damages, with the greatest increases for the largest awards. The court rejected this recommendation in favour of a more modest increase beginning with awards over £10,000 on a sliding scale up to an increase of the largest awards from £150,000 to £200,000. This increase has to be taken into account in the use of any reported decisions as authority for the conventional level of damages where a decision before March 2000 is to be relied on, but the effect is negligible for cases under about £30,000. The amount of the increase is regrettably imprecise in the judgment and the small illustrative graph that accompanies it is also unclear. With the caveat that it is not an exact science, suggested examples of revised awards are:

Old award	New award
20,000	20,500 (2.5%)
30,000	31,500 (5%)
40,000	44,000 (*Schofield's* case, 10% increase)
65,000	74,100 (14%)
80,000	95,000 (*Kent's* case, c. 19% increase)
100,000	122,000 (22%)
110,000	138,000 (*Ramsey's* case, c. 25% increase)
120,000	152,400 (27%)
135,000	175,000 (*Warren's* case, c. 30% increase)
150,000	200,000 (33%)

B. The Judicial Studies Board Guidelines

22.06 In 1992 this convenient guide to the level of injury damages was first published. The Judicial Studies Board (JSB) has responsibility for training judges and as the jurisdiction of district judges increased to take over a large amount of the work on the assessment of damages that was formerly undertaken by circuit judges, some assistance towards consistency of approach was required. The current version is the 7th edition, published in 2004, and setting awards up-to-date as at November 2004. As well as allowing for inflation, the *JSB Guidelines* take into account the effects of the decision in *Heil v Rankin* [2000] PIQR Q187 and this has made it a particularly valuable resource for assessing injury damages. The 7th edition of the *JSB Guidelines* is reproduced in full below.

The aim of the *JSB Guidelines* is to describe the actual current level of awards **22.07** being made by judges. The authors deny any ambition to influence the level of awards either up or down, either generally or in relation to specific injuries. It is therefore pointless to complain if certain kinds of injury seem to receive disproportionately mean or generous awards. The complaint, if there is one, must be directed to the judiciary.

At first the *JSB Guidelines* received a distinctly lukewarm welcome. The **22.08** traditional method for establishing an appropriate level of award was to look at previous decided cases. In *Arafa v Potter* [1994] PIQR Q73, Staughton LJ commented that the *JSB Guidelines* are not law and the law is still to be found in the cases; the Court of Appeal ought to look at the cases rather than the *JSB Guidelines*. The reliability of the *JSB Guidelines* was also somewhat shaken by the treatment of awards for VWF where the *JSB Guidelines* followed a first instance assessment that had been said to be too low (see the full discussion in *Kemp & Kemp* at H6A–002). These awards have now been revised to a proper level following a series of cases (see *Kemp & Kemp* at H6A–008).

With time and experience, the respect given to the *JSB Guidelines* has increased. **22.09** In practice, no assessment of damages takes place in any court without consideration of the appropriate bracket in the *JSB Guidelines*. Decided cases are then used for argument against this background. In the judgment in *Heil v Rankin* [2000] PIQR Q187, the *JSB Guidelines* featured strongly. They were used to demonstrate the change there had been in levels of awards generally (at Q209). Having decided that some levels of award should be increased, the court urged that it was highly desirable that the JSB should produce a new edition of the *Guidelines* as soon as possible (at Q210). In all of the individual cases the *JSB Guidelines* were specifically discussed, and the assessments by the Court of Appeal are striking for the lack of reliance on reported decisions in fixing the appropriate award before the application of their policy decision for a limited uplift in more serious cases.

C. Case Law Sources

A huge volume of case law is available to practitioners. In using these references **22.10** it is important to distinguish between decisions which are authoritative and decisions which are illustrative. Although it is interesting to the court and sometimes useful to the advocate to see what awards have been made in cases decided by district judges, their deputies and by recorders, these will be of illustrative value only unless a particular judge is known to have strong experience in personal injury claims. The decisions of circuit judges who are designated civil judges, High Court judges and the Court of Appeal are all entitled to be regarded as authoritative.

22.11 The principal source is *Kemp & Kemp*. Many of its reports fall into the illustrative category but it also collects numerous authoritative decisions that are not otherwise fully reported. Numerous decisions are also reported in *Butterworth's Personal Injury Litigation Service*, in *Current Law* and in the annual digest of *Halsbury's Laws of England*. Both *Kemp & Kemp* and *Current Law* are available in CD format so that the production of offprints for submission to the court is easy. In addition, many case reports and transcripts are available from online services such as Westlaw UK, LexisNexis, Lawtel, the Court Service and BAILII. In practice, most courts will be happy to look at any report in the course of an assessment. Advocates should bear in mind the limitations on the citation of excessive numbers of decisions that are not fully reported laid out in *Practice Direction* [2001] 2 All ER 510 which applies to all civil courts. Paragraph 6.2 of the *Practice Direction* specifically and exceptionally allows the citation of county court decisions to illustrate the conventional measure of damages in a personal injury case, but the spirit of the *Practice Direction* is to curtail reference to decisions which do not establish a legal point but merely illustrate the application of settled law.

D. Inflation

22.12 An award of damages should be expressed in the value of money at the date of the assessment. Inescapably, previous awards (and the figures in the *JSB Guidelines*) will have been expressed in money of a different value. Old awards should be increased in order to give a fair comparison. In *Heil v Rankin*, it was argued on behalf of the claimants that for a fair comparison with old awards to be made the court should not only look at changes in the Retail Prices Index (RPI) but also at the increase in the level of earnings, at the changes in the cost of living and the gross domestic product. This would result in larger increases in old awards. However, the Court of Appeal firmly decided that RPI should be the basis of comparison. In larger cases, the effect of a *Heil* uplift will also have to be taken into account.

22.13 There is a danger of being unduly concerned with inflation. The editors of *Kemp & Kemp* provide inflation increases for the *JSB Guidelines* during the life of each edition. But the assessment of injury damages is not a precise science as is shown by the fact that awards are invariably expressed in round figures. It is doubtful whether this degree of fine adjustment is realistic and where a decision is only one or two years old, it will rarely be necessary to make a specific calculation of the effect of inflation. The government has decided to favour the

Consumer Prices Index (CPI) measure of inflation over the RPI. This was formerly known as HICP but the baseline of 100 only goes back to 1996 so the usefulness of this measure for revaluing old awards will be limited. There is also a version of RPI which excludes house price inflation. It is suggested that in *Heil v Rankin* the adoption of simple RPI by the Court of Appeal was so forceful that it would not be appropriate to experiment with these alternative measures of inflation until some approval from the Court of Appeal is forthcoming.

22.14 The following case is used as an illustration of the calculation necessary to bring an old award up-to-date. In *Durrant v MacDonald* [1992] PIQR Q76, the claimant suffered a severe back injury and a disabling psychological injury. Judge J assessed injury damages at £32,500 on 28 January 1992. To bring this up-to-date, the first step is to find the equivalent at the date of *Heil v Rankin* decided on 23 March 2000. Over this period, the RPI increased from 135.6 to 168.4, so the award becomes £40,361 (32,500 × 168.4 ÷ 135.6). An award of this level should receive a 10% uplift (see *Schofield v Saunders* [2000] PIQR Q223, one of the *Heil* cases), so that the equivalent award after *Heil* is £44,397. If the RPI at the date for which the comparison is needed is now, say, 185, then the value of Judge J's award expressed in the value of money at the date of the comparison is £48,773 (44,397 × 185 ÷ 168.4).

E. Loss of Congenial Employment

22.15 It has become well established that a separate claim can be made for the loss of a congenial form of employment when a claimant is forced by his injuries to retire early or change to less enjoyable work. Awards tend to be around the £5,000 mark. They are not limited to any particular profession or occupation and have been awarded to claimants across a wide range of employment, but they seem to have been awarded most frequently to firemen. A convenient table of awards is at 5–251 of *Kemp & Kemp*.

22.16 *Hale v London Underground* [1993] PIQR Q30   The leading case in which Otton J recognized that loss of congenial employment had become recognized as a separate head of damage and he awarded £5,000 to a firefighter in his early forties (value in May 2000 about £6,000).

22.17 *Willbye v Gibbons* [2003] EWCA Civ 372; [2004] PIQR P227   The claimant suffered head injuries in a road accident when she was 12½ and could not pursue her ambition of training as a nursery nurse. The Court of Appeal reduced an award of £15,000 for loss of congenial employment to £5,000.

F. Public Policy and the Level of Injury Damages

22.18   Many lay people who become involved in injury claims are surprised by the low level of injury damages. In the age of a national lottery with prizes of more than £10 million, it takes an injury of some considerable severity and permanence to result in an award of £50,000 injury damages. There was a widespread expectation among practitioners that the recommendations of the Law Commission for a substantial general increase in awards would be implemented by the Court of Appeal. The Court of Appeal was persuaded against this mainly by the cost of claims that would fall on motor insurers and on the NHS. The issue must now be regarded as settled for the foreseeable future and the *Heil* uplift plus RPI is the basis on which future cases will be determined.

22.19   It remains the case that there are high awards of compensation, and the lay people who are surprised at low injury damages will have seen press reports of other awards of £1 or £2 million. However, these are cases where the bulk of the damages is for loss of earnings and for nursing care. For the catastrophically injured, a generous care regime is essential. However, as we will see in Chapter 25, the development of awards for family support in cases of less severely injured claimants has sometimes served to mask the low level of awards for the injury itself. It is not difficult to find that the claimant's spouse is awarded a far larger sum for looking after the claimant that the claimant receives for suffering the injury and disability.

22.20   The reason for the large sums awarded for family care is that these awards have come to be assessed in a mathematical way, taking a commercial cost on an annual basis, applying a discount for the gratuitous nature of the service but quantifying the claim with an actuarially precise multiplier, rather than assessing a lump sum of fair recompense for the burden that is taken on. Each year, month and day of care is separately valued. A similar mathematical approach has resulted in a significant increase in the level of awards for future loss of earnings, because actuarially accurate multipliers have proved to be significantly greater that the multipliers that used to result from the judge taking a conventional multiplier based on previous practice.

22.21   Against this background it is striking how little detailed analysis is involved in the assessment of injury damages. It remains a matter of judicial discretion. The days when it was thought impertinent for an advocate to suggest a specific figure have long passed, but in most cases the exercise of assessment is limited to the judge reading medical reports and a witness statement, looking at the *JSB Guidelines* and reading a handful of cases. While injury damages are based on convention, the judges do not apply a tariff but aim to take into account the effect of an injury on the individual. In practice, however, the variations made for individual circumstances, either up or down, are negligible and the system pays no more than lip service to the particular hardship of a disability sustained at a very young age or a disability which results in the loss of a lifetime hobby or interest.

There are three particular respects in which it is suggested that fairness to **22.22** claimants would be improved by greater particularity in the assessment of awards. The first is to take greater account of the age of the claimant. I do not suppose it is realistic to envisage, for the foreseeable future at least, a development towards awards based on an annual compensation figure and a multiplier, but it is very surprising how little awards to the elderly are reduced for their short duration and how little awards to the young for permanent disabilities are increased. A mid-range award of £50,000 for the amputation of a leg is worth £2,380 a year to a male claimant aged 60 with an expectation of life of 21 years but is worth only £833 a year to a male aged 20 with an expectation of life of 60 years, even though he has lost his most fit and active period of life; yet the court would be unlikely to reduce the award to the older man below £40,000 or to increase the award to the young man above £60,000.

The second type of case where a more detailed assessment might produce fairer **22.23** results is when the claimant suffers more than one injury. The risk of over-compensating because of an overlap is overstated. What usually happens in practice is that the most serious injury is taken as the basis for assessment and if there are other significant injuries that award will be slightly increased. This was the practical approach suggested by the Court of Appeal in *Durau v Evans* [1996] PIQR Q18. In rare cases where the second injury is of an entirely different character—for example a psychiatric injury—the court may set out a separate item in the final lump sum award but this is by no means common. It is interesting to compare the new Criminal Injuries Compensation tariff scheme, where 30% of the tariff is paid for a second distinct injury and 15% of the tariff for a third. This is one area where the tariff award system might even be fairer to claimants than the vagueness of the common law.

The third area where a more detailed approach would be fairer is in the attention **22.24** to be paid to the effects of the enjoyment of specific activities by individual claimants. At present we have the anomaly of compensation for the loss of congenial employment as a significant separate head of injury damages in appropriate cases, but no recognition is given to other equally compelling consequences which may affect individual claimants in other situations. A keen sportsman, dancer, or musician who loses the ability to enjoy a much loved pastime surely may suffer at least as great a loss of the quality of life as a firefighter who has to give up work, and the loss should be recognized in a similar way.

G. Judicial Studies Board Guidelines, 7th edn (2004)

1 INJURIES INVOLVING PARALYSIS

(a) **Quadriplegia**   £175,000 to £220,000

22.25 The level of the award within the bracket will be affected by the following considerations:

(i) the extent of any residual movement;
(ii) the presence and extent of pain;
(iii) depression;
(iv) age and life expectancy.

The top of the bracket will be appropriate only where there is significant effect on senses or ability to communicate. It will also often involve significant brain damage: see 2(A)(a).

(b) **Paraplegia**   £120,000 to £155,000

22.26 The level of the award within the bracket will be affected by the following considerations:

(i) the presence and extent of pain;
(ii) the degree of independence;
(iii) depression;
(iv) age and life expectancy.

The presence of increasing paralysis or the degree of risk that this will occur, for example, from syringomyelia, might take the case above this bracket. The latter might be the subject of a provisional damages order.

2 HEAD INJURIES

(A) BRAIN DAMAGE

(a) **Very Severe Brain Damage**   £155,000 to £220,000

22.27 In cases at the top of this bracket the injured person will have a degree of insight. There may be some ability to follow basic commands, recovery of eye opening and return of sleep and waking patterns and postural reflex movement. There will be little, if any, evidence of meaningful response to environment, little or no language function, double incontinence and the need for full-time nursing care.

The level of the award within the bracket will be affected by:

(i)   the degree of insight;
(ii) life expectancy;
(iii) the extent of physical limitations.

The top of the bracket will be appropriate only where there is significant effect on the senses and severe physical limitation.

Where there is a persistent vegetative state and/or death occurs very soon after the injuries were suffered and there has been no awareness by the injured person of his or her condition the award will be solely for loss of amenity and will fall substantially below the above bracket.

(b) Moderately Severe Brain Injury

£120,000 to £155,000

22.28

The injured person will be very seriously disabled. There will be substantial dependence on others and a need for constant professional and other care. Disabilities may be physical, for example, limb paralysis, or cognitive, with marked impairment of intellect and personality. Cases otherwise within (a) above may fall into this bracket if life expectancy has been greatly reduced.

The level of the award within the bracket will be affected by the following considerations:

(i)   the degree of insight;
(ii)   life expectancy;
(iii) the extent of physical limitations;
(iv)   the degree of dependence on others;
(v)   ability to communicate;
(vi)   behavioural abnormality;
(vii) epilepsy or a significant risk of epilepsy (unless a provisional damages order provides for this risk).

(c) Moderate Brain Damage

22.29

This category is distinguished from (b) by the fact that the degree of dependence is markedly lower.

(i)   Cases in which there is moderate to severe intellectual deficit, a personality change, an effect on sight, speech and senses with a significant risk of epilepsy and no prospect of employment. £82,000 to £120,000
(ii) Cases in which there is a moderate to modest intellectual deficit, the ability to work is greatly reduced if not removed and there is some risk of epilepsy (unless a provisional damages order provides for this risk). £50,000 to £82,000
(iii) Cases in which concentration and memory are affected, the ability to work is reduced, where there is a small risk of epilepsy and any dependence on others is very limited. £23,500 to £50,000

(d) Minor Brain Damage   £8,500 to £23,500

22.30   In these cases the injured person will have made a good recovery and will be able to take part in normal social life and to return to work. There may not have been a restoration of all normal functions so there may still be persisting problems such as poor concentration and memory or disinhibition of mood, which may interfere with lifestyle, leisure activities and future work prospects. At the top of this bracket there may be a small risk of epilepsy.

The level of the award within the bracket will be affected by:

   (i)   the extent and severity of the initial injury;
   (ii) the extent of any continuing, and possibly permanent, disability;
   (iii) the extent of any personality change;
   (iv) depression.

(B) MINOR HEAD INJURY   £1,250 to £7,000

22.31   In these cases brain damage, if any, will have been minimal.

The level of the award will be affected by the following considerations:

   (i)   the severity of the initial injury;
   (ii) the period taken to recover from any symptoms;
   (iii) the extent of continuing symptoms;
   (iv) the presence or absence of headaches.

The bottom of the bracket will reflect full recovery within a few weeks.

(C) EPILEPSY

22.32   **(a) Established Grand Mal**   £55,000 to £82,000

(b) Established Petit Mal   £30,000 to £71,500

The level of the award within these brackets will be affected by the following factors:

   (i)   whether attacks are successfully controlled by medication and the extent to which the need for medication is likely to persist;
   (ii) the extent to which the appreciation of life is blunted by such medication;
   (iii) the effect on working and/or social life;
   (iv) the existence of associated behavioural problems;
   (v)   the prognosis.

(c) Other Epileptic Conditions   £5,750 to £14,250

22.33   Cases where there are one or two discrete epileptic episodes, or a temporary resurgence of epilepsy, but there is no risk of further recurrence beyond that applicable to the population at large. The level of the award within the bracket will be affected by the extent of any consequences of the attacks on, for example, education, sporting activities, working and social life, and their duration.

3 PSYCHIATRIC DAMAGE

In part (A) of this chapter some of the brackets contain an element of **22.34**
compensation for post-traumatic stress disorder. This is of course not
a universal feature of cases of psychiatric injury and hence a number
of the awards upon which the brackets are based did not reflect it.
Where it does figure any award will tend towards the upper end of
the bracket. Cases where post-traumatic stress disorder is the sole
psychiatric condition are dealt with in part (B) of this chapter. Where
cases arise out of sexual and/or physical abuse in breach of parental,
family or other trust, involving victims who are young and/or vulnerable, awards will tend to be at the upper end of the relevant bracket
to take into account (A)(vii) below.

Part (C) of this chapter deals with various conditions under the **22.35**
generic heading 'Chronic Pain'. These are cases where there are
symptoms of pain without any, or any commensurate, organic basis.
Questions of causation inevitably arise in such cases, but it is not the
function of the Guidelines to consider them, and the figures given in
the various sections are on the basis that causation is established.
While the conditions dealt with in part (C) do not necessarily arise
out of psychiatric injury, they are dealt with here partly because they
almost always include an element of psychological damage and partly
for the convenience of users of the Guidelines, because symptoms
caused by these conditions can affect a variety of areas of an injured
person's anatomy. The figures given include compensation for any
physical injury and for any physical disability resulting from the
chronic pain.

(A) PSYCHIATRIC DAMAGE GENERALLY

The factors to be taken into account in valuing claims of this nature **22.36**
are as follows:

    (i)   the injured person's ability to cope with life and work;
    (ii) the effect on the injured person's relationships with
          family, friends and those with whom he or she comes into
          contact;
   (iii) the extent to which treatment would be successful;
   (iv) future vulnerability;
    (v) prognosis;
   (vi) whether medical help has been sought;
  (vii) (a) whether the injury results from sexual and/or physical
             abuse and/or breach of trust;
          (b) if so, the nature of the relationship between victim and
             abuser, the nature of the abuse, its duration and the
             symptoms caused by it.

(a) Severe   £30,000 to £63,000

In these cases the injured person will have marked problems with **22.37**
respect to factors (i) to (iv) above and the prognosis will be very poor.

(b) Moderately Severe £10,500 to £30,000

22.38 In these cases there will be significant problems associated with factors
(i) to (iv) above but the prognosis will be much more optimistic than
in (a) above. While there are awards which support both extremes of
this bracket, the majority are somewhere near the middle of the
bracket. Cases of work-related stress resulting in a permanent or long-
standing disability preventing a return to comparable employment
would appear to come within this category.

(c) Moderate £3,250 to £10,500

22.39 While there may have been the sort of problems associated with
factors (i) to (iv) above there will have been marked improvement by
trial and the prognosis will be good.

(d) Minor £800 to £3,250

22.40 The level of the award will take into consideration the length of the
period of disability and the extent to which daily activities and sleep
were affected. Awards have been made below this bracket in cases of
temporary 'anxiety'.

(B) POST-TRAUMATIC STRESS DISORDER

22.41 Cases within this category are exclusively those where there is a specific diagnosis of a reactive psychiatric disorder in which characteristic
symptoms are displayed following a psychologically distressing event
which was outside the range of normal human experience and which
would be markedly distressing to almost anyone. The guidelines
below have been compiled by reference to cases which variously reflect
the criteria established in the 4th edition of *Diagnostic and Statistical
Manual of Mental Disorders* (DSM-IV-TR). The symptoms affect
basic functions such as breathing, pulse rate and bowel and/or bladder
control. They also involve persistent re-experience of the relevant
event, difficulty in controlling temper, in concentrating and sleeping,
and exaggerated startle response.

(a) Severe £34,000 to £55,000

22.42 Such cases will involve permanent effects which prevent the injured
person from working at all or at least from functioning at anything
approaching the pre-trauma level. All aspects of the life of the injured
person will be badly affected.

(b) Moderately Severe £12,500 to £31,750

22.43 This category is distinct from (a) above because of the better prognosis which will be for some recovery with professional help. However, the effects are still likely to cause significant disability for the
foreseeable future. While there are awards which support both
extremes of this bracket, the majority are between £20,000 and
£25,000.

(c) Moderate £4,500 to £12,500

22.44 In these cases the injured person will have largely recovered and any
continuing effects will not be grossly disabling.

(d) Minor £2,150 to £4,500

22.45

In these cases a virtually full recovery will have been made within one to two years and only minor symptoms will persist over any longer period.

(C) CHRONIC PAIN

(a) Chronic Pain Syndrome **22.46**

(i) Severe £23,000 to £35,000

(ii) Moderate £6,000 to £18,000

(b) Fibromyalgia £19,000 to £35,000

(c) Chronic Fatigue Syndrome In the region of £27,500

(d) Reflex Sympathetic Dystrophy **22.47**

(Also called complex regional pain syndrome)

(i) Severe £28,000 to £55,000

(ii) Moderate £14,000 to £21,000

(e) Somatoform Disorder In the region of £25,000

4 INJURIES AFFECTING THE SENSES

(A) INJURIES AFFECTING SIGHT

(a) Total Blindness and Deafness In the region of £220,000

22.48

Such cases must be considered as ranking with the most devastating injuries.

(b) Total Blindness In the region of £147,500

(c) Loss of Sight in One Eye with Reduced Vision in the Remaining Eye

(i) Where there is serious risk of further deterioration in the remaining eye, going beyond some risk of sympathetic ophthalmia. £52,500 to £98,000 **22.49**

(ii) Where there is reduced vision in the remaining eye and/or additional problems such as double vision. £35,000 to £58,000

(d) Total Loss of One Eye £30,000 to £36,000

22.50

The level of the award within the bracket will depend on age and cosmetic effect.

(e) Complete Loss of Sight in One Eye £27,000 to £30,000

22.51

This award takes account of some risk of sympathetic ophthalmia. The upper end of the bracket is appropriate where there is scarring in the region of the eye which is not sufficiently serious to merit a separate award.

(f) Cases of serious but incomplete loss of vision in one eye without significant risk of loss or reduction of vision in the remaining eye, or where there is constant double vision.

£13,000 to £21,500

(g) Minor but permanent impairment of vision in one eye, including cases where there is some double vision, which may not be constant.

£6,750 to £11,500

(h) **Minor Eye Injuries**

£2,150 to £4,750

22.52 In this bracket fall cases of minor injuries, such as being struck in the eye, exposure to fumes including smoke, or being splashed by liquids, causing initial pain and some temporary interference with vision.

(i) **Transient Eye Injuries**

£1,250 to £2,150

22.53 In these cases the injured person will have recovered completely within a few weeks.

(B) DEAFNESS

22.54 The word 'deafness' is used to embrace total and partial hearing loss. In assessing awards for hearing loss regard must be had to the following:

  (i) whether the injury is one that has an immediate effect, allowing no opportunity to adapt, or whether it occurred over a period of time, as in noise exposure cases;
  (ii) whether the injury or disability is one which the injured person suffered at an early age so that it has had or will have an effect on his or her speech, or is one that is suffered in later life;
  (iii) whether the injury or disability affects balance;
  (iv) in cases of noise-induced hearing loss (NIHL) age is of particular relevance as noted in paragraph (d) below.

(a) **Total Deafness and Loss of Speech**

£60,000 to £77,000

22.55 Such cases arise, for example, where deafness has occurred at an early age (for example, rubella infection) so as to prevent or seriously to affect the development of normal speech.

(b) **Total Deafness**

£50,000 to £60,000

22.56 The lower end of the bracket is appropriate for cases where there is no speech deficit or tinnitus. The higher end is appropriate for cases involving both of these.

(c) **Total Loss of Hearing in One Ear**

£17,500 to £25,000

22.57 Cases will tend towards the higher end of the bracket where there are associated problems, such as tinnitus, dizziness or headaches.

(d) **Partial Hearing Loss/Tinnitus**

22.58 This category covers the bulk of deafness cases which usually result from exposure to noise over a prolonged period. The disability is not to be judged simply by the degree of hearing loss; there is often a degree of tinnitus present. Age is particularly relevant because impairment of hearing affects most people in the fullness of time and impacts both upon causation and upon valuation.

(i)	Severe tinnitus/hearing loss.	£16,000 to £25,000
(ii)	Moderate tinnitus/hearing loss.	£8,000 to £16,000
(iii)	Mild tinnitus with some hearing loss.	£6,750 to £8,000
(iv)	Slight or occasional tinnitus with slight hearing loss.	£4,000 to £6,750

(C) IMPAIRMENT OF TASTE AND SMELL

(a) Total Loss of Taste and Smell   In the region of £21,500   **22.59**

(b) Total Loss of Smell and Significant Loss of Taste   £18,000 to £21,500

It must be remembered that in nearly all cases of loss of smell there is some impairment of taste. Such cases fall into the next bracket.

(c) Loss of Smell   £13,500 to £18,000   **22.60**

(d) Loss of Taste   £10,500 to £13,500

5 INJURIES TO INTERNAL ORGANS

(A) CHEST INJURIES

This is a specially difficult area because the majority of awards relate to industrial *disease* (see (B) below) as distinct from traumatic *injury*. Cases of traumatic damage to, or loss of, a lung are comparatively rare: the range is as wide as £1,250 to £82,000.   **22.61**

The levels of awards within the brackets set out below will be affected by:

(i)	age and gender;	
(ii)	scarring;	
(iii)	the effect on the capacity to work and enjoy life;	
(iv)	the effect on life expectancy.	
	(a) The worst type of case will be of total removal of one lung and/or serious heart damage with serious and prolonged pain and suffering and permanent significant scarring.	£55,000 to £82,000
	(b) Traumatic injury to chest, lung(s) and/or heart causing permanent damage, impairment of function, physical disability and reduction of life expectancy.	£36,000 to £55,000
	(c) Damage to chest and lung(s) causing some continuing disability.	£17,500 to £30,000
	(d) A relatively simple injury (such as a single penetrating wound) causing some permanent damage to tissue but with no significant long-term effect on lung function.	£6,750 to £10,000
	(e) Toxic fume/smoke inhalation, leaving some residual damage, not serious enough to interfere permanently with lung function.	£3,000 to £6,750

(f) Injuries leading to collapsed lungs from which a full and uncomplicated recovery is made. £1,250 to £3,000

(g) Fractures of ribs, causing serious pain and disability over a period of weeks only. Up to £2,150

(B) LUNG DISEASE

22.62 The level of the appropriate award for lung disease necessarily, and often principally, reflects the prognosis for what is frequently a worsening condition and/or the risk of the development of secondary sequelae.

Most of the reported cases are of asbestos-related disease (as to which see (C) below) but, save for asthma (which is also dealt with separately in (D) below), the brackets set out are intended to encompass all other lung disease cases irrespective of causation. In many cases falling under this head provisional awards will be appropriate. At the upper end of the range where serious disabling consequences will already be present and the prognosis is likely to be relatively clear such an award may not be appropriate. Furthermore, in some cases awards may be enhanced where classifiable psychiatric illness is present.

22.63
(a) For a young person with serious disability where there is a probability of progressive worsening leading to premature death. £55,000 to £72,500

(b) Lung cancer (typically in an older person) causing severe pain and impairment both of function and of quality of life. The duration of pain and suffering accounts for variations within this bracket. See also paragraph (C)(b) below. £42,500 to £55,000

(c) Disease, e.g., emphysema, causing significant and worsening lung function and impairment of breathing, prolonged and frequent coughing, sleep disturbance and restriction of physical activity and employment. £30,000 to £43,750

(d) Breathing difficulties (short of disabling breathlessness) requiring fairly frequent use of an inhaler; where there is inability to tolerate a smoky environment and an uncertain prognosis but already significant effect on social and working life. £17,500 to £30,000

(e) Bronchitis and wheezing not causing serious symptoms; little or no serious or permanent effect on working or social life; varying levels of anxiety about the future. £11,500 to £17,500

(f) Some slight breathlessness with no effect on working life and the likelihood of substantial and permanent recovery within a few years of the exposure to the cause or the aggravation of an existing condition. £5,750 to £11,500

(g) Provisional awards for cases otherwise falling within (f), or the least serious cases within (e) where the provisional award excludes any risk of malignancy. £3,000 to £5,750

(h) Temporary aggravation of bronchitis or other chest problems resolving within a very few months. £1,250 to £3,000

(C) ASBESTOS-RELATED DISEASE

Mesothelioma, lung cancer and asbestosis are the most serious of these. Mesothelioma is typically of shorter duration than either of the other two and often proves fatal within a matter of months from first diagnosis. Lung cancer and asbestosis are likely to have a fatal outcome but the symptoms often endure for several years.

22.64

   (a) Mesothelioma causing severe pain and impairment of both function and quality of life. This may be of the pleura (the lung lining) or of the peritoneum (the lining of the abdominal cavity); the latter being typically more painful. The duration of pain and suffering accounts for variations within this bracket. For periods of up to 18 months, awards in the bottom half of the bracket may be appropriate; for longer periods of four years or more, an award at the top end. — **£45,000 to £70,000**

22.65

   (b) Lung cancer, again a disease proving fatal in most cases, the symptoms of which may not be as painful as those of mesothelioma, but more protracted. See also paragraph (B)(b) above. — **£42,500 to £55,000**

   (c) Asbestosis, causing impairment of the extremities of the lungs so that oxygen uptake to the blood stream is reduced. In the early stages the disease may be symptomless but progresses to cause severe breathlessness. Mobility is likely to become seriously impaired and quality of life reduced. Respiratory disability of between 10 and 20 per cent will probably attract an award in the region of £40,000. — **£26,500 to £58,000**

   (d) Pleural thickening, typically causing progressive symptoms of breathlessness by inhibiting expansion of the lungs (the so-called *cuirasse* restriction). Disease may gradually progress to cause more serious respiratory disability. — **£21,000 to £42,500**

   (e) Pleural plaques involving some, but limited, disability. May also be accompanied by psychological injury causing disability. — **£15,000 to £20,000**

   (f) Asymptomatic pleural plaques. — **£5,000 to £6,000**

   (g) Provisional awards for cases otherwise falling within (e) or (f) or the least serious cases within (d) where the provisional award excludes any risk of the development of mesothelioma, lung or other cancer or asbestosis. — **£5,000 to £25,000**

(D) ASTHMA

   (a) Severe and permanent disabling asthma, causing prolonged and regular coughing, disturbance of sleep, severe impairment of physical activity and enjoyment of life and where employment prospects, if any, are grossly restricted. — **£23,500 to £36,000**

22.66

   (b) Chronic asthma causing breathing difficulties, the need to use an inhaler from time to time and restriction of employment prospects, with uncertain prognosis. — **£14,250 to £23,500**

   (c) Bronchitis and wheezing, affecting working or social life, with the likelihood of substantial recovery within a few years of the exposure to the cause. — **£10,500 to £14,250**

(d) Relatively mild asthma-like symptoms often resulting, for instance, from exposure to harmful irritating vapour.	£5,750 to £10,500
(e) Mild asthma, bronchitis, colds and chest problems (usually resulting from unfit housing or similar exposure, particularly in cases of young children) treated by a general practitioner and resolving within a few months.	Up to £2,750

(E) REPRODUCTIVE SYSTEM: MALE

22.67   (a) Impotence

(i) Total impotence and loss of sexual function and sterility in the case of a young man.	**In the region of £80,000**

The level of the award will depend on:
        (1) age;
        (2) psychological reaction and the effect on social and domestic life.

(ii) Impotence which is likely to be permanent, in the case of a middle-aged man with children.	£23,500 to £43,750

(b) Cases of sterility usually fall into one of two categories: surgical, chemical and disease cases (which involve no traumatic injury or scarring) and traumatic injuries (frequently caused by assaults) which are often aggravated by scarring.

(i) The most serious cases merit awards approaching	£77,000
(ii) The bottom of the range is the case of the much older man and merits an award of about	£10,000
(c) An uncomplicated case of sterility without impotence and without any aggravating features for a young man without children.	£31,000 to £39,000
(d) A similar case but involving a family man who might have intended to have more children.	£13,000 to £17,000
(e) Cases where the sterility amounts to little more than an 'insult'.	**In the region of £3,500**

(F) REPRODUCTIVE SYSTEM: FEMALE

22.68   The level of awards in this area will typically depend on:

    (i) whether or not the affected woman already has children and/or whether the intended family was complete;
    (ii) scarring;
   (iii) depression or psychological scarring;
   (iv) whether a foetus was aborted.

22.69

(a) Infertility whether by reason of injury or disease, with severe depression and anxiety, pain and scarring.	£63,000 to £93,000
(b) Infertility without any medical complication and where the injured person already has children. The upper end of the bracket is appropriate in cases where there is significant psychological damage.	£10,000 to £20,000
(c) Infertility where the injured person would not have had children in any event (for example, because of age).	£3,500 to £7,000

(d) Failed sterilisation leading to unwanted pregnancy where there
is no serious psychological impact or depression.   **In the region of £5,500**

(G) DIGESTIVE SYSTEM

The risk of associated damage to the reproductive organs is frequently   **22.70**
encountered in cases of this nature and requires separate con-
sideration.

(a) Damage Resulting from Traumatic Injury

(i) Severe damage with continuing pain and discomfort.   £23,500 to £34,000   **22.71**

(ii) Serious non-penetrating injury causing long-standing or
permanent complications, for example, severe indigestion,
aggravated by physical strain.   £9,250 to £15,250

(iii) Penetrating stab wounds or industrial laceration or serious
seat-belt pressure cases.   £3,500 to £7,000

**(b) Illness/Damage Resulting from Non-traumatic Injury, e.g.
Food Poisoning**

There will be a marked distinction between those, comparatively rare,   **22.72**
cases having a long-standing or even permanent effect on quality of
life and those in which the only continuing symptoms may be allergy
to specific foods and the attendant risk of short-term illness.

(i) Severe toxicosis causing serious acute pain, vomiting, diarrhoea and fever, requiring hospital admission for some days
or weeks and some continuing incontinence, haemorrhoids
and irritable bowel syndrome, having a significant impact on
ability to work and enjoyment of life.   £21,000 to £32,000

(ii) Serious but short-lived food poisoning, diarrhoea and
vomiting diminishing over two to four weeks with some
remaining discomfort and disturbance of bowel function
and impact on sex life and enjoyment of food over a few
years.   £5,250 to £10,500

(iii) Food poisoning causing significant discomfort, stomach
cramps, alteration of bowel function and fatigue. Hospital
admission for some days with symptoms lasting for a few
weeks but complete recovery within a year or two.   £2,150 to £5,250

(iv) Varying degrees of disabling pain, cramps and diarrhoea
continuing for some days or weeks.   £500 to £2,150

(H) KIDNEY

(a) Serious and permanent damage to or loss of both kidneys.   £93,000 to £115,000   **22.73**

(b) Where there is a significant risk of future urinary tract infection or other total loss of natural kidney function.   Up to £35,000

Such cases will invariably carry with them substantial future medical
expenses, which in this field are particularly high.

(c) Loss of one kidney with no damage to the other.   £17,000 to £23,500

(I) BOWELS

22.74   (a) Total loss of natural function and dependence on colostomy, depending on age.   **Up to £82,000**

(b) Severe abdominal injury causing impairment of function and often necessitating temporary colostomy (leaving disfiguring scars) and/or restriction on employment and on diet.   **£24,500 to £38,000**

(c) Penetrating injuries causing some permanent damage but with an eventual return to natural function and control.   **£6,750 to £13,250**

(J) BLADDER

22.75   It is perhaps surprising that awards in cases of loss of bladder function have often been higher than awards for injury to the bowels. This is probably because bladder injuries frequently result from carcinogenic exposure. The reported decisions are seriously out of date and merely increasing them to reflect inflation may be misleading.

22.76   (a) Complete loss of function and control.   **Up to £77,000**

(b) Serious impairment of control with some pain and incontinence.   **£35,000 to £43,750**

(c) Where there has been almost a complete recovery but some fairly long-term interference with natural function.   **£13,000 to £17,000**

The cancer risk cases still occupy a special category and can properly attract awards at the top of the ranges even where natural function continues for the time being. However, these cases will now more appropriately be dealt with by provisional awards at a low level (£5,500) unless the foreseeable outcome is clear. Once the prognosis is firm and reliable the award will reflect any loss of life expectancy, the level of continuing pain and suffering and most significantly the extent to which the injured person has to live with the knowledge of the consequences which his or her death will have for others. The appropriate award for the middle-aged family man or woman whose life expectancy is reduced by 15 or 20 years is £30,000 to £43,750.

(K) SPLEEN

22.77   (a) Loss of spleen where there is continuing risk of internal infection and disorders due to the damage to the immune system.   **£11,500 to £14,500**

(b) Where the above risks are not present or are minimal.   **£2,250 to £4,750**

(L) HERNIA

22.78   (a) Continuing pain and/or limitation on physical activities, sport or employment, after repair.   **£8,000 to £13,250**

(b) Direct (where there was no pre-existing weakness) inguinal hernia, with some risk of recurrence, after repair.   **£3,750 to £5,000**

(c) Uncomplicated indirect inguinal hernia, possibly repaired, and with no other associated abdominal injury or damage.   **£1,850 to £4,000**

6 ORTHOPAEDIC INJURIES

(A) NECK INJURIES

There is a very wide range of neck injuries. Many are found in conjunction with back and shoulder problems.   **22.79**

At the highest level are injuries which shatter life and leave claimants very severely disabled. These may have a value of up to £85,000.

At the lowest level, claimants may suffer a minor strain, may not have time off work, and may suffer symptoms for a few weeks, justifying as little as £750.

(a) Severe

  (i) Neck injury associated with incomplete paraplegia or result-   **22.80**
ing in permanent spastic quadriparesis or where the injured person, despite wearing a collar 24 hours a day for a period of years, still has little or no movement in the neck and suffers severe headaches which have proved intractable.   **In the region of £82,000**

  (ii) Injuries which give rise to disabilities which fall short of those in (a)(i) above but which are of considerable severity; for example, permanent damage to the brachial plexus.   **£36,000 to £71,500**

  (iii) Injuries causing severe damage to soft tissues and/or ruptured tendons. They result in significant disability of a permanent nature. The precise award depends on the length of time during which the most serious symptoms are ameliorated, and on the prognosis.   **In the region of £30,000**

  (iv) Injuries such as fractures or dislocations which cause severe immediate symptoms and which may necessitate spinal fusion. They leave markedly impaired function or vulnerability to further trauma, and some limitation of activities.   **£13,500 to £18,000**

(b) Moderate

  (i) Cases involving whiplash or wrenching-type injury and   **22.81**
disc lesion of the more severe type resulting in cervical spondylosis, serious limitation of movement, permanent or recurring pain, stiffness or discomfort and the possible need for further surgery or increased vulnerability to further trauma.   **£7,500 to £13,750**

  (ii) Injuries which may have exacerbated or accelerated some pre-existing unrelated condition. There will have been a complete recovery or recovery to 'nuisance' level from the effects of the accident within a few years. This bracket will also apply to moderate whiplash injuries where the period of recovery has been fairly protracted and where there remains an increased vulnerability to further trauma.   **£4,250 to £7,750**

(c) Minor

22.82   Minor soft tissue and whiplash injuries and the like where symptoms are moderate:

(i)	and a full recovery takes place within about two years;	£2,500 to £4,250
(ii)	with a full recovery between a few weeks and a year.	£750 to £2,500

(B) BACK INJURIES

22.83   Relatively few back injuries which do not give rise to paralysis command awards above about £25,000. In those that do there are special features.

(a) Severe

22.84
(i)	Cases of the most severe injury which do not involve paralysis but where there may be very serious consequences not normally found in cases of back injury, such as impotence or double incontinence.	£55,000 to £93,000
(ii)	Cases which have special features taking them outside any lower bracket applicable to orthopaedic injury to the back. Such features include impaired bladder and bowel function, severe sexual difficulties and unsightly scarring and the possibility of future surgery.	In the region of £45,000
(iii)	Cases of disc lesions or fractures of discs or of vertebral bodies where, despite treatment, there remain disabilities such as continuing severe pain and discomfort, impaired agility, impaired sexual function, depression, personality change, alcoholism, unemployability and the risk of arthritis.	£21,500 to £38,000

(b) Moderate

22.85
(i)	Cases where any residual disability is of less severity than that in (a)(iii) above. The bracket contains a wide variety of injuries. Examples are a case of a crush fracture of the lumbar vertebrae where there is a substantial risk of osteoarthritis and constant pain and discomfort with impairment of sexual function; that of a traumatic spondylolisthesis with continuous pain and a probability that spinal fusion will be necessary; or that of a prolapsed intervertebral disc with substantial acceleration of back degeneration.	£15,250 to £21,500
(ii)	Many frequently encountered injuries to the back such as disturbance of ligaments and muscles giving rise to backache, soft tissue injuries resulting in exacerbation of an existing back condition or prolapsed discs necessitating laminectomy or resulting in repeated relapses. The precise figure depends upon the severity of the original injury and/or whether there is some permanent or chronic disability.	£6,750 to £15,250

(c) Minor

Strains, sprains, disc prolapses and soft tissue injuries from which a full recovery or recovery to 'nuisance' level has been made without surgery: **22.86**

(i) within about five years;	£4,250 to £7,500
(ii) within about two years.	Up to £4,250

(C) SHOULDER INJURIES

(a) Severe   £10,500 to £26,500

Often associated with neck injuries and involving damage to the brachial plexus (see (A)(a)(ii)) resulting in significant disability.   **22.87**

(b) Serious   £6,750 to £10,500

Dislocation of the shoulder and damage to the lower part of the brachial plexus causing pain in shoulder and neck, aching in elbow, sensory symptoms in the forearm and hand, and weakness of grip.   **22.88**

(c) Moderate   £4,250 to £7,000

Frozen shoulder with limitation of movement and discomfort with symptoms persisting for about two years.   **22.89**

(d) Minor

Soft tissue injury to shoulder with considerable pain but almost complete recovery: **22.90**

(i) in less than two years;	£2,500 to £4,500
(ii) within a year.	Up to £2,500

(e) Fracture of Clavicle   £2,750 to £6,500

The level of the award will depend on extent of fracture, level of disability, residual symptoms, and whether temporary or permanent, and whether union is anatomically displaced.   **22.91**

(D) INJURIES TO THE PELVIS AND HIPS

The most serious of injuries to the pelvis and hip can be as devastating as a leg amputation and accordingly will attract a similar award of damages. Such cases apart, the upper limit for these injuries will generally be in the region of £37,500. Cases where there are specific sequelae of exceptional severity would call for a higher award.   **22.92**

(a) Severe

(i) Extensive fractures of the pelvis involving, for example, dislocation of a low back joint and a ruptured bladder, or a hip injury resulting in spondylolisthesis of a low back joint with intolerable pain and necessitating spinal fusion. Inevitably there will be substantial residual disabilities such as a complicated arthrodesis with resulting lack of bladder and bowel control, sexual dysfunction or hip deformity making the use of a calliper essential; or may present difficulties for natural delivery.   £43,750 to £71,500   **22.93**

(ii) Injuries only a little less severe than in (a)(i) above but with particular distinguishing features lifting them above any lower bracket. Examples are: (a) fracture dislocation of the pelvis involving both ischial and pubic rami and resulting in impotence; or (b) traumatic myositis ossificans with formation of ectopic bone around the hip.   £34,000 to £43,750

(iii) Many injuries fall within this bracket: a fracture of the acetabulum leading to degenerative changes and leg instability requiring an osteotomy and the likelihood of hip replacement surgery in the future; the fracture of an arthritic femur or hip necessitating hip replacement; or a fracture resulting in a hip replacement which is only partially successful so that there is a clear risk of the need for revision surgery.   £21,500 to £28,500

(b) Moderate   £14,750 to £21,500

22.94   Significant injury to the pelvis or hip but any permanent disability is not major and any future risk not great.

(c) Injuries of Limited Severity   £6,750 to £14,750

22.95   These cases may involve hip replacement. Where it has been carried out wholly successfully the award will tend to the top of the bracket, but the bracket also includes cases where hip replacement may be necessary in the foreseeable future.

(d) Lesser Injuries

22.96   (i) Cases where despite significant injury there is little or no residual disability.   £2,150 to £7,000

(ii) Minor injuries with complete recovery.   Up to £2,150

(E) AMPUTATION OF ARMS

(a) Loss of Both Arms   £132,500 to £165,000

22.97   There is no recent case to offer guidance but the effect of such an injury is to reduce a person with full awareness to a state of considerable helplessness.

(b) Loss of One Arm

22.98   (i) **Arm Amputated at the Shoulder**   Not less than £75,000

(ii) **Above-elbow Amputation**   £60,000 to £71,500

A shorter stump may create difficulties in the use of a prosthesis. This will make the level of the award towards the top end of the bracket. Amputation through the elbow will normally produce an award at the bottom end of the bracket.

(iii) **Below-elbow Amputation**   £52,500 to £60,000

22.99   Amputation through the forearm with residual severe organic and phantom pains would attract an award at the top end of the bracket.

The value of such an injury depends upon:

(i) whether the amputation is above or below the elbow. The loss of the additional joint adds greatly to the disability;

  (ii) whether or not the amputation was of the dominant arm;
  (iii) the intensity of any phantom pains.

(F) OTHER ARM INJURIES

(a) Severe Injuries   £52,500 to £71,500

22.100

Injuries which fall short of amputation but which are extremely serious and leave the injured person little better off than if the arm had
been lost; for example, a serious brachial plexus injury.

(b) Injuries resulting in Permanent and Substantial Disablement   £21,500 to £33,000

22.101

Serious fractures of one or both forearms where there is significant
permanent residual disability whether functional or cosmetic.

(c) Less Severe Injury   £10,500 to £21,500

22.102

While there will have been significant disabilities, a substantial degree
of recovery will have taken place or will be expected.

(d) Simple Fractures of the Forearm   £3,650 to £10,500

22.103

Uncomplicated fractures of the radius and/or ulna with a complete
recovery within a short time would justify an award of £3,650.
Injuries resulting in modest residual disability or deformity would
merit an award towards the upper end of this bracket.

(G) INJURIES TO THE ELBOW

(a) A Severely Disabling Injury   £21,500 to £30,000   **22.104**

(b) Less Severe Injuries   £8,750 to £17,500

Injuries causing impairment of function but not involving major
surgery or significant disability.

(c) Moderate or Minor Injury   Up to £7,000

22.105

Most elbow injuries fall into this category. They comprise simple
fractures, tennis elbow syndrome and lacerations; i.e., those injuries
which cause no permanent damage and do not result in any permanent impairment of function.

(H) WRIST INJURIES

22.106

  (a) Injuries resulting in complete loss of function in the wrist, for
       example, where an arthrodesis has been performed.   £26,250 to £33,000
  (b) Injury resulting in significant permanent disability, but where
       some useful movement remains.   £13,500 to £21,500
  (c) Less severe injuries where these still result in some perman-
       ent disability as, for example, a degree of persisting pain and
       stiffness.   £6,750 to £13,500
  (d) An uncomplicated Colles' fracture.   **In the region of £4,000**
  (e) Very minor undisplaced or minimally displaced fractures and
       the like necessitating application of plaster or bandage for a
       matter of weeks and a full or virtual recovery within a matter of
       months.   £2,000 to £2,500

Where recovery from fracture or soft tissue injury takes longer but is complete, the award will rarely exceed £5,500.

(I) HAND INJURIES

22.107 The hands are cosmetically and functionally the most important component parts of the upper limbs. The loss of a hand is valued not far short of the amount which would be awarded for the loss of the arm itself. The upper end of any bracket will generally be appropriate where the injury is to the dominant hand.

(a) Total or Effective Loss of Both Hands £75,000 to £110,000

22.108 Serious injury resulting in extensive damage to both hands such as to render them little more than useless will justify an award of £75,000 or more. The top of the bracket is applicable where no effective prosthesis can be used.

(b) Serious Damage to Both Hands £30,000 to £46,500

22.109 Such injuries will have given rise to permanent cosmetic disability and significant loss of function.

(c) Total or Effective Loss of One Hand £52,500 to £60,000

22.110 This bracket will apply to a hand which was crushed and thereafter surgically amputated or where all fingers and most of the palm have been traumatically amputated. The upper end of the bracket is indicated where the hand so damaged was the dominant one.

(d) Amputation of Index and Middle and/or Ring Fingers £34,000 to £50,000

22.111 The hand will have been rendered of very little use and such grip as remains will be exceedingly weak.

(e) Serious Hand Injuries £16,000 to £34,000

22.112 Such injuries will, for example, have reduced the hand to about 50 per cent capacity. Included would be cases where several fingers have been amputated but rejoined to the hand leaving it clawed, clumsy and unsightly, or amputation of some fingers together with part of the palm resulting in gross diminution of grip and dexterity and gross cosmetic disfigurement.

(f) Less Serious Hand Injury £8,000 to £16,000

22.113 Such as a severe crush injury resulting in significantly impaired function without future surgery or despite operative treatment undergone.

(g) Moderate Hand Injury £3,500 to £7,250

22.114 Crush injuries, penetrating wounds, soft tissue type and deep lacerations. The top of the bracket would be appropriate where surgery has failed and permanent disability remains.

(h) Minor Hand Injuries £500 to £2,250

22.115 Injuries similar to but less serious than (g) above with recovery within a few months.

(i) Severe Fractures to Fingers	Up to £20,000	
These may lead to partial amputations and result in deformity, impairment of grip, reduced mechanical function and disturbed sensation.		**22.116**
(j) Total Loss of Index Finger	In the region of £10,000	**22.117**
(k) Partial Loss of Index Finger	£65,000 to £10,000	
This bracket also covers cases of injury to the index finger giving rise to disfigurement and impairment of grip or dexterity.		**22.118**
(l) Fracture of Index Finger	£5,000 to £6,500	
This level is appropriate where a fracture has mended quickly but grip has remained impaired, there is pain on heavy use and osteoarthritis is likely in due course.		**22.119**
(m) Total Loss of Middle Finger	In the region of £8,500	**22.120**
(n) Serious Injury to Ring or Middle Fingers	£8,000 to £9,000	
Fractures or serious injury to tendons causing stiffness, deformity and permanent loss of grip or dexterity will fall within this bracket.		**22.121**
(o) Loss of the Terminal Phalanx of the Ring or Middle Fingers	£2,150 to £4,000	**22.122**
(p) Amputation of Little Finger	£4,750 to £6,500	**22.123**
(q) Loss of Part of the Little Finger	£2,150 to £3,250	
This is appropriate where the remaining tip is sensitive.		**22.124**
(r) Amputation of Ring and Little Fingers	In the region of £12,000	**22.125**
(s) Amputation of the Terminal Phalanges of the Index and Middle Fingers	In the region of £13,500	
Such injury will involve scarring, restriction of movement and impairment of grip and fine handling.		**22.126**
(t) Fracture of One Finger	£1,500 to £2,600	
Depending upon recovery time.		**22.127**
(u) Loss of Thumb	£19,500 to £30,000	**22.128**
(v) Very Serious Injury to Thumb	£10,750 to £19,500	
This bracket is appropriate where the thumb has been severed at the base and grafted back leaving a virtually useless and deformed digit, or where the thumb has been amputated through the interphalangeal joint.		**22.129**
(w) Serious Injury to the Thumb	£6,750 to £9,250	
Such injuries may involve amputation of the tip, nerve damage or fracture necessitating the insertion of wires as a result of which the thumb is cold and ultra-sensitive and there is impaired grip and loss of manual dexterity.		**22.130**

(x) Moderate Injuries to the Thumb	£5,250 to £7,000

22.131 These are injuries such as those necessitating arthrodesis of the inter-phalangeal joint or causing damage to tendons or nerves. Such injuries result in impairment of sensation and function and cosmetic deformity.

22.132 (y) Severe Dislocation of the Thumb	£2,150 to £3,650

(z) Minor Injuries to the Thumb	In the region of £2,250

22.133 Such an injury would be a fracture which has recovered in six months except for residual stiffness and some discomfort.

(aa) Trivial Thumb Injuries	In the region of £1,250

22.134 These may have caused severe pain for a very short time but will have resolved within a few months.

(J) VIBRATION WHITE FINGER AND/OR HAND–ARM VIBRATION SYNDROME

22.135 Vibration White Finger and/or Hand–Arm Vibration Syndrome, caused by exposure to vibration, is a slowly progressive condition, the development and severity of which are affected by the degree of exposure, in particular the magnitude, frequency, duration and transmission of the vibration. The symptoms are similar to those experienced in the constitutional condition of Raynaud's phenomenon.

The Stockholm Workshop Scale is now the accepted table for grading the severity of the condition. The Scale classifies both the vascular and sensorineural components in two complementary tables. Individual assessment is made separately for each hand and for each finger. Any interference with work or social life is disregarded.

22.136 Accordingly, depending on individual circumstances, a lower award might be made despite significant disablement where, e.g., employment is unaffected, whilst a higher award might be attracted where there is a lesser disability but a consequential inability to pursue working life.

The vascular component is graded between Stage 0 (no attacks) through mild, moderate and severe to 4V (very severe) where there are frequent attacks affecting all phalanges of most fingers with atrophic changes in the fingertips.

22.137 The sensorineural component is graded between Stage 0SN (no symptoms) and 3SN (intermittent or persistent numbness, reduced tactile discrimination and/or manipulative dexterity).

The grade of disorder is indicated by the stage and number of affected fingers on both hands.

The assessment of damages depends upon the extent of the symptoms and their impact upon work and social life.

22.138 In a severe case, the injury may be regarded as damaging a hand rather than being confined to the fingers.

The brackets can best be defined and valued as follows:

(i)	Most Serious	£17,500 to £21,000
(ii)	Serious	£9,250 to £17,500
(iii)	Moderate	£4,750 to £9,250
(iv)	Minor	£1,500 to £4,750

(K) WORK-RELATED UPPER LIMB DISORDERS

This section covers a range of upper limb injury in the form of the following pathological conditions:

22.139

(a) Tenosynovitis: inflammation of synovial sheaths of tendons usually resolving with rest over a short period. Sometimes this condition leads to continuing symptoms of loss of grip and dexterity

(b) De Quervain's tenosynovitis: a form of tenosynovitis, rarely bilateral, involving inflammation of the tendons of the thumb.

(c) Stenosing tenosynovitis: otherwise, trigger finger/thumb: thickening tendons.

(d) Carpal tunnel syndrome: constriction of the median nerve of the wrist of thickening of surrounding tissue. It is often relieved by a decompression operation.

(e) Epicondylitis: inflammation in the elbow joint: medial = golfer's elbow; lateral = tennis elbow.

The brackets below apply to all these conditions but the level of the award is affected by the following considerations regardless of the precise condition:

(i)	are the effects bilateral or one sided?
(ii)	the level of symptoms, i.e., pain, swelling, tenderness, crepitus;
(iii)	the ability to work;
(iv)	the capacity to avoid the recurrence of symptoms;
(v)	surgery.

(a)	Continuing bilateral disability with surgery and loss of employment.	£12,000 to £12,500
(b)	Continuing, but fluctuating and unilateral symptoms.	£8,000 to £9,000
(c)	Symptoms resolving in the course of two years.	£4,750 to £5,250
(d)	Complete recovery within a short period.	£1,250 to £1,900

(L) LEG INJURIES

(a) Amputations

(i) Total Loss of Both Legs   £132,500 to £155,000   **22.140**

This is the appropriate award where both legs are lost above the knee and particularly if near to the hip leaving one or both stumps less than adequate to accommodate a useful prosthesis.

(ii) Below-knee Amputation of Both Legs   £110,000 to £147,500

The top of the bracket is appropriate where both legs are amputated just below the knee. Amputations lower down result in a lower award.

(iii) Above-knee Amputation of One Leg   £52,500 to £77,000

The area within the bracket within which the award should fall will depend upon such factors as the level of the amputation; the severity of phantom pains; whether or not there have been any problems with a prosthesis and any side effects such as depression or backache.

(iv) Below-knee Amputation of One Leg £50,000 to £71,500

The straightforward case of a below-knee amputation with no complications would justify an award at the bottom of this bracket. At or towards the top of the range would come the traumatic amputation which occurs in a devastating accident, where the injured person remained fully conscious, or cases where attempts to save the leg led to numerous unsuccessful operations so that amputation occurred years after the event.

(b) Severe Leg Injuries

22.141 **(i) The Most Serious Injuries short of Amputation** £52,500 to £74,000

Some injuries, although not involving amputation, are so severe that the courts have awarded damages at a comparable level. Such injuries would include extensive degloving of the leg, where there is gross shortening of the leg or where fractures have not united and extensive bone grafting has been undertaken.

(ii) Very Serious £30,000 to £46,500

Injuries leading to permanent problems with mobility, the need for crutches for the remainder of the injured person's life; injuries where multiple fractures have taken years to heal and have led to serious deformity and limitation of movement, or where arthritis has developed in a joint so that further surgical treatment is likely.

(iii) Serious £21,500 to £30,000

Serious injuries to joints or ligaments resulting in instability, prolonged treatment, a lengthy period of non-weight-bearing, the near certainty that arthritis will ensue; injuries involving the hip, requiring arthrodesis or hip replacement, extensive scarring. To justify an award within this bracket a combination of such features will generally be necessary.

(iv) Moderate £15,250 to £21,500

This bracket includes severe, complicated or multiple fractures. The level of an award within the bracket will be influenced by the period off work; the presence or risk of degenerative changes; imperfect union of fractures, muscle wasting; limited joint movements; instability in the knee; unsightly scarring or permanently increased vulnerability to future damage.

(c) Less Serious Leg Injuries

22.142 **(i) Fractures from which an Incomplete Recovery is Made** £10,000 to £15,250

The injured person will be left with a metal implant and/or defective gait, a limp, impaired mobility, sensory loss, discomfort or an exacerbation of a pre-existing disability.

(ii) Simple Fracture of a Femur with No Damage to Articular Surfaces £5,000 to £7,750

(iii) Simple Fractures and Soft Tissue Injuries   Up to £5,000

At the top of the bracket will come simple fractures of the tibia or fibula from which a complete recovery has been made. Below this level fall a wide variety of soft tissue injuries, lacerations, cuts, bruising or contusions, all of which have recovered completely or almost so and any residual disability is cosmetic or of a minor nature.

(M) KNEE INJURIES

Knee injuries fall within a bracket extending from a few hundred pounds for a simple twisting injury up to £50,000 or so.   **22.143**

(a) Severe

   (i) Serious knee injury where there has been disruption of the joint, gross ligamentous damage, lengthy treatment, considerable pain and loss of function and an arthrodesis or arthroplasty has taken place or is inevitable.   £38,000 to £52,500   **22.144**

  (ii) Leg fracture extending into the knee joint causing pain which is constant, permanent, limiting movement or impairing agility and rendering the injured person prone to osteoarthritis and the risk of arthroplasty.   £28,500 to £38,000

 (iii) Less severe injuries than those in (a)(ii) above and/or injuries which result in less severe disability. There may be continuing symptoms by way of pain and discomfort and limitation of movement or instability or deformity with the risk that degenerative changes may occur in the long term as a result of damage to the kneecap, ligamentous or meniscal injury or muscular wasting.   £14,750 to £23,500

(b) Moderate

   (i) Injuries involving dislocation, torn cartilage or meniscus or which accelerate symptoms from a pre-existing condition but which additionally result in minor instability, wasting, weakness or other mild future disability.   £8,000 to £14,750   **22.145**

  (ii) This bracket includes injuries similar to those in (b)(i) above, but less serious, and also lacerations, twisting or bruising injuries. Where recovery has been complete the award is unlikely to exceed £3,250. Where there is continuous aching or discomfort, or occasional pain, the award will be towards the upper end of the bracket.   Up to £7,500

(N) ANKLE INJURIES

The vast majority of ankle injuries are worth significantly less than £10,000.   **22.146**

(a) Very Severe   £27,500 to £38,000

Examples of injuries falling within this bracket are limited and unusual. They include cases of a transmalleolar fracture of the ankle with extensive soft-tissue damage resulting in deformity and the risk that any future injury to the leg might necessitate a below-knee amputation, or cases of bilateral ankle fractures causing degeneration of the joints at a young age so that arthrodesis is necessary.   **22.147**

(b) Severe   £17,500 to £27,500

22.148   Injuries necessitating an extensive period of treatment and/or a
lengthy period in plaster or where pins and plates have been inserted
and there is significant residual disability in the form of ankle instability, severely limited ability to walk. The level of the award within
the bracket will be determined in part by such features as a failed
arthrodesis, regular sleep disturbance, unsightly scarring and any need
to wear special footwear.

(c) Moderate   £7,250 to £14,750

22.149   Fractures, ligamentous tears and the like which give rise to less
serious disabilities such as difficulty in walking on uneven ground,
awkwardness on stairs, irritation from metal plates and residual
scarring.

(d) Modest Injuries   Up to £7,500

22.150   The less serious, minor or undisplaced fractures, sprains and ligamentous injuries. The level of the award within the bracket will be
determined by whether or not a complete recovery has been made
and, if recovery is incomplete, whether there is any tendency for the
ankle to give way, and whether there is scarring, aching or discomfort
or the possibility of later osteoarthritis.

Where recovery is within a year, the award is unlikely to exceed
£3,250.

(O) ACHILLES TENDON

(a) Most Serious   In the region of £20,000

22.151   Severance of the tendon and the peroneus longus muscle giving rise
to cramp, swelling and restricted ankle movement necessitating the
cessation of active sports.

(b) Serious   £13,500 to £16,500

22.152   Where complete division of the tendon has been successfully repaired
but there is residual weakness, a limitation of ankle movements, a
limp and residual scarring and where further improvement is unlikely.

(c) Moderate   £8,000 to £10,000

22.153   Complete division of the tendon but where its repair has left no
significant functional disability.

(d) Minor   £4,000 to £5,500

22.154   A turning of the ankle resulting in some damage to the tendon and a
feeling of being unsure of ankle support.

(P) FOOT INJURIES

(a) Amputation of Both Feet   £93,000 to £110,000

22.155   This injury is treated similarly to below-knee amputation of both legs
because the common feature is loss of a useful ankle joint.

(b) Amputation of One Foot   £46,000 to £60,000

This injury is also treated as similar to a below-knee amputation   **22.156**
because of the loss of the ankle joint.

(c) Very Severe   £46,000 to £60,000

To fall within this bracket the injury must produce permanent and   **22.157**
severe pain or really serious permanent disability. Examples would
include the traumatic amputation of the forefoot where there was a
significant risk of the need for a full amputation and serious exacerbation of an existing back problem, or cases of the loss of a substantial
portion of the heel so that mobility was grossly restricted.

(d) Severe   £25,000 to £37,000

Fractures of *both* heels or feet with a substantial restriction on   **22.158**
mobility or considerable or permanent pain. The bracket will also
include unusually severe injury to a single foot resulting, for example,
in heel fusion, osteoporosis, ulceration or other disability preventing
the wearing of ordinary shoes. It will also apply in the case of a drop
foot deformity corrected by a brace.

(e) Serious   £13,750 to £21,500

Towards the top end of the bracket fall cases such as those of grievous   **22.159**
burns to both feet requiring multiple operations and leaving dis-
figuring scars and persistent irritation. At the lower end of the bracket
would be those injuries less severe than in (d) above but leading to
fusion of foot joints, continuing pain from traumatic arthritis,
prolonged treatment and the future risk of osteoarthritis.

(f) Moderate   £7,500 to £13,750

Displaced metatarsal fractures resulting in permanent deformity and   **22.160**
continuing symptoms.

(g) Modest   Up to £7,500

Simple metatarsal fractures, ruptured ligaments, puncture wounds   **22.161**
and the like. Where there are continuing symptoms, such as a per-
manent limp, pain or aching, awards between £3,750 and £7,500
would be appropriate. Straightforward foot injuries such as fractures,
lacerations, contusions etc. from which complete or near complete
recovery is made would justify awards of £3,750 or less.

(Q) TOE INJURIES

(a) Amputation of All Toes   £20,000 to £31,000

The position within the bracket will be determined by, for example,   **22.162**
whether or not the amputation was traumatic or surgical and the
extent of the loss of the forefoot together with the residual effects on
mobility.

(b) Amputation of the Great Toe   In the region of £17,500   **22.163**

(c) Severe Toe Injuries   £7,500 to £10,500

22.164 This is the appropriate bracket for severe crush injuries, falling short of the need for amputation or necessitating only partial amputation. It also includes bursting wounds and injuries resulting in severe damage and in any event producing significant continuing symptoms.

(d) Serious Toe Injuries   £5,250 to £7,500

22.165 Such injuries will be serious injuries to the great toe or crush and multiple fractures of two or more toes. There will be some permanent disability by way of discomfort, pain or sensitive scarring to justify an award within this bracket. Where there have been a number of unsuccessful operations or persisting stabbing pains, impaired gait or the like the award will tend towards the top end of the bracket.

(e) Moderate Toe Injuries   Up to £5,250

22.166 These injuries include relatively straightforward fractures or the exacerbation of a pre-existing degenerative condition. Only £3,250 or less would be awarded for straightforward fractures of one or more toes with complete resolution within a short period of time and less still for minor injuries involving lacerations, cuts, contusions and bruises, in respect of all of which there would have been a complete or near complete recovery.

7 FACIAL INJURIES

22.167 The assessment of general damages for facial injuries is an extremely difficult task, there being three elements which complicate the award.

First, while in most of the cases dealt with below the injuries described are skeletal, many of them will involve an element of disfigurement or at least some cosmetic effect.

22.168 Second, in cases where there is a cosmetic element the courts have invariably drawn a distinction between the awards of damages to males and females, the latter attracting the higher awards.

Third, in cases of disfigurement there may also be severe psychological reactions which put the total award at the top of the bracket, or above it altogether.

22.169 The subject of burns is not dealt with separately. Burns of any degree of severity are particularly painful and disfiguring, and awards are invariably at the upper ends of the brackets, or above them altogether. The very worst burns may lead not only to considerable disfigurement and pain but to a variety of continuing physical and psychological injuries meriting very high awards.

(A) SKELETAL INJURIES

22.170 **(a) Le Fort Fractures of Frontal Facial Bones**   £13,250 to £20,000

(b) Multiple Fractures of Facial Bones   £8,000 to £13,250

22.171 Involving some facial deformity of a permanent nature.

(c) Fractures of Nose or Nasal Complex

22.172

(i) Serious or multiple fractures requiring a number of operations and/or resulting in permanent damage to airways and/or nerves or tear ducts and/or facial deformity. £5,750 to £12,750

(ii) Displaced fracture where recovery complete but only after surgery. £2,150 to £2,750

(iii) Displaced fracture requiring no more than manipulation. £1,400 to £1,700

(iv) Simple undisplaced fracture with full recovery. £1,000 to £1,350

(d) Fractures of Cheekbones

22.173

(i) Serious fractures requiring surgery but with lasting consequences such as paraesthesia in the cheeks or the lips or some element of disfigurement. £5,500 to £8,750

(ii) Simple fracture of cheekbones for which some reconstructive surgery is necessary but from which there is a complete recovery with no or only minimal cosmetic effects. £2,250 to £3,500

(iii) Simple fracture of cheekbone for which no surgery is required and where a complete recovery is effected. £1,350 to £1,600

(e) Fractures of Jaws

22.174

(i) Very serious multiple fractures followed by prolonged treatment and permanent consequences, including severe pain, restriction in eating, paraesthesia and/or the risk of arthritis in the joints. £16,750 to £25,000

(ii) Serious fracture with permanent consequences such as difficulty in opening the mouth or with eating or where there is paraesthesia in the area of the jaw. £10,000 to £16,750

(iii) Simple fracture requiring immobilisation but from which recovery is complete. £3,500 to £4,750

(f) Damage to Teeth

22.175

In these cases there will generally have been a course of treatment as a result of the initial injury. The amounts awarded will vary according to the extent and/or the degree of discomfort of such treatment. Any difficulty with eating increases the award. These cases may overlap with fractures of the jaw, meriting awards in the brackets for such fractures. Awards may be greater where the damage results in or is caused by protracted dentistry.

(i) Loss of or serious damage to several front teeth. £4,750 to £6,250

(ii) Loss of or serious damage to two front teeth. £2,250 to £4,000

(iii) Loss of or serious damage to one front tooth. £1,250 to £2,150

(iv) Loss of or damage to back teeth: per tooth: £600 to £1,000

(B) FACIAL DISFIGUREMENT

22.176

In this class of case the distinction between male and female and the subjective approach are of particular significance. Larger awards than those indicated may be justified if there have been many operations.

(a) Females

(i) Very Severe Scarring

£26,500 to £53,000 22.177

In a relatively young woman (teens to early 30s) where the cosmetic effect is very disfiguring and the psychological reaction severe.

(ii) Less Severe Scarring £16,500 to £26,500

Where the disfigurement is still substantial and where there is a significant psychological reaction.

(iii) Significant Scarring £10,000 to £16,500

Where the worst effects have been or will be reduced by plastic surgery leaving some cosmetic disability and where the psychological reaction is not great or, having been considerable at the outset, has diminished to relatively minor proportions.

(iv) Less Significant Scarring £2,150 to £7,750

In these cases there may be but one scar which can be camouflaged or, though there is a number of very small scars, the overall effect is to mar but not markedly to affect the appearance and the reaction is no more than that of an ordinarily sensitive young woman.

(v) Trivial Scarring £1,000 to £1,900

In these cases the effect is minor only.

(b) Males

22.178 **(i) Very Severe Scarring** £16,500 to £36,000

These are to be found especially in males under 30, where there is permanent disfigurement even after plastic surgery and a considerable element of psychological reaction.

(ii) Less Severe Scarring £10,000 to £16,500

This will have left moderate to severe permanent disfigurement.

(iii) Significant Scarring £5,000 to £10,000

Such scars will remain visible at conversational distances.

(iv) Less Significant Scarring £2,150 to £5,000

Such scarring is not particularly prominent except on close inspection.

(v) Trivial Scarring £1,000 to £1,900

In these cases the effect is minor only.

8 SCARRING TO OTHER PARTS OF THE BODY

22.179 This is an area in which it is not possible to offer much useful guidance. The principles are the same as those applied to cases of facial disfigurement. It must be remembered that many of the physical injuries already described involve some element of disfigurement and that element is of course taken into account in suggesting the appropriate bracket. There remain some cases where the element of disfigurement is the predominant one in the assessment of damages. Where the scarring is not to the face or is not usually visible then the awards will tend to be lower than those for facial or readily visible disfigurement.

A large proportion of awards for a number of noticeable laceration scars, or a single disfiguring scar, of leg(s) or arm(s) or hand(s) or back or chest (male), fall in the bracket of £4,250 to £7,500.

In cases where an exploratory laparotomy has been performed but no significant internal injury has been found, the award for the operation and the inevitable scar is in the region of £4,750.

22.180

A single noticeable scar, or several superficial scars, of leg(s) or arm(s) or hand(s), with some minor cosmetic deficit justifies £1,300 to £2,150.

As we have noted in Chapter 7, the effects of burns will normally be regarded as more serious since they tend to cause a greater degree of pain and may lead to continuing physical and psychological injury.

9 DAMAGE TO HAIR

(a) Damage to hair in consequence of defective permanent waving, tinting or the like, where the effects are dermatitis or tingling or 'burning' of the scalp causing dry, brittle hair, which breaks off and/or falls out, leading to distress, depression, embarrassment and loss of confidence, and inhibiting social life. In the more serious cases thinning continues and the prospects of regrowth are poor or there has been total loss of areas of hair and regrowth is slow.

22.181

£4,000 to £6,000

There may be a larger award in cases of psychological disability.

(b) Less serious versions of the above where symptoms are fewer or only of a minor character; also, cases where hair has been pulled out leaving bald patches. The level of the award will depend on the length of time taken before regrowth occurs.

£2,150 to £4,000

10 DERMATITIS

Apart from dermatitis of the scalp (see Chapter 9), most of the reported cases relate to dermatitis of the hands.

22.182

(a) Dermatitis of both hands, with cracking and soreness, affecting employment and domestic capability, possibly with some psychological consequences, lasting for some years, perhaps indefinitely.

£7,500 to £10,500

(b) Dermatitis of both hands, continuing for a significant period, but settling with treatment and/or use of gloves for specific tasks.

£4,750 to £6,250

(c) Itching, irritation of and/or rashes on one or both hands, but resolving within a few months with treatment.

£1,000 to £2,000

22.183   RETAIL PRICES INDEX

	Jan.	Feb.	March	April	May	June	July	Aug.	Sept.	Oct.	Nov.	Dec.
1987	100.0	100.4	100.6	101.8	101.9	101.9	101.8	102.1	102.4	102.9	103.4	103.3
1988	103.3	103.7	104.1	105.8	106.2	106.6	106.7	107.9	108.4	109.5	110.0	110.3
1989	111.0	111.8	112.3	114.3	115.0	115.4	115.5	115.8	116.6	117.5	118.5	118.8
1990	119.5	120.2	121.4	125.1	126.2	126.7	126.8	128.1	129.3	130.3	130.0	129.9
1991	130.2	130.9	131.4	133.1	133.5	134.1	133.8	134.1	134.6	135.1	135.6	135.7
1992	135.6	136.3	136.7	138.8	139.3	139.3	138.8	138.9	139.4	139.9	139.7	139.2
1993	137.9	138.8	139.3	140.6	141.1	141.0	140.7	141.3	141.9	141.8	141.6	141.9
1994	141.3	142.1	142.5	144.2	144.7	144.7	144.0	144.7	145.0	145.2	145.3	146.0
1995	146.0	146.9	147.5	149.0	149.6	149.8	149.1	149.9	150.6	149.8	149.8	150.7
1996	150.2	150.9	151.5	152.6	152.9	153.0	152.4	153.1	153.8	153.8	153.9	154.4
1997	154.4	155.0	155.4	156.3	156.9	157.5	157.5	158.5	159.3	159.5	159.6	160.0
1998	159.5	160.3	160.8	162.6	163.5	163.4	163.0	163.7	164.4	164.5	164.4	164.4
1999	163.4	163.7	163.7	165.2	165.6	165.6	165.1	165.5	166.2	166.5	166.7	167.3
2000	166.6	167.5	168.4	170.1	170.7	171.1	170.5	171.5	171.7	171.6	172.1	172.2
2001	171.1	172.0	176.2	173.1	174.2	174.4	173.6	173.3	174.0	174.6	173.4	174.3
2002	173.3	173.8	174.5	175.7	176.2	176.2	175.9	176.4	177.6	177.9	178.2	178.5
2003	178.4	179.3	179.9	181.2	181.5	181.3	181.3	181.6	182.5	182.6	182.7	183.5
2004	183.1	183.8	184.6	185.7	186.5	186.8						

23

MULTIPLIERS

A. The Purpose of Multipliers

By the time a trial date is reached, or the date of a determined effort to com- **23.01** promise a claim, it should be possible to calculate accurately the financial losses that have already been suffered by the claimant. The assessment of future loss and expense will, however, be uncertain. In almost all cases, a personal injury claim is resolved by a single, final payment even though in many cases of serious injury the losses will not have come to an end. There are exceptions to the award of a final lump sum. Section 2 of the Damages Act 1996 provides for structured settlements where the claimant recovers an income for life rather than a lump sum, by allowing the court to make a periodical payments order for damages, and s 2, as substituted by the Courts Act 2003, s 100 (when in force), will enable the court to impose such an order without the consent of the parties. In some cases a provisional award allows an additional payment to be made at a later date when a risk of a complication of an injury materializes and a new s 2B of the 1996 Act proposes a similar power of variation. However, these rules do not allow for orders comparable to matrimonial periodical payments which can be varied from time to time according to the changing needs and circumstances of the parties. There are real practical difficulties with structured settlements and they are only suitable in fairly large claims.

Apart from these special cases, which are unusual, the court will award a single, **23.02** final lump sum of damages which is paid now to compensate the claimant for losses which will occur in the future, sometimes many years away. The claimant can invest the damages until he needs to draw on the invested funds to compensate for his distant loss. The present value of a future loss is less than the nominal amount of the future loss because the claimant is entitled to keep the interest or dividend income and capital growth that his invested damages will earn over the period that goes by until they are needed. A final lump sum award cannot be increased or reduced later if the claimant's circumstances change: an assessment of the likely future events affecting the claimant has to be made at the time that the lump sum is assessed. The purpose of the multiplier system used by the court is to enable the court to make a fair assessment of the adjustment that should be made from the nominal loss to allow for the early receipt of damages and the assumptions made about the future.

23.03   For a single payment, such as the cost of an operation that will be required in 10 years time, the calculation of the benefit of investment income is relatively simple, but the most significant future losses in injury claims are for continuing losses or annual expenses such as a loss of income and pension or a continuing need for nursing care. Here the calculations are complex. The theoretical aim is to find the notional price to the claimant of an annuity that would meet his continuing loss and expense for the remainder of his life. Traditionally the court carried out a rather broad brush assessment. Today, a much more accurate assessment based on sound actuarial calculations can be made.

23.04   The Actuarial Tables for Use in Personal Injury and Fatal Accident Cases published by the Government Actuary's Department are commonly known as the Ogden Tables, taking the name of the late Sir Michael Ogden QC who chaired the Working Party which first drew up the tables and then fought for them to be accepted for use in personal injury litigation, a battle that was won in the House of Lords' decision *Wells v Wells* [1999] 1 AC 345. The purpose of the Ogden Tables is to fix a multiplier which will accurately take account of the claimant's expectation of life and the real return that will be received from his invested damages. The *multiplier* given by the tables is then applied to an annual rate of loss called the *multiplicand*, and the result should be a sum for investment from which the claimant could in theory draw his annual needs and be left with a nil balance on the day of his death.

23.05   Future loss claims are now invariably assessed with the use of the Ogden Tables, in spite of the extraordinary failure to bring into force s 10 of the Civil Evidence Act 1998 which would put this on a statutory footing.

23.06   *Wells v Wells* [1999] 1 AC 345   Multipliers for future loss should be based on the Ogden Tables, without any further general discount for uncertainty. Lord Lloyd at 378E: 'There is no purpose in the courts making as accurate a prediction as they can of the plaintiff's future needs if the resulting sum is arbitrarily reduced for no better reason than that the prediction might be wrong. A prediction remains a prediction. Contingencies should be taken into account when they work in one direction, but not where they cancel out.'

B. The Rate of Return

By the Damages (Personal Injury) Order 2001 the Lord Chancellor exercised **23.07** his power under s 1 of the Damages Act 1996 to fix the rate of return to be assumed from the investment of the sum awarded as general damages for future pecuniary loss in an action for personal injuries at 2.5%. The Order came into force on 28 June 2001.

The rate of return is of vital importance to the calculation of the appropriate **23.08** multiplier. The rate is the 'real' rate of return disregarding the part of the income or growth that does no more than allow for inflation: the multiplicand for future loss is set in terms of money values for the date of assessment. The Lord Chancellor was strongly influenced by the rate of return that a claimant can achieve by protecting himself against future inflation by investing in Index Linked Government Stock (ILGS). The actual investment return that the claimant will achieve, once his damages have been received, will depend on the degree of risk that he is willing to accept, so the argument is not only about the returns that are available in the financial market but also about the investment approach of the claimant that ought to be assumed for the purpose of the calculation. It is irrelevant for this purpose what the claimant will in fact do with his damages when he has received them: the multiplier cannot be challenged by proof that the claimant will in fact choose to invest in a different way.

For all practical purposes, the 'discount rate' of 2.5% fixed by the Lord Chancel- **23.09** lor applies across the board to all assessments of future loss in personal injury claims. There have been determined efforts to persuade the courts to apply a different rate, either because the reasoning of the Lord Chancellor was flawed, or because market conditions have changed since 2001, or because the expense of medical and nursing care is likely to increase by more than the general rate of inflation. Section 1(2) of the Damages Act 1996 provides that the prescribing of a rate by the Lord Chancellor shall not prevent the court taking a different rate of return into account if any party to the proceedings shows that it is more appropriate in the case in question. The courts have shown great reluctance to exercise this power to depart from the prescribed rate, and in everyday practice the 2.5% rate will always apply.

Claimants will sometimes think that the rate of return used by the court is **23.10** unfair because it fails to take account of future inflation. This is a misconception. The rate of return that has been fixed by the Lord Chancellor is a 'real' rate of return after allowing for future inflation. The advantage of ILGS, as the House of Lords recognized in *Wells v Wells* (above), is to provide clear evidence of a real rate of return in the marketplace, since protection against inflation is provided by the index linking. The nominal returns on a conventional investment will be greater, reflecting inflationary risk and investment risk.

23.11   *Cooke v United Bristol Healthcare* [2003] EWCA Civ 1370; [2004] 1 WLR 251   Claimants were refused permission to call expert evidence to show that future inflation in the cost of care was likely to be such that the application of the prescribed rate of return would leave the claimants undercompensated. The fixing of the 2.5% rate must be assumed to have taken account of the risks of future inflation and the multiplicand should always be based on the current costs at the date of trial.

C. Discount for Contingencies

23.12   The Ogden Tables make a mathematical calculation of the rate of return on invested damages, and apply the risk of mortality. The new 5th edition of the tables has shown some increase in the figures because of an increase in expectation of life. The tables do not take into account any other contingencies and it is therefore necessary to consider in every individual case whether some adjustment needs to be made.

23.13   When assessing a lifetime loss, the only relevant question is whether there are substantial grounds for assessing the expectation of life of the claimant as being greater or less than the average. It will usually be necessary for an argument of this kind to be supported by expert medical evidence rather than by generalized, amateur assumptions about lifestyle.

23.14   When assessing loss of earnings, the impact of contingencies other than mortality is much more significant. The prospect of the claimant continuing to receive a steady stream of earnings until normal retirement age is affected not only by the risk of mortality but also by the adverse risks such as the risk of injury, illness, dismissal, redundancy, or voluntary early retirement and by the positive chances such as promotion or work after normal retirement age. Most of the risks are adverse, and Section B of the Explanatory Notes to the Ogden Tables, paras 25–39, set out at **23.23** below, explains the approach that is recommended by the Working Party in order to take account of contingencies other than mortality. As the Notes indicate at para 25, it has been argued that the discounts proposed are not sufficient to take a realistic account of the contingencies of employment. However, the recommendations of the working party are still the best material available for practitioners.

D. Fatal Accident Claims

The Ogden Tables could be used in order to provide a more accurate assessment **23.15** of dependency in Fatal Accidents Act cases. In particular, the tables include a column of figures based on a nil rate of return which therefore enable calculation to be made taking account of the risk of mortality only, and the Working Party confirms that a more accurate calculation of dependency would be achieved by calculating the multiplier for future dependency from the date of trial, rather than from the date of death, since at the date of trial it is known that the dependant bringing the claim has survived until trial and therefore no discount for the dependent mortality should be made in respect of pre-trial dependency.

At the time of writing, the courts continue to follow the common law **23.16** approach laid down in *Cookson v Knowles* [1979] AC 556 rather than to allow dependency calculations to be undertaken by the Ogden Tables method. For this reason, the material in the Ogden Tables relating to fatal accidents has not been included here. Any change of practice on this issue will be set out in the updating website for this book, and if there is a change in favour of the Ogden Tables method, the material necessary to carry out the calculations will also be provided.

E. The Multipliers Provided Here

The Ogden Tables set out more information than is required in practice, and **23.17** cover a range of different rates of return and different retirement ages. In setting out the multipliers which are given in this chapter, the aim has been to present the multipliers that are likely to be needed often, and to set them out in a format which is easily accessible. It is inevitable that some subtleties are lost in this process of simplification.

It is only multipliers based on 2.5% that are relevant and it is only these **23.18** multipliers that have been included, with retirement ages of 60, 65, and 70 for both males and females. The full tables are widely available, and in due course will be posted on the website of the Government Actuary's Department at www.gad.gov.uk/, if other rates of return or other retirement ages arise.

For this edition, the tables include a multiplier for loss of earnings to age 60 and **23.19** age 65 adjusted for contingencies other than mortality. The main reason for the decision to include an adjusted multiplier is that this will act as a reminder to practitioners that an appropriate adjustment must be made. It would be wrong for the suggested adjustment to be applied in every case. The actual adjustment made will depend on the circumstances that apply to the individual claimant and the kind of employment that has been lost.

23.20 The guidance given in the Explanatory Notes is imprecise and for female claimants it is incomplete. First, there is a general adjustment for the uncertainties of employment. Secondly, there are different rates of adjustment for different levels of economic activity. In setting out typical adjusted multipliers in the tables which follow, a medium level of economic activity has been assumed, and the adjustments have been made on the following basis:

	Male		Female	
	65	60	65	60
16–19	0.98	0.99	0.97	0.98
20–27	0.98	0.99	0.97	0.98
28–32	0.97	0.98	0.96	0.98
33–37	0.96	0.98	0.94	0.95
38–42	0.96	0.97	0.92	0.93
43–47	0.95	0.96	0.89	0.90
48–52	0.93	0.94	0.89	0.90
53–57	0.90	0.93	0.92	0.94
58–62	0.90	0.93	0.92	0.94
63–65	0.90		0.92	

23.21 In addition, the Explanatory Notes in paras 35–39 invite two further adjustments: (1) to take account of the different risks of illness, injury and disability that arise in different kinds of work, and (2) to take account of the geographical region in which the claimant lives. No adjustment for these variations has been made in the tables at **23.23** follow.

23.22 The multipliers in the tables are calculated to two decimal places, which suggests a degree of scientific precision which may be unrealistic, particularly for earnings claims. In addition, they are calculated on the basis of complete years and if the assessment of damages does not happen at a time near to the claimant's birthday, it may be appropriate to interpolate a multiplier between two of the stated figures.

F. Table of Multipliers

Age		Lifetime Tables 1 & 2	Earnings to 70 Tables 11 & 12	Pension from 70 Tables 23 & 24	Earnings to 65 Tables 9 & 10	Adjusted earnings to 65 See 23.19	Pension from 65 Tables 21 & 22	Earnings to 60 Tables 7 & 8	Adjusted earnings to 60 See 23.19	Pension from 60 Tables 19 & 20	
Age 16	M	32.15	29.05	3.10	27.82	27.26	4.33	26.38	26.12	5.78	**23.23**
	F	33.05	29.39	3.66	28.10	27.25	4.95	26.60	26.07	6.45	
Age 17	M	31.94	28.77	3.18	27.51	26.96	4.43	26.03	25.77	5.91	
	F	32.86	29.11	3.75	27.79	26.96	5.07	26.26	25.73	6.60	
Age 18	M	31.73	28.48	3.25	27.19	22.65	4.54	25.67	25.41	6.06	
	F	32.67	28.83	3.84	27.48	26.66	5.19	25.90	25.38	6.76	
Age 19	M	31.52	28.19	3.33	26.87	26.33	4.64	25.31	25.06	6.20	
	F	32.47	28.54	3.93	27.16	26.35	5.31	25.54	25.03	6.93	
Age 20	M	31.30	27.90	3.40	26.55	26.02	4.75	24.95	24.70	6.35	
	F	32.27	28.25	4.02	26.85	26.03	5.44	25.17	24.67	7.09	
Age 21	M	31.08	27.60	3.48	26.21	25.69	4.87	24.57	24.32	6.51	
	F	32.06	27.94	4.11	26.49	25.70	5.57	24.80	24.30	7.26	
Age 22	M	30.85	27.29	3.56	25.87	25.35	4.98	24.19	23.95	6.66	
	F	31.84	27.63	4.21	26.14	25.36	5.70	24.41	23.92	7.44	
Age 23	M	30.62	26.97	3.65	25.52	25.01	5.10	23.79	23.55	6.82	
	F	31.63	27.32	4.31	25.79	25.02	5.84	24.01	23.62	7.62	
Age 24	M	30.38	26.64	3.73	25.16	24.66	5.22	23.39	23.16	6.99	
	F	31.40	26.99	4.41	25.42	24.66	5.98	23.60	23.13	7.80	
Age 25	M	30.13	26.31	3.82	24.79	24.29	8.35	22.98	22.75	7.15	
	F	31.17	26.65	4.51	25.05	24.30	6.12	23.18	22.72	7.99	
Age 26	M	29.88	25.97	3.91	24.41	23.92	5.47	22.55	22.32	7.33	
	F	30.98	26.31	4.62	24.67	23.93	6.26	22.75	22.29	8.18	
Age 27	M	29.62	25.62	4.00	24.02	23.54	5.60	22.12	21.90	7.50	
	F	30.69	25.96	4.73	24.28	23.55	6.41	22.32	21.87	8.37	
Age 28	M	29.36	25.27	4.09	23.63	22.92	5.73	21.68	21.25	7.68	
	F	30.44	25.60	4.84	23.88	22.92	6.56	21.87	21.43	8.57	

433

		Lifetime Tables 1 & 2	Earnings to 70 Tables 11 & 12	Pension from 70 Tables 23 & 24	Earnings to 65 Tables 9 & 10	Adjusted earnings to 65 See 23.19	Pension from 65 Tables 21 & 22	Earnings to 60 Tables 7 & 8	Adjusted earnings to 60 See 23.19	Pension from 60 Tables 19 & 20
Age 29	M	29.09	24.90	4.19	23.22	22.52	5.87	21.22	20.80	7.87
	F	30.18	25.23	4.95	23.46	22.52	6.72	21.40	20.97	8.78
Age 30	M	28.81	24.53	4.28	22.81	22.13	6.01	20.76	20.34	8.05
	F	29.92	24.85	5.07	23.04	22.12	6.88	20.93	20.51	8.99
Age 31	M	28.53	24.15	4.38	22.33	21.71	6.15	20.28	19.87	8.25
	F	29.65	24.47	8.18	22.61	21.71	7.04	20.45	20.04	9.20
Age 32	M	28.24	23.75	4.48	21.94	21.50	6.29	19.79	19.39	8.44
	F	29.37	24.07	5.30	22.17	21.28	7.20	19.95	19.55	9.42
Age 33	M	27.94	23.35	4.58	21.50	20.64	6.44	19.28	18.90	8.65
	F	29.09	23.67	5.43	21.72	20.42	7.37	19.45	18.57	9.65
Age 34	M	27.63	22.94	4.69	21.04	20.20	6.89	18.78	18.40	8.85
	F	28.80	23.25	5.55	21.26	19.98	7.75	18.93	17.98	9.88
Age 35	M	27.31	22.52	4.79	20.57	19.75	6.74	18.25	17.88	9.06
	F	28.51	22.83	5.68	20.78	19.53	7.72	18.39	17.47	10.11
Age 36	M	26.99	22.09	4.90	20.09	19.29	6.90	17.71	17.36	9.28
	F	28.20	22.39	5.81	20.30	19.08	7.91	17.85	16.96	10.35
Age 37	M	26.66	21.65	5.01	19.60	18.82	7.06	17.16	16.82	9.50
	F	27.89	21.95	5.94	19.80	18.61	8.09	17.29	16.43	10.60
Age 38	M	26.32	21.19	5.13	19.09	18.33	7.23	16.59	16.09	9.73
	F	27.57	21.49	6.08	19.29	17.75	8.28	16.72	15.55	10.85
Age 39	M	25.97	20.73	5.24	18.58	17.82	7.39	16.01	15.53	9.96
	F	27.25	21.03	6.22	18.77	17.27	8.48	16.14	15.01	11.11
Age 40	M	25.61	20.25	5.36	18.05	17.33	7.57	15.42	14.96	10.19
	F	26.92	20.55	6.36	18.24	16.78	8.68	15.54	14.45	11.38
Age 41	M	25.25	19.77	5.48	17.51	16.81	7.74	14.81	14.37	10.44
	F	26.58	20.07	6.51	17.70	16.28	8.88	14.93	15.88	11.65
Age 42	M	24.88	19.27	5.61	16.95	16.27	7.92	14.19	13.76	10.69
	F	26.23	19.57	6.66	17.14	15.77	9.09	14.30	13.30	11.93

		Lifetime Tables 1 & 2	Earnings to 70 Tables 11 & 12	Pension from 70 Tables 23 & 24	Earnings to 65 Tables 9 & 10	Adjusted earnings to 65 See 23.19	Pension from 65 Tables 21 & 22	Earnings to 60 Tables 7 & 8	Adjusted earnings to 60 See 23.19	Pension from 60 Tables 19 & 20
Age 43	M	24.50	18.77	5.73	16.39	15.57	8.11	13.55	13.01	10.94
	F	25.88	19.06	6.82	16.58	14.76	9.31	13.66	12.29	12.22
Age 44	M	24.11	18.25	5.86	15.81	15.02	8.30	12.90	12.38	11.21
	F	25.52	18.55	6.97	16.00	14.24	9.53	13.01	11.71	12.52
Age 45	M	23.72	17.72	6.00	15.22	14.46	8.50	12.24	11.75	11.48
	F	25.16	18.02	7.14	15.40	13.71	9.75	12.33	11.10	12.82
Age 46	M	23.32	17.19	6.13	14.62	13.89	8.70	11.56	11.10	11.76
	F	24.78	17.48	7.30	14.79	13.16	9.99	11.65	10.48	13.13
Age 47	M	22.92	16.64	6.28	14.01	13.31	8.91	10.86	10.43	12.05
	F	24.40	16.93	7.48	14.17	12.61	10.23	10.94	9.85	13.46
Age 48	M	22.51	16.08	6.42	13.38	12.44	9.12	10.15	9.54	12.35
	F	24.01	16.36	7.65	13.54	12.05	10.48	10.22	9.20	13.79
Age 49	M	22.08	15.51	6.57	12.74	11.85	9.34	9.42	9.34	12.66
	F	23.62	15.79	7.83	12.87	11.47	10.73	9.47	8.54	14.13
Age 50	M	21.65	14.93	6.72	12.08	11.23	9.57	8.67	8.15	12.98
	F	23.22	15.20	8.02	12.22	10.88	10.99	8.73	7.86	14.49
Age 51	M	21.21	14.33	6.88	11.41	10.61	9.80	7.91	7.44	13.31
	F	22.81	14.60	8.21	11.54	10.27	11.26	7.96	7.16	14.85
Age 52	M	20.76	13.72	7.04	10.72	9.97	10.04	7.12	6.69	13.64
	F	22.39	13.98	8.41	10.85	9.66	11.54	7.16	6.44	15.23
Age 53	M	20.32	13.09	7.21	10.01	9.01	10.29	6.31	5.81	13.99
	F	21.96	13.35	8.61	10.13	9.24	11.83	6.35	5.97	15.62
Age 54	M	19.84	12.46	7.38	9.29	8.36	10.55	5.48	5.04	14.36
	F	21.53	12.71	8.82	9.40	8.74	12.13	5.51	5.18	16.02
Age 55	M	19.37	11.81	7.56	8.55	7.69	10.82	4.63	4.26	14.74
	F	21.10	12.05	9.04	8.65	8.04	12.44	4.65	4.37	16.44
Age 56	M	18.89	11.15	7.75	7.79	7.01	11.10	3.76	3.46	15.14
	F	20.66	11.39	9.27	7.89	7.34	12.77	3.77	3.54	16.88

435

		Lifetime Tables 1 & 2	Earnings to 70 Tables 11 & 12	Pension from 70 Tables 23 & 24	Earnings to 65 Tables 9 & 10	Adjusted earnings to 65 See 23.19	Pension from 65 Tables 21 & 22	Earnings to 60 Tables 7 & 8	Adjusted earnings to 60 See 23.19	Pension from 60 Tables 19 & 20
Age 57	M	18.42	10.47	7.95	7.02	6.32	11.40	2.86	2.63	15.56
	F	20.21	10.70	9.51	7.11	6.63	13.10	2.87	2.70	17.34
Age 58	M	17.94	9.79	8.16	6.23	5.61	11.71	1.94	1.80	16.01
	F	19.76	10.00	9.75	6.30	5.80	13.46	1.94	1.82	17.82
Age 59	M	17.46	9.09	8.38	5.42	4.88	12.05	0.98	0.91	16.48
	F	19.30	9.29	10.01	5.48	5.04	13.82	0.99	0.93	18.31
Age 60	M	16.98	8.37	8.61	4.58	4.12	12.40			16.98
	F	18.84	8.55	10.28	4.63	4.26	14.21			18.84
Age 61	M	16.50	7.64	8.86	3.73	3.36	12.78			
	F	18.37	7.80	10.57	3.76	3.46	14.61			
Age 62	M	16.02	6.90	9.13	2.84	2.56	13.18			
	F	17.89	7.03	10.86	2.86	2.72	15.03			
Age 63	M	15.54	6.13	9.41	1.93	1.73	13.61			
	F	17.41	6.24	11.17	1.94	1.78	15.47			
Age 64	M	15.05	5.34	9.71	0.98	0.88	14.07			
	F	16.91	5.43	11.48	0.98	0.90	15.93			
Age 65	M	14.55	4.52	10.02			14.55			
	F	16.40	4.59	11.81			16.40			
Age 66	M	14.03	3.68	10.35						
	F	15.88	3.73	12.15						
Age 67	M	13.51	2.81	10.70						
	F	15.33	2.84	12.49						
Age 68	M	12.97	1.91	11.06						
	F	14.77	1.93	12.84						
Age 69	M	12.43	0.98	11.45						
	F	14.20	0.98	13.21						
Age 70	M	11.88		11.88						
	F	13.61		13.61						

LIFETIME MULTIPLIERS FOR CHILDREN (Tables 1 and 2)

23.24

Age	Multiplier Males	Females	Age	Multiplier Males	Females
0	34.76	35.35	8	33.70	34.41
1	34.79	35.38	9	33.52	34.26
2	34.65	35.26	10	33.34	34.09
3	34.51	35.13	11	33.16	33.93
4	34.36	34.99	12	32.96	33.76
5	34.20	34.86	13	32.77	33.59
6	34.04	34.71	14	32.57	33.41
7	33.87	34.56	15	32.36	33.23

LIFETIME MULTIPLIERS AFTER AGE 70 (Tables 1 and 2)

23.25

Age	Multiplier Males	Females	Age	Multiplier Males	Females
71	11.34	13.02	86	4.77	5.44
72	10.80	12.43	87	4.47	5.06
73	10.28	11.84	88	4.19	4.71
74	9.77	11.27	89	3.94	4.38
75	9.27	10.71	90	3.70	4.07
76	8.79	10.17	91	3.47	3.79
77	8.33	9.64	92	3.25	3.53
78	7.88	9.12	93	3.07	3.31
79	7.45	8.62	94	2.91	3.10
80	7.03	8.13	95	2.76	2.90
81	6.61	7.64	96	2.60	2.72
82	6.20	7.17	97	2.45	2.55
83	5.81	6.71	98	2.29	2.38
84	5.44	6.26	99	2.14	2.22
85	5.09	5.84	100	2.00	2.06

DISCOUNT FACTOR FOR DEFERMENT OF LOSS FOR A SPECIFIC PERIOD (Table 27)

23.26

Term							
1	0.9756	21	0.5954	41	0.3633	61	0.2217
2	0.9518	22	0.5809	42	0.3545	62	0.2163
3	0.9286	23	0.5667	43	0.3458	63	0.2111
4	0.9060	24	0.5529	44	0.3374	64	0.2059
5	0.8839	25	0.5394	45	0.3292	65	0.2009
6	0.8623	26	0.5262	46	0.3211	66	0.1960
7	0.8413	27	0.5134	47	0.3133	67	0.1912
8	0.8207	28	0.5009	48	0.3057	68	0.1865
9	0.8007	29	0.4887	49	0.2982	69	0.1820
10	0.7812	30	0.4767	50	0.2909	70	0.1776
11	0.7621	31	0.4651	51	0.2838	71	0.1732
12	0.7436	32	0.4538	52	0.2769	72	0.1690

DISCOUNT FACTOR FOR DEFERMENT OF LOSS FOR A SPECIFIC PERIOD (Table 27)—*continued*

Term

13	0.7254	33	0.4427	53	0.2702	73	0.1649
14	0.7077	34	0.4319	54	0.2636	74	0.1609
15	0.6905	35	0.4214	55	0.2572	75	0.1569
16	0.6736	36	0.4111	56	0.2509	76	0.1531
17	0.6572	37	0.4011	57	0.2448	77	0.1494
18	06412	38	0.3913	58	0.2388	78	0.1457
19	0.6255	39	0.3817	59	0.2330	79	0.1422
20	0 6103	40	0.3724	60	0.2273	80	0.1387

MULTIPLIERS FOR A SPECIFIC PERIOD OF YEARS
(excl risk of mortality) (Table 28)

23.27 Term

1	0.99	21	16.39	41	25.78	61	31.52
2	1.95	22	16.97	42	26.14	62	31.74
3	2.89	23	17.55	43	26.49	63	31.95
4	3.81	24	18.11	44	26.83	64	32.16
5	4.70	25	18.65	45	27.17	65	32.36
6	5.58	26	19.19	46	27.49	66	32.56
7	6.43	27	19.71	47	27.81	67	32.75
8	7.26	28	20.21	48	28.12	68	32.94
9	8.07	29	20.71	49	28.42	69	33.13
10	8.86	30	21.19	50	28.72	70	33.31
11	9.63	31	21.66	51	29.00	71	33.48
12	10.39	32	22.12	52	29.28	72	33.65
13	11.12	33	22.57	53	29.56	73	33.82
14	11.84	34	23.01	54	29.82	74	33.98
15	12.54	35	23.43	55	30.08	75	34.14
16	13.22	36	23.85	56	30.34	76	34.30
17	13.88	37	24.26	57	30.59	77	34.45
18	14.53	38	24.65	58	30.83	78	34.60
19	15.17	39	25.04	59	31.06	79	34.74
20	15.78	40	25.42	60	31.29	80	34.88

OGDEN TABLES: EXPLANATORY NOTES

SECTION B: CONTINGENCIES OTHER THAN MORTALITY

23.28   25. As stated in paragraph 20, the tables for loss of earnings (Tables 3 to 14) take no account of risks other than mortality. This section shows how the multipliers in these tables may be reduced to take account of risks other than mortality. This is based on work commissioned by the Institute of Actuaries and carried out by Professor S Haberman and Mrs D S F Bloomfield (*Work time lost to sickness, unemployment and stoppages: measurement and application* (1990), Journal of the Institute of Actuaries 117, 533–595). Although there was some debate within the actuarial profession about the details of this work, and in particular about the scope for developing it further, the findings were broadly accepted and were adopted by the Government Actuary and the other actuaries who were members of the Working Party when the Second Edition of the Tables was published.

26. Since the risk of mortality (including the risks of dying early or living longer) has already been taken into account in the tables, the principal contingencies in respect of which a further reduction is to be made, particularly for earnings loss up to retirement age, are illness and unemployment. Even with the effective disappearance of the 'job for life' there appears to be no scientific justification in the generality of cases for assuming significantly larger deductions than those given in this section. It should be noted that the authors of the 1990 paper (Professor Haberman and Mrs Bloomfield) wrote 'All the results discussed in this paper should be further qualified by the caveat that the underlying models . . . assume that economic activity rates and labour force separation and accession rated do not vary in the future from the bases chosen. As mentioned already in the text, it is unlikely to be true that the future would be free from marked secular trends.' The paper relied on Labour Force Surveys for 1973, 1977, 1981 and 1985 and English Life Tables No. 14 (1980–82). However, although it is now somewhat out of date, it is the best study presently available. Some related work has recently been published by Lewis, McNabb and Wass (*Methods of calculating damages for loss of future earnings*, Journal of Personal Injury Law, 2002 Number 2). It is hoped that further research into the impact of contingencies other than mortality will be carried out in the due course and the Ogden Working Party is in discussion with potential researchers in the hope of carrying this forward.

27. Specific factors in individual cases may necessitate larger reductions. By contrast, there will **23.29** also be cases where the standard multipliers should be increased, to take into account positive factors of lifestyle, employment prospects and life expectancy.

28. The extent to which the multiplier needs to be reduced will reflect individual circumstances such as occupation and geographical region. In the short term, levels of economic activity and unemployment, including time lost through industrial action, are relevant. Reductions may be expected to be smaller for clerical workers than for manual workers, for those living in the South rather than the North, and for those in 'secure' jobs and in occupations less affected by redundancy or industrial action.

29. The factors described in subsequent paragraphs are for use in calculating loss of earnings **23.30** up to retirement age. The research work did not investigate the impact of contingencies other than mortality on the value of future pension rights. Some reduction to the multiplier for loss of pension would often be appropriate when a reduction is being applied for loss of earnings. This may be less of a reduction than in the case of loss of earnings because of the ill-health contingency (as opposed to the unemployment contingency), particularly in cases where there are significant ill-health retirement pension rights. A bigger reduction may be necessary in cases where there is significant doubt whether pension rights would have continued to accrue (to the extent not already allowed for in the post-retirement multiplier) or in cases where there may be doubt over the ability of the pension fund to pay promised benefits. In the case of a defined contribution pension scheme, loss of pension rights may be able to be allowed for simply by increasing the future earnings loss (adjusted for contingencies other than mortality) by the percentage which the employer pays to the scheme in contributions.

30. The suggestions which follow are intended only to provide a 'ready reckoner', as opposed to precise figures.

The basic deduction for contingencies other than mortality

31. Subject to the adjustments which may be made as described below, the multiplier which **23.31** has been selected from the tables, i.e. in respect of risks of mortality only, should be reduced by *multiplying* it by a figure selected from the table below, under the heading 'Medium'.

Levels of economic activity and employment

23.32   32. The medium set of reductions is appropriate if it is anticipated that economic activity is likely to correspond to that in the 1970s and 1980s (ignoring periods of high and low unemployment). The high set is appropriate if higher economic activity and lower unemployment rates are anticipated. The low set is appropriate if lower economic activity and higher unemployment rates are anticipated.

TABLE A LOSS OF EARNINGS TO PENSION AGE 65 (MALES)

Age at date of trial	High	Medium	Low
20	0.99	0.98	0.97
25	0.99	0.98	0.96
30	0.99	0.97	0.95
35	0.98	0.96	0.93
40	0.98	0.96	0.92
45	0.97	0.95	0.90
50	0.96	0.93	0.87
55	0.95	0.90	0.82
60	0.95	0.90	0.81

Lower pension ages (Males)

23.33   33. The figures will be higher for a lower pension age. For example, if pension age is 60, the figures should be as shown in Table B.

TABLE B LOSS OF EARNINGS TO PENSION AGE 60 (MALES)

Age at date of trial	High	Medium	Low
20	0.99	0.99	0.98
25	0.99	0.99	0.97
30	0.99	0.98	0.97
35	0.99	0.98	0.96
40	0.98	0.97	0.94
45	0.98	0.96	0.93
50	0.97	0.94	0.92
55	0.96	0.93	0.88

Female lives

23.34   34. As a rough guide, for female lives between ages 35 and 55 with a pension age of 60, the figures should be as shown in Table C. As for males, the factors will be lower if the pension age is higher (e.g. 65) and higher if the pension age is lower (e.g. 55).

TABLE C LOSS OF EARNINGS TO PENSION AGE 60 (FEMALES)

Age at date of trial	High	Medium	Low
35	0.95	0.95	0.94
40	0.93	0.93	0.92
45	0.90	0.90	0.88
50	0.91	0.90	0.88
55	0.95	0.94	0.93

Variations by occupation

35. The risks of illness, injury and disability are less for persons in clerical or similar jobs, e.g. **23.35** civil servants, the professions and financial services industries, and greater for those in manual jobs, e.g. construction, mining, quarrying and ship-building. However, what matters is the precise nature of the work undertaken by the person in question, rather than the industry as such; for example, a secretary in the headquarters office of a large construction company may be at no greater risk than a secretary in a solicitor's office.

36. In less risky occupations the figures in Tables A to C should be *increased* by a maximum of the order of 0.01 up to age 40, rising to 0.03 at age 55.

37. In more risky occupations the figures in Tables A to C should be *reduced* by a maximum of the order of 0.01 at age 25, 0.02 at age 40 and 0.05 at age 55.

Variations by geographical region

38. For persons resident in the South East, East Anglia, South West and East Midlands, the **23.36** figures in Tables A to C should be *increased* by a maximum of the order of 0.01 up to age 40, rising to 0.03 at age 55.

39. For persons resident in the North, North West, Wales and Scotland, the figures in Tables A to C should be *reduced* by a maximum of the order of 0.01 at age 25, 0.02 at age 40 and 0.05 at age 55.

G. Expectation of Life

These figures are taken from the Interim Life Tables produced by the Govern- **23.37** ment Actuary's Department based on data for England and Wales for the years 1998 to 2000. The figures do not take account of projected improvements in mortality. Expectation of life is slightly shorter for Great Britain or the United Kingdom, but the difference is minimal. These are average figures and will need to be adjusted in a case where there are special factors affecting the individual.

The Expectation column gives the average expectation of life, that is, the average number of years that those exact age x will live thereafter. The Lifespan column gives the average expected age at death, that is, the age plus the expectation of life, for those who have attained age x.

23.38	Age	Male Expectation	Lifespan	Female Expectation	Lifespan	Age
	0	75.38	75.38	80.18	80.18	0
	1	74.86	75.86	79.59	80.59	1
	2	73.90	75.90	78.61	80.61	2
	3	72.92	75.92	77.63	80.63	3
	4	71.94	75.94	76.65	80.65	4
	5	70.95	75.95	75.66	80.66	5
	6	69.96	75.96	74.66	80.66	6
	7	68.97	75.97	73.67	80.67	7
	8	67.98	75.98	72.68	80.68	8
	9	66.98	75.98	71.69	80.69	9
	10	65.99	75.99	70.69	80.69	10
	11	65.00	76.00	69.70	80.70	11
	12	64.01	76.01	68.71	80.71	12
	13	63.02	76.02	67.72	80.72	13
	14	62.03	76.03	66.72	80.72	14
	15	61.04	76.04	65.73	80.73	15
	16	60.06	76.06	64.74	80.74	16
	17	59.08	76.08	63.76	80.76	17
	18	58.11	76.11	62.78	80.78	18
	19	57.15	76.15	61.79	80.79	19
	20	56.20	76.20	60.81	80.81	20
	21	55.24	76.24	59.83	80.83	21
	22	54.28	76.28	58.85	80.85	22
	23	53.32	76.32	57.87	80.87	23
	24	52.37	76.37	56.89	80.89	24
	25	51.41	76.41	55.90	80.90	25
	26	50.45	76.45	54.92	80.92	26
	27	49.49	76.49	53.94	80.94	27
	28	48.54	76.54	52.96	80.96	28
	29	47.58	76.58	51.98	80.98	29
	30	46.63	76.63	51.00	81.00	30
	31	45.67	76.67	50.02	81.02	31
	32	44.71	76.71	49.04	81.04	32
	33	43.76	76.76	48.07	81.07	33
	34	42.80	76.80	47.09	81.09	34
	35	41.84	76.84	46.12	81.12	35
	36	40.89	76.89	45.15	81.15	36
	37	39.94	76.94	44.18	81.18	37
	38	38.99	76.99	43.21	81.21	38
	39	38.04	77.04	42.25	81.25	39
	40	37.09	77.09	41.28	81.28	40
	41	36.14	77.14	40.33	81.33	41
	42	35.21	77.21	39.37	81.37	42
	43	34.27	77.27	38.42	81.42	43
	44	33.34	77.34	37.47	81.47	44
	45	32.41	77.41	36.53	81.53	45
	46	31.49	77.49	35.59	81.59	46
	47	30.57	77.57	34.65	81.65	47
	48	29.66	77.66	33.72	81.72	48
	49	28.76	77.76	32.79	81.79	49
	50	27.86	77.86	31.87	81.87	50
	51	26.97	77.97	30.96	81.96	51

Age	Male Expectation	Lifespan	Female Expectation	Lifespan	Age
52	26.08	78.08	30.04	82.04	52
53	25.20	78.20	29.14	82.14	53
54	24.33	78.33	28.23	82.23	54
55	23.47	78.47	27.34	82.34	55
56	22.62	78.62	26.46	82.46	56
57	21.79	78.79	25.57	82.57	57
58	20.96	78.96	24.70	82.70	58
59	20.15	79.15	23.84	82.84	59
60	19.35	79.35	22.99	92.99	60
61	18.56	79.56	22.14	83.14	61
62	17.79	79.79	21.30	83.30	62
63	17.03	80.03	20.48	83.48	63
64	16.28	80.28	19.66	83.66	64
65	15.55	80.55	18.85	83.85	65
66	14.84	80.84	18.06	84.06	66
67	14.14	81.14	17.28	84.28	67
68	13.47	81.47	16.51	84.51	68
69	12.81	81.81	15.76	84.76	69
70	12.17	82.17	15.03	85.03	70
71	11.55	82.55	14.31	85.31	71
72	10.96	82.96	13.61	85.61	72
73	10.39	83.39	12.94	85.94	73
74	9.84	83.84	12.28	86.28	74
75	9.31	84.31	11.64	86.64	75
76	8.81	84.81	11.02	87.02	76
77	8.32	85.32	10.42	87.42	77
78	7.85	85.85	9.83	87.83	78
79	7.40	86.40	9.26	88.26	79
80	6.97	86.97	8.71	88.71	80
81	6.55	87.55	8.18	89.18	81
82	6.16	88.16	7.68	89.68	82
83	5.80	88.80	7.21	90.21	83
84	5.46	89.46	6.76	90.76	84
85	5.15	90.15	6.34	91.34	85
86	4.86	90.86	5.94	91.94	86
87	4.60	91.60	5.58	92.58	87
88	4.35	92.35	5.25	93.25	88
89	4.13	93.13	4.95	93.95	89
90	3.93	93.93	4.67	94.67	90
91	3.74	94.74	4.39	95.39	91
92	3.51	95.51	4.10	96.10	92
93	3.32	96.32	3.84	96.84	93
94	3.14	97.14	3.60	97.60	94
95	2.96	97.96	3.36	98.36	95
96	2.81	98.81	3.15	99.15	96
97	2.66	99.66	2.98	99.98	97
98	2.55	100.55	2.83	100.83	98
99	2.47	101.47	2.68	101.68	99
100	2.37	102.37	2.53	102.53	100

24

LOSS OF EARNINGS AND PENSION

A. The Simple Loss of Earnings Claim

The aim of an award of compensation for a financial loss is to restore the victim **24.01** to the position as if the injury had not been sustained. In a simple case the computation of the loss of earnings is not unduly complex, but may require diligent investigation of the facts. With the case of a claimant who has a steady job but who has been so badly injured that there is no realistic prospect of him working again, the task is to assess the value of his earning capacity at the date of the assessment. The loss which can be claimed is the net loss after allowing for tax and National Insurance which would have been deducted from the earnings. It is necessary to make separate calculations for past and future loss, partly because the claimant is entitled to recover interest on an award for past loss, partly because he is entitled to the benefit of pay rises that he would have received between the date of the accident and the date of assessment, and partly because future loss must be discounted for early receipt by the use of an appropriate multiplier.

If earnings are variable because of overtime or shift patterns, it is a common **24.02** practice to take the average of the preceding 13 weeks in order to prove the level of pre-accident earnings, but a different period may be used if that is necessary to give an accurate figure for the rate of earnings that would have been received during the period of loss. Where the claim is brought against the employer, the employer's liability insurers will obtain and provide this information. In addition to pay, the rewards of an employment may include benefits which will have to be converted into a net cash equivalent such as luncheon vouchers, private health insurance, subsidized loans or the use of a company car. The claimant's solicitor should also establish from the employer whether there have been pay rises for which the claimant would have benefited. Unfortunately these do not always coincide with changes in tax rates in April each year, so there may be several steps to a calculation of the net loss of earnings over a prolonged period of absence. Where the calculation is done for a Schedule of Special Damages to accompany the Particulars of Claim, it should be carried up to a convenient date at around that time. Where the Schedule is revised in the run-up to a trial, it should be carried forward to the date of the trial window or the proposed trial date. At that point, the level of net annual earnings that has been reached will provide the multiplicand for the calculation of future loss. The multiplier is found from the Ogden Tables as explained in the previous chapter, and the computation of future loss is relatively straightforward.

24.03 No account is taken of future inflation, because part of the income of the invested compensation will allow for this. The multiplicand for future loss is the rate of earnings that the claimant would have been receiving the date of the assessment. However, real future changes, such as the likelihood of promotion, should be brought into the calculation. Again, the calculation should use the value of money at the date of the assessment. The net earnings after promotion should be the earnings of the post as at the date of the assessment. It is then up to the courts to decide how to bring the likelihood of promotion into the calculation, and the manner of doing so will depend on the degree of likelihood.

B. Tax and National Insurance

24.04 It is always necessary to deduct income tax and National Insurance contributions (NIC) from the calculation of lost earnings. This is because the receipt of damages by a claimant to compensate for a loss of earnings is not taxed as income (although the investment income later received from invested damages will be taxed). The rates and allowances are set out in the Reference Information in Chapter 49.

24.05 As a short cut, a reasonably accurate estimate of the deductions from gross earnings for income tax and National Insurance contributions can be made by applying a percentage deduction interpolated from the following table. This will not produce a net figure which is precisely accurate, but it will produce a figure which is sufficiently accurate to be suitable for most purposes. These figures are based on 2003–4 rates in round figures, on NIC rates for employees contracted out of SERPS. The percentages should make it possible to compute with acceptable accuracy the rate of net earnings from any annual figure for gross earnings.

APPROXIMATE LEVELS OF
DEDUCTION OF TAX AND NIC

Gross £	Net £	Net as %	
4,000	4,000	100	**24.06**
5,000	4,925	98.5	
6,000	5,731	95.5	
8,000	7,172	89.6	
10,000	8,544	85.5	
12,000	9,916	82.5	
14,000	11,288	80.5	
16,000	12,660	79.1	
18,000	14,032	78	
20,000	15,404	77	
24,000	18,148	75.5	
28,000	20,892	74.5	
32,000	23,725	74	
40,000	29,006	72.5	
50,000	34,906	69.8	
75,000	49,656	66.2	
100,000	64,406	64.4	

C. Pension Contributions

Most employees in permanent employment will be entitled to join a pension **24.07** scheme. The calculation of the loss of pension benefits is discussed at **24.33** below. For the purpose of calculating a loss of income, the treatment of pension contributions depends on the question whether the claimant is making a claim for the loss of pension benefits. If there is a claim for loss of pension benefits, then in calculating the net income, credit has to be given for the cost that the claimant would have incurred through making employee's contributions. If there is no claim for the loss of pension benefits, then the pension contributions are simply one of the ways that the claimant was choosing to spend his earnings, and there is no need to give credit for the contributions in the calculation of net earnings. If the pension scheme was building a money fund, it may be appropriate to treat the employer's contributions as a benefit of the employment to be added to the net earnings, rather than making a separate claim for loss of pension benefits.

D. Sick Pay

24.08   If, under the terms of the contract of employment, the employer pays sick pay to the claimant when he is absent from work as a result of the injury, then to the extent of the receipt of the sick pay, the claimant suffers no loss. In calculating the loss of earnings, credit must be given for the sick pay received.

24.09   Employers are responsible for paying Statutory Sick Pay to employees who are off work for up to 28 weeks. SSP is not a benefit to which the recoupment provisions apply. As with contractual sick pay, the claimant must give full credit for the SSP received from the employer when calculating the net loss of earnings.

24.10   There is an increasingly common complication in the treatment of sick pay received from an employer. An employer may make an arrangement in which the 'sick pay' received by the employee is described as a loan which is made on terms that the employee must repay the loan if he is successful in pursuing a third party for compensation in relation to the injury which caused the absence from work. The court will recognize an arrangement of this kind, and the claimant will be entitled to recover damages including the amounts to be repaid to the employer. It is essential that the character of the payment as a loan should be supported by a clear contract, either as a term of the conditions of employment or as a specific arrangement made at the time of the injury absence but before payment is made.

E. Uncertain or Fluctuating Earnings

24.11   Sometimes it is difficult to establish with accuracy the level of earnings that the claimant has lost. The burden of proof lies on the claimant. It may be possible to look at a much longer time span than the usual 13 weeks. The Inland Revenue may be able to provide details of earnings declared for tax purposes over previous years, if all other documentary evidence has been lost. With the self-employed, VAT records or bank account records may have to be analysed. If the difficulty is in an unpredictable pattern of overtime or shift payments, one solution may be to identify a colleague of the claimant, or a person who has taken over the claimant's job, and use his earnings as a comparison. However, there can be difficulties of confidentiality: if the other employee is not willing to allow his details to be used an employer might disclose pay records anonymously, but the claimant will have to trust that a fair comparison results.

24.12   Where the facts are so uncertain that they do not provide a clear annual loss on which a mathematical assessment can be made with a multiplier, the court may make a lump sum award in its place based on a broad estimate of the loss. It is usually in the claimant's interests to persuade the court to make a multiplier-type of award if possible.

Information about a claimant's employment history may be obtained, from **24.13** details of the full name, date of birth and National Insurance number of the claimant, from:

> Inland Revenue NI Contributions Office, Special Section A
> Bamburgh House BP1101, Benton Park View,
> Longbenton
> Newcastle upon Tyne NE98 1ZZ
> tel: 084591 55051; fax: 084591 55241

Blamire v South Cumbria HA [1993] PIQR Q1   The claimant, a nurse who **24.14** had injured her back, sought an award for future loss of earnings, but the judge held that the future risks were so incomparable that a multiplier approach was inappropriate and he awarded a lump sum of £25,000. It is often in the interests of defendants to rely on uncertainty of future prospects in this way because experience suggests that a lump sum is likely to be less than the outcome of a multiplier/multiplicand calculation.

Doyle v Wallace [1998] PIQR Q146   The claimant's injuries prevented her **24.15** training as a drama teacher, which was her ambition; if she had failed in this she would have done clerical work. The defendant argued that the claimant must prove on the balance of probabilities that she would have worked as a teacher, but the Court of Appeal held that, for a future loss, the claimant was entitled to be compensated for the loss of a chance. The trial judge had assessed the chance at 50% by taking the middle figure between earnings as a teacher and clerical earnings and the award was upheld.

Goldsborough v Thompson and Crowther [1996] PIQR Q86   A roofer suf- **24.16** fered a broken back. He was unfit for heavy work but capable of light work. He had been unable to return to work partly because his employer at the time of the accident had run out of work and would have made him redundant in any event before the trial date. The Court of Appeal upheld the award of £30,000 for the partial and uncertain future wage loss.

Amanpreet v Hunt [1995] PIQR Q56   The claimant was five years old when **24.17** she suffered a head injury with lasting neurological damage affecting her right limbs. There were several jobs she would be unable to do and using a computer was difficult. The Court of Appeal refused to apply a multiplier/multiplicand approach, but increased the award for reduced earning capacity from £5,000 to £12,500 (2004 value about £15,250).

24.18 *Langford v Hebran* [2001] EWCA Civ 361; [2001] PIQR Q160 The claimant was injured at the start of a promising professional career as a kick-boxer. An accountant set out a range of possible future careers and the court assessed the different probabilities of each of them in valuing the loss of the opportunity to pursue a kick-boxing career. The judgment of Ward LJ sets out the way in which such varying prospects of success should be considered.

F. Small Businesses and Partnerships

24.19 It is in small businesses or partnerships that the greatest difficulty can arise in the calculation of loss of earnings. The first reason is that the true income received by the claimant from the business may be much less easy to assess. The accounts may, for example, set out expenses such as depreciation or the use of an office at home which legitimately reduce the net profits for the purpose of taxation but which may result in an understatement of the true sums received in the owner's hands. It will often be reasonable to instruct an accountant to provide an opinion on the level of profits that would be likely to have continued but for the injury.

24.20 Secondly, the only loss that the claimant can recover is his own loss and no one except the injured person can bring a claim for loss resulting from the claimant's injury. Although there has been a significant departure from this rule in relation to the provision of family nursing care, it holds firm in relation to earnings. So if a business loses the services of a valuable employee, the business cannot claim for the loss that results: the loss is considered to be too remote. If illness throws exceptional burdens on the professional partners or fellow directors of the injured person, they cannot claim for the time spent in covering for the absence or for the expense incurred in employing a temporary locum. The injured person will be able to claim for the loss that represents his share of the partnership's loss, but the partners or shareholders cannot claim for their shares of the loss. The decision in *Hardwick v Hudson* (below) encourages making a formal contractual framework if, for example, the family and colleagues of the injured person give time and effort to make good the absence of the claimant from a business; although recovery in a claim will be limited to the claimant's share of the additional expense.

24.21 *Hardwick v Hudson* [1999] PIQR Q202 The claimant was a partner in a garage business who sustained a whiplash injury to his neck. He was off work for a period and then returned to undertake more administrative duties than before. Because of his injuries, the garage had employed an extra mechanic and his wife undertook increased clerical duties without increased pay. The court took a loss of business income represented by the cost of the extra mechanic (a cost incurred as a result of the injury) less part of the cost of that administrative clerk (work the claimant now did instead) but refused to make any award for the work done by the claimant's wife. The Court of Appeal regarded the award of damages for gratuitous nursing care as a special case and refused to apply the same flexible approach in a commercial environment. The wife could have charged for her services but there had been a deliberate choice to pay her at a rate just below the rate at which National Insurance contributions were payable.

Ward v Newalls Installation [1998] PIQR Q41   The claimant was in partner- **24.22** ship with another man; their wives became partners for tax reasons so that he was then only entitled to a quarter share of profits. However, the Court of Appeal awarded loss of earnings on the realistic basis of 50% of the profits because he had been responsible for 50% of the work; but the other working partner (and his wife) had no claim for the 50% of the loss of profits that they had suffered.

G. Alternative Work

If a claimant has a disability as a result of his injury, he may be unable to **24.23** continue with his pre-accident work but capable of undertaking alternative work. The claimant has a 'duty' to mitigate his loss, which means that the claimant is not entitled to receive damages to compensate for a loss which he might have avoided by acting reasonably. The defendant may therefore argue that a claimant did not act reasonably in resigning from his employment, or in changing his hours or the nature of his duties.

More often, the defendant will accept that a continuing disability may have **24.24** prevented the claimant from continuing in his pre-accident employment, but will argue that the claimant remains capable of pursuing some alternative form of employment, albeit with a lower level of skill or job satisfaction, or on a part-time basis. When an assessment of damages is imminent the claimant will naturally feel disinclined to make maximum effort in looking for new work. The assessment of the claimant's real prospects of finding alternative work is then a difficult task. In theory there are mundane jobs that can be undertaken in spite of significant disabilities, but they tend to be unrewarding both financially and in job satisfaction, and insecure. An employment consultant may be instructed to report to the court on the opportunities open to the claimant for retraining, the opportunities for finding suitable work, the availability of work, and the likely level of earnings. Employment consultants are not popular with district judges who make most case management decisions, and a judge who allows an employment consultant is likely to insist that a single expert should be jointly instructed. Without an employment consultant, the parties can rely on the statistics for average earnings set out in the New Earnings Survey, or on the rate of the National Minimum Wage.

H. New Earnings Survey

24.25   The full text of the New Earnings Survey can be found at www.statistics.gov.uk/statbase and in publications such as the Professional Negligence Bar Association's *Facts & Figures*. The survey is published annually by Sweet & Maxwell, but from 2004 will be in an altered form as the Annual Survey of Hours and Earnings (ASHE). This table sets out headline figures for earnings in the principal sub-groups in Tables A13 and A14 of the 2003 Survey, stating the average gross annual earnings for full-time adults from a sample of those whose pay was not affected by absence.

Occupation	Male £	Female £
Managers and senior officials		
Production managers	30,825	29,331
Functional managers	57,259	40,302
Quality and customer care managers	38,165	30,706
Financial institution and office managers	42,639	27,603
Managers in distribution, storage, and retail	29,714	18,288
Protective service officers	39,897	
Health and social services managers	34,814	26,182
Managers in agriculture and services	35,124	25,152
Managers in hospitality and leisure	24,593	20,443
Professional occupations		
Science professionals	34,891	28,848
Engineering professionals	32,303	27,178
ICT professionals	36,075	32,141
Medical practitioners	70,388	56,621
Teaching professionals	33,313	28,041
Research professionals	29,275	27,337
Legal professionals	52,776	44,424
Chartered and certified accountants	30,801	31,637
Architects, town planners, surveyors	34,244	28,157
Social workers	24,322	23,455
Clergy	18,586	
Librarians	24,116	21,074
Professional and technical occupations		
Science and engineering technicians	24,315	18,877
IT service delivery technicians	30,390	25,677
Nurses	24,779	23,296

Occupation	Male £	Female £
Physiotherapists		24,300
Police officers (Sergeant and below)	31,015	27,242
Graphic designers	26,366	22,880
Journalists and newspaper editors	33,103	
Train drivers	32,357	
Business and finance associates	43,714	29,759
Sales representatives	20,070	22,035
Administrative occupations		
Civil service executive officers	22,872	20,785
Local government clerical officers and assistants	21,073	16,772
Accounts and wages clerks	21,844	17,151
Filing and record clerks	19,406	15,170
Receptionists		12,820
Typists		14,224
Skilled trades		
Gardeners and groundsmen	15,404	
Metal forming, welding, etc	20,670	
Metal machining, fitting, and instrument making	23,472	
Vehicle trades	19,857	
Electrical trades	24,598	
Construction trades	21,291	
Textiles and garments trades	17,072	12,600
Printing trades	22,793	13,944
Food preparation trades	16,230	12,343
Personal service occupations		
Healthcare and personal services	15,874	13,536
Nursing auxiliaries	15,431	13,803
Care assistants at home carers	14,350	13,009
Dental nurses		12,775
Sports and leisure assistants	15,013	13,565
Hairdressers		10,812
Caretakers	15,142	12,697
Sales occupations		
Sales assistants and retail cashiers	15,246	11,882
Telephone salespersons	18,193	15,146
Process, plant, and machine operatives		
Process operatives	20,751	14,638
Plant and machine operatives	20,239	13,265
Assemblers and routine operatives	19,364	13,127
Construction operatives	23,928	
Scaffolders, stagers, riggers	26,244	
Transport drivers and operatives	18,943	14,809
Heavy goods vehicle drivers	20,780	
Van drivers	16,803	
Bus and coach drivers	17,037	

Occupation	Male £	Female £
Elementary occupations		
Farmworkers	16,003	
Building labourers	17,702	
Packers, bottlers, canners, fillers	15,037	12,892
Postal workers	18,899	19,215
Waiters, waitresses	12,802	10,029
Cleaners, domestics	13,969	10,937
Security guards	17,642	17,633
Shelf fillers	13,898	11,508
All occupations	28,065	20,314

I. National Minimum Wage

24.26

	Adult rate £	Development rate £
From 1 April 1999	3.60	3.00
From 1 June 2000		3.20
From 1 October 2000	3.70	
From 1 October 2001	4.10	3.50
From 1 October 2002	4.20	3.60
From 1 October 2003	4.50	3.80
From 1 October 2004	4.85	4.10

The adult rate applies to employees aged 22 and over. The development rate applies to employees aged 18 to 21 inclusive and to some older employees starting a new job with a new employer and receiving training. From 1 October 2004 a rate of £3.00 applies to employees aged 16 (above compulsory school leaving age) and 17.

J. Disability Discrimination Act 1995

24.27 The provisions of the Disability Discrimination Act 1995 ought to be of considerable practical assistance to claimants who are left with a long-term disability and who seek to return to work. In practice it often remains difficult for an applicant with a disability to compete fairly for employment.

1. Meaning of 'disability' and 'disabled person'

24.28 (1) Subject to the provisions of Schedule 1, a person has a disability for the purposes of this Act if he has a physical or mental impairment which has a substantial and long-term adverse effect on his ability to carry out normal day-to-day activities.

(2) In this Act 'disabled person' means a person who has a disability.

4. Discrimination against applicants and employees

24.29 (1) It is unlawful for an employer to discriminate against a disabled person—

(a) in the arrangements which he makes for the purpose of determining to whom he should offer employment;

(b) in the terms on which he offers that person employment; or

(c) by refusing to offer, or deliberately not offering, him employment.

(2) It is unlawful for an employer to discriminate against a disabled person whom he employs—

(a) in the terms of employment which he affords him;

(b) in the opportunities which he affords him for promotion, a transfer, training or receiving any other benefit;

(c) by refusing to afford him, or deliberately not affording him, any such opportunities; or

(d) by dismissing him, or subjecting him to any other detriment.

5. Meaning of 'discrimination'

(1) For the purposes of this Part, an employer discriminates against a disabled person if—   **24.30**

(a) for a reason which relates to the disabled person's disability, he treats him less favourably than he treats or would treat others to whom that reason does not or would not apply; and

(b) he cannot show that the treatment in question is justified.

(2) For the purposes of this Part, an employer also discriminates against a disabled person if—

(a) he fails to comply with a section 6 duty imposed on him in relation to the disabled person; and

(b) he cannot show that his failure to comply with that duty is justified.

(3) Subject to subsection (5), for the purposes of subsection (1) the treatment is justified if, but only if, the reason for it is both material to the circumstances of the particular case and substantial.

(4) For the purposes of subsection (2), failure to comply with a section 6 duty is justified if, but only if, the reason for the failure is both material to the circumstances of the particular case and substantial.

(5) If, in a case falling with subsection (1), the employer is under a section 6 duty in relation to the disabled person but fails without justification to comply with that duty, his treatment of that person cannot be justified under subsection (3) unless it would have been justified even if he had complied with a section 6 duty.

6. Duty of employer to make adjustments

(1) Where—   **24.31**

(a) any arrangements are made by or on behalf of an employer, or

(b) any physical feature of premises occupied by the employer,

place the disabled person concerned at a substantial disadvantage in comparison with persons who are not disabled, it is the duty of the employer to take such steps as it is reasonable, in all the circumstances of the case, for him to have to take in order to prevent the arrangements or feature having that effect.

(2) Subsection (1)(a) applies only in relation to—

(a) arrangements for determining to whom employment should be offered;

(b) any term, condition or arrangements on which employment, promotion, a transfer, training or any other benefit is offered or afforded.

(3) The following are examples of steps which an employer may have to take in relation to a disabled person in order to comply with subsection (1)—

(a) making adjustments to premises;

(b) allocating some of the disabled person's duties to another person;

(c) transferring him to fill an existing vacancy;

    (d) altering his working hours;

    (e) assigning him to a different place of work;

    (f) allowing him to be absent during working hours for rehabilitation, assessment or treatment;

    (g) giving him, or arranging for him to be given, training;

    (h) acquiring or modifying equipment;

    (i) modifying instructions or reference manuals;

    (j) modifying procedures for testing or assessment;

    (k) providing a reader or interpreter;

    (l) providing supervision.

(4) In determining whether it is reasonable for employer to have to take a particular step in order to comply with subsection (1), regard shall be had, in particular, to—

    (a) the extent to which taking the step would prevent the effect in question;

    (b) the extent to which it is practicable for the employer to take the step;

    (c) the financial and other costs which would be incurred by the employer in taking the step and the extent to which taking it would disrupt any of his activities;

    (d) the extent of the employer's financial and other resources;

    (e) the availability to the employer of financial or other assistance with respect to taking the step.

(7) Subject to the provisions of this section, nothing in this Part is to be taken to require an employer to treat a disabled person more favourably than he treats or would treat others.

(12) This section imposes duties only for the purpose of determining whether an employer has discriminated against the disabled person; and accordingly a breach of any such duty is not actionable as such.

K. Loss of Congenial Employment

24.32 If a claimant has to give up an enjoyable and personally rewarding occupation as a result of his injuries, he may be entitled to recover general damages for the loss of congenial employment. This head of claim is discussed at **22.15** above. A benchmark of about £5,000 for this head of damage may be inferred from the cases, which is appropriate for a claimant who particularly enjoyed his work and cannot now do anything comparable.

L. Loss of Pension

24.33 In most cases where there is a loss of earnings, there will also be a loss of pension benefits. The majority of people in employment and self-employment have the benefit of some kind of pension scheme which depends on contributions made during their working years. It is important that the loss of pension benefits should not be overlooked when a claim for the loss of earnings is being prepared.

24.34 Where a claim is made for the loss of pension benefits that the claimant will suffer in his retirement years, it is necessary to deduct the employee's pension contributions from the calculation of the net earnings that the employee would have received if he had not been injured.

Pension income is taxable. The loss to the claimant from having a reduced **24.35** pension is the net loss of income, and tax must be deducted, treating the lost income as the 'top slice' of the claimant's retirement income. If a person continues to work after normal retirement age, National Insurance contributions are no longer payable. After retirement age, most claimants will be entitled to receive a state retirement pension, which is also taxable. There are increased personal allowances for age, but it is usually the case that the full amount of pension income subject to a claim would be taxable at the standard rate.

M. Final Salary Schemes

Employees of central or local government, including employees in health and **24.36** education, will be entitled to pension benefits which are based on the years of service to calculate a fraction of final salary. Pensions of this kind used to be common in private employment also, but have increasingly been replaced by pension schemes in which contributions are paid into a fund and the pension income is determined by the size of the fund. When an injured claimant was a member of a final salary scheme, it is important to obtain full details of the scheme from the employer or from the pension trustees. There will usually be an explanatory booklet, which the claimant himself may have kept. But it is safer and easier to ask the trustees of the fund if they can indicate the level of lump-sum benefit and annual pension that the claimant now has, and the benefits he would have had if he had continued in his employment to normal retirement age. These figures are based on current day wage levels. Once these figures have been established, the Ogden Tables come into play. Table 27 will give the discount that has to be applied for the early receipt of the lost part of the lump-sum benefit and the pension tables, Tables 15–26, will give the current value of the reduced annual pension income.

The courts have tended to apply larger than usual discounts for uncertainty in **24.37** calculating pension claims. However, there is no logical reason to think that the uncertainties of the claimant achieving a full pension are any greater than the other uncertainties that apply to the assessment of the loss of earnings. The discount approaches 10% towards retirement years, but for a claimant who was injured when young, a lower level than this would be appropriate.

The pension scheme may also give benefits to the claimant resulting from the **24.38** need to retire early on grounds of ill health. Typically, there may be an ill-health pension until normal retirement age and a credit of some additional years' purchase to increase the level of retirement pension. Before retirement age, the ill-health pension is disregarded because it is treated as a benefit that the claimant has bought with his work in the same way that an insurance policy is bought. After retirement age, however, the claimant must give credit for the whole of his actual pension, including any increase or enhancement resulting from the injury.

24.39   *Parry v Cleaver* [1970] AC 1   This is the leading case on the calculation of loss of income. The claimant had contributed to a pension scheme under which he received ill-health benefits during the period of his loss of earnings. The House of Lords held that the benefits should be treated in a way similar to the proceeds of an insurance policy which is not to be offset against the claimant's claim for damages.

24.40   *Smoker v London Fire Authority* [1991] 2 AC 502   In this case the defendant unsuccessfully challenged the rule in *Parry v Cleaver*, seeking to rely on the fact that the claimant did not have to make financial contributions to the pension scheme. It was held that the claimant's work was the way in which he had paid for the benefit.

24.41   *Longden v British Coal* [1998] AC 653   On his early retirement the claimant received a lump sum under the pension scheme. It was held that the lump sum should be apportioned so that the claimant only has to give credit for the part of it that relates to post-retirement pension income and not for the part of it that relates to ill-health benefits before normal retirement age.

N. Money Purchase Schemes

24.42   Most pension schemes in the private sector now provide for contributions to be made to a pension fund administered by an independent financial provider. The most important loss that a claimant suffers is the loss of the employer's contributions to the fund, which will often be an entitlement to a percentage of gross earnings under the contract of employment. It is usually pointless and unrealistic to try to estimate the retirement benefits, or the contribution to the fund at the retirement date, that the employer's contributions would provide. It is more practical to treat the employer's contributions as a benefit of the employment and to claim the value of them as a benefit in kind when calculating the loss of earnings.

24.43   The employee may also contribute to the pension fund, either voluntarily or as the only terms on which pension benefits are available. However, no loss flows from the ceasing of these contributions. When the claimant receive damages for his loss of earnings, he is free to make an equivalent investment. Although there may be some loss of tax advantage, the great majority of claimants will, at least in theory, be able to obtain the same tax advantages by taking out a stakeholder pension scheme, which provides tax relief even to those who have no earned income.

O. Handicap in the Labour Market

A claim for handicap in the labour market is invariably known in legal jargon **24.44** as a claim for *Smith v Manchester* damages. Strictly speaking, such a claim arises where the claimant has suffered an injury which continues to impair his ability to carry out the tasks of his employment, but through good fortune or the forbearance of the employer the claimant has been able to continue in his pre-accident employment. There is no quantifiable present loss, but if the claimant were ever to lose this job, perhaps for a reason completely unrelated to his injury, he would find it more difficult to find a new job, at an equivalent rate of earnings, because of the effect of his injury. In practice, the title *Smith v Manchester* is often used to describe more broadly the range of future employment difficulties that the claimant may encounter.

The amount of a *Smith v Manchester* award is difficult to predict. The Court of **24.45** Appeal will not set out guidelines for assessment, and discourages an approach based on a multiple of annual earnings. Butler Sloss LJ said in *Tait v Pearson* [1996] PIQR Q92 that the task was 'to do what judges over the years have done, to pluck a figure from the air as best to provide an appropriate recognition that [the claimant] has a financial loss for the future'. In practice, the court is bound to have regard to the level of the claimant's net earnings and a rough idea of the difficulties the claimant would face in looking for work. It is good practice for the claimant, if possible, to establish an evidential basis for the claim by pointing to the possible time that might be taken in retraining or the possible reduced level of earnings. Defendants will focus on the double uncertainty of any loss: first, uncertainty whether the claimant's present job will in fact come to an end and, secondly, uncertainty whether the claimant who is coping at present will in fact have a longer job search or a reduction in earnings in a new job as a result of his injury.

Before a *Smith v Manchester* claim can succeed the claimant has to overcome a **24.46** threshold of showing that there is a real risk of losing his current employment and a real risk of subsequent difficulty. There is a burden of proof to be discharged and it is unwise to assume that the court will simply infer that every job must be at some risk and that every claimant with lasting symptoms must suffer an extended job search. The low level of award seen in some cases might suggest that some judges set the threshold fairly low, but in any case where this head of claim is likely to be important, the evidence must deal with the basic risks and difficulties.

24.47 *Smith v Manchester Corporation* (1974) 17 KIR 1   The claimant, a domestic worker in an old people's home, tripped and fell injuring her elbow. She suffered from a continuing disability but had been able to return to work. The employers undertook to keep her in employment for as long as they could properly do so. In spite of the undertaking, the Court of Appeal increased the award for loss of future earning capacity arising from the risk of future employment. The claimant was aged 49 and the normal retirement age would have been 60. The earnings were £16.50 a week or £585 a year and the award of £1,000 represented 14 months' net earnings.

24.48 *Moeliker v Reyolle & Co.* [1976] ICR 253   The first question is the risk that the claimant will be thrown on to the labour market. If the claimant does not cross the threshold of proving a real, rather than a fanciful risk, a claim does not arise. The second question is the assessment, which cannot be on a multiplier/multiplicand basis because of the uncertainties involved, but must have regard to the level of earnings, of the period of the claimant's working life that remains, the size of the risk that he may lose his job, the time the risk may arise and how far he would be handicapped by his disability in his individual circumstances. There must also be a discount for the immediate receipt of a certain lump sum.

24.49 *Foster v Tyne and Wear CC* [1986] 1 All ER 567   The claimant lorry driver, aged 35, seriously injured his left ankle. He rejected an offer of light work and returned to his pre-accident work but suffering increasing pain. His net earnings were £7,300 and a *Smith v Manchester* award of £35,000 was upheld by the Court of Appeal.

24.50 *Gunter v Nicholas* [1993] PIQR Q67   A wood machinist suffered damage to three fingers of his dominant right hand. He returned to work at the same firm, using a machine which required only left-hand dexterity. He was aged 34 at trial when the judge awarded £16,000 *Smith v Manchester* damages by reference to two years' net earnings. This was upheld by the Court of Appeal.

24.51 In a useful article at [2001] JPIL 37, Adam Chippindall suggests a formula for assessing—

   (a) the substance of the risk that the claimant will lose his current job;
   (b) the likely extra period out of work if the risk were to materialize;
   (c) the rate of current net earnings;
   (d) the years of working life remaining; and
   (e) a discount for early receipt from the mid-point of the period.

This helpfully focuses the mind on the relevant factual issues. The use of his arithmetical approach may become a useful tool in the argument, although it seems likely that the underlying uncertainties will mean that the final decision of the judge will never become an entirely arithmetical assessment.

25

NURSING AND CARING

A. Medical Treatment

The vast majority of accident victims receive NHS treatment in the immediate **25.01** aftermath of an accident. Unless they have private medical insurance, the question of private treatment at a later stage does not usually arise except for elective treatment for which the delays and restrictions on NHS treatment may be unacceptable, and if liability is not in issue an interim payment may be obtained to cover the cost. Where private treatment has been funded by the injured claimant's private health insurance it is likely that the terms of the policy will enable the insurer to require the claimant to pursue the reimbursement of its outlay and, as with an employer's recovery of contractual sick pay advanced under suitable terms, recovery is generally allowed. At the time of final assessment however, there is a considerable increase in the scope of treatment for which the cost of private medical treatment is sought and awarded. Where treatment will be needed in the future, an estimate of the current cost is obtained and discounted by the multiplier in the Ogden Tables, Table 27 (at **23.26** above), for a specific period of deferment. However, the courts are strongly resistant—as in *Cooke v United Bristol Healthcare* noted below on care costs—to making an allowance beyond inflation for the widely accepted likelihood that medical costs will increase at a faster rate than the general rate of inflation reflected in the Lord Chancellor's Order fixing the rate of return for future multipliers at 2.5%.

Section 2(4) of the Law Reform (Personal Injuries) Act 1948 provides that: **25.02**

> In an action for damages for personal injuries (including any such action arising out of a contract) there shall be disregarded in determining the reasonableness of any expenses, the possibility of avoiding those expenses or part of them by taking advantage of facilities available under the National Health Service Act 1977 . . .

25.03 This provision means that a defendant can never argue that a claim for the cost of private treatment is unreasonable on the ground that the claimant could as an alternative obtain the treatment free as an NHS patient. It does not mean that the cost of private treatment is always recoverable. It will only be recoverable if it is the genuine intention of the claimant, once in possession of damages sufficient to cover the cost, actually to receive treatment privately rather than as an NHS patient. In many cases there will be no difficulty in proving this intention, but defendants will be on their guard because once the damages have been paid, there is no requirement on the claimant that the damages should actually be spent on the need for which they were awarded. In practice there is little difficulty in recovering the cost of treatment for elective procedures for which there are very long NHS waiting lists, such as cosmetic surgery to improve scarring; on the other hand, special reasons would be needed to justify transferring to private care for the conclusion of a course of treatment that has begun in the NHS, for example planned follow up to a complex fracture.

25.04 *Woodrup v Nicol* [1993] PIQR Q104   The claimant would require future medical care, and claimed the cost of private treatment, but the trial judge found on the facts that for some of this care he would continue to receive NHS treatment. The Court of Appeal upheld an award of half the costs claimed. 'If on the balance of probabilities private facilities are not going to be used, for whatever reason, the [claimant] is not entitled to claim for an expense which he is not going to incur.'

B. Professional and Residential Care

25.05 Severely injured claimants may require care in a nursing home as well as medical treatment. They may be able to live at home with the help of regular nursing and, for example, help at night. The cost of private care is recoverable in the claim and the possible availability of NHS treatment or local authority social services care does not need to be brought into account. It is the cost of a full care regime to provide properly for severely disabled claimants that generates the largest claims.

25.06 A care regime as a resident in an institution will provide basic necessities such as food and laundry within the overall cost. The claimant would have had to pay for these even if he had not been injured. Section 5 of the Administration of Justice Act 1982 provides that:

In an action under the laws of England and Wales . . . for damages for personal injuries (including any such action arising out of a contract) any saving to the injured person which is attributable to his maintenance wholly or partly at public expense in a hospital, nursing home or other institution shall be set off against any income lost by him as a result of his injuries.

Although this deals specifically with provision at public expense, it reflects a general principle that the claimant can only recover his net loss so that if there are savings they should be offset against the loss. A person who can no longer drive and claims the cost of taxi fares for mobility must give credit for the saving that he no longer has the expense of running a car.

Where care is provided by a local authority (which will include any social **25.07** services provision), s 17 of the Health and Social Services and Social Security Adjudications Act 1983 provides that:

an authority providing a service . . . may recover such charge (if any) for it as they consider reasonable [but] if a person . . . satisfies the authority that his means are insufficient . . . the authority shall not require him to pay more for it than it appears to them that it is reasonably practicable for him to pay.

Avon CC v Hooper [1997] 1 WLR 1605   A child who suffered serious brain **25.08** damage was accommodated in a residential home at the expense of the local authority. When a claim for damages for clinical negligence which caused the brain damage was brought, the local authority made a claim for the cost of care. The negligence claim was settled on terms that the defendant agreed to meet future costs and gave an indemnity in respect of any liability for the cost of past care. In this action to recover the past cost, it was held that the cause of action held by the child had been sufficient to give the child the means to pay for the purpose of s 17 of the 1983 Act. The scope of the claim was however restricted by a limitation period of six years.

Firth v Ackroyd [2001] PIQR Q29   Where the statutory basis for the provision **25.09** of care is the National Assistance Act 1948, the liability to pay depends on regulations which incorporate the Income Support Regulations 1987 where the proceeds of a personal injury claim should be disregarded. In this case it was held that the local authority could not claim to be reimbursed out of the capital and thus the damages should not include either an award to meet the costs nor should a declaration of entitlement to an indemnity be given. Permission to appeal has, however, been granted.

Cooke v United Bristol Healthcare [2003] EWCA Civ 1370; [2004] PIQR **25.10** Q10   The claimants were refused permission to adduce expert accountancy evidence to show that the discount rate of 2.5% should not be applied in the assessment of future care costs because future increases in care costs were likely to outstrip inflation. The evidence would not amount to a case for exceptional treatment under s 1(2) of the Damages Act 1996 and the statutory rate of return must be used.

C. Recompense for Care Freely Given

25.11 An injured claimant who lives alone and requires paid help with the tasks of daily living such as dressing, washing and cooking, will need a complex and very expensive arrangement with several carers to attend on him for different purposes and at different times. For many claimants this is not necessary because friends and family make a commitment to help. A claimant is not bound to accept their help but most claimants would greatly prefer to be looked after at home by their families if institutional care can be avoided.

25.12 In *Hunt v Severs* (below) the House of Lords held that damages for the value of gratuitous family care should be awarded on the basis of an assessment of the commercial cost that would be incurred for the provision of such care by a professional carer, with a discount to reflect the free, family nature of the care and the fact that the carer does not have to incur expenses such as tax, National Insurance, or travel to work. Earlier cases suggested that the court was only concerned to make some reasonable recompense to the carer (*Housecroft v Burnett* below) and the claim should only be made in serious cases (*Mills v British Rail Engineering* [1992] PIQR Q130), but the recent cases summarized below show that a claim based on commercial cost and a discount can properly be made even in cases of modest and short-lived injury, although the amount allowed will be modest. The rate of discount is repeatedly said to be a matter for the discretion of the trial judge in the individual case, but in practice a discount of 25% has become very common unless there are special factors to be taken into account. However, in modest care claims the court may be specially liable to award a lump sum in round figures at rather less than the computed claim, as in the awards by Judge MacDuff that were approved in *Giambrone v JMC Holidays* (below).

25.13 The House of Lords also said in *Hunt v Severs* that damages for family care should be awarded to the claimant, but held in trust for the provider of the care. This trust may have been suggested mainly as a means of avoiding a liability which the House considered undeserving, because in that case the person providing the care was also the tortfeasor who had been responsible for causing the injuries. But in *H (A Child) v S* (below) the Court of Appeal held that there is a real trust which the court will enforce, and legal advisers should therefore be aware of the need to take account of the interest of the carer when formulating a claim of this kind, when reaching a compromise, and when giving the claimant advice on the way in which damages should be managed once received. Where a claim is brought on behalf of a child or patient, damages for past care belong to the carer and should be separated from the claimant's damages which are to be invested by the court. The courts have not yet grappled with the formidable practical difficulties that may arise if damages that have been awarded for future care are to be considered to be subject to a real trust in favour of the carer once a period of care has been provided.

Cunningham v Harrison [1973] QB 942   The claimant was permanently **25.14** paralysed in all four limbs and dependent on others for all personal care and for help with feeding. His wife cared for him devotedly. On advice, a contract for her services had been drawn up but this was rejected as unnecessary: if a wife renders services instead of a nurse, the injured person should recover compensation for the value of the services and hold it on trust for her.

Donnelly v Joyce [1974] QB 454   The claimant suffered serious leg **25.15** injuries and his mother gave up part-time work in order to look after him. The Court of Appeal upheld the award of a sum representing the mother's lost wages on the basis that the injury caused to the claimant included the need to be cared for.

Housecroft v Burnett [1986] 1 All ER 332   In a case of a tetraplegic claimant, **25.16** although the trial judge had heard detailed evidence of a commercial assessment of the cost of care, O'Connor LJ put the assessment more broadly:

> Once it is understood that this is an element in the award to the [claimant] to provide for the reasonable and proper care of the [claimant] and that a capital sum is to be available for this purpose, the court should look at it as a whole and consider whether on the facts of the case it is sufficient to enable the [claimant] among other things to make reasonable recompense to the relative.

Hunt v Severs [1994] 2 AC 350   The claimant was injured when she was a **25.17** pillion passenger on a motorcycle ridden negligently by the defendant, her boyfriend whom she later married. In her claim against him she claimed the value of his gratuitous nursing services. The House of Lords rejected this claim, preferring the trust basis of the carer's entitlement (*Cunningham* above) so that an award of damages for the care he provided would amount to an order that he should pay himself, which means that there is no recoverable loss. (This of course ignores the reality of payment by the motor insurer.)

Newman v Folkes [2002] EWCA Civ 591; [2002] PIQR Q2   The Court of **25.18** Appeal upheld an award for care based on commercial rate at a discount (but without weekend/holiday enhancement) where the claimant had suffered a severe change of personality which left him a very difficult, sometimes violent husband whose wife had developed sound techniques to deal with his behaviour.

25.19 *Evans v Pontypridd Roofing* [2001] EWCA Civ 1657; [2002] PIQR Q16 The claimant had suffered devastating arm and back injuries causing immobility and pain and severe depression. The Court of Appeal upheld an assessment of care by 24-hour basis rather than by considering the detailed services undertaken from time to time, and the use of the discount rate of 25%. Although it was stressed that the rate of discount is not to be fixed, but to be assessed separately for every case, in practice the rate of 25% has become extremely common.

25.20 *H (A Child) v S* [2002] EWCA Civ 792; [2003] PIQR Q1 In a fatal accident claim, the Court of Appeal approved the approach of assessing the loss of caring services by the deceased mother on the basis of an hourly rate for commercial care, and a discount, following the same approach as for the care needs of a living injured claimant. The court also held that the trust on which the claimant holds such damages on behalf of the carer, following *Hunt v Severs*, is a real trust which the court will enforce.

25.21 *Lowe v Guise* [2002] EWCA Civ 197; [2002] PIQR Q116 Before he was injured, the claimant provided gratuitous care to his disabled brother, but his injuries impaired his ability to do so, and his mother made up the difference. A claim was permitted for the care that the claimant could no longer provide, although his loss of earnings must be calculated on the basis that, but for the accident, he would continue to provide the full level of care.

25.22 *Giambrone v JMC Holidays* [2004] EWCA Civ 158; [2004] PIQR Q38 Several claims were brought together by families with children who had suffered gastroenteritis contracted while on holiday. They made modest claims for nursing care provided by the parents. The Court of Appeal rejected the defendant's argument that in principle a care claim should only be awarded in a case of serious injury (not following *Mills v British Rail Engineering*) and upheld the awards that had been made by Judge Macduff ([2003] 4 All ER 1212). He awarded simple lump sums at round figures significantly less than the claims presented by calculation of a commercial cost and a discount. For example, where the undiscounted commercial cost was £279, he awarded £175, and where the undiscounted cost was £518, he awarded £275. Brooke LJ at [33]: 'Any award for gratuitous care in excess of £50 a week at present values in a case in which a child suffering from gastroenteritis receives care from her family should be reserved for cases more serious than these. This sum represents, in my judgment, a fair and proportionate balance. . .'

25.23 Section 8 of the Administration of Justice Act 1982 provides for Scotland that the responsible person 'shall pay to the injured person by way of damages such sum as represents reasonable remuneration for those services and repayment of reasonable expenses incurred' and in *Hunt v Severs* (at 363B) this was treated as making the law of Scotland and England the same.

D. How Much

There are three steps to the assessment of how much should be awarded for **25.24** gratuitous care. Step one is to define precisely the nature of the care and the amount in terms of time reasonably spent in meeting the special needs of the injured person. Step two is to assess how much it would cost the injured person to employ a paid carer on a commercial basis to provide that level of care. Step three is to apply an appropriate discount to reflect the gratuitous nature of the care that is given freely and not on a commercial basis.

Step one, to define precisely the nature of the care and the amount in terms of **25.25** time reasonably devoted to meeting the special needs of the injured person, is in principle achieved by taking careful statements of evidence from the injured person and the carers setting out a daily routine and describing the tasks undertaken. The difficulty is that the assessment should be of the work attributable to the reasonable need for care, yet the family carer probably spends considerable amounts of time both on domestic work unrelated to specific care needs and on providing loving support and companionship beyond, at least in terms of time, what a commercial nurse would reasonably be engaged to do. In a case of serious injury therefore, it is far from straightforward to analyse the proper factual basis of care that is to be recompensed.

Step two, to assess how much it would cost the injured person to employ a paid **25.26** carer on a commercial basis to provide that level of care, is also difficult. It may be something which an experienced solicitor should be capable of undertaking once the facts are clear by consulting published rates for different kinds of care. Without knowing the detailed demands of the individual patient, however, this will always be an imprecise approach. Where the detailed requirements are known, a more accurate figure could be obtained by an estimate of costs from a local nursing agency.

The difficulty of making these assessments is the reason for the widespread use **25.27** of nursing care experts to assist in the quantification of serious care claims. An expert's report will provide a detailed account of the care regime that has been in place, but will additionally consider what level of care was reasonably required in the light of the injuries and level of disability, which may be more or less than what has so far been provided. It will assess a cost only for such care as is considered reasonably necessary. An expert will know which rates are appropriate and will present the court with a reasoned and reliable conclusion based on facts an expert has checked in answer to the first two steps of the inquiry. Although the CPR require judges to allow expert evidence only when it is necessary, the enormous value of professional care assessments in serious cases should make their continued employment welcome, though it is likely that they will often act as a single expert on joint instructions.

25.28 Step three, to apply an appropriate discount to reflect the gratuitous nature of the care that is given freely and not on a commercial basis, results in a discount from the commercial cost that is usually between 20% and 33%. The first reason for the discount is purely financial: a professional nurse may cost the patient the rates set out in answer to steps one and two but will herself benefit from less than this because of income tax, National Insurance contributions, and costs such as the cost of travel to work. It is the benefit to the carer that is relevant in this exercise and not the cost to the employer. Where the level of care is not great, it may be argued that the impact of tax would be negligible and a discount at the smaller end of the range would be appropriate. The second reason for a discount is that the payment is in fact recompense for care freely given for love rather than commercial remuneration.

25.29 In cases where there is a substantial care need, the joint instruction of a single care expert will often be appropriate and of considerable help to the parties and to the court in providing an appropriate answer to all of these questions except the issue of the discount: that is to say, such a report can be expected to provide a reasonably reliable analysis of the extent of the care need and a mathematical calculation of the commercial cost of obtaining care of the kind that is needed.

25.30 In cases where the care need is modest, so that instructions to an expert are not proportionate, the parties will have to put before the court a computation of care need and commercial cost, even if the court is likely to round the figures down to a convenient sum following *Giambrone* (above). In these cases of modest care need, it is suggested that the rates for local authority care workers negotiated by the National Joint Council, which are the rates recommended by Crossroads Caring for Carers (information available at www.crossroads.org.uk/), are likely to be appropriate.

National Joint Council Hourly Rates

25.31 The Spinal Point 8 salary scale is appropriate where the duties include domestic duties (for example, cleaning, cooking and washing), physical tasks approximating to home care (for example, dressing, washing, and feeding clients) and social duties (for example, talking with clients, helping clients to maintain contact with family, friends and community, assisting with shopping and recreation) aimed at creating a supportive homely atmosphere where clients can achieve maximum independence. These are the basic rates, without enhancement for evenings, weekends or holidays.

	£
From 1 April 1997	4.84
From 1 April 1998	4.98
From 1 April 1999	5.13
From 1 April 2000	5.29
From 1 April 2001	5.49
From 1 April 2002	5.65
From 1 October 2002	5.71
From 1 April 2003	5.90
From 1 April 2004	6.06
From 1 April 2005	6.24

25.32 *Fitzgerald v Ford* [1996] PIQR Q72   A discount of 25% from the commercial rate adopted by the Court of Appeal.

25.33 *Doyle v Wallace* [1998] PIQR Q146, 151   In a case of very serious injuries including brain damage where the claimant required constant attendance, the Court of Appeal described an hourly rate of £4 per hour after discount for nursing care as 'a very modest figure' and 'unassailable'. An RPI adjustment to late 2004 would increase this to just over £4.60 per hour.

25.34 *Burns v Davies* [1999] Lloyd's Med Rep 215   A discount of 20% adopted in place of the conventional 25% or 33% in view of the extreme difficulty of the mother's care and because no unsocial hours uplift was included in the commercial cost assessment.

E. Establishing a Regime

25.35 Where liability is in dispute and all issues are tried together, claimants sometimes find it difficult to persuade the court that a change to a more expensive regime, once there are funds to pay for it, will be reasonably necessary. Conversely, where a regime has in fact been put in place for the care of the claimant, defendants sometimes find it difficult to persuade the court that the arrangements are an unreasonably high expense. It is good tactics for a claimant to strive to put the appropriate regime into place before the assessment if possible, and where liability is not in dispute or has been resolved in a split trial, the power of the court to order interim payments should be used for this purpose.

25.36 *Campbell v Mylchreest* [1999] PIQR Q17   After the decision on liability, a severely brain damaged claimant sought an interim payment of £100,000 stating the intention to use the funds to set up a regime of increased home care instead of free NHS care. The defendant intended to argue at the assessment of damages that the home care was not reasonably necessary because of the severity of the claimant's injuries and if the interim payment were used to put the new regime in place there would not be a level playing field. In spite of this concern, the Court of Appeal approved the interim payment. In general, if the sum requested is well within the amount likely to be recovered, it is no concern of the court to know the use to which the money will be applied (*Stringman v McArdle* [1994] 1 WLR 1653).

F. Rehabilitation

25.37   It is obvious that it is in the interests of the defendant that a claimant should recover from his injuries as soon and as fully as possible. In human terms the same is also true of claimants, though they do not always recognize it: even though an early recovery may reduce the level of damages recovered, in the wider perspective damages are rarely an adequate compensation. A victim is nearly always better of financially, and in terms of well-being, in the quality of life and in the effect on those around him, by returning to work than by claiming compensation for having no work.

25.38   In recent years insurers have begun to take an increasingly interventionist approach to claimants with intractable injuries, encouraging them to seek treatment and help at the insurer's expense in the hope of promoting recovery. These steps have been formalized in a Code of Best Practice on Rehabilitation, Early Intervention and Medical Treatment in Personal Injury Claims launched in October 1999 and supported by many bodies concerned with injury claims from both sides. The Code urges solicitors and insurers to consider whether early treatment would be helpful and to arrange an independent assessment (at the insurer's expense) if this may be the case. The independent assessment cannot be used by either side in litigation, but insurers must consider whether to fund treatment recommended by the assessment.

25.39   Although the Code is well intentioned, it is capable of giving rise to difficult conflicts of interest. Inevitably it will apply chiefly in cases where primary liability is not in dispute. Where it is followed in cases where contributory negligence remains an issue, the claimant risks being drawn into expensive treatment he would not otherwise regard as worthwhile and for which he may end up having to pay a part of the cost. The claimant may be satisfied with his current medical advice and reluctant to cooperate with an assessment that may challenge the treatment regime he has been offered. The claimant may be fearful that if he does not follow a recommended treatment or therapy this may be held against him as a failure to mitigate his loss even though the therapy was not suggested by his own doctor.

G. The Rehabilitation Code

CODE OF BEST PRACTICE ON REHABILITATION, EARLY INTERVENTION AND MEDICAL TREATMENT IN PERSONAL INJURY CLAIMS

1. INTRODUCTION

1.1 It is recognised that, in many claims for damages for personal injuries, the claimant's **25.40** current medical situation, and/or the long-term prognosis, may be improved by appropriate medical treatment, including surgery, being given at the earliest practicable opportunity, rather than waiting until the claim has been settled. Similarly, claims may involve a need for non-medical treatment, such as physiotherapy, counselling, occupational therapy, speech therapy and so forth ('rehabilitation'): again, there is a benefit in these services being provided as early as practicable.

1.2 It is also recognised that (predominantly in cases of serious injury) the claimant's quality of life can be immediately improved by undertaking some basic home adaptations and/or by the provision of aids and equipment and/or appropriate medical treatment as soon as these are needed ('early intervention'), rather than when the claim is finally settled.

1.3 It is further recognised that, where these medical or other issues have been dealt with, there may be employment issues that can be addressed for the benefit of the claimant, to enable the claimant to keep his/her existing job, to obtain alternative suitable employment with the same employer or to retrain for new employment. Again, if these needs are addressed at the proper time, the claimant's quality of life and long-term prospects may be greatly improved.

1.4 Solicitors acting for claimants understand that, taking all these matters into account, they can achieve more for the claimant—by making rehabilitation available—than just the payment of compensation. The insurance industry realises that great benefit may be had in considering making funds available for these purposes.

1.5 The aim of this Rehabilitation Code is therefore to ensure that the claimant's solicitor and the insurer (and the insurer's solicitor or handling agent) both actively consider the use of rehabilitation services and the benefits of an early assessment of the claimant's needs. The further aim is that both should treat the possibility of improving the claimant's quality of life and their present and long-term physical and mental well-being as issues equally as important as the payment of just, full and proper compensation.

1.6 The report mentioned in section 6 of the Code focuses on the early assessment of the claimant's needs in terms of treatment and/or rehabilitation. The assessment report is not intended to determine the claimant's long-term needs for care or medical treatment, other than by way of general indication and comment.

2. THE CLAIMANT'S SOLICITOR'S DUTY

2.1 It shall be the duty of every claimant's solicitor to consider, from the earliest practicable **25.41** stage, and in consultation with the claimant and/or the claimant's family, whether it is likely or possible that early intervention, rehabilitation or medical treatment would improve their present and/or long-term physical or mental well-being. This duty is ongoing throughout the life of the case but is of most importance in the early stages.

2.2 It shall be the duty of a claimant's solicitor to consider, with the claimant and/or the claimant's family, whether there is an immediate need for aids, adaptations or other matters that would seek to alleviate problems caused by disability, and then to communicate with the insurer as soon as practicable about any rehabilitation needs, with a view to putting this Code into effect.

2.3 It shall not be the responsibility of the solicitor to decide on the need for treatment or rehabilitation or to arrange such matters without appropriate medical consultation. Such medical consultation should involve the claimant and/or the claimant's family, the claimant's primary care physician and, where appropriate, any other medical practitioner currently treating the claimant.

2.4 Nothing in this Code shall in any way affect the obligations placed on a claimant's solicitor by the Pre-Action Protocol for Personal Injury Claims ('the Protocol'). However, it must be appreciated that very early communication with the insurer will enable the matters dealt with here to be addressed more effectively.

2.5 It must be recognised that the insurer will need to receive from the claimant's solicitor sufficient information for the insurer to make a proper decision about the need for intervention, rehabilitation or treatment. To this extent, the claimant's solicitor must comply with the requirements of the Protocol to provide the insurer with full and adequate details of the injuries sustained by the claimant, the nature and extent of any, or any likely, continuing disability and any suggestions that may already have been made concerning rehabilitation and/or early intervention. There is no requirement under the Protocol, or this Code, for the claimant's solicitor to have obtained a full medical report. It is recognised that many cases will be identified for consideration under this Code before medical evidence has actually been commissioned.

3. THE INSURER

25.42   3.1 It shall be the duty of the insurer to consider, from the earliest practicable stage in any appropriate case, whether it is likely that the claimant will benefit in the immediate, medium or longer term from further medical treatment, rehabilitation or early intervention. This duty is ongoing throughout the life of the case but is of most importance in the early stages.

3.2 If the insurer considers that a particular claim might be suitable for intervention, rehabilitation or treatment, the insurer will communicate this to the claimant's solicitor as soon as practicable.

3.3 On receipt of such communication, the claimant's solicitor will immediately discuss these issues with the claimant and/or the claimant's family pursuant to his duty as set out above and, where appropriate, will seek advice from the claimant's treating physicians/surgeons.

3.4 Nothing in this or any other Code of Practice shall in any way modify the obligations of the insurer under the Protocol to investigate claims rapidly and in any event within three months (except where time is extended by the claimant's solicitor) from the date of the formal claim letter. It is recognised that, although the rehabilitation assessment can be done even where liability investigations are outstanding, it is essential that such investigations proceed with the appropriate speed.

4. ASSESSMENT

25.43   4.1 Unless the need for intervention, rehabilitation or treatment has already been identified by medical reports obtained and disclosed by either side, the need for and extent of such intervention, rehabilitation or treatment will be considered by means of an independent assessment.

4.2 'Independent assessment' in this context means that the assessment will be carried out by either:
   (a) One or more of the treating physicians/surgeons, or
   (b) By an agency suitably qualified and/or experienced in such matters, which is financially and managerially independent of the claimant's solicitor's firm and the insurers dealing with the claim.

4.3 It is essential that the process of assessment and recommendation be carried out by those who have an appropriate qualification (to include physiotherapists, occupational therapists, psychologists, psychotherapists and so forth). It would be inappropriate for assessments to be done by someone who does not have a medical or other appropriate qualification. Those doing the assessments should not only have an appropriate qualification but should have experience in treating the type of disability from which the individual claimant suffers.

5. THE ASSESSMENT PROCESS

5.1 Where possible, the agency to be instructed to provide the assessment should be agreed between the claimant's solicitor and the insurer. The instruction letter will be sent by the claimant's solicitor to the medical agency and a copy of the instruction letter will be sent to the insurer. **25.44**

5.2 The medical agency will be asked to interview the claimant at home (or in hospital, if the claimant is still in hospital, with a subsequent visit to the claimant's home) and will be asked to produce a report, which covers the following headings:
1. The injuries sustained by the claimant
2. The claimant's present medical condition (medical conditions that do not arise from the accident should also be noted where relevant to the overall picture of the claimant's needs)
3. The claimant's domestic circumstances (including mobility, accommodation and employment), where relevant
4. The injuries/disability in respect of which early intervention or early rehabilitation is suggested
5. The type of intervention or treatment envisaged
6. The likely cost
7. The likely short/medium-term benefit to the claimant

5.3 The report will not deal with diagnostic criteria, causation issues or long-term care requirements.

6. THE ASSESSMENT REPORT

6.1 The reporting agency will, on completion of the report, send copies to both the instructing solicitor and the insurer simultaneously. Both parties will have the right to raise queries on the report, disclosing such correspondence to the other party. **25.45**

6.2 It is recognised that for this independent assessment report to be of benefit to the parties, it should be prepared and used wholly outside the litigation process. Neither side can therefore rely on its contents in any subsequent litigation. With that strict proviso, to be confirmed in writing by the individual solicitor and insurer if required, the report shall be disclosed to both parties.

6.3 The report, any correspondence relating to it and any notes created by the assessing agency will be covered by legal privilege and will not under any circumstances be disclosed in any legal proceedings. Any notes or documents created in connection with the assessment process will not be disclosed in any litigation, and any person involved in the preparation of the report or involved in the assessment process shall not be a compellable witness at court.

6.4 The provision in paragraph 6.3 above as to treating the report, etc. as outside the litigation process is limited to the assessment report and any notes relating to it. Once the parties have agreed, following an assessment report, that a particular regime of rehabilitation or treatment should be put in place, the case management of that regime falls outside this Code and paragraph 6.3 does not therefore apply. Any notes and reports created during the subsequent case management will be governed by the usual principles relating to disclosure of documents and medical records relating to the claimant.

6.5 The insurer will pay for the report within 28 days of receipt.

6.6 The need for any further or subsequent assessment shall be agreed between the claimant's solicitor and the insurer. The provisions of this Code shall apply to such assessments.

7. RECOMMENDATIONS

25.46   7.1 When the assessment report is disclosed to the insurer, the insurer will be under a duty to consider the recommendations made and the extent to which funds will be made available to implement all or some of the recommendations. The insurer will not be required to pay for intervention or treatment that is unreasonable in nature, content or cost. The claimant will be under no obligation to undergo intervention, medical investigation or treatment that is unreasonable in all the circumstances of the case.

7.2 Any funds made available shall be treated as an interim payment on account of damages. However, if the funds are provided to enable specific intervention, rehabilitation or treatment to occur, the insurers warrant that they will not, in any legal proceedings connected with the claim, dispute the reasonableness of that treatment nor the agreed cost, provided of course that the claimant has had the recommended treatment.

26

FINANCIAL LOSSES AND EXPENSES

A. Special Needs

A seriously injured claimant may be helped by a wide range of aids and appliances and the cost of these can be included in any claim. The sort of claim where this will be a significant topic is likely also to be the sort of claim for which an expert apprasial of care costs will be helpful, and the expert will help by identifying and costing aids which are appropriate to the needs of the claimant. The yardstick for recovery is whether an item is reasonably necessary to help the claimant to manage with the disability caused by the injury. In difficult cases, for example where the claimant is so disabled that his ability to benefit from particular aids is in doubt, it may be necessary to address the question of need through the medical experts. The range of aids and appliances has grown to be very full and in the case of computer-aided or mechanical aids the cost is sometimes very great: an expense which is out of proportion to the benefit that will be derived from it may not be allowed. **26.01**

The method of claim usually involves a multiplier calculation based on the claimant's expectation of life, and the needs must therefore be converted into an annual expense. The initial acquisition cost is followed by an assessment of the durability and thus of the time before replacement. An aid that can be expected to last for five years is costed by allowing one-fifth of the expenditure in the list **26.02** of annual costs. The running and maintenance costs must similarly be turned into an annual figure. A multiplier is then applied in the usual way.

26.03 As always, it is the net added cost that must be assessed. If the claimant has sold a manual transmission car to buy an automatic car, the claim is limited to the added cost of the automatic and is not the entire cost of the new car.

26.04 Useful advice and assistance can be obtained from the Disabled Living Foundation at 380–384 Harrow Road, London W9 2HU (Helpline: 0845 130 9177; website: www.dlf.org.uk/).

26.05 *Woodrup v Nicol* [1993] PIQR Q104   A motor car is a wasting asset and the claimant was entitled to receive the net cost of a necessary car, giving credit for the value of the motorcycle he traded in, and the cost of replacing it over whatever period the judge chose, and it might not be right to make any deduction for the value of the value of the car at the end of the period.

26.06 *Goldfinch v Scannell* [1993] PIQR Q143   A severely injured claimant needed a new car and the assessment was based on the difference in depreciation between a new and a second-hand car, using as a multiplic-and a figure for annual capital depreciation taken from AA statistics.

B. Accommodation

26.07 The common situation is where a wheelchair dependent claimant has to move to a more expensive bungalow or a house with level approach and suitable adaptations. A special need for accommodation raises special problems because of the asset that is left in the hands of the claimant after taking account of his special needs.

26.08 *Roberts v Johnstone* [1989] QB 878   When a claimant needs to move to specially adapted accomodation, the cost should be divided between the expenses of moving house and adapting the new house, and the new capital asset in the greater value of the new house which will be an appreciating asset retained by the claimant. The expenses, so far as they do not increase the value of the house, will be recovered in full, but the cost of acquiring the asset should be not compensated by a payment of the cost incurred, but by a payment of the annual cost of tying up the capital in the property which should be taken as 2% a year (2.5% a year following the rate of return specified by the Damages (Personal Injury) Order 2001 made under the Damages Act 1996, s 1(1)).

26.09 Two comments may be made about the *Roberts v Johnstone* formula. First, for young claimants the resulting figure is not dramatically less than the capital cost incurred. At 2.5% a claimant aged 20 with a capital cost of £50,000 will recover

£1,250 × 30.74 = £38,425. Secondly, in spite of its attractive practical simplicity, the formula does not deal with the notional difficulty for a claimant at the end of his life who must have tied up in his house damages that he has been awarded, and may need, to spend to meet his other needs.

An example of an accommodation claim is as follows: **26.10**

	£	
(a) *Capital costs*		
Cost of purchase on bungalow	120,000	
Sale proceeds of former house	65,000	
Net capital investment	55,000	
Less value added by new conservatory	5,000	
Capital sum tied up	50,000	
Annual cost at 2.5% pa	1,250	
Multiplier for life (age 30)	25.60	
Roberts v Johnstone claim		35,275
(b) *Expenses of moving house*	£	
Estate agent on sale	1,645	
Surveyor fees	940	
Legal fees	705	
Stamp duty	1,200	
Removal costs	1,300	
Total for expenses of move		5,790
(c) *Costs of adaptation*	£	
Architect's fees	2,937	
Building costs for levelling access, wider doorways, adapted kitchen and bathroom, repositioned power points	10,575	
Redecoration	2,360	
Conservatory	10,000	
(adding £5,000 to the value, see above)		
Total for adaptation costs		20,935

Value of claim (the total of these three elements) is £62,000

In order to make the move, the claimant has to 'borrow' £20,000 from his other heads of damage.

C. Damaged Belongings

The normal measure of damages in a tort claim for a chattel which has been **26.11** destroyed is the market value of the chattel at the time of destruction. If the damage can be made good by repair, at a cost which is less than the market value, then the cost of repair is the usual measure of damages, together with any reduction in value resulting from the ownership of a chattel that has undergone repair.

In road accidents, clothing is often damaged, if not in the accident itself then in **26.12** the course of rescue and treatment. Rings may have to be cut off. Possessions kept in a vehicle may be lost or damaged. A motorcycle helmet may have to be replaced even if there is no obvious damage. For losses of this kind, repair is usually impracticable, and a market value based on the second-hand value of such items is not realistic. It is likely to be reasonable for the claimant to argue that he can only be returned to the position he would have been in if the accident had not happened by the purchase of new, replacement items. It may sometimes be appropriate, with items of high value and high depreciation, to make an allowance for the use of the item that the claimant enjoyed up to the date of the accident.

D. Damaged Vehicles

26.13   The same principles of law apply to the recovery of the value of a vehicle that has been damaged beyond economic repair, or the cost of repairing it. However, in the great majority of cases the vehicle damage will be assessed and agreed by insurance assessors and will not need to feature in the claim.

26.14   *Peyton v Brookes* [1974] RTR 169   The claimant alleged that his car, although excellently repaired, would be worth less as a result of having been involved in an accident. The claimant failed to establish that he had suffered such a loss, but the Court of Appeal observed that he would be entitled to recover the loss if it could be proved.

26.15   *O'Sullivan v Williams* [1992] 3 All ER 385   The claimant did not own the car she was driving but was authorized to use it by the owner, her boyfriend. This bailment was sufficient to entitle the driver to bring a claim for the damage to the car. It was not necessary for the owner to become a party.

26.16   The loss of the claimant's vehicle may lead to a number of consequential claims. The excess paid under the claimant's insurance is recoverable if he has had to pay it towards the cost of repair or replacement of his car. Storage charges may have been incurred while waiting for insurers to reach a decision about repair. However, care must be taken about wasted expenditure such as the car tax, insurance premium, or finance charges that had been paid for a vehicle which spends time off the road. These are expenses which the claimant would have incurred even if the car had not been damaged. The usual approach is to compensate the claimant for expenses incurred in finding alternative means of transport, such as hiring an alternative car or using public transport, and where this approach is adopted, there would be a double recovery if the standing costs of the damaged motor car were also recovered.

E. Car Hire, Credit Hire, and Credit Repair

It is reasonable for a claimant whose motor car is undergoing repair to hire a **26.17** replacement vehicle. In accordance with the general 'duty to mitigate' the claimant must act reasonably to keep the cost down, so the cost will not be fully recovered if the alternative vehicle is unreasonably expensive or is hired for an unreasonably long period of time. The cost incurred can be recovered unless the defendant proves a failure to mitigate.

In recent years credit hire companies have found a commercial opportunity to **26.18** hire cars to the victims of accidents who were not at fault but who might not otherwise have the means or inclination to hire a replacement vehicle. The credit hire companies offered hire vehicles to the victims of road accidents in circumstances where there was unlikely to be a dispute about liability, on the basis that the hire company would instigate proceedings for the recovery of the hire charges with the intention that the claimant would not have to meet the cost himself. The same approach has been extended to the repair cost. This practice led to fierce legal warfare between credit hire companies and motor insurers. The motor insurers were concerned about the provision of hire cars to people who might not have taken the step if they had had to pay for it themselves, and about the high costs involved. Broadly speaking, the outcome of much litigation has been that the courts have upheld arrangements for credit hire and repair, provided the amount is reasonable, and disputes are now much less common.

Giles v Thompson [1994] 1 AC 142   An agreement was not champertous and **26.19** illegal where a car hire company provided a vehicle to the claimant without charge on the basis that the charges would be recovered in an action for damages brought by the car hire company in the claimant's name; but no interest would be awarded on the amount since the claimant had not been expected to pay the hire charge during the course of the proceedings so she had not been kept out of any money.

Dimond v Lovell [2002] 1 AC 384   A credit hire agreement is subject to the **26.20** Consumer Credit Act 1974 and where the technical requirements under the Act concerning the execution of agreements had not been followed the agreement was unenforceable against the claimant who had therefore suffered no loss. Under an enforceable agreement the rate of hire would be limited to an ordinary market rate for car hire. The extra benefits in freedom from worry and nuisance of the credit hire agreement, represented by the greater cost of credit hire, were not recoverable.

Lagden v O'Connor [2003] UKHL 64; [2004] 1 AC 1067   The Court of **26.21** Appeal held that credit hire and credit repair agreements were not to be dismissed because they had been deliberately designed to fall outside the scope of the Consumer Credit Act and by requiring a payment to be made within 12 months the agreements were valid and enforceable exempt agreements; the claimants were entitled to recover 100% of the repair cost because this was the immediate damage caused by the accident even thought the repairer was content to receive 90% under the credit repair arrangement. The House of Lords dismissed the appeal: if through impecuniosity the claimant used a credit hire company, the defendant must take the claimant as he finds him. The cost of the credit hire was recoverable even though in general the reasonable cost of a hire car would be the spot or market rate.

F. Loss of Use of a Vehicle

26.22 A person who is deprived of the use of his motor car by damage suffered in an accident may, instead of hiring a replacement, put up with the inconvenience of managing without a motor car during the time that it takes to arrange for repair or replacement of the damaged car. There is no fixed measure of this type of loss, which will depend on the level of inconvenience suffered and the type of vehicle whose use has been lost in the particular case. It may be relevant to look at the cost the claimant has been incurring in order to be provided with the use of his car. Although it is not directly open to the claimant to recover the wasted standing costs on tax, insurance and finance charges, the level of such expenditure may be helpful in establishing the appropriate level of award when the claimant is deprived of the use of his car. In 1997 a district judge was reported to find that there was a going rate of about £50 a week (*Durbin v Lewis* [1997] CLY 1782). Awards in the region of £60 per week are now common. This is the rate that was proposed in a draft pre-action protocol for road traffic accidents. However, much depends on the circumstances, not only the expenses of the car of which the claimant has been deprived, but also the degree of inconvenience and restriction resulting from the temporary loss of the use of it.

G. Housekeeping Incapacity

26.23 A claimant who is unable to carry out the usual range of household duties as a result of injury and who therefore incurs expense in employing help with housekeeping or cleaning is entitled to recover the cost incurred. For the past loss, the actual expenditure will be recoverable, and for future loss the usual approach of fixing an annual multiplicand and an appropriate multiplier will be used. The only restrictions on the recovery of the expense are proof that the expense is attributable to the injuries sustained, and reasonableness of the expense so that it cannot be said that there has been a failure to mitigate the loss.

Instead of employing help, the claimant may be assisted by other members of **26.24** the family who do more than the usual share of household work. In principle, a claim can be made on their behalf, adopting the same approach as is taken with regard to the provision of nursing care, explained in Chapter 25. A loss of earnings suffered by other members of the family in order to do this will also be recoverable, but usually as an alternative to a valuation of the commercial cost of the hours spent and not in addition to it.

Where the housework simply is not done, because of the claimant's incapacity, **26.25** in principle no claim can be made in respect of past loss. In practice, such claims are often successful, and the distinction made in *Daly* (below) between past and future incapacity has been criticized (see, for example, *McGregor on Damages*, 17th edn at 35–048). In relation to the future, the court is not concerned with the way in which a claimant will spend his damages after they have been awarded, even though they will have been assessed on the basis of a particular future need, so damages will be awarded to reflect the need to employ help even if the claimant may choose subsequently to do without. It is not necessary for the claimant to prove an intention to employ help in accordance with the proposed award.

Daly v General Steam Navigation [1981] 1 WLR 120   The claimant house- **26.26** wife became incapable of undertaking housekeeping duties. Her husband assisted her and suffered a loss of part-time earnings. The Court of Appeal upheld an award for the future based on the cost of paying for housekeeping services which the claimant would need, because this was the proper measure of her damages even if the award might not be used for that purpose; but for the period before the trial when no expense had been incurred it was wrong to assess the damages by the figure it would have cost to employ someone. However, the same result was achieved by making awards for the loss of the husband's part-time earnings and an addition to the claimant's injury damages to compensate for her loss of capacity.

H. Gardening and DIY

The same principles apply to a claimant who is prevented by injury from carrying **26.27** out gardening, DIY or decorating activities. There is no standard level of award for this loss, and in each case it will depend on the past record of the claimant as a DIY enthusiast, the pre-accident frequency of home redecorations, the size of the garden, and so forth. In *Wells v Wells* [1998] PIQR Q58, the Court of

Appeal approved an award of £1,000 per year for DIY activities. The PNBA handbook, *Facts & Figures*, has publicized an unreported decision of May J (*Lawrence v Osborne*, 7 November 1997) in which it was apparently agreed by the defendant that £750 per year was an accepted standard figure for inability to perform DIY. These figures indicate the sort of award that might be agreed if the claim is supported by appropriate evidence, but they are no substitute for putting forward proper evidence to support the claim in each case.

26.28 The multiplier for a DIY claim will usually be something between the earnings multiplier to retirement age and the whole life multiplier to death, reflecting on the one hand the likelihood that a claimant is likely to have been less active and less competent in the last years of life even if the accident had not happened, but balancing this against the likelihood that the early years of retirement would have given increased time for this sort of activity before the onset of infirmity.

I. Spoilt Holidays

26.29 If the effects of an accident injury spoil the claimant's enjoyment of a holiday, this is a factor which should be taken into account in the assessment of general damages. It is tempting for the claimant to seek reimbursement for the cost of the holiday, particularly where a prospective holiday has to be cancelled and no refund can be obtained. This is however an expense which would have been incurred even if the accident had not happened and in principle therefore the costs of the holiday can only be used as evidence of the value the court should put on the loss of the enjoyment of it. In an appropriate case this evidence may of course be strongly persuasive.

J. Fuel Costs at Home

26.30 If the claimant is at home all day, kept relatively immobile as a result of disability, whereas before the accident he and his family would be out all day, there may be a significant increased cost in keeping the house warm during the daytime in winter months. The best evidence of this is a comparison of pre- and post-accident consumption from the fuel bills.

K. Travelling Expenses

26.31 A claimant is entitled to recover the cost of journeys that are undertaken as a result of the accident injuries sustained. For the most part such claims concern journeys for medical treatment. If a journey is undertaken by public transport, there is no difficulty about identifying the cost incurred. Considerable difficulty arises however when the claimant uses his own car.

It is very surprising that there has been no clear decision from the Court of Appeal to resolve the question whether the claimant is entitled to a rate per mile for the journeys that he undertakes based on the extra cost that he incurs for those journeys, or a rate based on the full cost of running his motor car. Detailed assessments of motoring costs show a very wide variation according to the type of car that is used, the size of the engine, and the fuel used. For example, complex calculations of standing costs and running cost per mile provided by the AA are set out in the PNBA handbook, *Facts & Figures*, Table I4. As a broad generalization, for a moderate-sized car undertaking a average annual mileage, running costs are in the region of 20p per mile while the combined standing costs and running costs are in the region of 35p to 40p per mile.

The Inland Revenue has a fixed profit scheme by which it is assumed for tax **26.32** purposes that there is no profit involved when an employer reimburses travelling expenses at a rate of 40p per mile for the first 10,000 miles, and 25p per mile thereafter. It is of course debatable whether this helps those who argue for the full rate of about 40p per mile as representing the real cost of the use of a car, or those who argue for a rate of 25p per mile as representing the actual increased expense to a claimant who has already incurred the fixed costs of providing the motor car.

Most claims for travelling expenses are put forward on the basis of a claim in the **26.33** region of 35p to 40p per mile, answered by an offer in the region of 20p to 25p per mile, and compromised somewhere in between. Legal principle would point to an award of the running cost only, since this is sufficient to put the claimant back in the position he would have been in if the accident had not happened. In practice, since the claimant puts his motor car at the disposal of the defendant whose wrongdoing caused the injury, and since the claimant using his own car incurs a cost which is likely to be significantly less, even on the full cost basis, than the use of public transport and taxis, it is suggested that an award representing the full cost of car use is appropriate unless the amount of travelling is very substantial. It is suggested that the Inland Revenue rate of 40p per mile currently provides a fair and reasonable indication of this cost.

L. Marriage Breakdown

Oakley v Walker (1977) 121 SJ 619   The claimant's disfigurement and change **26.34** of personality, as a result of the injuries he sustained in an accident, resulted in his wife leaving him and their children, and the husband was held entitled to recover the cost of providing home help and care for the children.

26.35 *Jones v Jones* [1985] QB 704   The claimant's severe injuries left him incapable of managing his affairs and his marriage broke up. The Court of Appeal held that the claimant was entitled to recover the costs of making a lump sum payment to his wife in divorce proceedings in order to provide her with a separate establishment (giving credit for a sum the claimant might have been expected to give his wife out of the damages awarded to him if they had stayed together) but the cost of providing maintenance and child support for his wife and children was not quantifiable and could not be recovered.

M. Credit for Savings

26.36 In principle, the claimant is entitled to recover his net loss, in order to be restored to the position he would have been in if the injury had not been sustained. This means that the claimant should give credit against claims of the kind described in this chapter, when another effect of his injury is to cause savings. For example, although there may be a claim for travelling on journeys related to the injury, there may be savings if the claimant is no longer able to make other journeys for recreation or to work. In practice, however, since the amounts are relatively small, and since the argument is extremely unattractive, insurers rarely seek to argue for an offset of this kind. However, claimants' advisers who have worked hard to maximize every arguable head of expense of this kind should be aware that they may be met with the suggestion that credit should be given for savings in living expenses that have been another consequence of the injury.

27

STATE AND OTHER BENEFITS

This chapter sets out the state benefits that may be available to an injured **27.01** person, and explains how these and other benefits will be treated in the calculation of damages in a compensation claim. As a separate issue, the compensation recovery scheme governs the recoupment of benefits at the ultimate expense of the defendant, and this is the subject of the next chapter. The recoupment of benefits operates outside the scope of the calculation of damages. It is necessary to understand how the recoupment will operate, but it is not necessary to include details of the recoupment in the calculation of damages.

A. State Benefits

In addition to tort compensation for claimants through the courts, there is a **27.02** no-fault system of state compensation for industrial accidents, and there is a universal system of state provision for the neediest in society, and both of these types of benefit can be of great immediate help to the victim of an accident alongside the prospect of eventually bringing a civil claim for damages.

(1) Statutory Sick Pay

Statutory Sick Pay (SSP) is a non-contributory taxable benefit paid by an **27.03** employer, in the same way as he pays wages, for up to 28 weeks where an employed person is unable to work because of sickness for at least four days in a row. There is no benefit for the first three days. Details of the means of proving sickness are for the employer to decide, but there is usually a system of self-certification for the first few days and a doctor's certificate is required for a longer absence. To qualify, the employee must be earning enough on average for his earnings to be above the lower limit for National Insurance purposes: at least £79 per week. Benefit is paid for a spell of sickness lasting up to 28 weeks, and spells with eight weeks or less between them are counted together as one. The standard rate for 2004–5 is £63.25, the same as the short-term higher rate of incapacity benefit (all rates are stated weekly). For sickness lasting for more than 28 weeks, or if SSP cannot be claimed, the claim becomes one for incapacity benefit. SSP is not included in the compensation recovery scheme, so the amount of SSP received from the employer must be taken into account as reducing the loss of earnings, just like contractual sick pay.

(2) Incapacity Benefit

27.04 Incapacity benefit is a contributory benefit paid after, or instead of, SSP. The short-term lower rate benefit is not taxable but the short-term higher rate and long-term benefits are taxable. Tax will only arise if the claimant has other income, and will be recovered by adjustment of the tax code for payment of that other income. This is the main benefit available to those who are incapable of work, and it is paid whatever the cause of the incapacity. The claimant must have paid National Insurance contributions and must be incapable of work because of sickness or disability for at least four days in a row. There are three rates of benefit, and other additions:

(a) Short-term lower rate is paid for up to 28 weeks instead of SSP, for example for someone who was self-employed or was not working when he became sick; the rate in 2004–5 is £53.50 a week.

(b) Short-term higher rate is paid after 28 weeks and up to 52 weeks; the rate in 2004–5 is £63.25 a week.

(c) Long-term rate is paid after 52 weeks; the rate in 2004–5 is £70.95 a week.

(d) Higher rates apply over pension age: the lower rate is £68.05 and the higher rate is £70.95.

(e) Supplements are paid at £14.90 if long-term incapacity begins under the age of 35 and £7.45 if it begins between 35 and 44.

(f) Dependency increases are available for those looking after dependent children or adults.

27.05 For the first 28 weeks, incapacity is measured against ability to work in the claimant's normal occupation. After 28 weeks, a Personal Capability Assessment will be carried out, and incapacity is measured against the ability to do all work. This involves an assessment, initially by questionnaire, of physical and mental capability and giving prescribed scores to different levels of restriction; a score of 15 or over amounts to incapability for work. Medical assessment may be required.

A recipient of incapacity benefit may not do any work, except that work for up **27.06** to 16 hours a week and up to £72 pay may be done if it is for therapeutic reasons only, on medical advice and with prior permission of the Benefits Agency. There is no limit on undertaking voluntary work, but permission of the Benefits Agency should be obtained beforehand.

(3) Industrial Injuries Disablement Benefit

Industrial injuries disablement benefit (IIDB) is a non-contributory tax-free **27.07** benefit paid to employees who suffer from injury or illness at work. The cause of disability must be an accident or illness at work, but entitlement does not depend on fault. In the case of illness it must be a disease, and incurred in an occupation, prescribed in Sch 1 to the Social Security (Industrial Injuries) (Prescribed Diseases) Regulations 1985. Payment cannot begin until 15 weeks after the accident or the onset of the disease. Some specific diseases may attract a payment when disability is assessed at a different level to the normal lower limit of 14%: the occupational death benefit is only paid if disablement is 20% or more and for pneumoconiosis and related lung diseases benefit is paid at over 1%. The amount paid depends on the seriousness of the disability, usually decided by a medical examination. For example, loss of sight or hearing or loss of both hands counts as 100%. Loss of an index finger or big toe will normally count as 14%. Between 14% and 19%, the 20% rate of benefit is paid; above that, benefit is added to the nearest 10%. The adult rates for 2004–5 are:

At 100%	£120.10 a week
At 90%	£108.09 a week
At 80%	£96.08 a week
At 70%	£84.07 a week
At 60%	£72.06 a week
At 50%	£60.05 a week
At 40%	£48.04 a week
At 30%	£36.03 a week
At 20%	£24.02 a week.

Lower rates apply to those under 18.

An additional constant attendance allowance may be paid to someone who was **27.08** 100% disabled and requiring constant attendance because of the loss of faculty: the higher rate is £96.20 and the lower rate is £48.10.

The self-employed are not covered, and are not entitled to receive IIDB. The **27.09** test is whether Class 1 NIC are paid. Most trainees on government schemes are not covered, but there is the Analogous Industrial Injuries Scheme administered by the Department of Work and Pensions which should provide an equivalent benefit.

(4) Disability Living Allowance

27.10 Disability living allowance (DLA) is paid for those who need help and care, having needed help for three months and being likely to go on needing it for at least another six months, where the need arises and the claim is made before the age of 65. Entitlement to DLA does not depend on having someone to provide the help that is needed: if the need exists there is no restriction on how the allowance is spent. There are two components, the care component and the mobility component, and there are different rates of payment for different levels of need. The mobility component can be used to support the provision of a motor car under the motability scheme. The rates for 2004–5 are:

    (a) care component highest level £58.80 a week, middle level £39.35 a week, lowest level of £15.55 a week;

    (b) mobility component higher level £41.05 a week, lower level £15.55 a week.

(5) Attendance Allowance

27.11 Attendance allowance is now limited to those over 65 who need help looking after themselves. For most claimants this benefit has been replaced by DLA. There is no mobility component. For 2004–5 the higher rate is £58.80 a week and the lower rate is £39.35 a week.

(6) Carer's Allowance

27.12 Carer's allowance is paid to someone between 16 and 65 who has no gainful employment and gives regular and substantial care to a person receiving the care component of DLA, attendance allowance or constant attendance allowance of IIDB. The basic rate is £44.35 a week, with an additional £26.54 for a dependent adult, £9.55 for a first child and £11.35 for other children.

(7) Bereavement

27.13 The three benefits available in respect of bereavement are:

    (a) a lump sum of £2,000,

    (b) a widowed parent's allowance at a rate of £79.60 a week plus £9.55 for the first child and £11.35 for other children,

    (c) a bereavement allowance paid for up to 52 weeks to a widow or widower over 45 years of age but under pension age, at a full rate from age 55 of £79.60 a week, reached in stages from £23.88 a week at age 45.

(8) Jobseeker's Allowance

Jobseeker's allowance is paid to the unemployed at a basic rate for 2004–5 of **27.14** £33.50 a week if under 18, £44.05 if aged 18 to 24 and £55.65 if aged 25 or over. An applicant must be actively seeking work, capable of work, and available for work. For an applicant with sufficient National Insurance contributions there is a flat rate for 26 weeks, which is not means tested, and then (or from the outset for the claimant with insufficient contributions) jobseeker's allowance becomes income based and similar to income support, with allowances for dependants and rules for the treatment of income and capital. Income-based jobseeker's allowance is a passport to other benefits such as free NHS treatment, housing benefit, and council tax benefit.

(9) Income Support

Income support is the provision for the elderly, sick and disabled, single parents **27.15** and carers but not for those who are simply unemployed. The benefit is means tested and based on needs. Recipients can work up to 16 hours a week. Capital over £3,000 is deemed to produce £1 income for each £250. A need level (the 'applicable amount') is ascertained from a system of allowances and premiums, and the benefit is paid to bring income from earnings, deemed income from capital and income from any other sources including child benefit up to the need level. The calculation of the applicable amount is too complex for restatement here. Payment of mortgage costs is restricted. Entitlement to income support is a passport to automatic entitlement to free NHS treatment, housing benefit, and council tax benefit.

A claimant in receipt of income support is likely to lose his entitlement on **27.16** means grounds once an award of personal injury damages has been received, and should therefore be advised to consider carefully the possibility of protecting his entitlement by putting the award of damages into a personal injury trust.

(10) Working Tax Credit

A person who works for at least 16 hours a week is entitled to claim working **27.17** tax credit (WTC) if he or she suffers from a disability, defined as a physical or mental disability which puts a person at a disadvantage in getting a job. The level of benefit increases in a case of severe disability, defined by the receipt of the highest rate of the care component of DLA. An applicant who is one of a couple, married or living together, must apply as a couple and the income of both partners is put together in calculating the entitlement.

To assess the amount of WTC, first assess the maximum amount of benefit to **27.18** which the applicant is entitled; secondly, work out the applicant's relevant income, which includes the earnings from employment; thirdly, compare the relevant income with the threshold amount for the tax credit of £5,060, and finally if the income exceeds the threshold, then calculate the excess and reduce the maximum amount of WTC by 37% of the excess.

27.19 The maximum amounts, some of which are alternatives, are as follows:

- a basic element of £1,525;
- a lone parent element of £1,500;
- a couple element of £1,500;
- a 30-hour element, for working at least 30 hours a week, of £620;
- a disability element of £2,040;
- a severe disability element of £865;
- a 50+ element for 16–29 hours of £1,045;
- a 50+ element for 30+ hours of £1,565.

27.20 For example, a single claimant with a job for 20 hours a week earning £6 an hour, £6,240 a year, has a maximum entitlement of £3,565: the basic element plus the disability element. His income exceeds the threshold of £5,060 by £1,180. His maximum entitlement will be reduced by 37% of the excess which is £436.60. His WTC is therefore £3,120.40.

27.21 WTC is not a benefit which is listed in Sch 2 to the Social Security (Recovery of Benefits) Act 1997. The treatment of the benefit is therefore governed by *Hodgson v Trapp* (below), and credit must be given by the claimant for the receipt of the benefit against a claim for both past and future loss of earnings.

B. Other Payments Resulting from the Injury

27.22 A claimant who is injured has other sources of support in addition to the potential proceeds of a claim for damages. The most important benefits are those outlined above, those received from the state. For these benefits, there is a special system to govern the way in which benefits should be treated in a claim, which is the subject of the next chapter. In addition to state benefits, there are many other payments and benefits which a claimant may receive. The basic common law rule is that damages in tort should represent the sum which will put the claimant into the position as if the wrong had not been done to him. A strict application of this rule would require the claimant to offset all other payments received as a result of his injury from the claim for damages. This is, broadly speaking, the approach of the Criminal Injuries Compensation Authority. The common law is not so severe and recognizes, for example, that it would be unacceptable to deprive someone of the benefit of an insurance policy for which he has paid a premium by setting off the proceeds of the insurance against a civil claim.

Hodgson v Trapp [1989] AC 807   While the recognized exceptions of **27.23** insurance benefits and charitable payments should be disregarded, the state benefits of attendance allowance and mobility allowance paid to the claimant as a result of the injury should be offset against the claim for the cost of care. The decision in this case has been overtaken by the scheme of the 1997 Act, but the principle remains to govern the treatment of benefits that are not covered by that Act.

(1) The Proceeds of Insurance

The proceeds of an insurance policy for which the claimant has paid the **27.24** premiums are not to be taken into account against his claim. Even though an injury may be the event leading to the payment, the payment is made as a result of the insurance contract and it should be the claimant rather than the defendant who benefits from the claimant's prudence.

(2) Charitable Payments

Charitable and benevolent payments from third parties are not to be taken **27.25** into account against a claim. Lord Reid in *Parry v Cleaver* [1970] AC 1 stated: 'It would be revolting to the ordinary man's sense of justice, and therefore contrary to public policy, that the sufferer should have his damages reduced so that he would gain nothing from the benevolence of his friends or relations or the public at large, and that the only gainer would be the wrongdoer.' Note the limits on the benevolence exception in *Pirelli v Gaca* noted below, where the payments are not received from a third party but from the defendant.

Redpath v Belfast & County Down Railway [1947] NI 167   The claimant was **27.26** the victim of a railway disaster who had received money from a distress fund. The court refused to deduct the payments from the claimant's damages.

(3) Pensions

An ill-health pension on early retirement caused by the effects of an accident **27.27** injury which is the subject of the claim need not be damages for loss of earnings. The principle was esta [1970] AC 1 mainly on the ground that, as with claimant has paid for the benefit by his pension cont↑ contrast, after normal retirement age the actual amount received under the pension scheme must be offset in full against the pension that the claimant would have received.

27.28   *Smoker v London Fire Authority* [1991] 2 AC 502   Even when the pension scheme of the claimant's employment was one to which the claimant was not required to contribute, none the less the principle of *Parry v Cleaver* applied and, up to normal retirement age, the benefits of the ill-health retirement provisions of the pension scheme would not be offset against a claim for loss of earnings.

27.29   *Longden v British Coal* [1998] AC 653   The incapacity pension is to be ignored during the claim for loss of earnings, but if the pension continues into retirement age it must be offset against the claim for the loss of retirement benefits. Therefore if the retirement benefits include a lump sum, and a lump sum was paid at the time of early retirement, there must be an apportionment between the part attributable to working life and the part attributable to the period of retirement and only the latter part is offset against a claim for loss of retirement benefits.

(4) Sick Pay

27.30   Where a claim is brought for loss of earnings, all the sums received from the employer during the period of the claim are to be offset against the loss, not only the contractual sick pay which the injured person is entitled to receive under the terms of his contract of employment, but also the SSP paid by the employer, which will not be subject to the recoupment scheme.

27.31   It is increasingly common for employers to limit the contractual liability for sick pay, but to protect their employees from hardship by making a loan equivalent to a rate of sick pay, on the basis that the loan will be repaid out of the recovery of damages if there is a successful claim against a third party. The practical effect is that the defendant will be liable to pay the full loss of earnings and will not be entitled to offset the 'sick pay', so that the claimant receives reimbursement which he must pay back to the employer and the loss falls on the tortfeasor rather than on the innocent employer. The character of the payments as a loan covered by an obligation of reimbursement should be established clearly in writing before the payments are made, either by an express provision in the contract of employment or by an agreement that is made at the commencement of such payments.

27.32   *Franklin v British Rail* [1994] PIQR P1   The claimant received sick pay which was subject to an obligation of reimbursement, following an accident at work for which his employer was liable. He agreed to repay the net sum that he had received. The Court of Appeal held that he was not obliged to reimburse the employers the tax and NIC in addition.

(5) Employers' Sickness Insurance

Employers may insure themselves against their liability to their employees and **27.33** may make a range of other insurance arrangements such as, for example an insurance policy, in order to be able to make an ex gratia payment to an injured employee, and then the benefit of the insurance policy will have to be offset.

Hussein v New Taplow Board Mills [1988] AC 514   The claimant's contract of **27.34** employment provided for indefinite sick pay on half wages, a non-contributory benefit. The defendant employer had taken out an insurance policy to protect its liability under the scheme. These payments were neither a pension nor a charitable benevolence, but sick pay which had to be deducted from the claim regardless of the fact that the defendant had insured against its liability.

Pirelli v Gaca [2004] EWCA Civ 373; [2004] PIQR Q49   The claimant had **27.35** to give credit against his loss of earnings for the proceeds of an insurance policy taken out by the employer to make an ex gratia payment for permanent total disability. As a matter of principle, ex gratia payments made by employer tort-feasors did not come within the benevolence exception. *McCamley v Cammell Laird Shipbuilders* [1990] 1 WLR 963, where a similar payment was treated as a benevolent payment, was wrong and should not be followed.

(6) Tax Rebates

If the claimant does not have his earnings made up by sick pay, a period of **27.36** absence from work is likely to result in a tax rebate, and this must be taken into account in calculating the loss of earnings since it is only the net loss that can be claimed.

(7) Redundancy Payments

Usually there is no connection between sustaining an injury and being made **27.37** redundant: the fact of an injury does not affect the employer's need for labour. In this normal case, where a redundancy intervenes to bring to an end the employment that the claimant held at the time of his injury, the redundancy will have to be taken into account in the calculation of any continuing loss of earnings because the claimant would have had to seek alternative work even if the accident had not happened, but since the claimant would have received his redundancy payment even if the accident had not happened, the payment will not be offset against the loss of earnings claimed.

Sometimes there may be a causal link between the injury and the redundancy. **27.38** For example, the claimant may decide to volunteer for redundancy because the continuing effects of his injury may have damaged his ability to do his job properly or with job satisfaction. In this case, the employee will be seeking to claim the earnings that he would have continued to receive if he had not accepted redundancy and if the accident had not happened, and he must therefore offset not only his likely actual earnings in any alternative employment, but also the redundancy payment that he receives, which would not have been received if the accident had not happened.

27.39 *Wilson v NCB* 1981 SLT 67   After his injury, the claimant was unable to work as a miner, but the employer protected his position and did not dismiss him. The mine where he was employed then closed. If he had not been injured, the claimant would have transferred his employment to a different mine. Because of his injuries, he accepted redundancy, and therefore the redundancy payment was deducted from the loss of earnings claim.

(8) Savings in Living Expenses

27.40 In principle, the claimant should give credit for any savings in his living expenses that result from his injuries, and they should be offset against the loss of income that he claims. For example, a claimant who can no longer work will no longer need a season ticket for the journey to work or the expense of car parking. In practice, such savings are not often pursued unless the amount is likely to be substantial. Where an injured claimant has to be cared for in an institution and claims for the full cost of this provision, an allowance for the saving in living expenses may well be merited. Section 5 of the Administration of Justice Act 1992 provides that in a claim for damages for personal injuries any saving to an injured person which is attributable to his maintenance wholly or partly at public expense in a hospital, nursing home, or other institution shall be set off against any income lost by him as a result of his injuries.

27.41 *Lim Poh Choo v Camden and Islington HA* [1980] AC 174   The way that credit for living expenses should be allowed is to deduct the domestic element from the amount that the claimant claims for earnings or care, rather than by calculating the costs that the claimant would have incurred if not injured.

(9) Local Authority Care

27.42 Once a claimant receives a large award of damages, he will become able to pay towards the cost of the benefits that he has received that have been provided by the local authority, which can then, subject to a six-year limitation period, retrospectively claim payment (*Avon CC v Hooper* [1997] 1 All ER 532 and the Health and Social Services and Social Security Adjudications Act 1983, s 17). A claimant should establish the intentions of the authority and include in the Particulars of Claim a claim for an indemnity against any charge that may be levied. This is a complex area of the law and the regulations are liable to change. Under sch 4 to the National Assistance (Assessment of Resources) Regulations

1992, as recently amended, capital that is held in a personal injury trust will be disregarded in assessing means in respect of long-term care fees.

C. Personal Injury Trusts

A seriously incapacitated claimant may receive means tested state benefits such **27.43** as income support, housing benefit, and council tax benefit. If the claimant then receives a capital sum such as an award of damages, it will be deemed to produce an income and an award (including an interim payment) may result in the loss of entitlement to these benefits. Capital in excess of £8,000 will result in the complete loss of entitlement. Spending the money so as to come below the limit may fall foul of the rules about deliberate deprivation of benefit.

Under the Income Support (General) Regulations 1987, Sch 10 the capital of a **27.44** personal injury trust is disregarded in the assessment of entitlement to means tested benefits. There is no deprivation of benefit by a person who places an award of damages into a trust. As noted above, a trust will also take capital out of the scope of means testing for the local authority care fees. As a result, every claimant who receives means tested benefits, or who may become entitled to means tested benefits in the future, should be advised to consider setting up a personal injury trust.

The rules about the capital of a personal injury trust enable the value of the trust **27.45** fund to be preserved, but it is then necessary to consider how the trust money will be spent. The treatment of income from the trust has been clarified by the Social Security Amendment (Personal Injury Payments) Regulations 2002. There is a partial disregard of income received by the claimant as beneficiary of the trust. The principle is that the income from the trust should not be used to meet everyday normal expenses of living which the means tested benefits are intended to cover. The effect of the 2002 Regulations is to disregard all payments that are made out of the trust which are used for purposes other than the normal expenses of daily living, and in addition to disregard £20 a week of income from the trust whatever it is spent on (which can, to this extent, include the normal expenses of daily living).

It continues to be necessary for the claimant to be careful that his spending of **27.46** money taken out of the trust does not leave him with assets in his own name that will give rise to problems over capital. However, this problem should be an avoidable one: the claimant's home and his personal chattels are disregarded for capital purposes, and the main purpose of taking money out of the trust will be to meet necessary expenses such as the cost of care and treatment, rather than to retain a capital asset.

27.47 If there is to be a trust, it should be set up before the award of damages is received. No court order is required, and there is no fixed form that the trust must take. The main advantage of a personal injury trust is the preservation of means tested benefits, but it may also be a reassurance to a claimant to have a professional trustee involved in the management of the damages. The disadvantages lie in the cost of administering the trust, and in the restriction on the beneficiary's freedom of action. Although a trust need not be a complicated matter, it is likely to need professional help in drawing up the trust and in preparing an annual tax return. Suitable trustees will have to be found, who will have important responsibilities for managing the investment of the trust fund and for making decisions about spending as well as the day-to-day administration. The claimant's freedom to spend his damages will be curtailed not only by the income support rules, but also by the involvement of trustees. It is of course a matter for an adult, capable claimant to decide whether a trust will be appropriate in his individual circumstances: as with structured settlements experience suggests that many claimants prefer to control their own money even at the cost of a financial penalty.

28

THE BENEFIT RECOUPMENT SYSTEM

A. The Scheme and How it Works

When an injured claimant receives welfare benefits and then makes a civil claim, **28.01** to the claimant it will seem that the welfare benefits are what he has paid his taxes and national insurance for, so that they should be disregarded just like the proceeds of a private accident insurance policy; to the defendant it will seem that the claimant is seeking double recovery because if the claimant receives the claimed loss of earnings in full as well as keeping the benefits he will be better off than if he had not been injured; and to the government it will seem that there is an opportunity to save public money on the ground that the wrongdoer should pay.

The current scheme is the third attempt at a workable compromise between **28.02** these points of view. The 1948 legislation required that one half of state benefits received should be deducted from a claim for a period of five years. This with hindsight can be seen to have been very advantageous for the claimant, who could receive benefits all his life but need only give credit against his lost earnings for a small amount of them, and for the defendant, who benefited from the credit given against the claim in so far as the claimant had to concede it. It was disadvantageous for the taxpayer and in 1989 a revolutionary scheme was introduced to make insurers (and thus insurance premium payers) foot the bill to a significant extent. This scheme worked frequent injustice to claimants, because it took no account of contributory negligence and allowed benefits to be offset against all heads of claim including injury damages. This could result in a worthless victory for a claimant who could see all his damages extinguished by the clawback of benefits by the Treasury. A small settlement up to £2,500 would escape the impact of the recoupment and there were many forced settlements at this level from which neither the parties nor the Treasury achieved a just result. The current scheme, contained in the Social Security (Recovery of Benefits) Act 1997 and regulations thereunder, has made the system more acceptable for claimants but has continued to throw the burden of providing for the victims of injuries heavily onto defendants' insurers. The five-year compromise remains however: benefits are recouped only up to the date of settlement or for five years, whichever is shorter. From that point on, and therefore in relation to all claims for future loss, benefits are disregarded and damages will be paid without deduction.

28.03   The scheme relies on the fact that virtually all injury compensation is paid by insurance companies. Before a compensator makes a compensation payment he must apply to the Compensation Recovery Unit (CRU) of the Department for Work and Pensions (DWP), Durham House, Washington, Tyne & Wear NE38 7SF (tel: 0191 225 2005), for a certificate of recoverable benefits. The name, address, date of birth, and National Insurance number of the claimant will have to be provided, together with details of the date and nature of the accident or injury. The certificate will list the types and amounts of benefits that have been paid to the claimant for up to five years from the date of the accident as a result of having sustained the injury in question. A copy will be sent to the claimant. The compensator may then, in making a compensation payment to the claimant, deduct from the payment those benefits which may be offset against the claimant's claim, and the compensator must then pay the sum shown in the certificate to the Secretary of State—even if this is more than he has been able to offset against the claim. If the compensator has failed to obtain a certificate, or has failed to make the offset when paying the claimant, he is still liable to pay the full amount of the certified benefits to the Department. Each certificate applies for a set period and when it has expired a new certificate must be obtained.

28.04   The reason the compensator may not be able to offset the whole amount of the benefits against the claim is that the different heads of a claim are treated separately. No benefits at all are offset against injury damages, which are thus 'ring-fenced'. Benefits are then offset against heads of damage for the kind of loss for which the benefit has been paid. Schedule 2 to the 1997 Act sets out the categories of benefits to be offset against three different heads of claim: (a) loss of earnings, (b) cost of care, and (c) loss of mobility. The full Schedule is a vital reference but looks complicated because the names of different benefits keep changing and the Schedule covers old ones as well as current ones. The principle is simply that benefits are offset against a claim for a matching loss, thus (ignoring historic benefits):

SCHEDULE 2

Head of compensation	Benefit (current types only)
Compensation for earnings lost during the relevant period	Disablement benefit
	Incapacity benefit
	Income support
	Jobseeker's allowance
Compensation for cost of care incurred during the relevant period	Attendance allowance
	Care component of disability living allowance
Compensation for loss of mobility during the relevant period	Mobility component of disability living allowance

Some short points on the working of the system: **28.05**

- (a) The relevant period for the recoupment system is five years, and this is the maximum period from the date of the accident or injury over which benefits will be subject to recoupment.

- (b) Recoupment comes to an earlier end during the five years at the point when the claim is paid and the recoupment is triggered, so the sooner a claim is paid the better for both claimant and defendant.

- (c) Because settlement or judgment will bring recoupment to an end, it is never necessary to take account of state benefits in calculating future loss.

- (d) Recoupment can therefore be ignored in the trial of the assessment of damages, as it takes effect outside the litigation by the defendant's deduction from the sum for which judgment is given (1997 Act, s 17).

- (e) SSP is mentioned in the Sch 2 table but note 2 makes clear that SSP has not been recouped since 6 April 1994; instead the claimant has to give credit for receiving it in the calculation of his loss of earnings.

- (f) Contributory negligence is ignored. The full amount of the benefits has to be recouped, and may be offset, even if the amount of damages is less than the claimant's full loss as a result of contributory negligence.

- (g) For a claimant with low or uncertain earnings and some contributory negligence, it is not uncommon for the offset of earnings type benefits to extinguish the claim for past loss of earnings. The defendant is still accountable to the DWP for the whole amount of the benefits.

- (h) If a defendant makes a Part 36 payment, he should obtain a certificate of recoverable benefits, pay in the net amount, and in the notice set out the details of the gross compensation payment offered, the benefits offset and the net amount paid into court.

- (i) If a defendant is awaiting a certificate so that he cannot yet make a payment into court, this is one of the rare cases where a written Part 36 offer can be effective in a money claim.

(j)   In *Oldham v Sharples* [1997] PIQR Q82, the claimant had won a useless victory because his award of damages was less than a criminal injuries compensation award so that the whole sum would have to be repaid to the Criminal Injuries Compensation Authority. He none the less was awarded his costs. Similarly, a claim which is successful but is extinguished for practical purposes by the impact of the recoupment provisions still carries an entitlement to costs.

(k)   The recoupment provisions do not apply to claims under the Fatal Accidents Act.

(l)   A claimant is entitled to ignore the benefits he has received in calculating the interest due on past losses, and can claim interest on the full sum (*Wisely v John Fulton* [2000] 2 All ER 545).

(m)   On the other hand, interest on an award is part of the compensation under the head of loss, so that if the amount the defendant has to repay is greater than the claimant's recovery, the offset may include an offset against interest also (*Griffiths v British Coal* [2001] PIQR Q119).

(n)   The 'cost' of care under Sch 2 includes an award of damages for gratuitous family care (*Griffiths*).

28.06   *Williams v Devon County Council* [2003] EWCA Civ 365; [2003] PIQR Q68   By para 10.3 of PD 36, a Part 36 Payment Notice must identify the benefits which the defendant has withheld under the Social Security (Recovery of Benefits) Act 1997. A finding of contributory negligence against the claimant does not reduce the benefits recoverable, although benefits can only be offset to the extent of the relevant head of damages. This case highlighted the need for the Notice to identify the categories of benefit and to ensure that the claimant was able to receive the amount of the general damages offered, without suffering an inappropriate reduction for recoupment. If the defendant relies on contributory negligence or partially disputes causation and makes a Part 36 payment on the basis of this case, the amount of benefits shown to have been deducted must be limited to the amount that is consistent with its case.

28.07   Certificates of recoverable benefits are not always correct. The argument is usually not about the mathematics of the benefits paid but about the cause of the payment. Recoupment applies where a payment is paid by the compensator 'in consequence of any accident, injury or disease' and benefits have been paid to the recipient 'in respect of the accident, injury or disease' (s 1). If there is an error in understating the amount of benefit, the parties are none the less entitled to rely on the certificate that has been issued. If there is an error in overstating the benefits, the parties will want the Secretary of State to review the certificate or, if that fails, will want to appeal against it. However, this can only be done after the claim has been resolved. A judicial finding that there has been no attributable loss under a certain head of claim will carry great weight. On the other hand, parties cannot assume that they can avoid recoupment by agreeing a particular basis of settlement, because such an agreement will not necessarily be taken at face value. In cases of dispute, a medical appeal tribunal may have to resolve the issue (see the Social Security and Child Support (Decisions and Appeals) Regulations 1999).

Bruce v Genesis Fast Food [2003] EWHC 788; [2004] PIQR P113   A consent **28.08** order on settlement of a personal injury claim recited the amount the defendant was entitled to withhold under the CRU certificate then in force. Subsequently the defendant successfully appealed against the certificate and a fresh certificate was issued for a much smaller sum. The defendant contended that the consent order determined the net amount that the claimant was entitled to receive, but the court held that the claimant was entitled to a recalculation of the amount to be deducted from the agreed gross amount after the new CRU certificate had been issued following the defendant's CRU appeal, so the claimant was entitled to an additional payment resulting from the appeal under reg 11(5) of the Social Security (Recovery of Benefits) Regulations 1997.

The outcome of this case resulted from the form of the consent order which **28.09** fixed the gross amount of the judgment in favour of the claimant. It is suggested that it is possible to devise a form of order on settlement which allows the claimant a fixed net sum regardless of the outcome of the defendant's CRU appeal, taking care to meet the terms of the 1997 Act and the 1997 Regulations.

B. Social Security (Recovery of Benefits) Act 1997

1. Cases in which this Act applies

(1) This Act applies in cases where—   **28.10**

(a) a person makes a payment (whether on his own behalf or not) to or in respect of any other person in consequence of any accident, injury or disease suffered by the other, and

(b) any listed benefits have been, or are likely to be, paid to or for the other during the relevant period in respect of the accident, injury or disease.

(2) The reference above to a payment in consequence of any accident, injury or disease is to a payment made—

(a) by or on behalf of a person who is, or is alleged to be, liable to any extent in respect of the accident, injury or disease, or

(b) in pursuance of a compensation scheme for motor accidents; but does not include a payment mentioned in Part I of Schedule 1.

(3) Subsection (1)(a) applies to a payment made—

(a) voluntarily, or in pursuance of a court order or an agreement, or otherwise, and

(b) in the United Kingdom or elsewhere.

(4) In a case where this Act applies—

(a) the 'injured person' is the person who suffered the accident, injury or disease,

(b) the 'compensation payment' is the payment within subsection (1)(a), and

(c) 'recoverable benefit' is any listed benefit which has been or is likely to be paid as mentioned in subsection (1)(b).

2. Compensation payments to which this Act applies

28.11   This Act applies in relation to compensation payments made on or after the day on which this section comes into force, unless they are made in pursuance of a court order or agreement made before that day.

3. 'The relevant period'

28.12   (1) In relation to a person ('the claimant') who has suffered any accident, injury or disease, 'the relevant period' has the meaning given by the following subsections.

(2) Subject to subsection (4), if it is a case of accident or injury, the relevant period is the period of five years immediately following the day on which the accident or injury in question occurred.

(3) Subject to subsection (4), if it is a case of disease, the relevant period is the period of five years beginning with the date on which the claimant first claims a listed benefit in consequence of the disease.

(4) If at any time before the end of the period referred to in subsection (2) or (3)—

(a) a person makes a compensation payment in final discharge of any claim made by or in respect of the claimant and arising out of the accident, injury or disease, or

(b) an agreement is made under which an earlier compensation payment is treated as having been made in final discharge of any such claim, the relevant period ends at that time.

4. Applications for certificates of recoverable benefits

28.13   (1) Before a person ('the compensator') makes a compensation payment he must apply to the Secretary of State for a certificate of recoverable benefits.

5. Information contained in certificates

28.14   (1) A certificate of recoverable benefits must specify, for each recoverable benefit—

(a) the amount which has been or is likely to have been paid on or before a specified date, and

(b) if the benefit is paid or likely to be paid after the specified date, the rate and period for which, and the intervals at which, it is or is likely to be so paid.

(2) In a case where the relevant period has ended before the day on which the Secretary of State receives the application for the certificate, the date specified in the certificate for the purposes of subsection (1) must be the day on which the relevant period ended.

(3) In any other case, the date specified for those purposes must not be earlier than the day on which the Secretary of State received the application.

(4) The Secretary of State may estimate, in such manner as he thinks fit, any of the amounts, rates or periods specified in the certificate.

(5) Where the Secretary of State issues a certificate of recoverable benefits, he must provide the information contained in the certificate to—

(a) the person who appears to him to be the injured person, or

(b) any person who he thinks will receive a compensation payment in respect of the injured person.

(6) A person to whom a certificate of recoverable benefits is issued or who is provided with information under subsection (5) is entitled to particulars of the manner in which any amount, rate or period specified in the certificate has been determined, if he applies to the Secretary of State for those particulars.

6. Liability to pay Secretary of State amount of benefits

(1) A person who makes a compensation payment in any case is liable to pay to the Secretary of State an amount equal to the total amount of the recoverable benefits.   **28.15**

(2) The liability referred to in subsection (1) arises immediately before the compensation payment or, if there is more than one, the first of them is made.

(3) No amount becomes payable under this section before the end of the period of 14 days following the day on which the liability arises.

(4) Subject to subsection (3), an amount becomes payable under this section at the end of the period of 14 days beginning with the day on which a certificate of recoverable benefits is first issued showing that the amount of recoverable benefit to which it relates has been or is likely to have been paid before a specified date.

7. Recovery of payments due under section 6

(1) This section applies where a person has made a compensation payment but—   **28.16**
    (a) has not applied for a certificate of recoverable benefits, or
    (b) has not made a payment to the Secretary of State under section 6 before the end of the period allowed under that section.

(2) The Secretary of State may—
    (a) issue the person who made the compensation payment with a certificate of recoverable benefits, if none has been issued, or
    (b) issue him with a copy of the certificate of recoverable benefits or (if more than one has been issued) the most recent one, and (in either case) issue him with a demand that payment of any amount due under section 6 be made immediately.

(3) The Secretary of State may, in accordance with subsection (4) and (5), recover the amount for which a demand for payment is made under subsection (2) from the person who made the compensation payment.

(4) If the person who made the compensation payment resides or carries on business in England and Wales and a county court so orders, any amount recoverable under subsection (3) is recoverable by execution issued from the county court or otherwise as if it were payable under an order of that court.

(5) If the person who made the payment resides or carries on business in Scotland, any amount recoverable under subsection (3) may be enforced in like manner as an extract registered decree arbitral bearing a warrant for execution issued by the sheriff court of any sheriffdom in Scotland.

(6) A document bearing a certificate which—
    (a) is signed by a person authorised to do so by the Secretary of State, and
    (b) states that the document, apart from the certificate, is a record of the amount recoverable under subsection (3), is conclusive evidence that that amount is so recoverable.

(7) A certificate under subsection (6) purporting to be signed by a person authorised to do so by the Secretary of State is to be treated as so signed unless the contrary is proved.

8. Reduction of compensation payment

(1) This section applies in a case where, in relation to any head of compensation listed in column 1 of Schedule 2—   **28.17**

(a) any of the compensation payment is attributable to the head, and

(b) any recoverable benefit is shown against that head in column 2 of the Schedule.

(2) In such a case, any claim of a person to receive the compensation payment is to be treated for all purposes as discharged if—

(a) he is paid the amount (if any) of the compensation payment calculated in accordance with this section, and

(b) if the amount of the compensation payment so calculated is nil, he is given a statement saying so by the person who (apart from this section) would have paid the gross amount of the compensation payment.

(3) For each head of compensation listed in column 1 of the Schedule for which paragraphs (a) and (b) of subsection (1) are met, so much of the gross amount of the compensation payment as is attributable to that head is to be reduced (to nil, if necessary) by deducting the amount of the recoverable benefit or, as the case may be, the aggregate amount of the recoverable benefits shown against it.

(4) Subsection (3) is to have effect as if a requirement to reduce a payment by deducting an amount which exceeds the payment were a requirement to reduce that payment to nil.

(5) The amount of the compensation payment calculated in accordance with this section is—

(a) the gross amount of the compensation payment, less

(b) the sum of the reductions made under subsection (3),

(and, accordingly, the amount may be nil).

9. Section 8: supplementary

28.18   (1) A person who makes a compensation payment calculated in accordance with section 8 must inform the person to whom the payment is made—

(a) that the payment has been so calculated, and

(b) of the date for payment by reference to which the calculation has been made.

(2) If the amount of a compensation payment calculated in accordance with section 8 is nil, a person giving a statement saying so is to be treated for the purposes of this Act as making a payment within section 1(1)(a) on the day on which he gives the statement.

(3) Where a person—

(a) makes a compensation payment calculated in accordance with section 8, and

(b) if the amount of the compensation payment so calculated is nil, gives a statement saying so, he is to be treated, for the purpose of determining any rights and liabilities in respect of contribution or indemnity, as having paid the gross amount of the compensation payment.

(4) For the purposes of this Act—

(a) the gross amount of the compensation payment is the amount of the compensation payment apart from section 8, and

(b) the amount of any recoverable benefit is the amount determined in accordance with the certificate of recoverable benefits.

10. Review of certificates of recoverable benefits

28.19   [(1) Any certificate of recoverable benefits may be reviewed by the Secretary of State—

(a) either within the prescribed period or in prescribed cases or circumstances; and

(b) either on an application made for the purpose or on his own initiative.]

(2) On a review under this section the Secretary of State may either—

(a) confirm the certificate, or

(b) (subject to subsection (3)) issue a fresh certificate containing such variations as he considers appropriate, [or

(c) revoke the certificate.].

(3) The Secretary of State may not vary the certificate so as to increase the total amount of the recoverable benefits unless it appears to him that the variation is required as a result of the person who applied for the certificate supplying him with incorrect or insufficient information.

11. Appeals against certificates of recoverable benefits

(1) An appeal against a certificate of recoverable benefits may be made on the ground—   **28.20**

(a) that any amount, rate or period specified in the certificate is incorrect, or

(b) that listed benefits which have been, or are likely to be, paid otherwise than in respect of the accident, injury or disease in question have been brought into account [or

(c) that listed benefits which have not been, and are not likely to be, paid to the injured person during the relevant period have been brought into account, or

(d) that the payment on the basis of which the certificate was issued is not a payment within section 1(1)(a)].

(2) An appeal under this section may be made by—

(a) the person who applied for the certificate of recoverable benefits, or

[(aa) (in a case where that certificate was issued under section 7(2)(a)) the person to whom it was so issued, or]

(b) (in a case where the amount of the compensation payment has been calculated under section 8) the injured person or other person to whom the payment is made.

(3) No appeal may be made under this section until—

(a) the claim giving rise to the compensation payment has been finally disposed of, and

(b) the liability under section 6 has been discharged.

(4) For the purposes of subsection (3)(a), if an award of damages in respect of a claim has been made under or by virtue of—

(a) section 32A(2)(a) of the Supreme Court Act 1981,

(b) section 12(2)(a) of the Administration of Justice Act 1982, or

(c) section 51(2)(a) of the Country Courts Act 1984,

(orders for provisional damages in personal injury cases), the claim is to be treated as having been finally disposed of.

(5) Regulations may make provision—

(a) as to the manner in which, and the time within which, appeals under this section may be made,

(b) as to the procedure to be followed where such an appeal is made, and

(c) for the purpose of enabling any such appeal to be treated as an application for review under section 10.

12. Reference of questions to medical appeal tribunal

[(1) The Secretary of State must refer an appeal under section 11 to an appeal tribunal.]   **28.21**

(3) In determining [any appeal under section 11], the tribunal must take into account any decision of a court relating to the same, or any similar, issue arising in connection with the accident, injury or disease in question.

(4) On [an appeal under section 11 an appeal tribunal] may either—

(a) confirm the amounts, rates and periods specified in the certificate of recoverable benefits, or

(b) specify any variations which are to be made on the issue of a fresh certificate under subsection (5) [or

(c) declare that the certificate of recoverable benefits is to be revoked.].

(5) When the Secretary of State has received [the decision of the tribunal on the appeal under section 11, he must in accordance with that decision] either—

(a) confirm the certificate against which the appeal was brought, or

(b) issue a fresh certificate [or

(c) revoke the certificate.].

(7) Regulations [. . .] may (among other things) provide for the non-disclosure of medical advice or medical evidence given or submitted following a reference under subsection (1).

13. Appeal to Social Security Commissioner

28.22   (1) An appeal may be made to a Commissioner against any decision of [an appeal tribunal] under section 12 on the ground that the decision was erroneous in point of law.

(2) An appeal under this section may be made by—

(a) the Secretary of State,

(b) the person who applied for the certificate of recoverable benefits, [. . .]

[(bb) (in a case where that certificate was issued under section 7(2)(a)) the person to whom it was so issued, or]

(c) (in a case where the amount of the compensation payment has been calculated in accordance with section 8) the injured person or other person to whom the payment is made.

14. Reviews and appeals: supplementary

28.23   (1) This section applies in cases where a fresh certificate of recoverable benefits is issued as a result of a review under Section 10 or an appeal under section 11.

(2) If—

(a) a person has made one or more payments to the Secretary of State under section 6, and

(b) in consequence of the review or appeal, it appears that the total amount paid is more than the amount that ought to have been paid, regulations may provide for the Secretary of State to pay the difference to that person, or to the person to whom the compensation payment is made, or partly to one and partly to the other.

(3) If—

(a) a person has made one or more payments to the Secretary of State under section 6, and

(b) in consequence of the review or appeal, it appears that the total amount paid is less than the amount that ought to have been paid, regulations may provide for that person to pay the difference to the Secretary of State.

(4) Regulations under this section may provide—

(a) for the re-calculation in accordance with section 8 of the amount of any compensation payment,

(b) for giving credit for amounts already paid, and

(c) for the payment by any person of any balance or the recovery from any person of any excess,

and may provide for any matter by modifying this Act.

15. Court orders

28.24   (1) This section applies where a court makes an order for a compensation payment to be made in any case, unless the order is made with the consent of the injured person and the person by whom the payment is to be made.

(2) The court must, in the case of each head of compensation listed in column 1 of Schedule 2 to which any of the compensation payment is attributable, specify in the order the amount of the compensation payment which is attributable to that head.

16. Payments into court

28.25   (1) Regulations may make provision (including provision modifying this Act) for any case in which a payment into court is made.

(2) The regulations may (among other things) provide—

(a) for the making of a payment into court to be treated in prescribed circumstances as the making of a compensation payment,

(b) for application for, and issue of, certificates of recoverable benefits, and

(c) for the relevant period to be treated as ending on a date determined in accordance with the regulations.

(3) Rules of court may make provision governing practice and procedure in such cases.

(4) This section does not extend to Scotland.

17. Benefits irrelevant to assessment of damages

In assessing damages in respect of any accident, injury or disease, the amount of any listed benefits paid or likely to be paid is to be disregarded.   **28.26**

18. Lump sum and periodical payments

(1) Regulations may make provision (including provision modifying this Act) for any case in which two or more compensation payments in the form of lump sums are made by the same person to or in respect of the injured person in consequence of the same accident, injury or disease.   **28.27**

(2) The regulations may (among other things) provide—

(a) for the re-calculation in accordance with Section 8 of the amount of any compensation payment,

(b) for giving credit for amounts already paid, and

(c) for the payment by any person of any balance or the recovery from any person of any excess.

(3) For the purposes of subsection (2), the regulations may provide for the gross amounts of the compensation payments to be aggregated and for—

(a) the aggregate amount to be taken to be the gross amount of the compensation payment for the purposes of section 8,

(b) so much of the aggregate amount as is attributable to a head of compensation listed in column 1 of Schedule 2 to be taken to be the part of the gross amount which is attributable to that head; and for the amount of any recoverable benefit shown against any head in column 2 of that Schedule to be taken to be the amount determined in accordance with the most recent certificate of recoverable benefits.

(4) Regulations may make provision (including provision modifying this Act) for any case in which, in final settlement of the injured person's claim, an agreement is entered into for the making of—

(a) periodical compensation payments (whether of an income or capital nature), or

(b) periodical compensation payments and lump sum compensation payments.

(5) Regulations made by virtue of subsection (4) may (among other things) provide—

(a) for the relevant period to be treated as ending at a prescribed time,

(b) for the person who is to make the payments under the agreement to be treated for the purposes of this Act as if he had made a single compensation payment on a prescribed date.

(6) A periodical payment may be a compensation payment for the purposes of this section even though it is a small payment (as defined in Part II of Schedule 1).

19. Payments by more than one person

(1) Regulations may make provision (including provision modifying this Act) for any case in which two or more persons ('the compensators') make compensation payments to or in respect of the same injured person in consequence of the same accident, injury or disease.   **28.28**

(2) In such a case, the sum of the liabilities of the compensators under section 6 is not to exceed the total amount of the recoverable benefits, and the regulations may provide for determining the respective liabilities under that section of each of the compensators.

(3) The regulations may (among other things) provide in the case of each compensator—

(a) for determining or re-determining the part of the recoverable benefits which may be taken into account in his case,

(b) for calculating or re-calculating in accordance with section 8 the amount of any compensation payment,

(c) for giving credit for amounts already paid, and

(d) for the payment by any person of any balance or the recovery from any person of any excess.

20. Amounts overpaid under section 6

28.29   (1) Regulations may make provision (including provision modifying this Act) for cases where a person has paid to the Secretary of State under section 6 any amount ('the amount of the overpayment') which he was not liable to pay.

(2) The regulations may provide—

(a) for the Secretary of State to pay the amount of the overpayment to that person, or to the person to whom the compensation payment is made, or partly to one and partly to the other, or

(b) for the receipt by the Secretary of State of the amount of the overpayment to be treated as the recovery of that amount.

(3) Regulations made by virtue of subsection (2)(b) are to have effect in spite of anything in section 71 of the Social Security Administration Act 1992 (overpayments—general).

(4) The regulations may also (among other things) provide—

(a) for the re-calculation in accordance with section 8 of the amount of any compensation payment,

(b) for giving credit for amounts already paid, and

(c) for the payment by any person of any balance or the recovery from any person of any excess.

(5) This section does not apply in a case where section 14 applies.

21. Compensation payments to be disregarded

28.30   (1) If, when a compensation payment is made, the first and second conditions are met, the payment is to be disregarded for the purposes of sections 6 and 8.

(2) The first condition is that the person making the payment—

(a) has made an application for a certificate of recoverable benefits which complies with subsection (3), and

(b) has in his possession a written acknowledgement of the receipt of his application.

(3) An application complies with this subsection if it—

(a) accurately states the prescribed particulars relating to the injured person and the accident, injury or disease in question, and

(b) specifies the name and address of the person to whom the certificate is to be sent.

(4) The second condition is that the Secretary of State has not sent the certificate to the person, at the address, specified in the application, before the end of the period allowed under section 4.

(5) In any case where—

(a) by virtue of subsection (1), a compensation payment is disregarded for the purposes of sections 6 and 8, but

(b) the person who made the compensation payment nevertheless makes a payment to the Secretary of State for which (but for subsection (1)) he would be liable under section 6, subsection (1) is to cease to apply in relation to the compensation payment.

(6) If, in the opinion of the Secretary of State, circumstances have arisen which adversely affect normal methods of communication—

(a) he may by order provide that subsection (1) is not to apply during a specified period not exceeding three months, and

(b) he may continue any such order in force for further periods not exceeding three months at a time.

22. Liability of insurers

(1) If a compensation payment is made in a case where—   **28.31**

(a) a person is liable to any extent in respect of the accident, injury or disease, and

(b) the liability is covered to any extent by a policy of insurance, the policy is also to be treated as covering any liability of that person under section 6.

(2) Liability imposed on the insurer by subsection (1) cannot be excluded or restricted.

(3) For that purpose excluding or restricting liability includes—

(a) making the liability or its enforcement subject to restrictive or onerous conditions,

(b) excluding or restricting any right or remedy in respect of the liability, or subjecting a person to any prejudice in consequence of his pursuing any such right or remedy, or

(c) excluding or restricting rules of evidence or procedure.

(4) Regulations may in prescribed cases limit the amount of the liability imposed on the insurer by subsection (1).

(5) This section applies to policies of insurance issued before (as well as those issued after) its coming into force.

(6) References in this section to policies of insurance and their issue include references to contracts of insurance and their making.

23. Provision of information

(1) Where compensation is sought in respect of any accident, injury or disease suffered by any   **28.32** person ('the injured person'), the following persons must give the Secretary of State the prescribed information about the injured person—

(a) anyone who is, or is alleged to be, liable in respect of the accident, injury or disease, and

(b) anyone acting on behalf of such a person.

(2) A person who receives or claims a listed benefit which is or is likely to be paid in respect of an accident, injury or disease suffered by him, must give the Secretary of State the prescribed information about the accident, injury or disease.

(3) Where a person who has received a listed benefit dies, the duty in subsection (2) is imposed on his personal representative.

(4) Any person who makes a payment (whether on his own behalf or not)—

(a) in consequence of, or

(b) which is referable to any costs (in Scotland. expenses) incurred by reason of,

any accident, injury or disease, or any damage to property, must, if the Secretary of State requests him in writing to do so, give the Secretary of State such particulars relating to the size and composition of the payment as are specified in the request.

(5) The employer of a person who suffers or has suffered an accident, injury or disease, and anyone who has been the employer of such a person at any time during the relevant period, must give the Secretary of State the prescribed information about the payment of statutory sick pay in respect of that person.

(6) In subsection (5) 'employer' has the same meaning as it has in Part XI of the Social Security Contributions and Benefits Act 1992.

(7) A person who is required to give information under this section must do so in the prescribed manner, at the prescribed place and within the prescribed time.

(8) Section 1 does not apply in relation to this section.

24. Power to amend Schedule 2

28.33   (1) The Secretary of State may by regulations amend Schedule 2.

(2) A statutory instrument which contains such regulations shall not be made unless a draft of the instrument has been laid before and approved by resolution of each House of Parliament.

28. The Crown

28.34   This Act applies to the Crown.

29. General interpretation

28.35   In this Act—

['appeal tribunal' means an appeal tribunal constituted under Chapter I of Part I of the Social Security Act 1998;]

'benefit' means any benefit under the Social Security Contributions and Benefits Act 1992, a jobseeker's allowance or mobility allowance,

['Commissioner' has the same meaning as in Chapter II of Part I of the Social Security Act 1998 (see section 39);]

'compensation scheme for motor accidents' means any scheme or arrangement under which funds are available for the payment of compensation in respect of motor accidents caused, or alleged to have been caused, by uninsured or unidentified persons,

'listed benefit' means a benefit listed in column 2 of Schedule 2,

'payment' means payment in money or money's worth, and related expressions are to be interpreted accordingly,

'prescribed' means prescribed by regulations, and

'regulations' means regulations made by the Secretary of State.

30. Regulations and orders

28.36   (1) Any power under this Act to make regulations or an order is exercisable by statutory instrument.

(2) A statutory instrument containing regulations or an order under this Act (other than regulations under section 24 or an order under section 34) shall be subject to annulment in pursuance of a resolution of either House of Parliament.

(3) Regulations under section 20, under section 24 amending the list of benefits in column 2 of Schedule 2 or under paragraph 9 of Schedule 1 may not be made without the consent of the Treasury.

(4) Subsections (4), (5), (6) and (9) of Section 189 of the Social Security Administration Act 1992 (regulations and orders—general) apply for the purposes of this Act as they apply for the purposes of that.

31. Financial arrangements

28.37   (1) There are to be paid out of the National Insurance Fund any expenses of the Secretary of State in making payments under section 14 or 20 to the extent that he estimates that those payments relate to sums paid out of that Fund.

(2) There are to be paid out of money provided by Parliament—

(a) any expenses of the Secretary of State in making payments under section 14 or 20 to the extent that he estimates that those payments relate to sums paid out of the Consolidated Fund, and

(b) (subject to subsection (1)) any other expenses of the Secretary of State incurred in consequence of this Act.

(3) Any sums paid to the Secretary of State under section 6 or 14 are to be paid—

(a) into the Consolidated Fund, to the extent that the Secretary of State estimates that the sums relate to payments out of money provided by Parliament, and

(b) into the National Insurance Fund, to the extent that he estimates that they relate to payments out of that Fund.

32. Power to make transitional, consequential etc. provisions

(1) Regulations may make such transitional and consequential provisions, and such savings, **28.38** as the Secretary of State considers necessary or expedient in preparation for, in connection with, or in consequence of—

(a) the coming into force of any provision of this Act, or

(b) the operation of any enactment repealed or amended by a provision of this Act during any period when the repeal or amendment is not wholly in force.

(2) Regulations under this section may (among other things) provide—

(a) for compensation payments in relation to which, by virtue of section 2, this Act does not apply to be treated as payments in relation to which this Act applies,

(b) for compensation payments in relation to which, by virtue of section 2, this Act applies to be treated as payments in relation to which this Act does not apply, and

(c) for the modification of any enactment contained in this Act or referred to in subsection (1)(b) in its application to any compensation payment.

SCHEDULES

Section 1   SCHEDULE I COMPENSATION PAYMENTS

PART I EXEMPTED PAYMENTS

1. Any small payment (defined in Part II of this Schedule).   **28.39**

2. Any payment made to or for the injured person under section 35 of the Powers of Criminal Courts Act 1973 or section 249 of the Criminal Procedure (Scotland) Act 1995 (compensation orders against convicted persons).

3. Any payment made in the exercise of a discretion out of property held subject to a trust in a case where no more than 50 per cent, by value of the capital contributed to the trust was directly or indirectly provided by persons who are, or are alleged to be, liable in respect of—

(a) the accident, injury or disease suffered by the injured person, or

(b) the same or any connected accident, injury or disease suffered by another.

4. Any payment made out of property held for the purposes of any prescribed trust (whether the payment also falls within paragraph 3 or not).

5. Any payment made to the injured person by an insurance company within the meaning of the Insurance Companies Act 1982 under the terms of any contract of insurance entered into between the injured person and the company before—

(a) the date on which the injured person first claims a listed benefit in consequence of the disease in question, or

(b) the occurrence of the accident or injury in question.

6. Any redundancy payment falling to be taken into account in the assessment of damages in respect of an accident, injury or disease.

7. So much of any payment as is referable to costs.

8. Any prescribed payment.

28.40 9.—(1) Regulations may make provision for compensation payments to be disregarded for the purposes of sections 6 and 8 in prescribed cases where the amount of the compensation payment, or the aggregate amount of two or more connected compensation payments, does not exceed the prescribed sum.

(2) A compensation payment disregarded by virtue of this paragraph is referred to in paragraph 1 as a 'small payment'.

(3) For the purposes of this paragraph—

(a) two or more compensation payments are 'connected' if each is made to or in respect of the same injured person and in respect of the same accident, injury or disease, and

(b) any reference to a compensation payment is a reference to a payment which would be such a payment apart from paragraph 1.

Section 8   Schedule 2 Calculation of Compensation Payment

28.41

(1) Head of compensation	(2) Benefit
1. Compensation for earnings lost during the relevant period	Disability working allowance Disablement pension payable under section 103 of the 1992 Act Incapacity benefit Income support Invalidity pension and allowance Jobseeker's allowance Reduced earnings allowance Severe disablement allowance Sickness benefit Statutory sick pay Unemployability supplement Unemployment benefit
2. Compensation for cost of care incurred during the relevant period	Attendance allowance Care component of disability living allowance Disablement pension increase payable under section 104 or 105 of the 1992 Act
3. Compensation for loss of mobility during the relevant period	Mobility allowance Mobility component of disability living allowance

Notes

1.—(1) References to incapacity benefit, invalidity pension and allowance, severe disablement allowance, sickness benefit and unemployment benefit also include any income support paid with each of those benefits on the same instrument of payment or paid concurrently with each of those benefits by means of an instrument for benefit payment.

(2) For the purpose of this Note, income support includes personal expenses addition, special transitional additions and transitional addition as defined in the Income Support (Transitional) Regulations 1987.

2. Any reference to statutory sick pay—

(a)includes only 80 per cent of payments made between 6 April 1991 and 5 April 1994, and

(b) does not include payments made on or after 6 April 1994.

3. In this Schedule 'the 1992 Act' means the Social Security Contributions and Benefits Act 1992.

C. PD 40B—Judgments and Orders

Adjustment of final judgment figure in respect of compensation recovery payments

5.1 In a final judgment where some or all of the damages awarded:

28.42

(1) fall under the heads of damage set out in column 1 of Schedule 2 to the Social Security (Recovery of Benefits) Act 1997 in respect of recoverable benefits received by the claimant set out in column 2 of that Schedule and

(2) where the defendant has paid to the Secretary of State the recoverable benefits in accordance with the certificate of recoverable benefits,

there should be stated in a preamble to the judgment or order the amount awarded under each head of damage and the amount by which it has been reduced in accordance with section 8 of and Schedule 2 to the Social Security (Recovery of Benefits) Act 1997.

29

FATAL ACCIDENTS ACT
CLAIMS ASSESSMENT

A. The Fatal Accidents Act

The Fatal Accidents Act 1976 (FAA) gives a statutory claim for loss of financial **29.01** dependency to the surviving dependants of a person who has died. There is no equivalent to such a claim at common law. The statutory claim is brought in respect of financial loss: by s 3(3) 'such damages may be awarded as are pro-portioned to the injury resulting from the death to the dependants'. Lord Wright said in *Davies v Powell Duffryn Collieries* [1942] AC 601: 'There is no question of what may be called sentimental damage, bereavement or pain and suffering. It is a hard matter of pounds, shillings and pence'. However, this is not the whole story. A limited class of people can also claim the statutory award for bereavement, currently £10,000. An FAA claim may be joined with a claim for the estate of the deceased person whose pain and suffering before death can be part of that claim. The pounds and pence of an FAA claim extend to putting a financial value on the care that children may need after the death of a parent including the incalculable loss of the special loving care given by a parent.

FAA claims are assessed by their own special rules, which can appear at first **29.02** sight rather complicated. The special rules include an unusually broad statutory disregard of other benefits received as a result of the death and freedom from the benefit recoupment system that applies to claims by living claimants. It is a legal framework characterized, more than in any other field of personal injury practice, by inconsistency between those topics where a broad brush approach is favoured, and those where detailed calculations are used, and by a generous principle of disregarding other benefits, which can lead to an appearance of double recovery. Once the principles have been understood, the computation of claims is not unduly difficult.

B. The Law Reform (Miscellaneous Provisions) Act

29.03 The Law Reform (Miscellaneous Provisions) Act 1934 provided for causes of action to survive for the benefit of the estate of the holder of a claim who dies before his claim has been resolved. Section 1 of the Act is set out in Chapter 19 above. A claim of this kind is conceptually quite different from an FAA claim. The substance is the claim which the deceased might himself have brought; the procedure is a claim brought by the personal representatives of the estate, who might be different from the dependants of the deceased; and the benefit of the claim goes to the beneficiaries of the estate of the deceased under his will or the rules of intestacy who, once again, might be different from the dependants of the deceased.

29.04 A claim under the 1934 Act is appropriate where there has been a significant interval between injury and death. A claim may arise for injury damages over this period, for care and for loss of earnings. A claim for injury damages in this context may arise in respect of loss of amenity even if there is no awareness to give rise to a claim for pain and suffering, but any claim of this kind can only be brought if there has been a significant period of survival. A claim can be brought in respect of funeral expenses, but this can also be pursued under the FAA claim, as long as it was a dependant who incurred the expenses.

29.05 *Hicks v Chief Constable of South Yorkshire* [1992] PIQR P433   The claimant died from asphyxia in the Hillsborough Stadium disaster. The evidence was of a loss of consciousness from crushing of the chest within a matter of seconds, and death within five minutes. On these facts, no award was to be made for pain and suffering and loss of amenity.

29.06 If there is to be a claim under the 1934 Act, it is usual for it to be combined in the same proceedings as an FAA claim. In order to bring such a claim it is necessary to have details of the representation of the estate. However, since the funeral expenses can usually be recovered under the FAA, it is usually not necessary to include a claim under the 1934 Act unless the deceased survived for a significant time after first sustaining injury.

C. The Multiplier

As with claims for living claimants, the future stream of loss is calculated with a **29.07** multiplier to assess the present value, taking account of the return on invested damages, the risks of mortality, and other contingencies. The return on invested damages is fixed under the Damages Act 1996 for this purpose at the usual rate of 2.5%. The risks and contingencies must allow, in this context, for the circumstances on both sides of the dependency relationship. The calculation must take into account the circumstances of the deceased, but equally a dependency on the earnings or services of the deceased will only continue so long as the dependant is there to receive them and so the mortality and circumstances of the dependants must also be taken into account. There is an additional factor in considering mortality. In a claim by a living claimant, at the date of trial it is a known fact that the risk of mortality has not materialized during the pre-trial period. In a dependency claim, the risk of mortality of the deceased applies to the whole of the dependency period from the date of death.

The conventional approach to fixing the multiplier for an FAA claim is to assess **29.08** a multiplier from the date of death, rather than from the date of trial. In calculating interest, the exact amount of time that has elapsed until the trial is treated as past loss and the balance of the whole multiplier is treated as future loss. The multiplier from the date of death can be calculated using the Ogden Tables as the starting point. However, the discounting of the basic figure will have to take account of the risk of mortality and other contingencies affecting the dependant as well as the deceased, and the duration of the dependency will be for joint lives and curtailed by the first death (as if this death had not happened) of either the deceased or the dependant.

Cookson v Knowles [1979] AC 556   In an FAA claim the court should assess **29.09** the claim as from the date of death, but should take into account known facts which have happened before the date of trial including, for the multiplicand, applying any increases in his net earnings that the deceased would have received. The multiplier is decided as at the date of death, although interest is to be awarded only on the part of the multiplier which has elapsed to the date of trial.

This method of deciding the multiplier has been criticized, and the members of **29.10** the Working Party compiling the Ogden Tables have proposed an alternative approach which is set out in the Introduction to the tables. The method involves assessing past loss of dependency as special damage, with an adjustment to allow for the risk of mortality of the deceased, and assessing future loss of dependency with a multiplier calculated from the date of trial using the actuarial information contained in the tables. The use of 0% tables to identify the risks of mortality is more accurate than the likely estimate of the judge. The use of this method of calculation usually results in a modest increase in the value of the dependency. However, the arithmetical accuracy of the new system has not yet overcome the authority of *Cookson v Knowles* (above) and at the time of writing it is still necessary to follow the conventional approach. If authority for the Ogden approach arises, full details will promptly be given on the updating website for this book.

29.11 *White v ESAB Group* [2002] PIQR Q76 (approved by the Court of Appeal in *ATH v MS* [2002] EWCA Civ 792; [2003] PIQR Q1 at [36])   The court is still bound by the authority of *Cookson v Knowles* (above) and *Graham v Dodds* [1983] 1 WLR 208 to assess multipliers in FAA claims from the date of death rather than in the manner recommended by the Ogden Tables Working Party.

D. Splitting the Multiplier

29.12 It is often necessary to assess the level of dependency at different figures for different stages of the projected future of the dependency relationship of the deceased. The dependency on an employed person will be split between working life and retirement. The dependency on a young employed person may need to be split between several steps of likely future promotion. The dependency on a spouse and parent must be divided between the years supporting a family with children and years when the children will no longer be dependent. It will be necessary to divide up the total future multiplier in a way which recognizes that dependency in the distant future will involve a much greater acceleration of receipt than dependency in the near future. The starting point is the use of Tables 27 and 28 of the Ogden Tables, although pure mathematical accuracy is usually unattainable in making the value of the various steps consistent with the overall multiplier. It is important to remember the underlying uncertainty of all factual projections about the future in fixing on steps in the multiplier that are reasonable and workable. Chances of promotion can alternatively be reflected by taking an increased multiplicand.

E. The Multiplicand: Financial Dependency

29.13 The multiplicand, in a case of dependency on income, is the net income of the deceased, less the amount of his income that he would have spent for his own benefit. Thus, income that he would have spent for the joint benefit of himself and his dependants is included in the dependency. You cannot live in half a house, so the income that is spent in supporting the provision of the family home is all part of the dependency of the rest of the family. In the same way, the services provided by the deceased in housekeeping, childcare, gardening and so forth are provided for the benefit of the whole household and form part of the dependency except in so far as the work would have been for the exclusive benefit of the deceased.

It is possible to attempt to calculate the value of the dependency by carrying out **29.14** a detailed analysis of the finances of the whole family of the deceased. In legal theory this is the right thing to do, and in view of the large amounts that can be involved in dependency claims it is surprising that the full exercise of analysis is not undertaken more frequently, if only as a cross-check. In practice, however, the multiplicand is usually decided using the *Harris* fraction (see below) which saves a great deal of legal trouble and expense.

Harris v Empress Motors [1983] 3 All ER 561   In a 'lost years' claim the Court **29.15** of Appeal approved a practical approach for assessing the proportion of the income of the deceased that would have been spent on his own needs: in the case of a couple, it is assumed that one third of the income would have been spent on the personal needs of the deceased, one-third of it would have been spent on the needs of the dependant and one-third would have been spent on joint needs, so that the dependency is two-thirds of the net income. When there are dependent children, the proportion spent on the needs of the deceased is taken to be one quarter, so that the dependency is three quarters of the net income.

The *Harris* fraction is only a rule of thumb, a guide to be applied in the normal **29.16** case. If the circumstances are out of the ordinary, the court will take account of this. For example, the proportion spent on the personal needs of the deceased might be taken at a smaller fraction of the income if there were a great many children in the family, or if the family income was relatively low, but might be a larger fraction of a high income. Unusual circumstances might be a good reason for turning to a detailed analysis of family finances, but in practice it is more common for the *Harris* fraction to be adjusted.

F. The Effect of the Income of the Survivor

Where a claim is made by a dependant who has his/her own income, that **29.17** income has to be taken into account in calculating the value of the dependency that has been lost. In a case which is assessed with the *Harris* fraction, a similar fraction of the income of the survivor will be taken to have been spent on the sole needs of the deceased before the death, so that part of the survivor's income is now available to support the surviving family.

29.18 *Coward v Comex Houlder Diving,* Independent, 25 July 1988; *Kemp & Kemp* at M2–207   The claimant's own earnings must be taken into account. In terms of a formula, the widow's dependency is two-thirds of the deceased's net earnings less one-third of her own earnings, or it is two-thirds of the joint earnings less her own earnings. The two calculations come to the same result.

29.19 This formula applies easily where the survivor has the same income before and after the death. If the survivor's income increases after the death, for example if financial necessity makes her go out to work for the first time, that additional income is likely to be disregarded under s 4 of the FAA because it arises as a result of the death. If the survivor's income ceases or is reduced after the death, for example because a mother now needs to devote more time to care for children after losing the father's contribution, the position in relation to dependency is unclear. The reality is that the family is now wholly dependent on the dependency claim and does not in fact have an income from the survivor, and it is suggested that the survivor's former income should be disregarded, whether or not the loss of the income is a result of the death. One way of approaching the problem would be to treat the additional care need as valued by reference to the lost income. Whether the survivor would be entitled to claim both a financial dependency unaffected by earnings she has given up, and a claim for the value of the deceased's lost care services, is a difficult and as yet unresolved question.

G. The Multiplicand: Services Dependency

29.20 The multiplicand for the dependency will also include the value of services that the deceased will no longer be able to provide to the dependants. In the case of the death of a parent, the services include the care of the children of the family. The basis of assessing the value of the services is derived from the way in which claims for an incapacitated living claimant are assessed.

29.21 First, therefore, the court will value the lost care of a mother in terms of the practical work she would have continued to provide: housekeeping, cooking, organizing clothes, transport, etc. In addition, it has come to be recognized that a child's dependency includes the special loving care that only a mother can give and that an additional award should be made for this loss.

29.22 *Spittle v Bunney* [1988] 1 WLR 847   In a claim for a child aged three following the death of her mother, the loss of the mother's services was assessed according to the net earnings of a full-time nanny in the early years of the child's life but this was less appropriate as the child grew older, and there should be included an element for the mother's services beyond the care a commercial nanny could provide.

ATH v MS [2002] EWCA Civ 792; [2003] PIQR Q1   In an FAA claim **29.23** following the death of the mother of young children, who were now in the care of their father, from whom she had been estranged, the lost services of the mother caring for the children were assessed according to an estimate of the hours of care and expert evidence of the commercial cost of such care. A parallel was drawn with *Hunt v Severs* [1994] 2 AC 350. Awards were also made for 'services only a mother can provide' of £3,500 for a child aged 11 at the date of his mother's death and £4,500 for a child aged eight.

H. Disregard of Benefits under FAA, s 4

Section 3(3) of the FAA provides that in assessing damages payable to a widow **29.24** for the death of her husband, the court must disregard her remarriage or her prospects of remarriage. In addition to this specific provision, s 4 provides that:

> In assessing damages in respect of a person's death in an action under this Act, benefits which have accrued or will or may accrue to any person from his estate or otherwise as a result of his death shall be disregarded.

These words are a 1982 amendment to words which previously limited the disregard to 'any insurance money, benefit, pension or gratuity' and the courts have interpreted the new words widely. The Law Commission in its November 1999 Report No 263 on claims for wrongful death recommended that s 4 should be reformed to return to a limited list of specific disregards, but at present neither Parliament nor the judicial interpretation of the FAA has moved in that direction.

Topp v London County Bus [1992] PIQR P206   A widower's prospects of **29.25** remarriage following the death of his wife are not disregarded under s 3(3), which applies only to widows, but the court should disregard them under s 4 anyway.

Where a child is cared for by an aunt, grandparent, or stepmother following the **29.26** death of the mother, the replacement care is generally disregarded because it is received by the child as a result of the death of the mother. It is the lost mother's care that is valued for the claim rather than the substitute care, but the outcome may well be the same. Where the new carer is a parent who was estranged from the mother and was not providing practical care or financial support before the death, then the same application of s 4 applies, but it seems that if the care of the children is simply continued by a parent who was sharing the care before the death it may be held that s 4 does not apply because this care is provided out of love and duty and not as a result of the death. The reported cases noted below concern estranged parents and it may be questioned how far this anomalous approach would be applied: it is suggested that the surviving parent's additional input of care should be regarded as arising as a result of the death and therefore to this extent the lost care of the deceased parent should be part of the dependency.

29.27 *Stanley v Saddique* [1992] QB 1   After the mother's death, the father met and married another woman who provided good care for the child: this care was disregarded because of the wide interpretation to be given to s 4. The dependency was based on the value of the (unsatisfactory) lost mother's care.

29.28 *Hayden v Hayden* [1992] 1 WLR 986   Conflicting reasons were given in the Court of Appeal for a decision in this case by the majority that the care of the child now provided by the father should be taken into account to extinguish the claim for loss of the deceased mother's services.

29.29 *L (A Child) v Barry May Haulage* [2002] PIQR Q35   The child was in the care of his mother at her home at the date of her death, and then moved to the care of his father who depended on state benefits and until her death had taken no part in the care of the child and had provided no financial support. In these circumstances, the care now provided by the father was to be disregarded. The judge observed that the position would have been different if at the date of the death there had been a prospect of the father providing care or financial support: to that extent, his care or financial support would have been taken into account.

29.30 *R v CICB, ex p K* [1999] QB 1131   Where the care of children had been taken over by their aunt and uncle following the death of their mother, the replacement parental services were to be disregarded under s 4.

29.31 *ATH v MS* (above)   Relying on the fact that there had been no likelihood of practical or financial support for the children from their father at the date of death, the support which they received after the accident was a benefit to be disregarded under s 4.

I. The Bereavement Award

29.32 The statutory bereavement award is £10,000 for deaths occurring after 1 April 2002. Before this date, the statutory sum was £7,500. The scope of those entitled to the bereavement award is much narrower than the scope of dependants. The claim can only be made (a) for the benefit of the wife or husband of the deceased (so there is no claim by an unmarried partner however strong the relationship) or (b) where the deceased was a minor who was never married, for the benefit of his parents if he was legitimate, and for the benefit of his mother if he was illegitimate (so there is no claim by a child for the death of a parent, there is no claim by the parents for the death of a child once the child is aged 18, and there is no claim by an unmarried father living in a settled long-term relationship with the mother or having parental responsibility). There are many claims for loss of dependency in which there is no one entitled to claim the bereavement award. It is not clear why the scope of those entitled to this award should be so limited, and there is a strong case for reform.

J. The Range of Dependants

A much wider range of people may qualify as dependants. A claim is not proved merely by being within the range of people who qualify as dependants, but only by proving in addition an actual dependency. Little purpose is served by limiting the class of potential dependants. In practice, almost all potential claims come within s 1(3)(a)–(g) which includes in the category of potential dependants former spouses, unmarried partners who have lived in the same household for at least two years, all ascendants and descendants, siblings, aunts and uncles, and children of others treated as a child of the family.   **29.33**

K. Apportionment between Dependants

Section 2 of the FAA envisages that a single action will be brought by a single claimant, but the action will be brought on behalf of all the persons who are dependants. The first opportunity to bring a claim is given to the executor or administrator of the estate, but any other dependant can take the initiative and bring a claim after six months. It is suggested that anyone who instigates proceedings as claimant ought to inform all the potential dependants of the intended claim, and has a responsibility to the dependants to protect and pursue their claims.   **29.34**

It is natural for each dependant to focus on the value of his share, but the nature of an FAA claim is first of all to establish the single amount of the financial and services support that the deceased would have provided and then to divide this up between the various dependants. As far as the defendant is concerned, he can treat an FAA claim as a single claim and need not be concerned with the question of apportionment between the dependants: s 3(6) allows a Part 36 payment to be made in one sum without specifying any person's share.   **29.35**

29.36 It is possible for the amount that is due to each dependant as a share of the overall dependency to be calculated accurately. In cases where the dependants do not all live together in one family unit, this may be necessary. It will not be an easy task: the *Harris* fraction takes a very broad brush approach to the impact of children on the total dependency, assuming a single family unit to exist, and it should not be assumed that the dependency of children is necessarily represented by the difference between two-thirds and three-quarters of the net income. Where there is more than one family unit however, it is likely that an assessment of child support in force at the date of the death, or an order for periodical payments after divorce, will provide a good indication of the likely level of continuing financial dependency.

29.37 In a family with children, the accurate calculation of the dependency of each child may be inappropriate and inconvenient. For example, in a claim for the death of a working father, a proportion of the total financial dependency will be attributable to all of the costs of housing, clothing, and feeding each of the children. If this full award is paid to each of the children, then it will have to be invested under the direction of the court or the Court of Protection, or managed by a receiver, and the mother will be encumbered with the cost and inconvenience of making repeated applications to the court or the receiver for payment of money which she could reasonably have been trusted to apply for the benefit of the children. Secondly, the younger the child, the longer the dependency and the greater the share, but it is often more appropriate in a family that each child should receive the same; this can be achieved if the court decides that it is appropriate to entrust the surviving parent with the bulk of the funds that will be used for the support of the family as a whole, and the parent agrees that notionally, part of his or her award should be used to make up the award for older children to the same amount as the award of the youngest.

29.38 Where there are dependent children, if the claim is settled the apportionment must be approved by the court. The approach to be taken must be discussed carefully with the claimant and fully explained to the court in the opinion that is provided under CPR PD 21, para 6.3.

L. Fatal Accidents Act 1976, ss 1–5

1. Right of action for wrongful act causing death

29.39   (1) If death is caused by any wrongful act, neglect or default which is such as would (if death had not ensued) have entitled the person injured to maintain an action and recover damages in respect thereof, the person who would have been liable if death had not ensued shall be liable to an action for damages, notwithstanding the death of the person injured.

    (2) Subject to section 1A(2) below, every such action shall be for the benefit of the dependants of the person ('the deceased') whose death has been so caused.

(3) In this Act 'dependant' means—

(a) the wife or husband or former wife or husband of the deceased;

(b) any person who—

(i) was living with the deceased in the same household immediately before the date of the death; and

(ii) had been living with the deceased in the same household for at least two years before that date; and

(iii) was living during the whole of that period as the husband or wife of the deceased;

(c) any parent or other ascendant of the deceased;

(d) any person who was treated by the deceased as his parent;

(e) any child or other descendant of the deceased;

(f) any person (not being a child of the deceased) who, in the case of any marriage to which the deceased was at any time a party, was treated by the deceased as a child of the family in relation to that marriage;

(g) any person who is, or is the issue of, a brother, sister, uncle or aunt of the deceased.

(4) The reference to the former wife or husband of the deceased in subsection (3)(a) above includes a reference to a person whose marriage to the deceased has been annulled or declared void as well as a person whose marriage to the deceased has been dissolved.

(5) In deducing any relationship for the purposes of subsection (3) above—

(a) any relationship by affinity shall be treated as a relationship of consanguinity, any relationship of the half blood as a relationship of the whole blood, and the stepchild of any person as his child, and

(b) an illegitimate person shall be treated as the legitimate child of his mother and reputed father.

(6) Any reference in this Act to injury includes any disease and any impairment of a person' physical or mental condition.

1A. Bereavement

(1) An action under this Act may consist of or include a claim for damages for bereavement. **29.40**

(2) A claim for damages for bereavement shall only be for the benefit—

(a) of the wife or husband of the deceased; and

(b) where the deceased was a minor who was never married—

(i) of his parents, if he was legitimate; and

(ii) of his mother, if he was illegitimate.

(3) Subject to subsection (5) below, the sum to be awarded as damages under this section shall be [£10,000].

(4) Where there is a claim for damages under this section for the benefit of both the parents of the deceased, the sum awarded shall be divided equally between them (subject to any deduction falling to be made in respect of costs not recovered from the defendant).

(5) The Lord Chancellor may by order made by statutory instrument, subject to annulment in pursuance of a resolution of either House of Parliament, amend this section by varying the sum for the time being specified in subsection (3) above.

2. Persons entitled to bring the action

(1) The action shall be brought by and in the name of the executor or administrator of the **29.41** deceased.

(2) If—

(a) there is no executor or administrator of the deceased, or

(b) no action is brought within six months after the death by and in the name of an executor or administrator of the deceased, the action may be brought by and in the name of all or any of the persons for whose benefit an executor or administrator could have brought it.

(3) Not more than one action shall lie for and in respect of the same subject matter of complaint.

(4) The plaintiff in the action shall be required to deliver to the defendant or his solicitor full particulars of the persons for whom and on whose behalf the action is brought and of the nature of the claim in respect of which damages are sought to be recovered.

3. Assessment of damages

29.42 (1) In the action such damages, other than damages for bereavement, may be awarded as are proportioned to the injury resulting from the death to the dependants respectively.

(2) After deducting the costs not recovered from the defendant any amount recovered otherwise than as damages for bereavement shall be divided among the dependants in such shares as may be directed.

(3) In an action under this Act where there fall to be assessed damages payable to a widow in respect of the death of her husband there shall not be taken into account the re-marriage of the widow or her prospects of re-marriage.

(4) In an action under this Act where there fall to be assessed damages payable to a person who is a dependant by virtue of section 1(3)(b) above in respect of the death of the person with whom the dependant was living as husband or wife there shall be taken into account (together with any other matter that appears to the court to be relevant to the action) the fact that the dependant had no enforceable right to financial support by the deceased as a result of their living together.

(5) If the dependants have incurred funeral expenses in respect of the deceased, damages may be awarded in respect of those expenses.

(6) Money paid into court in satisfaction of a cause of action under this Act may be in one sum without specifying any person's share.

4. Assessment of damages; disregard of benefits

29.43 In assessing damages in respect of a person's death in an action under this Act, benefits which have accrued or will or may accrue to any person from his estate or otherwise as a result of his death shall be disregarded.

5. Contributory negligence

29.44 Where any peson dies as the result partly of his own fault and partly of the fault of any other person or persons, and accordingly if an action were brought for the benefit of the estate under the Law Reform (Miscellaneous Provisions) Act 1934 the damages recoverable would be reduced under section 1(1) of the Law Reform (Contributory Negligence) Act 1945, any damages recoverable in an action under this Act shall be reduced to a proportionate extent.

30

PROVISIONAL DAMAGES

A. Provisional Awards: Basis and Assessment

30.01 The traditional method of compensating a claimant for a chance of future deterioration is to award an additional amount of damages for the chance as part of a single, final lump sum award. The added award is a proportion of the full damages which would compensate for the deterioration, and the proportion is decided according to the likelihood of the deterioration. The reasoning is often not made explicit: the judge simply announces that he has taken into account the risk of deterioration in making his award. On this basis, the assessment of damages will almost always be wrong. If the deterioration is avoided, the claimant has received too much; and if it does happen he has received too little.

30.02 With a provisional award, a lump sum award is assessed on the basis that the feared deterioration will not happen, and the claimant is given the right to return to court to seek an additional award if it does happen. The power to award provisional damages comes from s 32A of the Supreme Court Act 1981 and the similarly worded s 51 of the County Courts Act 1984. The procedure is in CPR Part 41 and its Practice Direction. The power arises when there is 'a chance that at some definite or indefinite time in the future the injured person will, as a result of the act or omission which gave rise to the cause of action, develop some serious disease or suffer some serious deterioration in his physical or mental condition.'

30.03 The typical case for a provisional award is an employee who has contracted asbestosis as a result of exposure to asbestos at work, often many years before. The disease may well be detected while symptoms are minimal and, because of limitation, there can be no delay in bringing a claim. The risks of later developing severe asbestosis, mesothelioma, lung cancer, laryngeal cancer and gastro-intestinal cancer are in such a case severe. These are specific and identifiable risks of developing distinct, new medical conditions.

30.04 By contrast, many orthopaedic injuries affecting the articular surface of a joint bring a risk of progressive future deterioration, usually through the onset of osteoarthritis. In these 'ordinary' and more common cases the courts have been reluctant to abandon the traditional final award which includes an allowance for the risk.

30.05 Sometimes the future deterioration would increase the severity of the injury and the level of injury damages but at the same time would reduce the expectation of life of the claimant and hence reduce the appropriate awards for loss of earnings or nursing care. The statute does not grapple with this issue: certainly the claimant cannot be made to repay any damages from a first award on this basis.

30.06 In practice, provisional awards are not popular with litigants. Except in a clear case such as asbestos exposure, claimants and insurers both usually prefer to bring a claim to an end rather than suffer continuing uncertainty. They do not share their lawyers' fondness for repetitive litigation, or for achieving an award whose technical correctness is intellectually satisfying. Where the feared deterioration would be painful and inconvenient rather than life threatening, claimants often prefer to take the chance of being over-compensated and are willing to run the risk of deterioration for this price. Even where a claim for a provisional award is argued, in only a small proportion of cases is such an award actually made. None the less in a suitable case a claimant's lawyer has a responsibility to discuss the possibility of such an award, and it may well be that if the traditional once-and-for-all approach were rigorously analysed it would be found to undercompensate the majority of those claimants who face a significant risk of late deterioration in their condition.

30.07 Only one application for additional damages can be made in relation to each specified chance of deterioration (CPR r 41.3(2)).

30.08 If a claimant is awarded provisional damages and later dies, a Fatal Accidents Act claim can still be brought in relation to the death but damages received under the first claim must be taken into account (Damages Act 1996, s 3).

30.09 *Thurman v Wiltshire HA* [1998] PIQR Q115   The defendant had failed to detect cervical cancer. Injury damages of £50,000 were awarded, with a provisional award allowing a further claim if there were to be a recurrence of cancer (without limit of time) or specified complications of radiotherapy (within ten years).

Ward v Newalls Insulation [1998] PIQR Q41   The claimant suffered severe **30.10** lung disease as a result of exposure to asbestos. He received an immediate provisional award of £40,000 and could reapply if he developed lung cancer or mesothelioma.

Wilson v Ministry of Defence [1991] 1 All ER 638   Scott Baker J refused to **30.11** make a provisional award to compensate for the risk that an ankle injury might lead to osteoarthritis, holding that the power to make a provisional award is discretionary and 'the section envisages a clear and severable risk rather than a continuing deterioration, as is the typical osteoarthritic picture'.

Molinari v Ministry of Defence [1994] PIQR Q33   A provisional award was **30.12** made and the court discussed, without resolving, the problem that would arise if a deterioration in the claimant's condition, while increasing the injury damages he should receive, at the same time reduced his other heads of damage, for example where a reduced life expectancy reduces the multiplier for care. This might in a strong case be a reason for refusing to make a provisional award.

Cowan v Kitson Insulations Ltd [1992] PIQR Q19   The claimant has the **30.13** right to insist on a single final award if he wishes, and cannot be compelled to seek a provisional award, even if the claim is suitable. If he wishes to have a final award he should not be penalized for his decision.

Pendleton v Stone [2001] EWCA Civ 1881; [2002] 1 WLR 1052   This was **30.14** one of the Fairchild appeals (see *Fairchild v Glenhaven Funeral Services Ltd*), with the difficulty of proving causation of mesothelioma. The Court of Appeal upheld a provisional award, holding that liability issues could be reconsidered if the disease developed on the basis of the evidence then available and the legal principles then applicable.

B. County Courts Act 1984, s 51

PROVISIONAL DAMAGES FOR PERSONAL INJURIES

51. Orders for provisional damages for personal injuries

(1) This section applies to an action for damages for personal injuries in which there is proved **30.15** or admitted to be a chance that at some definite or indefinite time in the future the injured person will, as a result of the act or omission which gave rise to the cause of action, develop some serious disease or suffer some serious deterioration in his physical or mental condition.

(2) Subject to subsection (4), as regards any action for damages to which this section applies in which a judgment is given in the county court, provision may be made by rules of court for enabling the court, in such circumstances as may be prescribed, to award the injured person—

(a) damages assessed on the assumption that the injured person will not develop the disease or suffer the deterioration in his condition; and

(b) further damages at a future date if he develops the disease or suffers the deterioration.

(3) Any rules made by virtue of this section may include such incidental, supplementary and consequential provisions as the rule committee may consider necessary or expedient.

(4) Nothing in this section shall be construed—

(a) as affecting the exercise of any power relating to costs, including any power to make county court rules relating to costs; or

(b) as prejudicing any duty of the court under any enactment or rule of law to reduce or limit the total damages which would have been recoverable apart from any such duty.

(5) In this section 'personal injuries' includes any disease and any impairment of a person's physical or mental condition.

C. CPR Part 41—Provisional Damages

41.1 Application and definitions

30.16 (1) This part applies to proceedings to which SCA s 32A or CCA s 51 applies.

(2) In this Part—

(a) 'SCA s 32A' means section 32A of the Supreme Court Act 1981;

(b) 'CCA s 51' means section 51 of the County Courts Act 1984; and

(c) 'award of provisional damages' means an award of damages for personal injuries under which

(i) damages are assessed on the assumption referred to in SCA s 32A or CCA s 51 that the injured person will not develop the disease or suffer the deterioration; and

(ii) the injured person is entitled to apply for further damages at a future date if he develops the disease or suffers the deterioration.

41.2 Order for an award of provisional damages

(1) The court may make an order for an award of provisional damages if—

(a) the particulars of claim include a claim for provisional damages; and

(b) the court is satisfied that SCA s 32A or CCA s 51 applies.

(Rule 16.4(1)(d) sets out what must be included in the particulars of claim where the claimant is claiming provisional damages)

(2) An order for an award of provisional damages—

(a) must specify the disease or type of deterioration in respect of which an application may be made at a future date;

(b) must specify the period within which such an application may be made; and

(c) may be made in respect of more than one disease or type of deterioration and may, in respect of each disease or type of deterioration, specify a different period within which a subsequent application may be made.

(3) The claimant may make more than one application to extend the period specified under paragraph (2)(b) or (2)(c).

41.3 Application for further damages

(1) The claimant may not make an application for further damages after the end of the period specified under rule 41.2(2), or such period as extended by the court.

(2) Only one application for further damages may be made in respect of each disease or type of deterioration specified in the award of provisional damages.

(3) The claimant must give at least 28 days' written notice to the defendant of his intention to apply for further damages.

(4) If the claimant knows—
   (a) that the defendant is insured in respect of the claim; and
   (b) the identity of the defendant's insurers,

he must also give at least 28 days' written notice to the insurers.

(5) Within 21 days after the end of the 28 day notice period referred to in paragraphs (3) and (4), the claimant must apply for directions.

(6) The rules in Part 25 about the making of an interim payment apply where an application is made under this rule.

D. PD 41—Provisional Damages

This Practice Direction supplements CPR Part 41 **30.17**

Claims for provisional damages

1.1 CPR Part 16 and the practice direction which supplements it set out information which must be included in the particulars of claim if a claim for provisional damages is made.

Judgment for an award of provisional damages

2.1 When giving judgment at trial the judge will: **30.18**
   (1) specify the disease or type of deterioration, or diseases or types of deterioration, which
      (a) for the purpose of the award of immediate damages it has been assumed will not occur, and
      (b) will entitle the claimant to further damages if it or they do occur at a future date,
   (2) give an award of immediate damages,
   (3) specify the period or periods within which an application for further damages may be made in respect of each disease or type of deterioration, and
   (4) direct what documents are to be filed and preserved as the case file in support of any application for further damages.

2.2 The claimant may make an application or applications to extend the periods referred to in paragraph 2.1(3) above.

2.3 A period specified under paragraph 2.1(3) may be expressed as being for the duration of the life of the claimant.

2.4 The documents to be preserved as the case file ('the case file documents') referred to in paragraph 2.1(4) will be set out in a schedule to the judgment as entered.

2.5 Causation of any further damages within the scope of the order shall be determined when any application for further damages is made.

2.6 A form for a provisional damages judgment is set out in the Annex to this practice direction.

The case file

3.1 The case file documents must be preserved until the expiry of the period or periods **30.19** specified or of any extension of them.

3.2 The case file documents will normally include:
   (1) the judgment as entered,
   (2) the statements of case,
   (3) a transcript of the judge's oral judgment,
   (4) all medical reports relied on, and

(5) a transcript of any parts of the claimant's own evidence which the judge considers necessary.

3.3 The associate/court clerk will:

(1) ensure that the case file documents are provided by the parties where necessary and filed on the court file,

(2) endorse the court file

(a) to the effect that it contains the case file documents, and

(b) with the period during which the case file documents must be preserved, and

(3) preserve the case file documents in the court office where the proceedings took place.

3.4 Any subsequent order:

(1) extending the period within which an application for further damages may be made, or

(2) of the Court of Appeal discharging or varying the provisions of the original judgment or of any subsequent order under sub-paragraph (1) above,

will become one of the case file documents and must be preserved accordingly and any variation of the period within which an application for further damages may be made should be endorsed on the court file containing the case file documents.

3.5 On an application to extend the periods referred to in paragraph 2.1(3) above a current medical report should be filed.

3.6 Legal representatives are reminded that it is their duty to preserve their own case file.

Consent orders

30.20 4.1 An application to give effect to a consent order for provisional damages should be made in accordance with CPR Part 23. If the claimant is a child or patient the approval of the court must also be sought and the application for approval will normally be dealt with at a hearing.

4.2 The order should be in the form of a consent judgment and should contain;

(1) the matters set out in paragraph 2.1(1) to (3) above, and

(2) a direction as to the documents to be preserved as the case file documents, which will normally be

(a) the consent judgment,

(b) any statements of case,

(c) an agreed statement of facts, and

(d) any agreed medical report(s).

4.3 The claimant or his legal representative must lodge the case file documents in the court office where the proceedings are taking place for inclusion in the court file. The court file should be endorsed as in paragraph 3.3(2) above, and the case file documents preserved as in paragraph 13(3) above.

Default judgment

30.21 5.1 Where a defendant:

(1) fails to file an acknowledgment of service in accordance with CPR Part 10, and

(2) fails to file a defence in accordance with CPR Part 15, within the time specified for doing so, the claimant may not, unless he abandons his claim for provisional damages, enter judgment in default but should make an application in accordance with CPR Part 23 for directions.

5.2 The Master or district judge will normally direct the following issues to be decided:

(1) whether the claim is an appropriate one for an award of provisional damages and if so, on what terms, and

(2) the amount of immediate damages.

5.3 If the judge makes an award of provisional damages, the provisions of paragraph 3 above apply.

ANNEX   EXAMPLE OF AN AWARD OF PROVISIONAL DAMAGES AFTER TRIAL   **30.22**

TITLE OF PROCEEDINGS

THIS CLAIM having been tried before [*title and name of judge*] without a jury at [the Royal Courts of Justice *or as may be*] and [*title and name of judge*] having ordered that judgment as set out below be entered for the claimant

IT IS ORDERED:

(1) that the defendant pay the claimant by way of immediate damages the sum of £ .... (being (i) £ .... for special damages and £ .... [agreed interest] [interest at the rate of .... from .... to .... (ii) £........................... for general damages and £ .... [agreed interest] [interest at the rate of 2% from .... to ....] and (iii) £........................... for loss of future earnings and/or earning capacity) on the assumption that the claimant would not at a future date as a result of the act or omission giving rise to the claim develop the following disease/type of deterioration namely [*set out disease or type of deterioration*]

(2) that if the claimant at a further date does develop that [disease] [type of deterioration] he should be entitled to apply for further damages provided that the application is made on or before [*set out period*]

(3) that the documents set out in the schedule to this order be filed on the court file and preserved as the case file until the expiry of the period set out in paragraph (2) above or of any extension of that period which has been ordered

(4) (costs)

SCHEDULE

(*list documents referred to in paragraph (3)*)

31

STRUCTURED SETTLEMENTS

A. Requirements for a Structured Settlement

It has been explained in Chapter 23 on multipliers how the court will usually **31.01** calculate a single lump sum award of damages to provide compensation to the claimant for the future losses and expenses that result from his injuries over the rest of his life. A conventional award of this kind gives parties the benefits of certainty and finality, but the claimant must then manage his damages so as to meet all of his needs, and runs the risk of finding that his funds have run out if the performance of his investments is disappointing, or if he survives longer than the expectation of life that was assumed when the damages were assessed.

A structured settlement is an arrangement in which a substantial part of **31.02** the claimant's lump sum award is exchanged for an annuity purchased by the defendant which provides the claimant with a guaranteed income for life.

The income from the annuity is free of tax and is disregarded in assessing **31.03** entitlement to means tested state benefits. It should in theory be possible for the claimant to receive a higher income than the investment return on an equivalent lump sum of damages, at a lower cost to the defendant, so that both sides gain from the tax benefit. In addition the claimant has the security of knowing that the income will continue for his lifetime and the funds will not run out.

Hitherto, structured settlements had only been possible by agreement. The **31.04** usual practice is for the lump sum award on a conventional basis to be agreed or decided by the court, and then for the parties to take some time to see whether suitable terms for a structured settlement can be negotiated. Specialist expert financial advice is essential. The structure can be based on seeing what annuity is available for the claimant after meeting the immediate capital need for expenditure on, for example, accommodation and equipment. Alternatively the structure can be based on assessing the income need of the claimant to meet living expenses and the cost of care, and finding what proportion of the total sum will be required to meet this need. Investment decisions then have to be made about the kind of funding and the kind of protection against inflation that is appropriate.

31.05 Unfortunately, most of the insurers have withdrawn from the market for structured settlements, leaving it very difficult for them in practice to be arranged, except for claims in which the National Health Service Litigation Authority (NHSLA) is involved.

31.06 The collapse in the insurance market has ironically come at the same time as two important recent changes have been introduced with the aim of encouraging the greater use of structured settlements. First, by amendment to PD 40C and PD 21 the rules now require that the possibility of making a structured settlement should be considered in every case in which the value of the claim for future loss is more than £500,000. Secondly, the Courts Act 2003, when in force, amends the Damages Act 1996 and the Income and Corporation Taxes Act 1988 so as to give the court the power to order periodical payments, effectively a structured settlement, even against the wishes of the parties. The amended provisions are impracticable, since the new s 2(3) of the 1996 Act provides that a court may not make an order for periodical payments unless satisfied that the continuity of payment under the order is reasonably secure, and this requires the availability of annuities on a similar basis to structured settlements. Since there are no insurers in the market to any significant extent, it is unlikely that either party will be able to demonstrate adequate security for future periodical payments under current market conditions. There will also be considerable difficulty about the extent to which the rate of periodical payments should be variable, the amendments being based on the limited power to take account of deterioration or improvement in the claimant's condition in terms that are similar to the conditions for a provisional damages award.

31.07 Under the Social Security Amendment (Personal Injury Payments) Regulations 2002 income from an annuity when there is a structured settlement, like income from a personal injury trust, will not affect the entitlement of the claimant to receive income support. This reverses the decision of the Court of Appeal in *B (A Child) v Secretary of State for Social Security* [2001] EWCA Civ 498; [2001] 1 WLR 1404.

B. PD 40C—Structured Settlements

Nature of structured settlement

1.1 A structured settlement is an order or agreement in settlement of a claim which includes, **31.08**
or consists of, payment by instalments over a specified period which may be for the remainder of
the claimant's life. The payments are either funded by an annuity from an insurance company
or, where the party paying is a government body, by payments direct from that body.

1.2 The part of such a settlement which is to be paid by periodical payments attracts tax
benefits and statutory guarantees of payment if entered into in accordance with the Damages Act
1996 and Income and Corporation Taxes Act 1988.

Considering the issue of a structured settlement

2.1 Parties should raise the question of a structured settlement in respect of future loss with **31.09**
the court during case management in every case where future loss is likely to equal or exceed
£500,000, and in any other case where a structured settlement might be appropriate. In addition,
the court may explore the issue of its own initiative.

2.2 In any such case, the reasonable cost of:
(1) financial advice from an independent financial adviser or accountant; and
(2) any reasonably necessary advice from a party's medical and legal advisers,
will be regarded as a cost in the litigation. Accordingly, those costs will be subject to general
rules on assessment of costs. To guard against the possibility of compromise of the necessary
impartiality, financial advice should not involve any implicit or explicit recommendation that the
adviser or his firm should be involved in future financial management on behalf of the claimant. It
should and in the case of a child or patient must be provided on a fee-paying basis, and should not
be dependent upon the receipt of a commission if that advice is followed. There is, however, no
bar to any adviser subsequently being involved in arranging a structured settlement or managing
any funds in consequence of the advice given.

2.3 This paragraph applies where the claimant is of full age and capacity. Where a judge has
found in favour of the claimant at trial and the claimant wishes and the defendant is prepared to
consider entering a structured settlement, the claimant or his legal representative should ask the
judge:
(1) not to enter judgment;
(2) to state the award to which he has found the claimant to be entitled, either by:
(a) identifying a lump sum consisting of the total amount of damages which in accordance with his judgment should be awarded; or
(b) identifying the annual amount of any recurring losses which it is anticipated will
continue for a future indefinite period separately from the balance of the award, stating the lump
sum amount of the balance of that award; and
(3) for an adjournment:
(a) for the purposes of drawing up a structured settlement; or
(b) where advice has not previously been sought, to enable advice to be sought as to
whether a structured settlement should be entered into.

2.4 In every case there is a claim in respect of a child or patient, the parties or their representatives must put before the court advice as to the general desirability and appropriateness of the
claimant entering into a structured settlement. Such advice must consist of or include the financial advice referred to at para. 2.2 above, which must consider the specific matters identified at
para. 5 below.

Consent order for a structured settlement

31.10   3.1 Where a claim settles before trial, an application should be made in accordance with Part 23 for the consent order embodying the structured settlement to be made, and for the approval of the structured settlement where the claimant is a child or patient.

3.2 If the claimant is not a child or patient, the consent order may be approved without a hearing.

Approval hearings

31.11   4.1 The annuity rate applicable to a structured settlement may remain available only for a short time. Therefore where a hearing is required, immediately on the issue of his application notice, the claimant or his legal representative should seek an early date for the hearing, being a date before the expiry of any period within which acceptance of that annuity rate is permitted.

4.2 For the purpose of such a hearing the following documents and evidence must be filed not later than midday on the day before the hearing:
    (1) counsel's or legal representative's opinion, together with the report of a financial adviser (as referred to in paragraph 2.2 above), considering:
        (a) the general desirability of entering into a structured settlement; and
        (b) the specific matters set out in paragraph 5 below;
    (2) a draft of the proposed agreement;
    (3) details of any assets available to the claimant other than the value of his claim; and
    (4) where the claimant is a patient, the approval or consent of the Court of Protection.

Contents of written advice

31.12   5 A written advice or report filed in accordance with para. 4.2(1) should specifically address the following matters:
    (1) whether or not the sum payable in compensation is sufficient to fund periodical payments, which will fully meet the anticipated annual and recurrent losses occasioned by the injury. This will in particular need to be considered where the damages are reduced by reference to factors such as contributory fault;
    (2) the balance between immediate payment by way of capital sum and subsequent periodical payments. In particular, where there is continuing expense of care, the amount of the periodic payments should aim to cover the anticipated costs, unless there is good reason to depart from this benchmark, whilst leaving an appropriate sum (whatever is reasonable, depending upon the circumstances of the case) to allow for unexpected contingencies. A proposal that the sums payable should in either respect be less than these benchmarks will require justification, though either may, of course, be greater. An example of this would be where periodical payments or a lump sum cover some or all of the claimant's probable loss of earned income. Another example would be where a lump sum includes payments in respect of pre-trial losses;
    (3) the balance between any of the different forms of structure and the reasons for striking that balance;
    (4) whether or not the amount of periodical payments to be made should be increased in steps, so that the payments would increase on the anticipated date that certain events with important financial consequences may occur. In any such case, the structured settlement should specify the event that will give rise to the proposed step increase. Where possible, the structured settlement should also specify the specific date of and the amount of the proposed step increase. Over-complication is to be avoided. Examples of events that may give rise to a step increase are where:
        (a) the child/patient becomes unable to care for him or herself independently in respect of:

> (i) mobility;
> (ii) toileting and bathing;
> (iii) dressing;

(b) gratuitous carers can no longer continue to provide care;

(c) the child/patient is able to work to some extent at the date of assessment of damages but later becomes unable to continue to work;

(d) some anticipated long-term therapy becomes necessary, at cost;

(e) the claimant is due to leave primary for secondary, or secondary for tertiary education;

(f) accommodation needs are anticipated to increase at a future date; and

(g) (in respect of income loss) it is anticipated that the claimant would have received a promotional increase in pay;

(5) whether there is sufficient flexbility within the balance between capital and income, and the nature of funding, to provide for anticipated needs throughout the claimant's lifetime; and

(6) the extent to which any arrangement for periodical payments may affect the ability of the claimant to receive income-related benefits otherwise provided at no or low cost by the State or by a relevant local authority.

Consideration of other means of meeting future income needs

31.13 6 Advisers should consider means of meeting future income needs other than or in addition to a structured settlement where these may be more appropriate. Such means may include an award of provisional damages, an indemnity, or an appropriate form of trust.

Obtaining Court of Protection approval

31.14 7.1 To obtain the approval of the Court of Protection the claimant's legal representative should lodge the documents and information set out in the above paragraphs together with a copy of the claim form and any statement of case filed in the proceedings in the Public Guardianship Office, Archway Tower, 2 Junction Road, London N19 5SZ by midday on the fourth day before the hearing.

7.2 If an application for the appointment of a receiver by the Court of Protection has not already been made:

(1) two copies of the application seeking his appointment (form CP1);

(2) a certificate of family and property (form CP5); and

(3) a medical certificate (form CP3),

should be lodged at the same time as the documents and information mentioned in paragraph 4.2 above. Forms CP1, CP3 and CP5 may be obtained from the address set out in paragraph 7.1.

Draft orders

31.15 8.1 Wherever possible a draft order should also be filed at the same time as the documents in paragraph 4.2 above.

8.2 Examples of structured settlement orders are set out in an annex to this practice direction. They may be adapted for use as individual circumstances require.

Obtaining payment out of money in court

31.16 9 Where it is necessary to obtain immediate payment out of money in court on the order being made, the claimant's legal representative should:

(1) notify the court office the day before the hearing so that the court is aware of the urgency; and

(2) bring to the hearing a completed Court Funds Office form 200 for authentication by the court upon the order being made.

ANNEX

Part 1: Structured Settlement Order

31.17 (Order to settle for a conventional sum and for an adjournment to seek advice on the formulation of a structured settlement)

Title of claim

UPON HEARING [Counsel] [Solicitor] for the Claimant and [Counsel] [Solicitor] for the Defendant

AND UPON the Defendant by [Counsel] [Solicitor] having undertaken to keep open an offer of £____ in full and final settlement of the claim and the Claimant having undertaken to limit the claim to £____

[**AND UPON** the Claimant's Solicitors' undertaking to instruct appropriate advisers to advise upon a structured settlement and to use their best endeavours promptly to make proposals to the Defendant's Solicitors as to the most equitable formulation of a structured settlement and after to seek (further directions/approval) from the Court if necessary) *(delete as required)*

IT IS ORDERED that this claim be adjourned [until *(date)*] [with permission to both parties to apply in respect of the further hearing relating to further directions providing for a structured settlement as undertaken by the Claimant's Solicitors] and that these proceedings be reserved to the *(trial judge)* unless otherwise ordered

AND IT IS ORDERED that the costs of these proceedings together with the costs relating to any proposal for a structured settlement be *(as ordered)*

Part 2: Structured Settlement Order

31.18 (Order giving effect to and approval of a structured settlement)

Title of Claim

UPON HEARING [Counsel] [Solicitor] for the Claimant and [Counsel] [Solicitor] for the Defendant and upon reading the advice(s) obtained on behalf of the Claimant as to the desirability and appropriateness of the terms in the Schedule to this Order ('the proposed terms') *(identifying the advice(s))*

AND UPON being satisfied that the terms of the Practice Direction supplementing CPR Part 40 in respect of structured settlements have been complied with

AND the Claimant and Defendant having agreed to the proposed terms

AND UPON the Judge having approved the terms of the draft Minute of Order, the Agreement and the Schedule to this Order

AND UPON the Claimant and the *(insurer/government department/self-funding body)* undertaking to execute the agreement this day

BY CONSENT

IT IS ORDERED

(1) that of the sum of £____ *(total sum in court)* now in Court standing to the credit of this claim the sum of £____ be paid out to *(insurers/payee, or as appropriate)* on behalf of the Defendant to provide payments as specified in the Payment Schedule to this Order

(2) (other relevant orders)

(3) that all further proceedings in this claim be stayed save for the purpose of carrying the terms into effect

(4) that the parties have permission to apply for the purpose of carrying the terms into effect.

(Attach proposed terms and set out any other terms of the settlement) **31.19**

C. Income and Corporation Taxes Act 1988, ss 329A and 329B

329AA. Personal injury damages in the form of periodical payments

(1) Where—

(a) an agreement is made settling a claim or action for damages for personal injury on terms   **31.20**
whereby the damages are to consist wholly or partly of periodical payments; or

(b) a court awarding damages for personal injury makes an order incorporating such terms,
the payments shall not for the purposes or income tax be regarded as the income of any of the
persons mentioned in subsection (2) below and accordingly shall be paid without any deduction
under section 348(1)(b) or 349(1).

(2) The persons referred to in subsection (1) above are—

(a) the person ('A') entitled to the damages under the agreement or order;

(b) any person who, whether in pursuance of the agreement or order or otherwise, receives
the payments or any of them on behalf of A;

(c) any trustee who, whether in pursuance of the agreement or order or otherwise, receives
the payments or any of them on trust for the benefit of A under a trust under which A is during
his lifetime the sole beneficiary.

(3) The periodical payments referred to in subsection (1) above, or any of them, may, if the
agreement or order mentioned in that subsection or a subsequent agreement so provides, consist
of payments under one or more annuities purchased or provided for, or for the benefit of, A by the
person by whom the payments would otherwise fall to he made.

(4) Sums paid to, or for the benefit of, A by a trustee or trustees shall not be regarded as his
income for the purposes of income tax if made out of payments which by virtue of this section are
not to be regarded for those purposes as income of the trustee or trustees.

(5) In this section 'personal injury' includes any disease and any impairment of a person's
physical or mental condition.

(6) For the purposes of this section a claim or action for personal injury includes—

(a) such a claim or action brought by virtue of the Law Reform '(Miscellaneous Provisions)
Act 1934;

(b) such a claim or action brought by virtue of the Law Reform (Miscellaneous Provisions)
Act (Northern Ireland) 1937;

(c) such a claim or action brought by virtue of the Damages (Scotland) Act 1976;

(d) a claim or action brought by virtue of the Fatal Accidents Act 1976:

(e) a claim or action brought by virtue of the Fatal Accidents (Northern Ireland) Order
1977.

(7) In relation to such an order as is mentioned in paragraph (b) of subsection (1) above
'damages' includes an interim payment which the court, by virtue of rules of court in that behalf,
orders the defendant to make to the plaintiff and where, without such an order, the defendant
agrees to make a payment on account of the damages that may be awarded against him in such an
action as is mentioned in paragraph (a) of that subsection, that paragraph shall apply to the
payment and the agreement as it applies to damages and to such an agreement as is there
mentioned.

(8) *(Applies to Scotland only.)*

329AB. Compensation for personal injury under statutory or other schemes

31.21   (1) Section 329AA applies to annuity payments under an award of compensation made under the Criminal Injuries Compensation Scheme as it applies to payments of damages in that form under such an agreement or order as is mentioned in subsection (1) of that section.

(2) In subsection (1) above 'the Criminal Injuries Compensation Scheme' means—

(a) the scheme established by arrangements made under the Criminal Injuries Compensation Act 1995; or

(b) arrangements made by the Secretary of State for compensation for criminal injuries and in operation before the commencement of that scheme.

(3) If it appears to the Treasury that any other scheme or arrangement, whether established by statute or otherwise, makes provision for the making of periodical payments by way of compensation for personal injury within the meaning of section 329AA, the Treasury may by order apply that section to those payments with such modifications as the Treasury consider necessary.

D. Damages Act 1996, ss 2, 4, 5–7

2. Consent orders for periodical payments

31.22   (1) A court awarding damages in an action for personal injury may, with the consent of the parties, make an order under which the damages are wholly or partly to take the form of periodical payments.

(2) In this section 'damages' includes an interim payment which the court, by virtue of rules of court on that behalf, orders the defendant to make to the plaintiff (or, in the application of this section to Scotland, the defender to make to the pursuer).

(3) This section is without prejudice to any powers exercisable apart from this section.

4. Enhanced protection for structured settlement annuitants

31.23   (1) In relation to an annuity purchased for a person pursuant to a structured settlement from an authorised insurance company within the meaning of the Policyholders Protection Act 1975 (and in respect of which that person as annuitant is accordingly the policyholder for the purposes of that Act) sections 10 and 11 of that Act (protection in the event of liquidation of the insurer) shall have effect as if any reference to ninety per cent of the amount of the liability, of any future benefit or of the value attributed to the policy were a reference to the full amount of the liability, benefit or value.

(2) Those sections shall also have effect as mentioned in subsection (1) above in ruation to an annuity purchased from an authorised insurance company within the meaning of the 1975 Act pursuant to any order incorporating terms corresponding to those of a structured settlement which a court makes when awarding damages for personal injury.

(3) Those sections shall also have effect as mentioned in subsection (1) above in relation to an annuity purchased from or otherwise provided by an authorised insurance company within the meaning of the 1975 Act pursuant to terms corresponding to those of a structured settlement contained in an agreement made by—

(a) the Motor Insurers' Bureau; or

(b) a Domestic Regulations Insurer, in respect of damages for personal injury which the Bureau or Insurer undertakes to pay in satisfaction of a claim or action against an uninsured driver.

(4) In subsection (3) above 'the Motor Insurers' Bureau' means the company of that name incorporated on 14th June 1946 under the Companies Act 1929 and 'a Domestic Regulations

Insurer' has the meaning given in the Bureau's Domestic Regulations.

(5) This section applies if the liquidation of the authorised insurance company begins (within the meaning of the 1975 Act) after the coming into force of this section irrespective of when the annuity was purchased or provided.

5. Meaning of structured settlement

(1) In section 4 above a 'structured settlement' means an agreement settling a claim or action **31.24** for damages for personal injury on terms whereby—

(a) the damages are to consist wholly or partly of periodical payments; and

(b) the person to whom the payments are to be made is to receive them as the annuitant under one or more annuities purchased for him by the person against whom the claim or action is brought or, if he is insured against the claim, by his insurer.

(2) The periodical payments may be for the life of the claimant, for a specified period or of a specified number or minimum number or include payments of more than one of those descriptions.

(3) The amounts of the periodical payments (which need not be at a uniform rate or payable at uniform intervals) may be—

(a) specified in the agreement, with or without provision for increases of specified amounts or percentages; or

(b) subject to adjustment in a specified manner so as to preserve their real value; or

(c) partly specified as mentioned in paragraph (a) above and partly subject to adjustment as mentioned in paragraph (b) above.

(4) The annuity or annuities must be such as to provide the annuitant with sums which as to amount and time of payment correspond to the periodical payments described in the agreement.

(5) Payments in respect of the annuity or annuities may be received on behalf of the annuitant by another person or received and held on trust for his benefit under a trust of which he is, during his lifetime, the sole beneficiary.

(6) The Lord Chancellor may by an order made by statutory instrument provide that there shall for the purposes of this section be treated as an insurer any body specified in the order, being a body which, though not an insurer, appears to him to fulfil corresponding functions in relation to damages for personal injury claimed or awarded against persons of any class or description, and the reference in subsection (1)(b) above to a person being insured against the claim and his insurer shall be construed accordingly.

(7) In the application of subsection (6) above to Scotland for the reference to the Lord Chancellor there shall be substituted a reference to the Secretary of State.

(8) Where—

(a) an agreement is made settling a claim or action for damages for personal injury on terms whereby the damages are to consist wholly or partly of periodical payments;

(b) the person against whom the claim or action is brought (or, if he is insured against the claim, his insurer) purchases one or more annuities; and

(c) a subsequent agreement is made under which the annuity is, or the annuities are, assigned in favour of the person entitled to the payments (so as to secure that from a future date he receives the payments as the annuitant under the annuity or annuities), then, for the purposes of section 4 above, the agreement settling the claim or action shall be treated as a structured settlement and any such annuity assigned in favour of that person shall be treated as an annuity purchased for him pursuant to the settlement.

(9) Subsections (2) to (7) above shall apply to an agreement to which subsection (8) above applies as they apply to a structured settlement as defined in subsection (1) above (the reference in subsection (6) to subsection (1)(b) being read as a reference to subsection (8)(b)).

6. Guarantees for public sector settlements

31.25   (1) This section applies where—

(a) a claim or action for damages for personal injury is settled on terms corresponding to those of a structured settlement as defined in section 5 above except that the person to whom the payments are to be made is not to receive them as mentioned in subsection (1)(b) of that section; or

(b) a court awarding damages for personal injury makes an order incorporating such terms.

(2) If it appears to a Minister of the Crown that the payments are to be made by a body in relation to which he has, by virtue of this section, power to do so, he may guarantee the payments to be made under the agreement or order.

(3) The bodies in relation to which a Minister may give such a guarantee shall, subject to subsection (4) below, be such bodies as are designated in relation to the relevant government department by guidelines agreed upon between that department and the Treasury.

(4) A guarantee purporting to be given by a Minister under this section shall not be invalidated by any failure on his part to act in accordance with such guidelines as are mentioned in subsection (3) above.

(5) A guarantee under this section shall be given on such terms as the Minister concerned may determine but those terms shall in every case require the body in question to reimburse the Minister, with interest, for any sums paid by him in fulfilment of the guarantee.

7. Interpretation

31.26   (1) Subject to subsection (2) below, in this Act 'personal injury' includes any disease and any impairment of a person's physical or mental condition and references to a claim or action for personal injury include references to such a claim or action brought by virtue of the Law Reform (Miscellaneous Provisions) Act 1934 and to a claim or action brought by virtue of the Fatal Accidents Act 1976.

E. Courts Act 2003, ss 100 and 101

DAMAGES

100. Periodical payments

31.27   (1) For section 2 of the Damages Act 1996 (c. 48) (periodical payments by consent) substitute—

'2. Periodical payments

(1) A court awarding damages for future pecuniary loss in respect of personal injury—

(a) may order that the damages are wholly or partly to take the form of periodical payments, and

(b) shall consider whether to make that order.

(2) A court awarding other damages in respect of personal injury may, if the parties consent, order that the damages are wholly or partly to take the form of periodical payments.

(3) A court may not make an order for periodical payments unless satisfied that the continuity of payment under the order is reasonably secure.

(4) For the purpose of subsection (3) the continuity of payment under an order is reasonably secure if—

(a) it is protected by a guarantee given under section 6 of or the Schedule to this Act,

(b) it is protected by a scheme under section 213 of the Financial Services and Markets Act 2000 (compensation) (whether or not as modified by section 4 of this Act), or

(c) the source of payment is a government or health service body.

(5) An order for periodical payments may include provision—

(a) requiring the party responsible for the payments to use a method (selected or to be selected by him) under which the continuity of payment is reasonably secure by virtue of subsection (4);

(b) about how the payments are to be made, if not by a method under which the continuity of payment is reasonably secure by virtue of subsection (4);

(c) requiring the party responsible for the payments to take specified action to secure continuity of payment, where continuity is not reasonably secure by virtue of subsection (4);

(d) enabling a party to apply for a variation of provision included under paragraph (a), (b) or (c).

(6) Where a person has a right to receive payments under an order for periodical payments, or where an arrangement is entered into in satisfaction of an order which gives a person a right to receive periodical payments, that person's right under the order or arrangement may not be assigned or charged without the approval of the court which made the order; and—

(a) a court shall not approve an assignment or charge unless satisfied that special circumstances make it necessary, and

(b) a purported assignment or charge, or agreement to assign or charge, is void unless approved by the court.

(7) Where an order is made for periodical payments, an alteration of the method by which the payments are made shall be treated as a breach of the order (whether or not the method was specified under subsection (5)(b)) unless—

(a) the court which made the order declares its satisfaction that the continuity of payment under the new method is reasonably secure,

(b) the new method is protected by a guarantee given under section 6 of or the Schedule to this Act,

(c) the new method is protected by a scheme under section 213 of the Financial Services and Markets Act 2000 (compensation) (whether or not as modified by section 4 of this Act), or

(d) the source of payment under the new method is a government or health service body.

(8) An order for periodical payments shall be treated as providing for the amount of payments to vary by reference to the retail prices index (within the meaning of section 833(2) of the Income and Corporation Taxes Act 1988) at such times, and in such a manner, as may be determined by or in accordance with Civil Procedure Rules.

(9) But an order for periodical payments may include provision—

(a) disapplying subsection (8), or

(b) modifying the effect of subsection (8).

2A. Periodical payments: supplementary

(1) Civil Procedure Rules may require a court to take specified matters into account in considering—

(a) whether to order periodical payments;

(b) the security of the continuity of payment;

(c) whether to approve an assignment or charge.

(2) For the purposes of section 2(4)(c) and (7)(d) "government or health service body" means a body designated as a government body or a health service body by order made by the Lord Chancellor.

(3) An order under subsection (2)—

(a) shall be made by statutory instrument, and

(b) shall be subject to annulment in pursuance of a resolution of either House of Parliament.

(4) Section 2(6) is without prejudice to a person's power to assign a right to the scheme manager established under section 212 of the Financial Services and Markets Act 2000.

(5) In section 2 "damages" includes an interim payment which a court orders a defendant to make to a claimant.

(6) In the application of this section to Northern Ireland—

(a) a reference to Civil Procedure Rules shall be taken as a reference to rules of court, and

(b) a reference to a claimant shall be taken as a reference to a plaintiff.

(7) Section 2 is without prejudice to any power exercisable apart from that section.

2B. Variation of orders and settlements

(1) The Lord Chancellor may by order enable a court which has made an order for periodical payments to vary the order in specified circumstances (otherwise than in accordance with section 2(5)(d)).

(2) The Lord Chancellor may by order enable a court in specified circumstances to vary the terms on which a claim or action for damages for personal injury is settled by agreement between the parties if the agreement—

(a) provides for periodical payments, and

(b) expressly permits a party to apply to a court for variation in those circumstances.

(3) An order under this section may make provision—

(a) which operates wholly or partly by reference to a condition or other term of the court's order or of the agreement;

(b) about the nature of an order which may be made by a court on a variation;

(c) about the matters to be taken into account on considering variation;

(d) of a kind that could be made by Civil Procedure Rules or, in relation to Northern Ireland, rules of court (and which may be expressed to be with or without prejudice to the power to make those rules).

(4) An order under this section may apply (with or without modification) or amend an enactment about provisional or further damages.

(5) An order under this section shall be subject to any order under section 1 of the Courts and Legal Services Act 1990 (allocation between High Court and county courts).

(6) An order under this section—

(a) shall be made by statutory instrument,

(b) may not be made unless the Lord Chancellor has consulted such persons as he thinks appropriate,

(c) may not be made unless a draft has been laid before and approved by resolution of each House of Parliament, and

(d) may include transitional, consequential or incidental provision.

(7) In subsection (4)—

"provisional damages" means damages awarded by virtue of subsection (2)(a) of section 32A of the Supreme Court Act 1981 or section 51 of the County Courts Act 1984 (or, in relation to Northern Ireland, paragraph 10(2)(a) of Schedule 6 to the Administration of Justice Act 1982), and "further damages" means damages awarded by virtue of subsection (2)(b) of either of those sections (or, in relation to Northern Ireland, paragraph 10(2)(b) of Schedule 6 to the Administration of Justice Act 1982).'

(2) In section 329AA of the Income and Corporation Taxes Act 1988 (c. 1) (periodical payments)—

(a) for subsection (1) substitute—

'(1) Periodical payments shall not for the purposes of income tax be regarded as the income of any of the persons mentioned in subsection (2) below (and shall be paid without deduction under section 348(1)(b) or 349(1)).

(1A) In subsection (1) "periodical payments" means periodical payments made pursuant to—

(a) an order of a court in so far as it is made in reliance on section 2 of the Damages Act 1996 (including an order as varied), or

(b) an agreement in so far as it settles a claim or action for damages in respect of personal injury (including an agreement as varied).',

(b) in subsection (3) for 'if the agreement or order mentioned in that subsection or a subsequent agreement so provides,' substitute 'if the order, agreement or undertaking mentioned in subsection (1A), or a varying order, agreement or undertaking, so provides or permits,',

(c) in subsection (6) after 'claim or action for' insert 'damages in respect of',

(d) for subsection (7) substitute—

'(7) For the purposes of subsection (1A) above—

(a) the reference to an order of a court made in reliance on section 2 of the Damages Act 1996 includes an order of a court outside the United Kingdom which is similar to an order made in reliance on that section,

(b) the reference to an agreement settling a claim or action includes a reference to an agreement to make payments on account of damages that may be awarded in a claim or action, and

(c) the reference to an agreement in so far as it settles a claim or action for damages in respect of personal injury also includes a reference to an undertaking given by the Motor Insurers' Bureau (being the company of that name incorporated on 14th June 1946 under the Companies Act 1929), or an Article 75 insurer under the Bureau's Articles of Association, in relation to a claim or action in respect of personal injury.', and

(e) omit subsection (8).

(3) In section 329AB(1) of that Act (statutory compensation) for 'subsection (1)' substitute 'subsection (1A)'.

(4) In this section—

(a) subsection (1) shall extend only to England and Wales and Northern Ireland, and

(b) the remainder shall extend to the whole of the United Kingdom.

101. Periodical payments: security

(1) For sections 4 and 5 of the Damages Act 1996 (c. 48) (enhanced protection for structured settlement annuitant) substitute— **31.28**

'**4. Enhanced protection for periodical payments**

(1) Subsection (2) applies where—

(a) a person has a right to receive periodical payments, and

(b) his right is protected by a scheme under section 213 of the Financial Services and Markets Act 2000 (compensation), but only as to part of the payments.

(2) The protection provided by the scheme shall extend by virtue of this section to the whole of the payments.

(3) Subsection (4) applies where—

(a) one person ("the claimant") has a right to receive periodical payments from another person ("the defendant"),

(b) a third person ("the insurer") is required by or in pursuance of an arrangement entered into with the defendant (whether or not together with other persons and whether before or after the creation of the claimant's right) to make payments in satisfaction of the claimant's right or for the purpose of enabling it to be satisfied, and

(c) the claimant's right to receive the payments would be wholly or partly protected by a scheme under section 213 of the Financial Services and Markets Act 2000 if it arose from an arrangement of the same kind as that mentioned in paragraph (b) but made between the claimant and the insurer.

(4) For the purposes of the scheme under section 213 of that Act—

(a) the claimant shall be treated as having a right to receive the payments from the insurer under an arrangement of the same kind as that mentioned in subsection (3)(b),

(b) the protection under the scheme in respect of those payments shall extend by virtue of this section to the whole of the payments, and

(c) no person other than the claimant shall be entitled to protection under the scheme in respect of the payments.

(5) In this section "periodical payments" means periodical payments made pursuant to—

(a) an order of a court in so far as it is made in reliance on section 2 above (including an order as varied), or

(b) an agreement in so far as it settles a claim or action for damages in respect of personal injury (including an agreement as varied).

(6) In subsection (5)(b) the reference to an agreement in so far as it settles a claim or action for damages in respect of personal injury includes a reference to an undertaking given by the Motor Insurers' Bureau (being the company of that name incorporated on 14th June 1946 under the Companies Act 1929), or an Article 75 insurer under the Bureau's Articles of Association, in relation to a claim or action in respect of personal injury.'

(2) In section 6(1) of the Damages Act 1996 (c. 48) (guarantee for public sector settlement) for the words 'on terms corresponding to those of a structured settlement as defined in section 5 above except that the person to whom the payments are to be made is not to receive them as mentioned in subsection (1)(b) of that section' substitute 'on terms whereby the damages are to consist wholly or partly of periodical payments'.

(3) In paragraph 1(a) of the Schedule to that Act (guarantee by Northern Ireland Department for public sector settlement) for the words 'on terms corresponding to those of a structured settlement as defined in section 5 of this Act except that the person to whom the payments are to be made is not to receive them as mentioned in subsection (1)(b) of that section' substitute 'on terms whereby the damages are to consist wholly or partly of periodical payments'.

32

INVESTMENT ADVICE

A. Investment Advice

A lump sum award of damages to a badly injured claimant will put into his **32.01** hands a large sum of money which is assessed on the basis that it will be sufficient to provide for his needs for the rest of his lifetime. Most claimants will be inexperienced in managing large sums, and will need help. In the management of their day-to-day practical needs, the reasonableness of appointing a case manager has achieved widespread acceptance for claimants who cannot manage their own affairs. This has become a common feature of claims for seriously injured claimants and the award of damages on a multiplier basis for this purpose is often agreed. Why should the same not apply to the need for sound financial advice?

The decisions on this topic (at first instance) exclude a claim for financial advice **32.02** because the loss is too remote and a line has to be drawn somewhere. In *Francis v Bostock, The Times,* 9 November 1985, Russell J refused to make an award for the cost of professional financial advice on the ground that this was consistent with the rule that the court is not concerned with the way the claimant actually chooses to spend his award after it has been paid. In *Cunningham v Camberwell HA* [1992] PIQR Q1, Owen J made an award for the cost of accountancy services which the Court of Protection would require, and in *Anderson v Davis* [1992] PIQR Q87 Rodger Bell QC awarded £400 a year for the cost of professional advice on financial management by analogy with the recovery of Court of Protection fees. However, in *Routledge v Mackenzie* [1994] PIQR Q49, Otton J refused to make any award, adopting the reasoning of *Francis v Bostock*. Now that the statutory rate of return is based on that which can be achieved by investment in Index Linked Government Securities there is even less reason for the adult claimant of full capacity to recover the cost of active investment management, and this potential head of claim is now closed.

32.03   *Page v Plymouth Hospitals NHS Trust* [2004] EWHC 1154; [2004] 3 All ER 367   Liability was admitted in a claim where damages were likely to be at least £2 million. On a preliminary issue on the question whether the claimant was entitled to damages for the projected cost of investment management, Davis J held that the argument amounted to an attack on the discount rate. The Lord Chancellor had taken into account the cost of investment advice when setting the discount rate in 2001, which had the benefit of certainty, and the claimant was not entitled to recover the cost of investment advice and fund management charges.

B. The Court of Protection

32.04   The Court of Protection deals with the property of patients, i.e. those who are incapable of managing their own affairs because of mental incapacity. Its powers are derived from Part VII of the Mental Health Act 1983. Any solicitor acting for a claimant to whom this jurisdiction may apply, particularly a claimant who has suffered brain damage, should at an early stage have addressed the question whether the claimant should proceed with a litigation friend. As soon as there is a prospect of recovering money for the claimant, even by an interim payment, the issue needs to be reconsidered. If the claimant is or may be incapable, contact the Master of the Court of Protection at Public Guardianship Office, Archway Tower, 2 Junction Road, London N19 5SZ (tel: 0845 330 2900; fax: 0870 739 5780; website: www.guardianship.gov.uk). This is imperative: although there is some flexibility about the final arrangements that may be made for managing the claimant's financial affairs, at the first stage neither a solicitor nor a litigation friend may deal with a patient's money without involving the Court of Protection and the appointment of a receiver, unless the sum involved is less than £20,000 and can be dealt with by local court order under CPR PD 21, para 11.2(2). Although CPR Part 21 deals with court approval of settlements, the approval of the Court of Protection may be required in addition.

32.05   An award of more than £30,000 will be transferred to the Court of Protection and the litigation friend will be ordered to apply for the appointment of a receiver. The receiver will carry out the day-to-day administration of the fund under the supervision of the Court of Protection. It can be a burdensome task. The litigation friend is often appointed, but any other relative or friend could be chosen and where the circumstances make it appropriate, either because of the size of the fund, the complexity of the claimant's needs or the lack of any other obviously suitable candidate, a professional person such as a solicitor or accountant may act as receiver and receive professional fees for doing so. A third possibility is the appointment of the Public Trustee as receiver, in which case the fees payable are significantly greater.

The fees of the Court of Protection are recoverable as special damage and should **32.06** be included in a claim. Likewise, if there is to be the appointment of a lay or professional receiver, the costs of the receivership are recoverable. Details of the fees of the Court of Protection are given in Part XVII of the Court of Protection Rules 2001 (as amended), and the Master of the Court of Protection has set out details of fixed costs of receivership that have been agreed with the Law Society in a Practice Note dated 7 December 2002.

Cassel v Riverside HA [1992] PIQR Q168   The Court of Appeal held that an **32.07** apportionment of liability applied to reduce the award for the costs of the Court of Protection as it applied to any head of damages, even though the costs were those applicable to the reduced fund. This principle will apply to any case where there is contributory negligence.

C. Special Needs Trusts

Provided the court gives its approval, it is possible to arrange for the manage- **32.08** ment of a patient's affairs under a trust so that the costs of the Court of Protection are not incurred. There is no technical restriction of such trusts to claims for patients and the cost of necessary advice might be generally recoverable.

A special needs trust is a mechanism under s 96(1)(d) of the Mental Health Act **32.09** 1983 and the Social Security Contributions and Benefits Act 1992 for investing the resources of a patient in such a way that the capital is disregarded for the purpose of assessing entitlement to income support and other means tested benefits. Careful analysis of the financial circumstances of the claimant and the likely purpose of expenditure of the resources of the trust will be required before the Court of Protection will regard a trust as in the patient's best interests. It is usually in cases where the award of damages is relatively small, so that the preservation of an entitlement to benefits is correspondingly more significant, that a special needs trust will be appropriate. A helpful Guidance Note (1996) from the Master of the Court of Protection is reproduced in *Facts & Figures* at H5 p 214. The main advantage of a trust is that the income from the trust will be disregarded in assessing the claimaint's entitlement to means tested benefits: see the discussion of personal injury trusts at **27.43** above.

D. CPR Part 21—Children and Patients, r 21.11

21.11 Control of money recovered by or on behalf of child or patient

32.10 (1) Where in any proceedings—

(a) money is recovered by or on behalf of or for the benefit of a child or patient; or

(b) money paid into court is accepted by or on behalf of a child or patient, the money shall be dealt with in accordance with directions given by the court under this rule and not otherwise.

(2) Directions given under this rule may provide that the money shall be wholly or partly paid into court and invested or otherwise dealt with.

E. PD 21—Children and Patients, paras 6, 8, and 11

Settlement or compromise by or on behalf of a child or patient

32.11 6.1 Where a claim by or on behalf of a child or patient has been dealt with by agreement prior to the start of proceedings and only the approval of the court to the agreement is sought, the claim:

(1) must be made using the Part 8 procedure,

(2) must include a request for approval of the settlement or compromise, and

(3) in addition to the details of the claim, must set out the terms of the settlement or compromise or have attached to it a draft consent order form N292.

6.2 In order to approve the settlement or compromise, the information concerning the claim that the court will require will include:

(1) whether and to what extent the defendant admits liability,

(2) the age and occupation (if any) of the child or patient,

(3) the litigation friend's approval of the proposed settlement or compromise, and

(4) in a personal injury case arising from an accident—

(a) the circumstances of the accident,

(b) any medical reports,

(c) where appropriate, a schedule of any past and future expenses and losses claimed and any other relevant information relating to personal injury as set out in the practice direction which supplements Part 16 (statements of case), and

(d) where considerations of liability are raised—

(i) any evidence or police reports in any criminal proceedings or in an inquest, and

(ii) details of any prosecution brought.

6.3 (1) An opinion on the merits of the settlement or compromise given by counsel or solicitor acting for the child or patient should, except in very clear cases, be obtained.

(2) A copy of the opinion and, unless the instructions on which it was given are sufficiently set out in it, a copy of the instructions, must also be supplied to the court.

6.4 Applications for the approval of a settlement or compromise will normally be heard by a Master or district judge.

(For information about structured settlements see the practice direction on structured settlements supplementing Part 40 (judgments and orders))

(For information about provisional damages claims see Part 41 and PD 41.)

Control of money recovered by or on behalf of a child or patient

8.1 Money recovered or paid into court on behalf of or for the benefit of a child or patient shall **32.12**
be dealt with in accordance with directions of the court under rule 21.11.

8.2 The court:
(1) may direct the money to be paid into the High Court for investment,
(2) may also direct that certain sums be paid direct to the child or patient, his litigation
friend or his legal representative for the immediate benefit of the child or patient or for expenses
incurred on his behalf, and
(3) may direct the applications in respect of the investment of the money be transferred to a
local district registry.

8.3 The master or district judge will consider the general aims to be achieved for the money in
court (the fund) by investment and will give directions as to the type of investment.

8.4 Where a child is also a patient, and likely to remain so on reaching full age, his fund should
be administered as a patient's fund.

8.5 Where a child or patient is legally aided the fund will be subject to a first charge under s 16
of the Legal Aid Act 1988 (the legal aid charge) and an order for the investment of money on the
child or patient's behalf must contain a direction to that effect.

Investment on behalf of a patient

11.1 The Court of Protection is responsible for protecting the property of patients and is **32.13**
given extensive powers to do so under the Mental Health Act 1983. Fees are charged for the
administration of funds by the Court of Protection and these should be provided for in any
settlement.

11.2 Where the sum to be administered is:
(1) over £30,000, the order approving the settlement will contain a direction to the litigation friend to apply to the Court of Protection for the appointment of a receiver, after which the
fund will be transferred to the Court of Protection,
(2) under £20,000, it may be retained in court and invested in the same way as the fund of a
child, or
(3) in intermediate cases the advice of the Master of the Court of Protection should be
sought.

11.3 A form of order transferring the fund to the Court of Protection is set out in practice
form N292.

11.4 In order for the Court Funds Office to release a fund which is subject to the legal aid
charge to the Court of Protection the litigation friend or his legal representative should provide
the appropriate area office of the Legal Aid Board with an undertaking in respect of a sum to cover
their costs, following which the area office will advise the Court Funds Office in writing of that
sum, enabling them to transfer the balance to the Court of Protection on receipt of a CFO form
200 payment schedule authorized by the court.

11.5 The CFO form 200 should be completed and presented to the court where the settlement or trial took place for authorisation, subject to paragraphs 11.6 and 11.7 below.

11.6 Where the settlement took place in the Royal Courts of Justice the CFO form 200 should
be completed and presented for authorisation:
(1) on behalf of a child, in the Masters' Secretary's Office, Room E214, and
(2) on behalf of a patient, in the Action Department, Room E15.

11.7 Where the trial took place in the Royal Courts of Justice the CFO form 200 is completed
and authorised by the court officer.

F. Court of Protection Fees

32.14 See the Court of Protection Rules 2001 (as amended) and **32.06** above.

The rules also provide for various transaction fees too complex to include here. Details are at para 6B-318 of the *White Book*.

33

INTERIM PAYMENTS

A. Entitlement and Requirements for Interim Payments

The process of claiming damages can take a long time. Lawyers are often blamed **33.01** for this. Sometimes the accusation is just, but sometimes there are good reasons for delay. In particular, some injuries require prolonged treatment with an uncertain outcome, and the final extent of recovery cannot be ascertained until some time has passed. Since a final lump sum award cannot be altered subsequently in the light of events, it would be unjust to make a final assessment of damages before the true extent of the injury has become clear. Where liability is not disputed it would be very harsh if the claimant could not obtain some money on account. Lost wages may have to be paid so that the mortgage is kept up-to-date, and funds may be required for medical treatment. None the less, in simple cases where there is no medical reason for delay, the court will often prefer to arrange an early assessment date rather than accept the inevitability of delay and order an interim payment.

In order to be entitled to an interim payment in a personal injury claim the **33.02** claimant must first show that liability has been admitted, or judgment has been entered, or that the claimant would obtain a judgment for substantial damages at trial. The latter is in effect the same test as for summary judgment. Secondly, the claimant must show that the defendant is to be indemnified by an insurer or by the MIB or is a public body. Once these hurdles have been overcome, the court 'may' make an order but 'must not order an interim payment of more than a reasonable proportion of the likely amount of the final judgment'. Although there is power to order the repayment of an award that turns out to have been unduly generous, the likelihood is that the money will have been spent, and the court is always anxious therefore not to risk getting into the position where repayment has to be considered.

33.03 Where there are several defendants, CPR r 25.7(3) is a useful simplification for claimants: as long as all the defendants satisfy the insurer, MIB or public body condition, an order can be made against any of them if the court is satisfied that the claimant would obtain substantial damages against at least one of them.

33.04 Contributory negligence does not stand in the way of a finding of liability so if primary liability is clear, the court may still make an order. However, an allegation of contributory negligence will be relevant to the assessment of the reasonable proportion of the damages claimed that can properly be ordered.

33.05 A payment into court may be referred to by the claimant in making the application (*Fryer v London Transport, The Times*, 4 December 1982 and *Kemp & Kemp* at 12–222). This would disqualify the judge on the application from hearing the final assessment of damages.

33.06 The rules about interim payments are set out in CPR Part 25 (for the relevant part of which, see below). An application must be supported by evidence which must (PD 25B, para 2.1) include details of:

    (a) the sum of money sought;
    (b) the items or matters in respect of which the sum is sought;
    (c) the sum for which final judgment is likely to be given;
    (d) the reasons for believing that the qualifying conditions are satisfied;
    (e) in personal injury claims, details of past and future special damages;
    (f) in fatal claims, details of the dependants and the nature of the claim.

33.07 The second item in the list is an open invitation to claimants to specify the particular needs or expenses on which a payment would be spent. It is often tactful to include any such considerations, but it is not, as a matter of law, necessary to have any particular purpose in mind and in *Stringman v McArdle* [1994] 1 WLR 1653 the Court of Appeal stressed that the court need not be concerned at all with the way in which an adult claimant intends to spend the damages paid.

33.08 *Stringman v McArdle* [1994] 1 WLR 1653 Interim payments having been provided for the purchase of a house, the judge refused a further interim payment for the adaptation of the house holding that the proposals were unreasonably expensive. The Court of Appeal ordered the payment sought, taking account of the fact that any expenditure would be approved by the Court of Protection but also stating that a claimant did not need to prove any particular need in order to be entitled to an interim payment as long as the threshold requirements of liability were satisfied and the amount sought was no more than a reasonable proportion of the damages likely to be recovered.

Campbell v Mylchreest [1999] PIQR Q17   An interim payment was ordered **33.09** which the claimant intended to use to set up arrangements for home visits from hospital. Even though the defendant would contend at trial that this expenditure was not reasonable, and complained that it was premature to make the payment because there would not be a level playing field at trial, there seemed no real doubt that some home visits would be part of the care plan for the claimant's future and the interim payment was upheld.

Bristow v Judd [1993] PIQR Q117   An interim payment will be taken first as **33.10** a payment towards special damages and, if it exceeded the past expenses at the date of payment could then in the discretion of the court be taken to be paid on account of general damages. From the date that the payment was received, it should be taken into account in the calculation of interest, but since interest was a matter of discretion, no hard and fast rule suitable for every case could be laid down.

British and Commonwealth Holdings v Quadrax Holdings [1989] QB 842 **33.11** The Court of Appeal held that it would be inconsistent and wrong to order an interim payment at the same time as giving leave to defend on an application for summary judgment.

B. County Courts Act 1984, s 50

INTERIM PAYMENTS IN PENDING PROCEEDINGS

50. Orders for interim payment

(1) Provision may be made by rules of court for enabling the court, in such circumstances as **33.12** may be prescribed, to make an order requiring a party to the proceedings to make an interim payment of such amount as may be specified in the order, with provision for the payment to be made to such other party to the proceedings as may be so specified or, if the order so provides, by paying it into court.

(2) Any rules of court which make provision in accordance with subsection (1) may include provision for enabling a party to any proceedings who, in pursuance of such an order, has made an interim payment to recover the whole or part of the amount of the payment in such circumstances, and from such other party to the proceedings, as may be determined in accordance with the rules.

(3) Any rules made by virtue of this section may include such incidental, supplementary and consequential provisions as the rule committee may consider necessary or expedient.

(4) Nothing in this section shall be construed as affecting the exercise of any power relating to costs, including any power to make county court rules relating to costs.

(5) In this section 'interim payment', in relation to a party to any proceedings, means a payment on account of any damages, debt or other sum (excluding any costs) which that party may be held liable to pay to or for the benefit of another party to the proceedings if a final judgment or order of the court in the proceedings is given or made in favour of that other

party; and any reference to a party to any proceedings includes a reference to any person who for the purposes of the proceedings acts as next friend or guardian of a party to the proceedings.

C. CPR Part 25—Interim Remedies

25.1 Orders for Interim Remedies

33.13   (1) The court may grant the following interim remedies—
    (k) an order (referred to as an order for interim payment) under rule 25.6 for payment by a defendant on account of any damages, debt or other sum (except costs) which the court may hold the defendant liable to pay;

25.2 Time when an order for an interim remedy may be made

33.14   (1) An order for an interim remedy may be made at any time, including—
    (a) before proceedings are started; and
    (b) after judgment has been given.

(Rule 7.2 provides that proceedings are started when the court issues a claim form)

    (2) However—
    (a) paragraph (1) is subject to any rule, practice direction or other enactment which provides otherwise;
    (b) the court may grant an interim remedy before a claim has been made only if—
        (i) the matter is urgent; or
        (ii) it is otherwise desirable to do so in the interests of justice; and
    (c) unless the court otherwise orders, a defendant may not apply for any of the orders listed in rule 25.1(1) before he has filed either an acknowledgment of service or a defence.

(Part 10 provides for filing an acknowledgment of service and Part 15 for filing a defence)

    (3) Where the court grants an interim remedy before a claim has been commenced, it may give directions requiring a claim to be commenced.

    (4) In particular, the court need not direct that a claim be commenced where the application is made under section 33 of the Supreme Court Act 1981 or section 52 of the County Courts Act 1984 (order for disclosure, inspection etc. before commencement of a claim).

25.3 How to apply for an interim remedy

33.15   (1) The court may grant an interim remedy on an application made without notice if it appears to the court that there are good reasons for not giving notice.

    (2) An application for an interim remedy must be supported by evidence, unless the court orders otherwise.

    (3) If the applicant makes an application without giving notice, the evidence in support of the application must state the reasons why notice has not been given.

(Part 3 lists general powers of the court)

(Part 23 contains general rules about making an application)

25.6 Interim payments—general procedure

33.16   (1) The claimant may not apply for an order for an interim payment before the end of the period for filing an acknowledgment of service applicable to the defendant against whom the application is made.

(Rule 10.3 sets out the period for filing an acknowledgment of service)

(Rule 25.1 (1)(k) defines an interim payment)

(2) The claimant may make more than one application for an order for an interim payment.

(3) A copy of an application notice for an order for an interim payment must—
   (a) be served at least 14 days before the hearing of the application; and
   (b) be supported by evidence.

(4) If the respondent to an application for an order for an interim payment wishes to rely on written evidence at the hearing, he must—
   (a) file the written evidence; and
   (b) serve copies on every other party to the application,

at least 7 days before the hearing of the application.

(5) If the applicant wishes to rely on written evidence in reply, he must—
   (a) file the written evidence; and
   (b) serve a copy on the respondent,

at least 3 days before the hearing of the application.

(6) This rule does not require written evidence—
   (a) to be filed if it has already been filed; or
   (b) to be served on a party on whom it has already been served.

(7) The court may order an interim payment in one sum or in instalments.

(Part 23 contains general rules about applications)

25.7 Interim payments—conditions to be satisfied and matters to be taken into account

(1) The court may make an order for an interim payment only if—   **33.17**
   (a) the defendant against whom the order is sought has admitted liability to pay damages or some other sum of money to the claimant;
   (b) the claimant has obtained judgment against that defendant for damages to be assessed or for a sum of money (other than costs) to be assessed;
   (c) except where paragraph (3) applies, it is satisfied that, if the claim went to trial, the claimant would obtain judgment for a substantial amount of money (other than costs) against the defendant from whom he is seeking an order for an interim payment; or
   (d) the following conditions are satisfied—
      (i) the claimant is seeking an order for possession of land (whether or not any other order is also sought); and
      (ii) the court is satisfied that, if the case went to trial, the defendant would be held liable (even if the claim for possession fails) to pay the claimant a sum of money for the defendant's occupation and use of the land while the claim for possession was pending.

(2) In addition, in a claim for personal injuries the court may make an order for an interim payment of damages only if—
   (a) the defendant is insured in respect of the claim;
   (b) the defendant's liability will be met by—
      (i) an insurer under section 151 of the Road Traffic Act 1988; or
      (ii) an insurer acting under the Motor Insurers Bureau Agreement, or the Motor Insurers Bureau where it is acting itself; or
   (c) the defendant is a public body.

(3) In a claim for personal injuries where there are two or more defendants, the court may make an order for the interim payment of damages against any defendant if—

(a) it is satisfied that, if the claim went to trial, the claimant would obtain judgment for substantial damages against at least one of the defendants (even if the court has not yet determined which of them is liable); and

(b) paragraph (2) is satisfied in relation to each of the defendants.

(4) The court must not order an interim payment of more than a reasonable proportion of the likely amount of the final judgment.

(5) The court must take into account—

(a) contributory negligence; and

(b) any relevant set-off or counterclaim.

25.8 Powers of court where it has made an order for interim payment

33.18 (1) Where a defendant has been ordered to make an interim payment, or has in fact made an interim payment (whether voluntarily or under an order), the court may make an order to adjust the interim payment.

(2) The court may in particular—

(a) order all or part of the interim payment to be repaid;

(b) vary or discharge the order for the interim payment;

(c) order a defendant to reimburse, either wholly or partly, another defendant who has made an interim payment.

(3) The court may make an order under paragraph (2)(c) only if—

(a) the defendant to be reimbursed made the interim payment in relation to a claim in respect of which he has made a claim against the other defendant for a contribution, indemnity or other remedy; and

(b) where the claim or part to which the interim payment relates has not been discontinued or disposed of, the circumstances are such that the court could make an order for interim payment under rule 25.7.

(4) The court may make an order under this rule without an application by any party if it makes the order when it disposes of the claim or any part of it.

(5) Where—

(a) a defendant has made an interim payment; and

(b) the amount of the payment is more than his total liability under the final judgment or order,

the court may award him interest on the overpaid amount from the date when he made the interim payment.

25.9 Restriction on disclosure of an interim payment

33.19 The fact that a defendant has made an interim payment, whether voluntarily or by court order, shall not be disclosed to the trial judge until all questions of liability and the amount of money to be awarded have been decided unless the defendant agrees.

D. PD 25B—Interim Payments

33.20 This practice direction supplements CPR Part 25

General

1.1 Rule 25.7 sets out the conditions to be satisfied and matters to be taken into account before the court will make an order for an interim payment.

1.2 The permission of the court must be obtained before making a voluntary interim payment in respect of a claim by a child or patient.

Evidence

2.1 An application for an interim payment of damages must be supported by evidence dealing **33.21** with the following:

    (1) the sum of money sought by way of an interim payment,

    (2) the items or matters in respect of which the interim payment is sought,

    (3) the sum of money for which final judgment is likely to be given,

    (4) the reason for believing that the conditions set out in rule 25.7 are satisfied,

    (5) any other relevant matters,

    (6) in claims for personal injuries, details of special damages and past and future loss, and

    (7) in a claim under the Fatal Accidents Act 1976, details of the person(s) on whose behalf the claim is made and the nature of the claim.

2.2 Any documents in support of the application should be exhibited, including, in personal injuries claims, the medical report(s).

2.3 If a respondent to an application for an interim payment wishes to rely on written evidence at the hearing he must comply with the provisions of rule 25.6(4).

2.4 If the applicant wishes to rely on written evidence in reply he must comply with the provisions of rule 25.6(5).

Interim payment where account to be taken

2A.1 This section of this practice direction applies if a party seeks an interim payment under r. **33.22** 25.7(1)(b) where the court has ordered an account to be taken.

2A.2 If the evidence on the application for interim payment shows that the account is bound to result in a payment to the applicant the court will, before making an order for interim payment, order that the liable party pay to the applicant 'the amount shown by the account to be due'.

Instalments

3 Where an interim payment is to be paid in instalments the order should set out: **33.23**

    (1) the total amount of the payment,

    (2) the amount of each instalment,

    (3) the number of instalments and the date on which each is to be paid, and

    (4) to whom the payment should be made.

Compensation recovery payments

4.1 Where in a claim for personal injuries there is an application for an interim payment of **33.24** damages:

    (1) which is other than by consent,

    (2) which fails under the heads of damage set out in column 1 of Schedule 2 of the Social Security (Recovery of Benefits) Act 1997 in respect of recoverable benefits received by the claimant set out in column 2 of that Schedule, and

    (3) where the defendant is liable to pay recoverable benefits to the Secretary of State,

the defendant should obtain from the Secretary of State a certificate of recoverable benefits.

4.2 A copy of the certificate should be filed at the hearing of the application for an interim payment.

4.3 The order will set out the amount by which the payment to be made to the claimant has been reduced according to the Act and the Social Security (Recovery of Benefits) Regulations 1997.

4.4 The payment made to the claimant will be the net amount but the interim payment for the purposes of paragraph 5 below will be the gross amount.

Adjustment of final judgment figure

33.25   5.1 In this paragraph 'judgment' means:
    (1) any order to pay a sum of money,
    (2) a final award of damages,
    (3) an assessment of damages.

5.2 In a final judgment where an interim payment has previously been made which is less than the total amount awarded by the judge, the order should set out in a preamble:
    (1) the total amount awarded by the judge, and
    (2) the amounts and dates of the interim payment(s).

5.3 The total amount awarded by the judge should then be reduced by the total amount of any interim payments, and an order made for entry of judgment and payment of the balance.

5.4 In a final judgment where an interim payment has previously been made which is more than the total amount awarded by the judge, the order should set out in a preamble:
    (1) the total amount awarded by the judge, and
    (2) the amounts and dates of the interim payment(s).

5.5 An order should then be made for repayment, reimbursement, variation or discharge under rule 25.8(2) and for interest on an overpayment under rule 25.8(5).

5.6 PD 40B provides further information concerning adjustment of the final judgment sum.

34

INTEREST

All claims for damages attract simple interest and the rules for the calculation of **34.01** interest are relatively straightforward.

A. General Damages

Interest on general damages is assessed at 2% a year from the date on which the **34.02** claim form was served on the defendant.

The reason for allowing interest at this rate is that it represents the value to **34.03** the claimant of being kept out of his compensation from the date when the defendant ought to have paid him compensation in response to a properly formulated claim. The reason interest is limited to this rate is that the damages awarded keep pace with the value of money and are assessed at trial in the value of money prevailing at the date of trial rather than at the date of injury or the date of the commencement of the claim.

The period runs from the date of service of the proceedings on the established **34.04** authority of the House of Lords' decision in *Wright v BRB* [1983] 2 AC 773 which has been consistently followed ever since. The editors of the *White Book* at 7.0.4 have suggested that interest ought to run from an earlier date (perhaps the date of the first letter of claim under the relevant protocol) in order to encourage negotiation and discourage the early issue and service of proceedings with a view to protecting the right to interest. It is suggested that this is rarely a problem in practice and the rule about interest is too firmly established to be altered except by a change of the rules or legislation or a House of Lords' decision.

B. Special Damages

34.05 Interest on special damages is assessed at the special account rate for the period of the loss. The special account rate was 8% from 1993 until 31 July 1999, was 7% from 1 August 1999 until 31 January 2002 and has been 6% since 1 February 2002.

34.06 For continuous losses through the period from the accident to trial, for example a loss of earnings when the claimant has not returned to work, the practice is to calculate interest on the whole loss at half the rate—that is, at 4% until 31 July 1999 and 3.5% until 31 January 2002 and at 3% thereafter—rather than carry out a complex calculation year by year on the increasing loss to arrive at broadly the same result. However, this is (it is submitted) a simplifying approach to the arithmetic rather than a rule of law, and where the losses occur soon after injury and then cease, for example where the claimant recovers and is able to return to work after a few weeks, the full interest rate can be claimed from the date of the loss, or more exactly from the date which is the mid-point of the period of loss.

34.07 The reason for allowing interest at the higher special account rate is that special damages are awarded in money values expressed at the date of the loss so that the award of interest must not only compensate for the delay in payment but also for the loss in the value of the money over the period of delay.

34.08 Under CPR r 16.4(2)(b) (*Blackstone's Civil Practice 2004* 1451) where Particulars of Claim make a claim for a specified amount of money, the claim for interest must state the percentage rate at which interest is claimed, the date from which it is claimed, the date on which it is calculated (not later than the date on which the claim form is issued), the total amount of interest claimed to the date of calculation, and the daily rate at which interest accrues after that date. It is sometimes argued that interest cannot be awarded on special damages in a personal injury claim unless this mandatory rule has been followed. It is suggested that it this not an appropriate approach to take in the majority of personal injury claims, where the special damages claimed in a schedule do not have the certainty or finality of a claim for a commercial debt, but are subject to the decision of the court and are likely to change in the period leading up to the assessment of damages.

34.09 *Jefford v Gee* [1970] 2 QB 130   The leading case on all aspects of entitlement to interest. Lord Denning MR stated, at 147A:

The special damages should be dealt with on broad lines. The amounts of interest at stake are not large enough to warrant minute attention to detail. Losses, expenditure and receipts should all go into one pool. In all ordinary cases we should have thought that it would be fair to award interest on the total sum of special damages from the date of the accident until the date of trial at half the rate allowed on other damages.

Lord Denning's broad brush approach to amounts not large enough to warrant minute attention to detail does not reflect the reasonable desire of practitioners to get the interest right when it is capable of being calculated correctly, and the reference to half the rate is considered to have been derived from the fact that there was in Mr Jefford's case a continuing stream of loss of wages up to the trial date.

Dexter v Courtaulds Ltd [1984] 1 WLR 372   In a case where the period off **34.10** work had been brief, the Court of Appeal refused to apply the approach of awarding the full rate from the mid-point of the loss. The court held that the *Jefford v Gee* approach should apply in ordinary personal injury cases, but in special circumstances a different approach might be justified and if that was to be argued the reasons should be stated.

Prokop v DHSS [1985] CLY 1037   A decision of the Court of Appeal which **34.11** limited the half rate approach to cases of continuous losses. May LJ said:

> If there is any general view in any quarter that interest on special damages is in any event to be calculated at half rate, when the losses do not continue from accident to trial, then I think that is wrong and should not be followed. (quoted by Patrick Curran QC in *Personal Injuries Handbook*, p 279)

In practice this view has prevailed and interest is routinely awarded on one-off or short-term losses at the full rate from the date of loss or the mid-point of the period of loss, as long as the advocates are prepared to carry out the arithmetic.

Wadey v Surrey CC [2000] 1 WLR 820   The receipt of benefits that will be **34.12** recouped under the Social Security Administration Act 1997 should be ignored in the calculation of interest so that (contrary to the usual principle) the claimant is entitled to interest on the full loss of earnings.

Griffiths v British Coal [2001] PIQR Q119   Where the claimant's receipt of **34.13** relevant state benefits was greater than his loss of earnings, the defendant's entitlement under the recoupment scheme of the Social Security (Recovery of Benefits) Act 1997 to deduct the amount of state benefits from the claimant's damages for loss of earnings included an entitlement to make the deduction from interest awarded on the claimant's loss of earnings.

Wisley v John Fulton (Plumbers) Ltd [2000] 1 WLR 820   Where the defen- **34.14** dant was entitled to reduce the amount payable to the claimant in accordance with a CRU certificate, the Social Security (Recovery of Benefits) Act 1997 required the court to disregard the benefits in assessing the claim and therefore the certified benefits should be disregarded in calculating the interest the claimant was entitled to recover on special damages, which should therefore be calculated on the gross amount.

34.15 Under s 329 of the Income and Corporation Taxes Act 1988, neither damages nor interest awarded in a judgment will be treated as income for tax purposes.

C. Delay

34.16 The award of interest is not a matter of discretion but a legal entitlement under s 35A of the Supreme Court Act 1981 or s 69 of the County Courts Act 1984. None the less, the court has a discretion to disallow part of the claim for interest if the claimant has been guilty of delay (see, for example, *Read v Harris* [1993] PIQR Q25 and *Nash v Southmead HA* [1993] PIQR Q156). In any such case the delay will usually have been the fault of the claimant's lawyers rather than of the claimant personally, and a finding to disallow interest in this way will result in a need for a candid explanation and perhaps a recommendation to the claimant to seek other advice. Indeed, a finding to disallow interest might be indicative of negligence in the conduct of the claim. It is likely that the worst examples of delay will no longer be encountered because the court takes much greater responsibility under the CPR for making and enforcing a timetable to avoid unnecessary delay.

D. Interest on a Successful Part 36 Offer

34.17 If a claimant is successful in beating a Part 36 offer, CPR r 36.21 provides for the award of special interest on the sum recovered and costs from the last date for acceptance of the offer at a rate not exceeding the base rate plus 10%. The court will make such an order unless it considers it unjust to do so. This can be a valuable addition to the claim. Base rates have fluctuated as shown by the table below.

Starting from	Base rate	Base + 10%	Days at this rate
07.01.1999	6.0	16%	28
04.02.1999	5.5	15.5%	63
08.04.1999	5.25	15.25%	63
10.06.1999	5.0	15%	90
08.09.1999	5.25	15.25%	57

Starting from	Base rate	Base + 10%	Days at this rate
04.11.1999	5.5	15.5%	70
13.01.2000	5.75	15.75%	28
10.02.2000	6.0	16%	366
08.02.2001	5.75	15.75%	56
05.04.2001	5.5	15.5%	35
10.05.2001	5.25	15.25%	84
02.08.2001	5.0	15%	47
18.09.2001	4.75	14.75%	16
04.10.2001	4.5	14.5%	35
08.11.2001	4.0	14%	455
06.02.2003	3.75	13.75%	154
10.07.2003	3.5	13.5%	119
06.11.2003	3.75	13.75%	91
05.02.2004	4.0	14%	91
06.05.2004	4.25	14.25%	35
10.06.2004	4.5	14.5%	

E. Procedure

34.18 The right to receive interest comes from stature: in the High-Court, from the Supreme Court Act 1981, s 35A and in the county court from the County Courts Act 1984, s 69.

34.19 CPR r 16.4(2) requires the statement of case to include a statement as to interest sought. This must state the basis on which interest is sought, i.e. a reference to the relevant statutory provision, and a detailed calculation where a specific sum is claimed. Even though special damages may be calculated carefully, in a personal injury claim general damages cannot be specified as a specific sum of money. The requirement to state the precise amount claimed and the continuing daily rate is aimed more at claims for debt or commercial damages and in practice it is rare for interest on special damages to be stated so fully as to comply with the rule. It is suggested that a form of statement of case along the following lines will be appropriate:

> The claimant claims interest on any award of damages under section 69 of the County Courts Act 1984 at such rate and for such period as may be just, including interest on special damages at the full special account rate from the date on which each loss was incurred.

34.20 In addition to a claim of this kind in the body of the statement of case, a claim for interest should be included in the prayer, or summary, at the conclusion. There is no point in calculating interest in a schedule of special damages to be served with the particulars of claim, though it would be sensible to mention the claim briefly. When a final schedule of special damages is prepared, which is calculated to the expected date of trial or the trial window, it is then appropriate for the claimant to set out the rates of interest that will be claimed on both general and special damages, and to give the detailed calculations relied on. The defendant can then raise any disagreement in the counter-schedule.

F. Supreme Court Act 1981, s 35A

35A. Power of High Court to award interest on debts and damages

34.21   (1) Subject to rules of court, in proceedings (whenever instituted) before the High Court for the recovery of a debt or damages there may be included in any sum for which judgment is given simple interest, at such rate as the court thinks fit or as rules of court may provide, on all or any part of the debt or damages in respect of which judgment is given, or payment is made before judgment, for all or any part of the period between the date when the cause of action arose and—

    (a) in the case of any sum paid before judgment, the date of the payment; and

    (b) in the case of the sum for which judgment is given, the date of the judgment.

(2) In relation to a judgment given for damages for personal injuries or death which exceed £200 subsection (1) shall have effect—

    (a) with the substitution of 'shall be included' for 'may be included'; and

    (b) with the addition of 'unless the court is satisfied that there are special reasons to the contrary' after 'given', where first occurring.

G. CPR Part 16—Statements of Case, r 16.4

16.4 Contents of the particulars of claim

34.22   (1) Particulars of claim must include—

    (a) a concise statement of the facts on which the claimant relies;

    (b) if the claimant is seeking interest, a statement to that effect and the details set out in paragraph (2);

(2) If the claimant is seeking interest he must—

    (a) state whether he is doing so—

        (i) under the terms of a contract;

        (ii) under an enactment and if so which; or

        (iii) on some other basis and if so what that basis is; and

    (b) if the claim is for a specified amount of money, state—

        (i) the percentage rate at which interest is claimed;

        (ii) the date from which it is claimed;

        (iii) the date to which it is calculated, which must not be later than the date on which the claim form is issued;

        (iv) the total amount of interest claimed to the date of calculation; and

        (v) the daily rate at which interest accrues after that date.

Part D

PROCEDURE

35

FUNDING OF CLAIMS

A. Access to Justice

Lawyers do not act out of love, but in return for payment. Litigation will always **35.01** involve expense and risk. Yet personal injury claims have reached the surprising position that a claimant with a sound case can expect to be able to pursue a compensation claim at minimal expense and risk. The keys to this are the development of the conditional fee agreement (CFA) and the exclusion of the claimant whose case is of uncertain merit.

CFAs became a part of the funding of civil claims with the Courts and Legal **35.02** Services Act 1990. Where a claim is successful a CFA allows the claimant's lawyer to add to his normal fees an added element of profit called a success fee to make up for the loss on unsuccessful claims in which no fees will be recovered. As originally conceived, CFAs made the success fee a deduction from the damages recovered. CFAs became central to the funding of personal injury claims with the changes made under the Access to Justice Act 1999, implemented in April 2000, which brought the withdrawal of legal aid from personal injury claims but changed the CFA system so that the success fee, and the insurance premium against liability for adverse costs, could be included in the costs recoverable from the opponent in a successful claim. This change allowed lawyers to offer 'no win, no fee' arrangements to injured claimants under which the claimant would be entitled to the whole of the award of damages. The aim was to make the recovery of compensation accessible to all, not only those who might have qualified on means grounds for legal aid. The effect was to pass all the costs onto insurers including, indirectly, the costs of unsuccessful claims, since the justification for success fees is to make up for the loss suffered by lawyers under CFA cases which fail.

35.03 In widening access to the courts, the introduction of CFAs must be considered a success: anyone who is injured and who has a sound case on liability can now expect to be able to pursue a claim, either by the protection of an existing legal expenses insurance policy or by a CFA. A claimant can obtain the help of a specialist solicitor, without needing to fund the costs of the litigation or to run the risk of adverse costs liability. However, a claimant whose claim is not likely to succeed will find it difficult to find a solicitor (and a cost liability insurer) willing to take the risk of failure. Therefore the ease of access for those with good claims has been at the expense of those with doubtful claims even when severely injured. This dichotomy is illustrated by the emergence of commercial claims management companies hoping to profit from handling straightforward claims such as rear-end road traffic collisions: it is perhaps a sign of maturity that so many of these companies have failed.

35.04 The 2000 change to CFA funding came hard on the heels of the introduction of the Woolf reforms which provided a new procedural code for civil proceedings, including the innovations of pre-trial protocols and Part 36 incentives to settle. The last five years have been a time of considerable difficulty and uncertainty for both claimants and defendants. There has been much wasteful litigation about costs and success fees although there has been a gradual and much needed improvement in the CFA regime with the new simplified CFAs and the fixing of staged success fees for routine cases. These allow only modest additional fees where claims settle early, but add further heavy costs to penalize defendants who dispute a claim to trial without success. The scale of the changes that have been necessary makes it reasonable to question whether the reforms might have been less painful if they had been more carefully considered in the first place; but the system is undoubtedly in better shape now.

B. Traditional Terms of Engagement

35.05 There is nothing to stop an injured person instructing a solicitor on the traditional basis of a retainer in which the client is liable to pay the costs of his solicitor and the disbursements incurred on his behalf, and is liable to meet any adverse costs awarded to the opponent in the litigation, but hopes that the claim will be successful and that this will result in an order requiring the opponent to meet his costs. In a claim where the merits are strong, an arrangement of this kind will avoid the complications and uncertainties of a CFA, and in a claim where the merits are weak the solicitor and costs liability insurer may be unwilling to take the risks involved in a CFA so that a traditional engagement of this kind may be the only way that legal representation can be obtained. The intending claimant would be wise, however, to heed the risks which have dissuaded the solicitor from entering into a CFA, because the potential financial cost of an unsuccessful claim will run into many thousands of pounds. A solicitor has a duty under the Solicitors' Costs Information and Client Care Code 1999 to discuss funding arrangements and to explain the options that are available, including the possibility of a CFA. Since a CFA will provide equal benefits of professional representation at a much reduced risk, it is difficult to envisage circumstances in which a client with a sound claim would be well advised to instruct a solicitor on the traditional basis.

C. Before the Event Insurance

The prospective claimant may have the benefit of insurance which gives protec-   **35.06**
tion against the legal costs involved in pursuing a claim. It is common for legal expenses insurance to be sold alongside motor insurance policies and as an additional benefit in household insurance policies. It may be that the expenses can be met by a policy held by somebody else, for example the householder where the client lives or the driver of a vehicle in which the client was a passenger. Such policies are described as 'before the event' insurance because they have been taken out before, and without reference to, the accident or event giving rise to the proposed claim. Where the client has cover available under a before the event policy, it will usually be unreasonable to incur the added cost of the additional liability for a success fee and insurance premium that would arise under a CFA, so if before the event insurance is available the client is likely to be, in practice, required to use it to pursue the claim: this will be undertaken by the traditional instruction of a solicitor under the protection of the insurance, without entitlement to a success fee. The drawback is that under many such policies, it is necessary to instruct one of the solicitors introduced by the insurer rather than a solicitor of the policyholder's choice.

Sarwar v Alam [2001] EWCA Civ 1401; [2001] 4 All ER 541   Usually it is   **35.07**
not reasonable to enter into a CFA if the claimant has other sources of funding such as legal expenses insurance. In this case, because of the potential conflict of interest, the claimant who had been a passenger was entitled to make a CFA and did not need to use the legal expenses insurance that was available to him under the defendant driver's motor insurance policy. However, solicitors should make a standard practice of asking to see any motor or household or other insurance policy that might provide legal expenses cover before entering into a CFA.

D. Public Funding

35.08 Legal aid became 'public funding' under the Community Legal Service in 2000, and for all practical purposes public funding was withdrawn for the support of personal injury claims. (It is still possible to obtain public funding for representation at an inquest where exceptional circumstances arise, and it is still possible to obtain public funding for the initial investigation of clinical negligence claims.) For those who qualify for legal aid, this was a baffling reform since the net amount of public money spent on supporting personal injury claims was extremely small and the upheaval that has been caused by the introduction of CFAs has been extremely great. For the many who failed to qualify for legal aid on means grounds, although having such a modest income and such modest resources that instructing a solicitor privately was not a practical proposition, there is no doubt that the introduction of CFAs and the development of before the event insurance have increased the real prospects of being able to afford to pursue a claim, provided it is of sufficient merit.

35.09 There is however one category of claimant that has been severely disadvantaged by the withdrawal of public funding from personal injury claims. Someone who has been very severely injured is likely to be unable to work and is therefore likely to have qualified on means grounds for legal aid. Such a person will have a strong and obvious need for access to the court to pursue a claim for much needed compensation, which should surely be made easy in a civilized society which requires universal liability insurance for motorists and employers. However, to pursue such a claim will require a heavy investment in work and in disbursements for medical and expert reports and will involve a significant risk of incurring a large adverse costs liability. When such a claimant has an arguable but difficult claim on liability, the merits may be sufficient to have previously attracted public funding, but the difficulties may be sufficient to deter a sensible and businesslike solicitor from taking the risks of a CFA and, perhaps more important, may make it impossible for after the event insurance cover against adverse costs to be obtained, so that litigation becomes impracticable. It is questionable whether this is a result which was intended or foreseen at the time of the withdrawal of legal aid. One cannot escape the suspicion that the primary motive behind the reform was simply to transfer the costs of personal injury litigation wholly to insurers.

E. CFAs and After the Event Insurance

A success fee is not necessary under a CFA, but the usual arrangement for a **35.10** personal injury claim on behalf of a claimant is an agreement that no fees will be due if the claim fails, but the full fees, together with a success fee expressed as a percentage of the fees, will be paid if the claim is successful. The success fee is not expressed as a proportion of the damages recovered, but as a percentage of the normal costs, and in the majority of claims the rate of success fee will be fixed by the rules and will depend on the stage of the claim when settlement or judgment is achieved. The success fee will be included in the costs recovered from the unsuccessful opponent, although it is possible that the client may be liable to pay any part of the costs and the success fee that cannot be so recovered.

Since June 2003 CPR r 43.2 (3) (*Blackstone* 1705) and reg 3A of the Con- **35.11** ditional Fee Agreements Regulations 2000 (*Blackstone* 2676) have allowed a simplified form of CFA in which the solicitor agrees to limit the entitlement to costs and success fee to the amount recovered from the opponent in the proceedings, and with the protection that this gives to the claimant, the requirements as to explanation and notification for such an agreement are less burdensome than under the original 1995 Regulations. This sensible reform reflects the reality of most CFA arrangements and provides a useful measure of consumer protection because clients can now expect to be assured, in a competitive marketplace, that the solicitor will not only work on a 'no win, no fee' basis but will also promise that the whole of the damages awarded by the court or achieved by a negotiated settlement will be received by the client.

CFAs can be made by both solicitors and barristers, but the agreement made by **35.12** the client will be with the solicitor and it will be the solicitor who, in turn, may make a CFA with the barrister who is instructed. Because barristers are usually instructed in a much smaller number of cases, and in those cases which raise questions of difficulty, it is more difficult for them to undertake CFAs on a commercially sensible basis and the Bar Council continues to press for barristers usually to be engaged on the basis that their fees should be treated as a disbursement, like the fees of expert witnesses.

An important step in creating a viable system of 'no win, no fee' litigation was, **35.13** under the Access to Justice Act 1999, s 29, to enable the court to award a successful claimant the cost of the premium for an insurance policy against the risk of incurring a liability for costs in the proceedings. Without insurance, a CFA only deals with half of the risk facing a claimant, the risk of having to pay the costs of his own solicitor if the claim is unsuccessful leaving the client exposed to liability for the costs of the successful opponent. With insurance comes peace of mind, and with the rule that the insurance premium may be payable only on success and at the conclusion of the case, the claimant can pursue a claim safe in the knowledge that there should be no risk attached to failure, and no charge on the damages awarded save for the risk that (under the 2000 Regulations) there might be an element of the success fee which the court disallows but which the solicitor is entitled to pursue against the client. Such policies are known as after the event (ATE) insurance and they are an essential part of the CFA framework.

35.14   It is important to comply with the formal requirements for a CFA. The regulations make demanding requirements at the stage when an agreement is made and notice of the existence of a CFA and insurance must be given at the earliest possible stage. There were many technical challenges to costs liability brought by defendant insurers, based on technical infringement of the requirements of the regulations which was said to render the agreement unenforceable against the client and therefore, under the indemnity principle, unenforceable against the defendant, so that no costs at all were payable. The Court of Appeal has introduced a sensible and workable test, whether the particular departure from a requirement under the 2000 Regulations or the 1990 Act, either on its own or in conjunction with any other such departure, has had a materially adverse effect on the protection afforded to the client or on the proper administration of justice: *Hollins v Russell* [2003] EWCA Civ 718; [2003] 1 WLR 2487. This decision, coupled with the introduction of simplified CFAs where entitlement to costs is limited to the recovery from the opponent, represent considerable strides towards a workable and fair system for funding claims.

35.15   Claims arising out of road accidents and accidents at work are now governed by levels of success fees that are fixed by CPR Part 45, Part III in the case of road accidents and by an agreement in the Civil Justice Council in the case of employers' liability accidents. Outside these categories of claim, and notably in occupational disease claims, the CFA will have to specify the success fee as a percentage uplift on basic fees based on the perceived chances of success and subject to review by the court. The opponent must be given notice of the existence of a CFA at the earliest possible opportunity, but need not be told the level of the success fee, which would unavoidably hint at the assessment of the prospects of success that the claimant's solicitor has made. At the end of the case, if the parties do not agree, the court will assess the level of success fee that is reasonable as part of the costs liability of the unsuccessful defendant, following the guidance in paras 11.7–11.9 of PD About Costs (*Blackstone* 1747). The trend in such cases is towards staged success fees which reflect the approach taken in the Civil Justice Council. A modest success fee (awarded on a modest level of cost) will apply when a claim is settled at an early stage, with increasing fees as the defence of the claim continues, and much more, usually 100%, will be appropriate for a case that proceeds to a fully defended trial.

F. Collective CFAs

Trade unions have for many years filled an important role by supporting **35.16** compensation claims for accidents suffered by their members, primarily for claims arising out of accidents at work but often extending to claims of all kinds and to include the family of the member concerned. An injured person who has such support available to him may find that it was unreasonable to enter into a private CFA agreement with a private solicitor. He can expect the details of funding to be negotiated between his union and the solicitor to whom he is introduced, and he need not be concerned with the details. Handling a great many claims, generally through association with a limited number of solicitors' firms, bulk providers of work of this kind are able to enter into a global agreement under the Collective Conditional Fee Agreements Regulations 2000, although it is necessary for a principle of personal liability of the client to be retained, even if this is only technical, so that the indemnity principle is not infringed.

Thornley v Lang [2003] EWCA Civ 1484; [2004] 1 WLR 378 Insurers **35.17** objected to paying the success fee under a valid collective CFA because the requirements of the Conditional Fee Agreements Regulations 2000 had not been complied with. The Court of Appeal held that the regimes were mutually exclusive, so the requirements of the CFA Regulations had no application. Under the agreement, the claimant was liable to pay the solicitors appointed by the union, although he would be indemnified by the union. This did not infringe the indemnity principle. The success fee was recoverable.

36

BEFORE COURT PROCEEDINGS BEGIN

A. Investigation of the Facts

It is a guiding principle of the Woolf reforms that claims should be conducted **36.01** with a view to reaching a settlement wherever possible without the need to issue court proceedings. Work to establish the merits and value of a claim must therefore be done on both sides without waiting for the framework of litigation.

The first step in preparing a claim must be a careful investigation of the facts. A **36.02** broad outline will have been necessary in order to arrange appropriate funding for the claim, but it is important to get the details right and to record them from the outset. One of the most potent ways in which a client's credibility can be weakened is by putting forward, perhaps accidentally, accounts of the facts on different occasions which are inconsistent in detail. Under the CPR, with the use of pre-action protocols, parties are encouraged to investigate and prepare the details of claims more thoroughly before the issue of proceedings than used to be the case. A witness statement should be prepared on behalf of the client at an early stage. The availability of evidence from witnesses should be established, and initial statements obtained. In a road accident or a workplace accident claim, it will be of great assistance if the client can obtain photographs of the scene of the accident, or to draw a clear plan. In a road traffic accident claim, if the police attended it is vital to attain a copy of the police accident report. In a workplace accident, there may have been an investigation by the Health and

Safety Executive, so that a factual report and helpful photographs may be available. After a fatal accident, there may have been an inquest, and the coroner will provide a copy of the evidence to any properly interested person.

36.03 From the outset, the client should be advised to keep receipts and a careful record of any expenditure that might be included in the claim for financial loss. The client should be advised of the obligation to disclose copies of all documents that are relevant under the test for standard disclosure, and it is never too soon for the client to get into the habit of providing documents. The client should also be advised of the need to take reasonable steps to keep losses to a minimum and in consequence of the possible need to justify the claims for expenses that are to be put forward.

B. Pre-action Disclosure

36.04 It is possible to apply for disclosure of documents before proceedings have started and the procedure is governed by CPR r 31.16 (*Blackstone's Civil Practice 2004* 1594; hereafter *Blackstone*). An application can be made where the applicant and the respondent are likely to be parties to subsequent proceedings. The order can only be made in respect of documents which would be covered by the obligation of standard disclosure in CPR r 31.6: a party must disclose the documents on which he relies, documents which adversely affect his own case, documents which adversely affect another party's case, and documents which support another party's case. The best indication of the scope of documents which may reasonably be sought is the list of documents set out in Annex B of the pre-action protocol. Finally, the court may only make an order of disclosure before the proceedings have started if it is desirable in order to dispose fairly of the anticipated proceedings, to assist the dispute to be resolved without proceedings, or to save costs.

36.05 In personal injury claims, the jurisdiction of the court to order pre-action disclosure is related to the disclosure obligation on a defendant who does not admit liability under the procedures of the relevant protocol. The legal test for pre-action disclosure is strict, but in practice the court will quite readily grant an order for disclosure (with costs) against an intended defendant who has failed to carry out the obligation of disclosure under paras 3.10–3.12 of the personal injury protocol without giving any good reason. Where the defendant has complied with the protocol, the general rule under CPR r 48.1 is that the person giving pre-action disclosure is entitled to the costs of doing so.

C. Obtaining Medical Evidence

A medical report will be required at some stage of every claim. The steps that it **36.06** is reasonable to take at an early stage in relation to medical evidence will depend on the nature of the claim. Where injuries are serious, and treatment is continuing at the time when a letter of claim is to be written, it may be too early for medical evidence to be obtained. In straightforward claims, the personal injury protocol encourages a process which will ensure that if possible the claimant instructs an expert acceptable to the defendant, or that an expert is jointly instructed. If the claimant has recovered from his injuries, there is no need for delay in obtaining a report, once a suitable expert has been agreed. For this purpose it is the responsibility of the claimants to organize access to the relevant medical records.

D. Compliance with the Pre-action Protocol

There are three pre-action protocols potentially relevant to personal injury **36.07** claims. For the majority of claims, the protocol for personal injury claims will apply and this protocol is reproduced in full at **36.15** below. A relatively new protocol for disease and illness claims came into force on 8 December 2003 and this protocol is reproduced in full at **36.47** below. In addition, there is a protocol for the resolution of clinical disputes (*Blackstone* 2207). The personal injury protocol is expressed to be directly applicable to accident claims with a value of less than £15,000 which are likely to be allocated to the fast track. However, parties are encouraged to act in accordance with the protocol so far as is appropriate in cases of great value. The protocol for disease and illness claims is similar in style to the personal injury protocol, but recognizes that the complexity of such claims may well make the fast track inappropriate and require that increased attention should be given to disclosure, which should extend to occupational records, including occupational health records, to be disclosed by the defendant as well as medical records in relation to the injury which the claimant may obtain. The protocol also recognizes that expert evidence is likely to be more extensive and more controversial in claims for disease or illness.

The court would expect parties to have complied in substance with the terms **36.08** of an approved protocol and compliance is one of the matters which has to be set out in the allocation questionnaire. Where there is an unreasonable failure to comply with the protocol, the court can punish the failure by sanctions including costs. For example, if proceedings would have been unnecessary if a protocol had been followed, a party at fault may have to pay the costs of the proceedings, may have to pay them on an indemnity basis, or may be penalized with interest. These powers are sanctions set out in the Practice Direction on Protocols (*Blackstone* 2193).

E. The Letter of Claim

36.09   The letter of claim is an important document, which merits considerable care. The allegations provide the basis on which the defendant will consider liability under the protocol, and the clearest allegations will have the best prospect of provoking an admission. The letter of claim is an open document, on which the claimant may be cross-examined to attack his credibility if there is a significant discrepancy between the case advanced in the letter and the case subsequently advanced in the statement of case, witness statement, or oral evidence. There are specimens of the letter of claim in the protocols, which should provide the starting point for the letter of claim when the protocol applies, but which should be adapted to the demands of the particular case.

F. Early Settlement Offers

36.10   In cases of serious injury it is likely that the letter of claim will be sent long before it is possible to come to an accurate opinion on the value of the claim. In cases where this is possible, the claimant is entitled to put added pressure on the defendant by making an offer of settlement at the same time. An offer can be made either limited to a specific issue such as liability or contributory negligence, or in terms of a global settlement figure, or both. CPR Part 36 does not come into force until the proceedings have begun, but the court later deciding issues of costs and interest will be required to take into account any offer of settlement, so there is much to be said for an early offer which will be in place throughout any subsequent proceedings. The formal requirements of CPR Part 36 should be complied with so that the defendant is aware of the risk on costs and interest which may arise, and the information about the claim that is provided by the letter of claim or otherwise must be sufficient to enable the defendant to make a reasonably reliable estimate of the value of the claim, otherwise the benefits of an effective offer may not be awarded.

36.11   The defendant can also make an early offer of settlement, hoping that the risk on costs will discourage the claimant from issuing proceedings. Where an offer is made before the commencement of proceedings, the value of it will be lost in a later argument on costs unless the defendant pays at least as much as the offered amount into court as soon as the proceedings are served.

G. Notice to Insurers in Road Traffic Accident Claims

Under s 151 of the Road Traffic Act 1988 a motor insurer is obliged to satisfy a **36.12** judgment obtained against the insured person even if the insurer may have grounds to avoid or cancel the policy, but under s 152, this liability only arises if notice has been given to the insurer of the bringing of the proceedings, and the notice was given within seven days after the commencement of the proceedings in which the judgment was given. In every road traffic accident claim, such notice should be given as a matter of invariable practice. The letter of claim does not amount to notice of the proceedings. The only safe course is to ensure that formal written notice is given to the insurer by letter at the time of issuing the claim form. The insurer does not waive the requirement of notice by its involvement in the defence of the claim on the merits.

There are also complex and important requirements in the MIB Agreements in **36.13** relation to obtaining information about insurance and giving written notice of the commencement of the proceedings. There are no short cuts, and a careful study of the requirements of the agreements, which are set out in full in Chapter 8, is essential.

H. Early Preparation on Damages

The protocols do not require the letter of claim to be accompanied by detailed **36.14** information about special damages. The personal injury protocol envisages this only in response to an admission of liability. At the outset of the claim, it is understandable that the main interest should be to establish the extent of agreement or dispute about liability. However, it is good practice to begin the assessment of damages as soon as possible. If the letter of claim can be accompanied by an initial Schedule of Special Damages, this will assist the defendant to understand the value of the claim that is likely to be put forward, it will demonstrate to the court that the claimant is doing his best to give early disclosure of the nature of the case, it will impose on the claimant the discipline of providing instructions and documents to support the claim at an early stage, it may increase the likelihood of an early negotiated settlement, and it will save time later if proceedings are necessary.

I. Pre-action Protocol for Personal Injury Claims

1 INTRODUCTION

36.15   1.1 Lord Woolf in his final Access to Justice Report of July 1996 recommended the development of pre-action protocols:

'To build on and increase the benefits of early but well informed settlement which genuinely satisfy both parties to dispute.'

1.2 The aims of pre-action protocols are:
- more pre-action contact between the parties
- better and earlier exchange of information
- better pre-action investigation by both sides
- to put the parties in a position where they may be able to settle cases fairly and early without litigation
- to enable proceedings to run to the court's timetable and efficiently, if litigation does become necessary.

1.3 The concept of protocols is relevant to a range of initiatives for good litigation and pre-litigation practice, especially:
- predictability in the time needed for steps pre-proceedings
- standardisation of relevant information, including documents to be disclosed.

1.4 The courts will be able to treat the standards set in protocols as the normal reasonable approach to pre-action conduct. If proceedings are issued, it will be for the court to decide whether non-compliance with a protocol should merit adverse consequences. Guidance on the court's likely approach will be given from time to time in practice directions.

1.5 If the court has to consider the question of compliance after proceedings have begun, it will not be concerned with minor infringements, e.g. failure by a short period to provide relevant information. One minor breach will not exempt the 'innocent' party from following the protocol. The court will look at the effect of non-compliance on the other party when deciding whether to impose sanctions.

2 NOTES OF GUIDANCE

36.16   2.1 The protocol has been kept deliberately simple to promote ease of use and general acceptability. The notes of guidance which follow relate particularly to issues which arose during the piloting of the protocol.

Scope of the protocol

36.17   2.2 This protocol is intended to apply to all claims which include a claim for personal injury (except industrial disease claims) and to the entirety of those claims: not only to the personal injury element of a claim which also includes, for instance, property damage.

2.3 This protocol is primarily designed for those road traffic, tripping and slipping and accident at work cases which include an element of personal injury with a value of less than £15,000 which are likely to be allocated to the fast track. This is because time will be of the essence, after proceedings are issued, especially for the defendant, if a case is to be ready for trial within 30 weeks of allocation. Also, proportionality of work and costs to the value of what is in dispute is particularly important in lower value claims. For some claims within the value 'scope' of the fast track some flexibility in the timescale of the protocol may be necessary; see also paragraph 3.8.

2.4 However, the 'cards on the table' approach advocated by the protocol is equally appropriate to some higher value claims. The spirit, if not the letter of the protocol, should still be followed for multi-track type claims. In accordance with the sense of the civil justice reforms, the court will expect to see the spirit of reasonable pre-action behaviour applied in all cases, regardless of the existence of a specific protocol. In particular with regard to personal injury cases worth more than £15,000, with a view to avoiding the necessity of proceedings parties are expected to comply with the protocol as far as possible e.g. in respect of letters before action, exchanging information and documents agreeing experts.

2.5 The timetable and the arrangements for disclosing documents and obtaining expert evidence may need to be varied to suit the circumstances of the case. Where one or both parties consider the detail of the protocol is not appropriate to the case, and proceedings are subsequently issued, the court will expect an explanation as to why the protocol has not been followed, or has been varied.

Early notification

2.6 The claimant's legal representative may wish to notify the defendant and/or his insurer as soon as they know a claim is likely to be made, but before they are able to send a detailed letter of claim, particularly for instance, when the defendant has no or limited knowledge of the incident giving rise to the claim or where the claimant is incurring significant expenditure as a result of the accident which he hopes the defendant might pay for, in whole or in part. If the claimant's representative chooses to do this, it will not start the timetable for responding. **36.18**

The letter of claim

2.7 The specimen letter of claim at Annex A will usually be sent to the individual defendant. In practice, he/she may have no personal financial interest in the financial outcome of the claim/dispute because he/she is insured. Court imposed sanctions for non-compliance with the protocol may be ineffective against an insured. This is why the protocol emphasises the importance of passing the letter of claim to the insurer and the possibility that the insurance cover might be affected. If an insurer receives the letter of claim only after some delay by the insured, it would not be unreasonable for the insurer to ask the claimant for additional time to respond. **36.19**

Reasons for early issue

2.8 The protocol recommends that a defendant be given three months to investigate and respond to a claim before proceedings are issued. This may not always be possible, particularly where a claimant only consults a solicitor close to the end of any relevant limitation period. In these circumstances, the claimant's solicitor should give as much notice of the intention to issue proceedings as is practicable and the parties should consider whether the court might be invited to extend time for service of the claimant's supporting documents and for service of any defence, or alternatively, to stay the proceedings while the recommended steps in the protocol are followed. **36.20**

Status of letters of claim and response

2.9 Letters of claim and response are not intended to have the same status as a statement of case in proceedings. Matters may come to light as a result of investigation after the letter of claim has been sent, or after the defendant has responded, particularly if disclosure of documents takes place outside the recommended three-month period. These circumstances could mean that the 'pleaded' case of one or both parties is presented slightly differently than in the letter of claim and response. It would not be consistent with the spirit of the protocol for a party to 'take a point' on this in the proceedings, provided that there was no obvious intention by the party who changed their position to mislead the other party. **36.21**

Disclosure of documents

36.22   2.10 The aim of the early disclosure of documents by the defendant is not to encourage 'fishing expeditions' by the claimant, but to promote an early exchange of relevant information to help in clarifying or resolving issues in dispute. The claimant's solicitor can assist by identifying in the letter of claim or in a subsequent letter the particular categories of documents which they consider are relevant.

Experts

36.23   2.11 The protocol encourages joint selection of, and access to, experts. Most frequently this will apply to the medical expert, but on occasions also to liability experts, e.g. engineers. The protocol promotes the practice of the claimant obtaining a medical report, disclosing it to the defendant who then asks questions and/or agrees it and does not obtain his own report. The protocol provides for nomination of the expert by the claimant in personal injury claims because of the early stage of the proceedings and the particular nature of such claims. If proceedings have to be issued, a medical report must be attached to these proceedings. However, if necessary after proceedings have commenced and with the permission of the court, the parties may obtain further expert reports. It would be for the court to decide whether the costs of more than one expert's report should be recoverable.

2.12 Some solicitors choose to obtain medical reports through medical agencies, rather than directly from a specific doctor or hospital. The defendant's prior consent to the action should be sought and, if the defendant so requests, the agency should be asked to provide in advance the names of the doctor(s) whom they are considering instructing.

Negotiations/settlement

36.24   2.13 Parties and their legal representatives are encouraged to enter into discussions and/or negotiations prior to starting proceedings. The protocol does not specify when or how this might be done but parties should bear in mind that the courts increasingly take the view that litigation should be a last resort, and that claims should not be issued prematurely when a settlement is in reasonable prospect.

Stocktake

36.25   2.14 Where a claim is not resolved when the protocol has been followed, the parties might wish to carry out a 'stocktake' of the issues in dispute, and the evidence that the court is likely to need to decide those issues, before proceedings are started. Where the defendant is insured and the pre-action steps have been conducted by the insurer, the insurer would normally be expected to nominate solicitors to act in the proceedings and the claimant's solicitor is recommended to invite the insurer to nominate solicitors to act in the proceedings and do so 7–14 days before the intended issue date.

3 THE PROTOCOL

Letter of claim

36.26   3.1 The claimant shall send to the proposed defendant two copies of a letter of claim, immediately sufficient information is available to substantiate a realistic claim and before issues of quantum are addressed in detail. One copy of the letter is for the defendants, the second for passing on to his insurers.

3.2 The letter shall contain a **clear summary of the facts** on which the claim is based together with an indication of the **nature of any injuries** suffered and of **any financial loss incurred**. In cases of road traffic accidents, the letter should provide the name and address of the hospital where treatment has been obtained and the claimant's hospital reference number.

3.3 Solicitors are recommended to use a **standard format** for such a letter—an example is at Annex A: this can be amended to suit the particular case.

3.4 The letter should ask for **details of the insurer** and that a copy should be sent by the proposed defendant to the insurer where appropriate. If the insurer is known, a copy shall be sent directly to the insurer. Details of the claimant's National Insurance number and date of birth should be supplied to the defendant's insurer once the defendant has responded to the letter of claim and confirmed the identity of the insurer. This information should not be supplied in the letter of claim.

3.5 **Sufficient information** should be given in order to enable the defendant's insurer solicitor to commence investigations and at least put a broad valuation on the 'risk'.

3.6 The **defendant should reply within 21 calendar days** of the date of posting of the letter identifying the insurer (if any). If there has been no reply by the defendant or insurer within 21 days, the claimant will be entitled to issue proceedings.

3.7 The **defendant** ('s insurers) will have a **maximum of three months** from the date of acknowledgment of the claim **to investigate**. No later than the end of that period the defendant (insurer) shall reply, stating whether liability is denied and, if so, giving reasons for their denial of liability.

3.8 Where the accident occurred outside England and Wales and/or where the defendant is outside the jurisdiction, the time periods of 21 days and three months should normally be extended up to 42 days and six months.

3.9 Where **liability is admitted**, the presumption is that the defendant will be bound by this admission for all claims with a total value of up to £15,000.

Documents

3.10 If the **defendant denies liability**, he should enclose with the letter of reply, **documents** in his possession which are **material to the issues** between the parties, and which would be likely to be ordered to be disclosed by the court, either on an application for pre-action disclosure, or on disclosure during proceedings. **36.27**

3.11 Attached at Annex B are **specimen**, but non-exhaustive, **lists** of documents likely to be material in different types of claim. Where the claimant's investigation of the case is well advanced, the letter of claim could indicate which classes of documents are considered relevant for early disclosure. Alternatively these could be identified at a later stage.

3.12 Where the defendant admits primary liability, but alleges contributory negligence by the claimant, the defendant should give reasons supporting those allegations and disclose those documents from Annex B which are relevant to the issues in dispute. The claimant should respond to the allegations of contributory negligence before proceedings are issued.

Special damages

3.13 The claimant will send to the defendant as soon as practicable a Schedule of Special Damages with supporting documents, particularly where the defendant has admitted liability. **36.28**

Experts

3.14 Before any party instructs an expert he should give the other party a list of the **name**(s) of **one or more experts** in the relevant speciality whom he considers are suitable to instruct. **36.29**

3.15 Where a medical expert is to be instructed the claimant's solicitor will organise access to relevant medical records—see specimen letter of instruction at Annex C.

3.16 **Within 14 days** the other party may indicate **an objection** to one or more of the named experts. The first party should then instruct a mutually acceptable expert. It must be emphasised that if the claimant nominates an expert in the original letter of claim, the defendant has 14 days to object to one or more of the named experts after expiration of the period of 21 days within which he has to reply to the letter of claim, as set out in paragraph 3.6.

3.17 If the second party objects to all the listed experts, the parties may then instruct **experts of their own choice**. It would be for the court to decide subsequently, if proceedings are issued, whether either party had acted unreasonably.

3.18 If the **second party does not object to an expert nominated**, he shall not be entitled to rely on his own expert evidence within that particular speciality unless:

(a) the first party agrees,

(b) the court so directs, or

(c) the first party's expert report has been amended and the first party is not prepared to disclose the original report.

3.19 **Either party may send to an agreed expert written questions** on the report, relevant to the issues, via the first party's solicitors. The expert should send answers to the questions separately and directly to each party.

3.20 The cost of a report from an agreed expert will usually be paid by the instructing first party: the costs of the expert replying to questions will usually be borne by the party which asks the questions.

3.21 Where the defendant admits liability in whole or in part, before proceedings are issued, any medical report obtained by agreement under this protocol should be disclosed to the other party. The claimant should delay issuing proceedings for 21 days from disclosure of the report, to enable the parties to consider whether the claim is capable of settlement. The Civil Procedure Rules Part 36 permit claimants and defendants to make offers to settle pre-proceedings. Parties should always consider before issuing if it is appropriate to make a Part 36 offer. If such an offer is made, the party making the offer must always supply sufficient evidence and/or information to enable the offer to be properly considered.

ANNEX A LETTER OF CLAIM

36.30 To

Defendant

Dear Sirs

Re: **Claimant's full name**
      Claimant's full address
      Claimant's Clock or Works Number
      Claimant's Employer (*name and address*)

We are instructed by the above named to claim damages in connection with *an accident at work/ road traffic accident/tripping accident* on   day of   (*year*) at (*place of accident which must be sufficiently detailed to establish location*)

Please confirm the identity of your insurers. Please note that the insurers will need to see this letter as soon as possible and it may affect your insurance cover and/or the conduct of any subsequent legal proceedings if you do not send this letter to them.

The circumstances of the accident are:—
(*brief outline*)

The reason why we are alleging fault is:
(*simple explanation e.g. defective machine, broken ground*)

A description of our clients' injuries is as follows:—
(*brief outline*)

(*In cases of road traffic accidents*)
Our client (*state hospital reference number*) received treatment for the injuries at (*name and address of hospital*).

He is employed as (*occupation*) and has had the following time off work (*dates of absence*). His approximate weekly income is (*insert if known*).

If you are our client's employers, please provide us with the usual earnings details which will enable us to calculate his financial loss.

We are obtaining a police report and will let you have a copy of the same upon your undertaking to meet half the fee.

We have also sent a letter of claim to (*name and address*) and a copy of that letter is attached. We understand their insurers are (*name, address and claims number if known*).

At this stage of our enquiries we would expect the documents contained in parts (*insert appropriate parts of standard disclosure list*) to be relevant to this action.

A copy of this letter is attached for you to send to your insurers. Finally we expect an acknowledgment of this letter within 21 days by yourselves or your insurers.

Yours faithfully

ANNEX B STANDARD DISCLOSURE LISTS FAST TRACK DISCLOSURE

ROAD TRAFFIC ACCIDENT CASES

Section A

In all cases where liability is at issue—   **36.31**
    (i) Documents identifying nature, extent and location of damage to defendant's vehicle where there is any dispute about point of impact.
    (ii) MOT certificate where relevant.
    (iii) Maintenance records where vehicle defect is alleged or it is alleged by defendant that there was an unforeseen defect which caused or contributed to the accident.

Section B

Accident involving commercial vehicle as potential defendant—
    (i) Tachograph charts or entry from individual control book.
    (ii) Maintenance and repair records required for operators' licence where vehicle defect is alleged or it is alleged by defendants that there was an unforeseen defect which caused or contributed to the accident.

Section C

Cases against local authorities where highway design defect is alleged—
    (i) Documents produced to comply with Section 39 of the Road Traffic Act 1988 in respect of the duty designed to promote road safety to include studies into road accidents in the relevant area and documents relating to measures recommended to prevent accidents in the relevant area.

HIGHWAY TRIPPING CLAIMS

Documents from Highway Authority for a period of 12 months prior to the accident—   **36.32**
    (i) Records of inspection for the relevant stretch of highway.
    (ii) Maintenance records including records of independent contractors working in relevant area.
    (iii) Records of the minutes of Highway Authority meetings where maintenance or repair policy has been discussed or decided.

(iv) Records of complaints about the state of highways.

(v) Records of other accidents which have occurred on the relevant stretch of highway.

WORKPLACE CLAIMS

36.33   (i) Accident book entry.

(ii) First aider report.

(iii) Surgery record.

(iv) Foreman/supervisor accident report.

(v) Safety representatives accident report.

(vi) RIDDOR report to HSE.

(vii) Other communications between defendants and HSE.

(viii) Minutes of Health and Safety Committee meeting(s) where accident/matter considered.

(ix) Report to DSS.

(x) Documents listed above relative to any previous accident/matter identified by the claimant and relied upon as proof of negligence.

(xi) Earnings information where defendant is employer.

Documents produced to comply with requirements of the Management of Health and Safety at Work Regulations 1992—

(i) Pre-accident Risk Assessment required by Regulation 3.

(ii) Post-accident Re-Assessment required by Regulation 3.

(iii) Accident Investigation Report prepared in implementing the requirements of Regulations 4, 6 and 9.

(iv) Health Surveillance Records in appropriate cases required by Regulation 5.

(v) Information provided to employees under Regulation 8.

(vi) Documents relating to the employees health and safety training required by Regulation 11.

WORKPLACE CLAIMS—DISCLOSURE WHERE SPECIFIC REGULATIONS APPLY

Section A—Workplace (Health Safety and Welfare) Regulations 1992

36.34   (i) Repair and maintenance records required by Regulation 5.

(ii) Housekeeping records to comply with the requirements of Regulation 9.

(iii) Hazard warning signs or notices to comply with Regulation 17 (Traffic Routes).

Section B—Provision and Use of Work Equipment Regulations 1992

36.35   (i) Manufacturers' specifications and instructions in respect of relevant work equipment establishing its suitability to comply with Regulation 5.

(ii) Maintenance log/maintenance records required to comply with Regulation 6.

(iii) Documents providing information and instructions to employees to comply with Regulation 8.

(iv) Documents provided to the employee in respect of training for use to comply with Regulation 9.

(v) Any notice, sign or document relied upon as a defence to alleged breaches of Regulations 14 to 18 dealing with controls and control systems.

(vi) Instruction/training documents issued to comply with the requirements of Regulation 22 insofar as it deals with maintenance operations where the machinery is not shut down.

(vii) Copies of markings required to comply with Regulation 23.

(viii) Copies of warnings required to comply with Regulation 24.

Section C—Personal Protective Equipment at Work Regulations 1992

(i) Documents relating to the assessment of the Personal Protective Equipment to comply **36.36** with Regulation 6.

(ii) Documents relating to the maintenance and replacement of Personal Protective Equipment to comply with Regulation 7.

(iii) Record of maintenance procedures for Personal Protective Equipment to comply with Regulation 7.

(iv) Records of tests and examinations of Personal Protective Equipment to comply with Regulation 7.

(v) Documents providing information, instruction and training in relation to the Personal Protective Equipment to comply with Regulation 9.

(vi) Instructions for use of Personal Protective Equipment to include the manufacturers' instructions to comply with Regulation 10.

Section D—Manual Handling Operations Regulations 1992

(i) Manual Handling Risk Assessment carried out to comply with the requirements of **36.37** Regulation 4(1)(b)(i).

(ii) Re-assessment carried out post-accident to comply with requirements of Regulation 4(1)(b)(i).

(iii) Documents showing the information provided to the employee to give general indications related to the load and precise indications on the weight of the load and the heaviest side of the load if the centre of gravity was not positioned centrally to comply with Regulation 4(1)(b)(iii).

(iv) Documents relating to training in respect of manual handling operations and training records.

Section E—Health and Safety (Display Screen Equipment) Regulations 1992

(i) Analysis of work stations to assess and reduce risks carried out to comply with the **36.38** requirements of Regulation 2.

(ii) Re-assessment of analysis of work stations to assess and reduce risks following development of symptoms by the claimant.

(iii) Documents detailing the provision of training including training records to comply with the requirements of Regulation 6.

(iv) Documents providing information to employees to comply with the requirements of Regulation 7.

Section F—Control of Substances Hazardous to Health Regulations 1988

(i) Risk assessment carried out to comply with the requirements of Regulation 6. **36.39**

(ii) Reviewed risk assessment carried out to comply with the requirements of Regulation 6.

(iii) Copy labels from containers used for storage handling and disposal of carcinogenics to comply with the requirements of Regulation 7(2A)(h).

(iv) Warning signs identifying designation of areas and installations which may be contaminated by carcinogenics to comply with the requirements of Regulation 7(2A)(h).

(v) Documents relating to the assessment of the Personal Protective Equipment to comply with Regulation 7(3A).

(vi) Documents relating to the maintenance and replacement of Personal Protective Equipment to comply with Regulation 7(3A).

(vii) Record of maintenance procedures for Personal Protective Equipment to comply with Regulation 7(3A).

(viii) Records of tests and examinations of Personal Protective Equipment to comply with Regulation 7(3A).

(ix) Documents providing information, instruction and training in relation to the Personal Protective Equipment to comply with Regulation 7(3A).

(x) Instructions for use of Personal Protective Equipment to include the manufacturers' instructions to comply with Regulation 7(3A).

(xi) Air monitoring records for substances assigned a maximum exposure limit or occupational exposure standard to comply with the requirements of Regulation 7.

(xii) Maintenance examination and test of control measures records to comply with Regulation 9.

(xiii) Monitoring records to comply with the requirements of Regulation 10.

(xiv) Health surveillance records to comply with the requirements of Regulation 11.

(xv) Documents detailing information, instruction and training including training records for employees to comply with the requirements of Regulation 12.

(xvi) Labels and Health and Safety data sheets supplied to the employers to comply with the CHIP Regulations.

Section G—Construction (Design and Management) Regulations 1994

36.40   (i) Notification of a project form (HSE F10) to comply with the requirements of Regulation 7.

(ii) Health and Safety Plan to comply with requirements of Regulation 15.

(iii) Health and Safety file to comply with the requirements of Regulations 12 and 14.

(iv) Information and training records provided to comply with the requirements of Regulation 17.

(v) Records of advice from and views of persons at work to comply with the requirements of Regulation 18.

Section H—Pressure Systems and Transportable Gas Containers Regulations 1989

36.41   (i) Information and specimen markings provided to comply with the requirements of Regulation 5.

(ii) Written statements specifying the safe operating limits of a system to comply with the requirements of Regulation 7.

(iii) Copy of the written scheme of examination required to comply with the requirements of Regulation 8.

(iv) Examination records required to comply with the requirements of Regulation 9.

(v) Instructions provided for the use of operator to comply with Regulation 11.

(vi) Records kept to comply with the requirements of Regulation 13.

(vii) Records kept to comply with the requirements of Regulation 22.

Section I—Lifting Plant and Equipment (Records of Test and Examination etc.) Regulations 1992

36.42   (i) Record kept to comply with the requirements of Regulation 6.

Section J—The Noise at Work Regulations 1989

36.43   (i) Any risk assessment records required to comply with the requirements of Regulations 4 and 5.

(ii) Manufacturers' literature in respect of all ear protection made available to claimant to comply with the requirements of Regulation 8.

(iii) All documents provided to the employee for the provision of information to comply with Regulation 11.

Section K—Construction (Head Protection) Regulations 1989

    (i) Pre-accident assessment of head protection required to comply with Regulation 3(4).   **36.44**

    (ii) Post-accident re-assessment required to comply with Regulation 3(5).

Section L—The Construction (General Provisions) Regulations 1961

    (i) Report prepared following inspections and examinations of excavations etc. to comply   **36.45** with the requirements of Regulation 9.

    (ii) Report prepared following inspections and examinations of work in cofferdams and caissons to comply with the requirements of Regulations 17 and 18.

N.B. Further Standard Discovery lists will be required prior to full implementation.

ANNEX C LETTER OF INSTRUCTION TO MEDICAL EXPERT

Dear Sir,   **36.46**
Re: (*Name and Address*)
D.O.B.—
Telephone No.—
Date of Accident—

We are acting for the above named in connection with injuries received in an accident which occurred on the above date. The main injuries appear to have been (**main injuries**).

We should be obliged if you would examine our Client and let us have a full and detailed report dealing with any relevant pre-accident medical history, the injuries sustained, treatment received and present condition, dealing in particular with the capacity for work and giving a prognosis.

It is central to our assessment of the extent of our Client's injuries to establish the extent and duration of any continuing disability. Accordingly, in the prognosis section we would ask you to specifically comment on any areas of continuing complaint or disability or impact on daily living. If there is such continuing disability you should comment upon the level of suffering or inconvenience caused and, if you are able, give your view as to when or if the complaint or disability is likely to resolve.

Please send our Client an appointment direct for this purpose. Should you be able to offer a cancellation appointment please contact our Client direct. We confirm we will be responsible for your reasonable fees.

We are obtaining the notes and records from our Client's GP and Hospitals attended and will forward them to you when they are to hand/or please request the GP and Hospital records direct and advise that any invoice for the provision of these records should be forwarded to us.

In order to comply with Court Rules we would be grateful if you would insert above your signature a statement that the contents are true to the best of your knowledge and belief.

In order to avoid further correspondence we can confirm that on the evidence we have there is no reason to suspect we may be pursuing a claim against the hospital or its staff.

We look forward to receiving your report within __ weeks. If you will not be able to prepare your report within this period please telephone us upon receipt of these instructions.

When acknowledging these instructions it would assist if you could give an estimate as to the likely time scale for the provision of your report and also an indication as to your fee.

Yours faithfully

J. Pre-action Protocol for Disease and Illness Claims

1 INTRODUCTION

36.47   1.1 Lord Woolf in his *Final Report* of July 1996 recommended the development of protocols: 'to build on and increase the benefits of early but well-informed settlements which genuinely satisfy both parties to a dispute'.

1.2 The aims of these protocols are:
- more contact between the parties;
- better and earlier exchange of information;
- better investigation by both sides;
- to put the parties in a position where they may be able to settle cases fairly and early without litigation;
- to enable proceedings to run to the court's timetable and efficiently, if litigation does become necessary.

1.3 The concept of protocols is relevant to a range of initiatives for good claims practice, especially:
- predictability in the time needed for steps to be taken;
- standardisation of relevant information, including documents to be disclosed.

1.4 The courts will be able to treat the standards set in protocols as the normal reasonable approach. If proceedings are issued, it will be for the court to decide whether non-compliance with a protocol should merit adverse consequences. Guidance on the court's likely approach will be given from time to time in practice directions.

1.5 If the court has to consider the question of compliance after proceedings have begun, it will not be concerned with minor infringements, e.g., failure by a short period to provide relevant information. One minor breach will not exempt the 'innocent' party from following the protocol. The court will look at the effect of non-compliance on the other party when deciding whether to impose sanctions.

2 NOTES OF GUIDANCE

Scope of the Protocol

36.48   2.1 This protocol is intended to apply to all personal injury claims where the injury is not as the result of an accident but takes the form of an illness or disease.

2.2 This protocol covers disease claims which are likely to be complex and frequently not suitable for fast track procedures even though they may fall within fast track limits. Disease for the purpose of this protocol primarily covers any illness physical or psychological, any disorder, ailment, affliction, complaint, malady, or derangement other than a physical or psychological injury solely caused by an accident or other similar single event.

2.3 This protocol is not limited to diseases occurring in the workplace but will embrace diseases occurring in other situations for example through occupation of premises or the use of products. It is not intended to cover those cases, which are dealt with as a 'group' or 'class' action.

2.4 The 'cards on the table' approach advocated by the personal injury protocol is equally appropriate to disease claims. The spirit of that protocol, and of the clinical negligence protocol is followed here, in accordance with the sense of the civil justice reforms.

2.5 The timetable and the arrangements for disclosing documents and obtaining expert evidence may need to be varied to suit the circumstances of the case. If a party considers the detail of the protocol to be inappropriate they should communicate their reasons to all of the parties at that stage. If proceedings are subsequently issued, the court will expect an explanation as to why the protocol has not been followed, or has been varied. In a terminal disease claim with short life expectancy, for instance for a claimant who has a disease such as mesothelioma, the timescale of the protocol is likely to be too long. In such a claim, the claimant may not be able to follow the protocol and the defendant would be expected to treat the claim with urgency.

3 THE AIMS OF THE PROTOCOL

3.1 The *general* aims of the protocol are: **36.49**
- to resolve as many disputes as possible without litigation;
- where a claim cannot be resolved to identify the relevant issues which remain in dispute.

3.2 The *specific* objectives are:

Openness

- to encourage early communication of the perceived problem between the parties or their insurers;
- to encourage employees to voice any concerns or worries about possible work-related illness as soon as practicable;
- to encourage employers to develop systems of early reporting and investigation of suspected occupational health problems and to provide full and prompt explanations to concerned employees or former employees;
- to apply such principles to perceived problems outside the employer/employee relationship, for example occupiers of premises or land and producers of products;
- to ensure that sufficient information is disclosed by both parties to enable each to understand the other's perspective and case, and to encourage early resolution;

Timeliness

- to provide an early opportunity for employers (past or present) or their insurers to identify cases where an investigation is required and to carry out that investigation promptly;
- to encourage employers (past or present) or other defendants to involve and identify their insurers at an early stage;
- to ensure that all relevant records including health and personnel records are provided to employees (past or present) or their appointed representatives promptly on request, by any employer (past or present) or their insurers. This should be complied with to a realistic timetable;
- to ensure that relevant records which are in the claimant's possession are made available to the employers or their insurers by claimants or their advisers at an appropriate stage;
- to proceed on a reasonable timetable where a resolution is not achievable to lay the ground to enable litigation to proceed at a reasonable and proportionate cost, and to limit the matters in contention;
- to communicate promptly where any of the requested information is not available or does not exist;
- to discourage the prolonged pursuit of unmeritorious claims and the prolonged defence of meritorious claims;
- to encourage all parties, at the earliest possible stage, to disclose voluntarily any additional documents which will assist in resolving any issue.

4 THE PROTOCOL

This protocol is not a comprehensive code governing all the steps in disease claims. Rather it   **36.50**
attempts to set out *a code of good practice* which parties should follow.

Obtaining occupational records including health records

36.51   4.1 In appropriate cases, a *potential claimant* may request occupational records including health records and personnel records before sending a letter of claim.

4.2 Any request for records by the *potential claimant* or his adviser should *provide sufficient information* to alert the *potential defendant* or his insurer where a possible disease claim is being investigated. Annex A1 provides a suggested form for this purpose for use in cases arising from employment. Similar forms can be prepared and used in other situations.

4.3 The copy records should be provided *within a maximum of 40 days* of the request at no cost. Although these will primarily be occupational records, it will be good practice for a *potential defendant* to disclose product data documents identified by a *potential claimant* at this stage which may resolve a causation issue.

4.4 In the rare circumstances that the *potential defendant* or his insurer is in difficulty in providing information quickly details should be given of what is being done to resolve it with a reasonable time estimate for doing so.

4.5 If the *potential defendant* or his insurer fails to provide the records including health records within 40 days and fails to comply with para. 4.4 above, the *potential claimant* or his adviser may then apply to the court for an *order for pre-action disclosure*. The CPR make pre-action applications to the court easier. The court also has the power to impose costs sanctions for unreasonable delay in providing records.

5 COMMUNICATION

36.52   5.1 If either the *potential claimant* or his adviser considers *additional records are required from a third party*, such as records from previous employers or general practitioner records, in the first instance these should be requested by the *potential claimant* or their advisers. Third party record holders would be expected to cooperate. The CPR enable parties to apply to the court for pre-action disclosure by third parties.

5.2 As soon as the records have been received and analysed, the *potential claimant* or his adviser should consider whether a claim should be made. General practitioner records will normally be obtained before a decision is reached.

5.3 If a decision is made not to proceed further at this stage against a party identified as a *potential defendant*, the *potential claimant* or his adviser should notify that *potential defendant* as soon as practicable.

6 LETTER OF CLAIM

36.53   6.1 Where a decision is made to make a claim, the claimant shall send to the proposed defendant two copies of a letter of claim, as soon as sufficient information is available to substantiate a realistic claim and before issues of quantum are addressed in detail. One copy is for the defendants, the second for passing on to his insurers.

6.2 This letter shall contain a *clear summary of the facts* on which the claim is based, including details of the illness alleged, and the *main allegations of fault*. It shall also give details of present condition and prognosis. The *financial loss* incurred by the claimant should be outlined. Where the case is funded by a conditional fee agreement, notification should be given of the existence of the agreement and where appropriate, that there is a success fee and insurance premium, although not the level of the success fee or premium.

6.3 Solicitors are recommended to use *a standard format* for such a letter—an example is at annex B: this can be amended to suit the particular case, for example, if the client has rehabilitation needs these can also be detailed in the letter.

6.4 A *chronology* of the relevant events (e.g. dates or periods of exposure) should be provided. In the case of alleged occupational disease an appropriate employment history should also be provided, particularly if the claimant has been employed by a number of different employers and the illness in question has a long latency period.

6.5 The letter of claim should identify any *relevant documents*, including health records not already in the defendant's possession e.g. any relevant general practitioner records. These will need to be disclosed in confidence to the nominated insurance manager or solicitor representing the defendant following receipt of their letter of acknowledgment. Where the action is brought under the Law Reform (Miscellaneous Provisions) Act 1934 or the Fatal Accidents Act 1976 then *relevant documents* will normally include copies of the death certificate, the post mortem report, the inquest depositions and if obtained by that date the grant of probate or letters of administration.

6.6 The letter of claim should indicate whether a claim is also being made against any *other potential defendant* and identify any known insurer involved.

6.7 Sufficient information should be given to enable the defendant's insurer/solicitor to commence *investigations* and at least to put a broad valuation on the 'risk'.

6.8 It is not a requirement for the claimant to provide *medical evidence* with the letter of claim, but the claimant may choose to do so in very many cases.

6.9 *Letters of claim and response* are not intended to have the same *status* as a statement of case in proceedings. Matters may come to light as a result of investigation after the letter of claim has been sent, or after the defendant has responded, particularly if disclosure of documents takes place outside the recommended three-month period. These circumstances could mean that the 'pleaded' case of one or both parties is presented slightly differently than in the letter of claim or response. It would not be consistent with the spirit of the protocol for a party to 'take a point' on this in the proceedings, provided that there was no obvious intention by the party who changed their position to mislead the other party.

6.10 *Proceedings should not be issued until after three months from the date of acknowledgment* (see para. 7), unless there is a limitation problem and/or the claimant's position needs to be protected by early issue (see para. 2.5).

7 THE RESPONSE

7.1 The defendant should *send an acknowledgment within 21 calendar days* of the date of **36.54** posting of the letter of claim, identifying the liability insurer (if any) who will be dealing with the matter and, if necessary, identifying specifically any significant omissions from the letter of claim. If there has been no acknowledgment by the defendant or insurer within 21 days, the claimant will be entitled to issue proceedings.

7.2 The identity of all relevant insurers, if more than one, should be notified to the claimant by the insurer identified in the acknowledgment letter, within one calendar month of the date of that acknowledgment.

7.3 The defendant or his representative should, *within three months of the date of the acknowledgment letter*, provide a *reasoned answer*:
- if the *claim is admitted*, they should say so in clear terms;
- if only *part of the claim is admitted* they should make clear which issues of fault and/or causation and/or limitation are admitted and which remain in issue and why;
- if the *claim is not admitted in full*, they should explain why and should, for example, include comments on the employment status of the claimant (including job description(s) and details of the department(s) where the claimant worked), the allegations of fault, causation and of limitation, and if a synopsis or chronology of relevant events has been provided and is disputed, their version of those events;

- if the *claim is not admitted in full*, the defendant should enclose with his letter of reply *documents* in his possession which are *material to the issues* between the parties and which would be likely to be ordered to be disclosed by the court, either on an application for pre-action disclosure, or on disclosure during proceedings. Reference can be made to the documents annexed to the personal injury protocol;
- where more than one defendant receives a letter of claim, the timetable will be activated for each defendant by the date on the letter of claim addressed to them. If any defendant wishes to extend the timetable because the number of defendants will cause complications, they should seek agreement to a different timetable as soon as possible.

7.4 If the parties reach agreement on liability and/or causation, but time is needed to resolve other issues including the value of the claim, they should aim to agree a reasonable period.

7.5 Where it is not practicable for the defendant to complete his investigations within three months, the defendant should indicate the difficulties and outline the further time needed. Any request for an extension of time should be made, with reasons, as soon as the defendant becomes aware that an extension is needed and normally before the three-month period has expired. Such an extension of time should be agreed in circumstances where reasonable justification has been shown. Lapse of many years since the circumstances giving rise to the claim does not, by itself, constitute reasonable justification for further time.

7.6 Where the relevant negligence occurred outside England and Wales and/or where the defendant is outside the jurisdiction, the time periods of 21 days and three months should normally be extended up to 42 days and six months.

8 SPECIAL DAMAGES

36.55   8.1 The claimant will send to the defendant as soon as practicable a schedule of special damages with supporting documents, particularly where the defendant has admitted liability.

9 EXPERTS

36.56   9.1 In disease claims expert opinions will usually be needed:
- on knowledge, fault and causation;
- on condition and prognosis;
- to assist in valuing aspects of the claim.

9.2 The civil justice reforms and the CPR encourage economy in the use of experts and a less adversarial expert culture. It is recognised that in disease claims, the parties and their advisers will require flexibility in their approach to expert evidence. Decisions on whether experts might be instructed jointly, and on whether reports might be disclosed sequentially or by exchange, should rest with the parties and their advisers. Sharing expert evidence may be appropriate on various issues including those relating to the value of the claim. However, this protocol does not attempt to be prescriptive on issues in relation to expert evidence.

9.3 Obtaining expert evidence will often be an expensive step and may take time, especially in specialised areas where there are limited numbers of suitable experts. Claimants, defendants and their advisers, will therefore need to consider carefully how best to obtain any necessary expert help quickly and cost-effectively.

9.4 The protocol recognises that a flexible approach must be adopted in the obtaining of medical reports in claims of this type. There will be very many occasions where the claimant will need to obtain a medical report before writing the letter of claim. In such cases the defendant will be entitled to obtain their own medical report. In some other instances it may be more appropriate to send the letter of claim before the medical report is obtained. Defendants will usually need to see a medical report before they can reach a view on causation.

9.5 Where the parties agree the nomination of a single expert is appropriate, before any party instructs an expert he should give the other party a list of the *name(s) of one or more experts* in the relevant speciality whom he considers are suitable to instruct. The parties are encouraged to agree the instruction of a single expert to deal with discrete areas such as cost of care.

9.6 *Within 14 days* the other party may indicate an objection to one or more of the named experts. The first party should then instruct a mutually acceptable expert. If the Claimant nominates an expert in the original letter of claim, the 14 days is in addition to the 21 days in para. 7.1.

9.7 If the second party objects to all the listed experts, the parties may then instruct *experts of their own choice.* It would be for the court to decide subsequently, if proceedings are issued, whether either party had acted unreasonably.

9.8 If the *second party does not object to an expert nominated,* he shall not be entitled to rely on his own expert evidence within that particular speciality unless:
    (a) the first party agrees,
    (b) the court so directs, or
    (c) the first party's expert report has been amended and the first party is not prepared to disclose the original report.

9.9 *Either party may send to an agreed expert written questions* on the report, relevant to the issues, via the first party's solicitors. The expert should send answers to the questions separately and directly to each party.

9.10 The cost of a report from an agreed expert will usually be paid by the instructing first party: the costs of the expert replying to questions will usually be borne by the party which asks the questions.

9.11 Where the defendant admits liability in whole or in part, before proceedings are issued, any medical report obtained under this protocol which *the claimant* relies upon, should be disclosed to the other party.

9.12 Where the defendant admits liability in whole or in part before proceedings are issued, any medical report obtained under this protocol which *the defendant* relies upon, should be disclosed to the claimant.

10 RESOLUTION OF ISSUES

10.1 Part 36 of the CPR enables claimants and defendants to make formal offers to settle **36.57** before proceedings are started. Parties should consider making such an offer, since to do so often leads to settlement. If such an offer is made, the party making the offer must always supply sufficient evidence and/or information to enable the offer to be properly considered.

10.2 Where a claim is not resolved when the protocol has been followed, the parties might wish to carry out a 'stocktake' of the issues in dispute, and the evidence that the court is likely to need to decide those issues, before proceedings are started.

10.3 Prior to proceedings it will be usual for all parties to disclose those expert reports relating to liability and causation upon which they propose to rely.

10.4 The claimant should delay issuing proceedings for 21 days from disclosure of reports to enable the parties to consider whether the claim is capable of settlement.

10.5 Where the defendant is insured and the pre-action steps have been conducted by the insurer, the insurer would normally be expected to nominate solicitors to act in the proceedings and the claimant's solicitor is recommended to invite the insurer to nominate solicitors to act in the proceedings and to do so seven to 14 days before the intended issue date.

11 LIMITATION

36.58   11.1 If by reason of complying with any part of this protocol a claimant's claim may be time-barred under any provision of the Limitation Act 1980, or any other legislation which imposes a time limit for bringing an action, the claimant may commence proceedings without complying with this protocol. In such circumstances, a claimant who commences proceedings without complying with all, or any part, of this protocol may apply to the court on notice for directions as to the timetable and form of procedure to be adopted, at the same time as he requests the court to issue proceedings. The court will consider whether to order a stay of the whole or part of the proceedings pending compliance with this protocol.

ANNEX A LETTER REQUESTING OCCUPATIONAL
RECORDS INCLUDING HEALTH RECORDS

36.59   Dear Sirs,

We are acting on behalf of the above-named who has developed the following *(disease)*. We are investigating whether this disease may have been caused:

- during the course of his employment with [you] [*(name of employer if different)*;
- whilst at your premises at *(address)*;
- as a result of your product *(name)*.

We are writing this in accordance with the Pre-action Protocol for Disease and Illness Claims.

We seek the following records:

(details, e.g., personnel, occupational health)

Please note your insurers may require you to advise them of this request.

We enclose a request form and expect to receive the records within 40 days.

If you are not able to comply with this request within this time, please advise us of the reason.

Yours faithfully

ANNEX A1 APPLICATION ON BEHALF OF A POTENTIAL CLAIMANT
FOR USE WHERE A DISEASE CLAIM IS BEING INVESTIGATED

36.60   This should be completed as fully as possible.

Company

Name

Address

1 (a) Full name of claimant (including previous surnames)

1 (b) Address now

1 (c) Address at date of termination of employment, if different

1 (d) Date of birth (and death, if applicable)

1 (e) National Insurance number, if available

2 Department(s) where claimant worked

3 This application is made because the claimant is considering:
   (a) a claim against you as detailed in point 4YES/NO
   (b) pursuing an action against someone elseYES/NO

4 If the answer to point 3(a) is 'Yes' details of:
   (a) the likely nature of the claim, e.g., dermatitis

    (b) grounds for the claim, e.g., exposure to chemical

    (c) approximate dates of the events involved

 5 If the answer to point 3(b) is 'Yes' insert:

    (a) the names of the proposed defendants

    (b) have legal proceedings been started?YES/NO

    (c) if appropriate, details of the claim and action number

 6 Any other relevant information or documents requested

Signature of solicitor

Name

Address

Ref.

Telephone number

Fax number

I authorise you to disclose all of your records relating to me/the claimant to my solicitor and to your legal and insurance representatives.

Signature of claimant

Signature of personal representative where claimant has died

ANNEX B TEMPLATE FOR LETTER OF CLAIM

To Defendant **36.61**

Dear Sirs

Re: *(Claimant's full name)*

(Claimant's full address)

National Insurance number:

Date of birth:

Clock or works number:

Employer: *(name and address)*

We are instructed by the above named to claim damages in connection with a claim for:

(specify occupational disease)

We are writing this letter in accordance with the Pre-action Protocol for Disease and Illness Claims.

Please confirm the identity of your insurers. Please note that your insurers will need to see this letter as soon as possible and it may affect your insurance cover if you do not send this to them.

The Claimant was employed by you *(if the claim arises out of public or occupiers' liability give appropriate details)* as *(job description)* from *(date)* to *(date)*. During the relevant period of his employment he worked:

(description of precisely where the claimant worked and what he did to include a description of any machines used and details of any exposure to noise or substances)

The circumstances leading to the development of this condition are as follows:

(give chronology of events)

The reason why we are alleging fault is:

(details should be given of contemporary and comparable employees who have suffered from similar problems if known; any protective equipment provided; complaints; the supervisors concerned, if known)

Our client's employment history is attached.

[We have also made a claim against:

(insert details)

Their insurers' details are:

(insert if known)]

We have the following documents in support of our client's claim and will disclose these in confidence to your nominated insurance manager or solicitor when we receive their acknowledgment letter:

(e.g., occupational health notes; GP notes)

[We have obtained a medical report from *(name)* and will disclose this when we receive your acknowledgment of this letter.

(This is optional at this stage.)]

From the information we presently have:

  (i) the Claimant first became aware of symptoms on *(insert approximate date)*;

  (ii) the Claimant first received medical advice about those symptoms on *(insert date)* *(give details of advice given if appropriate)*;

  (iii) the Claimant first believed that those symptoms might be due to exposure leading to this claim on *(insert approximate date)*.

A description of our client's condition is as follows:

(this should be sufficiently detailed to allow the defendant to put a broad value on the claim)

He has the following time off work:

(insert dates)

He is presently employed as a *(job description)* and his average net weekly income is £ __.

If you are our client's employers, please provide us with the usual earnings details, which will enable us to calculate his financial loss.

[Please note that we have entered into a conditional fee agreement with our client dated ___ in relation to this claim which provides for a success fee within the meaning of section 58(2) of the Courts and Legal Services Act 1990. Our client has taken out an insurance policy dated with *(name of insurance company)* to which section 29 of the Access to Justice Act 1999 applies in respect of this claim.]

A copy of this letter is attached for you to send to your insurers. Finally we expect an acknowledgment of this letter within 21 days by yourselves or your insurers.

Yours faithfully

37

THE CIVIL PROCEDURE RULES

This chapter provides an outline of some key provisions of the CPR. Space does **37.01** not permit the inclusion of the full text of the rules and Practice Directions, but commentary is no substitute for a careful study of the original text and cross-references have therefore been included to the relevant passages in *Blackstone's Civil Practice 2004* (hereafter *Blackstone*). The current version of the CPR can also be accessed at www.dca.gov.uk/civil/procrules_fin/current.htm. This narrative should not be thought sufficient on its own: its purpose is to direct readers to the relevant sources where the answers will be found.

A characteristic of the CPR is that it is necessary to look up almost everything **37.02** twice. The Rules are divided into 75 Parts, each covering a separate topic, and each part comprises the rules on that topic followed by a Practice Direction which restates or explains or develops the rules.

A. The Overriding Objective

The CPR begin in Part 1 with a statement of the Overriding Objective (*Black-* **37.03** *stone* 1314), a mission statement which identifies two themes of the new rules. First, r 1.1(2) identifies the requirement of proportionality, that the parties, their legal advisers and the courts should devote to each case only the amount of work and effort that is proportionate to the value and importance of the case. Simple claims of modest value do not merit the commitment of resources involved in providing the best obtainable representation, expert evidence or judicial input. In order to keep the parties on an equal footing the courts will not only disallow the recovery of extravagant costs but will intervene to prevent a wealthy party from relying on materials such as expert evidence obtained at disproportionate expense. Secondly, judges, instead of being limited to deciding the issues put before them by the parties or their representatives, have a duty of actively managing cases, which sometimes means imposing a framework for the disposal of a claim that is contrary to the wishes of the legal representatives on both sides, but is intended to protect the interests of the litigants and of the system as a whole. This greater role for judicial discretion makes it less easy to predict the way cases will be dealt with.

B. High Court and County Court

37.04 The CPR provide a unified set of rules for civil claims proceeding in both the High Court and the county court, but the two levels of court continue to have separate existence. It is difficult to see why it has been thought appropriate to continue with this distinction, which serves little useful purpose for litigants. In London High Court claims will usually proceed in the Royal Court of Justice but outside London the local offices, staff and district judges will usually be the same people for both courts. A personal injury claim proceeding in the High Court will often be tried by a circuit judge appointed under s 9 of the Supreme Court Act 1981 rather than by a High Court judge.

37.05 There is no clear-cut rule to determine the level of value or difficulty which may make a personal injury claim suitable to proceed in the High Court. PD 7 (How to Start Proceedings) provides the only guidance in the CPR and para 2.2 of that Practice Direction (*Blackstone* 1397) provides that a personal injury claim with a value below £50,000 cannot be started in the High Court, but in practice the unlimited jurisdiction of the county court in claims for damages means that the threshold is much higher than this, and it would be unusual for a claim with a value below £250,000 to begin in the High Court unless it has some special features of difficulty. A claim started in the county court can be transferred later to the High Court if it continues to be defended and has a value or difficulty which make this appropriate. The incentives to encourage litigants to start in the right court include the risk of bearing the costs of a transfer later (Part 30, *Blackstone* 1587), the risk of being penalized in the costs of the whole claim under s 51(8) and (9) of the Supreme Court Act 1981 (*Blackstone* 2897) and the risk of being struck out if the court concludes that there was an inappropriate tactical motive, rather than a genuine mistake (*Restick v Criskmore* [1994] 1 WLR 420).

C. Geographical Jurisdiction

A claimant is entitled to issue a claim form in any court, regardless of the place **37.06** in which the cause of action arose or place where the defendant resides. The rule for automatic transfer of claims to the defendant's home court in r 26.2 applies only to claims for a specified sum of money, and not to a claim for damages. The criteria for transfer under r 30.3 (*Blackstone* 1588) require the court to consider whether a different court would be more convenient or fair for hearings. This covers the convenience of everybody involved and not just the defendant, who, in most personal injury claims, will be represented by insurers and solicitors and will have no argument of convenience in favour of his home court unless there is a real likelihood of a trial. If the claimant's solicitors find it more convenient to issue proceedings in their local court it is reasonable to do so.

D. General Rules about Service

In personal injury claims, difficulties about service are rare, because almost all **37.07** claims are pursued with the help of solicitors and almost all claims are defended by insurers who will nominate solicitors to accept service during the pre-action protocol procedures. By r 6.4 (*Blackstone* 1364) where a solicitor is authorized to accept service and has notified the party serving the document in writing that he is so authorized, a document must be served on the solicitor, unless personal service is required by some specific rule (*Nanglegan v Royal Free Hampstead NHS Trust* [2001] EWCA Civ 127; [2002] 1 WLR 1043). Rule 6.5(4) allows a document to be served by first class post, by leaving it at the place of service, through a document exchange, by fax, or by other means of electronic communication (*Blackstone* 1365). If a solicitor has not been authorized to accept service, the place for service will be the usual or last known residence of an individual or the place of business of a firm or company, as set out in r 6.5(6).

Rule 6.7 (*Blackstone* 1366) sets out the time at which service by different **37.08** methods is deemed to have occurred:

First class post	The second day after it was posted
Document exchange	The second day after it was left at the document exchange

Delivering the document to or leaving it at a permitted address	The day after it was delivered to or left at the permitted address
Fax	If it is transmitted on a business day before 4 pm, on that day, *or*
	In any other case, on the business day after the day on which it is transmitted
Other electronic method	The second day after the day on which it is transmitted.

E. Rules about Time

37.09 The calculation of time is governed by r 2.8 (*Blackstone* 1318). In calculating a period for doing any act that is expressed as a number of days, the computation is of clear days, so that the day on which the period begins and the day on which an event will happen at the end of the period are both disregarded. Saturdays, Sundays and bank holidays do not count in a period of five days or less. If the court office is closed on the last day, the act is in time if it is done on the next day on which the court office is open. In *Anderton v Clwyd CC* [2002] EWCA Civ 933; [2002] 1 WLR 1374 the Court of Appeal decided that r 2.8(4) applies only to time for doing any act, so that Saturdays, Sundays and bank holidays are to be included as days when deemed service can take place even though the deemed period for service is less than five days. A month is a calendar month.

F. Starting a Claim

37.10 CPR Part 7.2 provides that a claim is started by issuing a claim form (*Blackstone* 1394). The style is set out in Form N1 and the content of the claim form is considered in the next chapter. Once the form has been completed, it is sent or taken to court office and the court will then note the date of issue on the form itself. A list of court addresses is included in Chapter 49 below.

37.11 The date of the issue of the claim form is important (a) in order to determine whether a claim has been issued in time for purposes of limitation, and (b) because there is a strict time limit for serving the claim form, which runs from the date of issue. By r 7.5 (*Blackstone* 1395) the time limit is four months (six months for service out of the jurisdiction).

37.12 A claimant who has entered into a conditional fee agreement before starting the proceedings must file and serve notice of the arrangement (Form N251) when he issues the claim form (PD Costs para 19.2, *Blackstone* 1753).

G. Service of the Claim Form

A claim cannot proceed until the claim form has been served on the defendant. **37.13**
The Rules are unusually severe about this, and give the court only a very
restricted power to allow the claimant to escape from the consequences of failing
to serve within the four-month time limit. There are special rules about the
service of a claim form in rr 6.13–6.16 (*Blackstone* 1368). Rule 6.7 (above)
deeming the time of service applies. If a claim form is not served within four
months after the date of issue, the claim cannot proceed because the claimant
will find it extremely difficult to obtain an extension of time under r 7.6
(*Blackstone* 1395). An application may be made to extend the period within
which the claim form may be served, but if the application is not made until the
period for service has expired the court may make such an order only if (a) the
court has been unable to serve the claim form, or (b) the claimant has taken all
reasonable steps to serve the claim form but has been unable to do so, and (c) in
either case, the claimant has acted promptly in making the application. If the
limitation period has expired the claimant will be unable to start again, and will
have an unanswerable claim against his solicitor for the loss of the action. Almost
all other procedural mistakes can be remedied by the wide case management
powers of the court under r 3.1 (*Blackstone* 1326) but a failure to serve the claim
form cannot. The service of the claim form should never be left to the last day
and a deliberate decision to take advantage of the four months allowed can be
dangerous.

Godwin v Swindon BC [2001] EWCA Civ 1478; [2002] 1 WLR 997   The **37.14**
claim form was served by first class post on Thursday, arriving on Friday, which
was the last day to comply with the four-month limit. However, by r 6.7 it
was irrebuttably to be presumed that the claim form arrived on the following
Monday, out of time, and the action was struck out.

Anderton v Clwyd CC [2002] 1 WLR 1371   The severity of the rule in *Godwin* **37.15**
was upheld in the interests of certainty. The deemed day of service cannot be
displaced by proof of actual receipt on an earlier day, although deemed service
can take place at the weekend which saved the action in this case.

Cranfield v Bridgegrove [2003] EWCA Civ 656; [2003] 1 WLR 2441   Five **37.16**
more appeals on service of the claim form, covering the power to dispense with
service, the circumstances in which the court is 'unable' to serve, and service at a
last known residence after the defendant is no longer there.

Hastroodi v Hancock [2004] EWCA Civ 652; [2004] 3 All ER 530   The claim **37.17**
was issued eight days before the expiry of the limitation period. One working
day before the expiry of the validity of the claim form the claimant applied

without notice for an extension of time for service. The only reason for failing to serve the claim form in time was the incompetence of the claimant's solicitors. Even though the application was made before the expiry of the period, in the circumstances an extension of time should not be granted.

H. Statements of Truth

37.18 Formal documents deployed in the pursuit or defence of the claim must be verified by a statement of truth in accordance with Part 22 and PD 22 (*Blackstone* 1498). Although the formal requirements vary slightly, this requirement applies to all statements of case, amendments, schedules, responses to a request for further information, applications, witness statements and expert reports. The requirement was extended to schedules and counter-schedules with effect from 8 December 2003.

37.19 The effect of a statement of truth is first, to ensure that parties and their representatives take the assertions that are put forward in litigation seriously, so as to restrain exaggerated and unfounded claims. Secondly, by r 32.6 (*Blackstone* 1601) a document that has been verified by a statement of truth can be used as evidence in the course of the proceedings, except at the final trial, without needing further verification.

37.20 Rule 32.14 (*Blackstone* 1602) provides that if a person makes, or causes to be made, a false statement in a document verified by a statement of truth without an honest belief in its truth, he may be subject to proceedings for contempt of court, although such proceedings can only be brought by the Attorney General or with the permission of the court.

37.21 At its simplest, the form of a statement of truth required by PD 22 (*Blackstone* 1500) is 'I believe that the facts stated in this [Particulars of Claim] [witness statement] are true'. The document containing these words must be signed (r 22.1(6)). In proceedings brought on behalf of a child or patient, it is the litigation friend who should sign in place of the child or patient. In addition, a statement of case, a response to a request for further information, or an application may have a statement of truth that is signed by the legal representative of the party rather than by the party himself, in which case the form of the statement is 'The [claimant] believes . . .'. A statement of truth verifying a witness statement must be signed by the witness and a statement of truth verifying an expert report must be signed by the expert.

37.22 In personal injury claims the defendant is often a company or corporation and the statement of truth may be made by a person in a senior position (PD 22 para 3.5) or by an insurer with a financial interest in the result of the proceedings (para 3.6A) or by a legal representative. The legal representative must state the capacity in which he signs and the name of his firm, but signs in his own name and not in the name of his firm or employer. He need not state that he is authorized to make the statement of truth. His signature is taken as his statement that the client on whose behalf he has signed has authorized him to do so, that before signing he had explained to the client that in signing the statement of truth he would be confirming the client's belief that the facts stated in the document, and that before signing he had informed the client of the possible consequences to the client if it subsequently appears that the client did not have an honest belief in the truth of these facts (para 3.8). Thus, where a legal representative signs the statement of truth on a statement of case it should refer to the client's belief, and he should (a) sign it (b) print his name (c) state the capacity in which he signs and (d) state the name of his firm.

I. Multiple Parties

Rule 19.1 (*Blackstone* 1467) permits any number of claimants or defendants to be joined as parties to a claim. In personal injury claims, it is not unusual to have several defendants to a single claim, and the court will have jurisdiction to apportion responsibility between defendants who are jointly liable for the same damage under the Civil Liability (Contribution) Act 1978 without the need for any further statements of case between the defendants beyond their defences to the claim. **37.23**

Where a defendant wishes to bring a cross-claim against the claimant, the procedural requirements under Part 20 and PD 20 (*Blackstone* 1481) allow for the counterclaim to be made with the defence but otherwise treat the counterclaim as a separate claim. In addition Part 20 governs a claim for contribution or indemnity in respect of the claim that a defendant may wish to make against a person other than the claimant, what used to be known as third party proceedings. The terminology and procedure for Part 20 claims are some of the least successful parts of the CPR. **37.24**

J. Civil Liability (Contribution) Act 1978, ss 1–7

1. Entitlement to contribution

(1) Subject to the following provisions of this section, any person liable in respect of any damage suffered by another person may recover contribution from any other person liable in respect of the same damage (whether jointly with him or otherwise). **37.25**

(2) A person shall be entitled to recover contribution by virtue of subsection (1) above notwithstanding that he has ceased to be liable in respect of the damage in question since the time

when the damage occurred, provided that he was so liable immediately before he made or was ordered or agreed to make the payment in respect of which the contribution is sought.

(3) A person shall be liable to make contribution by virtue of subsection (1) above notwith-standing that he has ceased to be liable in respect of the damage in question since the time when the damage occurred, unless he ceased to be liable by virtue of the expiry of a period of limitation or prescription which extinguished the right on which the claim against him in respect of the damage was based.

(4) A person who has made or agreed to make any payment in bona fide settlement or compromise of any claim made against him in respect of any damage (including a payment into court which has been accepted) shall be entitled to recover contribution in accordance with this section without regard to whether or not he himself is or ever was liable in respect of the damage, provided, however, that he would have been liable assuming that the factual basis of the claim against him could be established.

(5) A judgment given in any action brought in any part of the United Kingdom by or on behalf of the person who suffered the damage in question against any person from whom contribution is sought under this section shall be conclusive in the proceedings for contribution as to any issue determined by that judgment in favour of the person from whom the contribution is sought.

(6) References in this section to a person's liability in respect of any damage are references to any such liability which has been or could be established in an action brought against him in England and Wales by or on behalf of the person who suffered the damage; but it is immaterial whether any issue arising in any such action was or would be determined (in accordance with the rules of private international law) by reference to the law of a country outside England and Wales.

2. Assessment of contribution

37.26   (1) Subject to subsection (3) below, in any proceedings for contribution under section 1 above the amount of the contribution recoverable from any person shall be such as may be found by the court to be just and equitable having regard to the extent of that person's responsibility for the damage in question.

(2) Subject to subsection (3) below, the court shall have power in any such proceedings to exempt any person from liability to make contribution or to direct that the contribution to be recovered from any person shall amount to a complete indemnity.

(3) Where the amount of the damages which have or might have been awarded in respect of the damage in question in any action brought in England and Wales by or on behalf of the person who suffered it against the person from whom the contribution is sought was or would have been subject to—

(a) any limit imposed by or under any enactment or by any agreement made before the damage occurred;

(b) any reduction by virtue of section 1 of the Law Reform (Contributory Negligence) Act 1945 or section 5 of the Fatal Accidents Act 1976; or

(c) any corresponding limit or reduction under the law of a country outside England and Wales;

the person from whom the contribution is sought shall not by virtue of any contribution awarded under section 1 above be required to pay in respect of the damage a greater amount than the amount of those damages as so limited or reduced.

3. Proceedings against persons jointly liable for the same debt or damage

37.27   Judgment recovered against any person liable in respect of any debt or damage shall not be a bar to an action, or to the continuance of an action, against any person who is (apart from any such bar) jointly liable with him in respect of the same debt or damage.

4. Successive actions against persons liable (jointly or otherwise) for the same damage

If more than one action is bought in respect of any damage by or on behalf of the person by whom **37.28**
it was suffered against persons liable in respect of the damage (whether jointly or otherwise) the
plaintiff shall not be entitled to costs in any of those actions, other than that in which judgment is
first given, unless the court is of the opinion that there was reasonable ground for bringing the
action.

5. Application to the Crown

Without prejudice to section 4(1) of the Crown Proceedings Act 1947 (indemnity and contri- **37.29**
bution), this Act shall bind the Crown, but nothing in this Act shall be construed as in any way
affecting Her Majesty in Her private capacity (including in right of Her Duchy of Lancaster) or
the Duchy of Cornwall.

6. Interpretation

(1) A person is liable in respect of any damage for the purposes of this Act if the person who **37.30**
suffered it (or anyone representing his estate or dependants) is entitled to recover compensation
from him in respect of that damage (whatever the legal basis of his liability, whether tort, breach of
contract, breach of trust or otherwise).

(2) References in this Act to an action brought by or on behalf of the person who suffered any
damage include references to an action brought for the benefit of his estate or dependants.

(3) In this Act 'dependants' has the same meaning as in the Fatal Accidents Act 1976.

(4) In this Act, except in section 1(5) above, 'action' means an action brought in England and
Wales.

7. Savings

(3) The right to recover contribution in accordance with section 1 above supersedes any right, **37.31**
other than an express contractual right, to recover contribution (as distinct from indemnity)
otherwise than under this Act in corresponding circumstances; but nothing in this Act shall
affect—

(a) any express or implied contractual or other right to indemnity; or

(b) any express contractual provision regulating or excluding contribution; which would
be enforceable apart from this Act (or render enforceable any agreement for indemnity or contribution which would not be enforceable apart from this Act).

K. Joining a Defendant after Three Years

A special rule applies when a claimant seeks to join a new defendant into an **37.32**
existing claim after the primary limitation period has expired. When issuing a
claim form for the first time outside the primary limitation period, the claimant
is entitled to issue the claim and the defence of limitation then arises if the point
is taken in the defence. However, the claimant is not entitled to issue a claim
against an additional defendant in the same way. Rule 19.5 (*Blackstone* 1468)
permits the court to add or substitute a party in a claim for personal injuries
where the court directs that s 11 or 12 of the Limitation Act 1980 shall not
apply to the claim by or against a new party. Thus the claimant must issue
an application to disapply the primary limitation period and serve it on the

proposed new defendant, and the limitation issue must be resolved by the court in favour of the claimant before permission can be given for the new defendant to be joined and for the claim form and statements of case to be amended accordingly.

L. Bankrupt Claimants

37.33 By s 306 of the Insolvency Act 1986 a bankrupt's estate vests automatically in the trustee of the bankrupt immediately on his appointment taking effect. No formal document is needed to make the transfer of all the property of the bankrupt and the definition of property in s 436 of the 1986 Act includes 'things in action'. At common law, however, the property of the bankrupt does not include damages for bodily pain and a bankrupt claimant would be free to bring a claim limited to damages for pain and suffering and loss of amenity without reference to his trustee (*Heath v Tang* [1993] 1 WLR 1421). However, a claim for loss of earnings referable to the period of the bankruptcy is part of the property of the bankrupt. A cause of action in respect of such loss vests in the trustee under s 306. A cause of action for personal injury which includes both injury damages and a claim for loss of earnings will be a mixed claim, arising out of a single cause of action which therefore vests in the trustee. If the trustee pursues such a claim, any damages received which do not form part of the estate of the bankrupt but are personal to the claimant will be held on a constructive trust for the claimant. If the claimant takes an assignment of the cause of action from the trustee and pursues the claim himself, it will usually be on terms providing that the claimant can retain the damages personal to him, but must account to the trustee for damages which form part of the property in his estate, principally his loss of earnings for the period of the bankruptcy. It is suggested that the damage which will form part of the property of the bankrupt will in such cases be limited to loss of earnings during the period of the bankruptcy and interest. Injury damages, reimbursement of expenses made necessary by the injury, and damages for gratuitous care by the claimant's family, as well as claims for future loss of earnings and pension after the date of discharge, will be the personal claim of the bankrupt.

37.34 *Ord v Upton* [2000] Ch 352   The claimant pursued a claim for damages for negligent medical treatment. The claim included general damages for pain and suffering, and loss of earnings both past and future. The Court of Appeal held that the single cause of action was included in the bankrupt's property, but the action was hybrid, and in part personal so far as it related to the body and mind of the applicant. The cause of action vested in the trustee, but the trustee held on a constructive trust the right to receive damages for pain and suffering and loss of amenity, and damages for future loss of earnings after the date of the claimant's discharge from the bankruptcy.

M. Companies that Have Been Dissolved

A difficulty which arises quite often in disease claims dealing with periods of **37.35** employment many years ago is to find the defendant. The Association of British Insurers may be able to circulate the details of a company in order to assist the claimant to trace the relevant employers' liability insurer. Even when the insurer has been identified however, the claim cannot be pursued in legal proceedings without a defendant to sue, which technically must be the former employer rather than the insurer even though it will be the insurer alone which will deal with the claim. If the company has been dissolved, it will be necessary to make an application to restore the name of the company to the register for the purpose of bringing the claim. The claim is made under s 653 of the Companies Act 1985 and may be made at any time within 20 years from the date when the dissolution of the company was published in the *London Gazette*. The procedure is the subject of a Practice Note at [1974] 1 WLR 1459.

N. Group Litigation

There are special rules that govern the conduct of litigation when there are a **37.36** number of claims which all give rise to common issues of fact or law which have to be decided by the court. These are set out at rr 19.11–19.15 and PD 19B (*Blackstone* 1472). Such cases are rare and are beyond the scope of this everyday book.

38

STATEMENTS OF CASE

A. Format

38.01 Statements of case are court documents, which should be prepared in a form which complies with the requirements of PD 5 (*Blackstone's Civil Practice 2004* 1353; hereafter *Blackstone*). They should:

(a) be written on A4 paper,
(b) have a margin not less than 3.5 cm,
(c) be typed,
(d) be bound securely together,
(e) have pages numbered consecutively,
(f) be divided into numbered paragraphs, and
(g) have all numbers, including dates, expressed as figures.

The heading of all statements of case should set out the name of the court, the claim number, and the title of the proceedings which gives the full names of all the parties. Statements of case drafted by a legal representative should contain his or her signature or the name of the firm. Statements of case should be verified by a statement of truth.

B. The Claim Form

38.02 A claim form must (PD 7, para 3.1, *Blackstone* 1398) be completed on the standard Form N1. The claimant must show the details of the court in which the claim is to be issued, the full name and address of the claimant, the claimant's address for service, the capacity of the claimant when he is a child or patient with a litigation friend or sues in a representative capacity, and the full name and address of the defendant. If a personal injury claim is to be issued in the High Court the claim form must include a statement 'My claim includes a claim for personal injuries and the value of the claim is £50,000 or more'.

38.03   The claim form must include a statement of the value. A personal injury claim will not be for a specific amount, since general damages are in the discretion of the court, so the value will be 'not more than £5,000', 'more than £5,000 but not more than £15,000' or 'more than £15,000'. These categories represent the usual scope of the small claims track, the fast track and the multi-track respectively, but a claimant issuing a claim for more than £15,000 may wish to impose an upper limit on the value of the claim because this will be relevant to the amount of the issue fee that will be payable.

38.04   An issue fee will be due according to the value of the claim stated in the claim form. The issue fees from April 2003 are:

Up to £300	£30
£300 to £500	£50
£500 to £1,000	£80
£1,000 to £5,000	£120
£5,000 to £15,000	£250
£15,000 to £50,000	£400
£50,000 to £100,000	£600
£100,000 to £150,000	£700
More than £150,000 or unlimited	£800

38.05   In addition to the usual statement of the overall value of the claim, PD 7, para 3.8 requires that if a claim for damages for personal injuries is started in the county court, the claim form must also state whether or not the claimant expects to recover more than £1,000 in respect of pain, suffering and loss of amenity.

38.06   The claim form must contain 'brief details' of the claim, and may contain the Particulars of Claim. Alternatively, the Particulars of Claim can be set out in a separate document which may be served with the claim form, or must otherwise be served within 14 days after the date on which the claim form is served. Except in the most straightforward road traffic accident case, it will usually be appropriate for the Particulars of Claim for a personal injury action to be a separate document. The brief details of the claim set out on the first page of the claim form need then only identify the nature of the claim in very general terms, setting out the date of the cause of action if possible and the nature of the remedy claimed.

A claim form must be verified by a statement of truth.   **38.07**

C. Particulars of Claim

In the Particulars of Claim, the claimant must set out concisely the nature of his   **38.08** claim. The technical importance of pleadings has diminished in modern litigation, now that the nature of the claim will have been disclosed to the defendant in considerable detail in the letter of claim sent in accordance with the Protocol before proceedings are commenced, and will be further explained by the disclosure of witness statements and expert reports by the time the case is considered at trial. None the less it is important that the Particulars of Claim set out the basis of the claim in a manner that is technically correct, and as a subsidiary purpose it is helpful to remember that the Particulars of Claim may be the first document to be read by the trial judge in preparation for the hearing so that it will be helpful to the cause if they put forward the case in a clear, competent, and attractive manner.

There are general rules for the content of the Particulars of Claim in r 16.4   **38.09** (*Blackstone* 1451) and there are specific rules for matters that should be included in Particulars of Claim for personal injury claims and fatal accident claims in PD 16 (Statements of Case) (*Blackstone* 1455). In particular, in a personal injury claim the Particulars of Claim must state the claimant's date of birth, must contain brief details of the claimant's personal injuries, must be accompanied by a medical report (assuming that medical evidence is to be relied on which, in all but the most trivial cases, will be essential) and must have attached to them a schedule giving details of any past and future expenses and losses which are claimed.

In setting out the facts, a chronological order is best, and in setting out the law, a   **38.10** logical sequence of duty, breach of duty, and damage is required. It is helpful to break the document up into separate paragraphs for each separate allegation, so that it will be easy for the defendant to answer in a way which makes it clear which matters are agreed and which matters are in dispute. The traditional practice of pleading involves setting out particularized allegations of breach of duty and of damage, and this approach is generally followed in the drafting of Particulars of Claim under the CPR although there is no longer any technical requirement for this form of presentation to be adopted. It is suggested that the traditional form of technically correct pleading is particularly appropriate to claims arising out of industrial accidents, whereas a simple narrative of events will suffice in a straightforward road accident case. Sometimes, in a simple case, the claimant's witness statement can be prepared in a way which allows it to be used as the Particulars of Claim as well.

D. Defence

38.11   The defendant cannot simply put the whole claim in dispute. Rule 16.5 (*Blackstone* 1452) requires that he must give a meaningful response to the allegations that have been made by setting out a detailed defence, stating which of the allegations in the Particulars of Claim he denies, which allegations he is unable to admit or deny but requires the claimant to prove, and which allegations he admits. Where the defendant denies an allegation, he must state his reasons for doing so, and if he intends to put forward a different version of events from that given by the claimant, he must state his own version.

38.12   The status of an allegation made in the Particulars of Claim that has not been dealt with in the defence is that by r 16.5(5) (*Blackstone* 1452) it is taken to be admitted.

38.13   It is good practice for the defence to follow the Particulars of Claim paragraph by paragraph, dealing in turn with each allegation. It is no longer the rule that the defendant need not answer particulars of the allegations in the Particulars of Claim in detail. On an issue where the defendant has the burden of proof, the facts must be set out in the defence. For example, if the claimant alleges the breach of a regulation which imposes a duty on the employer 'as far as is reasonably practicable', the defendant will not be entitled to advance a case showing that he had done all that was reasonably practicable unless the defence has set out in detail the facts that are relied on. If contributory negligence is alleged, it is usual to make the case in the form of detailed particulars. If a failure to mitigate loss is alleged, the defendant has the burden of proof and the case must be pleaded. If there is an allegation that the claimant has deliberately exaggerated his disability or that the claim is in some respects fraudulent, again full details of the allegation should be set out in the defence.

E. Reply

38.14   Although a reply to the defence is permitted under r 15.8 (*Blackstone* 1448) statements of case beyond a defence have become very rare in personal injury claims. The status of an allegation in the defence which raises matters that were not specifically covered by the Particulars of Claim is that, unlike allegations overlooked in the defence, by r 16.7(1) (*Blackstone* 1452) they are not taken to be admitted so the claimant is not prejudiced if they go unanswered unless the defence has raised a new issue which is not covered by the Particulars of Claim and the claimant needs to rely on additional facts in order to respond to it.

If a claim has been started more than three years after the cause of action   **38.15** accrued, it may be defeated by the defence of limitation. This defence does not arise unless the point is taken by the defendant: it is a procedural defence rather than a matter of substantive law. The issue of limitation is sometimes doubtful, for example in disease cases where the claimant's date of knowledge may be uncertain or where there are strong grounds for disapplying the primary limitation period under s 33 of the Limitation Act 1980. A claimant may therefore reasonably serve Particulars of Claim which do not deal with the date of knowledge or with s 33, in the hope that the defendant may not take the point. When the defence relies on limitation the claimant does not need to amend the Particulars of Claim but may raise the limitation matters, including the application under s 33, by way of a reply.

F. Further Information

The power to obtain further information about the other party's statement of   **38.16** case is contained in Part 18 and PD 18 (*Blackstone* 1463). The purpose of the request for further information must be to clarify, or to give additional information about, any matter which is in dispute in the proceedings. A request should be confined to matters which are reasonably necessary and proportionate to enable the party making the request to prepare his own case or to understand the case he has to meet. An application to the court should not be made until the party has made a request in correspondence, but that request should be made in a formal document or, if it is contained in the letter, should be made with sufficient formality to mark it out from routine correspondence, in a letter clearly marked as a request made under Part 18 which deals with no other matters.

The response to a request must be in writing, dated and signed by the party   **38.17** giving the response or by his legal representative. It should set out the text of the separate paragraph of the request and then set out under each paragraph the response that is given to it. A response should be verified by a statement of truth.

Requests for further information, like questions to experts, can be highly effective in some cases to expose the weaknesses of the opponent's case.

G. Amendment

38.18 The rules about amendment are contained in Part 17 and PD 17 (*Blackstone* 1460). Once a statement of case has been served, it can only be amended by consent or with the permission of the court. The amended statement of case must be marked to show the date of amendment, and need not then include the text that has been deleted unless the court directs that this should be shown (PD 17, para 2.2). Amendments can be indicated by a numerical code. In practice, however, amended statements of case are usually prepared in the traditional manner, with the deleted text struck through and the new text underlined. The deletion and underlining may be in colour: red for the first amendment, green for the second, violet for the third, and yellow for the fourth.

38.19 *Binks v Securicor* [2003] EWCA Civ 993; [2003] 1 WLR 2557   The claimant based his claim on a version of the facts which the trial judge did not accept. The defendant's version of the facts also gave the claimant a basis on which liability could be established. The trial judge refused to allow the claimant to depart from his statement of case or to amend to plead the alternative version. The Court of Appeal said that this was the wrong approach and was inconsistent with the requirement in the overriding objective of dealing with the claim justly. The amendment should have been allowed and the claimant should have been excused under r 22.1(2) from giving a statement of truth.

38.20 *Maguire v Molin* [2002] EWCA Civ 1083; [2003] PIQR P8   The claim was issued with a value limited to £15,000 and allocated to the fast track. At trial the claimant applied to amend by deleting the limitation and to serve a revised schedule bringing the value of the claim to more than £80,000. The Court of Appeal held that the trial judge was entitled to conclude that it would be wrong to hear such an increased claim in the fast track and to refuse both applications.

38.21 After the limitation period has expired, the scope of amendment that the court will permit is limited to matters arising out of the same facts (r 17.4(2)) and an amendment for the purpose of adding a new party can only be undertaken if the court has disapplied the primary limitation period (r 19.5(4), *Blackstone* 1469).

H. Specimen Statements of Case

(1) Specimen of Brief Details for the Claim Form

38.22 The claimant claims damages and interest for personal injuries sustained in a road traffic accident at High Street, Casterbridge on 15 January 2004 caused by the negligent driving of the defendant.

(2) Particulars of Claim—Simple Road Traffic Accident

1. On Wednesday 14 August 2003 I was driving my Ford Escort car H123 ABC and I had **38.23** stopped at the traffic lights at the junction of High Street, Casterbridge with Station Road when Mr Brian Smith carelessly drove into the back of my car in his Vauxhall Astra car N456 DEF.

2. As a result of the collision I suffered a whiplash injury which was painful for three weeks. I took two days off work, and visited a physiotherapist on three occasions. I attach a letter from my GP Dr William Jones dated 9 October 2003 which describes my injury, and a list of my loss of earnings and out of pocket expenses. My date of birth is 2 February 1968.

3. I claim damages for my injury and my financial loss, and interest.

(3) Particulars of Claim—Road Traffic Accident

IN THE MELCHESTER COUNTY COURT **38.24**

Between:

ELIZABETH SMALLBURY   Claimant

and

RICHARD HILL   Defendant

PARTICULARS OF CLAIM

1. On the 17 October 2003 the claimant was lawfully driving her Ford Escort motor car registration number H123 ABD south on the A483 Melchester to Sandbourne road at Bramshurst and she was approaching a right-hand bend when a Ford Transit van registration number F880 BPR driven in the opposite direction by the defendant crossed onto the claimant's side of the road and collided with her car.

2. The accident was caused by the negligence of the defendant.

Particulars of Negligence

(1) He crossed onto the wrong side of the road.
(2) He drove too fast around a sharp left-hand bend.
(3) He lost control of his vehicle.
(4) He failed to observe the presence of mud and water on the road.
(5) He failed to heed a sign beside the road 'Mud on road'.
(6) He failed to slow down to the speed suitable for a sharp bend on a muddy road.
(7) He collided with the claimant's car.

3. On 12 December 2003 at the Melchester Magistrates' Court the defendant was convicted of the offence of careless driving. The conviction is relevant to the issue of negligence.

4. By an open letter dated 6 May 2004 the insurers of the defendant accepted liability for the accident.

5. As a result of the accident the claimant has suffered personal injury, loss and damage.

Particulars of Injury

The claimant, who was born on 15 February 1964, sustained severe injuries to her right leg with fractures to the tibia and fibula and ligament damage to the knee joint; a fracture of the right ulna; a soft tissue injury to her neck; bruising to her chest; and many superficial abrasions and bruises. She was trapped in her car for half an hour until cut free by the fire brigade. She has suffered a moderately severe post-traumatic stress disorder. Details of her injuries, treatment and prognosis are given on the following medical reports, copies of which are attached:

(a) Mr James Herring FRCS, consultant orthopaedic surgeon, dated 13 September 2003 and 4 July 2004.

(b) Dr Christine Wellbeloved, consultant psychiatrist, dated 3 August 2004.

The claimant has continuing weakness and restriction of mobility as a result of her leg injuries. She has lost a congenial form of employment in outdoor farm work, and she would be handicapped in the labour market.

Particulars of Special Damage

Please see the schedule attached.

6. The claimant claims interest on any award of damages under section 69 of the County Courts Act 1984 at such rate and for such period as may be just, including interest on special damages at the full special account rate from the date on which each loss was sustained.

A N D the claimant claims damages and interest.

Charles Wilson

Statement of Truth

I believe that the facts stated in these Particulars Claim are true

Signed:

(4) Defence to the Road Accident Claim

38.25 [Title as for the claim]

1. It is admitted that the collision took place between the claimant's car and the defendant's van at the time and place alleged.

2. For the purpose of this action only, the defendant admits liability for the collision.

3. The defendant can neither admit nor deny the matters set out on the medical report obtained on behalf of the claimant and the matters set out in the Schedule of Special Damages. The defendant is unable to serve a Counter-schedule at present and wishes to obtain his own medical evidence.

4. An entitlement to interest is admitted in principle.

[Statement of truth]

(5) Particulars of Claim—Back Strain from Slipping and Lifting

IN THE CASTERBRIDGE COUNTY COURT **38.26**

Between:

JOSEPH WILLIAMS

Claimant

and

CASTERBRIDGE MANUFACTURING LIMITED

Defendant

PARTICULARS OF CLAIM

1. At all relevant times the claimant was employed by the defendant as a machine operator at the defendant's factory at South Street, Casterbridge.

2. The Workplace (Health, Safety and Welfare) Regulations 1992 applied to the claimant's work.

3. On 19 April 2003 in the course of his employment the claimant was required to carry a box of materials to the No 6 machine but as he walked along the gangway towards the machine his right foot slipped on a puddle of oil that had escaped from the reservoir of No 2 machine and he fell to the ground, suffering a heavy blow to his lower back.

4. The accident was caused by the breach of statutory duty and/or negligence of the defendant, its employees or agents.

Particulars of Breach of Duty

(1) Contrary to regulation 12(3) of the Workplace (Health, Safety and Welfare) Regulations 1992 and negligently, failing to keep the surface of the traffic route free from oil, a substance which might cause the claimant to slip.

(2) Failing adequately to maintain the machine so as to prevent the escape of oil.

(3) Failing to operate a suitable and sufficient system for the inspection and cleaning of the gangway.

(4) Failing to heed the significance of an escape of oil from the machine on 17 April 2003 which was reported to the foreman Mr David who made arrangements for it to be cleared up.

(5) Failing to provide for the claimant a safe place of work.

5. As a result of the accident the claimant has suffered personal injury, loss and damage.

Particulars of Injury

The claimant, who was born on the 30 January 1958, suffered a strain to the soft tissues of his lower back. He was absent from work for four weeks and has only been able to return to light and part-time duties.

The claimant's continuing employment is at risk and he is handicapped in the labour market.

Details of the claimant's injury, treatment and prognosis are given on the medical report of Mr Cecil White dated 7 June 2004, a copy of which is attached.

623

Particulars of Special Damage

Please see the schedule attached.

6. The claimant claims interest on any award of damages, pursuant to section 69 of the County Courts Act 1984, at such rate and for such period as may be just, including interest on special damages at the full special account rate from the date on which each loss was sustained.

    A N D the claimant claims damages and interest.

Susan Green

Statement of truth

I believe that the facts stated in these Particulars of Claim are true.

Signed:

38.27 **(6) Defence to the Back Injury Claim**

[Title as for the claim]

1. The defendant admits that the claimant has made a complaint of having suffered a fall on 19 April 2003, but does not admit the happening or circumstances of any accident and puts the claimant to proof.

2. The defendant admits that there had been a small seepage of oil from the No 2 machine but the seepage did not extend into the gangway.

3. The defendant will contend that it had taken all reasonably practicable steps to prevent any seepage of oil onto the gangway.

    (1) The defendant employed a full-time cleaner who was responsible for sweeping the gangway at least three times a day and who was available to clear up any spillage that might occur.

    (2) The No 2 machine was stripped down and thoroughly inspected by the defendant's staff during 18 April 2003. New seals were fitted to the reservoir and there was no seepage of oil when the machine was started at the beginning of work on 19 April 2003.

    (3) The operator of the machine had inspected the area around the machine less than 30 minutes before the claimant claims to have suffered his fall and observed no seepage.

    (4) In the circumstances there is nothing further the defendant could reasonably have done to keep the gangway clear.

4. If the claimant proves that he suffered a fall in the circumstances alleged, his accident was caused wholly or in part by his own negligence.

Particulars of Contributory Negligence

    (1) He stepped onto the spillage of oil.

    (2) He failed to look where he was going.

    (3) He failed to observe the spillage when he had walked the other way along the gangway and he failed to report it or to clear it up.

5. The defendant will contend that even if he did suffer a fall, the claimant suffered no significant injury on Friday 19 April 2003. He worked until the end of his shift without making any complaint and his first complaint, when he made an entry in the accident book, was when he arrived for work on 22 April.

624

6. The claimant had a substantial previous history of back pain, including an absence from work for three weeks attributed to back pain in March 2002. The defendant will seek to have the claimant examined by an orthopaedic surgeon instructed on the defendant's behalf and makes no admissions as to the nature, seriousness, and causation of any injury suffered by the claimant.

7. In April 2003 the claimant was subject to two written warnings because of his poor attendance record. His employment is likely to have come to an end within six months in any event.

8. The claimant has failed to take reasonable steps to mitigate his loss. The defendant offered the claimant the opportunity of lighter full-time work in the stores department but the claimant refused the offer.

9. An entitlement to interest is admitted in principle.

Statement of Truth

The defendant believes that the facts stated in this Defence are true.

Signed:

Name in print:

Position held:

39

SCHEDULES AND COUNTER-SCHEDULES

A. Schedules of Special Damages

39.01 Every compensation claim will need a Schedule of Special Damages. In every assessment of damages, the Schedule of Special Damages and the counter-schedule will be the main working documents. In every detailed negotiation, these documents will be the first point of reference for assessing the value of the claim. It is hard to overstate the importance of getting the schedule right.

39.02 The expression 'Special Damages' refers to financial losses and expenses which are capable of being calculated in arithmetic, unlike general damages which are the heads of damage which must be assessed by the judgment of the court such as damages for pain and suffering and loss of amenity, and damages for loss of a congenial form of employment. Even in a case of minor injury, there are likely to be some incidental expenses to be recovered. In a case of serious injury, the Schedule of Special Damages is a vitally important document for the proper presentation of the claim with regard to the amount of damages. The preparation of the schedule is perhaps the most underrated task of the claimant's lawyer. A schedule which is carefully considered and attractively presented can make a real difference to the sucess of the claim. In the same way, a counter-schedule which is carefully considered and realistic is vital to the effective defence of an overstated claim.

39.03 There are three stages of a claim at which a schedule of financial loss will be required. First, para 3.13 of the Pre-action Protocol for Personal Injury says that the claimant will send the defendant a Schedule of Special Damages with supporting documents as soon as practicable, particularly when the defendant has admitted liability. Secondly, by para 4.2 of PD 16, a schedule must be served with the Particulars of Claim giving details of any past and future expenses and losses which the claimant claims. It will often be possible to use the same schedule as that which was served in accordance with the protocol. Thirdly, in every serious case there will have been significant changes in the case on special damages between the preparation of the Particulars of Claim and the time when a trial or assessment of damages is approaching and, although there is nothing in the CPR which automatically provides for it, a final, revised schedule calculated to the trial date will be invariably be required.

39.04 In relation to liability issues, the trend of modern litigation has been to make the detailed accuracy of the statements of case something which is less and less important, because the opponent and the court have many other sources from which the claimant's case can be understood, principally the letter of claim, the witness statements and the expert reports, and the requirement of the overriding objective that the court should deal justly with cases will inhibit the court from rejecting a claim on technical grounds relating to the pleadings, or refusing a necessary amendment. In relation to quantum issues, however, the trend has been on the opposite direction, and it will be difficult for the claimant at an assessment of damages to pursue any claim which goes beyond the calculations and heads of damage set out in the schedule, and it will be difficult for the defendant to resile from concessions that have been made in the counter-schedule.

39.05 There are some losses which are a matter of patience and diligence in obtaining the necessary evidence, but which then become a matter of arithmetic about which there can be little argument. In most cases, the claimant's loss of earnings ought to fall into this category. It is necessary to obtain from the claimant's employer full details of the pay and benefits of his employment, and of any wage increases that would have applied to his continuing work, but once the details have been obtained the final figures should be clear. A letter from the employer setting out the details can be attached to the schedule (and is admissible in evidence as a hearsay statement under the Civil Evidence Act 1995).

39.06 Other heads of loss are more open to debate and this is where careful judgment has to be exercised in the preparation of the schedule. The claimant's lawyer will naturally be inclined to state the value of the claim at its highest. However, overstatement or exaggeration can backfire. First, if the court making an assessment comes to the conclusion that a head of claim has been overstated without justification, not only will that head of damages be considered with a more than usually critical eye, but also the credibility of the schedule as a whole may suffer.

Secondly, there may be a costs penalty under CPR r 44.5 if the court considers that a claim has been exaggerated. Thirdly, the schedule must be verified with a statement of truth. Although strictly speaking this verifies only the statements of fact that are made in the schedule and not the legal arguments, the claimant will be vulnerable in cross-examination if a schedule that has been verified by him or on his instructions is seen to be unsupportable on careful scrutiny.

Similar considerations apply to counter-schedules. Reasoned and moderate **39.07** objections will carry far more weight than the outright dismissal of sensible claims. A narrative explanation of the reasons for disputing a claim made in the schedule will be more persuasive than a curt 'not agreed'. It is particularly important to explain clearly any objections which are based on a specific case on the facts, for example concerning a likelihood of promotion, or an allegation that disability has been overstated in the light of surveillance evidence, or an allegation of malingering. Where the claimant has wholly failed to support a minor head of claim with proper evidence, but some loss is likely to have been incurred, it is attractive to offer a reasonable compromise, accepting that it would not be proportionate to insist on strict proof. The counter-schedule also has to be verified with a statement of truth, so credibility will be lost if sensible claims are unreasonably rejected.

B. Drafting Schedules and Counter-schedules

The key to the skill of drafting good schedules and counter-schedules is to **39.08** remember their primary purpose as working documents for the court at an assessment of damages. There is no single approach which is right for every case, and there is scope for developing a personal style. However, the aim should always be clarity and accuracy. The following hints may not apply to every case, but may provide a good starting point.

With Schedules of Special Damages, it is helpful to begin with a chronology of **39.09** key dates and a narrative introduction to explain the facts on which the calculations have been based. It is helpful to divide the schedule into sections, using clear headings. It is also a good idea to remove long, detailed calculations to an appendix, for example calculations of net income or the list of journeys for which travel expenses are claimed. It is common for a schedule to be divided into two parts, covering the past and future claims through each head of damage. This is convenient for the calculation of interest, but it is suggested that in a long schedule it is more appropriate, and more helpful to the court, to set out the whole of the case on each head of damage both past and future at the same place, including within the section a division between past and future loss. There is no point in including interest calculations in a schedule that is to be served under the protocol, or with Particulars of Claim, but the final revision of the schedule will be undertaken at a time when the trial date, or at least a trial window, will be known and therefore the rate of interest to be claimed on both general and special damages can be calculated. Unless the claims are very simple, it is helpful to end with a summary.

39.10 With counter-schedules, it is again helpful to begin with a narrative introduction which explains the extent to which the basis of the claimant's schedule is agreed, and the extent to which it is in dispute, and which explains the basis of fact on which the counter-schedule has been prepared. Even if the manner in which the schedule has been prepared is unsatisfactory, it is usually better for the counter-schedule to be reactive and to answer the points in the schedule in the same sequence and against the same numbering and headings. Indeed, in a complicated case it will be helpful to prepare a counter-schedule in the form of a Scott Schedule, a single document which sets out in a series of columns a description of each item claimed, the amount of the claim, the response of the defendant, and a blank column for the judge to complete.

39.11 In most schedules, there is much to be said for omitting all references to pence. The exception to this is a claim of moderate value where the pence in the weekly or monthly value of a loss or expense that is to be increased by a large multiplier may be significant. For example, 75p a week in a claim of the multiplier of 25 will add £975 to a claim. Generally however, a very meticulous approach to arithmetic is likely to be out of step with the vagueness of the fundamental factual assumptions on which the arithmetic is based, and a rounding up or down to the nearest pound is fair.

39.12 The following is a checklist of potential heads of damage:

> Loss of earnings
>> Earnings lost through absence
>> Sick pay repayable to the employer
>> Loss of overtime
>> Loss of bonus
>> Loss of promotion prospects
>> *Smith v Manchester* loss
>> Loss of congenial employment
> Loss of pension benefits
> Loss of benefits in kind, for example company car
> Loss of wages for family carers
> Recompense for family care
> Cost of nursing care and respite care
> Cost when family will no longer be able to help

    Commercial basis of home care
    Residential care
Cost of special accommodation
Cost of medical treatment
Prescription charges
Cost of over the counter medicines
Cost of swimming or gym to keep fit
Expenses to cope with disability
Extra home heating costs
Cost of special diet
Help with housework
Help with decorating
Help with gardening
Help with house maintenance
Help with car maintenance
Wasted expense, for example non-refundable holiday deposit
Travel for treatment
Travel for relatives to visit
Car parking at hospital
Damaged clothing
Damaged jewellery
Court of Protection costs

39.13 There is no provision under the rules for details of a claim for injury damages to be included in a schedule or counter-schedule. At the early stages of the claim it will usually be better to say nothing about general damages, since the medical evidence may well be incomplete and the claimant may reasonably wish to wait for the defendant to make an offer. However, when a final schedule is prepared shortly before the trial, different considerations apply, and it may well be helpful if both parties include the salient points from the medical evidence, the relevant bracket under the *JSB Guidelines*, any authorities to be relied upon, and a figure or a bracket for injury damages.

C. Specimen Schedule and Counter-schedule

IN THE MELCHESTER COUNTY COURT   Case No MC 048862

Between: **39.14**

ELIZABETH SMALLBURY   Claimant

and

RICHARD HILL   Defendant

REVISED SCHEDULE OF SPECIAL DAMAGES

Date of accident	17.10.02
Claimant's date of birth	15.02.77
Claimant's age at accident	25
Proposed trial date	19.03.05
Claimant's age at trial	28

1. Basis of calculations

The Claimant used to enjoy a vigorous outdoor lifestyle with a close association with Chene Manor Stables where she had worked since the age of 17 years. She sustained injuries, principally to her right leg, in the accident on 17.10.02. She was in hospital for three weeks, and was discharged to her parents' home where she was cared for over the following two months. On 07.01.03 she returned to her own home and on 21.01.03 she returned to her work as a stable hand and farm worker restricted to light duties. She has enjoyed some gradual improvement in her symptoms but there is significant permanent restriction and weakness in her right leg. Riding horses is difficult and competitive riding is impossible. The Claimant is now limited to office work, which she dislikes and for which she is paid less and her quality of life has been seriously damaged.

2. Injury damages

The principal injuries are (i) to the right leg and knee and (ii) moderately severe post-traumatic stress disorder and depressive illness. The medical evidence on which the claimant relies comprises the following reports:

[list the up-to-date reports]

The appropriate bracket of the *JSB Guidelines* for the leg injury is 6(M)(a)(ii) £2,500 to £38,000. The bracket for the psychiatric injury is the lower end of 3(B)(b) £12,500 to £31,750. There is no overlap of these two main injuries.

The Claimant has lost the enjoyment of her previous lifestyle and her principal recreation of horseriding.

The Claimant contends that a reasonable award of injury damages would be £45,000.

The Claimant also seeks damages for the loss of a congenial employment.

3. Past loss of earnings

On 04.03.03 she attempted the physical work of her normal job but was unable to cope and on 28.03.03 she transferred to full-time office work in the same farm business.

Loss of earnings during absence and part-time working £1,489.

On changing jobs on 28.03.03 the Claimant's net earnings were reduced by £65.70 per month. Reduced earnings to trial 23.5 months × £65.70 = £1,544

The calculation of these sums is set out in Annex 1.

4. Recompense for past care

Gratuitous care by the Claimant's parents

5 hours a day for 2 weeks at £6 an hour: 70 hours £420

3 hours a day for 6 weeks at £6 an hour: 126 hours £756

Continuing at 2 hours a week for help with heavy housework and gardening 116 weeks at £12 a week £1,392

Total for past care £2,568

5. Incidental expenses

(a) Travel Car journeys to hospital for follow-up treatment and physiotherapy, travel to work which before the accident would have been by bicycle, and to social activities. Details are set out in Annex 2 and amount to 746 miles. Journeys were in a 1.8 litre Ford car and a rate of 35p per mile is claimed: £261.10

(b) Treatment and Prescriptions Details are set out in Annex 3: £74.30

(c) Damaged clothing: Details are set out in Annex 4: £135.00

6. Interest

(a) On general damages at 2% from the date of the service of the Claim Form on 17.04.04: 18 months, rate 3%

(b) On special damages at half special account rate namely 3% from the date of the accident on 17.10.02: 2 years 5 months, rate 7.25%

7. Multipliers for future loss

Age at trial 28 years

For the Claimant's working life to age 60:

> Ogden Table 8 gives 21.84
> Table A adjustment for contingencies 0.98
> No Table C adjustment for age 28
> Occupation adjustment deduct 0.01
> Geographical adjustment (SW) add 0.01
> Multiplier $21.84 \times 0.98 = 21.4$

Lifetime multiplier

> Ogden Table 2: 30.44

8. Future loss of earnings

(a) Partial earnings loss at £65.70 net per month = £788 a year × 20: £15,760

(b) *Smith v Manchester* damages: The Claimant has lost the only employment field in which she had real aptitude. Her clerical skills are poor. If she lost her present job, she would struggle to find work in the open labour market. Her current net annual earnings are £11,500 and she has 32 years of working life to age 60. It would be appropriate to award the equivalent of two years' net income: £23,000.

(c) Three months off work is likely if, as predicted, the Claimant requires a total knee replacement at the age of 55: loss of 3 months' net earnings £2,875 discount factor 0.4502 (Table 27): £1,294

9. Future housework and gardening

The Claimant will continue to need help with heavy housework and gardening for 2 hours a week at £6 = £624 a year × 30.44 = £18,994.56.

10. Future treatment

The agreed medical opinion (see joint statement of orthopaedic experts at page 105 of the Trial Bundle) is that a total knee replacement is likely to be required at around the age of 60. The cost of treatment is £7,500 (letter 15.11.03 from Melchester Nuffield Hospital attached). Discount factor as above 0.4502: £3,376

11. Summary

£   for the court

Injury damages
Past loss of earnings
Past care
Incidental expenses
Interest

Future loss of earnings
Future housework and gardening
Future treatment

Total   £

I believe that the facts stated in this Schedule of Special Damages are true

Signed ....

IN THE MELCHESTER COUNTY COURT   Case No MC 048862

39.15   Between:

ELIZABETH SMALLBURY   Claimant

and

RICHARD HILL   Defendant

DEFENDANT'S COUNTER-SCHEDULE

Pain and Suffering and Loss of Amenity

The Claimant's assessment is excessive. A good though imperfect recovery from the leg injury has been achieved. The Claimant can ride horses recreationally, she can walk without limitation, can swim and has played tennis. The appropriate JSB category is (M)(a)(iii) Less Severe £14,750 to £23,500 and not the category claimed. The Claimant suffered a depressive episode but the defendant relies on the psychiatric opinion of Dr Charles that there was no true post-traumatic stress disorder; the depressive illness was of short duration and has now resolved. £17,500 allowed

Past Loss of Earnings

The first loss of £2,489 is agreed.
The claimed reduction in earnings is disputed, The pre-accident wages details show a very variable pattern of overtime and basic pay was less than current earnings.
Reduced earnings: nil

Past Care

The hours claimed for the first two months are agreed.
The rate of £6 is excessive for gratuitous care. The care need was for home care and not skilled nursing. This is more than a commercial rate and that rate should be discounted. The Defendant proposes £4 an hour producing £784 allowed for the first two periods.

Continuing care: the need is overstated. Gardening help is not required in winter months. The rate of £6 is excessive and £4 is proposed. 2 hours for 20 weeks and 1 hour for 32 weeks, annual rate $72 \times £4 = £288$, for 116 weeks to trial £642 allowed.

Expenses

Not agreed but in the interests of proportionality the defendant offers £300.

Interest

Agreed

Multipliers

The Claimant was engaged in a high-risk occupation. Allowance should be made for the possibility of a career break for a family. An earnings multiplier of 18 is appropriate.

The lifetime multiplier is applied only to help with housework and gardening. Help would be needed in old age in any case. The multiplier to age 70 is appropriate Table 12, 25.6.

Future Loss of Earnings

A continuing partial loss is disputed, as above.

A potential handicap in the labour market is admitted but the value is small. The Claimant will have developed good office skills and familiarity with the business in which she works. Her injury does not interfere with her current work. She has a permanent job with a good employer and there is no evidence that her job is or will be at risk. The small risk is adequately reflected by an award of £2,000.

Future Household Work and Gardening

As above, agreed to the extent of £288 × 23.5 = £6,768.

Future Treatment

The Claimant has received all her treatment to date as a NHS patient. It is disputed that she would have private treatment. If this intention were proved, the cost of treatment and the discount are agreed.

Statements of truth

The defendant believes that the facts stated in this counter-schedule are true

Signed:

Name in print:

Name of firm:

Position held:

40

CASE MANAGEMENT

A. Court Control

One of the key themes of Lord Woolf's reforms is that courts should carry out **40.01** active case management. CPR r 1.4(1) (*Blackstone's Civil Practice 2004* 1314; hereafter *Blackstone*) requires that the court must further the overriding objective by actively managing cases and the extensive general powers of the court are set out in Part 3 (*Blackstone* 1326). The court does not need to depend on applications made by the parties, but can make an order of its own initiative and can do so without a hearing provided a party affected by the order has the opportunity to apply to have it set aside or altered and the order so provides (r 3.3, *Blackstone* 1327). Where hearings are necessary, they can be carried out by telephone rather than requiring personal attendance of all the parties at the court office.

B. Allocation to Track

When a claim is started by the claimant, by the issue of the claim form, one of **40.02** the first case management steps that the court will take is to ensure that the claim is allocated to the appropriate court and to the appropriate track. Case management at this early stage is governed by Part 26 (*Blackstone* 1541). There is an opportunity under r 26.4 for the parties to ask for the case to be stayed, for one month in the first instance, while they try to settle the case by negotiation, by alternative dispute resolution or by other means. If the case has been issued in a local court which is not a civil trial centre, the court will also consider whether the claim should be transferred to the appropriate trial centre, at that stage or subsequently.

40.03 Every claim must be allocated to one of the three tracks, the small claims track, the fast track or the multi-track. The approach is set out in r 26.6 (*Blackstone* 1543). The most important criterion is the value of the claim, although the court will also take into account any other circumstances. The small claims track is suitable for personal injury claims with a value up to £5,000 where damages for pain and suffering and loss of amenity are likely to be not more than £1,000; the fast track is suitable for claims with a value between £5,000 and £15,000 where it is likely that the trial will last no more than one day and that oral evidence from expert witnesses will not be required; and the multi-track is suitable for claims which do not meet these criteria and in particular for those with a value in excess of £15,000. However, where a claim is straight-forward but the value is unclear, it is not unusual for allocation to the fast track to be made for a case which turns out to have a value in excess of £15,000: neither the statement of value on the claim form nor the allocation to the fast track will prevent the court from making an award of the damages that are properly due, even if they exceed £15,000. By r 16.3(7) (*Blackstone* 1451) 'The statement of value in the claim form does not limit the power of the court to give judgment for the amount which it finds the claimant is entitled to'.

40.04 The procedure is for the court office to require each of the parties to complete an allocation questionnaire (Form N150) once a defence has been filed. The questionnaire requires the parties to confirm their compliance with any relevant pre-action protocol, to give basic information about the likely future conduct of the case and to set out their proposals about the track that may be suitable and any directions that should be given. At the same time the parties will be required to file an estimate of past and future costs in accordance with section 6 of the Practice Direction on Costs (*Blackstone* 1743) and the estimate must also be shown to the client.

40.05 Where liability is admitted, and judgment is given for an amount to be decided by the court, it is on the making of this 'relevant order' that the court may give directions for the claim to be listed for a disposal hearing or a hearing of the assessment of damages and allocated to a track (PD 26, para 12.2, *Blackstone* 1553). There is no formal limit to the jurisdiction of a district judge on an assessment of damages in any track, but cases involving substantial damages or complex issues are usually heard by a circuit judge.

C. The Small Claims Track

The basis for allocating a claim to the small claims track is given at r 26.6(1) **40.06**
(*Blackstone* 1543) amplified by the discussion in section 8 of PD 26 (*Blackstone*
1551). Once allocated to the small claims track, the procedure is governed by
Part 27 and PD 27 (*Blackstone* 1555, 1560).

The financial limit of claims and the small claims track mean that this track will **40.07**
only be relevant for a case of minor injury which has completely recovered, or
when the claimant chooses to limit injury damages to £1,000. These circumstances are most likely to arise when minor personal injury has accompanied
property damage and financial loss, for example a simple road traffic accident in
which the major issues are vehicle damage, car hire, or loss of earnings within
the £5,000 limit. As an indication of the very minor nature of an injury to
which no more than £1,000 in injury damages would be appropriate, note that,
for example, under the *JSB Guidelines* a trivial thumb injury at 6(I)(aa) has a
recommended award in the region of £1,250, and a simple undisplaced broken
nose with full recovery at 7(A)(c)(iv) has a bracket of £1,000 to £1,350. Thus,
any claim involving a real injury is excluded from the small claims track.

A claim in the small claims track should be dealt with quickly, cheaply and **40.08**
informally. After allocation, the court will fix a date for the final hearing and
give directions. Standard directions are set out in the appendix to PD 27 (*Blackstone* 1562). The parties will be required to exchange all the documents that they
intend to rely on at the hearing. Although there can be a preliminary hearing,
this will only happen if it is necessary. At the final hearing, the proceedings will
be informal, the strict rules of evidence will not apply, evidence need not be
taken on oath, and the court has a complete discretion about the method of
proceeding. However, a reasoned decision must be given.

The recovery of costs by the successful party is strictly limited in the small **40.09**
claims track by r 27.14 (*Blackstone* 1558). The fixed costs of issue under r 45.2
(*Blackstone* 1714) can be recovered, and the court can in addition make orders
in respect of court fees and witness expenses, subject to restrictions in para 7
of PD 27 (*Blackstone* 1561) but the costs of legal representation cannot be
recovered unless the paying party has behaved unreasonably.

D. The Fast Track

Personal injury claims of relatively modest value are part of the staple diet of the **40.10**
fast track. The basis for allocation to the fast track is set out in r 26.6(4) and (5)

(*Blackstone* 1543): a claim outside the small claims track, with a value not more than £15,000, the trial of which is likely to last no longer than one day, having a limited need for expert evidence, with no more than one expert per party in no more than two expert fields (and in practice, in personal injury claims, probably no expert evidence except the written report and answers to questions from a single, jointly instructed medical expert). The principles of allocation are developed in section 9 of PD 26 (*Blackstone* 1551) and the rules for the management of proceedings on the fast track are given in Part 28 and PD 28 (*Blackstone* 1566). Standard directions for proceedings in the fast track are suggested in the appendix to PD 28 (*Blackstone* 1573).

40.11 A claim in the fast track will be dealt with in accordance with the legal rules of general application regarding disclosure, evidence, experts, and trial procedure, but with the exercise of the discretion of the court in controlling these matters so as to ensure that the time taken and the expenditure of legal costs will be proportionate to resolving a claim in which the issues are likely to be relatively straightforward and the value relatively modest. The court will give directions on allocation, and usually in response to the filing of pre-trial checklists, but will decide on directions as a paper exercise without a hearing as far as possible. On allocation to the fast track, a trial date, or a trial window of up to three weeks, will be fixed so as to be not later than 30 weeks from the date of the directions order. The full range of interim applications can be made in a fast track case, but whatever complications arise, the court will always be extremely reluctant to adjourn the trial date that was fixed at the outset: PD 28, para 5.4(6) (*Blackstone* 1571) 'Litigants and lawyers must be in no doubt that the court will regard the postponement of the trial as an order of last resort'. The timescale assumes that a great deal of preparatory work will have been undertaken between the parties in advance to identify the issues and exchange relevant documents in accordance with the pre-action protocol. Directions will provide a timetable for disclosure, the exchange of witness statements, expert evidence, and pre-trial checklists.

40.12 The costs of proceedings in the fast track are subject to the general rule that the unsuccessful party is liable to pay the costs of the successful party. There are two important rules of practice which qualify this. First, the costs will generally be assessed summarily by the court at the conclusion of the trial, if there is a trial. In the absence of an effective Part 36 settlement offer, the question of proportionality is likely to be important in this assessment. Secondly, while there is at present no fixed or standard amount for the costs incurred up to trial, the costs of the trial itself are limited in accordance with Part 46 (*Blackstone* 1719).

E. The Multi-track

Proceedings on the multi-track are governed by Part 29 and PD 29 (*Blackstone* **40.13**
1577). This is the track for claims where the difficulty of the issues or the value
of the claim make it proportionate for greater individual attention to be given
to the preparations for trial, and for the amount of the trial costs to be freed
from the limitations of fixed costs. It is less easy to generalize about the way in
which the case will be managed, because there will be a greater willingness of the
court to deal with case management hearings attended by legal representatives,
resulting in orders tailored to the needs of the individual case.

F. Pre-trial Checklists

In fast track and multi-track claims, the rules provide for the completion of pre- **40.14**
trial checklists by the parties in the final stages of preparation for the trial. The
standard form is Form N170. The standard fast track directions (PD 28 section
6; *Blackstone* 1572) provide for each party to file a pre-trial checklist no later
than eight weeks before the trial date or the beginning of the trial window, and
in the multi-track the checklist will be sent out by the court unless some order
has been made dispensing with the need for it. The purpose of the checklist is
to help in ensuring that the case will be ready for trial by confirming that all
outstanding orders have been complied with, and that the necessary steps such
as the joint meeting of experts or the updating of the Schedule of Special
Damages are on course to be carried out. The filing of the checklist is also a
trigger for an obligation to file an updated estimate of costs. The usefulness of
pre-trial checklists depends on the extent to which there have been hearings and
active correspondence about the progress of the case, and if the court is dealing
with case management in the presence of the parties' representatives when the
trial date is in view, it will often be considered that checklists will serve no useful
purpose and can safely be dispensed with.

G. Case Management Conferences and Pre-trial Reviews

In the small claims track and the fast track, the court will strive to deal with case **40.15**
management questions on paper, without requiring the parties to incur the costs
of attending at the court, and often of the court's own initiative. If discussion is
necessary, arrangements may be made for a case management conference to be
held by telephone. In the multi-track, by contrast, an important aspect of active
case management under the CPR is for case management conferences to be

held, attended by the parties, when the court will not only consider applications that are made by the parties, and the directions they propose, but will endeavour to identify the real issues between the parties and the appropriate means of resolving them, and to set out a timetable for the future steps that the court decides will be necessary. Case management in the multi-track is governed by Part 29 and PD 29 (*Blackstone* 1577). Where a party has a legal representative, the representative must be familiar with the case and must have sufficient authority to deal with any issues that are likely to arise. The parties must consider whether it would be helpful to the court for the claimant to prepare a short case summary with a chronology, a statement of the factual issues agreed and in dispute, and a statement of the evidence likely to be required.

40.16 A pre-trial review is a hearing which shares with the case management conference the purpose of ensuring that the case will be properly prepared for trial on the date that has been fixed, but which differs in that the focus is on the management of the forthcoming trial rather than on the general management of resolving the issues in dispute, so that the date of the pre-trial review is fixed by reference to the trial date (usually about ten weeks beforehand) and the review will be conducted where possible by the trial judge.

H. Split Trial

40.17 An important case management issue which frequently arises in personal injury claims is the possibility of separating the issues of liability and quantum. Every claim raises these two separate issues. In cases of serious injury, it is not appropriate to decide the quantum of damages until the claimant's treatment has been completed, and sufficient time has gone by to enable the medical experts and the court to make a reliable assessment of the long-term prospects for the future. Liability issues by contrast can only suffer from delay which is likely to impair the accuracy of the recollections of witnesses even when it has been possible to capture their early recollections in detailed witness statements.

40.18 These considerations make a separate, early trial of liability attractive in many cases of lasting injury, where there is a real dispute about liability. If liability is resolved in favour of the claimant, it will then be possible for interim payments to be ordered, which can in turn greatly assist the claimant in achieving the best possible rehabilitation at the earliest possible time. On the other hand, if liability is resolved in favour of the defendant, the insurer will be spared at an early stage the pressure to fund assessment, treatment, and rehabilitation under the Rehabilitation Code (see **25.40** above).

40.19 However, before separate trials of liability and quantum are ordered it is necessary to consider whether the two issues may be so inter-related that separate trial is inappropriate. This may arise where the credibility of the claimant's evidence is central to both issues and will be challenged at both hearings: for example, video evidence on quantum may lead the defendant to allege that the claimant has been lying about his injuries in a case where the proof of liability depends on the credibility of the claimant's own account of the events which happened. Another situation where separate trials may be inappropriate is where complex issues of causation turn on the detailed findings about liability. The advantages of a speedy trial of liability must be set against the likely increase in costs, and the likely increase in the overall delay before reaching a final conclusion in the case, if two final hearings become necessary rather than one. The reality of personal injury litigation is that the proportion of claims resolved on any issue by a fully contested hearing is tiny. For these reasons, although there may be a superficial attraction to a speedy trial of liability in many cases, in practice the court will be cautious and will not make such an order unless satisfied that it is really appropriate.

I. Disobedience to Orders

Guidance on the approach that the court will take in order to deal with a failure **40.20** to comply with case management directions is given in section 5 of PD 28 (*Blackstone* 1571) in relation to fast track claims, and section 7 of PD 29 (*Blackstone* 1584) in relation to the multi-track. General powers to extend or abridge time and a general power to impose conditions are given by r 3.1 (*Blackstone* 1326) but an application for an extension is always more attractive if it is made before the time limit has expired.

The most serious sanction in the power of the court for failure to comply **40.21** with a rule, practice direction, or court order is the striking out of the whole or part of the statement of case of the defaulting party under r 3.4(2)(c) (*Blackstone* 1328). Since an order of this kind deprives the party in default of access to the court for a hearing of his claim on the merits, it is a sanction of last resort which is reserved for the most serious or repeated acts of disobedience.

Faced with an opponent in default of an order, the innocent party should first **40.22** write a letter asking for the default to be rectified within a short reasonable period and warning of an intention to apply for an order if the default is not remedied. If there is continuing default, the innocent party may apply for an order. Such an application must be made without delay. A priority will be to ensure that the trial date does not have to be postponed.

The court has a range of sanctions at its disposal, including: **40.23**

(a) the power to make an 'unless' order (examples are given at section 8 of PD 14B) (*Blackstone* 1686);

(b) power to make an order about costs liability, including indemnity basis costs and costs payable immediately;

(c) the striking out of part of a case;

(d) refusing permission to update a case;

(e) refusing or limiting permission to call expert evidence disclosed late;

(f) making an order requiring the payment of money into court;

(g) awarding interest at higher or lower rates than normal.

40.24 A party in breach of an order which makes the party subject to a sanction must apply for relief from the sanction, or else by r 3.8 (*Blackstone* 1329) the sanction will automatically take effect; and the court will take into account the matters set out in r 3.9 (*Blackstone* 1330) in deciding whether and on what terms to grant relief. An application of this kind must be supported by evidence.

J. Summary Judgment, Default Judgment, and Striking Out

40.25 The court has power to dispose of a hopeless case or defence by pre-emptive order without the necessity of a trial, and one of the aims of judicial case management in the CPR was to be an increased willingness of the courts to use these powers. The court can therefore strike out a hopeless statement of case which fails to make out a claim that is good in law and the court can give a default judgment where the defendant fails to defend the claim. Where a form of defence is put forward but the defence is hopeless, the court has power to strike it out or, where the defence has no real prospect of success and there is no other reason for holding a trial, the court can give summary judgment to the claimant. Equally a defendant can apply for summary judgment when the claim, or a part of the claim, has no real prospect of success and the court can do so of its own initiative. These steps can apply to the whole of the claim or the defence or only to a specific issue. For example, liability issues in personal injury claims may be suitable for summary judgment but the amount of damages will still have to be decided by the court.

40.26 Applications for default judgment are governed by Part 12 and PD 12 (*Blackstone* 1430). Applications for summary judgment are governed by Part 24 and PD 24 (*Blackstone* 1514). If the defendant fails to file an acknowledgement of service or a defence, the claimant should apply for judgment in default; the claimant can only apply for summary judgment after the defendant has filed either an acknowledgement or a defence. Such an application should be made as soon as possible and preferably before the claimant returns the allocation questionnaire. The application should be made by an application notice in accordance with

Part 23 (*Blackstone* 1504) which must be supported by evidence. There is an extended notice period of 14 days and the respondent's evidence must be filed at least seven days before the hearing, and any further evidence in reply from the applicant at least three days before the hearing (rr 24.4 and 24.5). The evidence in support should state and explain the belief that there is no defence to the claim that has a reasonable prospect of success. The content of the evidence will depend on the circumstances of the case but might, for example, include the police accident report in a road accident case or the report of an employer's inquiry into the circumstances of a workplace accident if it is contended that the basic facts make out an unanswerable case and yet liability remains in dispute after the protocol procedures have been followed.

The test for giving summary judgment under r 24.2 is that, as the case may be, **40.27** the claimant has no real prospect of succeeding on the claim or issue, or the defendant has no real prospect of defending the claim or issue, and in either case there is no other compelling reason why the case or issue should be disposed of at a trial.

Swain v Hillman [2001] 1 All ER 91 The words 'no real prospect of **40.28** succeeding' speak for themselves and need no amplification. But, explaining them, Lord Woolf said that 'real' points to a realistic rather than a fanciful prospect of success. A summary judgment application should not become a mini trial.

K. Admissions

Where a fact is formally admitted in a statement of case the admission is binding **40.29** and can provide the basis for the granting of judgment. The admission can only be withdrawn by amendment of the statement of case, which, once the statement of case has been served, requires the permission of the court or the consent of all the parties (r 17.1, *Blackstone* 1460). Rule 14.1(2) provides that notice of an admission must be in writing, such as in a statement of case or by a letter.

Informal admissions can be highly significant but take effect as matters of **40.30** evidence only. The weight to be given to the admission may vary according to the circumstances and according to the knowledge and authority of the person whose admission is relied on. It is open to the party alleged to have made an admission to seek to explain it and to argue that in spite of the earlier admission the court should reach a different conclusion.

Difficulties arise with admissions made by insurers or solicitors in claims above **40.31** fast-track value when responding to a letter of claim, before a claim form has been issued. Such admissions are often made in formal, open correspondence in circumstances where it is plain that they have been given only after an investigation of the claim and with the purpose of curtailing the expenditure of costs by the claimant in continuing to investigate and prepare the evidence for a liability dispute. Paragraph 3.9 of the protocol for personal injury claims deals with the defendant's response to the claim and says that 'Where liability is admitted the presumption is that the defendant will be bound by this admission for all claims with a total value of up to £15,000.' It is likely that the court would strike out a defence disputing liability after an admission had been given under the protocol, unless the defendant could put forward a good explanation for its change of mind. For claims above £15,000 in value there is no such restriction and the defendant will usually be entitled to defend the claim. It will rarely be possible for the claimant so show that the change of mind has caused sufficient prejudice to estop the defendant from defending.

40.32 *Gale v Superdrug Stores* [1996] 1 WLR 1089   Before proceedings were issued the defendant admitted liability and made interim payments. When proceedings were issued the defendant put in a defence which the claimant applied to strike out. In the absence of clear prejudice to the claimant the defendant was held to be entitled to change its mind.

40.33 *Mallia v Islington LBC* [2002] 1 CL 40   The defendant sought to resile from an admission of liability without giving any reason for making the admission in the first place or for withdrawing it. The circuit judge upheld the decision to refuse to allow the defendant to withdraw the admission.

L. Discontinuance

40.34 Once a claim has been commenced and the court has managed it with a time-table for pre-trial procedures and eventual trial, the orders must be obeyed and the costs of the litigation being incurred on both sides will continue to increase. A claimant who then decides that the merits of his claim are poor, perhaps in the light of the evidence or documents disclosed, will seek to negotiate a suitable compromise but may be faced with a defendant who will make no concessions and expects to proceed to trial. Discontinuance allows the claimant to bring a claim to an end, accepting liability for the defendant's costs of the action, but preventing any further costs being incurred and retaining the power to bring a fresh action based on the same facts once the costs have been paid. The rules about discontinuance are in Part 38 (*Blackstone* 1664).

M. Staying Proceedings

According to the CPR Glossary (*Blackstone* 2009), a stay 'imposes a halt on **40.35** proceedings, apart from taking any steps allowed by the rules or the terms of the stay. Proceedings can be continued if a stay is lifted'. One of the questions raised in the allocation questionnaire is whether the parties wish there to be a stay for a month while they seek to negotiate a settlement (r 26.4, *Blackstone* 1542). If it is necessary for reasons of limitation to issue a claim before the procedures of the relevant protocol have been followed, a stay may be ordered to enable the usual exchanges to take place within the timescale of the protocol in the hope of reducing costs. Further proceedings in a claim are automatically stayed by the acceptance of a settlement offer or payment under r 36.15 (*Blackstone* 1649). A consent order made in settlement of a claim will often be made on terms that provide for a stay of the proceedings rather than the entry of judgment.

The imposition of a stay is the means by which the courts enforce a decision **40.36** that the claimant ought reasonably to submit himself to a medical examination on behalf of the defendant: *Edmeads v Thames Board Mills* [1969] 2 QB 67. The claimant cannot be directly compelled to submit to the mechanics of a medical examination: for example, the trivial physical demands would probably amount to an unlawful assault without his consent to them. The procedure for the defendant is to apply for an order to stay further proceedings on the claim unless the claimant submits to the examination. The court will then decide whether the request for examination is one which the claimant cannot reasonably refuse. Now that the court has responsibility for case management which includes control of all matters relating to expert evidence, such an application is likely to follow a decision by the court that in principle the defendant should be entitled to adduce the evidence in question and the issue of the reasonableness of the claimant's refusal will be the subject of that decision; therefore applications for stay are now much less common than they were before the CPR but also more straightforward since the key question of reasonableness should already have been decided.

41

DISCLOSURE

A. The Disclosure List

41.01 The obligation to disclose all relevant documents to the other side and to the court, whether they help or hinder a person's case, is a central feature of civil litigation. The Civil Procedure Rules do not weaken this obligation, but they do seek to limit the scope of disclosure to what is readily available or really needed and therefore to keep the cost and time devoted to disclosure proportionate to the needs of the case. The rules also make it explicit that the duty of disclosure continues throughout the life of a case and does not end with the completion of inspection.

41.02 An order for standard disclosure will usually be made at the first occasion of case management by the court. Each party must carry out a reasonable search for relevant documents, list the documents on a form that is provided to the other side, and allow the other party to inspect them, usually by providing photocopies. The documents to be disclosed are those on which the party relies, and those which are relevant because they adversely affect his own case, adversely affect another party's case or support another party's case. Thus a document need not be disclosed if it relates to the subject matter of the action but has no bearing on the strength of the case of any party to the action. In giving disclosure, a party should set out the limits of the search for documents that has been undertaken and provision is made for this in the standard form N265. The scope of the search can be challenged by the other party by applying for an order for specific disclosure: at this stage the court will consider whether a reasonable search has been undertaken applying the criteria in CPR r 31.7(2).

41.03 A list of documents must be supported by a disclosure statement. This requirement bears a family likeness to the support of statements of case, applications and witness statements with a statement of truth. It is the legal representative's responsibility to ensure that the person making the disclosure statement understands the duty of disclosure. However, the responsibility for signing the statement lies with the party and this has introduced a significant responsibility for corporate defendants in employment cases which raise issues of system or previous complaint.

41.04 Once documents have been disclosed their status in the evidence has often in the past been left poorly defined. The documents are often put into the trial bundle and discussed in the course of a trial without any clear thought being given to the evidential status that they have, or the extent to which the contents can be relied on as proof of the facts stated in them without having been confirmed by the maker of the document. Rule 32.19 provides that a party is deemed to admit the authenticity of any document that is disclosed to him unless he serves a notice requiring it to be proved. PD 39, para 3.9 (*Blackstone* 1670) goes further in relation to trial bundles: where possible parties should agree that the documents in the trial bundle are authentic, and should agree that they may be treated as evidence of the facts stated in them even if no notice has been served under the Civil Evidence Act 1995. Coupled with the abolition of the rule against hearsay evidence, the practical effect is that any documents included in the disclosure lists can be put before the court and the statements embodied in the documents become part of the evidence in the case. The weight to be given to them will of course vary according to the circumstances, and a party who seeks to rely on a crucial statement in a document will often be wise to serve a witness statement and call the maker at trial rather than relying on the contents of the document only; but this will go to weight rather than admissibility. Often hearsay notices should be served in respect of the contents but in practice, since there is no sanction of inadmissibility when no notice has been given, the service of notices is infrequent.

B. Pre-action and Non-party Disclosure

41.05 In most personal injury claims, disclosure of the most significant documents will take place before court proceedings begin, under the arrangements made in the Pre-action Protocol for Personal Injury Claims. Where the operation of the protocol has failed to provide a prospective claimant with the information necessary to investigate a case, it is possible to seek an order for pre-action disclosure under r 31.16. Once proceedings are under way, the duty to give formal disclosure and inspection of documents will arise, but it now arises on an order of the court rather than automatically on the close of statements of case. In addition, it is possible under r 31.17 to obtain an order during the proceedings for disclosure to be given by someone who is not a party to the litigation, and a witness summons requiring the production of documents can be obtained under r 34.2 (*Blackstone* 1620).

C. Privilege

The first category of document to be included in the list is the documents being 41.06 disclosed. For a claimant this may include, for example, photographs of the scene, a police accident report, documents and receipts proving expenditure and loss of earnings; for a defendant it may include for example the accident book entry in relation to a workplace accident, or the documents relating to an internal inquiry.

The second category in the list is for relevant documents which are in the 41.07 control of the party making the list, but for which the party objects to disclosure. The usual ground is a claim to privilege of which there are two relevant kinds: first, documents which have formed part of confidential correspondence between a party and his solicitor for legal advice, to which privilege from production is allowed regardless of whether there are court proceedings afoot; and secondly, a wider range of correspondence and advice between a solicitor and others such as potential witnesses, experts and counsel as well as with his client, when they come into being in relation to litigation that is contemplated or in progress. Under r 35.10(3) (*Blackstone* 1639) instructions to an expert are not privileged but will not normally be disclosed. Sometimes a document may have two purposes: for example, a responsible employer will carry out an inquiry into the circumstances of any serious accident for the purpose of running the business properly, preventing a recurrence and identifying any shortcomings in the organization; the documents generated will not be protected by privilege unless the defence to a potential claim was the dominant purpose of the inquiry.

A claim to privilege does not lessen the duty to disclose the existence of a 41.08 document. It is only the inspection of the document which is protected. It is only when the other party knows of the existence of a document for which privilege is claimed that he can consider whether the claim to privilege should be challenged. It was common practice under the old rules to list privileged documents in only the most general terms rather than specifying what the individual documents or classes of document are. In many run-of-the-mill cases this is acceptable, saves costs and does no harm, but the practice ought not to be used to conceal the existence of a document in respect of which the possessor should know that the claim to privilege might be questioned, and it is to be hoped that more candour will be expected under the CPR.

41.09   If privileged documents are accidentally sent to the opposing party, the court will require that they be returned and will grant an injunction against the use of them by the recipient, who ought, if the mistake is appreciated, immediately return them: (*Darby v Weldon (No. 8)* [1991] 1 WLR 73 applied under the CPR 1998 in *Breeze v Stacey, The Times*, 8 July 1999). Rule 31.20 provides that a document inadvertently allowed to be inspected may only be used with the permission of the court.

41.10   *R v Derby Magistrates, ex p B* [1996] AC 487   A case which affirms the complete confidentiality of legal professional privilege between a lawyer and client in any circumstances of seeking legal advice, even in a trial for murder where the accused seeks disclosure in relation to statements made by a crucial witness for the Crown to the witness's solicitor.

41.11   *General Mediterranean Holdings v Patel* [2000] 1 WLR 272   Legal professional privilege gives everyone a fundamental right to confidential communication with his lawyer, and the rules which then (but no longer) required disclosure of the solicitor's papers in a wasted costs application were *ultra vires*. Disclosure of documents protected by privilege would not be ordered.

41.12   *Waugh v British Rail* [1980] AC 521   An employer's inquiry report into a fatal accident was prepared both for the purpose of obtaining legal advice in an anticipated claim and for the purpose of the operation and safety of the railway; since litigation was not the dominant purpose, the report was not protected by privilege and had to be disclosed.

D. Surveillance Videos

41.13   When I started in practice, before the popularity of video cameras, a local orthopaedic surgeon was well known for watching claimants approach and leave his consulting room and including in his report a comment on whether they showed the same limp as they had shown during the formal examination. This concern for finding the truth was notable because it was fairly rare, and still many doctors make it clear that a medico-legal report is based on the assumption that the complaints are true and they try not to be drawn into arguments about exaggeration and malingering. Now however the secret filming of claimants, not by doctors but by inquiry agents, has become a common feature of claims about persistent disability, and on occasions a very effective weapon for insurers confronting a claim of disability that seems disproportionate to the physical injury sustained.

41.14   The disclosure obligation applies to video recordings as well as to paper documents. A document is defined in r 31.4 as anything on which data is recorded. It follows that a defendant in possession of a surveillance video at the time of making a list of documents should disclose its existence. Further, the obligation of disclosure is, by r 31.11, a continuing obligation and a video ought to be disclosed when it is received, even though privilege may be claimed for it. The risk from non-disclosure is under r 31.21 that the court may not give permission for the video to be admitted in evidence.

Not all videos are hostile in intent. For a severely injured claimant, the **41.15** preparation of a video to show a typical daily routine (mobility, feeding and so forth) can be a powerful way to set the evidence of doctors and therapists in context. Such films are unlikely to be controversial and the claimant's advisers need only remember the requirement to give advance notice and inspection under r 33.6 (*Blackstone* 1617).

Videos taken by defendants or insurers are likely to prove more controversial. **41.16** In addition to the requirements of r 33.6 for advance disclosure at the time of serving witness statements, the ordinary rules of disclosure under Part 31 apply to limit the scope for the old-fashioned practice of ambushing the claimant with the video film after he has committed himself to his evidence in chief. The existence of the video has to be disclosed even if the content may not be shown. If the purpose of the video is not simply to show how well the claimant is able to move but also to show that he has lied to the medical experts about his disability, that amounts to an allegation of fraud, which ought to be specifically stated in the defence under PD 16, para 9.2 (*Blackstone* 1457). An application may be made in advance, without notice to the claimant, for permission to withhold disclosure and except in the most unusual case the court is likely to insist on a 'cards on the table' approach with early disclosure rather than allowing the forensic theatricality of a cross-examination ambush.

A defendant has to consider carefully the tactics of obtaining videos. They **41.17** potentially serve two purposes. The first is simply to illustrate the activities undertaken by the claimant when he believes he is unobserved: how easily he walks, whether he carries shopping, controls a strongly pulling dog, or digs his garden in spite of the injury of which he complains. Such evidence can be helpful to set the claimant's complaints of constant pain and disability into the context of a tolerably active way of life. The second purpose of a video, however, is to identify the claimant who is deliberately exaggerating the extent of his difficulties. Where this is suspected, it is best to carry out the surveillance close in time to an account given to a doctor or some other statement of disability given in the claimant's own words. If, for example, the claimant tells the doctor he cannot play golf but has been filmed on the golf course only a few days earlier, the point will be powerfully made and the risk of making a false accusation because of the variability of the disability over time will be reduced.

In a very strong case very effective results can still be obtained from withholding the video until trial, as the outcome of *Birch v Hales Containers* (see below) shows. More often, however, the court will refuse to grant the necessary order and it may be that in the ordinary case of exaggeration rather than out and out dishonesty, the early disclosure of the video will in fact lead to an earlier settlement and a realistic outcome. Current practice often involves defendants taking a calculated risk by withholding disclosure of video films until a few weeks before trial and then combining late disclosure of videos with a realistic payment into court. Although this practice is a breach of the spirit of the CPR on disclosure, it is an effective means of promoting realistic settlements.

41.18 *Digby v Essex CC* [1994] PIQR P53   Non-disclosure in advance can only be justified where there is a clear and categorical case of malingering advanced by the defendant and the disclosure of the video would allow the claimant to doctor his evidence. A medical opinion that there is no organic basis for the symptoms complained of is not sufficient to meet this test.

41.19 *Khan v Armaguard* [1994] 1 WLR 1204   This remains the leading decision in favour of the current 'cards on the table' approach, that permission to defendants to withhold disclosure of a video until trial should only be granted in the rarest and most exceptional circumstances and the existence of an allegation of malingering is not sufficient.

41.20 *Birch v Hale Containers* [1996] PIQR P307   The video in this case was of unusually powerful nature and the defendant obtained a without notice order permitting non-disclosure. When the video was produced at trial, the judge refused the claimant an adjournment and proceeded to award low damages. The Court of Appeal emphasized that the *Khan* approach is good law but since the defendants had obtained an order permitting non-disclosure the result stood. The court also commented that the video was a document which should have been disclosed even if privilege was claimed. The Court of Appeal was unimpressed by the claimant's complaint that non-disclosure lost the claimant the chance to accept a payment into court which would have been much too high!

41.21 *Rall v Hume* [2001] EWCA Civ 146; [2001] 3 All ER 248   The defendant obtained significant video evidence, but delayed in disclosing it to the claimant. By the time the defendant applied for permission, the admission of the evidence would have required the adjournment of the trial date. However, there had been no deliberate delay in disclosure so as to achieve surprise. The Court of Appeal held that it would usually be in the interests of justice to allow cross-examination of the claimant on video evidence which undermined the claimant's case to an extent that would substantially reduce the award of damages, provided there was no trial by ambush. By careful case management of the trial, selection of the key passages to be viewed at trial, and advance viewing of the video by all the witnesses, it should be possible for the trial to proceed as planned, so the video evidence could be admitted.

Uttley v Uttley [2002] PIQR P123   The defendant obtained significant video **41.22** evidence, but did not disclose it until the claimant had served an up-to-date witness statement and Schedule of Special Damages, which was long overdue and had been frequently requested. On seeing the video, the claimant accepted earlier payment into court, but objected to paying the defendant's costs for a period when the defendant was in possession of the video but had not disclosed it. The court held that the defendant's tactic was reasonable and the usual order for costs should apply.

Jones v University of Warwick [2003] EWCA Civ 151; [2003] PIQR **41.23** P382   The defendant had obtained significant video evidence by its agent using a trick to gain entry to the claimant's home and film her there. The defendant admitted that this had been a trespass and admitted that, since the medical experts had seen the video, if the video could not be admitted in evidence new experts would have to be instructed. The Court of Appeal held that the video evidence should be admitted, but marked its disapproval of the behaviour on behalf of the defendant by a costs sanction.

E. CPR Part 31—Disclosure and Inspection of Documents

31.1 Scope of this Part

(1) This Part sets out rules about the disclosure and inspection of documents.   **41.24**

(2) This Part applies to all claims except a claim on the small claims track.

31.2 Meaning of disclosure

A party discloses a document by stating that the document exists or has existed.   **41.25**

31.3 Right of inspection of a disclosed document

(1) A party to whom a document has been disclosed has a right to inspect that document **41.26** except where—
    (a) the document is no longer in the control of the party who disclosed it;
    (b) the party disclosing the document has a right or a duty to withhold inspection of it; or
    (c) paragraph (2) applies.

(Rule 31.8 sets out when a document is in the control of a party)

(Rule 31.19 sets out the procedure for claiming a right or duty to withhold inspection)

(2) Where a party considers that it would be disproportionate to the issues in the case to permit inspection of documents within a category or class of document disclosed under rule 31.6(b)—
    (a) he is not required to permit inspection of documents within that category or class; but
    (b) he must state in his disclosure statement that inspection of those documents will not be permitted on the grounds that to do so would be disproportionate.

(Rule 31.6 provides for standard disclosure)

(Rule 31.10 makes provision for a disclosure statement)

(Rule 31.12 provides for a party to apply for an order for specific inspection of documents)

31.4 Meaning of document

41.27 In this Part—

    'document' means anything in which information of any description is recorded; and

    'copy', in relation to a document, means anything onto which information recorded in the document has been copied, by whatever means and whether directly or indirectly.

31.5 Disclosure limited to standard disclosure

41.28 (1) An order to give disclosure is an order to give standard disclosure unless the court directs otherwise.

    (2) The court may dispense with or limit standard disclosure.

    (3) The parties may agree in writing to dispense with or to limit standard disclosure.

(The court may make an order requiring standard disclosure under rule 28.3 which deals with directions in relation to cases on the fast track and under rule 29.2 which deals with case management in relation to cases on the multi-track)

31.6 Standard disclosure—what documents are to be disclosed

41.29 Standard disclosure requires a party to disclose only—

    (a) the documents on which he relies; and

    (b) the documents which—

      (i) adversely affect his own case;

      (ii) adversely affect another party's case; or

      (iii) support another party's case; and

    (c) the documents which he is required to disclose by a relevant practice direction.

31.7 Duty of search

41.30 (1) When giving standard disclosure, a party is required to make a reasonable search for documents falling within rule 31.6(b) or (c).

    (2) The factors relevant in deciding the reasonableness of a search include the following—

    (a) the number of documents involved;

    (b) the nature and complexity of the proceedings;

    (c) the ease and expense of retrieval of any particular document; and

    (d) the significance of any document which is likely to be located during the search.

    (3) Where a party has not searched for a category or class of document on the grounds that to do so would be unreasonable, he must state this in his disclosure statement and identify the category or class of document.

(Rule 31.10 makes provision for a disclosure statement)

31.8 Duty of disclosure limited to documents which are or have been in a party's control

41.31 (1) A party's duty to disclose documents is limited to documents which are or have been in his control.

    (2) For this purpose a party has or has had a document in his control if—

    (a) it is or was in his physical possession;

    (b) he has or has had a right to possession of it; or

    (c) he has or has had a right to inspect or take copies of it.

31.9 Disclosure of copies

(1) A party need not disclose more than one copy of a document. **41.32**

(2) A copy of a document that contains a modification, obliteration or other marking or feature—

(a) on which a party intends to rely; or

(b) which adversely affects his own case or another party's case or supports another party's case;

shall be treated as a separate document.

(Rule 31.4 sets out the meaning of a copy of a document)

31.10 Procedure for standard disclosure

(1) The procedure for standard disclosure is as follows. **41.33**

(2) Each party must make and serve on every other party, a list of documents in the relevant practice form.

(3) The list must identify the documents in a convenient order and manner and as concisely as possible.

(4) The list must indicate—

(a) those documents in respect of which the party claims a right or duty to withhold inspection; and

(b) (i) those documents which are no longer in the party's control; and

(ii) what has happened to those documents.

(Rule 31.19(3) and (4) require a statement in the list of documents relating to any documents inspection of which a person claims he has a right or duty to withhold)

(5) The list must include a disclosure statement.

(6) A disclosure statement is a statement made by the party disclosing the documents—

(a) setting out the extent of the search that has been made to locate documents which he is required to disclose;

(b) certifying that he understands the duty to disclose documents; and

(c) certifying that to the best of his knowledge he has carried out that duty.

(7) Where the party making the disclosure statement is a company, firm, association or other organisation, the statement must also—

(a) identify the person making the statement; and

(b) explain why he is considered an appropriate person to make the statement.

(8) The parties may agree in writing—

(a) to disclose documents without making a list; and

(b) to disclose documents without the disclosing party making a disclosure statement.

(9) A disclosure statement may be made by a person who is not a party where this is permitted by a relevant practice direction.

31.11 Duty of disclosure continues during proceedings

(1) Any duty of disclosure continues until the proceedings are concluded. **41.34**

(2) If documents to which that duty extends come to a party's notice at any time during the proceedings, he must immediately notify every other party.

31.12 Specific disclosure or inspection

(1) The court may make an order for specific disclosure or specific inspection.

(2) An order for specific disclosure is an order that a party must do one or more of the following things—

    (a) disclose documents or classes of documents specified in the order;

    (b) carry out a search to the extent stated in the order;

    (c) disclose any documents located as a result of that search.

(3) An order for specific inspection is an order that a party permit inspection of a document referred to in rule 31.3(2).

(Rule 31.3(2) allows a party to state in his disclosure statement that he will not permit inspection of a document on the grounds that it would be disproportionate to do so)

31.13 Disclosure in stages

41.35 The parties may agree in writing, or the court may direct, that disclosure or inspection or both shall take place in stages.

31.14 Documents referred to in statements of case etc.

41.36   (1) A party may inspect a document mentioned in—

    (a) a statement of case;

    (b) a witness statement;

    (c) a witness summary; or

    (d) an affidavit.

(2) Subject to rule 35.10(4), a party may apply for an order for inspection of any document mentioned in an expert's report which has not already been disclosed in the proceedings.

(Rule 35.10(4) makes provision in relation to instructions referred to in an expert's report)

31.15 Inspection and copying of documents

41.37 Where a party has a right to inspect a document—

    (a) that party must give the party who disclosed the document written notice of his wish to inspect it;

    (b) the party who disclosed the document must permit inspection not more than 7 days after the date on which he received the notice; and

    (c) that party may request a copy of the document and, if he also undertakes to pay reasonable copying costs, the party who disclosed the document must supply him with a copy not more than 7 days after the date on which he received the request.

(Rule[s] 31.3 and 31.14 deal with the right of a party to inspect a document)

31.16 Disclosure before proceedings start

41.38   (1) This rule applies where an application is made to the court under any Act for disclosure before proceedings have started.

(2) The application must be supported by evidence.

(3) The court may make an order under this rule only where—

    (a) the respondent is likely to be a party to subsequent proceedings;

    (b) the applicant is also likely to be a party to those proceedings;

    (c) if proceedings had started, the respondent's duty by way of standard disclosure, set out in rule 31.6, would extend to the documents or classes of documents of which the applicant seeks disclosure; and

    (d) disclosure before proceedings have started is desirable in order to—

        (i) dispose fairly of the anticipated proceedings;

        (ii) assist the dispute to be resolved without proceedings; or

        (iii) save costs.

(4) An order under this rule must—
(a) specify the documents or the classes of documents which the respondent must disclose; and
(b) require him, when making disclosure, to specify any of those documents—
(i) which are no longer in his control; or
(ii) in respect of which he claims a right or duty to withhold inspection.
(5) Such an order may—
(a) require the respondent to indicate what has happened to any documents which are no longer in his control; and
(b) specify the time and place for disclosure and inspection.

31.17 Orders for disclosure against a person not a party

(1) This rule applies where an application is made to the court under any Act for disclosure by **41.39** a person who is not a party to the proceedings.

(2) The application must be supported by evidence.

(3) The court may make an order under this rule only where—
(a) the documents of which disclosure is sought are likely to support the case of the applicant or adversely affect the case of one of the other parties to the proceedings; and
(b) disclosure is necessary in order to dispose fairly of the claim or to save costs.

(4) An order under this rule must—
(a) specify the documents or the classes of documents which the respondent must disclose; and
(b) require the respondent, when making disclosure, to specify any of those documents—
(i) which are no longer in his control; or
(ii) in respect of which he claims a right or duty to withhold inspection.
(5) Such an order may—
(a) require the respondent to indicate what has happened to any documents which are no longer in his control; and
(b) specify the time and place for disclosure and inspection.

31.18 Rules not to limit other powers of the court to order disclosure

Rules 31.16 and 31.17 do not limit any other power which the court may have to order— **41.40**
(a) disclosure before proceedings have started; and
(b) disclosure against a person who is not a party to proceedings.

31.19 Claim to withhold inspection or disclosure of a document

(1) A person may apply, without notice, for an order permitting him to withhold disclosure of **41.41** a document on the ground that disclosure would damage the public interest.

(2) Unless the court orders otherwise, an order of the court under paragraph (1)—
(a) must not be served on any other person; and
(b) must not be open to inspection by any person.

(3) A person who wishes to claim that he has a right or a duty to withhold inspection of a document, or part of a document, must state in writing—
(a) that he has such a right or duty; and
(b) the grounds on which he claims that right or duty.

(4) The statement referred to in paragraph (3) must be made—
(a) in the list in which the document is disclosed; or
(b) if there is no list, to the person wishing to inspect the document.

(5) A party may apply to the court to decide whether a claim made under paragraph (3) should be upheld.

(6) For the purpose of deciding an application under paragraph (1) (application to withhold disclosure) or paragraph (3) (claim to withhold inspection) the court may—

(a) require the person seeking to withhold disclosure or inspection of a document to produce that document to the court; and

(b) invite any person, whether or not a party, to make representations.

(7) An application under paragraph (1) or paragraph (5) must be supported by evidence.

(8) This Part does not affect any rule of law which permits or requires a document to be withhold from disclosure or inspection on the ground that its disclosure or inspection would damage the public interest.

31.20 Restriction on use of a privileged document inspection of which has been inadvertently allowed

41.42 Where a party inadvertently allows a privileged document to be inspected, the party who has inspected the document may use it or its contents only with the permission of the court.

31.21 Consequence of failure to disclose documents or permit inspection

41.43 A party may not rely on any document which he fails to disclose or in respect of which he fails to permit inspection unless the court gives permission.

31.22 Subsequent use of disclosed documents

41.44 (1) A party to whom a document has been disclosed may use the document only for the purpose of the proceedings in which it is disclosed, except where—

(a) the document has been read to or by the court, or referred to, at a hearing which has been held in public;

(b) the court gives permission; or

(c) the party who disclosed the document and the person to whom the document belongs agree.

(2) The court may make an order restricting or prohibiting the use of a document which has been disclosed, even where the document has been read to or by the court, or referred to, at a hearing which has been held in public.

(3) An application for such an order may be made—

(a) by a party; or

(b) by any person to whom the document belongs.

31.23 False disclosure statements

41.45 (1) Proceedings for contempt of court may be brought against a person if he makes, or causes to be made, a false disclosure statement, without an honest belief in its truth.

(2) Proceedings under this rule may be brought only—

(a) by the Attorney General; or

(b) with the permission of the court.

F. PD 31—Disclosure and Inspection

General

1.1 The normal order for disclosure will be an order that the parties give standard **41.46**
disclosure.

1.2 In order to give standard disclosure the disclosing party must make a reasonable search for
documents falling within the paragraphs of rule 31.6.

1.3 Having made the search the disclosing party must (unless rule 31.10(8) applies) make a list
of the documents of whose existence the party is aware that fall within those paragraphs and
which are or have been in the party's control (see rule 31.8).

1.4 The obligations imposed by an order for standard disclosure may be dispensed with or
limited either by the court or by written agreement between the parties. Any such written
agreement should be lodged with the court.

The search

2 The extent of the search which must be made will depend upon the circumstances of the case **41.47**
including, in particular, the factors referred to in rule 31.7(2). The parties should bear in mind the
overriding principle of proportionality (see rule 1.1(2)(c)). It may, for example, be reasonable to
decide not to search for documents coming into existence before some particular date, or to limit
the search to documents in some particular place or places, or to documents falling into particular
categories.

The list

3.1 The list should be in Form N265. **41.48**

3.2 In order to comply with rule 31.10(3) it will normally be necessary to list the documents in
date order, to number them consecutively and to give each a concise description (e.g. letter,
claimant to defendant). Where there is a large number of documents all falling into a particular
category the disclosing party may list those documents as a category rather than individually
e.g. 50 bank statements relating to account number _at _ Bank, _ 19_ to _19_; or, 35 letters
passing between _ and _ between _ 19_ and _ 19 _.

3.3 The obligations imposed by an order for disclosure will continue until the proceedings
come to an end. If, after a list of documents has been prepared and served, the existence of further
documents to which the order applies comes to the attention of the disclosing party, the party
must prepare and serve a supplemental list.

Disclosure statement

4.1 A list of documents must (unless rule 31.10(8)(b) applies) contain a disclosure statement **41.49**
complying with rule 31.10. The form of disclosure statement is set out in the Annex to this
practice direction.

4.2 The disclosure statement should:

(1) expressly state that the disclosing party believes the extent of the search to have been
reasonable in all the circumstances, and

(2) in setting out the extent of the search (see rule 31.10(6)) draw attention to any particular
limitations on the extent of the search which were adopted for proportionality reasons and give
the reasons why the limitations were adopted, e.g. the difficulty or expense that a search not
subject to those limitations would have entailed or the marginal relevance of categories of documents omitted from the search.

4.3 Where rule 31.10(7) applies, the details given in the disclosure statement about the person making the statement must include his name and address and the office or position he holds in the disclosing party.

4.4 If the disclosing party has a legal representative acting for him, the legal representative must endeavour to ensure that the person making the disclosure statement (whether the disclosing party or, in a case to which rule 31.10(7) applies, some other person) understands the duty of disclosure under Part 31.

4.5 If the disclosing party wishes to claim that he has a right or duty to withhold a document, or part of a document, in his list of documents from inspection (see rule 31.19(3)), he must state in writing:
> (1) that he has such a right or duty, and
> (2) the grounds on which he claims that right or duty.

4.6 The statement referred to in paragraph 4.5 above should normally be included in the disclosure statement and must identify the document, or part of a document, to which the claim relates.

4.7 An insurer or the Motor Insurers' Bureau may sign a disclosure statement on behalf of a party where the insurer or the Motor Insurers' Bureau has a financial interest in the result of proceedings brought wholly or partially by or against that party. Rule 31.10(7) and paragraph 4.3 above shall apply to the insurer or the Motor Insurers' Bureau making such a statement.

Specific disclosure

41.50   5.1 If a party believes that the disclosure of documents given by a disclosing party is inadequate he may make an application for an order for specific disclosure (see rule 31.12).

5.2 The application notice must specify the order that the applicant intends to ask the court to make and must be supported by evidence (see rule 31.12(2) which describes the orders the court may make).

5.3 The grounds on which the order is sought may be set out in the application notice itself but if not there set out must be set out in the evidence filed in support of the application.

5.4 In deciding whether or not to make an order for specific disclosure the court will take into account all the circumstances of the case and, in particular, the overriding objective described in Part 1. But if the court concludes that the party from whom specific disclosure is sought has failed adequately to comply with the obligations imposed by an order for disclosure (whether by failing to make a sufficient search for documents or otherwise) the court will usually make such order as is necessary to ensure that those obligations are properly complied with.

Claims to withhold disclosure or inspection of a document

41.51   6.1 A claim to withhold inspection of a document, or part of a document, disclosed in a list of documents does not require an application to the court. Where such a claim has been made, a party who wishes to challenge it must apply to the court (see rule 31.19(5)).

6.2 Rule 31.19(1) and (6) provide a procedure enabling a party to apply for an order permitting disclosure of the existence of a document to be withheld.

Inspection of documents mentioned in expert's report (rule 31.4(e))

41.52   7 Reference should be made to PD 35 for provisions dealing with applications to inspect these documents.

8 Attention is drawn to r. 31.23 which sets out the consequences of making a false disclosure statement without an honest belief in its truth, and to the procedure set out in PD 32, para. 27.

ANNEX   DISCLOSURE STATEMENT

I, the above named claimant [or defendant] [if party making disclosure is a company, firm or other organization identify here who the person making the disclosure statement is and why he is the appropriate person to make it] state that I have carried out a reasonable and proportionate search to locate all the documents which I am required to disclose under the order made by the court on   day of   . I did not search:

41.53

(1) for documents predating ....,

(2) for documents located elsewhere than ....,

(3) for documents in categories other than ....

I certify that I understand the duty of disclosure and to the best of my knowledge I have carried out that duty. I certify that the list above is a complete list of all documents which are or have been in my control and which I am obliged under the said order to disclose.

G. County Courts Act 1984, s 53

53. Power of court to order disclosure of documents, inspection of property etc. in proceedings for personal injuries or death

(2) On the application, in accordance with rules of court, of a party to any proceedings, a county court shall, in such circumstances as may be prescribed, have power to order a person who is not a party to the proceedings and who appears to the court to be likely to have in his possession, custody or power any documents which are relevant to an issue arising out of the said claim—

41.54

(a) to disclose whether those documents are in his possession, custody or power; and

(b) to produce such of those documents as are in his possession, custody or power to the applicant or, on such conditions as may be specified in the order,—

(i) to the applicant's legal advisers; or

(ii) to the applicant's legal advisers and any medical or other professional adviser of the applicant; or

(iii) if the applicant has no legal adviser, to any medical or other professional adviser of the applicant.

(3) On the application, in accordance with rules of court, of a party to any proceedings, a county court shall, in such circumstances as may be prescribed, have power to make an order providing for any one or more of the following matters, that is to say—

(a) the inspection, photographing, preservation, custody and detention of property which is not the property of, or in the possession of, any party to the proceedings but which is the subject-matter of the proceedings or as to which any question arises in the proceedings;

(b) the taking of samples of any such property as is mentioned in paragraph (a) and the carrying out of any experiment on or with any such property.

(4) The preceding provisions of this section are without prejudice to the exercise by a county court of any power to make orders which is exercisable apart from those provisions.

42

EXPERTS

A. Who Can Give Expert Evidence?

An expert is a witness who, because of his special knowledge and experience, is **42.01** entitled to give the court admissible evidence of his own opinion on a matter in dispute. An ordinary or 'lay' witness is not allowed to express his opinion, but should only give evidence about the facts. There are no specific rules which define the qualification of an expert to be regarded as such, but the proposed expert must have a high degree of specialist skill and knowledge in the particular subject, and it must be knowledge which the court does not otherwise have: so, for example, expert evidence is not admissible on the credibility of witnesses or on matters of English law. The area in which the expert witness is entitled to express an opinion is the area of his expertise, and opinions which the expert may express in passing about the law, the facts, or the other aspects of the case should carry no weight.

Liverpool RC Archdiocesan Trustees v Goldberg (No. 3) [2001] 1 WLR 2337 **42.02** A person who has a relationship with a party on whose instructions he reports is not a suitable person to be an independent expert. In this case the expert was a colleague in chambers with the barrister defendant and if the case had not settled before judgment, such expert evidence would not have been admitted.

42.03 Every personal injury claim is likely to require an expert opinion from a doctor to assist the court with the nature and effect of the injuries sustained by the claimant. Medical evidence is usually obtained from a consultant in the relevant specialty, although in cases of minor injury doctors of lower seniority may be appropriate and may be willing to cover a wider range. Some personal injury claims may require expert evidence in other fields. In a claim for an accident at work, expert evidence from a consulting engineer may be required to explain to the court the machinery and processes which led to the risk of injury. In a claim for a road traffic accident an expert in accident reconstruction may sometimes (but rarely) be required to interpret the factual evidence. In a claim for serious injuries, experts may be needed to assist on quantum by identifying the nursing, therapeutic, and housing needs of the claimant and the likelihood of finding alternative employment.

42.04 In straightforward personal injury claims it is tempting to assume that the consultant who has been responsible for treatment will be the person best placed to give an expert report for the court. The temptation should be resisted. A treating doctor will have a relationship with a patient which may make it more difficult for the doctor to report with true objectivity; and the demands of objective reporting to the court may interfere with the therapeutic relationship with the patient. For therapeutic reasons the doctor may wish to encourage the patient with an optimistic prognosis, whereas the court needs to know the full range of risks and concerns for the future. The treating doctor may have a useful role to play in forming a treatment plan, but it is better to obtain the basic medical report from a new and independent doctor.

B. Changes under the Civil Procedure Rules

42.05 The changes made under the CPR were intended to address a number of perceived problems with expert evidence. Experts were instructed when they were not always necessary, experts tended to be partisan towards the interest of the party instructing them, and the volume of expert evidence added substantially, and to an extent that was not proportionate to the benefit gained from their input, to the cost and delay of litigation and to the habit of the parties arguing rather than seeking agreement.

42.06 First, under the CPR the court has taken control of expert evidence. Under the overriding objective, the court must seek to deal with cases justly and in ways which put the parties on an equal footing, save expense and are proportionate to the nature of the case. The parties need permission to adduce any expert evidence and the court has power to control the manner in which expert evidence is adduced and the cost of it.

Secondly, the CPR further provide that the expert owes his primary duty to the court and not to the party who has instructed him and who is responsible for payment of his fee. This rule applies even when there are separate experts instructed by the parties under the protection of privilege. **42.07**

Thirdly, the CPR introduce the single expert jointly instructed by both parties. This innovation has been an outstanding and surprising success, giving the court necessary and impartial expert input at reasonable expense where the issues are relatively uncontroversial or where the amount in dispute is relatively low. Part of the success is attributable to the willingness of the court to allow a party to go on to instruct a separate expert where there is a sensible reason for being unable to accept the opinion of a jointly instructed single expert. **42.08**

Fourthly, the CPR move the focus away from a system where the court will resolve a dispute between experts by hearing oral evidence from the competing experts at trial, towards a system of resolving such disputes as far as possible ahead of the trial, by encouraging parties to ask questions of experts in writing in response to their reports, and by ensuring that in any case where there is more than one expert in the same discipline, the experts will hold a discussion before the trial in which they must identify the matters on which they are able to agree and the matters which remain in dispute. **42.09**

Fifthly, the court is able to insist that expert evidence will be given only in a written report rather than by the attendance of the expert at trial, even when the opinion of the expert is disputed by one of the parties. This power is particularly important in the fast track as a way of overriding legal sensitivities in the interests of resolving a dispute briskly and at reasonable cost. **42.10**

Expert evidence is governed by Part 35 and PD 35, which are set out below. The Code of Guidance on Expert Evidence is also reproduced later in this chapter. The Academy of Experts has also produced a code of guidance, available at www.academy-expert.org, and there are procedures governing the use of expert evidence in the personal injury protocol (*Blackstone* 2199) with a model form letter of instruction for medical experts at Annex C (*Blackstone* 2205), in the clinical negligence protocol (*Blackstone* 2213), in the disease and illness protocol (*Blackstone* 2243) and in the Queen's Bench Guide (*Blackstone* 2458). **42.11**

C. The Expert's Role and Duty

A general statement of the responsibilities of an expert witness is set out in PD 35, section 1, restating the principles derived from CPR r 35.3 and *The Ikarian Reefer* [1993] 2 Lloyd's Rep 68: **42.12**

1. It is the duty of an expert to help the court on matters within his own expertise. This duty is paramount and overrides any obligation to the person from whom the expert has received instructions or by whom he is paid.
2. Expert evidence should be the independent product of the expert uninfluenced by the pressures of litigation.
3. An expert should assist the court by providing objective, unbiased opinion on matters within his expertise, and should not assume the role of an advocate.
4. An expert should consider all material facts, including those which might detract from his opinion.
5. An expert should make it clear
   (a) when a question or issue falls outside his expertise, and
   (b) when he is not able to reach a definite opinion, for example because he has insufficient information.
6. If, after producing a report, an expert changes his view on any material matter, such change of view should be communicated to all the parties without delay and, when appropriate, to the court.

42.13 *Vernon v Bosley (No. 2)* [1999] QB 18   Principle 6 above imposes responsibilities on legal representatives, who are likely to be the means of making the communication of a change of the expert's view. The claimant called expert evidence to prove a psychiatric injury, but three weeks before the trial the same expert had expressed a far more optimistic prognosis when called for the claimant in a separate case about the care of his children. The Court of Appeal held that the claimant's legal representatives had been wrong not to disclose the reports that the psychiatrist had given in the other case and a new trial was ordered.

D. Case Management of Expert Evidence

42.14 The court will limit expert evidence to that which is reasonably required to resolve the proceedings. This limiting principle is the opening salvo of Part 35. First, it means that expert evidence must be necessary. There are fields in which expert evidence has in the past been common but where the court may consider that the expert is dealing with matters which can be addressed from the court's own knowledge and experience, supplemented by materials available to legal representatives from public documents, internet searches, and publications such as the PNBA's handbook *Facts & Figures*. Accident reconstruction evidence and expert evidence on employment and care issues in claims of moderate value are often disallowed in accordance with this trend. Secondly, it means that a single expert may be sufficient rather than separate experts instructed by each party.

Liddell v Middleton [1996] PIQR P36   A prophetic case decided before the **42.15** new CPR in which the Court of Appeal deplored the unnecessary use of road accident reconstruction experts and set out the limits of the proper scope of an expert report—which did not extend to commenting on the credibility of the statements of factual witnesses.

No party can put forward expert evidence without the court's permission **42.16** (r 35.4). On the other hand, the claimant must obtain an expert medical report in time to attach it to his Particulars of Claim. The personal injury protocol envisages that the letter of claim will list the names of one or more experts that the claimant considers suitable. The defendant can indicate an objection within 14 days and the claimant should then instruct a mutually acceptable expert. When the claimant has done so, there is a presumption in the fast track that the defendant will not be entitled to obtain its own expert evidence within that specialist field. This is therefore a process of joint selection rather than joint instruction, carried out before the commencement of proceedings.

Carlson v Townsend [2001] EWCA Civ 511; [2001] 1 WLR 2415   The **42.17** claimant proposed three possible medical experts in accordance with the protocol. The defendant objected to one and the claimant obtained a report from one of the others named. However, the claimant decided not to disclose that report but obtained a report from a new expert, not one of those originally suggested, and the defendant then sought disclosure of the first report. The first report had not been not obtained on joint instructions and the claimant had not waived privilege; obtaining the second report was a breach of the protocol, but insisting on disclosure of the first report was not a sanction available to the court for that breach.

Once the proceedings have been started, the court has control. A party pro- **42.18** posing to rely on expert evidence must apply for permission, stating the field of expertise and where practicable identifying the proposed expert. If the other party also wishes to rely on expert evidence in the same specialist field, the court may order that there should be joint instructions to a single expert and the preamble to PD 35 indicates that, consistent with the duty to restrict expert evidence to no more than that which is reasonably required, 'where possible, matters requiring expert evidence should be dealt with by a single expert'. The allocation questionnaire requires parties to identify any expert evidence they wish to use, identifying the experts and the field of expertise, and in appropriate cases this will lead to permission granted on paper. In the fast track the court will need good reasons if permission is sought for separate experts. In the multi-track, the court is more likely to agree that parties should instruct separate experts on matters which lie at the heart of the dispute and on matters which are likely to involve a range of expert opinions, but may still limit the parties to a single jointly instructed expert on subsidiary issues or on matters of quantum. Where separate experts are instructed, the court is likely to direct a simultaneous exchange of their reports, and if there is disagreement the court will direct that there must be a discussion between the experts in accordance with r 35.12 for the purpose of setting out the issues on which they agree and the issues on which they disagree with a summary of their reasons for disagreeing.

42.19   *Daniels v Walker* [2000] 1 WLR 1382   The defendant agreed to joint instruction of a single care expert, but when the report was received the defendant disagreed with the care regime proposed and wished to instruct its own expert. Lord Woolf MR said at 1387E: 'The correct approach is to regard the instruction of an expert jointly by the parties as the first step in obtaining expert evidence on a particular issue. It is to be hoped that in the majority of cases it will not only be the first step but the last step. If having obtained a joint expert's report a party for reasons which are not fanciful wishes to obtain further information before making a decision as to whether there is a particular part (or indeed the whole) of the expert's report which he may wish to challenge, then they should, subject to the discretion of the court, be permitted to obtain that evidence.'

E. Expert Reports

42.20   The formal requirements of an expert report are set out in r 35.10 and PD 35, para 2. An expert report must be addressed to the court and not to a party from whom the expert has received his instructions. The report must give details of the expert's qualifications. The report must give details of any literature or other material which the expert has relied on in making the report. The report must contain a statement setting out the substance of all facts and instructions given to the expert which are material to the opinions expressed in the report or upon which his opinions are based. The report must make clear which of the facts stated in the report are within the expert's own knowledge. The report must say who carried out any examination, measurement, test, or experiment which the expert has used for the report, give the qualifications of that person, and say whether or not the test or experiment has been carried out under the expert's supervision. The report must contain a summary of the conclusions reached. If the expert is not able to give his opinion without qualification, the report must state the qualification. At the end of an expert report there must be a statement that the expert understands his duty to the court and has complied with that duty.

These requirements are matters of form rather than substance. In addition **42.21**
under PD 35, para 2.2(6) the report of an expert must, where there is a range of
opinion on the matters dealt with in the report, summarize the range of opinion
and give reasons for his own opinion. This can be a troublesome requirement. It
is useful when the subject matter of the report is truly a matter on which the
range of expert opinion lies at the heart of the dispute. For example, in a clinical
negligence claim, there may be a range of clinical practice and if the procedure
in question is said to fall outside the scope of acceptable practice it is vital for the
court to understand fully all the relevant clinical approaches. On the other
hand, the rule cannot have been intended to require an expert to set out all the
points on which he can foresee that he might be cross-examined at trial, but
then to state that the opinion he has expressed is correct.

F. The Single Joint Expert

There can be difficulties in managing the appointment of a single joint expert, **42.22**
particularly when one or both of the parties had wished to instruct a separate
expert. However, the rules allow the court to direct that there should be a single
expert and if there is no agreement, the rules allow for the court to select the
expert, or to devise the manner of selecting the expert, and to give instructions
about the investigations the expert should carry out and about his fees.
Although it may be easier for the expert to receive a single letter of instruction,
since he is to be a 'joint' expert, r 35.8(1) provides for each of the instructing
parties to give his own instructions to the expert, provided a copy of the instructions is sent at the same time to the other instructing party. The report prepared
by a single jointly instructed expert must comply with the same rules as to the
form and content of his report as an expert who is separately instructed.

A single joint expert owes duties to all parties and to the court. Since there will **42.23**
not be another expert to disagree with, the evidence of a single joint expert is
likely to be given in writing only, in the report and the answers to questions,
although it remains possible for the court to order that a single joint expert
should attend the trial to be cross-examined. However, neither of the parties
is entitled to have any private communication with a single joint expert so it
is not possible to canvass matters in advance with a single joint expert in
correspondence or at a conference under the protection of legal privilege.

G. Examination by Medical Experts

The defendant cannot arrange for a claimant to undergo a medical examination, **42.24**
or obtain sight of the claimant's medical records, unless the claimant gives

consent. However, if the claimant fails to give consent to reasonable investigations on behalf of the defendant, the claim may be stayed (*Edmeades v Thames Board Mills* [1969] 2 QB 67). The issue will be decided on the basis of what it is reasonable to expect the claimant to undergo. The nature of the claim, the reasons for refusal and the invasiveness, risk, or pain of the procedure will be relevant. In a case of complex injuries, the claimant may be required to undergo examinations across a range of specialties, but it would require special circumstances for the court to require the claimant to undergo a second examination after the defendant had decided not to rely on the opinion of another expert in the same specialty who had already examined him (but see *Beck v Ministry of Defence* below).

H. Questions to Experts

42.25 Under r 35.6 a party may put written questions about an expert report to any expert who was instructed by another party or to a single joint expert. The questions should be for the purpose of clarification of the report only, unless the court or the other party agrees to allow wider questions. Questions may be put once only and must be put within 28 days of the service of the expert's report. The answers given by the expert are treated as part of the report. The ability to ask questions can be a useful forensic tool and is especially important in cases where the court is unlikely to give permission for the expert to give oral evidence at trial. In practice, the 'clarification' of the report is often interpreted quite widely to allow searching questions about the interpretation of the materials seen by the expert or about new information. It is common, for example, to ask a medical expert to review his opinion on the severity of injury in the light of significant video surveillance even though this goes further than clarifying the original report. An expert who concedes in answer to questions that there is a range of opinions and alternative interpretations demonstrates a potential vulnerability to cross-examination and although this may be no more than the expert would have conceded in cross-examination at trial, to have the concession in writing ahead of the trial may contribute to the process of narrowing the area of disagreement and achieving a settlement.

I. Discussions between Experts

42.26 Litigators trained in the old ways have been uncomfortable—as a sweeping generalization—about losing control of expert evidence to the court, but have been somewhat reassured by the fact that the evidence of a separately instructed expert remains privileged until the report is disclosed. Correspondence and discussion in conference with the expert is permitted. The Code of Guidance, para 17 suggests that an expert must not be asked to amend, expand, or alter any part of his report in a manner which distorts the expert's true opinion, but may be invited to amend or expand the report to ensure accuracy and internal consistency, completeness, relevance to the issues, and clarity. The expert must state the substance of all the instructions that he has received, but need not disclose the detail or the copy documents, and the option remains of deciding not to disclose or rely on the opinion of the expert.

Where separate experts hold a discussion, litigators again feel uncomfortable **42.27** because of the loss of control. It is the experts, performing their duty to the court, who are responsible for carrying out the discussion and reporting the outcome. The expert cannot be protected from making rash or unwelcome concessions by having a lawyer at his elbow. Indeed, the point of these discussions is precisely to give the expert the opportunity to make any concessions that are proper, however tactically unwelcome this may be to the party who instructed the expert. Litigators often try to retain control by insisting that the joint discussion should be conducted under an agenda drawn up by lawyers and answering (only) specific questions put forward by the lawyers. These precautions are sometimes appropriate, where it is necessary to ensure that the experts give workable answers on issues which require legal precision, such as may arise, for example, where there is a complex dispute about causation. For the most part, however, experts in personal injury litigation quickly develop a sufficient understanding of the legal principles to be able to work out for themselves the nature of the issues their discussion should address. In the great majority of cases therefore, it is suggested that confining the expert by an external agenda is more likely to do harm than good since it may discourage the experts from expressing their full opinions to the court in their own way.

The joint statement which results from a discussion may express the agreement **42.28** of the experts, in which case the expert will find it very difficult to advance a contrary view at trial, but the agreement does not bind the party who instructed the expert unless the party expressly agrees to be bound by it. The discussion between the experts is held 'without prejudice' so, while an expert may be cross-examined about the content of the joint statement, he may not be cross-examined about the content of the discussion that led to it.

J. Privilege

No question of privilege can arise in relation to the instructions and report of **42.29** a single joint expert, since all of the material passing to and from the expert must be copied and shared between all the parties and the court.

42.30 Where separate experts are instructed, communications with the expert are protected by privilege until the report from the expert is disclosed in the course of the litigation, even though this rule is in conflict with the 'cards on the table' approach encouraged by the CPR. If an expert's report is disclosed, it must contain a statement setting out the substance of all material instructions on the basis of which the report was written, but the court will not normally order the disclosure of the instructions or permit cross-examination about the instructions unless there are reasonable grounds to consider that the statement of instructions was accurate or incomplete. If the report is not disclosed, because the instructing party decides not to rely on the evidence of the expert, the opinion of the expert is privileged and the opponent is not entitled to disclosure of it, neither should a requirement of disclosure be imposed on the consent of the claimant to attend a medical examination.

42.31 *Beck v Ministry of Defence* [2003] EWCA Civ 1043; [2004] PIQR P1   The court overrode the usual rule of privilege. The defendant lost confidence in the expert psychiatrist it had instructed to examine the claimant and required the claimant to undergo a second examination. The court ordered that this additional expert evidence would only be permitted on condition that the report of the first expert was disclosed.

K. CPR Part 35—Experts and Assessors

35.1 Duty to restrict expert evidence

42.32 Expert evidence shall be restricted to that which is reasonably required to resolve the proceedings.

35.2 Interpretation

42.33 A reference to an 'expert' in this Part is a reference to an expert who has been instructed to give or prepare evidence for the purpose of court proceedings.

35.3 Experts—overriding duty to the court

42.34   (1) It is the duty of an expert to help the court on the matters within his expertise.

(2) This duty overrides any obligation to the person from whom he has received instructions or by whom he is paid.

35.4 Court's power to restrict expert evidence

42.35   (1) No party may call an expert or put in evidence an expert's report without the court's permission.

(2) When a party applies for permission under this rule he must identify—
(a) the field in which he wishes to rely on expert evidence; and
(b) where practicable the expert in that field on whose evidence he wishes to rely.

(3) If permission is granted under this rule it shall be in relation only to the expert named or the field identified under paragraph (2).

(4) The court may limit the amount of the expert's fees and expenses that the party who wishes to rely on the expert may recover from any other party.

35.5 General requirement for expert evidence to be given in a written report

(1) Expert evidence is to be given in a written report unless the court directs otherwise.   **42.36**

(2) If a claim is on the fast track, the court will not direct an expert to attend a hearing unless it is necessary to do so in the interests of justice.

35.6 Written questions to experts

(1) A party may put to—   **42.37**
    (a) an expert instructed by another party; or
    (b) a single joint expert appointed under rule 35.7, written questions about his report.

(2) Written questions under paragraph (1)—
    (a) may be put once only;
    (b) must be put within 28 days of service of the expert's report; and
    (c) must be for the purpose only of clarification of the report, unless in any case—
        (i) the court gives permission; or
        (ii) the other party agrees.

(3) An expert's answers to questions put in accordance with paragraph (1) shall be treated as part of the expert's report.

(4) Where—
    (a) a party has put a written question to an expert instructed by another party in accordance with this rule; and
    (b) the expert does not answer that question, the court may make one or both of the following orders in relation to the party who instructed the expert—
        (i) that the party may not rely on the evidence of that expert; or
        (ii) that the party may not recover the fees and expenses of that expert from any other party.

35.7 Court's power to direct that evidence is to be given by a single joint expert

(1) Where two or more parties wish to submit expert evidence on a particular issue, the court   **42.38**
may direct that the evidence on that issue is to given by one expert only.

(2) The parties wishing to submit the expert evidence are called 'the instructing parties'.

(3) Where the instructing parties cannot agree who should be the expert, the court may—
    (a) select the expert from a list prepared or identified by the instructing parties; or
    (b) direct that the expert be selected in such other manner as the court may direct.

35.8 Instructions to a single joint expert

(1) Where the court gives a direction under rule 35.7 for a single joint expert to be used, each   **42.39**
instructing party may give instructions to the expert.

(2) When an instructing party gives instructions to the expert he must, at the same time, send a copy of the instructions to the other instructing parties.

(3) The court may give directions about—
    (a) the payment of the expert's fees and expenses; and
    (b) any inspection, examination or experiments which the expert wishes to carry out.

(4) The court may, before an expert is instructed—
    (a) limit the amount that can be paid by way of fees and expenses to the expert; and
    (b) direct that the instructing parties pay that amount into court.

(5) Unless the court otherwise directs, the instructing parties are jointly and severally liable for the payment of the expert's fees and expenses.

35.9 Power of court to direct a party to provide information

42.40   Where a party has access to information which is not reasonably available to the other party, the court may direct the party who has access to the information to—

(a) prepare and file a document recording the information; and

(b) serve a copy of that document on the other party.

35.10 Contents of report

42.41   (1) An expert's report must comply with the requirements set out in the relevant practice direction.

(2) At the end of an expert's report there must be a statement that—

(a) the expert understands his duty to the court; and

(b) he has complied with that duty.

(3) The expert's report must state the substance of all material instructions, whether written or oral, on the basis of which the report was written.

(4) The instructions referred to in paragraph (3) shall not be privileged against disclosure but the court will not, in relation to those instructions—

(a) order disclosure of any specific document; or

(b) permit any questioning in court, other than by the party who instructed the expert,

unless it is satisfied that there are reasonable grounds to consider the statement of instructions given under paragraph (3) to be inaccurate or incomplete.

35.11 Use by one party of expert's report disclosed by another

42.42   Where a party has disclosed an expert's report, any party may use that expert's report as evidence at the trial.

35.12 Discussions between experts

42.43   (1) The court may, at any stage, direct a discussion between experts for the purpose of requiring the experts to—

(a) identify and discuss the expert issues in the proceedings; and

(b) where possible, reach an agreed opinion on those issues.

(2) The court may specify the issues which the experts must discuss.

(3) The court may direct that following a discussion between the experts they must prepare a statement for the court showing—

(a) those issues on which they agree; and

(b) those issues on which they disagree and a summary of their reasons for disagreeing.

(4) The content of the discussion between the experts shall not be referred to at the trial unless the parties agree.

(5) Where experts reach agreement on an issue during their discussions, the agreement shall not bind the parties unless the parties expressly agree to be bound by the agreement.

35.13 Consequence of failure to disclose expert's report

42.44   A party who fails to disclose an expert's report may not use the report at the trial or call the expert to give evidence orally unless the court gives permission.

35.14 Expert's right to ask court for directions

42.45   (1) An expert may file a written request for directions to assist him in carrying out his function as an expert.

(2) An expert may request directions under paragraph (1) without giving notice to any party.

(3) The court, when it gives directions, may also direct that a party be served with—

(a) a copy of the directions; and

(b) a copy of the request for directions.

L. PD 35—Experts and Assessors

Part 35 is intended to limit the use of oral expert evidence to that which is reasonably required. In addition, where possible, matters requiring expert evidence should be dealt with by a single expert. Permission of the court is always required either to call an expert or to put an expert's report in evidence.

Form and content of expert's reports

1.1 An expert's report should be addressed to the court and not to the party from whom the expert has received his instructions.   **42.46**

1.2 An expert's report must:

(1) give details of the expert's qualifications,

(2) give details of any literature or other material which the expert has relied on in making the report,

(3) say who carried out any test or experiment which the expert has used for the report and whether or not the test or experiment has been carried out under the expert's supervision,

(4) give the qualifications of the person who carried out any such test or experiment, and

(5) where there is a range of opinion on the matters dealt with in the report—

(i) summarise the range of opinion, and

(ii) give reasons for his own opinion,

(6) contain a summary of the conclusions reached,

(7) contain a statement that the expert understands his duty to the court and has complied with that duty (rule 35.10(2)), and

(8) contain a statement setting out the substance of all material instructions (whether written or oral). The statement should summarise the facts and instructions given to the expert which are material to the opinions expressed in the report or upon which those opinions are based (rule 35.10(3)).

1.3 An expert's report must be verified by a statement of truth as well as containing the statements required in paragraph 1.2(7) and (8) above.

1.4 The form of the statement of truth is as follows:

'I believe that the facts I have stated in this report are true and that the opinions I have expressed are correct.'

1.5 Attention is drawn to rule 32.14 which sets out the consequences of verifying a document containing a false statement without an honest belief in its truth.

1.6 In addition, an expert's report should comply with the requirements of any approved expert's protocol.

Information

2 Under r. 35.9 the court may direct a party with access to information which is not reasonably available to another party to serve on that other party a document which records the information.   **42.47**

The document served must include sufficient details of all the facts, tests, experiments and assumptions which underlie any part of the information to enable the party on whom it is served to make, or to obtain, a proper interpretation of the information and an assessment of its significance.

Instructions

42.48   3 The instructions referred to in paragraph 1.2(8) will not be protected by privilege (see rule 35.10(4)). But cross-examination of the expert on the contents of his instructions will not be allowed unless the court permits it (or unless the party who gave the instructions consents to it). Before it gives permission the court must be satisfied that there are reasonable grounds to consider that the statement in the report of the substance of the instructions is inaccurate or incomplete. If the court is so satisfied, it will allow the cross-examination where it appears to be in the interests of justice to do so.

Questions to experts

42.49   4.1 Questions asked for the purpose of clarifying the expert's report (see rule 35.6) should be put, in writing, to the expert not later than 28 days after receipt of the expert's report (see paragraphs 1.2 to 1.5 above as to verification).

4.2 Where a party sends a written question or questions direct to an expert, a copy of the questions should, at the same time, be sent to the other party or parties.

4.3 The party or parties instructing the expert must pay any fees charged by that expert for answering questions put under rule 35.6. This does not affect any decision of the court as to the party who is ultimately to bear the expert's costs.

Single expert

42.50   5 Where the court has directed that the evidence on a particular issue is to be given by one expert only (rule 35.7) but there are a number of disciplines relevant to that issue, a leading expert in the dominant discipline should be identified as the single expert. He should prepare the general part of the report and be responsible for annexing or incorporating the contents of any reports from experts in other disciplines.

M. Code of Guidance on Expert Evidence

42.51   This Code of Guidance was issued in December 2001. It was prepared by a Working Party for the Head of Civil Justice. It describes general principles which apply to all the courts in which personal injury claims are likely to be litigated. Most of it is uncontroversial, but note:

(a) In para 4, the Working Party envisages that there may be circumstances in which privileged communications with experts may have to be disclosed in the course of litigation.

(b) The requirements of para 16, including the requirement for a report to contain a declaration of compliance with the Code, are mandatory.

(c) Paragraphs 39 and 40 forbid separate communications between a single joint expert and one party without first inviting the other party to participate.

CODE OF GUIDANCE ON EXPERT EVIDENCE

Preamble

In framing this Code, the Working Party has taken account of the Civil Procedure Rules (CPR) **42.52**
and the Practice Directions as they exist on 1 December 2001, together with any case law on their
interpretation. The Code of Guidance is designed to help experts and those instructing them in all
cases where CPR applies. It is intended to facilitate better communication and dealings both
between the expert and the instructing party and between the parties; as such it is drawn in
general terms so as to provide guidance for every court of law in the civil jurisdiction and in every
type of civil litigation.

Part 35 of the CPR applies in every case where an expert is instructed to give or prepare evidence
for the purpose of court proceedings. Part 35 is of limited application in the small claims court
where, with some exceptions, its provisions do not apply.

Assistance from an expert may be needed at various stages of a dispute and for different purposes.
An expert always owes a duty to exercise reasonable care and skill to the person instructing him or
her, and to comply with any relevant professional code of ethics.

However, where the expert is instructed to give or prepare evidence for the purpose of court
proceedings, rather than to give advice before they have started, Part 35 applies. Under Part
35.3(1) the expert owes a duty to help the court on matters within his expertise, and this duty
overrides any obligation to the person from whom the expert has received instructions or by
whom the expert is paid.

The extent to which the rules may require the expert to disclose to the court, and to other parties
to court proceedings, matters which would otherwise be confidential to the client and privileged
from disclosure is dealt with in paragraphs 3 and 4 below.

Part I—Experts

1. An expert witness in under an overriding duty to help the court to deal with the case 'justly'. **42.53**
That is the overriding obligation of the court under Part 1.1(1) and it is further defined in
Part 1.1(2) as follows:
    '1.1(2) Dealing with a case justly includes, so far as is practicable—
        (a) ensuring that the parties are on an equal footing
        (b) saving expense
        (c) dealing with the case in ways which are proportionate—
            (i) to the amount of money involved
            (ii) too the importance of the case
            (iii) to the complexity of the issues, and
            (iv) to the financial position of each party
        (d) ensuring that it is dealt with expeditiously and fairly; and
        (e) allotting to it an appropriate share of the court's resources . . .'

2. Some courts have published their own Guides which supplement the CPR for proceedings
in those courts. These contain provisions affecting expert evidence and an expert witness should
be familiar with them when they are relevant to his evidence.

3. Any advice given by an expert before court proceedings are started is likely to be confidential
to the client and privileged from disclosure to other parties. But where the expert is asked to give
or prepare evidence for the purpose of court proceedings, so that Part 35 applies, s/he is required
to state the substance of the instructions s/he has received. The Court has power to order the
expert to disclose what his or her instructions were.

4. Although the point has yet to be definitively decided, the power to order disclosure may in
certain circumstances extend to instructions or advice that were privileged when they were given.

5. The expert should also be aware that any failure by him to comply with the Rules of court orders or any excessive delay for which the expert is responsible may result in the party who instructed him being penalised in costs and even in extreme cases being debarred from placing the expert's evidence before the court.

Appointment

42.54 6. Those intending to instruct an expert to give or prepare evidence for the purpose of court proceedings should consider whether evidence from that expert is appropriate, taking account of the principles set out in Parts 1 and 35 of the CPR, and in particular whether:

(a) the evidence is relevant to a matter which is in dispute between the parties. An expert witness may be able to

(i) give relevant opinion evidence

(ii) help to establish relevant facts

(iii) identify issues which require decision by the court, and

(iv) explore areas where agreement may be possible;

(b) the expert has expertise relevant to the issue on which an opinion is sought

(c) the expert has the experience, expertise and training appropriate to the value, complexity and importance of the case

(d) the objects referred to under (a) can be achieved by the appointment of a single joint expert

(e) the expert will be able to

(i) produce a report

(ii) deal with questions for or by other experts, and

(iii) have discussions with other experts

all within a reasonable time and at a cost proportionate to the matters in issue; and

(f) the expert will be available to attend the trial, if his attendance is required.

7. Those instructing experts should also bear in mind:

(a) that no party can call an expert or put in evidence an expert's report without the court's permission, and

(b) that the court may limit the amount of an expert's fees and expenses that the party who wishes to rely on the expert may recover from any other party.

Terms of appointment

42.55 8. Terms of appointment should be agreed at the outset and should include:

(a) the basis of the expert's charges (either daily or hourly rates and an estimate of the time likely to be required, or a fee for the services)

(b) any travelling expenses and other disbursements

(c) rates for attendance at court and provisions for payment on late notice of cancellation of a court hearing

(d) time for delivery of a report

(e) time for making payment, and

(f) whether fees are to be paid by a third party.

When necessary, arrangements should be made for dealing with questions to experts and discussions between experts, including any directions given by the court, and provision should be made for the cost of this work.

Payment

42.56 9. Payments contingent upon the nature of the expert's advice given in legal proceedings, or upon the outcome of the case, must not be offered or accepted. To do so would contravene the expert's overriding duty to the court.

Deferment of payment

10. Agreement to delay payment of an expert's fee until after the conclusion of the case is **42.57**
permissible as long as the amount of the fee does not depend on the outcome of the case.

Instructions

11. Those instructing experts should ensure that they give clear instructions, including the **42.58**
following:

(a) basic information, such as names, addresses, telephone numbers, dates of birth and dates
of incidents

(b) the nature and extent of expertise that is called for

(c) the purpose of requesting the advice or report, a description of the matter to be
investigated, the principal known issues and the identity of all parties

(d) the statement(s) of case (if any), those documents which form part of standard disclosure
and witness statements which are relevant to the advice or report

(e) where proceedings have not been started, whether proceedings are being contemplated
and, if so, whether the expert is asked only for advice, and

(f) where proceedings have been started, the date of any hearing and in which court and to
which track they have been allocated.

12. Experts who do not receive clear instructions should request clarification and indicate that
they are not prepared to act unless and until such clear instructions are received.

13. Experts must neither express an opinion outside the scope of their field of expertise, nor
accept any instructions to do so. Experts must not accept instructions if they are not satisfied they
can comply with any orders that have been made. Where an expert has already been instructed,
the expert should notify those instructing him/her immediately if the expert considers s/he may
not be able to comply with an order.

The expert's report

14. In preparing their reports, experts   **42.59**

(a) should maintain professional objectivity and impartiality at all times

(b) in addressing questions of fact and opinion, should keep the two separate and discrete,
and

(c) where there are facts in dispute—

(i) should not express a view in favour of one or other disputed set of facts, unless,
because of their particular learning and experience, they perceive one set of facts as being
improbable or less probable, in which case they may express that view, and should give reasons,
and

(ii) should express separate opinions on every set of facts in dispute.

Information

15. All experts' reports should contain the following information: **42.60**

(a) the expert's academic and professional qualifications

(b) a statement of the source of instructions and the purpose of the advice or report

(c) a chronology of relevant events

(d) a statement of the methodology used, in particular what laboratory or other tests (if any)
were employed, by whom and under whose supervision

(e) details of the documents or any other evidence upon which any aspects of the advice or
report is based

(f) relevant extracts of literature or any other material which might assist the court in
deciding the case, and

(g) a summary of conclusions reached.

Content of report

42.61 16. In providing a report experts:

(a) must address it to the court and not to any of the parties

(b) must include a statement setting out the substance of all instructions (whether written or oral). The statement should summarise the facts and instructions given to the expert which are material to the opinions expressed in the report or upon which those opinions are based

(c) where there is a range of opinion in the matters dealt with in the report, give

(i) a summary of the range of opinion, and

(ii) the reasons for his own opinion

(d) must express any qualification of, or reservation to, their opinion

(e) if such opinion was not formed independently, should make clear the source of the opinion

(f) must declare that the report has been prepared in accordance with this Code and the requirements of the Civil Procedure Rules, and

(g) must include a statement of truth, as required by PD 35 para. 1.3.

Amendment

42.62 17. Experts

(a) must not be asked to, and must not, amend, expand or alter any part of the report in a manner which distorts the expert's true opinion, but

(b) may be invited to amend or expand a report to ensure accuracy and internal consistency, completeness, relevance to the issues and clarity.

18. Before disclosure of any report, the expert should be given the opportunity to review, and if necessary, update the contents of the report.

Procedure

42.63 19. Experts should

(a) be kept informed adequately about any deadlines for the preparation of their advice or reports

(b) be advised promptly about any timetable for the proceedings set by the court, or any changes thereto

(c) be provided without delay with further or updated instructions where the progress of the case requires this, and

(d) be provided with any order or notice making any provision in relation to expert evidence.

20. Following completion of the report, experts should be:

(a) advised as soon as reasonably practicable of the following:

(i) whether, and if so when, the report will be disclosed to the other party, and

(ii) if so disclosed, the date of disclosure

(b) given the opportunity to consider and comment on other reports which deal with the same issues, and

(c) kept informed of the progress of the action, including any amendments to the statements of case relevant to the expert's opinion.

21. Experts should communicate promptly with those instructing them any change of opinion and the reasons therefor.

22. The court has power to direct a party to provide information to which it has access and which is not reasonably available to the other party. If the expert requires further information for the purposes of his report which s/he thinks may fall within this category, s/he should notify those instructing him accordingly.

23. Experts may file with the court a written request for directions to assist them in carrying out their function as experts, and they may do so without giving notice to any party.

Questions for experts

24. A party may put written questions to another party's expert about that expert's report:　　**42.64**
　　(a) for the purpose of clarifying the report in accordance with Rule 35.6, and
　　(b) within the time limits prescribed within Rule 35.6(2) and Practice Direction 4.1 [i.e. within 28 days of the service of the report], or
　　(c) otherwise as the court may direct or the parties agree.

Any such questions should be answered within 28 days unless the court directs otherwise. The expert's reply shall be treated as part of the expert's report. If experts have any queries or concerns in respect of questions put by a party they should in the first instance seek clarification from those instructing them. Where a party puts a written question to an expert instructed by another party in accordance with Rule 35.6(2) and the expert does not answer the question, the court may order that the party who instructed the expert may not rely on the evidence of that expert or that the party may not recover the expert's fees and expenses from any other party.

Conferences and discussions

25. The parties and their lawyers should seek to reach agreement about, and consider taking　**42.65** steps to clarify, the issues by way of:
　　(a) conference or discussion with the experts, and/or
　　(b) discussion between experts for opposing parties in order to narrow the issues and identify:
　　　　(i) the extent of the agreement between experts
　　　　(ii) the points of disagreement and the reasons for disagreement
　　　　(iii) action, if any, which may be taken to resolve the outstanding points of disagreement, and
　　　　(iv) any issues not raised in the agenda for discussion and the extent to which these issues may be agreed.

26. The parties, their lawyers and experts should co-operate to produce concise agendas for any discussion between experts, which should, so far as possible:
　　(a) be circulated 28 days before the date fixed for the discussion
　　(b) be agreed 7 days before the date fixed for the discussion
　　(c) consist of questions which are clearly stated and apply, where necessary, the correct legal test
　　(d) consist of questions which, by their nature, are closed, that is to say, capable of being answered 'yes' or 'no', and
　　(e) include questions which enable the experts to state the reasons for their agreement or disagreement.

27. The discussions may take place face to face or by any other appropriate means proportionate to the circumstances of the case and the Court track. Lawyers will not normally be present at such discussions. If lawyers do attend they should not normally intervene save to answer questions put to them by the experts or to advise them on the law.

28. If there has been a discussion, a statement of the areas of and the reasons for agreement and disagreement should be prepared and agreed. This should be done at the meeting or, in the event of discussion at a distance, promptly between the experts, usually before the discussion is concluded. This statement may have to be produced to the court, but shall not be binding on the parties. A copy of the statement shall be provided to the parties. The content of the discussion between the experts may not be referred to in court unless the parties expressly agree. The parties should consider making such an agreement and record it or any failure to agree in the statement.

29. Those instructing experts must not give, and experts must not accept, instructions not to reach agreement at such discussions on areas within the competence of experts.

Attendance at trial

42.66   30. The parties should consider whether the use of available audio-visual facilities might avoid unnecessary attendance at court by the experts without compromising a party's presentation of its case.

31. Those instructing experts should inform them promptly whether attendance at trial will be required, and if so inform them of the date and venue fixed for the hearing of the case. In applying to fix dates for the trial, those instructing experts should, as far as possible, take account of the availability of experts.

32. Experts must take all steps to ensure availability to attend court but should be alerted to the fact that a solicitor may need to serve a witness summons in the event of difficulties.

33. If a party wishes its experts to attend a hearing in a fast track claim, the burden is on that party to persuade the court that the case is so exceptional that the overriding objective requires such attendance.

Part II—Single joint experts

42.67   34. The court has power to direct the appointment of a single joint expert selected by the parties. The court may also select the expert to be appointed, if the parties cannot agree who it should be, and may give directions regarding the amount and payment of the expert's fees.

35. The spirit as well as the letter of Parts 35.7 and 35.8 call upon the parties to consider from the outset of the proceedings whether appointment of a single joint expert is appropriate (paragraph 6(d) above). The courts encourage such appointments particularly in cases where the sums involved are not large and the issues are not complex.

36. The appointment of a single joint expert does not prevent a party from instructing his own expert to advise him.

37. A party may propose the appointment as single joint expert of an expert who has already advised him in the case, but this may mean disclosing to the other party any privileged or confidential information the expert has received and any advice s/he has given.

38. Parties should bear in mind that a single joint expert may be appointed to deal with some but not all of the issues requiring expert evidence, with a view to promoting agreement on those issues and narrowing the scope of expert evidence. In a case involving a number of disciplines, a single joint expert in the dominant discipline may be appointed to co-ordinate a single report.

39. The parties may send separate instructions to a single joint expert, but if they do, they must provide a copy to the other party. Wherever possible instructions should be agreed, and they should be in writing. Instructions should comply strictly with the provisions relating to parties' experts. In the event of any meeting with the single joint expert an opportunity must be offered to the other parties and their legal representatives to attend the meeting.

40. The single joint expert owes the same duties of professional competence as does an expert instructed by one of the parties, and the same overriding duty to the court. The conduct of the single joint expert should be determined by the principles of fairness and transparency. The expert should not communicate with or meet either party independently of the others. The expert's report should comply strictly with the provisions relating to those of parties' experts set out under paragraphs 14 to 16 above, and the expert may be questioned and must provide answers in the same manner as set out in paragraph 24 above.

41. If the single joint expert is unable to prepare a report within the terms of reference of both parties the expert should, as a first step, seek the help of the parties to resolve the conflict. If this is unsuccessful, the single joint expert may seek directions from the court.

42. The single joint expert may also seek further information and directions from the court as set out in paragraphs 22 and 23 above.

43

APPLICATIONS, EVIDENCE, AND TRIAL

A. Applications

After the defendant has responded to the claim by serving a defence, the next **43.01** step will be an allocation decision. On allocating a case to the fast track the court will give standard directions and will try to deal with any further issues that arise before trial by considering matters on paper without the necessity for hearing. If a claim is allocated to the multi-track, the court will fix a date for a case management conference when the whole range of case management directions will be considered and the court will take whatever steps are necessary to resolve the issues between the parties in a sensible, fair and proportionate manner. Rule 1.4(2)(i) (*Blackstone's Civil Practice 2004* 1315; hereafter *Blackstone*) requires the court to deal with as many aspects of the case as it can on the same occasion. A further opportunity for case management may arise at a later case management conference or pre-trial review. Many of the case management issues that arise in the course of a case may be resolved in this way without the need for a specific application to be made. However, if one of the parties wishes to apply for an interim remedy or to ask the court to give specific directions at any stage of the case an application can be made. For example an application should be made if a party wishes to have permission to amend its statement of case, or wishes to obtain an order for specific disclosure, or an interim payment, or a variation in the directions that have been given about expert evidence.

43.02   The general rules about applications are in Part 23 and PD 23 (*Blackstone* 1504). Other rules deal with specific kinds of application: Part 24 (*Blackstone* 1514) covers applications for summary judgment; Part 25 (*Blackstone* 1519) covers applications for interim remedies and r 25.6 (*Blackstone* 1521) and PD 25B (*Blackstone* 1539) cover applications for an interim payment; r 31.12 (*Blackstone* 1593) covers applications for specific disclosure.

43.03   There is a standard form for an application notice, Form N244, which is in three parts. Part A provides for a statement of the nature of the order that the applicant is seeking and a brief explanation of the reasons for seeking the order. Whenever possible a draft order should be attached to the application. Part B identifies the evidence to be relied on. It is usually necessary to support an application with evidence to set out the facts. By r 32.2(1)(b) the evidence at the hearing of an application will be given in writing and not orally. The applicant can rely on a witness statement prepared for the application and on any other document such as a statement of case which has been verified by a statement of truth. Part C provides a page on which a brief statement in support of the application can be written. In a straightforward application it is more convenient to use Part C rather than to create another separate document, but in a complex application where it is necessary to rely on the history of the case it will be better for a full narrative statement to be prepared as a separate document without pressure of space. The application must be signed and the evidence in support of the application must be verified by a statement of truth. An application should be served at least three clear days before the hearing date, and as soon as practicable after it is filed. A respondent should serve any evidence to be relied on in response to the application as soon as possible.

43.04   Under r 23.8 the court may deal with an application without a hearing, and under PD 23, section 6 the court may order that an application should be dealt with by a telephone hearing. The disadvantages of the telephone hearing are that the participants lose all the non-verbal communication that makes a court hearing interesting so that discussion tends to be rather stilted, and the participants are limited to referring to the documents that have been exchanged in advance without the opportunity to deal with any difficulties that might arise during the hearing by reference to other documents or correspondence. The advantage of a telephone hearing is that it saves the time and expense of travel to court for the advocates. Opinions among practitioners and judges vary about the effectiveness of telephone hearings, and there is no doubt that a face-to-face hearing is a more satisfactory way of dealing with complex or difficult issues. This is, however, an area in which the legal profession has to live with a procedure which is less than ideal, in the interests of proportionality.

43.05   Before the hearing of any application, in both the fast track and the multi-track, which is expected to last no more than a day, statements of costs for the purpose of summary assessment should be filed and served at least 24 hours in advance, and at the end of the application the court will usually deal summarily with the costs of the application. Although it is possible for the court to order that the costs should be 'in the case' the court will usually consider the application as a separate episode in the litigation and make an order with respect to the costs incurred based on the merits and the outcome of the application. This practice has acted as a powerful tool to reduce the number of unnecessary applications being made. The costs will not usually be payable until the conclusion of the case, and an order for payment forthwith usually marks disapproval of the paying party.

B. Witness Statements

The preparation of witness statements is a crucially important stage in litigation. **43.06** Courts can only act on the basis of evidence. The witness statement is, in modern civil court procedure, the evidence of the witness. The witness statement will take the place of evidence in chief. It must cover all of the issues on which evidence is necessary. By r 32.5(3) (*Blackstone* 1601) the witness statement will stand as the evidence in chief of the witness, and oral evidence, if the court gives permission, will be limited to amplifying the witness statement and giving evidence of new matters which have arisen since the witness statement was served. The scope of the evidence is limited by the scope of the witness statement. The purpose of exchanging witness statements is to avoid trial by ambush, and if a significant matter has been left out of the witness statement it is likely to be impossible to introduce it at the trial. A careful balance has to be struck between providing a statement which is reasonably concise and yet ensuring that all necessary matters are covered. Any significant new matters should be set out in an additional witness statement in advance of the trial rather than relying on the discretion of the court to allow oral evidence.

The use of witness statements is governed by r 32.5 (*Blackstone* 1601) and the **43.07** form of witness statements is governed by PD 32, sections 17–25 (*Blackstone* 1608). The witness statement should be written, if practicable, in the witness's own words (para 18.1) and it is usually convenient to follow a chronological order (para 19.2). A witness statement must be verified by a statement of truth.

If it is not possible to serve the witness statement from a person whom a party **43.08** intends to call at trial, r 32.9 (*Blackstone* 1601) allows that party to apply without notice for permission to serve a witness summary instead, setting out the evidence to be included or the matters on which the party proposes to question the witness. This is the procedure which should be followed if, for example, a reluctant witness refuses to sign a witness statement and will be ordered to attend the trial by a witness summons.

C. Evidence of the Facts

43.09 At trial, evidence of the facts will be given by witnesses, and by r 32.2(1)(a) (*Blackstone* 1600) the general rule is that the witness will give oral evidence in public. The witness statement will stand as the evidence in chief supplemented by such amplification and updating as the court may allow. The witness may then be cross-examined, for the purpose of challenging and undermining the case of the party calling the witness, and advancing if possible the case of the cross-examining party. Leading questions may be asked, that is to say, questions which suggest an answer to the witness. 'It was raining, wasn't it?' is a leading question; 'What was the weather like?' is not. It is common to seek to undermine a witness by finding discrepancies between different accounts that the witness has given on different occasions or conflicts between his evidence and other contemporaneous documents. After cross-examination, the party who called the witness is entitled to re-examine. The scope of re-examination should be limited to matters raised with the witness in cross-examination, and leading questions should not be asked.

43.10 It is the responsibility of an advocate in cross-examination to put his party's case to the witness. However, it is questionable whether this rule continues to serve a useful purpose. When there was no advance exchange of witness statements, case summaries, or skeleton arguments, and a defendant was allowed to plead a bare denial in his defence, the witnesses might be called on behalf of the claimant when neither they nor the advocate knew in any detail what evidence was to come in opposition, so the obligation of the defendant's advocate to put his case to the witnesses was necessary to ensure that they would be given the chance to have their say on any relevant matters.

43.11 The rules about witness summonses to enforce the attendance of the witness at trial are contained in Part 34 and PD 34 (*Blackstone* 1620).

D. Hearsay Evidence

43.12 The rule at trial is that the evidence of a witness of fact should be given orally on the basis of the witness statement that has been exchanged. Typically this will be a direct account of what the witness saw and heard happen. Hearsay evidence is second-hand evidence which seeks to prove what happened by giving someone else's account of it. The common law was suspicious of hearsay evidence and held it to be inadmissible except in very rare circumstances. The Civil Evidence Act 1995 has thrown off all these restrictions and has made all hearsay evidence admissible in all civil proceedings. There is a requirement under s 2 of the 1995

Act and r 33.2 (*Blackstone* 1616) for written notice to be given of the intention to adduce hearsay evidence, but if notice has not been given, the evidence is still admissible and the sanction for failing to serve a notice is in the weight that may be given to the evidence and a risk on costs. Therefore if a witness cannot attend, his witness statement can be put in evidence under the 1995 Act. If a contemporaneous document contains a description of an accident, or if an inquiry was undertaken immediately afterwards, the facts stated in such documents can be admitted in evidence under the 1995 Act. The greatest weight will be given to the evidence of a witness who attends the trial and who remains convincing after cross-examination; the weight to be given to hearsay evidence will vary enormously according to the circumstances and nature of the evidence in question.

The power to admit a hearsay statement does not make it acceptable to dispense **43.13** with the attendance of witnesses. In deciding the weight to be given to a hearsay statement, the court will have in mind the general rule that witnesses of fact should attend for cross-examination. Rule 33.4 (*Blackstone* 1617) enables the other party to call a witness whose statement has been served as hearsay evidence, for the purpose of cross-examining the witness on the content of the statement; and r 33.5 envisages that the other party might wish to call evidence to attack the credibility of a hearsay witness and requires that advance notice of this should be given. If the absence of a hearsay notice has prevented the other party from following these steps in the expectation that the witness will be called, the other party will have strong grounds for seeking an adjournment or for arguing that the weight to be given to the evidence should be negligible.

E. Documentary Evidence

Rule 32.19 (*Blackstone* 1603) provides that a party shall be deemed to admit the **43.14** authenticity of the documents disclosed to him under Part 31 unless he serves notice that he wishes the documents to be proved at trial. Section 8 of the Civil Evidence Act 1995 allows a statement contained in a document to be proved by the production of the document itself or by a copy of the document at any number of removes from the original. In addition, s 9 allows any document which is part of the records of a business or of a public authority to be received in evidence without further proof. Thus, where there is no dispute about the authenticity of the original, the copy documents that have been disclosed by the parties are invariably included in the trial bundles for the court and treated as evidence in the case without requiring further proof. Rule 33.6 (*Blackstone* 1617) provides for notice to be given in advance by a party who intends to rely on evidence such as a plan, photograph, or model which is not part of the witness statements or expert reports that have been exchanged.

F. Trial Bundles

43.15 It will be the responsibility of the claimant's solicitor to prepare the bundles for use at trial. The content of the trial bundle should be agreed in advance, and r 39.5(2) (*Blackstone* 1667) requires the bundle to be filed at court not more than seven days and not less than three days before the start of the trial. Guidance on the content of bundles is given in PD 39, section 3 (*Blackstone* 1670). The claimant's solicitor should bear in mind that care invested in the preparation of the bundle will pay a large dividend in the happiness of the trial judge if the bundle is accurately paginated, with clear legible copies, arranged in a logical order, and containing, in respect of disclosed documents, medical records and correspondence, no greater number than the documents which are relevant to the hearing.

G. Skeleton Arguments

43.16 It has become customary for advocates to add to the proliferation of documents generated by litigation by preparing a skeleton argument in advance of every trial and substantial application. Standard directions in the fast track allow for a direction to be given that a case summary outlining the matters still in issue and referring where appropriate to the relevant documents shall be included in the trial bundle. A Practice Direction on citation of authorities dated 9 April 2001 reported at [2001] 1 WLR 1001 records the duty of advocates to draw to the attention of the court any authority not cited by an opponent which is adverse to the case being advanced, subject to which the Practice Direction forbids citation of applications attended by one party only, applications for permission to appeal, and decisions on applications that only decide that the application is arguable. It forbids citation of county court cases unless they are cited to illustrate the conventional measure of damages in a personal injury case, or to demonstrate current authority at that level when no decision at a higher level is available. When citing an authority an advocate is required to state in a skeleton argument the proposition of law that the authority demonstrates and the part of the judgment which supports that proposition. The citation of more than one authority must be explained, and any list of authorities must have a certificate by the advocate that these requirements have been complied with. Paragraph 7.11.12 of the Queen's Bench Guide (*Blackstone* 2461) indicates that a skeleton argument should:

(1) concisely summarise the party's submissions in relation to each of the issues,

(2) cite the main authorities relied on, which may be attached,

(3) contain a reading list and an estimate of the time it will take the Judge to read,

(4) be as brief as the issues allow and not normally be longer than 20 pages of double-spaced A4 paper,

(5) be divided into numbered paragraphs and paged consecutively,

(6) avoid formality and use understandable abbreviations, and

(7) identify any core documents which it would be helpful to read beforehand.

H. Procedure at Trial

43.17 It is for the party who has the burden of proof, nearly always the claimant, to begin. It is usual to begin with an opening speech, but if a reading of the trial bundle and skeleton argument has made an opening unnecessary, the court can dispense with it under PD 28, para 8.2 for the fast track (*Blackstone* 1567) and PD 29, para 10.2 in the multi-track (*Blackstone* 1586). A short opening is often useful to indicate the extent to which further discussion may have narrowed the issues between the parties.

43.18 After the opening, the evidence of witnesses on behalf of the claimant, including the claimant himself, will be called and the witnesses in turn will be cross-examined. Where there is more than one defendant, they will cross-examine in the order in which they are joined in the claim form unless some different order is directed by the judge. If there is documentary evidence contained in the trial bundle on which the claimant relies, it may be appropriate for the advocate to make clear exactly what is relied on as evidence in support of the claim. Sometimes, although rarely, there may be other exhibits to be put in evidence, or the judge may be asked to leave the courtroom and view the scene of the accident or the machinery involved. When the claimant has called all the evidence on which he relies, he will close his case, and the defendant can, if he wishes, call evidence in support of the defence. The advocates for each party will then be entitled to make a closing speech. Unlike criminal trials, the speech for the defendant is given first, unless the defendant has called no evidence in which case he is entitled to the last word. After closing speeches, the judge will give judgment and will then deal with the drafting of an appropriate order and issues of costs.

43.19 This is the standard framework, but it can be adjusted to meet the needs of a particular case in the absolute discretion of the judge. For example, it is often agreed that expert evidence should be heard in one block, so that the claimant's expert in a particular field is immediately followed by the defendant's expert taken out of turn. If time runs out, the judge may invite closing speeches in writing, and the judgment may be given in writing leaving the issues of drafting and costs to be resolved at a later hearing if they cannot be agreed in the light of the judgment.

I. Submission 'No Case to Answer'

43.20 At the close of the claimant's case, the defendant may submit that there is no case to answer. In civil cases there was a formal rule prior to the CPR that the defendant must be 'put to his election' which means that if the defendant elected to make the submission but was unsuccessful, he would not then be entitled to adduce evidence in support of the defence. If the defendant elects to make a submission, the court is deciding the matter with the benefit of all the evidence that there will be in the case, so the issue for the court is whether the claimant has established his case by the evidence called, on the balance of probabilities. With the introduction of the CPR there were suggestions that under the new and more flexible case management powers given to the court, it might no longer be appropriate to put the defendant to his election. Orthodoxy has been firmly reapplied by the Court of Appeal and a judge should always put the defendant to his election when a submission of 'No case' is advanced.

43.21 *Boyce v Wyatt Engineering* [2001] EWCA Civ 692; [2001] CP Rep 87 and *Benham v Kythira Investments* [2003] EWCA Civ 1794; (2004) 154 NLJ 21   There are good reasons for the rule requiring that a defendant should be put to his election before making a submission of 'No case to answer', and only in rare and unusual circumstances, for example if the judge can conclude that there is nothing in the defendant's evidence that could affect the view he has taken at first of the claimant's case, would it be proper to hear a submission without doing so.

J. Civil Evidence Act 1995, ss 1–10, 13, 14

1. Admissibility of hearsay evidence

43.22   (1) In civil proceedings evidence shall not be excluded on the ground that it is hearsay.

(2) In this Act—

(a) 'hearsay' means a statement made otherwise than by a person while giving oral evidence in the proceedings which is tendered as evidence of the matters stated; and

(b) references to hearsay include hearsay of whatever degree.

(3) Nothing in this Act affects the admissibility of evidence admissible apart from this section.

(4) The provisions of sections 2 to 6 (safeguards and supplementary provisions relating to hearsay evidence) do not apply in relation to hearsay evidence admissible apart from this section, notwithstanding that it may also be admissible by virtue of this section.

2. Notice of proposal to adduce hearsay evidence

(1) A party proposing to adduce hearsay evidence in civil proceedings shall, subject to the **43.23** following provisions of this section, give to the other party or parties to the proceedings—

(a) such notice (if any) of that fact, and

(b) on request, such particulars of or relating to the evidence, as is reasonable and practicable in the circumstances for the purpose of enabling him or them to deal with any matters arising from its being hearsay.

(2) Provision may be made by rules of court—

(a) specifying classes of proceedings or evidence in relation to which subsection (1) does not apply, and

(b) as to the manner in which (including the time within which) the duties imposed by that subsection are to be complied with in the cases where it does apply.

(3) Subsection (1) may also be excluded by agreement of the parties; and compliance with the duty to give notice may in any case be waived by the person to whom notice is required to be given.

(4) A failure to comply with subsection (1), or with rules under subsection (2)(b), does not affect the admissibility of the evidence but may be taken into account by the court—

(a) in considering the exercise of its powers with respect to the course of proceedings and costs, and

(b) as a matter adversely affecting the weight to be given to the evidence in accordance with section 4.

3. Power to call witness for cross-examination on hearsay statement

Rules of court may provide that where a party to civil proceedings adduces hearsay evidence of a **43.24** statement made by a person and does not call that person as a witness, any other party to the proceedings may, with the leave of the court, call that person as a witness and cross-examine him on the statement as if he had been called by the first-mentioned party and as if the hearsay statement were his evidence in chief.

4. Considerations relevant to weighing of hearsay evidence

(1) In estimating the weight (if any) to be given to hearsay evidence in civil proceedings the **43.25** court shall have regard to any circumstances from which any inference can reasonably be drawn as to the reliability or otherwise of the evidence.

(2) Regard may be had, in particular, to the following—

(a) whether it would have been reasonable and practicable for the party by whom the evidence was adduced to have produced the maker of the original statement as a witness;

(b) whether the original statement was made contemporaneously with the occurrence or existence of the matters stated;

(c) whether the evidence involves multiple hearsay;

(d) whether any person involved had any motive to conceal or misrepresent matters;

(e) whether the original statement was an edited account, or was made in collaboration with another or for a particular purpose;

(f) whether the circumstances in which the evidence is adduced as hearsay are such as to suggest an attempt to prevent proper evaluation of its weight.

5. Competence and credibility

(1) Hearsay evidence shall not be admitted in civil proceedings if or to the extent that it is **43.26** shown to consist of, or to be proved by means of, a statement made by a person who at the time he made the statement was not competent as a witness.

For this purpose 'not competent as a witness' means suffering from such mental or physical infirmity, or lack of understanding, as would render a person incompetent as a witness in civil proceedings; but a child shall be treated as competent as a witness if he satisfies the requirements of section 96(2) (a) and (b) of the Children Act 1989 (conditions for reception of unsworn evidence of child).

(2) Where in civil proceedings hearsay evidence is adduced and the maker of the original statement, or of any statement relied upon to prove another statement, is not called as a witness—

(a) evidence which if he had been so called would be admissible for the purpose of attacking or supporting his credibility as a witness is admissible for that purpose in the proceedings; and

(b) evidence tending to prove that, whether before or after he made the statement, he made any other statement inconsistent with it is admissible for the purpose of showing that he had contradicted himself.

Provided that evidence may not be given of any matter of which, if he had been called as a witness and had denied that matter in cross-examination, evidence could not have been adduced by the cross-examining party.

6. Previous statements of witnesses

43.27   (1) Subject as follows, the provisions of this Act as to hearsay evidence in civil proceedings apply equally (but with any necessary modifications) in relation to a previous statement made by a person called as a witness in the proceedings.

(2) A party who has called or intends to call a person as a witness in civil proceedings may not in those proceedings adduce evidence of a previous statement made by that person, except—

(a) with the leave of the court, or

(b) for the purpose of rebutting a suggestion that his evidence has been fabricated.

This shall not be construed as preventing a witness statement (that is, a written statement of oral evidence which a party to the proceedings intends to lead) from being adopted by a witness in giving evidence or treated as his evidence.

(3) Where in the case of civil proceedings section 3, 4 or 5 of the Criminal Procedure Act 1865 applies, which make provision as to—

(a) how far a witness may be discredited by the party producing him,

(b) the proof of contradictory statements made by a witness, and

(c) cross-examination as to previous statements in writing, this Act does not authorize the adducing of evidence of a previous inconsistent or contradictory statement otherwise than in accordance with those sections.

This is without prejudice to any provision made by rules of court under section 3 above (power to call witness for cross-examination on hearsay statement).

(4) Nothing in this Act affects any of the rules of law as to the circumstances in which, where a person called as a witness in civil proceedings is cross-examined on a document used by him to refresh his memory, that document may be made evidence in the proceedings.

(5) Nothing in this section shall be construed as preventing a statement of any description referred to above from being admissible by virtue of section 1 as evidence of the matters stated.

7. Evidence formerly admissible at common law

43.28   (1) The common law rule effectively preserved by section 9(1) and (2)(a) of the Civil Evidence Act 1968 (admissibility of admissions adverse to a party) is superseded by the provisions of this Act.

(2) The common law rules effectively preserved by section 9(1) and (2)(b) to (d) of the Civil Evidence Act 1968, that is, any rule of law whereby in civil proceedings—

(a) published works dealing with matters of a public nature (for example, histories, scientific works, dictionaries and maps) are admissible as evidence of facts of a public nature stated in them,

(b) public documents (for example, public registers, and returns made under public authority with respect to matters of public interest) are admissible as evidence of facts stated in them, or

(c) records (for example, the records of certain courts, treaties, Crown grants, pardons and commissions) are admissible as evidence of facts stated in them,

shall continue to have effect.

(3) The common law rules effectively preserved by section 9(3) and (4) of the Civil Evidence Act 1968, that is, any rule of law whereby in civil proceedings—

(a) evidence of a person's reputation is admissible for the purpose of proving his good or bad character, or

(b) evidence of reputation or family tradition is admissible—

(i) for the purpose of proving or disproving pedigree or the existence of a marriage, or

(ii) for the purpose of proving or disproving the existence of any public or general right or of identifying any person or thing,

shall continue to have effect in so far as they authorize the court to treat such evidence as proving or disproving that matter.

Where any such rule applies, reputation or family tradition shall be treated for the purposes of this Act as a fact and not as a statement or multiplicity of statements about the matter in question.

(4) The words in which a rule of law mentioned in this section is described are intended only to identify the rule and shall not be construed as altering it in any way.

8. Proof of statements contained in documents

(1) Where a statement contained in a document is admissible as evidence in civil proceedings, **43.29** it may be proved—

(a) by the production of that document, or

(b) whether or not that document is still in existence, by the production of a copy of that document or of the material part of it, authenticated in such manner as the court may approve.

(2) It is immaterial for this purpose how many removes there are between a copy and the original.

9. Proof of records of business or public authority

(1) A document which is shown to form part of the records of a business or public authority **43.30** may be received in evidence in civil proceedings without further proof.

(2) A document shall be taken to form part of the records of a business or public authority if there is produced to the court a certificate to that effect signed by an officer of the business or authority to which the records belong.

For this purpose—

(a) a document purporting to be a certificate signed by an officer of a business or public authority shall be deemed to have been duly given by such an officer and signed by him; and

(b) a certificate shall be treated as signed by a person if it purports to bear a facsimile of his signature.

(3) The absence of an entry in the records of a business or public authority may be proved in civil proceedings by affidavit of an officer of the business or authority to which the records belong.

(4) In this section—

'records' means records in whatever form;

'business' includes any activity regularly carried on over a period of time, whether for profit or not, by any body (whether corporate or not) or by an individual;

'officer' includes any person occupying a responsible position in relation to the relevant activities of the business or public authority or in relation to its records; and

'public authority' includes any public or statutory undertaking, any government department and any person holding office under Her Majesty.

(5) The court may, having regard to the circumstances of the case, direct that all or any of the above provisions of this section do not apply in relation to a particular document or record, or description of documents or records.

10. Admissibility and proof of Ogden Tables

43.31   (1) The actuarial tables (together with explanatory notes) for use in personal injury and fatal accident cases issued from time to time by the Government Actuary's Department are admissible in evidence for the purpose of assessing, in an action for personal injury, the sum to be awarded as general damages for future pecuniary loss.

(2) They may be proved by the production of a copy published by Her Majesty's Stationery Office.

(3) For the purposes of this section—

(a) 'personal injury' includes any disease and any impairment of a person's physical or mental condition; and

(b) 'action for personal injury' includes an action brought by virtue of the Law Reform (Miscellaneous Provisions) Act 1934 or the Fatal Accidents Act 1976.

Note: at the date of writing, this section is not in force

43.32   [**11. Meaning of 'civil proceedings'**]

[**12. Provisions as to rules of court**]

13. Interpretation

43.33   In this Act—

'document' means anything in which information of any description is recorded, and 'copy', in relation to a document, means anything onto which information recorded in the document has been copied, by whatever means and whether directly or indirectly;

'hearsay' shall be construed in accordance with section 1(2);

'oral evidence' includes evidence which, by reason of a defect of speech or hearing, a person called as a witness gives in writing or by signs;

'the original statement', in relation to hearsay evidence, means the underlying statement (if any) by—

(a) in the case of evidence of fact, a person having personal knowledge of that fact, or

(b) in the case of evidence of opinion, the person whose opinion it is; and 'statement' means any representation of fact or opinion, however made.

14. Savings

43.34   (1) Nothing in this Act affects the exclusion of evidence on grounds other than that it is hearsay.

This applies whether the evidence falls to be excluded in pursuance of any enactment or rule of law, for failure to comply with rules of court or an order of the court, or otherwise.

(2) Nothing in this Act affects the proof of documents by means other than those specified in section 8 or 9.

43.35   [**15. Consequential amendments and repeals**]

[**16. Short title, commencement and extent**]

44

LIMITATION

A. The Limitation Act

Because of the difficulty for the courts in dealing fairly with very stale claims, **44.01** and the injustice to those against whom claims might be brought after memories have faded and relevant documents have been lost, there is a time limit imposed on the bringing of proceedings. If the time limit is exceeded, the wrongdoer can rely on this as a defence to escape a claim, no matter how good the merits of the claim might be. The modern statutory basis for the time limits for bringing a legal claim is the Limitation Act 1980. For personal injury claims the rules include a discretionary element first introduced in 1963. The Law Commission (Consultation Paper No. 270, 10 July 2001) has suggested that all limitation rules might be simplified and this discretion be removed in favour of a 30-year long stop.

The first step in applying the time limit rules under the 1980 Act is to decide the **44.02** date on which the claimant's cause of action accrued. This is the date when all the elements of the cause of action have come into existence. For example, as we saw in Chapter 2, damage is an essential element in the tort of negligence, so a cause of action does not accrue in negligence until the breach of the duty of care has resulted in damage. On the other hand, awareness of the damage is not an element of the tort, so that a cause of action may accrue when an injury is sustained even though, for example in the case of an occupational disease, the victim at the time is unaware of sustaining it: this is the reason for the complexity of the knowledge provisions of the Act.

The 1980 Act works in this way. First, under s 2, there is a general time limit for **44.03** actions in tort of six years from the date on which the cause of action accrued.

Next, under s 11, this is varied to a shorter time limit of three years which applies to 'any action for damages for negligence, nuisance or breach of duty . . . where the damages claimed . . . consist of or include damages in respect of personal injuries'. For the vast majority of injury claims, therefore, the time limit is that a claim must be started within three years from the date of the accident. The definition catches most but not all claims for damages for personal injuries: it does not cover claims for intentional injury or assault, malicious prosecution or false imprisonment, and it does not cover claims against lawyers or other advisers for negligently or in breach of contract failing to pursue a client's personal injury claim properly. For these claims the ordinary time limit in tort or contract of six years applies.

B. Date of Knowledge

44.04 The first relaxation of the three-year rule is that it is not only counted from the date when the cause of action accrued. The starting date for counting the three years may alternatively be a later date on which the claimant first had the elements of knowledge set out in s 14(1). If the claimant can show that his date of knowledge is later than the date on which the cause of action accrued, he is entitled as of right to rely on the later date as the start of the three-year period. The court has no discretion about it.

44.05 It is important to look at s 14 carefully when an issue of knowledge arises. It is a very specific kind of knowledge, and must not be treated as merely 'knowing you have a claim'. The section defines a date of knowledge as the claimant first knowing he has suffered an injury that is attributable to the cause of action. This is not at all the same thing as knowing that there could be a viable claim: indeed knowledge of the legal grounds for a possible claim in relation to the injury is expressly made irrelevant, as the decision in *Dobbie v Medway Health Authority* [1994] 1 WLR 1234 illustrates (see below).

44.06 Section 14 is not easy to apply and there have been many arguments about the level of understanding of the facts about the cause of an injury that is sufficient to start the three-year time period running. This summary is taken from the judgment of Brooke LJ in *Spargo v North Essex HA* [1997] PIQR P235 at P242:

> (1) The knowledge required to satisfy section 14(1)(b) is a broad knowledge of the essence of the causally relevant act or omission to which the injury is attributable.
>
> (2) 'Attributable' in this context means 'capable of being attributed to', in the sense of being a real possibility.
>
> (3) A [claimant] has the requisite knowledge when she knows enough to make it reasonable for her to begin to investigate whether or not she has a case against

the defendant. Another way of putting this is to say that she will have such knowledge if she so firmly believes that her condition is capable of being attributed to an act or omission which she can identify (in broad terms) that she goes to a solicitor to seek advice about making a claim for compensation.

(4) On the other hand she will not have the requisite knowledge if she thinks she knows the acts or omissions she should investigate but in fact is barking up the wrong tree; or if her knowledge of what the defendant did or did not do is so vague or general that she cannot fairly be expected to know what she should investigate; or if her state of mind is such that she thinks her condition is capable of being attributed to the act or omission alleged to constitute negligence, but she is not sure about this, and would need to check with an expert before she could be properly said to know that it was.

C. Discretionary Extension

The other relaxation of the three-year rule is that, in cases to which the three-year period applies, the court has a broad discretion under s 33 of the Act to allow an action to proceed even if it has been started after the expiry of the primary three-year period, if it is equitable to do so. There is no limit to the scope of this discretion, although the length of the delay is one of the factors that the court must take into account in deciding whether to exercise it. The court does not only consider the delay from the claimant's point of view. If the delay has made it more difficult for the defendant to respond to the claim, for example because witnesses cannot be traced or have died, that will be an important consideration. It is common for a claimant who starts a claim more than three years after his injury to couple an application under s 33 with a claim to be entitled to rely on a later date of knowledge under s 14. The existence of the discretionary power has been accompanied by—and has perhaps influenced—a fairly strict and restrictive approach to questions of knowledge.   **44.07**

The discretion to allow a late claim to proceed can only be exercised when a claim was never started in time. It cannot be used to have a second attempt at a claim which was previously issued in time but has failed before reaching trial on the merits because of a breach of court rules.   **44.08**

In a case such as assault to which the six-year period applies, there is no equivalent of the s 33 discretion. They are not actions for negligence for which there would be a provision under ss 14A and 14B, inserted by the Latent Damage Act 1986, to allow an alternative starting date based on a later date of knowledge, subject to a time limit of three years from the date of knowledge, and an overall long stop time limit of 15 years. In such cases the six-year time limit is absolute.   **44.09**

Special rules apply under s 10 to claims for contribution between wrongdoers both liable for the same injury, under s 11A to claims under the Consumer   **44.10**

Protection Act 1987 and under s 12 to claims under the Fatal Accidents Act 1976.

D. Procedure

44.11 The step which has to be taken in order to comply with a time limit is the commencement of a claim. Proceedings start when the claim form is received by the court office but when the date is critical care is needed to ensure that this date is recorded (see PD 7, para 5.1). The day of the accident is not included: *Marren v Dawson Bentley* [1961] 2 QB 135 shows that when the claimant was injured during 8 November 1954, a claim that was started on 8 November 1957 was in time. If the court office is closed on the last day, a claim issued on the next opening of the office will be too late, but the shortness of the delay would give a good chance that the court would allow the action to proceed under s 33 of the Act.

44.12 Limitation is a defence and not a rule of law: it is for the defendant to take the point that the action is barred by the provisions of the Act, and if the defence is not stated the action must proceed. It is therefore possible for the parties to agree to extend the limitation period if, for example, a defendant insurer who is in negotiations to settle a claim wishes to avoid the costs of proceedings being incurred by the claimant.

44.13 Where the limitation period is about to expire, there may not be sufficient time to follow the procedure in the Pre-action Protocol for Personal Injury Claims of letter of claim and a three-month period to allow for a reasoned response. In that situation, the Personal Injury Protocol, para 2.8 suggests that:

> the claimant's solicitor should give as much notice of the intention to issue proceedings as is practicable and the parties should consider whether the court might be invited to extend time for service of the claimant's supporting documents and for service of any defence, or alternatively, to stay the proceedings while the recommended steps in the protocol are followed.

44.14 Disputes about limitation, and applications for the exercise of discretion under s 33, can be left open to trial but are very commonly decided at an early stage of a case as a preliminary issue. Before the CPR, tactical considerations might enter this decision, but district judges are usually keen to have these issues resolved as soon as possible and active case management makes it a rarity for any uncertainties of limitation to remain unresolved until final trial. In the county court a preliminary issue should be tried by a circuit judge unless the parties agree otherwise.

Claims in civil litigation are governed by the 1980 Act. Note however that the **44.15** Athens Convention on travel by sea and the Warsaw Convention on travel by air apply shorter and less flexible time limits for international travel and restrictions on the level of compensation.

Cartledge v Jopling [1963] AC 758   The date for the accrual of a cause of **44.16** action is the date on which the damage was sustained and not the date on which the claimant knew of the damage.

Marren v Dawson Bentley & Co. [1961] 2 QB 135   The day of the accident is **44.17** not included in calculating time, so when the claimant was injured during 8 November 1954, a claim that was started on 8 November 1957 was in time.

Letang v Cooper [1965] 1 QB 232   The allegation was that the defendant **44.18** carelessly drove over the claimant. Proceedings were issued after four years alleging both negligence and trespass. The claimant's claim was struck out: for negligently caused injury the cause of action must be negligence.

Stubbings v Webb [1993] AC 498   A claim of deliberate assault in the form of **44.19** sexual abuse was struck out because cases of deliberate injury are subject to the six-year limitation period and ss 11, 14 and 33 of the 1980 Act do not apply.

Seymour v Williams [1995] PIQR P470   A somewhat bizarre consequence of **44.20** *Stubbings v Webb*: while the claim against the perpetrator of sexual abuse was struck out, a claim against the other parent for breach of a parental duty to protect the child from the same abuse was allowed to proceed.

Walkley v Precision Forgings [1979] 1 WLR 606   Where the claimant started a **44.21** claim within the limitation period but failed to proceed with it and started a new claim, s 33 could not apply to the new claim because it was not the limitation period but the claimant's own failure to pursue the first claim that was the cause of the claimant's prejudice.

Nash v Eli Lily [1993] 1 WLR 782   A person who thinks her condition is **44.22** capable of being attributed to drugs she had taken but realized that her belief should be confirmed by a doctor did not have knowledge of attribution for the purpose of s 14(1). The court refused to exercise the s 33 discretion in favour of the claimants.

Thompson v Brown [1981] 1 WLR 744   The leading case on s 33, emphasiz- **44.23** ing the breadth of the court's discretion. The claimant's failure to issue in time was the result of his solicitor's negligence but his remedy against his own solicitor, though relevant, was not a complete answer and the claim was allowed to proceed (see *Corbin v Penfold Metallising* below).

Dobbie v Medway HA [1994] 1 WLR 1234   In April 1973 the claimant was **44.24** admitted to hospital for removal of a lump in her left breast. The surgeon at the defendant's hospital removed the whole breast because he suspected cancer. No proper investigation was carried out. In fact the lump was benign. The claimant suffered a psychological injury as a result of the mastectomy. In 1988 she became aware through media reports that her breast need not have been removed and in 1989 she began a claim, alleging negligent removal of the breast before microscopic examination of the lump showed cancer. She relied on s 14, arguing that she did not know crucial facts until she knew that the surgeon had done something wrong in proceeding straight to the removal of her breast without further examination. The Court of Appeal held that she knew of her injury, the removal of her breast, at the time of the operation and there is no requirement that she should know that her injury was actionable or tortious. Sir Thomas Bingham MR said:

> This condition is not satisfied when a man knows that he has a disabling cough or shortness of breath but does not know that his injured condition has anything to do with his working conditions. It is satisfied when he knows that his injured condition is capable of being attributed to his working conditions, even though he has no inkling that his employer may have been at fault.

The claimant applied under s 33 but this also failed. The delay was very long, the health authority was prejudiced by the delay, and the claimant could have sought advice earlier than she did.

44.25 *Parry v Clwyd HA* [1997] PIQR P1   The claimant succeeded on s 14 knowledge: her and her mother's ordinary understanding was not enough to fix her with actual knowledge of the attribution of her cerebral palsy to the management of the claimant's delivery at birth until a television programme explained the possibility; and it was only the knowledge of the claimant herself that was relevant.

44.26 *Spargo v North Essex HA* [1997] PIQR P235   The claimant failed on s 14 knowledge: the writ was not issued until seven years after the claimant first consulted a solicitor stating her clear lay opinion about the mistaken diagnosis for which she claimed and its effects on her, and this showed a sufficient level of knowledge.

44.27 *Hayes v Pilkington Glass* [1998] PIQR P303   A claimant with Vibration White Finger did not have the relevant knowledge until causation was confirmed by a medical expert even though he agreed he had consulted the solicitors who arranged the examination because he thought he had suffered a work-related injury.

44.28 *Irshadi v Ali* [1999] Lloyd's Rep 301   A claimant suffering from industrial deafness was held not to have relevant knowledge of causation until his suspicions were confirmed by a medical expert. Suspicion does not amount to knowledge.

Sneizek v Bundy [2000] PIQR P213   A claimant does not have relevant **44.29** knowledge for s 14 where he believes he may have, or probably has, an injury attributable to his working conditions but is not sure until he has expert advice. This claimant however was sure that he had an attributable injury more than three years before issue (and remained sure of it in spite of expert evidence to the contrary). He failed under s 14 but was allowed to proceed under s 33.

Henderson v Temple Pier [1998] 1 WLR 1540   A claimant is fixed with **44.30** knowledge of facts ascertainable by expert advice which it is reasonable to seek. When solicitors failed to make reasonably diligent inquiries to discover the identity of the defendant, the claimant could not rely on her lack of knowledge. See also, on a solicitor's failure to obtain a police accident report, *Copeland v Smith* [2000] 1 WLR 1371.

Corbin v Penfold Metallising, The Times, 2 May 2000   A contrast with **44.31** *Henderson,* here under s 33. The claimant's date of knowledge of an occupational chest disease was in March 1993. He consulted solicitors promptly but they failed to issue a claim until September 1996. In applying the s 33 discretion, the claimant was not responsible for the failings of his solicitor and since the five and a half months' delay had caused no difficulties and the claimant himself had acted promptly, the claim was allowed to proceed.

Steeds v Peverel Management [2001] EWCA Civ 419; *The Times,* 16 May **44.32** 2001   Where the claimant is not himself at fault but his solicitor failed to issue proceedings in time, there being no prejudice as a result of the delay, the delay could not be held against the claimant and his action should be allowed to proceed.

Das v Ganju [1999] PIQR P260   The claimant in a s 33 application was **44.33** not fixed with the consequences of misleading advice from her own solicitors and counsel when she had acted properly herself throughout and her clinical negligence claim was allowed to proceed after 18 years.

Hughes v Jones [1996] PIQR P380   A pre-CPR decision that a preliminary **44.34** issue under the Limitation Act 1980 in the county court is a final issue and should be tried by a circuit judge rather than a district judge.

Young v Western Power Distribution [2003] EWCA Civ 1034; [2003] 1 WLR **44.35** 2868   Mr Young was exposed to asbestos during his work. In 1993 asbestos-related malignant mesothelioma was diagnosed and proceedings were issued, but the action was discontinued on medical evidence which questioned the diagnosis. After his death in 1999 the diagnosis was confirmed. The widow's claim under the FAA was barred by the principle in *Walkley v Precision Forgings* (above).

44.36 *Various claimants v Bryn Alan Community Homes* [2003] EWCA Civ 85; [2004] 2 All ER 716   This is a guideline case on the approach to limitation in claims arising out of physical and sexual abuse in children's homes many years before resulting in immediate and delayed psychiatric symptoms.

44.37 *McDonnell v Congregation of Christian Brothers Trustees* [2003] UKHL 63; [2004] 1 AC 1101   A claim for abuse suffered between 1941 and 1951 was statute barred because the claim had accrued under the Limitation Act 1939 and the subsequent discretion, although retrospective for cases in negligence with a three-year limitation period, did not extend to claims of assault which were subject to a six-year time limit.

44.38 *Buckler v J F Finnegan* [2004] EWCA Civ 920   The claimant was diagnosed with pleural thickening in 1991 having been employed by the defendant in the early 1970s. He knew that he could sue but decided that it was not worthwhile. The claimant issued proceedings in April 2003 having been told that he had plural plaques (see **d.105**), wrongly believing that his condition had deteriorated. The Court of Appeal held that the judge had been wrong to disapply the limitation period.

E. Limitation Act 1980

PART I

1. Time limits under Part I subject to extension or exclusion under Part II

44.39   (1) This Part of this Act gives the ordinary time limits for bringing actions of the various classes mentioned in the following provisions of this Part.

(2) The ordinary time limits given in this Part of this Act are subject to extension or exclusion in accordance with the provisions of Part II of this Act.

2. Time limit for actions founded on tort

44.40   An action founded on tort shall not be brought after the expiration of six years from the date on which the cause of action accrued.

10. Special time limit for claiming contribution

44.41   (1) Where under section 1 of the Civil Liability (Contribution) Act 1978 any person becomes entitled to a right to recover contribution in respect of any damage from any other person, no action to recover contribution by virtue of that right shall be brought after the expiration of two years from the date on which that right accrued.

(2) For the purposes of this section the date on which a right to recover contribution in respect of any damage accrues to any person (referred to below in this section as 'the relevant date') shall be ascertained as provided in subsections (3) and (4) below.

(3) If the person in question is held liable in respect of that damage—
   (a) by a judgment given in any civil proceedings; or
   (b) by an award made on any arbitration;

the relevant date shall be the date on which the judgment is given, or the date of the award (as the case may be).

For the purposes of this subsection no account shall be taken of any judgment or award given or made on appeal in so far as it varies the amount of damages awarded against the person in question.

(4) If, in any case not within subsection (3) above, the person in question makes or agrees to make any payment to one or more persons in compensation for that damage (whether he admits any liability in respect of the damage or not), the relevant date shall be the earliest date on which the amount to be paid by him is agreed between him (or his representative) and the person (or each of the persons, as the case may be) to whom the payment is to be made.

(5) An action to recover contribution shall be one to which sections 28, 32 and 35 of this Act apply, but otherwise Parts II and III of this Act (except sections 34, 37 and 38) shall not apply for the purposes of this section.

11. Special time limit for actions in respect of personal injuries

(1) This section applies to any action for damages for negligence, nuisance or breach of duty **44.42** (whether the duty exists by virtue of a contract or of provision made by or under a statute or independently of any contract or any such provision) where the damages claimed by the plaintiff for the negligence, nuisance or breach of duty consist of or include damages in respect of personal injuries to the plaintiff or any other person.

(1A) This section does not apply to any action brought for damages under section 3 of the Protection from Harassment Act 1997.

(3) An action to which this section applies shall not be brought after the expiration of the period applicable in accordance with subsection (4) or (5) below.

(4) Except where subsection (5) below applies, the period applicable is three years from—
  (a) the date on which the cause of action accrued; or
  (b) the date of knowledge (if later) of the person injured.

(5) If the person injured dies before the expiration of the period mentioned in subsection (4) above, the period applicable as respects the cause of action surviving for the benefit of his estate by virtue of section 1 of the Law Reform (Miscellaneous Provisions) Act 1934 shall be three years from—
  (a) the date of death; or
  (b) the date of the personal representative's knowledge, whichever is the later.

11A. Actions in respect of defective products

(1) This section shall apply to an action for damages by virtue of any provision of Part I of the **44.43** Consumer Protection Act 1987.

(2) None of the time limits given in the preceding provisions of this Act shall apply to an action to which this section applies.

(3) An action to which this section applies shall not be brought after the expiration of the period of ten years from the relevant time within the meaning of section 4 of the said Act of 1987; and this subsection shall operate to extinguish a right of action and shall do so whether or not that right of action had accrued, or time under the following provisions of this Act had begun to run, at the end of the said period of ten years.

(4) Subject to subsection (5) below, an action to which this section applies in which the damages claimed by the plaintiff consist of or include damages in respect of personal injuries to the plaintiff or any other person or loss of or damage to any property shall not be brought after the expiration of the period of three years from whichever is the later of—

(a) the date on which the cause of action accrued; and

(b) the date of knowledge of the injured person or, in the case of loss of or damage to property, the date of knowledge of the plaintiff or (if earlier) of any person in whom his cause of action was previously vested.

(5) If in a case where the damages claimed by the plaintiff consist of or include damages in respect of personal injuries to the plaintiff or any other person the injured person died before the expiration of the period mentioned in subsection (4) above, that subsection shall have effect as respects the cause of action surviving for the benefit of his estate by virtue of section 1 of the Law Reform (Miscellaneous Provisions) Act 1934 as if for the reference to that period there were substituted a reference to the period of three years from whichever is the later of—

(a) the date of death; and

(b) the date of the personal representative's knowledge.

(6) For the purposes of this section 'personal representative' includes any person who is or has been a personal representative of the deceased, including an executor who has not proved the will (whether or not he has renounced probate) but not anyone appointed only as a special personal representative in relation to settled land; and regard shall be had to any knowledge acquired by any such person while a personal representative or previously.

(7) If there is more than one personal representative and their dates of knowledge are different, subsection (5)(b) above shall be read as referring to the earliest of those dates.

(8) Expressions used in this section or section 14 of this Act and in Part I of the Consumer Protection Act 1987 have the same meanings in this section or that section as in that Part; and section 1(1) of that Act (Part I to be construed as enacted for the purpose of complying with the product liability Directive) shall apply for the purpose of construing this section and the following provisions of this Act so far as they relate to an action by virtue of any provision of that Part as it applies for the purpose of construing that Part.

12. Special time limit for actions under Fatal Accidents legislation

44.44   (1) An action under the Fatal Accidents Act 1976 shall not be brought if the death occurred when the person injured could no longer maintain an action and recover damages in respect of the injury (whether because of a time limit in this Act or in any other Act, or for any other reason).

Where any such action by the injured person would have been barred by the time limit in section 11 or 11A of this Act, no account shall be taken of the possibility of that time limit being overridden under section 33 of this Act.

(2) None of the time limits given in the preceding provisions of this Act shall apply to an action under the Fatal Accidents Act 1976, but no such action shall be brought after the expiration of three years from—

(a) the date of death; or

(b) the date of knowledge of the person for whose benefit the action is brought;

whichever is the later.

(3) An action under the Fatal Accidents Act 1976 shall be one to which sections 28, 33 and 35 of this Act apply, and the application to any such action of the time limit under subsection (2) above shall be subject to section 39; but otherwise Parts II and III of this Act shall not apply to any such action.

13. Operation of time limit under section 12 in relation to different dependants

44.45   (1) Where there is more than one person for whose benefit an action under the Fatal Accidents Act 1976 is brought, section 12(2)(b) of this Act shall be applied separately to each of them.

(2) Subject to subsection (3) below, if by virtue of subsection (1) above the action would be outside the time limit given by section 12(2) as regards one or more, but not all, of the persons for

whose benefit it is brought, the court shall direct that any person as regards whom the action would be outside that limit shall be excluded from those for whom the action is brought.

(3) The court shall not give such a direction if it is shown that if the action were brought exclusively for the benefit of the person in question it would not be defeated by a defence of limitation (whether in consequence of section 28 of this Act or an agreement between the parties not to raise the defence, or otherwise).

14. Definition of date of knowledge for purposes of sections 11 and 12

(1) Subject to subsection (1A) below, in sections 11 and 12 of this Act references to a person's **44.46** date of knowledge are references to the date on which he first had knowledge of the following facts—
    (a) that the injury in question was significant; and
    (b) that the injury was attributable in whole or in part to the act or omission which is alleged to constitute negligence, nuisance or breach of duty; and
    (c) the identity of the defendant; and
    (d) if it is alleged that the act or omission was that of a person other than the defendant, the identity of that person and the additional facts supporting the bringing of an action against the defendant;

and knowledge that any acts or omissions did or did not, as a matter of law, involve negligence, nuisance or breach of duty is irrelevant.

[(1A) In section 11A of this Act and in section 12 of this Act so far as that section applies to an action by virtue of section 6(1)(a) of the Consumer Protection Act 1987 (death caused by defective product) references to a person's date of knowledge are references to the date on which he first had knowledge of the following facts—
    (a) such facts about the damage caused by the defect as would lead a reasonable person who had suffered such damage to consider it sufficiently serious to justify his instituting proceedings for damages against a defendant who did not dispute liability and was able to satisfy a judgment; and
    (b) that the damage was wholly or partly attributable to the facts and circumstances alleged to constitute the defect; and
    (c) the identity of the defendant;

but, in determining the date on which a person first had such knowledge there shall be disregarded both the extent (if any) of that person's knowledge on any date of whether particular facts or circumstances would or would not, as a matter of law, constitute a defect and, in a case relating to loss of or damage to property, any knowledge which that person had on a date on which he had no right of action by virtue of Part I of that Act in respect of the loss or damage.]

(2) For the purposes of this section an injury is significant if the person whose date of knowledge is in question would reasonably have considered it sufficiently serious to justify his instituting proceedings for damages against a defendant who did not dispute liability and was able to satisfy a judgment.

(3) For the purposes of this section a person's knowledge includes knowledge which be might reasonably have been expected to acquire—
    (a) from facts observable or ascertainable by him; or
    (b) from facts ascertainable by him with the help of medical or other appropriate expert advice which it is reasonable for him to seek;

but a person shall not be fixed under this subsection with knowledge of a fact ascertainable only with the help of expert advice so long as he has taken all reasonable steps to obtain (and, where appropriate, to act on) that advice.

14A. Special time limit for negligence actions where facts relevant to cause of action are not known at date of accrual

44.47   (1) This section applies to any action for damages for negligence, other than one to which section 11 of this Act applies, where the starting date for reckoning the period of limitation under subsection (4)(b) below falls after the date on which the cause of action accrued.

(2) Section 2 of this Act shall not apply to an action to which this section applies.

(3) An action to which this section applies shall not be brought after the expiration of the period applicable in accordance with subsection (4) below.

(4) That period is either—
    (a) six years from the date on which the cause of action accrued; or
    (b) three years from the starting date as defined by subsection (5) below, if that period expires later than the period mentioned in paragraph (a) above.

(5) For the purposes of this section, the starting date for reckoning the period of limitation under subsection (4)(b) above is the earliest date on which the plaintiff or any person in whom the cause of action was vested before him first had both the knowledge required for bringing an action for damages in respect of the relevant damage and a right to bring such an action.

(6) In subsection (5) above' the knowledge required for bringing an action for damages in respect of the relevant damage' means knowledge both—
    (a) of the material facts about the damage in respect of which damages are claimed; and
    (b) of the other facts relevant to the current action mentioned in subsection (8) below.

(7) For the purposes of subsection (6)(a) above, the material facts about the damage are such facts about the damage as would lead a reasonable person who had suffered such damage to consider it sufficiently serious to justify his instituting proceedings for damages against a defendant who did not dispute liability and was able to satisfy a judgment.

(8) The other facts referred to in subsection (6)(b) above are—
    (a) that the damage was attributable in whole or in part to the act or omission which is alleged to constitute negligence: and
    (b) the identity of the defendant; and
    (c) if it is alleged that the act or omission was that of a person other than the defendant, the identity of that person and the additional facts supporting the bringing of an action against the defendant.

(9) Knowledge that any acts or omissions did or did not, as a matter of law, involve negligence is irrelevant for the purposes of subsection (5) above.

(10) For the purposes of this section a person s knowledge includes knowledge which he might reasonably have been expected to acquire—
    (a) from facts observable or ascertainable by him; or
    (b) from facts ascertainable by him with the help of appropriate expert advice which it is reasonable for him to seek;

but a person shall not be taken by virtue of this subsection to have knowledge of a fact ascertainable only with the help of expert advice so long as he has taken all reasonable steps to obtain (and, where appropriate, to act on) that advice.

PART II

28. Extension of limitation period in case of disability

44.48   (1) Subject to the following provisions of this section, if on the date when any right of action accrued for which a period of limitation is prescribed by this Act, the person to whom it accrued

708

was under a disability, the action may be brought at any time before the expiration of six years from the date when he ceased to be under a disability or died (whichever first occurred) notwithstanding that the period of limitation has expired.

(2) This section shall not affect any case where the right of action first accured to some person (not under a disability) through whom the person under a disability claims.

(3) When a right of action which has accrued to a person under a disability accrues, on the death of that person while still under a disability, to another person under a disability, no further extension of time shall be allowed by reason of the disability of the second person.

(4A) If the action is one to which section 4A of this Act applies, subsection (1) above shall have effect—

(a) in the case of an action for libel or slander, as if for the words from 'at any time' to 'occurred)' there were substituted the words 'by him at any time before the expiration of one year from the date on which he ceased to be under a disability'; and

(b) in the case of an action for slander of title, slander of goods or other malicious falsehood, as if for the words 'six years' there were substituted the words 'one year'.

(5) If the action is one to which section 10 of this Act applies, subsection (1) above shall have effect as if for the words 'six years' there were substituted the words 'two years'.

(6) If the action is one to which section 11 or 12(2) of this Act applies, subsection (1) above shall have effect as if for the words 'six years' there were substituted the words 'three years'.

(7) If the action is one to which section 11A of this Act applies or one by virtue of section 6(1)(a) of the Consumer Protection Act 1987 (death caused by defective product), subsection (1) above—

(a) shall not apply to the time limit prescribed by subsection (3) of the said section 11A or to that time limit as applied by virtue of section 12(1) of this Act; and

(b) in relation to any other time limit prescribed by this Act shall have effect as if for the words 'six years' there were substituted the words 'three years'.

28A. Extension for cases where the limitation period is the period under section 14A(4)(b)

(1) Subject to subsection (2) below, if in the case of any action for which a period of limitation is prescribed by section 14A of this Act—   **44.49**

(a) the period applicable in accordance with subsection (4) of that section is the period mentioned in paragraph (b) of that subsection;

(b) on the date which is for the purposes of that section the starting date for reckoning that period the person by reference to whose knowledge that date fell to be determined under subsection (5) of that section was under a disability; and

(c) Section 28 of this Act does not apply to the action;

the action may be brought at any time before the expiration of three years from the date when he ceased to be under a disability or died (whichever first occurred) notwithstanding that the period mentioned above has expired.

(2) An action may not be brought by virtue of subsection (1) above after the end of the period of limitation prescribed by section 14B of this Act.

33. Discretionary exclusion of time limit for actions in respect of personal injuries or death

(1) If it appears to the court that it would be equitable to allow an action to proceed having regard to the degree to which—   **44.50**

(a) the provisions of section 11 [or 11A] or 12 of this Act prejudice the plaintiff or any person whom he represents; and

(b) any decision of the court under this subsection would prejudice the defendant or any person whom he represents;

the court may direct that those provisions shall not apply to the action, or shall not apply to any specified cause of action to which the action relates.

[(1A) The court shall not under this section disapply—

(a) subsection (3) of section 11A; or

(b) where the damages claimed by the plaintiff are confined to damages for loss of or damage to any property, any other provision in its application to an action by virtue of Part I of the Consumer Protection Act 1987.]

(2) The court shall not under this section disapply section 12(1) except where the reason why the person injured could no longer maintain an action was because of the time limit in section 11 [or subsection (4) of section 11A].

If, for example, the person injured could at his death no longer maintain an action under the Fatal Accidents Act 1976 because of the time limit in Article 29 in Schedule 1 to the Carriage by Air Act 1961, the court has no power to direct that section 12(1) shall not apply.

(3) In acting under this section the court shall have regard to all the circumstances of the case and in particular to—

(a) the length of, and the reasons for, the delay on the part of the plaintiff;

(b) the extent to which, having regard to the delay, the evidence adduced or likely to be adduced by the plaintiff or the defendant is or is likely to be less cogent than if the action had been brought within the time allowed by section 11 [, by section 11A] or (as the case may be) by section 12;

(c) the conduct of the defendant after the cause of action arose, including the extent (if any) to which he responded to requests reasonably made by the plaintiff for information or inspection for the purpose of ascertaining facts which were or might be relevant to the plaintiff's cause of action against the defendant;

(d) the duration of any disability of the plaintiff arising after the date of the accrual of the cause of action;

(e) the extent to which the plaintiff acted promptly and reasonably once he knew whether or not the act or omission of the defendant, to which the injury was attributable, might be capable at that time of giving rise to an action for damages;

(f) the steps, if any, taken by the plaintiff to obtain medical, legal or other expert advice and the nature of any such advice he may have received.

(4) In a case where the person injured died when, because of section 11 [or subsection (4) of section 11A], he could no longer maintain an action and recover damages in respect of the injury, the court shall have regard in particular to the length of, and the reasons for, the delay on the part of the deceased.

(5) In a case under subsection (4) above, or any other case where the time limit, or one of the time limits, depends on the date of knowledge of a person other than the plaintiff, subsection (3) above shall have effect with appropriate modifications, and shall have effect in particular as if references to the plaintiff included references to any person whose date of knowledge is or was relevant in determining a time limit.

(6) A direction by the court disapplying the provisions of section 12(1) shall operate to disapply the provisions to the same effect in section 1(1) of the Fatal Accidents Act 1976.

(7) In this section 'the court' means the court in which the action has been brought.

(8) References in this section to section 11 [or 11A] include references to that section as extended by any of the preceding provisions of this Part of this Act or by any provision of Part III of this Act.

35. New claims in pending actions: rules of court

(1) For the purposes of this Act, any new claim made in the course of any action shall be **44.51** deemed to be a separate action and to have been commenced—

(a) in the case of a new claim made in or by way of third party proceedings, on the date on which those proceedings were commenced; and

(b) in the case of any other new claim, on the same date as the original action.

(2) In this section a new claim means any claim by way of set-off or counter-claim, and any claim involving either—

(a) the addition or substitution of a new cause of action; or

(b) the addition or substitution of a new party;

and 'third party proceedings' means any proceedings brought in the course of any action by any party to the action against a person not previously a party to the action, other than proceedings brought by joining any such person as defendant to any claim already made in the original action by the party bringing the proceedings.

(3) Except as provided by section 33 of this Act or by rules of court, neither the High Court nor any county court shall allow a new claim within subsection (1)(b) above, other than an original set-off or counterclaim, to be made in the course of any action after the expiry of any time limit under this Act which would affect a new action to enforce that claim.

For the purposes of this subsection, a claim is an original set-off or an original counterclaim if it is a claim made by way of set-off or (as the case may be) by way of counterclaim by a party who has not previously made any claim in the action.

(4) Rules of court may provide for allowing a new claim to which subsection (3) above applies to be made as there mentioned, but only if the conditions specified in subsection (5) below are satisfied, and subject to any further restrictions the rules may impose.

(5) The conditions referred to in subsection (4) above are the following—

(a) in the case of a claim involving a new cause of action, if the new cause of action arises out of the same facts or substantially the same facts as are already in issue on any claim previously made in the original action; and

(b) in the case of a claim involving a new party, if the addition or substitution of the new party is necessary for the determination of the original action.

(6) The addition or substitution of a new party shall not be regarded for the purposes of subsection (5)(b) above as necessary for the determination of the original action unless either—

(a) the new party is substituted for a party whose name was given in any claim made in the original action in mistake for the new party's name; or

(b) any claim already made in the original action cannot be maintained by or against an existing party unless the new party is joined or substituted as plaintiff or defendant in that action.

(7) Subject to subsection (4) above, rules of court may provide for allowing a party to any action to claim relief in a new capacity in respect of a new cause of action notwithstanding that he had no title to make that claim at the date of the commencement of the action.

This subsection shall not be taken as prejudicing the power of rules of court to provide for allowing a party to claim relief in a new capacity without adding or substituting a new cause of action.

(8) Subsections (3) to (7) above shall apply in relation to a new claim made in the course of third party proceedings as if those proceedings were the original action, and subject to such other modifications as may be prescribed by rules of court in any case or class of case.

37. Application to the Crown and the Duke of Cornwall

44.52   (1) Except as otherwise expressly provided in this Act, and without prejudice to section 39, this Act shall apply to proceedings by or against the Crown in like manner as it applies to proceedings between subjects.

38. Interpretation

44.53   (1) In this Act, unless the context otherwise requires—
    'personal injuries' includes any disease and any impairment of a person's physical or mental condition, and 'injury' and cognate expressions shall be construed accordingly;

(2) For the purposes of this Act a person shall be treated as under a disability while he is an infant, or of unsound mind.

(3) For the purposes of subsection (2) above a person is of unsound mind if he is a person who, by reason of mental disorder within the meaning of the [Mental Health Act 1983] is incapable of managing and administering his property and affairs.

(4) Without prejudice to the generality of subsection (3) above, a person shall be conclusively presumed for the purposes of subsection (2) above to be of unsound mind—
    (a) while he is liable to be detained or subject to guardianship under [the Mental Health Act 1983 (otherwise than by virtue of section 35 or 89)];. . .

39. Saving for other limitation enactments

44.54   This Act shall not apply to any action or arbitration for which a period of limitation is prescribed by or under any other enactment (whether passed before or after the passing of this Act) or to any action or arbitration to which the Crown is a party and for which, if it were between subjects, a period of limitation would be prescribed by or under any such other enactment.

45

CHILDREN AND PATIENTS

A. Definitions and General Principles

The legal system gives special protection to children and the mentally incapable. **45.01** They must have the support of a competent adult in legal proceedings, and any compromise of a claim can only take effect if the court approves it as reasonable. The procedural rules which provide this protection are in CPR Part 21.

A child is a person under the age of 18 years. The general rule is that a child **45.02** must sue or be sued with a litigation friend; however the CPR have introduced the innovation of permitting a child to apply for an order under r 21.2(3) to allow the child to proceed without a litigation friend. There is no guidance in the Rules or the Practice Direction on the circumstances where this will be appropriate but it will surely apply only to older 'children' who persuade the court that they can deal responsibly with the case, or in the case of a defence that the effective defendant is an insurer. Many 16 and 17-year-olds are well able to understand and conduct litigation. There is a broadly comparable power under s 41(4) of the Children Act 1989 and rr 4.11 and 9.2A of the Family Proceedings Rules 1991 for a child to be separately represented if he has sufficient understanding, but takeup has been low and the same is likely to be true of this power. In the family jurisdiction permission to dispense with a guardian was refused to an 11-year-old in *Re S* [1993] Fam 263 but granted to a 15-year-old in *Re H* [1993] 2 FLR 552.

A patient is a person who is incapable of managing and administering his **45.03** property and affairs by reason of mental disorder under the Mental Health Act 1983. It is possible for a person to be able to manage his property and simple affairs hitherto but to become incapable of managing them with the prospect that his affairs will include handling a substantial award of compensation. In any case where the possibility arises that a client may suffer from mental incapacity, whether as a consequence of the accident injury or generally, a medical opinion should immediately be sought either from the client's general practitioner or from an expert instructed to assess the client's mental state. Where the advice is that the client is not capable, an appropriate person must be sought to act as litigation friend, and as soon as there is the prospect of money being received, even as an interim payment to defray specific expenses such as for residential care or treatment, the Court of Protection must be contacted in addition.

45.04 The compromise of a claim by a child or a patient must be approved by the court before it can take effect. Proceedings brought solely to seek approval provide the only situation in which CPR Part 8 proceedings are likely to arise in personal injury litigation. This is a unique occasion when one side is prevented from seeing material that is before the judge. It is usual to provide for the court a written opinion setting out advice on the merits of a proposed settlement. This will inevitably refer to matters such as the potential difficulties in establishing liability, or in suffering a finding of contributory negligence, and a candid opinion of quantum. Such advice is privileged, and the submission of the opinion to the court in the context of an approval hearing does not operate to waive privilege. If the court decides that the settlement is not in the best interests of the child or patient, the case will have to proceed to a hearing (or an improved offer). The defendant therefore does not see the claimant's opinion that is submitted to the judge; naturally it follows that any subsequent trial must be before a different judge.

45.05 The management of compensation received for a child or patient must always be approved by the court. Where the sum received is small it may be possible simply to provide for the money to be invested for the child in a building society or similar savings account by the litigation friend. If it is a larger sum, the bulk will be paid into court and held in an investment account until the child is 18, though a sum can be paid out immediately for the child if appropriate. For a patient, sums under £20,000 may be invested by the court in the same way as a child's damages. Sums over £30,000 must be managed by applying to the Court of Protection for a receiver to be appointed. In between these figures the court making the order has a discretion as to what should be done.

45.06 The staff of the Court of Protection are generally helpful and can be contacted at Archway Tower, 2 Junction Road, London N19 5SZ, DX 141150 Archway 2 (tel: 0845 330 2900; fax: 020 7664 7705; website www.guardianship.gov.uk).

45.07 *Masterman-Lister v Brutton & Co.* [2002] EWCA Civ 1889; [2003] PIQR P310   The Court of Appeal gave important guidance on the question of deciding when a litigant is a patient. In 1987 the claimant settled a claim arising out of a road traffic accident. In 1993 he sued his former solicitors for negligence and claimed that the settlement was not binding because he had been a patient and the settlement had not been approved by the court. The court commented on the absence of any satisfactory mechanism under the rules for arriving at a judicial decision on the question. There is a presumption in favour of capacity. Capacity depends on the time and context of asking the question, so the issue is capacity to understand and give instructions in the litigation rather than capacity to manage affairs generally. The fact that a claimant might be incapable of managing a large award of damages does not mean that he is incapable of conducting the litigation leading to the award.

Drinkall v Whitwood [2003] EWCA Civ 1547; [2004] 1 WLR 462   An agree-   **45.08** ment to settle a claim for a child is not binding until it has been approved by the court. Although the rule exists for the protection of the child, its effect is to allow a defendant of full capacity to resile from an agreement before court approval. The representatives of the child should therefore consider issuing proceedings for the approval of the settlement as soon as possible, even if it deals with only a part of the claim such as liability.

B. CPR Part 21—Children and Patients

21.1 Scope of this Part

(1) This Part—   **45.09**
　　(a) contains special provisions which apply in proceedings involving children and patients; and
　　(b) sets out how a person becomes a litigation friend.

(2) In this Part—
　　(a) 'child' means a person under 18; and
　　(b) 'patient' means a person who by reason of mental disorder within the meaning of the Mental Health Act 1983 is incapable of managing and administering his property and affairs.

21.2 Requirement for litigation friend in proceedings by or against children and patients

(1) A patient must have a litigation friend to conduct proceedings on his behalf.   **45.10**

(2) A child must have a litigation friend to conduct proceedings on his behalf unless the court makes an order under paragraph (3).

(3) The court may make an order permitting the child to conduct proceedings without a litigation friend.

(4) An application for an order under paragraph (3)—
　　(a) may be made by the child;
　　(b) if the child already has a litigation friend, must be made on notice to the litigation friend; and
　　(c) if the child has no litigation friend, may be made without notice.

(5) Where—

    (a) the court has made an order under paragraph (3); and

    (b) it subsequently appears to the court that it is desirable for a litigation friend to conduct the proceedings on behalf of the child,

the court may appoint a person to be the child's litigation friend.

21.3 Stage of proceedings at which a litigation friend becomes necessary

45.11   (1) This rule does not apply where the court has made an order under rule 21.2(3).

(2) A person may not, without the permission of the court—

    (a) make an application against a child or patient before proceedings have started; or

    (b) take any step in proceedings except—

        (i) issuing and serving a claim form; or

        (ii) applying for the appointment of a litigation friend under rule 21.6, until the child or patient has a litigation friend.

(3) If a party becomes a patient during proceedings, no party may take any step in the proceedings without the permission of the court until the patient has a litigation friend.

(4) Any step taken before a child or patient has a litigation friend shall be of no effect unless the court otherwise orders.

21.4 Who may be a litigation friend without a court order

45.12   (1) This rule does not apply if the court has appointed a person to be a litigation friend.

(2) A person authorised under Part VII of the Mental Health Act 1983 to conduct legal proceedings in the name of a patient or on his behalf is entitled to be the litigation friend of the patient in any proceedings to which his authority extends.

(3) If nobody has been appointed by the court or, in the case of a patient, authorised under Part VII, a person may act as a litigation friend if he—

    (a) can fairly and competently conduct proceedings on behalf of the child or patient;

    (b) has no interest adverse to that of the child or patient; and

    (c) where the child or patient is a claimant, undertakes to pay any costs which the child or patient may be ordered to pay in relation to the proceedings, subject to any right he may have to be repaid from the assets of the child or patient.

21.5 How a person becomes a litigation friend without a court order

45.13   (1) If the court has not appointed a litigation friend, a person who wishes to act as a litigation friend must follow the procedure set out in this rule.

(2) A person authorised under Part VII of the Mental Health Act 1983 must file an official copy of the order or other document which constitutes his authorisation to act.

(3) Any other person must file a certificate of suitability stating that he satisfies the conditions specified in rule 21.4(3).

(4) A person who is to act as a litigation friend for a claimant must file—

    (a) the authorisation; or

    (b) the certificate of suitability,

at the time when the claim is made.

(5) A person who is to act as a litigation friend for a defendant must file—

    (a) the authorisation; or

    (b) the certificate of suitability, at the time when he first takes a step in the proceedings on behalf of the defendant.

(6) The litigation friend must—

(a) serve the certificate of suitability on every person on whom, in accordance with rule 6.6 (service on parent, guardian etc.), the claim form should be served; and

(b) file a certificate of service when he files the certificate of suitability.

(Rule 6.10 sets out the details to be contained in a certificate of service)

21.6 How a person becomes a litigation friend by court order

(1) The court may make an order appointing a litigation friend.

(2) An application for an order appointing a litigation friend may be made by—

(a) a person who wishes to be the litigation friend; or

(b) a party.

(3) Where—

(a) a person makes a claim against a child or patient;

(b) the child or patient has no litigation friend;

(c) the court has not make an order under rule 21.2(3) (order that a child can act without a litigation friend); and

(d) either—

(i) someone who is not entitled to be a litigation friend files a defence; or

(ii) the claimant wishes to take some step in the proceedings,

the claimant must apply to the court for an order appointing a litigation friend for the child or patient.

(4) An application for an order appointing a litigation friend must be supported by evidence.

(5) The court may not appoint a litigation friend under this rule unless it is satisfied that the person to be appointed complies with the conditions specified in rule 21.4(3).

21.7 Courts power to change litigation friend and to prevent person acting as litigation friend

(1) The court may—

(a) direct that a person may not act as a litigation friend;

(b) terminate a litigation friend's appointment;

(c) appoint a new litigation friend in substitution for an existing one.

(2) An application for an order under paragraph (1) must be supported by evidence.

(3) The court may not appoint a litigation friend under this rule unless it is satisfied that the person to be appointed complies with the conditions specified in rule 21.4(3).

21.8 Appointment of litigation friend by court order—supplementary

(1) An application for an order under rule 21.6 or 21.7 must be served on every person on whom, in accordance with rule 6.6 (service on parent, guardian etc.), the claim form should be served.

(2) Where an application for an order under rule 21.6 is in respect of a patient, the application must also be served on the patient unless the court orders otherwise.

(3) An application for an order under rule 21.7 must also be served on—

(a) the person who is the litigation friend, or who is purporting to act as the litigation friend, when the application is made; and

(b) the person who it is proposed should be the litigation friend, if he is not the applicant.

(4) On an application for an order under rule 21.6 or 21.7, the court may appoint the person proposed or any other person who complies with the conditions specified in rule 21.4(3).

45.14

45.15

45.16

21.9 Procedure where appointment of litigation friend ceases

45.17   (1) When a child who is not a patient reaches the age of 18, a litigation friend's appointment ceases.

(2) When a party ceases to be a patient, the litigation friend's appointment continues until it is ended by a court order.

(3) An application for an order under paragraph (2) may be made by—
    (a) the former patient;
    (b) the litigation friend; or
    (c) a party.

(4) The child or patient in respect of whom the appointment to act has ceased must serve notice on the other parties—
    (a) stating that the appointment of his litigation friend to act has ceased;
    (b) giving his address for service; and
    (c) stating whether or not he intends to carry on the proceedings.

(5) If he does not do so within 28 days after the day on which the appointment of the litigation friend ceases the court may, on application, strike out any claim or defence brought by him.

(6) The liability of a litigation friend for costs continues until—
    (a) the person in respect of whom his appointment to act has ceased serves the notice referred to in paragraph (4); or
    (b) the litigation friend serves notice on the parties that his appointment to act has ceased.

21.10 Compromise etc. by or on behalf of child or patient

45.18   (1) Where a claim is made—
    (a) by or on behalf of a child or patient; or
    (b) against a child or patient,

no settlement, compromise or payment and no acceptance of money paid into court shall be valid, so far as it relates to the claim by, on behalf of or against the child or patient, without the approval of the court.

(2) Where—
    (a) before proceedings in which a claim is made by or on behalf of, or against a child or patient (whether alone or with any other person) are begun, an agreement is reached for the settlement of the claim; and
    (b) the sole purpose of proceedings on that claim is to obtain the approval of the court to a settlement or compromise of the claim,

the claim must—
    (i) be made using the procedure set out in Part 8 (alternative procedure for claims); and
    (ii) include a request to the court for approval of the settlement or compromise.

(Rule 48.5 contains provisions about costs where money is payable to a child or patient)

21.11 Control of money recovered by or on behalf of child or patient

45.19   (1) Where in any proceedings—
    (a) money is recovered by or on behalf of or for the benefit of a child or patient; or
    (b) money paid into court is accepted by or on behalf of a child or patient, the money shall be dealt with in accordance with directions given by the court under this rule and not otherwise.

(2) Directions given under this rule may provide that the money shall be wholly or partly paid into court and invested or otherwise dealt with.

21.12 Appointment of guardian of child's estate

(1) The court may appoint the Official Solicitor to be a guardian of a child's estate where—

    (a) money is paid into court on behalf of the child in accordance with directions given under rule 21.11 (control of money received by a child or patient);

    (b) the Criminal Injuries Compensation Board or the Criminal Injuries Compensation Authority notifies the court that it has made or intends to make an award to the child;

    (c) a court or tribunal outside England and Wales notifies the court that it has ordered or intends to order that money be paid to the child;

    (d) the child is absolutely entitled to the proceeds of a pension fund; or

    (e) in any other case, such an appointment seems desirable to the court.

(2) The court may not appoint the Official Solicitor under this rule unless—

    (a) the persons with parental responsibility (within the meaning of section 3 of the Children Act 1989) agree; or

    (b) the court considers that their agreement can be dispensed with.

(3) The Official Solicitor's appointment may continue only until the child reaches 18.

45.20

C. PD 21—Children and Patients

General

1.1 In this practice direction 'child' means a person under 18 years old and 'patient' means a person who by reason of mental disorder within the meaning of the Mental Health Act 1983 is incapable of managing and administering his own affairs.

1.2 A patient must bring or defend proceedings by a litigation friend (see paragraph 2 below for the definition of a litigation friend).

1.3 In the proceedings referred to in paragraph 1.2 above the patient should be referred to in the title as 'A.B. (by C.D. his litigation friend)'.

1.4 A child must bring or defend proceedings by a litigation friend unless the court has made an order permitting the child to do so on his own behalf.

1.5 Where:

    (1) the child has a litigation friend, the child should be referred to in the title to proceedings as 'A.B. (a child by C.D. his litigation friend)', and

    (2) the child is conducting proceedings on his own behalf, the child should be referred to in the title as 'A.B. (a child)'.

1.6 The approval of the court must be obtained if a settlement of a claim by or against a child or patient is to be valid. A settlement includes an agreement on a sum to be apportioned to a dependent child under the Fatal Accidents Act 1976.

1.7 The approval of the court must also be obtained before making a voluntary interim payment to a child or patient.

(Rule 39.2(3) provides for a hearing or part of a hearing to be in private)

45.21

The litigation friend

2.1 It is the duty of a litigation friend fairly and competently to conduct proceedings on behalf of a child or patient. He must have no interest in the proceedings adverse to that of the child or patient and all steps and decisions he takes in the proceedings must be taken for the benefit of the child or patient.

2.2 A person may become a litigation friend:

45.22

    (1) of a child—

        (a) without a court order under the provisions of rule 21.5, or

        (b) by a court order under rule 21.6, and

    (2) of a patient

        (a) by authorisation under Part VII of the Mental Health Act 1983, or

        (b) by a court order under rule 21.6.

2.3 In order to become a litigation friend without a court order the person who wishes to act as litigation friend must:

    (1) if he wishes to act on behalf of a patient, file an official copy of the order or other document which constitutes the authorisation referred to in paragraph 2.2(2)(a) above, or

    (2) if he wishes to act on behalf of a child, or on behalf of a patient without the authorisation referred to in (1) above, file a certificate of suitability—

        (a) stating that he consents to act,

        (b) stating that he knows or believes that the [claimant] [defendant] is a [child] [patient],

        (c) in the case of a patient, stating the grounds of his belief and if his belief is based upon medical opinion attaching any relevant document to the certificate,

        (d) stating that he can fairly and competently conduct proceedings on behalf of the child or patient and has no interest adverse to that of the child or patient,

        (e) where the child or patient is a claimant, undertaking to pay any costs which the child or patient may be ordered to pay in relation to the proceedings, subject to any right he may have to be repaid from the assets of the child or patient, and

        (f) which he has signed in verification of its contents.

2.4 The litigation friend must serve a certificate of suitability:

    (1) in the case of a child (who is not also a patient) on one of the child's parents or guardians or if there is no parent or guardian, on the person with whom the child resides or in whose care the child is, and

    (2) in the case of a patient on the person authorised under Part VII of the Mental Health Act 1983 to conduct proceedings on behalf of the patient or if there is no person so authorised, on the person with whom the patient resides or in whose care the patient is.

2.4A The litigation friend is not required to serve the documents referred to in paragraph 2.3(2)(c) when he serves a certificate of suitability on the person to be served under paragraph 2.4.

2.5 The litigation friend must file either the certificate of suitability together with a certificate of service of it, or the authorisation referred to in paragraph 2.31(1) above:

    (1) where the litigation friend is acting on behalf of a claimant, when the claim form is issued, and

    (2) where the litigation friend is acting on behalf of a defendant, when he first takes a step in the action.

Application for a court order appointing a litigation friend

45.23   3.1 Rule 21.6 sets out who may apply for an order appointing a litigation friend.

3.2 An application should be made in accordance with Part 23 and must be supported by evidence.

3.3 The application notice must be served:

    (1) on the persons referred to in paragraph 2.4 above, and

    (2) where the application is in respect of a patient, on the patient unless the court orders otherwise.

3.4 The evidence in support must satisfy the court that the proposed litigation friend:

    (1) consents to act,

    (2) can fairly and competently conduct proceedings on behalf of the child or patient,

(3) has no interest adverse to that of the child or patient, and

(4) where the child or patient is a claimant, undertakes to pay any costs which the child or patient may be ordered to pay in relation to the proceedings, subject to any right he may have to be repaid from the assets of the child or patient.

3.5 Where a claimant wishes to take a step in proceedings against a child or patient who does not have a litigation friend he must apply to the court for an order appointing a litigation friend.

3.6 The proposed litigation friend must satisfy the conditions in paragraph 3.4(1), (2) and (3) above and may be one of the persons referred to in paragraph 2.4 above where appropriate, or otherwise may be the Official Solicitor. Where it is sought to appoint the Official Solicitor, provision should be made for payment of his charges.

Change of litigation friend and prevention of person acting as litigation friend

4.1 Rule 21.7(1) states that the court may: **45.24**
    (1) direct that a person may not act as a litigation friend,
    (2) terminate a litigation friend's appointment,
    (3) substitute a new litigation friend for an existing one.

4.2 Where an application is made for an order under rule 21.7(1), the application notice must set out the reasons for seeking it. The application must be supported by evidence.

4.3 If the order sought is the substitution of a new litigation friend for an existing one, the evidence must satisfy the court of the matters set out in paragraph 3.4 above.

4.4 The application notice must be served:
    (1) on the persons referred to in paragraph 2.4 above, and
    (2) on the litigation friend or person purporting to act as litigation friend.

Procedure where the need for a litigation friend has come to an end

5.1 Rule 21.9 deals with the situation where the need for a litigation friend comes to an end **45.25** during the proceedings because either:
    (1) a child who is not also a patient reaches the age of 18 (full age) during the proceedings,
or
    (2) a patient ceases to be a patient (recovers).

5.2 A child on reaching full age must serve on the other parties to the proceedings and file with the court a notice:
    (1) stating that he has reached full age,
    (2) stating that his litigation friend's appointment has ceased,
    (3) giving an address for service, and
    (4) stating whether or not he intends to carry on with or continue to defend the proceedings.

5.3 If the notice states that the child intends to carry on with or continue to defend the proceedings he shall subsequently be described in the proceedings as:
    'A.B. (formerly a child but now of full age)'

5.4 Whether or not a child having reached full age serves a notice in accordance with rule 21.9(4)(a) and paragraph 5.2(2) above, a litigation friend may at any time after the child has reached full age serve a notice on the other parties that his appointment has ceased.

5.5 The liability of a litigation friend for costs continues until a notice that his appointment to act has ceased is served on the other parties.

5.6 Where a patient recovers, an application under rule 21.9(3) must be made for an order under rule 21.9(2) that the litigation friend's appointment has ceased.

5.7 The application must be supported by the following evidence:

(1) a medical report indicating that the patient has recovered and that he is capable of managing and administering his property and affairs,

(2) where the patient's affairs were under the control of the Court of Protection, a copy of the order or notice discharging the receiver, and

(3) if the application is made by the patient, a statement whether or not he intends to carry on with or continue to defend the proceedings.

5.8 An order under rule 21.9(2) must be served on the other parties to the proceedings. The patient must file with the court a notice;

(1) stating that his litigation friend's appointment has ceased,

(2) giving an address for service, and

(3) stating whether or not he intends to carry on with or continue to defend the proceedings.

Settlement or compromise by or on behalf of a child or patient

45.26
6.1 Where a claim by or on behalf of a child or patient has been dealt with by agreement prior to the start of proceedings and only the approval of the court to the agreement is sought, the claim:

(1) must be made using the Part 8 procedure,

(2) must include a request for approval of the settlement or compromise, and

(3) in addition to the details of the claim, must set out the terms of the settlement or compromise or have attached to it a draft consent order in practice form N292.

6.2 In order to approve the settlement or compromise, the information concerning the claim that the court will require will include:

(1) whether and to what extent the defendant admits liability,

(2) the age and occupation (if any) of the child or patient,

(3) the litigation friend's approval of the proposed settlement or compromise, and

(4) in a personal injury case arising from an accident—

(a) the circumstances of the accident,

(b) any medical reports,

(c) where appropriate, a schedule of any past and future expenses and losses claimed and any other relevant information relating to personal injury as set out in the practice direction which supplements Part 16 (statements of case), and

(d) where considerations of liability are raised—

(i) any evidence or police reports in any criminal proceedings or in an inquest, and

(ii) details of any prosecution brought.

6.3 (1) An opinion on the merits of the settlement or compromise given by counsel or solicitor acting for the child or patient should, except in very clear cases, be obtained.

(2) A copy of the opinion and, unless the instructions on which it was given are sufficiently set out in it, a copy of the instructions, must also be supplied to the court.

6.4 In any case where future loss is likely to equal or exceed £500,000, and in any other case in which the court considers it might be appropriate, the court will need to be satisfied that consideration has been given to entering into a structured settlement. A copy of written financial advice, together with any other relevant written material such as counsel's opinion and any relevant medical opinion must be supplied to the court. The advice(s) should consider the matters specifically identified by the practice direction on structured settlements supplementing Part 40 (Judgments and Orders).

6.5 Applications for the approval of a settlement or compromise will normally be heard by a Master or district judge.

(For information about structured settlements see the practice direction on structured settlements supplementing Part 40 (judgments and orders))

(For information about provisional damages claims see Part 41 and PD 41)

Apportionment under the Fatal Accidents Act 1976

45.27 7.1 A judgment on or settlement in respect of a claim under the Fatal Accidents Act 1976 must be apportioned between the persons by or on whose behalf the claim has been brought.

7.2 Where a claim is brought on behalf of a dependent child or children, the money apportioned to any child must be invested on his behalf in accordance with rules 21.10 and 21.11 and paragraphs 8 and 9 below.

7.3 In order to approve an apportionment of money to a dependent child, the court will require the following information;
    (1) the matters set out in paragraph 6.2(1),(2) above, and
    (2) in respect of the deceased
    (a) where death was caused by an accident, the matters set out in paragraph 6.2(3)(a),(b) and (c) above, and
    (b) his future loss of earnings, and
    (3) the extent and nature of the dependency.

Control of money recovered by or on behalf of a child or patient

45.28 8.1 Money recovered or paid into court on behalf of or for the benefit of a child or patient shall be dealt with in accordance with directions of the court under rule 21.11.

8.2 The court:
    (1) may direct the money to be paid into the High Court for investment,
    (2) may also direct that certain sums be paid direct to the child or patient, his litigation friend or his legal representative for the immediate benefit of the child or patient or for expenses incurred on his behalf, and
    (3) may direct the applications in respect of the investment of the money be transferred to a local district registry.

8.3 The master or district judge will consider the general aims to be achieved for the money in court (the fund) by investment and will give directions as to the type of investment.

8.4 Where a child is also a patient, and likely to remain so on reaching full age, his fund should be administered as a patient's fund.

8.5 Where a child or patient is legally aided the fund will be subject to a first charge under s. 16 of the Legal Aid Act 1988 (the legal aid charge) and an order for the investment of money on the child or patient's behalf must contain a direction to that effect.

Guardian's accounts

45.29 9 Paragraph 8 of PD 40 deals with the approval of the accounts of a guardian of assets of a child.

Investment on behalf of a child

45.30 10.1 At the hearing of the application for the approval of the agreement the litigation friend or his legal representative should provide a CFO form 320 (request for investment) for completion by the Master or district judge.

10.2 On receipt of that form in the Court Funds Office the investment managers of the Public Trust Office will make the appropriate investment.

10.3 Where an award of damages for a child is made at trial the trial judge may direct:

(1) the money to be paid into court and placed in the special investment account, and

(2) the litigation friend to make an application to a Master or district judge for further investment directions.

10.4 If the money to be invested is very small the court may order it to be paid direct to the litigation friend to be put into a building society account (or similar) for the child's use.

10.5 If the money is invested in court it must be paid out to the child when he reaches full age.

Investment on behalf of a patient

45.31   11.1 The Court of Protection is responsible for protecting the property of patients and is given extensive powers to do so under the Mental Health Act 1983. Fees are charged for the administration of funds by the Court of Protection and these should be provided for in any settlement.

11.2 Where the sum to be administered is:

(1) over £30,000, the order approving the settlement will contain a direction to the litigation friend to apply to the Court of Protection for the appointment of a receiver, after which the fund will be transferred to the Court of Protection,

(2) under £20,000, it may be retained in court and invested in the same way as the fund of a child, or

(3) in intermediate cases the advice of the Master of the Court of Protection should be sought.

11.3 A form of order transferring the fund to the Court of Protection is set out in practice form N292.

11.4 In order for the Court Funds Office to release a fund which is subject to the legal aid charge to the Court of Protection the litigation friend or his legal representative should provide the appropriate area office of the Legal Aid Board with an undertaking in respect of a sum to cover their costs, following which the area office will advise the Court Funds Office in writing of that sum, enabling them to transfer the balance to the Court of Protection on receipt of a CFO form 200 payment schedule authorised by the court.

11.5 The CFO form 200 should be completed and presented to the court where the settlement or trial took place for authorisation, subject to paragraphs 11.6 and 11.7 below.

11.6 Where the settlement took place in the Royal Courts of Justice the CFO form 200 should be completed and presented for authorisation:

(1) on behalf of a child, in the Masters' Secretary's Office, Room E214, and

(2) on behalf of a patient, in the Action Department, Room E15.

11.7 Where the trial took place in the Royal Courts of Justice the CFO form 200 is completed and authorised by the court officer.

Payment out of funds in court

45.32   12.1 Applications to a Master or district judge;

(1) for payment out of money from the fund for the benefit of the child, or

(2) to vary an investment strategy,

may be dealt with without a hearing unless the court directs otherwise.

12.2 When the child reaches full age, his fund in court:

(1) where it is a sum of money will be paid out to him, and

(2) where it is in the form of investments other than money (for example shares or unit trusts), will be transferred into his name.

12.3 An application for payment out of funds being administered by the Court of Protection must be made to the Court of Protection.

(For further information on payments into and out of court see PD 36 and PD 37)

46

SETTLEMENT AND PART 36

A. Background

Most cases settle. This is particularly the case with personal injury claims. This **46.01** is a good thing (except for the lawyers) as long as the settlement is on proper terms and is not an undervalue of a claim, which a claimant is compelled to accept because of a fear of the barriers such as cost, delay and uncertainty which stand in the way of taking a claim to court. When a claim is settled, the assessment of the claim is in the hands of the lawyers rather than the court; much depends on the skill and experience of the legal advisers and their resistance to the conflicts of interest which increasingly arise in practice.

Because of the cost involved in taking a claim to trial, the rules about costs **46.02** have been traditionally used to encourage settlement or, in the absence of a settlement, to protect a litigant who acts reasonably. The standard rule in civil litigation is that the loser must pay the costs of the winner. This rule strongly discourages unmeritorious claims and unmeritorious defences. In claims of moderate value it is not difficult for the costs of a case which goes to a full trial to exceed the amount in issue in the claim.

A refinement to the rule that the loser pays the costs came, long before the CPR, **46.03** with the rules about payments into court. If a defendant admitted that a claim had merit but disputed the amount claimed, he might end up ordered to make a payment to the claimant, which made it look as if he was the loser, while in reality he had successfully argued down the value of the claim to a sum he was always willing to pay. The rules allowed him to make a formal settlement offer (formal, but secret as far as the trial judge was concerned) by making a payment into court during the proceedings, and this had the effect of moving the goal-posts for the purpose of deciding at the end of the case which party was really the loser. If the claimant recovered no more than the sum the defendant had paid into court, but the claimant had rejected, then from the date of the payment into court the defendant would be treated as the winner and the claimant would have to pay the defendant's costs. This could be a powerful factor in the tactics of litigation, and some of the saddest tragedies of litigation have been cases of claims of merit where the well deserved benefits of victory were extinguished by the impact of costs because a well judged payment into court had been unwisely rejected.

B. CPR Part 36

46.04 The CPR have developed the rules about payments into court into a more sophisticated code which is driven not only by an aim to protect the reasonable litigant faced with an unreasonable opponent, but also quite openly to put pressure on parties to settle their claims rather than having them decided by the court. The new rules provide for settlement offers to be made before court proceedings begin, which will be taken into account in deciding liability for costs, so that the entire costs of the case may be at risk. The rules also now provide for the first time a mechanism for claimants to make settlement offers which put a different but more subtle pressure on defendants by a risk of the award of special interest and indemnity costs. However, this has been achieved at the price of simplicity and the rules have become technical and complex.

46.05 The key points to note under CPR Part 36 are:

(a) The requirements for the form and content of an offer letter are strict (rr 36.5 and 36.10). In spite of the generally broad discretion on costs and the overriding objective, there will be real doubt about achieving the benefits of an offer if the letter is not written precisely in accordance with the rules.

(b) If the formalities are correct, the rules state that the court *will* make the orders provided unless it considers it unjust to do so.

(c) The benefits of a successful Part 36 offer for a claimant are:
(i) interest at up to base rate plus 10% on the whole sum recovered (not just the parts of the award which carry normal interest);
(ii) interest at that rate on costs; and
(iii) indemnity costs rather than standard basis costs.

The base rate is 4.5% at the time or writing. A table of rates is set out at 34.17.

(d) The benefits of a successful use of Part 36 can be considerable. It is important for a claimant's advisers to consider continually whether a sufficient assessment of the claim can be made to allow a Part 36 offer to be put forward, and the earlier the better; a wise defendant will have a system in place to make a realistic written offer as soon as a claim can be evaluated and to follow this up with a prompt payment into court.

(e) The 21-day period for acceptance runs from the date on which the offer, or notice of the payment, is received by the offeree (r 36.8).

(f) In a money claim, which covers almost all personal injury claims, a defendant must make a payment into court (a Part 36 payment rather than a Part 36 offer) and a written offer will not do. However, a payment can only be made after the proceedings have begun. A defendant can make a written offer before the start of proceedings, in the form required by r 36.10, and must then make a payment of at least as much as the written offer within 14 days of service of the claim form. The defendant will then be able to rely on the pre-action offer.

(g) If a Part 36 offer/payment is accepted by the claimant within 21 days, no order of the court is needed and the claimant becomes automatically entitled to his costs.

(h) If a Part 36 offer/payment is not accepted within the period of 21 days, it can still be accepted if costs are agreed or ordered by the court. The usual order in this situation would be that the offeree is entitled to his costs up to the date of the offer and is liable for the offeror's costs between offer and acceptance.

(i) Once a payment into court has been made, the payer will need permission to withdraw it, which is not likely to be granted unless there has been a significant change of circumstances (*Sherratt v Bromley* [1985] 1 QB 1038).

46.06 *Petrograde v Texaco* [2001] 4 All ER 853   The claimant succeeded in improving on its Part 36 offer on an application for summary judgment. Rule 36.21 applies only at trial, but even so the Court of Appeal held that the court's discretion on costs and interest, and the requirement under r 44.3(4)(c) to have regard to any admissible offer made, should have led the court to award the claimant costs on the indemnity basis and an enhanced rate of interest.

46.07 *Williams v Devon County Council* [2003] EWCA Civ 365; [2003] PIQR Q68   The Part 36 payment notice must identify the benefits which the defendant withholds under the Social Security (Recovery of Benefits) Act 1997. A finding of contributory negligence against the claimant does not reduce the benefits recoverable, although benefits can only be offset to the extent of the relevant head of damages. This case highlighted the need for the notice to identify the categories of benefit and to ensure that the claimant was able to receive the amount of the general damages offered, without suffering an inappropriate reduction for recoupment. If the defendant relies on contributory negligence or partially disputes causation, and makes a Part 36 payment on the basis of this case, the amount of benefits shown to have been deducted must be limited to the amount that is consistent with its case.

46.08 *Mitchell v James* [2002] EWCA Civ 997; [2003] 2 All ER 1064   The claimant made a written offer of settlement terms, which included an offer to pay his own costs, and relied on this offer on costs in claiming Part 36 benefits. The Court of Appeal upheld the trial judge's refusal to give effect to the Part 36 offer, because Part 36 is concerned only with the substance of the dispute and not with matters of costs. (This is an accurate reading of the rules, but the impact of costs is so significant in the negotiation of settlements that it has a regrettable outcome.)

46.09 *Scammell v Dicker* [2001] 1 WLR 631   Even though the rules require that a Part 36 offer letter should state that the offer remains open for acceptance for 21 days after it has been made, the claimant is entitled to withdraw his offer at any time, even before the 21 days have gone by, if it has not yet been accepted.

46.10 *Huck v Robson* [2002] EWCA Civ 398; [2002] 3 All ER 263   In a road accident claim with a dispute on liability, before proceedings were started the claimant offered to settle for 95% and at trial succeeded in recovering 100%. The Court of Appeal held that (1) the offer should be given effect even though it was made before proceedings began, and (2) it was not unjust to give effect to an offer at 95% even though this was not an order that the court was likely to make at trial. 5% is a substantial discount for settlement. The comments of the court suggest, however, that an offer must amount to a genuine concession for settlement, so that an offer of 99.9% would not be effective.

46.11 *Ford v GKR Construction* [2000] 1 WLR 1397   The claimant recovered £89,323 when the defendant had paid into court £95,000. However the claim was only reduced below the level of the payment because the defendant had used the interval between the days of a drawn-out hearing to obtain surveillance evidence and additional medical evidence, evidence which could easily have been obtained in advance of the trial. In a striking example of the flexible approach to costs under the CPR the Court of Appeal upheld the decision to order that the defendant should pay the claimant's costs in full in spite of the Part 36 payment.

46.12 *P & O Nedlloyd v Utaniko* [2003] EWCA Civ 174; [2003] 1 Lloyd's Rep 265   The claimant succeeded at trial, beating its Part 36 offer and receiving costs on the indemnity basis as a result. The defendant brought an unsuccessful appeal. The Court of Appeal refused to award the claimant costs of the appeal on the indemnity basis relying on the same Part 36 offer. A separate offer should have been made in relation to the appeal.

Blackham v Entrepose UK [2004] EWCA Civ 1109   The question whether **46.13** the claimant has beaten a Part 36 payment by the judgment awarded at trial requires the comparison of the amount of damages in the payment and in the award, disregarding interest. The lapse of time before trial may make it seem that the claimant has recovered a larger award than the offer, because of the increase in the entitlement of interest, but in this case when interest was disregarded the claimant had not beaten the offer.

C. Settlement

The settlement of a claim takes effect as a contract. In a case involving a person **46.14** under 18 years of age or a person who is incapable of managing his own affairs, a settlement will not be binding until the court has approved the terms agreed (see Chapter 45). In ordinary cases however, a settlement is achieved by the normal contractual requirement for an offer and a corresponding, unequivocal acceptance. It is common for a settlement to be incorporated in an order made by the court by consent but this is not necessary in order for a settlement to bind the parties.

Solicitors and barristers have an implied authority to reach an agreement to **46.15** compromise an action. This means that the opponent does not need to concern himself with the question whether the litigant has agreed to the terms: if the lawyer purports to reach a settlement as his client's agent, the settlement will be binding and if the lawyer was acting without instructions or contrary to his instructions, the remedy for the litigant has to be against his own lawyer rather than by challenging the settlement.

D. Privilege

The law encourages parties to negotiate a settlement and facilitates the process **46.16** by granting the protection of secrecy from the trial judge to any communication that takes place as part of an attempt to negotiate a settlement. It is common for lawyers to add the phrase 'without prejudice' to correspondence in which concessions are expressed with a view to negotiating. These archaic words mean that this secrecy, the privilege from disclosure, is claimed for the letter. As a matter of law however, these words are neither necessary nor sufficient. A letter which is written in a genuine attempt to negotiate will be privileged whether or not it carries these words, and a letter which is not an attempt to negotiate will not be privileged even if it carries these words.

E. Offers to Settle and Payments into Court—CPR Parts 36 and 37 and Practice Directions

CPR PART 36—OFFERS TO SETTLE AND PAYMENTS INTO COURT

36.1 Scope of this Part

46.17   (1) This Part contains rules about—

(a) offers to settle and payments into court; and

(b) the consequences where an offer to settle or payment into court is made in accordance with this Part.

(2) Nothing in this Part prevents a party making an offer to settle in whatever way he chooses, but if that offer is not made in accordance with this Part, it will only have the consequences specified in this Part if the court so orders.

(Part 36 applies to Part 20 claims by virtue of rule 20.3)

36.2 Part 36 offers and Part 36 payments—general provisions

46.18   (1) An offer made in accordance with the requirements of this Part is called—

(a) if made by way of a payment into court, 'a Part 36 payment';

(b) otherwise 'a Part 36 offer'.

(Rule 36.3 sets out when an offer has to be made by way of a payment into court)

(2) The party who makes an offer is the 'offeror'.

(3) The party to whom an offer is made is the 'offeree'.

(4) A Part 36 offer or a Part 36 payment—

(a) may be made at any time after proceedings have started; and

(b) may be made in appeal proceedings.

(5) A Part 36 offer or a Part 36 payment shall not have the consequences set out in this Part while the claim is being dealt with on the small claims track unless the court orders otherwise.

(Part 26 deals with allocation to the small claims track)

(Rule 27.2 provides that Part 36 does not apply to small claims)

36.3 A defendant's offer to settle a money claim requires a Part 36 payment

46.19   (1) Subject to rules 36.5(5) and 36.23, an offer by a defendant to settle a money claim will not have the consequences set out in this Part unless it is made by way of a Part 36 payment.

(2) A Part 36 payment may only be made after proceedings have started.

(Rule 36.5(5) permits a Part 36 offer to be made by reference to an interim payment)

(Rule 36.10 makes provision for an offer to settle a money claim before the commencement of proceedings)

(Rule 36.23 makes provision for where benefit is recoverable under the Social Security (Recovery of Benefit) Act 1997)

36.4 Defendants offer to settle the whole of a claim which includes both a money claim and a non-money claim

46.20   (1) This rule applies where a defendant to a claim which includes both a money claim and a non-money claim wishes—

(a) to make an offer to settle the whole claim which will have the consequences set out in this Part; and

(b) to make a money offer in respect of the money claim and a non-money offer in respect of the non-money claim.

(2) The defendant must—

(a) make a Part 36 payment in relation to the money claim; and

(b) make a Part 36 offer in relation to the non-money claim.

(3) The Part 36 payment notice must—

(a) identify the document which sets out the terms of the Part 36 offer; and

(b) state that if the claimant gives notice of acceptance of the Part 36 payment he will be treated as also accepting the Part 36 offer.

(Rule 36.6 makes provision for a Part 36 payment notice)

(4) If the claimant gives notice of acceptance of the Part 36 payment, he shall also be taken as giving notice of acceptance of the Part 36 offer in relation to the non-money claim.

36.5 Form and content of a Part 36 offer

(1) A Part 36 offer must be in writing.   **46.21**

(2) A Part 36 offer may relate to the whole claim or to part of it or to any issue that arises in it.

(3) A Part 36 offer must—

(a) state whether it relates to the whole of the claim or to part of it or to an issue that arises in it and if so to which part or issue;

(b) state whether it takes into account any counterclaim; and

(c) if it is expressed not to be inclusive of interest, give the details relating to interest set out in rule 36.22(2).

(4) A defendant may make a Part 36 offer limited to accepting liability up to a specified proportion.

(5) A Part 36 offer may be made by reference to an interim payment.

(Part 25 contains provisions relating to interim payments)

(6) A Part 36 offer made not less than 21 days before the start of the trial must—

(a) be expressed to remain open for acceptance for 21 days from the date it is made; and

(b) provide that after 21 days the offeree may only accept it if—

(i) the parties agree the liability for costs; or

(ii) the court gives permission.

(7) A Part 36 offer made less than 21 days before the start of the trial must state that the offeree may only accept it if—

(a) the parties agree the liability for costs; or

(b) the court gives permission.

(Rule 36.8 makes provision for when a Part 36 offer is treated as being made)

(8) If a Part 36 offer is withdrawn it will not have the consequences set out in this Part.

36.6 Notice of a Part 36 payment

(1) A Part 36 payment may relate to the whole claim or part of it or to an issue that arises in it.   **46.22**

(2) A defendant who makes a Part 36 payment must file with the court a notice ('Part 36 payment notice') which—

(a) states the amount of the payment;

(b) states whether the payment relates to the whole claim or to part of it or to any issue that arises in it and if so to which part or issue;

(c) states whether it takes into account any counterclaim;

(d) if an interim payment has been made, states that the defendant has taken into account the interim payment; and

(e) if it is expressed not to be inclusive of interest, gives the details relating to interest set out in rule 36.22(2).

(Rule 25.6 makes provision for an interim payment)

(Rule 36.4 provides for further information to be included where a defendant wishes to settle the whole of a claim which includes a money claim and a non-money claim)

(Rule 36.23 makes provision for extra information to be included in the payment notice in a case where benefit is recoverable under the Social Security (Recovery of Benefit) Act 1997)

(3) The offeror must—

(a) serve the Part 36 payment notice on the offeree; and

(b) file a certificate of service of the notice.

. . .

(Rule 6.10 specifies what must be contained in a certificate of service)

(5) A Part 36 payment may be withdrawn or reduced only with the permission of the court.

36.7 Offer to settle a claim for provisional damages

46.23   (1) A defendant may make a Part 36 payment in respect of a claim which includes a claim for provisional damages.

(2) Where he does so, the Part 36 payment notice must specify whether or not the defendant is offering to agree to the making of an award of provisional damages.

(3) Where the defendant is offering to agree to the making of an award of provisional damages the payment notice must also state—

(a) that the sum paid into court is in satisfaction of the claim for damages on the assumption that the injured person will not develop the disease or suffer the type of deterioration specified in the notice;

(b) that the offer is subject to the condition that the claimant must make any claim for further damages within a limited period; and

(c) what that period is.

(4) Where a Part 36 payment is—

(a) made in accordance with paragraph (3); and

(b) accepted within the relevant period in rule 36.11,

the Part 36 payment will have the consequences set out in rule 36.13, unless the court orders otherwise.

(5) If the claimant accepts the Part 36 payment he must, within 7 days of doing so, apply to the court for an order for an award of provisional damages under rule 41.2.

(Rule 41.2 provides for an order for an award of provisional damages)

(6) The money in court may not be paid out until the court has disposed of the application made in accordance with paragraph (5).

36.8 Time when a Part 36 offer or a Part 36 payment is made and accepted

46.24   (1) A Part 36 offer is made when received by the offeree.

(2) A Part 36 payment is made when written notice of the payment into court is served on the offeree.

(3) An improvement to a Part 36 offer will be effective when its details are received by the offeree.

(4) An increase in a Part 36 payment will be effective when notice of the increase is served on the offeree.

(5) A Part 36 offer or Part 36 payment is accepted when notice of its acceptance is received by the offeror.

36.9 Clarification of a Part 36 offer or a Part 36 payment notice

(1) The offeree may, within 7 days of a Part 36 offer or payment being made, request the offeror to clarify the offer or payment notice. **46.25**

(2) If the offeror does not give the clarification requested under paragraph (1) within 7 days of receiving the request, the offeree may, unless the trial has started, apply for an order that he does so.

(3) If the court makes an order under paragraph (2), it must specify the date when the Part 36 offer or Part 36 payment is to be treated as having been made.

36.10 Court to take into account offer to settle made before commencement of proceedings

(1) If a person makes an offer to settle before proceedings are begun which complies with the provisions of this rule, the court will take that offer into account when making any order as to costs. **46.26**

(2) The offer must—
    (a) be expressed to be open for at least 21 days after the date it was made;
    (b) if made by a person who would be a defendant were proceedings commenced, include an offer to pay the costs of the offeree incurred up to the date 21 days after the date it was made; and
    (c) otherwise comply with this Part.

(3) If the offeror is a defendant to a money claim—
    (a) he must make a Part 36 payment within 14 days of service of the claim form; and
    (b) the amount of the payment must be not less than the sum offered before proceedings began.

(4) An offeree may not, after proceedings have begun, accept—
    (a) an offer made under paragraph (2); or
    (b) a Part 36 payment made under paragraph (3),
without the permission of the court.

(5) An offer under this rule is made when it is received by the offeree.

36.11 Time for acceptance of a defendant's Part 36 offer or Part 36 payment

(1) A claimant may accept a Part 36 offer or a Part 36 payment made not less than 21 days before the start of the trial without needing the court's permission if he gives the defendant written notice of acceptance not later than 21 days after the offer or payment was made. **46.27**

(Rule 36.13 sets out the costs consequences of accepting a defendant's offer or payment without needing the permission of the court)

(2) If—
    (a) a defendant's Part 36 offer or Part 36 payment is made less than 21 days before the start of the trial; or
    (b) the claimant does not accept it within the period specified in paragraph (1)—
        (i) if the parties agree the liability for costs, the claimant may accept the offer or payment without needing the permission of the court;
        (ii) if the parties do not agree the liability for costs the claimant may only accept the offer or payment with the permission of the court.

(3) Where the permission of the court is needed under paragraph (2) the court will, if it gives permission, make an order as to costs.

36.12 Time for acceptance of a claimant's Part 36 offer

46.28   (1) A defendant may accept a Part 36 offer made not less than 21 days before the start of the trial without needing the court's permission if he gives the claimant written notice of acceptance not later than 21 days after the offer was made.

(Rule 36.14 sets out the costs consequences of accepting a claimant's offer without needing the permission of the court)

(2) If—
(a) a claimant's Part 36 offer is made less than 21 days before the start of the trial; or
(b) the defendant does not accept it within the period specified in paragraph (1)—
(i) if the parties agree the liability for costs, the defendant may accept the offer without needing the permission of the court;
(ii) if the parties do not agree the liability for costs the defendant may only accept the offer with the permission of the court.
(3) Where the permission of the court is needed under paragraph (2) the court will, if it gives permission, make an order as to costs.

36.13 Costs consequences of acceptance of a defendant's Part 36 offer or Part 36 payment

46.29   (1) Where a Part 36 offer or a Part 36 payment is accepted without needing the permission of the court the claimant will be entitled to his costs of the proceedings up to the date of serving notice of acceptance.

(2) Where—
(a) a Part 36 offer or a Part 36 payment relates to part only of the claim; and
(b) at the time of serving notice of acceptance the claimant abandons the balance of the claim,

the claimant will be entitled to his costs of the proceedings up to the date of serving notice of acceptance, unless the court orders otherwise.

(3) The claimant's costs include any costs attributable to the defendant's counterclaim if the Part 36 offer or the Part 36 payment notice states that it takes into account the counterclaim.

(4) Costs under this rule will be payable on the standard basis if not agreed.

36.14 Costs consequences of acceptance of a claimant's Part 36 offer

46.30   Where a claimant's Part 36 offer is accepted without needing the permission of the court the claimant will be entitled to his costs of the proceedings up to the date upon which the defendant serves notice of acceptance.

36.15 The effect of acceptance of a Part 36 offer or a Part 36 payment

46.31   (1) If a part 36 offer or Part 36 payment relates to the whole claim and is accepted, the claim will be stayed.

(2) In the case of acceptance of a Part 36 offer which relates to the whole claim—
(a) the stay will be upon the terms of the offer; and
(b) either party may apply to enforce those terms without the need for a new claim.

(3) If a Part 36 offer or a Part 36 payment which relates to part only of the claim is accepted—
(a) the claim will be stayed as to that part; and
(b) unless the parties have agreed costs, the liability for costs shall be decided by the court.

(4) If the approval of the court is required before a settlement can be binding, any stay which would otherwise arise on the acceptance of a Part 36 offer or a Part 36 payment will take effect only when that approval has been given.

(5) Any stay arising under this rule will not affect the power of the court—

(a) to enforce the terms of a Part 36 offer;

(b) to deal with any question of costs (including interest on costs) relating to the proceedings;

(c) to order payment out of court of any sum paid into court.

(6) Where—

(a) a Part 36 offer has been accepted; and

(b) a party alleges that—

(i) the other party has not honoured the terms of the offer; and

(ii) he is therefore entitled to a remedy for breach of contract,

the party may claim the remedy by applying to the court without the need to start a new claim unless the court orders otherwise.

36.16 Payment out of a sum in court on the acceptance of a Part 36 payment

Where a Part 36 payment is accepted the claimant obtains payment out of the sum in court by **46.32** making a request for payment in the practice form.

36.17 Acceptance of a Part 36 offer or a Part 36 payment made by one or more, but not all, defendants

(1) This rule applies where the claimant wishes to accept a Part 36 offer or a Part 36 payment **46.33** made by one or more, but not all, of a number of defendants.

(2) If the defendants are sued jointly or in the alternative, the claimant may accept the offer or payment without needing the permission of the court in accordance with rule 36.11(1) if—

(a) he discontinues his claim against those defendants who have not made the offer or payment; and

(b) those defendants give written consent to the acceptance of the offer or payment.

(3) If the claimant alleges that the defendants have a several liability to him the claimant may—

(a) accept the offer or payment in accordance with rule 36.11(1); and

(b) continue with his claims against the other defendants if he is entitled to do so.

(4) In all other cases the claimant must apply to the court for—

(a) an order permitting a payment out to him of any sum in court; and

(b) such order as to costs as the court considers appropriate.

36.18 Other cases where a court order is required to enable acceptance of a Part 36 offer or a Part 36 payment

(1) Where a Part 36 offer or a Part 36 payment is made in proceedings to which rule 21.10 **46.34** applies—

(a) the offer or payment may be accepted only with the permission of the court; and

(b) no payment out of any sum in court shall be made without a court order.

(Rule 21.10 deals with compromise etc. by or on behalf of a child or patient)

(2) Where the court gives a claimant permission to accept a Part 36 offer or payment after the trial has started—

(a) any money in court may be paid out only with a court order; and

(b) the court must, in the order, deal with the whole costs of the proceedings.

(3) Where a claimant accepts a Part 36 payment after a defence of tender before claim has been put forward by the defendant, the money in court may be paid out only after an order of the court.

(Rule 37.3 requires a defendant who wishes to rely on a defence of tender before claim to make a payment into court)

36.19 Restriction on disclosure of a Part 36 offer or a Part 36 payment

46.35 (1) A Part 36 offer will be treated as 'without prejudice except as to costs'.

(2) The fact that a Part 36 payment has been made shall not be communicated to the trial judge until all questions of liability and the amount of money to be awarded have been decided.

(3) Paragraph (2) does not apply—

(a) where the defence of tender before claim has been raised;

(b) where the proceedings have been stayed under rule 36.15 following acceptance of a Part 36 offer or Part 36 payment; or

(c) where—

(i) the issue of liability has been determined before any assessment of the money claimed; and

(ii) the fact that there has or has not been a Part 36 payment may be relevant to the question of the costs of the issue of liability.

36.20 Costs consequences where claimant fails to do better than a Part 36 offer or a Part 36 payment

46.36 (1) This rule applies where at trial a claimant—

(a) fails to better a Part 36 payment; or

(b) fails to obtain a judgment which is more advantageous than a defendant's Part 36 offer.

(2) Unless it considers it unjust to do so, the court will order the claimant to pay any costs incurred by the defendant after the latest date on which the payment or offer could have been accepted without needing the permission of the court.

(Rule 36.11 sets out the time for acceptance of a defendant's Part 36 offer or Part 36 payment)

36.21 Costs and other consequences where claimant does better than he proposed in his Part 36 offer

46.37 (1) This rule applies where at trial—

(a) a defendant is held liable for more; or

(b) the judgment against a defendant is more advantageous to the claimant, than the proposals contained in a claimant's Part 36 offer.

(2) The court may order interest on the whole or part of any sum of money (excluding interest) awarded to the claimant at a rate not exceeding 10% above base rate for some or all of the period starting with the latest date on which the defendant could have accepted the offer without needing the permission of the court.

(3) The court may also order that the claimant is entitled to—

(a) his costs on the indemnity basis from the latest date when the defendant could have accepted the offer without needing the permission of the court; and

(b) interest on those costs at a rate not exceeding 10% above base rate.

(4) Where this rule applies, the court will make the orders referred to in paragraphs (2) and (3) unless it considers it unjust to do so.

(Rule 36.12 sets out the latest date when the defendant could have accepted the offer)

(5) In considering whether it would be unjust to make the orders referred to in paragraphs (2) and (3) above, the court will take into account all the circumstances of the case including—

(a) the terms of any Part 36 offer;

(b) the stage in the proceedings when any Part 36 offer or Part 36 payment was made;

(c) the information available to the parties at the time when the Part 36 offer or Part 36 payment was made; and

(d) the conduct of the parties with regard to the giving or refusing to give information for the purposes of enabling the offer or payment into court to be made or evaluated.

(6) Where the court awards interest under this rule and also awards interest on the same sum and for the same period under any other power, the total rate of interest may not exceed 10% above base rate.

36.22 Interest

(1) Unless—   **46.38**

(a) a claimant's Part 36 offer which offers to accept a sum of money; or

(b) a Part 36 payment notice,

indicates to the contrary, any such offer or payment will be treated as inclusive of all interest until the last date on which it could be accepted without needing the permission of the court.

(2) Where a claimant's Part 36 offer or Part 36 payment notice is expressed not to be inclusive of interest, the offer or notice must state—

(a) whether interest is offered; and

(b) if so, the amount offered, the rate or rates offered and the period or periods for which it is offered.

36.23 Deduction of benefits

(1) This rule applies where a payment to a claimant following acceptance of a Part 36 offer **46.39** or Part 36 payment into court would be a compensation payment as defined in section 1 of the Social Security (Recovery of Benefits) Act 1997.

(2) A defendant to a money claim may make an offer to settle the claim which will have the consequences set out in this Part, without making a Part 36 payment if—

(a) at the time he makes the offer he has applied for, but not received, a certificate of recoverable benefit; and

(b) he makes a Part 36 payment not more than 7 days after he receives the certificate.

(Section 1 of the 1997 Act defines 'recoverable benefit')

(3) A Part 36 payment notice must state—

(a) the amount of gross compensation;

(b) the name and amount of any benefit by which that gross amount is reduced in accordance with section 8 and Schedule 2 to the 1997 Act; and

(c) that the sum paid in is the net amount after deduction of the amount of benefit.

(4) For the purposes of rule 36.20, a claimant fails to better a Part 36 payment if he fails to obtain judgment for more than the gross sum specified in the Part 36 payment notice.

(5) Where—

(a) a Part 36 payment has been made; and

(b) application is made for the money remaining in court to be paid out,

the court may treat the money in court as being reduced by a sum equivalent to any further recoverable benefits paid to the claimant since the date of payment into court and may direct payment out accordingly.

PD 36—OFFERS TO SETTLE AND PAYMENTS INTO COURT

Part 36 Offers and Part 36 payments

46.40   1.1 A written offer to settle a claim or part of a claim or any issue that arises in it made in accordance with the provisions of Part 36 is called:

(1) if made by way of a payment into court, a Part 36 payment, or

(2) if made otherwise, a Part 36 offer.

1.2 A Part 36 offer or Part 36 payment has the costs and other consequences set out in rules 36.13, 36.14, 36.20 and 36.21.

1.3 An offer to settle which is not made in accordance with Part 36 will only have the consequences specified in that Part if the court so orders and will be given such weight on any issue as to costs as the court thinks appropriate.

Parties and Part 36 offers

46.41   2.1 A Part 36 offer, subject to paragraph 3 below, may be made by any party.

2.2 The party making an offer is the 'offeror' and the party to whom it is made is the 'offeree'.

2.3 A Part 36 offer may consist of a proposal to settle for a specified sum or for some other remedy.

2.4 A Part 36 offer is made when received by the offeree.

2.5 An improvement to a Part 36 offer is effective when its details are received by the offeree.

Parties and Part 36 payments

46.42   3.1 An offer to settle for a specified sum made by a defendant must, in order to comply with Part 36, be made by way of a Part 36 payment into court.

3.2 A Part 36 payment is made when the Part 36 payment notice is served on the claimant.

3.3 An increase to a Part 36 payment will be effective when notice of the increase is served on the claimant.

(For service of the Part 36 payment notice see rule 36.6(3) and (4).)

3.4 A defendant who wishes to withdraw or reduce a Part 36 payment must obtain the court's permission to do so.

3.5 Permission may be obtained by making an application in accordance with Part 23 stating the reasons giving rise to the wish to withdraw or reduce the Part 36 payment.

Making a Part 36 payment

46.43   4.1 To make a Part 36 payment the defendant must file the following documents:

(1) where that court is a county court or a district registry—

(a) the Part 36 payment notice, and

(b) the payment, usually a cheque made payable to Her Majesty's Pay-master General,

with the court, and

(2) where that court is the Royal Courts of Justice—

(a) the Part 36 payment notice with the court, and

(b) the payment, usually a cheque made payable to the Accountant General of the Supreme Court, and

(c) a sealed copy of the Claim Form,

(d) the Court Funds Office form 100 with the Court Funds Office.

Part 36 Offers and Part 36 payments—general provisions

5.1 A Part 36 offer or a Part 36 payment notice must: **46.44**

    (1) state that it is a Part 36 offer or that the payment into court is a Part 36 payment, and

    (2) be signed by the offeror or his legal representative.

5.2 The contents of a Part 36 offer must also comply with the requirements of rule 36.5(3), (5) and (6).

5.3 The contents of a Part 36 payment notice must comply with rule 36.6(2) and, if rule 36.23 applies, with rule 36.23(3).

5.4 A Part 36 offer or Part 36 payment will be taken to include interest unless it is expressly stated in the offer or the payment notice that interest is not included, in which case the details set out in rule 36.22(2) must be given.

5.5 Where a Part 36 offer is made by a company or other corporation, a person holding a senior position in the company or corporation may sign the offer on the offeror's behalf, but must state the position he holds.

5.6 Each of the following persons is a person holding a senior position:

    (1) in respect of a registered company or corporation, a director, the treasurer, secretary, chief executive, manager or other officer of the company or corporation, and

    (2) in respect of a corporation which is not a registered company, in addition to those persons set out in (1), the mayor, chairman, president, town clerk or similar officer of the corporation.

Clarification of Part 36 offer or payment

6.1 An offeree may apply to the court for an order requiring the offeror to clarify the terms of **46.45** a Part 36 offer or Part 36 payment notice (a clarification order) where the offeror has failed to comply within 7 days with a request for clarification.

6.2 An application for a clarification order should be made in accordance with Part 23.

6.3 The application notice should state the respects in which the terms of the Part 36 offer or Part 36 payment notice, as the case may be, are said to need clarification.

Acceptance of a Part 36 offer or payment

7.1 The times for accepting a Part 36 offer or a Part 36 payment are set out in rules 36.11 and **46.46** 36.12.

7.2 The general rule is that a Part 36 offer or Part 36 payment made more than 21 days before the start of the trial may be accepted within 21 days after it was made without the permission of the court. The costs consequences set out in rules 36.13 and 36.14 will then come into effect.

7.3 A Part 36 offer or Part 36 payment made less than 21 days before the start of the trial cannot be accepted without the permission of the court unless the parties agree what the costs consequences of acceptance will be.

7.4 The permission of the court may be sought:

    (1) before the start of the trial, by making an application in accordance with Part 23, and

    (2) after the start of the trial, by making an application to the trial judge.

7.5 If the court gives permission it will make an order dealing with costs and may order that, in the circumstances, the costs consequences set out in rules 36.13 and 36.14 will apply.

7.6 Where a Part 36 offer or Part 36 payment is accepted in accordance with rule 36.11(1) or rule 36.12(1) the notice of acceptance must be sent to the offeror and filed with the court.

7.7 The notice of acceptance:

    (1) must set out—

(a) the claim number, and

(b) the title of the proceedings,

(2) must identify the Part 36 offer or Part 36 payment notice to which it relates, and

(3) must be signed by the offeree or his legal representative (see paragraphs [5.5 and 5.6] above).

7.8 Where:

(1) the court's approval, or

(2) an order for payment of money out of court, or

(3) an order apportioning money in court—

(a) between the Fatal Accidents Act 1976 and the Law Reform (Miscellaneous Provisions) Act 1934, or

(b) between the persons entitled to it under the Fatal Accidents Act 1976, is required for acceptance of a Part 36 offer or Part 36 payment, application for the approval or the order should be made in accordance with Part 23.

7.9 The court will include in any order made under paragraph 7.8 above a direction for;

(1) the payment out of the money in court, and

(2) the payment of interest.

7.10 Unless the parties have agreed otherwise:

(1) interest accruing up to the date of acceptance will be paid to the offeror, and

(2) interest accruing as from the date of acceptance until payment out will be paid to the offeree.

7.11 A claimant may not accept a Part 36 payment which is part of a defendant's offer to settle the whole of a claim consisting of both a money and a non-money claim unless at the same time he accepts the offer to settle the whole of the claim. Therefore:

(1) if a claimant accepts a Part 36 payment which is part of a defendant's offer to settle the whole of the claim, or

(2) if a claimant accepts a Part 36 offer which is part of a defendant's offer to settle the whole of the claim,

the claimant will be deemed to have accepted the offer to settle the whole of the claim.

(See paragraph 8 below for the method of obtaining money out of court.)

Payment out of court

46.47   8.1 To obtain money out of court following acceptance of a Part 36 payment, the claimant should file a request for payment with the court.

8.2 The request for payment should contain the following details:

(1) where the party receiving the payment—

(a) is legally represented—

(i) the name, business address and reference of the legal representative, and

(ii) the name of the bank and the sort code number, the title of the account and the account number where the payment is to be transmitted, and

(2) where the party is acting in person—

(a) his name and address, and

(b) his bank account details as in (ii) above.

8.3 Where the request for payment is made to the Royal Courts of Justice, the claimant should also complete Court Funds Office form 201 and file it in the Court Funds Office.

8.4 Subject to paragraph 8.5(1) and (2), if a party does not wish the payment to be transmitted into his bank account or if he does not have a bank account, he may send a written request to the Accountant-General for the payment to be made to him by cheque.

8.5 Where a party seeking payment out of court has provided the necessary information, the payment:

(1) where a party is legally represented, must be made to the legal representative,

(2) if the party is not legally represented but is, or has been, in receipt of legal aid in respect of the proceedings and a notice to that effect has been filed, should be made to the Legal Aid Board by direction of the court,

(3) where a person entitled to money in court dies without having made a will and the court is satisfied—

(a) that no grant of administration of his estate has been made, and

(b) that the assets of his estate, including the money in court, do not exceed in value the amount specified in any order in force under section 6 of the Administration of Estates (Small Payments) Act 1965,

may be ordered to be made to the person appearing to have the prior right to a grant of administration of the estate of the deceased, e.g. a widower, widow, child, father, mother, brother or sister of the deceased.

Foreign currency

9.1 Money may be paid into court in a foreign currency: **46.48**

(1) where it is a Part 36 payment and the claim is in a foreign currency, or

(2) under a court order.

9.2 The court may direct that the money be placed in an interest bearing account in the currency of the claim or any other currency.

9.3 Where a Part 36 payment is made in a foreign currency and has not been accepted within 21 days, the defendant may apply for an order that the money be placed in an interest bearing account.

9.4 The application should be made in accordance with Part 23 and should state:

(1) that the payment has not been accepted in accordance with rule 36.11, and

(2) the type of currency on which interest is to accrue.

Compensation recovery

10.1 Where a defendant makes a Part 36 payment in respect of a claim for a sum or part of a **46.49**
sum:

(1) which fails under the heads of damage set out in column 1 of Schedule 2 of the Social Security (Recovery of Benefits) Act 1997 in respect of recoverable benefits received by the claimant as set out in column 2 of that Schedule, and

(2) where the defendant is liable to pay recoverable benefits to the Secretary of State,

the defendant should obtain from the Secretary of State a certificate of recoverable benefits and file the certificate with the Part 36 payment notice.

10.2 If a defendant wishes to offer to settle a claim where he has applied for but not yet received a certificate of recoverable benefits, he may, provided that he makes a Part 36 payment not more than 7 days after he has received the certificate, make a Part 36 offer which will have the costs and other consequences set out in rules 36.13 and 36.20.

10.3 The Part 36 payment notice should state in addition to the requirements set out in rule 36.6(2):

(1) the total amount represented by the Part 36 payment (the gross compensation),

(2) that the defendant has reduced this sum by £   , in accordance with section 8 of and Schedule 2 to the Social Security (Recovery of Benefits) Act 1997, which was calculated as follows:

Name of benefit   Amount

and

(3) that the amount paid in, being the sum of £ ___ is the net amount after the deduction of the amount of benefit.

10.4 On acceptance of a Part 36 payment to which this paragraph relates, a claimant will receive the sum in court which will be net of the recoverable benefits.

10.5 In establishing at trial whether a claimant has bettered or obtained a judgment more advantageous than a Part 36 payment to which this paragraph relates, the court will base its decision on the gross sum specified in the Part 36 payment notice.

General

46.50   11.1 Where a party on whom a Part 36 offer, a Part 36 payment notice or a notice of acceptance is to be served is legally represented, the Part 36 offer, Part 36 payment notice and notice of acceptance must be served on the legal representative.

11.2 In a claim arising out of an accident involving a motor vehicle on a road or in a public place:

(1) where the damages claimed include a sum for hospital expenses, and

(2) the defendant or his insurer pays that sum to the hospital under section 157 of the Road Traffic Act 1988,

the defendant must give notice of that payment to the court and all the other parties to the proceedings.

11.3 Money paid into court:

(1) as a Part 36 payment which is not accepted by the claimant, or

(2) under a court order,

will be placed after 21 days in a basic account (subject to paragraph 11.4 below) for interest to accrue.

11.4 Where money referred to in paragraph 11.3 above is paid in in respect of a child or patient it will be placed in a special investment account for interest to accrue.

(PD 21 contains information about the investment of money in court in respect of a child or patient)

(PD 40B and PD 40C contain information about adjustment of the judgment sum in respect of recoverable benefits, and about structured settlements)

(PD 41 contains information about provisional damages awards)

CPR PART 37—MISCELLANEOUS PROVISIONS ABOUT PAYMENTS INTO COURT

37.1 Money paid into court under a court order—general

46.51   (1) When a party makes a payment into court under a court order, the court will give notice of the payment to every other party.

(2) Money paid into court under a court order may not be paid out without the court's permission except where—

(a) the defendant treats the money as a Part 36 payment under rule 37.2; and

(b) the claimant accepts the Part 36 payment without needing the permission of the court.

(Rule 36.11 sets out when the claimant can accept a Part 36 payment without needing the permission of the court)

37.2 Money paid into court may be treated as a Part 36 payment

46.52   (1) Where a defendant makes a payment into court following an order made under rule 3.1(3) or 3.1(5) he may choose to treat the whole or any part of the money paid into court as a Part 36 payment.

(Rule 36.2 defines a Part 36 payment)

742

(2) To do this he must file a Part 36 payment notice.

(Rule 36.6 sets out what a Part 36 payment notice must contain and provides for the court to serve it on the other parties)

(3) If he does so Part 36 applies to the money as if he had paid it into court as a Part 36 payment.

37.4 Proceedings under Fatal Accidents Act 1976 and Law Reform (Miscellaneous Provisions) Act 1934—apportionment by court

(1) Where—   **46.53**
    (a) a claim includes claims arising under—
        (i) the Fatal Accidents Act 1976; and
        (ii) the Law Reform (Miscellaneous Provisions) Act 1934;
    (b) a single sum of money is paid into court in satisfaction of those claims; and
    (c) the money is accepted,
the court shall apportion the money between the different claims.

(2) The court shall apportion money under paragraph (1)—
    (a) when it gives directions under rule 21.11 (control of money received by a child or patient); or
    (b) if rule 21.11 does not apply, when it gives permission for the money to be paid out of court.

(3) Where, in an action in which a claim under the Fatal Accidents Act 1976 is made by or on behalf of more than one person—
    (a) a sum in respect of damages is ordered or agreed to be paid in satisfaction of the claim; or
    (b) a sum of money is accepted in satisfaction of the claim,
the court shall apportion it between the persons entitled to it unless it has already been apportioned by the court, a jury, or agreement between the parties.

PD 37—MISCELLANEOUS PROVISIONS ABOUT PAYMENTS INTO COURT

For information about payments into and out of court in relation to offers to settle see Part 36 and the Practice Direction which supplements it.

Payments into court under an order

1.1 Where money is paid into court under an order, the party making the payment should: **46.54**
    (1) lodge his payment, and
    (2) file a copy of the order directing payment into court.

1.2 Where the order is made in a county court or district registry the payment will usually be made by cheque payable to Her Majesty's Paymaster General.

1.3 Where the order is made in the Royal Courts of Justice, the payment will usually be made by cheque payable to the Accountant-General of the Supreme Court, and should be:
    (1) accompanied by
        (a) a completed Court Funds Office form 100 or 101, and
        (b) a sealed copy of the order, and
    (2) lodged in the Court Funds Office.

A copy of the Court Funds Office receipt should be filed in the appropriate court office in the Royal Courts of Justice.

[Defence of tender]

General

46.55   3.1 Where money is paid into court:

(1) under an order permitting a defendant to defend or to continue to defend under r 37.2(1), or

(2) in support of a defence of tender under r. 37.3,

the party making the payment may, if a defendant, choose to treat the whole or any part of the money as a Part 36 payment.

3.2 In order to do so the defendant must file a Part 36 payment notice in accordance with r. 36.6 (see also PD 36, para. 5).

3.3 Rule 37.4 deals with the apportionment of money paid into court in respect of claims arising under:

(1) the Fatal Accidents Act 1976, and

(2) the Law Reform (Miscellaneous Provisions) Act 1934.

(See also PD 36, para. 7.8)

Payment out of court

46.56   4.1 Except where money which has been paid into court is treated as a Part 36 payment and can be accepted by the claimant without needing the court's permission, the court's permission is required to take the money out of court.

4.2 Permission may be obtained by making an application in accordance with Part 23. The application notice must state the grounds on which the order for payment out is sought. Evidence of any facts on which the applicant relies may also be necessary.

4.3 To obtain the money out of court the applicant must comply with the provisions of PD 36, para. 8, where they apply.

Foreign currency

46.57   5 For information on payments into court made in a foreign currency, see PD 36, para. 9.

47

COSTS

A. General Principles

The central principle about liability for costs is that the unsuccessful party will **47.01** be ordered to pay the costs of the successful party. This general rule is restated in r 44.3(2) (*Blackstone's Civil Practice 2004* 1706; hereafter *Blackstone*). However the CPR have introduced greater flexibility, and therefore uncertainty, both as to the question where liability for costs will fall and as to the amount that will be ordered to be paid. Costs are a matter of discretion, but the discretion must be exercised judicially, on proper grounds relevant to the facts of the case.

The flexibility arises from r 44.3(4)–(6) (*Blackstone* 1707) by which the court **47.02** is required to have regard to all the circumstances including the conduct of all the parties, the outcome on parts of the case as well as the totality, and any admissible offers to settle. These matters must always be considered even if the outcome of the consideration is a simple order that costs will follow the event in accordance with the general rule. If the consideration of these matters leads the court to make a different order, there is a wide range of orders that can be made falling short of a full award of costs, apportioning liability by periods of time, by amount, by a fraction, or by particular parts or steps in the proceedings.

The CPR have also seen an increased importance being given to the distinction **47.03** between costs assessed on the standard basis and costs assessed on the indemnity basis. It is plain that an assessment on the standard basis is likely to result in an award which falls substantially short of the litigant's actual liability for the fees of his legal representatives, even though the implication of this is that costs must have been incurred which were not reasonably necessary and proportionate in order to pursue the claim. A successful claimant may also receive a success fee under a conditional fee agreement; however, the proper purpose of success fees is to compensate for the loss incurred in cases which are unsuccessful. Before the CPR, costs could only be obtained on the indemnity basis where the conduct of the paying party was open to serious criticism. This use of the power to award indemnity basis costs continues, but in addition the provision for indemnity costs under Part 36 following a claimant's successful settlement offer has led the courts to be more willing to make an award of costs on the indemnity basis without misconduct. On the indemnity basis there is a good prospect that the litigant's actual liability for the fees of his legal representatives will be met in full, because considerations of proportionality do not arise (r 44.5, *Blackstone* 1709).

47.04 The detailed rules about costs take up Parts 43–48 of the CPR. A lengthy Practice Direction about Costs (*Blackstone* 1735) supplements Parts 43–48 and amounts to a comprehensive guide to issues about costs. There is also a series of model bills of costs.

B. Fixed Costs

47.05 Nearly all applications for costs needed to be assessed by the court if there is no agreement between the parties. Although there continues to be pressure in some quarters for a regime of fixed costs in lower value claims, as Lord Woolf initially proposed, progress has been slow. There are fixed costs which apply on the commencement of a claim which is resolved at an early stage and on the entry of judgment, set out in Part 45 (*Blackstone* 1713) and PD Costs, sections 24 and 25 (*Blackstone* 1761). These are the costs allowed in the small claims track. Rules 45.7–45.14 (*Blackstone* 1716) also set out predictable costs to be awarded in cost only proceedings in road traffic accident claims with agreed damages of less than £10,000. In the fast track the amount of costs to be awarded for advocacy at the trial is fixed by r 46.2 (*Blackstone* 1719) but the other costs of the proceedings are variable and will be assessed at the end of the case.

C. Estimates of Costs

47.06 One of the ways in which the CPR aim to control the costs of litigation is by requiring solicitors to keep track of the costs incurred and the projected future costs of a claim. The main rules about estimates of costs are in section 6 of PD

Costs (*Blackstone* 1743). An estimate of base costs and disbursements can be ordered by the court at any stage but in particular the rules require that an estimate of base costs and disbursements already incurred and to be incurred must be filed by a party's solicitor with the allocation questionnaire in any claim outside the scope of the small claims track, and the estimate must also be served on the other parties and on the client. Then on filing a pre-trial checklist in any claim on the fast track or the multi-track, an updated estimate of costs must be filed with the court and served on the other parties and on the client. Compliance with these obligations is not in practice reliable.

The estimate of costs is not decisive of the amount that may be recovered on assessment at a later stage, but para 6.6 of PD Costs (*Blackstone* 1743) provides that on an assessment of costs the court may have regard to any estimate previously filed by any party in the same proceedings, and the estimate may be taken into account as a factor, among others, when assessing the reasonableness of any costs claimed. **47.07**

Leigh v Michelin Tyre plc [2003] EWCA Civ 1766; [2004] 1 WLR 846   The claimant's cost estimate at allocation had been £6,000 but after settlement the bill was £21,740 and the award was £20,490. On the defendant's appeal, it was held that the cost estimate had been hopelessly inadequate and the discrepancy had not been properly explained, but a more accurate estimate would not have made any difference to the case management, and the costs as assessed were reasonable and proportionate. The claimant was not bound by the original estimate and was entitled to the assessed costs. A significant discrepancy between an estimate and a bill of costs may call for an explanation, without which the court would be entitled to conclude that the costs claimed are unreasonable. **47.08**

D. Orders for Costs

The forms of order about costs that are commonly made are explained in PD Costs, para 8.5 (*Blackstone* 1744): **47.09**

'Costs' or 'Costs in any event' means that the party in whose favour the order is made is entitled to the costs in respect of the part of the proceedings to which the order relates, whatever other costs orders are made in the proceedings.

'Costs in the case' or 'Costs in the application' means that the party in whose favour the court makes an order for costs at the end of the proceedings is entitled to his costs of the part of the proceedings to which the order relates.

'Costs reserved' means that the decision about costs is deferred to a later occasion, but if no later order is made the costs will be costs in the case.

'Claimant's/Defendant's costs in the case/application' means that if the party in whose favour the costs order is made is awarded costs at the end of the proceedings, that party is entitled to his costs of the part of the proceedings to which the order relates. If any other party is awarded costs at the end of the proceedings, the party in whose favour the final costs order is made is not liable to pay the costs of any other party in respect of a part of the proceedings to which the order relates.

'Costs thrown away' means that where, for example, a judgment or order is set aside, the party in whose favour the costs order is made is entitled to the costs which have been incurred as a consequence. This includes the costs of:

(a) preparing for and attending any hearing at which the judgment or order which has been set aside was made;

(b) preparing for and attending any hearing to set aside the judgment or order in question;

(c) preparing for and attending any hearing at which the court orders the proceedings or the part in question to be adjourned;

(d) any steps taken to enforce a judgment or order which has subsequently been set aside.

'Costs of and caused by' means that where, for example, the court makes this order on an application to amend a statement of case, the party in whose favour the costs order is made is entitled to the costs of preparing for and attending the application and the costs of any consequential amendments to his own statement of case.

'Costs here and below' means that the party in whose favour the costs order is made is entitled not only to his costs in respect of the proceedings in which the court makes the order but also to his costs of the proceedings in any lower court.

'No order as to costs' or 'Each party to pay his own costs' means that each party is to bear his own costs of the part of the proceedings to which the order relates whatever costs order the court makes at the end of the proceedings.

E. Summary Assessment

47.10 Where costs are to be assessed by the court, there can be a summary assessment at the conclusion of the hearing, or there can be a detailed assessment as a separate procedure after the conclusion of the case. Summary assessment will allow only a brief consideration of the items claimed, but it will provide an effective and proportionate means of dealing with the assessment of costs in relatively straightforward and moderate value claims. PD Costs, section 13 (*Blackstone* 1748) sets out the rules for summary assessment, and para 13.2 makes it the general rule that there will be a summary assessment at the conclusion of a fast track trial, dealing with the costs of the whole claim, and at the conclusion of any application lasting no more than a day, when the assessment will only deal with the costs of the application unless the outcome has disposed of the whole claim, in which case the assessment can deal with the costs of the whole claim.

The parties must prepare in advance a statement of costs which will be the basis **47.11** of the summary assessment. The statement should be prepared in accordance with Form N260, giving the information set out in para 13.5(2) of PD Costs, which must be filed with the court and served on the other parties at least 24 hours before the date fixed for the hearing. The accuracy of this statement is clearly important: it must be verified by the signature of the party or his legal representative, which operates as the solicitor's certificate as an officer of the court that the schedule is accurate and claims no more than the client's liability to his solicitor (the indemnity principle). The summary assessment takes into account proportionality, but should involve a reasoned consideration of the costs set out in the schedule rather than the arbitrary substitution of an alternative figure. If the proceedings have involved any unusual factors which have resulted in costs being incurred at a higher level than would be normal, it is important to ensure that the advocate at the hearing is given sufficient information to be able to explain and justify the claims made in the schedule. The summary assessment can include the assessment of any additional liability, that is to say the success fee and insurance premium under a conditional fee agreement.

MacDonald v Taree Holdings [2001] CPLR 431   It is a disproportionate **47.12** response to a failure to serve a schedule of costs in time to hold that this results in the loss of all entitlement to costs or a detailed assessment. The court should consider adjourning to give the paying party time to consider the statement of costs. However, the failure to serve a schedule would be taken into account in the summary assessment.

F. Detailed Assessment

A detailed assessment of costs will be necessary when there is no summary **47.13** assessment and the parties are unable to agree. Therefore it applies to claims which are resolved by settlement without the need for a final hearing, and to cases on the multi-track for which a summary assessment will be inappropriate. The procedure for detailed assessment is set out in Part 47 (*Blackstone* 1722) and in PD Costs sections 31–47 (*Blackstone* 1764–1776). These rules set out a detailed code for the preparation of a bill of costs in the standard form consistent with the requirements of PD Costs section 4 (*Blackstone* 1737) and as demonstrated in the precedents of bills of costs which follow PD Costs (*Blackstone* CD-ROM). The paying party will respond to the bill with Points of Dispute and the receiving party is entitled to serve a reply if appropriate. The hearing follows, in which the costs judge decides whether costs were reasonably incurred or were reasonable and proportionate in amount, having regard to all the circumstances and in particular the factors set out in r 44.5(3) (*Blackstone* 1709). The costs judge will also deal with the costs of the assessment itself, and r 47.19 (*Blackstone* 1728) allows for written offers of settlement to be made in relation to the assessment by a procedure comparable with Part 36. A detailed assessment will not usually be carried out until after the proceedings have reached a conclusion, although the court has a power to make an order for payment on account under r 44.3(8) (*Blackstone* 1707) which is frequently exercised when a decision on liability for costs has been made, subject to detailed assessment.

G. Success Fees and Insurance Premiums

47.14 Many personal injury claims are pursued on behalf of the claimant under a conditional fee agreement or a collective conditional fee agreement. If the claim is successful and the appropriate formalities have been complied with, the claimant is entitled to recover on the assessment of costs not only the normal or 'base' costs of the claim but also the additional liability consisting of the percentage success fee claimed by the claimant's solicitor and the insurance premium (or the charge of an approved membership organization such as a trade union) giving protection against a liability for adverse costs. The additional liability cannot be assessed until the conclusion of the proceedings, even if some of the base costs may have been assessed during the course of the proceedings. The general rules about costs and funding arrangements can be found at r 44.3A and B (*Blackstone* 1707), r 44.15 (*Blackstone* 1712), and in PD Costs at paras 11.8– 11.11 (*Blackstone* 1747) and section 19 (*Blackstone* 1752). The level of success fees has now been fixed by the rules for road traffic accidents. By r 45.16 the success fee for solicitors is 100% where the claim concludes at trial, or 12.5% where the claim concludes before a trial has commenced or the dispute is settled before a claim is issued. Levels of success fee for employers liability claims have been agreed in the Civil Justice Council but have not yet been incorporated in the rules.

H. Refusing Alternative Dispute Resolution

Halsey v Milton Keynes NHS Trust [2004] EWCA Civ 576   Rule 44.5(3)(ii)   **47.15**
requires the court when deciding costs to have regard to the efforts made, if any,
before and during the proceedings in order to try to resolve the dispute. Where
one party refuses to agree to alternative dispute resolution (ADR), this will only
have an impact on liability for costs if the refusing party's refusal was unreasonable. The burden is on the unsuccessful party to show why there should be a
departure from the general rule that costs should follow the event. The court
should bear in mind the advantages of ADR, and should take into account the
nature of the dispute, the merits of the case, the extent to which other settlement methods have been attempted, whether the costs of ADR would be disproportionately high, whether the delay involved in ADR would be prejudicial,
whether ADR had a reasonable prospect of success, and whether it had been
encouraged by the court. The court cannot compel parties to follow ADR,
which would be an unacceptable constraint on the right of access to the court
contrary to Article 6 of the European Convention on Human Rights.

I. Wasted Costs

A legal representative whose improper, unreasonable, or negligent conduct has   **47.16**
resulted in costs being unnecessarily incurred may be the subject of an order for
'wasted costs' under s 51(6) of the Supreme Court Act 1981, implemented by
r 48.7 (*Blackstone* 1733) and section 53 of PD Costs (*Blackstone* 1779). In order
to discourage disproportionate satellite litigation, the test is a high one.

Ridehalgh v Horsefield [1994] Ch 205   This is the leading case on the test for   **47.17**
deciding whether conduct is improper, unreasonable, or negligent. Unreasonable conduct includes that which is designed to harass the other side rather than
advance the resolution of the case, and it makes no difference that the conduct is
the product of excessive zeal and not improper motive.

An application for wasted costs is not normally made until the end of the   **47.18**
proceedings, and the legal representative whose conduct is challenged must be
given an opportunity to respond to the application. The legal representative will
need the consent of his client in order to divulge to the court matters that are
covered by privilege in answering the application.

48

APPEALS

The rules are to be found in the Access to Justice Act 1999, the Access to Justice **48.01** (Destination of Appeals) Order 2000, CPR Part 52, and PD 52. As ever with the Civil Procedure Rules, you need fingers in at least two places to understand the rules.

A. Permission to Appeal

Every appeal relevant to personal injury cases requires permission. The test for **48.02** granting permission on a first appeal is that *the appeal would have a real prospect of success*. This test is not intended to exclude any reasonably arguable appeal. By contrast, the stricter test for permission to make a second appeal to the Court of Appeal is intended to prevent many appeals.

The overriding objective applies, and in case management appeals it is also **48.03** relevant to the grant of permission:

(a) whether the significance of the issue justifies the costs;
(b) whether the significance of the issue justifies the procedural con-sequences, for example, loss of a trial date;
(c) whether it would be more convenient to decide the issue at trial.

Permission can be limited in scope, for example to a specific defined issue, and **48.04** can be granted subject to conditions. The lower court and the appeal court can each grant permission. Application should first be made orally to the lower court at the hearing to be appealed but there is no sanction except the loss of opportunity if this is not done.

48.05   If the trial court refuses permission to appeal, *the time limit for applying to the appeal court for permission is 14 days* from the lower court decision unless the lower court directs otherwise. It is always sensible to ask for an extension of time because a good deal of paperwork will have to be prepared in order to apply to the appeal court for permission, but the lower court should not direct a time of more than 28 days. The appeal court can grant an extension but the parties cannot do this by agreement. In *Customs & Excise v Eastwood Care Homes* [2001] CP Rep 18, the court took a flexible approach.

48.06   A standard form appellant's notice must be used, to include an application for permission if this is to be made to the appeal court. Permission can be decided on paper, but if it is refused an oral hearing can be requested. If the appeal court refuses permission at an oral hearing, there is no further appeal from this decision.

48.07   At the end of a hearing an advocate who wishes to appeal should:

(a) apply orally for permission; and at the same time
(b) apply for an extension of time to 28 days, to renew the application for permission if refused by the lower court or to obtain a transcript and serve an appellant's notice if granted; and
(c) apply for a stay of the order granted: permission to appeal does not operate as a stay of the order and if a stay is not granted the successful party is entitled to enforce the order made regardless of the intention to appeal. In general a stay is likely to be granted if permission to appeal has been granted, but not otherwise.

48.08   For a second appeal to the Court of Appeal, permission to appeal can only be granted by the Court of Appeal. The criteria are that the appeal *would raise an important point of principle or practice, or there is some other compelling reason* for the Court of Appeal to hear it. This is intended to be a high hurdle. Second appeals are to be rare.

48.09   *P & O Nedlloyd v Utaniko* [2003] EWCA Civ 174; [2003] 1 Lloyd's Rep 265   The claimant succeeded at trial, beating its Part 36 offer and receiving costs on the indemnity basis as a result. The defendant brought an unsuccessful appeal. The Court of Appeal refused to award the claimant costs of the appeal on the indemnity basis relying on the same Part 36 offer. A separate offer should have been made in relation to the appeal.

B. Procedure

It is necessary to file at the appeal court with the appellant's notice a full bundle **48.10** including a transcript or reliable record of the decision appealed and a skeleton argument for the appeal. The front loading of work applies to appeals as it does to the new procedure for actions.

The documents must be served on the respondent in seven days. Any **48.11** respondent's notice must be served in 14 days from notice of the grant of permission and a respondent's skeleton argument must be filed in 21 days from service of the appellant's skeleton (normally with the appeal notice). A respondent's notice is needed if the respondent also wishes to appeal against the order (for which he also needs permission), or if he wishes to argue that the decision of the lower court should be upheld on different grounds. This applies at all levels of appeal court, not just the Court of Appeal.

C. Grounds of Appeal

The grounds of a first appeal are that the decision of the lower court was **48.12**

(a) wrong, or
(b) unjust because of a serious procedural or other irregularity.

As a general rule an appeal will take the form of a review of the decision of the lower court, though there is power to order a rehearing if it is in the interests of justice. A review means that the appeal court will consider the record of the evidence at the lower court, will draw any proper inferences from that evidence, but will not hear the witnesses again or admit any new evidence.

The same ground for deciding an appeal applies to all appeals. The old rule **48.13** that interlocutory appeals take the form of a rehearing and a fresh exercise of discretion has gone. The issue is now whether the lower court's exercise of discretion 'has exceeded the generous ambit within which a reasonable disagreement is possible' (Brooke LJ in the leading case of *Tanfern Ltd v Cameron-Macdonald* [2000] 1 WLR 1311 at para 32, quoting *G v G* [1985] 1 WLR 647).

This new approach means that even in case management issues, since the **48.14** appeal court will review the decision of the lower court rather than make its own decision, it is crucial to provide the appeal court with an accurate record of the reasons for the decision of the lower court. Every judicial decision has to include a clear statement of the reasons for the decision, not least as a part of the requirement for a fair trial under the Human Rights Act 1998 and Article 6 of the European Convention on Human Rights. There ought to be a tape recording made of all civil court proceedings and one of the first and urgent steps to be taken in any appeal is to obtain a transcript. Ask the County Court Office for Form 107. It may take some days to obtain a transcript, and a clear handwritten note of the judgment will be invaluable for preparing the grounds of appeal.

48.15 Fresh evidence can only be admitted with permission. Criteria similar to those in *Ladd v Marshall* [1954] 1 WLR 1489, interpreted alongside the overriding objective, are likely to apply and to restrict the discretion to exceptional cases. The *Ladd v Marshall* conditions are that the evidence:

    (a) could not have been obtained with reasonable diligence for use at the trial;

    (b) is such that if given it would probably have an important influence on the result of the case, though it need not be decisive;

    (c) is such as is presumably to be believed, apparently credible though it need not be incontrovertible.

48.16 *Hertfordshire Investments v Bubb*, *The Times*, 31 August 2000 In an application to introduce fresh evidence on an appeal, there may be greater indulgence to a party at the early stages of a case when it is more understandable if all relevant evidence had not been collected at the time of the lower court's decision.

48.17 There is a power to leapfrog an appeal to the Court of Appeal. A lower court can order that an appeal be transferred to the Court of Appeal on the same grounds as the Court of Appeal would apply; but the Master of the Rolls can send it back if he does not agree that a Court of Appeal hearing is appropriate. This is a power which might be exercised, for example, when an appeal raises an issue of importance or controversy such that the view of the Court of Appeal ought to be given quickly, and it enables the appeal to leapfrog over the first appeal level to circuit judge or High Court judge with a saving of costs and time.

48.18 Appeals to the House of Lords are not affected by the Civil Procedure Rules and are so rare that the rules are not considered here. The House of Lords is the second venue for an appeal from a High Court judge in a multi-track final decision. A point of law of general public importance must be certified by the Court of Appeal or the House of Lords. The detailed procedures require specialist research and are included in volume 2 of the *White Book*.

If an appeal is granted, the appeal court has very wide and flexible powers **48.19** including all the case management powers of the lower court.

D. To which Court does an Appeal Lie?

The major change in the new rules is that there is now an increased range of **48.20** appeals made to a single High Court judge rather than to the Court of Appeal.

(1) Small Claims Cases

The same principles now apply to small claims appeals as to the other tracks. **48.21** Appeal from a district judge is to a circuit judge, and where an appeal is dismissed at a hearing, from circuit judge to the Court of Appeal subject to the restrictions on second appeals. When a circuit judge hears a small claim, appeal is to a High Court judge.

(2) Fast Track Cases

Appeal from a district judge is to a circuit judge, with a second appeal to the **48.22** Court of Appeal subject to the restrictions on second appeals. (However, there is no further appeal from a circuit judge refusing permission to appeal at a hearing.) When a circuit judge hears a fast track claim, appeal is to a single High Court judge.

(3) Multi-track Cases

It is necessary to decide whether the decision to be appealed is a final decision. A **48.23** final decision is one which finally determines (subject to appeal and costs) the entire proceedings whichever way the court decides the issues before it. Where a trial has been split into parts, a decision is final at the conclusion of a hearing which, if it had been made at the conclusion of an all embracing hearing, would have been final (art 1(2) of the Destination of Appeals Order 2000). This cumbersome rule has the effect that a decision on any component of a split trial of liability, limitation or assessment of damages is treated as final. However, the precise scope of the rule is not easy to define. An order striking out proceedings, or striking out a statement of case, or giving summary judgment clearly is not final, because the decision only ends the case if it is decided in one of the possible ways.

(4) Multi-track Case Final Decisions

Whether from district judge, Master, circuit judge, or High Court judge, **48.24** whether High Court or county court, first appeal is to the Court of Appeal and second appeal is to the House of Lords.

(5) Multi-track Cases Other than Final Decisions

48.25 A first appeal lies:

    (a) from a district judge in the county court to a circuit judge;

    (b) from a district judge in the High Court to a High Court judge;

    (c) from a circuit judge in the county court to a High Court judge; and

    (d) from a High Court judge to the Court of Appeal.

Special rules apply to an appeal from a costs officer on a detailed assessment. Permission to appeal is not required, an appeal lies to a circuit judge and is a rehearing.

48.26 The guideline case is *Tanfern Ltd v Cameron-Macdonald* [2000] 1 WLR 1311.

E. CPR Part 52—Appeals

I GENERAL RULES ABOUT APPEALS

52.1 Scope and interpretation

48.27   (1) The rules in this Part apply to appeals to—

        (a) the civil division of the Court of Appeal;

        (b) the High Court; and

        (c) a county court.

    (2) This Part does not apply to an appeal in detailed assessment proceedings against a decision of an authorised court officer.

(Rules [47.21 to 47.23] deal with appeals against a decision of an authorised court officer in detailed assessment proceedings)

    (3) In this Part—

        (a) 'appeal' includes an appeal by way of case stated;

        (b) 'appeal court' means the court to which an appeal is made;

        (c) 'lower court' means the court, tribunal or other person or body from whose decision an appeal is brought;

        (d) 'appellant' means a person who brings or seeks to bring an appeal;

        (e) 'respondent' means—

            (i) a person other than the appellant who was a party to the proceedings in the lower court and who is affected by the appeal; and

            (ii) a person who is permitted by the appeal court to be a party to the appeal; and

        (f) 'appeal notice' means an appellant's or respondent's notice.

    (4) This Part is subject to any rule, enactment or practice direction which sets out special provisions with regard to any particular category of appeal.

52.2 Parties to comply with the practice direction

48.28 All parties to an appeal must comply with the relevant practice direction.

52.3 Permission

48.29   (1) An appellant or respondent requires permission to appeal—

        (a) where the appeal is from a decision of a judge in a county court or the High Court, except where the appeal is against—

(i) a committal order;

(ii) a refusal to grant habeas corpus; or

(iii) a secure accommodation order made under section 25 of the Children Act 1989; or

(b) as provided by the relevant practice direction.

(2) An application for permission to appeal may be made—

(a) to the lower court at the hearing at which the decision to be appealed was made; or

(b) to the appeal court in an appeal notice.

(3) Where the lower court refuses an application for permission to appeal, a further application for permission to appeal may be made to the appeal court.

(4) Where the appeal court, without a hearing, refuses permission to appeal, the person seeking permission may request the decision to be reconsidered at a hearing.

(5) A request under paragraph (4) must be filed within 7 days after service of the notice that permission has been refused.

(6) Permission to appeal will only be given where—

(a) the court considers that the appeal would have a real prospect of success; or

(b) there is some other compelling reason why the appeal should be heard.

(7) An order giving permission may—

(a) limit the issues to be heard; and

(b) be made subject to conditions.

52.4 Appellant's notice

(1) Where the appellant seeks permission from the appeal court it must be requested in the appellant's notice.

48.30

(2) The appellant must file the appellant's notice at the appeal court within—

(a) such period as may be directed by the lower court; or

(b) where the court makes no such direction, 14 days after the date of the decision of the lower court that the appellant wishes to appeal.

(3) Unless the appeal court orders otherwise, an appeal notice must be served on each respondent—

(a) as soon as practicable; and

(b) in any event not later than 7 days,

after it is filed.

52.5 Respondent's notice

(1) A respondent may file and serve a respondent's notice.

48.31

(2) A respondent who—

(a) is seeking permission to appeal from the appeal court; or

(b) wishes to ask the appeal court to uphold the order of the lower court for reasons different from or additional to those given by the lower court, must file a respondent's notice.

(3) Where the respondent seeks permission from the appeal court it must be requested in the respondent's notice.

(4) A respondent's notice must be filed within—

(a) such period as may be directed by the lower court; or

(b) where the court makes no such direction, 14 days, after the date in paragraph (5).

(5) The date referred to in paragraph (4) is—

(a) the date the respondent is served with the appellant's notice where—

(i) permission to appeal was given by the lower court; or

(ii) permission to appeal is not required;

(b) the date the respondent is served with notification that the appeal court has given the appellant permission to appeal; or

(c) the date the respondent is served with notification that the application for permission to appeal and the appeal itself are to be heard together.

(6) Unless the appeal court orders otherwise a respondent's notice must be served on the appellant and any other respondent—

(a) as soon as practicable; and

(b) in any event not later than 7 days, after it is filed.

52.6 Variation of time

48.32   (1) An application to vary the time limit for filing an appeal notice must be made to the appeal court.

(2) The parties may not agree to extend any date or time limit set by—

(a) these Rules;

(b) the relevant practice direction; or

(c) an order of the appeal court or the lower court.

(Rule 3.1(2)(a) provides that the court may extend or shorten the time for compliance with any rule, practice direction or court order (even if an application for extension is made after the time for compliance has expired))

(Rule 3.1(2)(b) provides that the court may adjourn or bring forward a hearing)

52.7 Stay

48.33   Unless—

(a) the appeal court or the lower court orders otherwise; or

(b) the appeal is from the Immigration Appeal Tribunal,

an appeal shall not operate as a stay of any order or decision of the lower court.

52.8 Amendment of appeal notice

48.34   An appeal notice may not be amended without the permission of the appeal court.

52.9 Striking out appeal notices and setting aside or imposing conditions on permission to appeal

(1) The appeal court may—

(a) strike out the whole or part of an appeal notice;

(b) set aside permission to appeal in whole or in part;

(c) impose or vary conditions upon which an appeal may be brought.

(2) The court will only exercise its powers under paragraph (1) where there is a compelling reason for doing so.

(3) Where a party was present at the hearing at which permission was given he may not subsequently apply for an order that the court exercise its powers under sub-paragraphs (1)(b) or (1)(c).

52.10 Appeal court's powers

48.35   (1) In relation to an appeal the appeal court has all the powers of the lower court.

(2) The appeal court has power to—

(a) affirm, set aside or vary any order or judgment made or given by the lower court;

(b) refer any claim or issue for determination by the lower court;

(c) order a new trial or hearing;

(d) make orders for the payment of interest;

(e) make a costs order.

(3) In an appeal from a claim tried with a jury the Court of Appeal may, instead of ordering a new trial—

(a) make an order for damages; or

(b) vary an award of damages made by the jury.

(4) The appeal court may exercise its powers in relation to the whole or part of an order of the lower court.

52.11 Hearing of appeals

(1) Every appeal will be limited to a review of the decision of the lower court unless— **48.36**

(a) a practice direction makes different provision for a particular category of appeal; or

(b) the court considers that in the circumstances of an individual appeal it would be in the interests of justice to hold a re-hearing.

(2) Unless it orders otherwise, the appeal court will not receive—

(a) oral evidence; or

(b) evidence which was not before the lower court.

(3) The appeal court will allow an appeal where the decision of the lower court was—

(a) wrong; or

(b) unjust because of a serious procedural or other irregularity in the proceedings in the lower court.

(4) The appeal court may draw any inference of fact which it considers justified on the evidence.

(5) At the hearing of the appeal a party may not rely on a matter not contained in his appeal notice unless the appeal court gives permission.

52.12 Non-disclosure of Part 36 offers and payments

(1) The fact that a Part 36 offer or Part 36 payment has been made must not be disclosed to **48.37** any judge of the appeal court who is to hear or determine—

(a) an application for permission to appeal; or

(b) an appeal,

until all question (other than costs) have been determined.

(2) Paragraph (1) does not apply if the Part 36 offer or Part 36 payment is relevant to the substance of the appeal.

(3) Paragraph (1) does not prevent disclosure in any application in the appeal proceedings if disclosure of the fact that a Part 36 offer or Part 36 payment has been made is properly relevant to the matter to be decided.

II SPECIAL PROVISIONS APPLYING TO THE COURT OF APPEAL

52.13 Second appeals to the Court

(1) Permission is required from the Court of Appeal for any appeal to that court from a **48.38** decision of a county court or the High Court which was itself made on appeal.

(2) The Court of Appeal will not give permission unless it considers that—

(a) the appeal would raise an important point of principle or practice; or

(b) there is some other compelling reason for the Court of Appeal to hear it.

52.14 Assignment of appeals to the Court of Appeal

48.39   (1) Where the court from or to which an appeal is made or from which permission to appeal is sought ('the relevant court') considers that—

(a) an appeal which is to be heard by a county court or the High Court would raise an important point of principle or practice; or

(b) there is some other compelling reason for the Court of Appeal to hear it, the relevant court may order the appeal to be transferred to the Court of Appeal.

(The Master of the Rolls has the power to direct that an appeal which would be heard by a county court or the High Court should be heard instead by the Court of Appeal—see section 57 of the Access to Justice Act 1999)

(2) The Master of the Rolls or the Court of Appeal may remit an appeal to the court in which the original appeal was or would have been brought.

F. PD 52—Appeals

SECTION I—GENERAL PROVISIONS ABOUT APPEALS

48.40   2.1 This practice direction applies to all appeals to which Part 52 applies except where specific provision is made for appeals to the Court of Appeal.

2.2 For the purpose only of appeals to the Court of Appeal from cases in family proceedings this practice direction will apply with such modifications as may be required.

Routes of appeal

48.41   2A.1 Subject to paragraph 2A.2, the following table sets out to which court or judge an appeal is to be made (subject to obtaining any necessary permission):

Decision of:	*Appeal made to:*
District judge of a county court	Circuit judge
Master or district judge of the High Court	High Court judge
Circuit judge	High Court judge
High Court judge	Court of Appeal

2A.2 Where the decision to be appealed is a final decision:

(a) in a Part 7 claim allocated to the multi-track; or

(b) made in specialist proceedings (under the Companies Acts 1985 or 1989 or to which Sections I, II or III of Part 57 or any of Parts 58 to 63 apply),

the appeal is to be made to the Court of Appeal (subject to obtaining any necessary permission).

2A.3 A 'final decision' is a decision of a court that would finally determine (subject to any possible appeal or detailed assessment of costs) the entire proceedings whichever way the court decided the issues before it.

2A.4 A decision of a court is to be treated as a final decision for routes of appeal purposes where it:

(a) is made at the conclusion of part of a hearing or trial which has been split into parts; and

(b) would, if it had been made at the conclusion of that hearing or trial, have been a final decision.

2A.5 An order made:

(a) on a summary or detailed assessment of costs; or

(b) on application to enforce a final decision,

is not a 'final decision' and any appeal from such an order will follow the appeal routes set out in the table in paragraph 2A.1.

2A.6 (1) Where the decision to be appealed is a final decision in a Part 8 claim treated as allocated to the multi-track under rule 8.9(c), the court to which the permission application is made should, if permission is given, and unless the appeal would lie to the Court of Appeal in any event, consider whether to order the appeal to be transferred to the Court of Appeal under rule 52.14.

(2) An appeal against a final decision on a point of law in a case which did not involve any substantial dispute of fact would normally be a suitable appeal to be so transferred.

Grounds for appeal

3.1 Rule 52.11(3)(a) and (b) sets out the circumstances in which the appeal court will allow an appeal. **48.42**

3.2 The grounds of appeal should—

(1) set out clearly the reasons why rule 52.11(3)(a) or (b) is said to apply;

and

(2) specify, in respect of each ground, whether the ground raises an appeal on a point of law or is an appeal against a finding of fact.

Permission to appeal

4.1 Rule 52.3 sets out the circumstances when permission to appeal is required. **48.43**

4.2 The permission of:

(a) the Court of Appeal; or

(b) Where the lower court's rules allow, the lower court,

is required for all appeals to the Court of Appeal except as provided by statute or rule 52.3.

(The requirement of permission to appeal may be imposed by a practice direction—see rule 52.3(1)(b))

4.3 Where the lower court is not required to give permission to appeal, it may give an indication of its opinion as to whether permission should be given.

(Rule 52.1(3)(c) defines 'lower court')

Appeals from case management decisions

4.4 Case management decisions include decisions made under rule 3.1(2) and decisions about: **48.44**

(1) disclosure

(2) filing of witness statements or experts' reports

(3) directions about the timetable of the claim

(4) adding a party to a claim

(5) security for costs.

4.5 Where the application is for permission to appeal from a case management decision, the court dealing with the application may take into account whether:

(1) the issue is of sufficient significance to justify the costs of an appeal;

(2) the procedural consequences of an appeal (e.g. loss of trial date) outweigh the significance of the case management decision;

(3) it would be more convenient to determine the issue at or after trial.

Court to which permission to appeal application should be made

4.6 An application for permission should be made orally at the hearing at which the decision to be appealed against is made. **48.45**

4.7 Where:

(a) no application for permission to appeal is made at the hearing; or

(b) the lower court refuses permission to appeal,

an application for permission to appeal may be made to the appeal court in accordance with rules 52.3(2) and (3).

4.8 There is no appeal from a decision of the appeal court to allow or refuse permission to appeal to that court (although where the appeal court, without a hearing, refuses permission to appeal, the person seeking permission may request that decision to be reconsidered at a hearing). See section 54(4) of the Access to Justice Act and rule 52.3(2), (3), (4) and (5).

Second appeals

48.46 4.9 An application for permission to appeal from a decision of the High Court or a county court which was itself made on appeal must be made to the court of Appeal.

4.10 If permission to appeal is granted the appeal will be heard by the Court of Appeal.

Consideration of permission without a hearing

48.47 4.11 Applications for permission to appeal may be considered by the appeal court without a hearing.

4.12 If permission is granted without a hearing the parties will be notified of that decision and the procedure in paragraphs 6.1 to 6.7 will then apply.

4.13 If permission is refused without a hearing the parties will be notified of that decision with the reasons for it. The decision is subject to the appellant's right to have it reconsidered at an oral hearing. This may be before the same judge.

4.14 A request for the decision to be reconsidered at an oral hearing must be filed at the appeal court within seven days after service of the notice that permission has been refused. A copy of the request must be served by the appellant on the respondent at the same time.

Permission hearing

48.48 4.14A (1) This paragraph applies where an appellant, who is represented, makes a request for a decision to be reconsidered at an oral hearing.

(2) The appellant's advocate must, at least 4 days before the hearing, in a brief written statement—

(a) inform the court and the respondent of the points which he proposes to raise at the hearing;

(b) set out his reasons why permission should be granted notwithstanding the reasons given for the refusal of permission; and

(c) confirm, where applicable, that the requirements of paragraph 4.17 have been complied with (appellant in receipt of services funded by the Legal Services Commission).

4.15 Notice of a permission hearing will be given to the respondent but he is not required to attend unless the court requests him to do so.

4.16 If the court requests the respondent's attendance at the permission hearing, the appellant must supply the respondent with a copy of the appeal bundle (see paragraph 5.6A) within 7 days of being notified of the request, or such other period as the court may direct. The costs of providing that bundle shall be borne by the appellant initially, but will form part of the costs of the permission application.

Appellants in receipt of services funded by the Legal Services Commission applying for permission to appeal

48.49 4.17 Where the appellant is in receipt of services funded by the Legal Services Commission (or legally aided) and permission to appeal has been refused by the appeal court without a hearing, the appellant must send a copy of the reasons the appeal court gave for refusing permission to the relevant office of the Legal Services Commission as soon as it has been received from the court. The court will require confirmation that this has been done if a hearing is requested to reconsider the question of permission.

Limited permission

4.18 Where a court under rule 52.3(7) gives permission to appeal on some issues only, it will—   **48.50**

  (1) refuse permission on any remaining issues; or

  (2) reserve the question of permission to appeal on any remaining issues to the court hearing the appeal.

4.19 If the court reserves the question of permission under paragraph 4.18(2), the appellant must, within 14 days after service of the court's order, inform the appeal court and the respondent in writing whether he intends to pursue the reserved issues. If the appellant does intend to pursue the reserved issues, the parties must include in any time estimate for the appeal hearing, their time estimate for the reserved issues.

4.20 If the appeal court refuses permission to appeal on the remaining issues without a hearing and the applicant wishes to have that decision reconsidered at an oral hearing, the time limit in rule 52.3(5) shall apply. Any application for an extension of this time limit should be made promptly. The court hearing the appeal on the issues for which permission has been granted will not normally grant, at the appeal hearing, an application to extend the time limit in rule 52.3(5) for the remaining issues.

4.21 If the appeal court refuses permission to appeal on remaining issues at or after an oral hearing, the application for permission to appeal on those issues cannot be renewed at the appeal hearing. See section 54(4) of the Access to Justice Act 1999.

Appellant's notice

5.1 An appellant's notice [N161] must be filed and served in all cases. Where an application for permission to appeal is made to the appeal court it must be applied for in the appellant's notice.   **48.51**

[Human rights]

Extension of time for filing appellant's notice

5.2 If an appellant requires an extension of time for filing his notice the application must be made in the appellant's notice. The notice should state the reason for the delay and the steps taken prior to the application being made.   **48.52**

5.3 Where the appellant's notice includes an application for an extension of time and permission to appeal has been given or is not required the respondent has the right to be heard on that application. He must be served with a copy of the appeal bundle (see paragraph 5.6A). However, a respondent who unreasonably opposes an extension of time runs the risk of being ordered to pay the appellant's costs of that application.

5.4 If an extension of time is given following such an application the procedure at paragraphs 6.1 to 6.6 applies.

Applications

5.5 Notice of an application to be made to the appeal court for a remedy incidental to the appeal (e.g. an interim remedy under rule 25.1 or an order for security for costs) may be included in the appeal notice or in a Part 23 application notice.   **48.53**

Documents

48.54   5.6 (1) This paragraph applies to every case except where the appeal—

(a) relates to a claim allocated to the small claims track; and

(b) is being heard in a county court or the High Court.

(Paragraph 5.8 applies where this paragraph does not apply)

(2) The appellant must file the following documents together with an appeal bundle (see paragraph 5.6A) with his appellant's notice—

(a) two additional copies of the appellant's notice for the appeal court; and

(b) one copy of the appellant's notice for each of the respondents;

(c) one copy of his skeleton argument for each copy of the appellant's notice that is filed (see paragraph 5.9);

(d) a sealed copy of the order being appealed;

(e) a copy of any order giving or refusing permission to appeal, together with a copy of the judge's reasons for allowing or refusing permission to appeal;

(f) any witness statements or affidavits in support of any application included in the appellant's notice.

5.6A (1) An appellant must include in his appeal bundle the following documents:

(a) a sealed copy of the appellant's notice;

(b) a sealed copy of the order being appealed;

(c) a copy of any order giving or refusing permission to appeal, together with a copy of the judge's reasons for allowing or refusing permission to appeal;

(d) any affidavit or witness statement filed in support of any application included in the appellant's notice;

(e) a copy of his skeleton argument;

(f) a transcript or note of judgment (see paragraph 5.12), and in cases where permission to appeal was given by the lower court or is not required those parts of any transcript of evidence which are directly relevant to any question at issue on the appeal;

(g) the claim form and statements of case (where relevant to the subject of the appeal);

(h) any application notice (or case management documentation) relevant to the subject of the appeal;

(i) in cases where the decision appealed was itself made on appeal (eg from district judge to circuit judge), the first order, the reasons given and the appellant's notice used to appeal from that order;

(j) in the case of judicial review or a statutory appeal, the original decision which was the subject of the application to the lower court;

(k) in cases where the appeal is from a Tribunal, a copy of the Tribunal's reasons for the decision, a copy of the decision reviewed by the Tribunal and the reasons for the original decision and any document filed with the Tribunal setting out the grounds of appeal from that decision;

(l) any other documents which the appellant reasonably considers necessary to enable the appeal court to reach its decision on the hearing of the application or appeal; and

(m) such other documents as the court may direct.

(2) All documents that are extraneous to the issues to be considered on the application or the appeal must be excluded. The appeal bundle may include affidavits, witness statements, summaries, experts' reports and exhibits but only where these are directly relevant to the subject matter of the appeal.

(3) Where the appellant is represented, the appeal bundle must contain a certificate signed by his solicitor, counsel or other representative to the effect that he has read and understood paragraph (2) above and that the composition of the appeal bundle complies with it.

5.7 Where it is not possible to file all the above documents, the appellant must indicate which documents have not yet been filed and the reasons why they are not currently available. The appellant must then provide a reasonable estimate of when the missing document or documents can be filed and file them as soon as reasonably practicable.

Small claims

5.8 (1) This paragraph applies where—   **48.55**
  (a) the appeal relates to a claim allocated to the small claims track; and
  (b) the appeal is being heard in a county court or the High Court.
(2) The appellant must file the following documents with his appellant's notice—
    (a) a sealed copy of the order being appealed; and
    (b) any order giving or refusing permission to appeal, together with a copy of the reasons for that decision.
(3) The appellant may, if relevant to the issues to be determined on the appeal, file any other document listed in paragraph 5.6 or 5.6A in addition to the documents referred to in sub-paragraph (2).
(4) The appellant need not file a record of the reasons for judgment of the lower court with his appellant's notice unless sub-paragraph (5) applies.
(5) The court may order a suitable record of the reasons for judgment of the lower court (see paragraph 5.12) to be filed—
    (a) to enable it to decide if permission should be granted; or
    (b) if permission is granted to enable it to decide the appeal.

Skeleton arguments

5.9 (1) the appellant's notice must, subject to (2) and (3) below, be accompanied by a skeleton   **48.56**
argument. Alternatively the skeleton argument may be included in the appellant's notice. Where the skeleton argument is so included it will not form part of the notice for the purposes of rule 52.8.
(2) Where it is impracticable for the appellant's skeleton argument to accompany the appellant's notice it must be filed and served on all respondents within 14 days of filing the notice.
(3) An appellant who is not represented need not file a skeleton argument but is encouraged to do so since this will be helpful to the court.

Content of skeleton arguments   5.10 (1) A skeleton argument must contain a numbered list of   **48.57**
the points which the party wishes to make. These should both define and confine the areas of controversy. Each point should be stated as concisely as the nature of the case allows.
(2) A numbered point must be followed by a reference to any document on which the party wishes to rely.
(3) A skeleton argument must state, in respect of each authority cited—
    (a) the proposition of law that the authority demonstrates; and
    (b) the parts of the authority (identified by page or paragraph references) that support the proposition.
(4) If more than one authority is cited in support of a given proposition, the skeleton argument must briefly state the reason for taking that course.
(5) The statement referred to in sub-paragraph (4) should not materially add to the length of the skeleton argument but should be sufficient to demonstrate, in the context of the argument—
    (a) the relevance of the authority or authorities to that argument; and
    (b) that the citation is necessary for a proper presentation of that argument.
(6) The cost of preparing a skeleton argument which—
    (a) does not comply with the requirements set out in this paragraph; or

(b) was not filed within the time limits provided by this Practice Direction (or any further time granted by the court),

will not be allowed on assessment except to the extent that the court otherwise directs.

5.11 The appellant should consider what other information the appeal court will need. This may include a list of persons who feature in the case or glossaries of technical terms. A chronology of relevant events will be necessary in most appeals.

Suitable record of the judgment

48.58 5.12 Where the judgment to be appealed has been officially recorded by the court, an approved transcript of that record should accompany the appellant's notice. Photocopies will not be accepted for this purpose. However, where there is no officially recorded judgment the following documents will be acceptable:

48.59 **Written judgments** (1) Where the judgment was made in writing a copy of that judgment endorsed with the judge's signature.

48.60 **Note of judgment** (2) When judgment was not officially recorded or made in writing a note of the judgment (agreed between the appellant's and respondent's advocates) should be submitted for approval to the judge whose decision is being appealed. If the parties cannot agree on a single note of the judgment, both versions should be provided to that judge with an explanatory letter. For the purpose of an application for permission to appeal the note need not be approved by the respondent or the lower court judge.

48.61 **Advocates' notes of judgments where the appellant is unrepresented** (3) When the appellant was unrepresented in the lower court it is the duty of any advocate for the respondent to make his/her note of judgment promptly available, free of charge to the appellant where there is no officially recorded judgment or if the court so directs. Where the appellant was represented in the lower court it is the duty of his/her own former advocate to make his/her note available in these circumstances. The appellant should submit the note of judgment to the appeal court.

48.62 **Reasons for judgment in tribunal cases** (4) A sealed copy of the tribunal's reasons for the decision.

5.13 An appellant may not be able to obtain an official transcript or other suitable record of the lower court's decision within which the appellant's notice must be filed. In such cases the appellant's must still be completed to the best of the appellant's ability on the basis of the documentation available. However it may be amended subsequently with the permission of the appeal court.

Advocates' notes of judgment

48.63 5.14 Advocates' brief (or, where appropriate, refresher) fee includes:
(1) remuneration for taking a note of the judgment of the court;
(2) having the note transcribed accurately;
(3) attempting to agree the note with the other side if represented;
(4) submitting the note to the judge for approval where appropriate;
(5) revising it if so requested by the judge;
(6) providing any copies required for the appeal court, instructing solicitors and lay client;
and
(7) providing a copy of his note to an unrepresented appellant.

Transcripts or notes of evidence

5.15 When the evidence is relevant to the appeal an official transcript of the relevant evidence **48.64** must be obtained. Transcripts or notes of evidence are generally not needed for the purpose of determining an application for permission to appeal.

Notes of evidence

5.16 If evidence relevant to the appeal was not officially recorded, a typed version of the **48.65** judge's notes of evidence must be obtained.

Transcripts at public expense

5.17 Where the lower court or the appeal court is satisfied that an unrepresented appellant is **48.66** in such poor financial circumstances that the cost of a transcript would be an excessive burden the court may certify that the cost of obtaining one official transcript should be borne at public expense.

5.18 In the case of a request for an official transcript of evidence or proceedings to be paid for at public expense, the court must also be satisfied that there are reasonable grounds for appeal. Whenever possible a request for a transcript at public expense should be made to the lower court when asking for permission to appeal.

Filing and service of appellant's notice

5.19 Rule 52.4 sets out the procedure and time limits for filing and serving an appellant's **48.67** notice. The appellant must file the appellant's notice at the appeal court within such period as may be directed by the lower court which should not normally exceed 28 days or, where the lower court directs no such period, within 14 days of the date of the decision that the appellant wishes to appeal.

5.20 Where the lower court judge announces his decision and reserves the reasons for his judgment or order until a later date, he should, in the exercise of powers under rule 52.4(2)(a), fix a period for filing the appellant's notice at the appeal court that takes this into account.

5.21 (1) Except where the appeal court orders otherwise a sealed copy of the appellant's notice, including any skeleton arguments must be served on all respondents in accordance with the timetable prescribed by rule 52.4(3) except where this requirement is modified by paragraph 5.9(2) in which case the skeleton argument should be served as soon as it is filed.

(2) The appellant must, as soon as practicable, file a certificate of service of the documents referred to in paragraph (1).

5.22 Unless the court otherwise directs a respondent need not take any action when served with an appellant's notice until such time as notification is given to him that permission to appeal has been given.

5.23 The court may dispense with the requirement for service of the notice on a respondent. Any application notice seeking an order under rule 6.9 to dispense with service should set out the reasons relied on and be verified by a statement of truth.

5.24 (1) Where the appellant is applying for permission to appeal in his appellant's notice, he must serve on the respondents his appellant's notice and skeleton argument (but not the appeal bundle), unless the appeal court directs otherwise.

(2) Where permission to appeal—

(a) has been given by the lower court; or

(b) is not required,

the appellant must serve the appeal bundle on the respondents with the appellant's notice.

Amendment of appeal notice

48.68   5.25 An appeal notice may be amended with permission. Such an application to amend and any application in opposition will normally be dealt with at the hearing unless that course would cause unnecessary expense or delay in which case a request should be made for the application to amend to be heard in advance.

Procedure after permission is obtained

48.69   6.1 This paragraph sets out the procedure where:
(1) permission to appeal is given by the appeal court; or
(2) the appellant's notice is filed in the appeal court and:
(a) permission was given by the lower court; or
(b) permission is not required.

6.2 If the appeal court gives permission to appeal, the appeal bundle must be served on each of the respondents within seven days of receiving the order giving permission to appeal.

6.3 The appeal court will send the parties—
(1) notification of—
(a) the date of the hearing or the period of time (the 'listing window') during which the appeal is likely to be heard; and
(b) in the Court of Appeal, the date by which the appeal will be heard (the 'hear-by date');
(2) where permission is granted by the appeal court a copy of the order giving permission to appeal; and
(3) any other directions given by the court.

6.3A (1) Where the appeal court grants permission to appeal, the appellant must add the following documents to the appeal bundle—
(a) the respondent's notice and skeleton argument (if any);
(b) those parts of the transcripts of evidence which are directly relevant to any question at issue on the appeal;
(c) the order granting permission to appeal and, where permission to appeal was granted at an oral hearing, the transcript (or note) of any judgment which was given; and
(d) any document which the appellant and respondent have agreed to add to the appeal bundle in accordance with paragraph 7.11.
(2) Where permission to appeal has been refused on a particular issue, the appellant must remove from the appeal bundle all documents that are relevant only to that issue.

Appeal questionnaire in the Court of Appeal

48.70   6.4 The Court of Appeal will send an appeal questionnaire to the appellant when it notifies him of the matters referred to in paragraph 6.3.

6.5 The appellant must complete and lodge the appeal questionnaire within 14 days of the date of the letter of notification of the matters in paragraph 6.3. The appeal questionnaire must contain:
(1) if the appellant is legally represented, the advocate's time estimate for the hearing of the appeal;
(2) where a transcript of evidence is relevant to the appeal; confirmation that a transcript of evidence has been ordered where this is not already in the bundle of documents;
(3) confirmation that copies of the appeal bundle are being prepared and will be held ready for the use of the Court of Appeal and an undertaking that they will be supplied to the court on request. For the purpose of these bundles photocopies of the transcripts will be accepted;
(4) confirmation that copies of the appeal questionnaire and the appeal bundle have been served on the respondents and the date of that service.

Time estimates   6.6 The time estimate included in an Appeal Questionnaire must be that of **48.71** the advocate who will argue the appeal. It should exclude the time required by the court to give judgment. If the respondent disagrees with the time estimate, the respondent must inform the court within seven days of receipt of the Appeal Questionnaire. In the absence of such notification the respondent will be deemed to have accepted the estimate proposed on behalf of the appellant.

Respondent

7.1 A respondent who wishes to ask the appeal court to vary the order of the lower court in any **48.72** way must appeal and permission will be required on the same basis as for an appellant.

7.2 A respondent who wishes only to request that the appeal court upholds the judgment or order of the lower court whether for the reasons given in the lower court or otherwise does not make an appeal and does not therefore require permission to appeal in accordance with rule 52.3(1).

7.3 (1) A respondent who wishes to appeal or who wishes to ask the appeal court to uphold the order of the lower court for reasons different from or additional to those given by the lower court must file a respondent's notice.

(2) If the respondent does not file a respondent's notice, he will not be entitled, except with the permission of the court, to rely on any reason not relied on in the lower court.

7.3A Paragraphs 5.1A, 5.1B and 5.2 of this practice direction (Human Rights and extension for time for filing appellant's notice) also apply to a respondent and a respondent's notice.

Time limits

7.4 The time limits for filing a respondent's notice are set out in rule 52.5(4) and (5).   **48.73**

7.5 Where an extension of time is required the extension must be requested in the respondent's notice and the reasons why the respondent failed to act within the specified time must be included.

Respondent's skeleton argument

7.6 Except where paragraph 7.7A applies, the respondent must provide a skeleton argu- **48.74** ment for the court where he proposes to address arguments to the court. The respondent's skeleton argument may be included within a respondent's notice. Where a skeleton argument is included within a respondent's notice it will not form part of the notice for the purposes of rule 52.8.

7.7 (1) A respondent who—
    (a) files a respondent's notice; but
    (b) does not include his skeleton argument within that notice,
must file and serve his skeleton argument within 14 days of filing the notice.

(2) A respondent who does not file a respondent's notice but who files a skeleton argument must file and serve that skeleton argument at least 7 days before the appeal hearing.
(Rule 52.5(4) sets out the period for filing and serving a respondent's notice)

7.7A (1) Where the appeal relates to a claim allocated to the small claims track and is being heard in a county court or the High Court, the respondent may file a skeleton argument but is not required to do so.

(2) A respondent who is not represented need not file a skeleton argument but is encouraged to do so in order to assist the court.

7.7B. The respondent must—
    (1) serve his skeleton argument on—
        (a) the appellant; and

(b) any other respondent,

at the same time as he files it at the court; and

    (2) file a certificate of service.

48.75 **Content of skeleton arguments** 7.8 A respondent's skeleton argument must conform to the directions at paragraphs 5.10 and 5.11 with any necessary modifications. It should, where appropriate, answer the arguments set out in the appellant's skeleton argument.

Applications within respondent's notices

48.76   7.9 A respondent may include an application within a respondent's notice in accordance with paragraph 5.5 above.

Filing respondent's notices and skeleton arguments

48.77   7.10 (1) The respondent must file the following documents with his respondent's notice in every case:

    (a) two additional copies of the respondent's notice for the appeal court; and

    (b) one copy each for the appellant and any other respondents.

    (2) The respondent may file a skeleton argument with his respondent's notice and—

    (a) where he does so he must file two copies; and

    (b) where he does not do so he must comply with paragraph 7.7.

7.11 If the respondent wishes to rely on any documents which he reasonably considers necessary to enable the appeal court to reach its decision on the appeal in addition to those filed by the appellant, he must make every effort to agree amendments to the appeal bundle with the appellant.

7.12 (1) If the representatives for the parties are unable to reach agreement, the respondent may prepare a supplemental bundle.

    (2) If the respondent prepares a supplemental bundle he must file it, together with the requisite number of copies for the appeal court, at the appeal court—

    (a) with the respondent's notice; or

    (b) if a respondent's notice is not filed, within 21 days after he is served with the appeal bundle.

    7.13 The respondent must serve—

    (1) the respondent's notice;

    (2) his skeleton argument (if any); and

    (3) the supplemental bundle (if any), on—

    (a) the appellant; and

    (b) any other respondent,

at the same time as he files them at the court.

Appeals to the High Court

48.78 **Application** 8.1 This paragraph applies where an appeal lies to a High Court judge from the decision of a country court or a district judge of the High Court.

8.2 The following table sets out the following venues for each circuit—

    (a) Appeal centres—court centres where appeals to which this paragraph applies may be filed, managed and heard.

    (b) Hearing-only centres—court centres where appeals to which this paragraph applies may be heard by order made at an appeal centre (see paragraph 8.10).

Circuit	Appeal centres	Hearing-only centres
Midland Circuit	Birmingham Nottingham	Lincoln Leicester Northampton Stafford
North Eastern Circuit	Leeds Newcastle Sheffield	Teesside
Northern Circuit	Manchester Liverpool Preston	Carlisle
Wales and Chester Circuit	Cardiff Swansea Chester	
Western Circuit	Bristol Exeter Winchester	Truro Plymouth
South Eastern Circuit	*Central London:* Royal Courts of Justice	
	Provincial: Lewes Luton Norwich Reading	Oxford Chelmsford St Albans Maidstone

Venue for appeals and filing of notices on circuits other than the South Eastern Circuit

8.3 Paragraphs 8.4 and 8.5 apply where the lower court is situated on a circuit other than the South Eastern Circuit.

8.4 The appellant's notice must be filed at an appeal centre on the circuit in which the lower court is situated. The appeal will be managed and heard at that appeal centre unless the appeal court orders otherwise.

8.5 A respondent's notice must be filed at the appeal centre where the appellant's notice was filed unless the appeal has been transferred to another appeal centre, in which case it must be filed at that appeal centre.

Venue for appeals and filing of notices on the South Eastern Circuit

8.6 Paragraphs 8.7 and 8.8 apply where the lower court is situated on the South Eastern **48.79** Circuit.

8.7 The appellant's notice must be filed at an appeal centre on the South Eastern Circuit. The appeal will be managed and heard at the Royal Courts of Justice unless the appeal court orders otherwise. An order that an appeal is to be managed or heard at another appeal centre may not be made unless the consent of the Presiding Judge of the circuit in charge of civil matters has been obtained.

8.8 A respondent's notice must be filed at the Royal Courts of Justice unless the appeal has been transferred to another appeal centre, in which case it must be filed at that appeal centre.

General provisions

48.80   8.9 The appeal court may transfer an appeal to another appeal centre (whether or not on the same circuit). In deciding whether to do so the court will have regard to the criteria in rule 30.3 (criteria for a transfer order). The appeal court may do so either on application by a party or of its own initiative. Where an appeal is transferred under this paragraph, notice of transfer must be served on every person on whom the appellant's notice has been served. An appeal may not be transferred to an appeal centre on another circuit, either for management or hearing, unless the consent of the Presiding Judge of that circuit in charge of civil matters has been obtained.

8.10 Directions may be given for—
   (a) an appeal to be heard at a hearing only centre; or
   (b) an application in an appeal to be heard at any other venue,

instead of at the appeal centre managing the appeal.

8.11 Unless a direction has been made under 8.10, any application in the appeal must be made at the appeal centre where the appeal is being managed.

8.12 The appeal court may adopt all or any part of the procedure set out in paragraphs 6.4 to 6.6.

8.13 Where the lower court is a county court:
   (1) appeals and applications for permission to appeal will be heard by a High Court Judge or by a person authorised under paragraphs (1), (2) or (4) of the Table in section 9(1) of the Supreme Court Act 1981 to act as a judge of the High Court; and
   (2) other applications in the appeal may be heard and directions in the appeal may be given either by a High Court Judge or by any person authorised under section 9 of the Supreme Court Act 1981 to act as a judge of the High Court.

8.14 In the case of appeals from Masters or district judges of the High Court, appeals, applications for permission and any other applications in the appeal may be heard and directions in the appeal may be given by a High Court Judge or by any person authorised under section 9 of the Supreme Court Act 1981 to act as a judge of the High Court.

Appeals to a judge of a county court from a district judge

48.81   8A.1 The designated civil judge in consultation with his presiding judges has responsibility for allocating appeals from decisions of district judges to circuit judges.

Re-hearings

48.82   9.1 The hearing of an appeal will be a re-hearing (as opposed to a review of the decision of the lower court) if the appeal is from the decision of a minister, person or other body and the minister, person or other body—
   (1) did not hold a hearing to come to that decision; or
   (2) held a hearing to come to that decision, but the procedure adopted did not provide for the consideration of evidence.

Appeals transferred to the Court of Appeal

48.83   10.1 Where an appeal is transferred to the Court of Appeal under rule 52.14 the Court of Appeal may give such additional directions as are considered appropriate.

Applications

48.84   11.1 Where a party to an appeal makes an application whether in an appeal notice or by Part 23 application notice, the provisions of Part 23 will apply.

11.2 The applicant must file the following documents with the notice—

(1) one additional copy of the application notice for the appeal court and one copy for each of the respondents;

(2) where applicable a sealed copy of the order which is the subject of the main appeal;

(3) a bundle of documents in support which should include:

(a) the Part 23 application notice;

(b) any witness statements and affidavits filed in support of the application notice.

Disposing of applications or appeals by consent

Dismissal of applications or appeals by consent

12.1 These paragraphs do not apply where any party to the proceedings is a child or patient. **48.85**

12.2 Where an appellant does not wish to pursue an application or an appeal, he may request the appeal court for an order that his application or appeal be dismissed. Such a request must contain a statement that the appellant is not a child or patient. If such a request is granted it will usually be on the basis that the appellant pays the costs of the application or appeal.

12.3 If the appellant wishes to have the application or appeal dismissed without costs, his request must be accompanied by a consent signed by the respondent or his legal representative stating that the respondent is not a child or patient and consents to the dismissal of the application or appeal without costs.

12.4 Where a settlement has been reached disposing of the application or appeal, the parties may make a joint request to the court stating that none of them is a child or patient, and asking that the application or appeal be dismissed by consent. If the request is granted the application or appeal will be dismissed.

Allowing unopposed appeals or applications on paper

13.1 The appeal court will not normally make an order allowing an appeal unless satisfied that **48.86** the decision of the lower court was wrong, but the appeal court may set aside or vary the order of the lower court with consent and without determining the merits of the appeal, if it is satisfied that there are good and sufficient reasons for doing so. Where the appeal court is requested by all parties to allow an application or an appeal the court may consider the request on the papers. The request should state that none of the parties is a child or patient and set out the relevant history of the proceedings and the matters relied on as justifying the proposed order and be accompanied by a copy of the proposed order.

Procedure for structured settlements and consent orders involving a child or patient

13.2 Settlements relating to appeals and applications where one of the parties is a child or a **48.87** patient and structured settlements which are agreed upon at the appeal stage require the court's approval.

Child

13.3 In cases involving a child a copy of the proposed order signed by the parties' solicitors **48.88** should be sent to the appeal court, together with an opinion from the advocate acting on behalf of the child.

Patient

13.4 Where a party is a patient the same procedure will be adopted, but the documents filed **48.89** should also include any relevant reports prepared for the Court of Protection and a document evidencing formal approval by that court where required.

Structured settlements

48.90   13.5 Where a structured settlement has been negotiated in a case which is under appeal the documents filed should include those which would be required in the case of a structured settlement dealt with at first instance. Details can be found in the Practice Direction which supplements CPR Part 40.

Summary assessment of costs

48.91   14.1 Costs are likely to be assessed by way of summary assessment at the following hearings:
(1) contested directions hearings;
(2) applications for permission to appeal at which the respondent is present;
(3) dismissal list hearings in the Court of Appeal at which the respondent is present;
(4) appeals from case management decisions; and
(5) appeals listed for one day or less.

14.2 Parties attending any of the hearings referred to in paragraph 14.1 should be prepared to deal with the summary assessment.

Other special provisions regarding the Court of Appeal

Filing of documents

48.92   15.1 (1) The documents relevant to proceedings in the Court of Appeal, Civil Division must be filed in the Civil Appeals Office Registry, Room E307, Royal Courts of Justice, Strand, London, WC2A 2LL.

(2) The Civil Appeals Office will not serve documents and where service is required by the CPR or this practice direction it must be effected by the parties.

Core bundles

48.93   15.2 In cases where the appeal bundle comprises more than 500 pages, exclusive of transcripts, the appellant's solicitors must, after consultation with the respondent's solicitors, also prepare and file with the court, in addition to copies of the appeal bundle (as amended in accordance with paragraph 7.11) the requisite number of copies of a core bundle.

15.3 (1) The core bundle must be filed within 28 days of receipt of the order giving permission to appeal or, where permission to appeal was granted by the lower court or is not required, within 28 days of the date of service of the appellant's notice on the respondent.

(2) The core bundle—
(a) must contain the documents which are central to the appeal; and
(b) must not exceed 150 pages.

Preparation of bundles

48.94   15.4 The provisions of this paragraph apply to the preparation of appeal bundles, supplemental respondents' bundles where the parties are unable to agree amendments to the appeal bundle, and core bundles.

(1) **Rejection of bundles.** Where documents are copied unnecessarily or bundled incompletely, costs may be disallowed. Where the provisions of this Practice Direction as to the preparation or delivery of bundles are not followed the bundle may be rejected by the court or be made the subject of a special costs order.

(2) **Avoidance of duplication.** No more than one copy of any document should be included unless there is a good reason for doing otherwise (such as the use of a separate core bundle—see paragraph 15.2).

(3) **Pagination**
(a) Bundles must be paginated, each page being numbered individually and consecutively. The pagination used at trial must also be indicated. Letters and other documents should

normally be included in chronological order. (An exception to consecutive page numbering arises in the case of core bundles where it may be preferable to retain the original numbering.)

(b) Page numbers should be inserted in bold figures at the bottom of the page and in a form that can be clearly distinguished from any other pagination on the document.

(4) **Format and presentation**

(a) Where possible the documents should be in A4 format. Where a document has to be read across rather than down the page, it should be so placed in the bundle as to ensure that the text starts nearest the spine.

(b) Where any marking or writing in colour on a document is important, the document must be copied in colour or marked up correctly in colour.

(c) Documents which are not easily legible should be transcribed and the transcription marked and placed adjacent to the document transcribed.

(d) Documents in a foreign language should be translated and the translation marked and placed adjacent to the document translated. The translation should be agreed or, if it cannot be agreed, each party's proposed translation should be included.

(e) The size of any bundle should be tailored to its contents. A large lever arch file should not be used for just a few pages nor should files of whatever size be overloaded.

(f) Where it will assist the Court of Appeal, different sections of the file may be separated by cardboard or other tabbed dividers so long as these are clearly indexed. Where, for example, a document is awaited when the appeal bundle is filed, a single sheet of paper can be inserted after a divider, indicating the nature of the document awaited. For example, 'Transcript of evidence of Mr J Smith (to follow)'.

(5) **Binding**

(a) All documents, with the exception of transcripts, must be bound together. This may be in a lever arch file, ring binder or plastic folder. Plastic sleeves containing loose documents must not be used. Binders and files must be strong enough to withstand heavy use.

(b) Large documents such as plans should be placed in an easily accessible file. Large documents which will need to be opened up frequently should be inserted in a file larger than A4 size.

(6) **Indices and labels**

(a) An index must be included at the front of the bundle listing all the documents and providing the page references for each. In the case of documents such as letters, invoices or bank statements, they may be given a general description.

(b) Where the bundles consist of more than one file, an index to all the files should be included in the first file and an index included for each file. Indices should, if possible, be on a single sheet. The full name of the case should not be inserted on the index if this would waste space. Documents should be identified briefly but properly.

(7) **Identification**

(a) Every bundle must be clearly identified, on the spine and on the front cover, with the name of the case and the Court of Appeal's reference. Where the bundle consists of more than one file, each file must be numbered on the spine, the front cover and the inside of the front cover.

(b) Outer labels should use large lettering eg 'Appeal Bundle A' or 'Core Bundle'. The full title of the appeal and solicitors' names and addresses should be omitted. A label should be used on the front as well as on the spine.

(8) **Staples etc.** All staples, heavy metal clips etc, must be removed.

(9) **Statements of case**

(a) Statements of case should be assembled in 'chapter' form—i.e claim followed by particulars of claim, followed by further information, irrespective of date.

(b) Redundant documents, eg particulars of claim overtaken by amendments, requests for further information recited in the answers given, should generally be excluded.

(10) **New Documents**

(a) Before a new document is introduced into bundles which have already been delivered to the court, steps should be taken to ensure that it carries an appropriate bundle/page number so that it can be added to the court documents. It should not be stapled and it should be prepared with punch holes for immediate inclusion in the binders in use.

(b) If it is expected that a large number of miscellaneous new documents will from time to time be introduced, there should be a special tabbed empty loose-leaf file for that purpose. An index should be produced for this file, updated as necessary.

(11) **Inter-solicitor correspondence.** Since inter-solicitor correspondence is unlikely to be required for the purposes of an appeal, only those letters which will need to be referred to should be copied.

(12) **Sanctions for non-compliance.** If the appellant fails to comply with the requirements as to the provision of bundles of documents, the application or appeal will be referred for consideration to be given as to why it should not be dismissed for failure to so comply.

Master in the Court of Appeal, Civil Division

48.95 15.5 When the Head of the Civil Appeals Office acts in a judicial capacity pursuant to rule 52.16, he shall be known as Master. Other eligible officers may also be designated by the Master of the Rolls to exercise judicial authority under rule 52.16 and shall then be known as Deputy Masters.

Respondent to notify Civil Appeals Office whether he intends to file respondent's notice

48.96 15.6 A respondent must, no later than 21 days after the date he is served with notification that—

(1) permission to appeal has been granted; or

(2) the application for permission to appeal and the appeal are to be heard together,

inform the Civil Appeals Office and the appellant in writing whether—

(a) he proposes to file a respondent's notice appealing the order or seeking to uphold the order for reasons different from, or additional to, those given by the lower court; or

(b) he proposes to rely on the reasons given by the lower court for its decision.

(Paragraph 15.11B requires all documents needed for an appeal hearing, including a respondent's skeleton argument, to be filed at least 7 days before the hearing)

Listing and hear-by dates

48.97 15.7 The management of the list will be dealt with by the listing officer under the direction of the Master.

15.8 The Civil Appeals List of the Court of Appeal is divided as follows:

- *The applications list*—applications for permission to appeal and other applications.
- *The appeals list*—appeals where permission to appeal has been given or where an appeal lies without permission being required where a hearing date is fixed in advance. (Appeals in this list which require special listing arrangements will be assigned to the special fixtures list.)
- *The expedited list*—appeals or applications where the Court of Appeal has directed an expedited hearing. The current practice of the Court of Appeal is summarized in *Unilever plc v Chefaro Proprietaries Ltd (Practice Note)* [1995] 1 WLR 24.
- *The stand-out list*—appeals or applications which, for good reason, are not at present ready to proceed and have been stood out by judicial direction.
- *The special fixtures list*—[see paragraph 15.9A(1) below].
- *The second fixtures list*—if an appeal is designated as a 'second fixture' it means that a hearing date is arranged in advance on the express basis that the list is fully booked for the period in question and therefore the case will be heard only if a suitanlble gap occurs in the list.

- *The short-warned list*—appeals which the court considers may be prepared for the hearing by an advocate other than the one originally instructed with a half day's notice, or such other period as the court may direct.

Special provisions relating to the short-warned list

15.9 (1) Where an appeal is assigned to the short-warned list, the Civil Appeals Office will notify the parties' solicitors in writing. The court may abridge the time for filing any outstanding bundles in an appeal assigned to this list.

    (2) The solicitors for the parties must notify their advocate and their client as soon as the Civil Appeals Office notifies them that the appeal has been assigned to the short-warned list.

    (3) The appellant may apply in writing for the appeal to be removed from the short-warned list within 14 days of notification of its assignment. The application will be decided by a Lord Justice, or the Master, and will only be granted for the most compelling reasons.

    (4) The Civil Appeals Listing Officer may place an appeal from the short-warned list 'on call' from a given date and will inform the parties' advocates accordingly.

    (5) An appeal which is 'on call' may be listed for hearing on half a day's notice or such longer period as the court may direct.

    (6) Once an appeal is listed for hearing from the short warned list it becomes the immediate professional duty of the advocate instructed in the appeal, if he is unable to appear at the hearing, to take all practicable measures to ensure that his lay client is represented at the hearing by an advocate who is fully instructed and able to argue the appeal.

48.98

Special provisions relating to the special fixtures list

15.9A (1) The special fixtures list is a sub-division of the appeals list and is used to deal with appeals that may require special listing arrangements, such as the need to list a number of cases before the same constitution, in a particular order, during a particular period or at a given location.

    (2) The Civil Appeals Office will notify the parties' representatives, or the parties if acting in person, of the particular arrangements that will apply. The notice—

        (a) will give details of the specific period during which a case is scheduled to be heard; and

        (b) may give directions in relation to the filing of any outstanding documents.

    (3) The listing officer will notify the parties' representatives of the precise hearing date as soon as practicable. While every effort will be made to accommodate the availability of counsel, the requirements of the court will prevail.

48.99

Requests for directions

15.10 To ensure that all requests for directions are centrally monitored and correctly allocated, all requests for directions or rulings (whether relating to listing or any other matters) should be made to the Civil Appeals Office. Those seeking directions or rulings must not approach the supervising Lord Justice either directly, or via his or her clerk.

48.100

Bundles of authorities

15.11 (1) Once the parties have been notified of the date fixed for the hearing, the appellant's advocate must, after consultation with his opponent, file a bundle containing photocopies of the authorities upon which each side will rely at the hearing.

    (2) The bundle of authorities should, in general—

        (a) have the relevant passages of the authorities marked;

        (b) not include authorities for propositions not in dispute; and

        (c) not contain more than 10 authorities unless the scale of the appeal warrants more extensive citation.

48.101

(3) The bundle of authorities must be filed—

    (a) at least 7 days before the hearing; or

    (b) where the period of notice of the hearing is less than 7 days, immediately.

(4) If, through some oversight, a party intends, during the hearing, to refer to other authorities the parties may agree a second agreed bundle. The appellant's advocate must file this bundle at least 48 hours before the hearing commences.

(5) A bundle of authorities must bear a certification by the advocates responsible for arguing the case that the requirements of sub-paragraphs (3) to (5) of paragraph 5.10 have been complied with in respect of each authority included.

Supplementary skeleton arguments

48.102   15.11A (1) A supplementary skeleton argument on which the appellant wishes to rely must be filed at least 14 days before the hearing.

(2) A supplementary skeleton argument on which the respondent wishes to rely must be filed at least 7 days before the hearing.

(3) All supplementary skeleton arguments must comply with the requirements set out in paragraph 5.10.

(4) At the hearing the court may refuse to hear argument from a party not contained in a skeleton argument filed within the relevant time limit set out in this paragraph.

Papers for the appeal hearing

48.103   15.11B (1) All the documents which are needed for the appeal hearing must be filed at least 7 days before the hearing. Where a document has not been filed 10 days before the hearing a reminder will be sent by the Civil Appeals Office.

(2) Any party who fails to comply with the provisions of paragraph (1) may be required to attend before the Presiding Lord Justice to seek permission to proceed with, or to oppose, the appeal.

Disposal of bundles of documents

48.104   15.11C (1) Where the court has determined a case, the official transcriber will retain one set of papers. The Civil Appeals Office will destroy any remaining sets of papers not collected within 21 days of—

    (a) where one or more parties attend the hearing, the date of the court's decision;

    (b) where there is no attendance, the date of the notification of court's decision.

(2) The parties should ensure that bundles of papers supplies to the court do not contain original documents (other than transcripts). The parties must ensure that they—

    (a) bring any necessary original documents to the hearing; and

    (b) retrieve any original documents handed up to the court before leaving the court.

(3) The court will retain application bundles where permission to appeal has been granted. Where permission is refused the arrangements in sub-paragraph (1) will apply.

(4) Where a single Lord Justice has refused permission to appeal on paper, application bundles will not be destroyed until after the time limit for seeking a hearing has expired.

Availability of reserved judgments before hand down

48.105   15.12 This section applies where the presiding Lord Justice is satisfied that the result of the appeal will attract no special degree of confidentiality or sensitivity.

15.13 A copy of the written judgment will be made available to the parties' legal advisers by 4 p.m. on the second working day before judgment is due to be pronounced or such other period as the court may direct. This can be shown, in confidence, to the parties but only for the purpose of obtaining instructions and on the strict understanding that the judgment, or its effect, is not to be disclosed to any other person. A working day is any day on which the Civil Appeals Office is open for business.

15.14 The appeal will be listed for judgment in the cause list and the judgment handed down at the appropriate time.

Attendance of advocates on the handing down of a reserved judgment

15.15 Where any consequential orders are agreed, the parties' advocates need not attend on **48.106** the handing down of a reserved judgment. Where an advocate does attend the court may, if it considers such attendance unnecessary, disallow the costs of the attendance. If the parties do not indicate that they intend to attend, the judgment may be handed down by a single member of the court.

Agreed orders following judgment

15.16 The parties must, in respect of any draft agreed orders— **48.107**
    (a) fax a copy to the clerk to the presiding Lord Justice; and
    (b) file four copies in the Civil Appeals Office,

no later than 12 noon on the working day before the judgment is handed down.

15.17 A copy of a draft order must bear the Court of Appeal case reference, the date the judgment is to be handed down and the name of the presiding Lord Justice.

Corrections to the draft judgment

15.18 Any proposed correction to the draft judgment should be sent to the clerk to the judge **48.108** who prepared the draft with a copy to any other party.

Application for leave to appeal

15.19 Where a party wishes to apply for leave to appeal to the House of Lords under section 1 **48.109** of the Administration of Justice (Appeals) Act 1934 the court may deal with the application on the basis of written submissions.

15.20 A party must, in relation to his submission—
    (a) fax a copy to the clerk to the presiding Lord Justice; and
    (b) file four copies in the Civil Appeals Office,

no later than 12 noon on the working day before the judgment is handed down.

15.21 A copy of a submission must bear the Court of Appeal case reference, the date the judgment is to be handed down and the name of the presiding Lord Justice.

G. CPR Part 47—Procedure for Detailed Assessment of Costs and Default Provisions

VIII APPEALS FROM AUTHORIZED COURT OFFICERS IN DETAILED ASSESSMENT PROCEEDINGS

47.20 Right to appeal **48.110**

(1) Any party to detailed assessment proceedings may appeal against a decision of an authorised court officer in those proceedings.

(2) For the purposes of this Section, a LSC funded client or an assisted person is not a party to detailed assessment proceedings.

(Part 52 sets out general rules about appeals)

47.21 Court to hear appeal

An appeal against a decision of an authorised court officer is to a costs judge or a district judge of the High Court.

47.22 Appeal procedure

(1) The appellant must file an appeal notice within 14 days after the date of the decision he wishes to appeal against.

(2) On receipt of the appeal notice, the court will—

(a) serve a copy of the notice on the parties to the detailed assessment proceedings; and

(b) give notice of the appeal hearing to those parties.

47.23 Powers of the Court on Appeal

On an appeal from an authorised court officer the court will—

(a) re-hear the proceedings which gave rise to the decision appealed against; and

(b) make any order and give any directions as it considers appropriate.

H. Access to Justice Act 1999, s 55

55. Second appeals

48.111   (1) Where an appeal is made to a county court or the High Court in relation to any matter, and on hearing the appeal the court makes a decision in relation to that matter, no appeal may be made to the Court of Appeal from that decision unless the Court of Appeal considers that—

(a) the appeal would raise an important point of principle or practice, or

(b) there is some other compelling reason for the Court of Appeal to hear it.

(2) This section does not apply in relation to an appeal in a criminal cause or matter.

49

REFERENCE INFORMATION

A. Calendar 2000 to 2007

2000

49.01

January

M		3	10	17	24	31
T		4	11	18	25
W		5	12	19	26
T		6	13	20	27
F		7	14	21	28
S	1	8	15	22	29
S	2	9	16	23	30

February

M		7	14	21	28
T	1	8	15	22	29
W	2	9	16	23
T	3	10	17	24
F	4	11	18	25
S	5	12	19	26
S	6	13	20	27

March

M		6	13	20	27
T		7	14	21	28
W	1	8	15	22	29
T	2	9	16	23	30
F	3	10	17	24	31
S	4	11	18	25
S	5	12	19	26

April

M	3	10	17	24
T	4	11	18	25
W	5	12	19	26
T	6	13	20	27
F	7	14	21	28
S	1	8	15	22	29
S	2	9	16	23	30

May

M	1	8	15	22	29
T	2	9	16	23	30
W	3	10	17	24	31
T	4	11	18	25
F	5	12	19	26
S	6	13	20	27
S	7	14	21	28

June

M		5	12	19	26
T		6	13	20	27
W		7	14	21	28
T	1	8	15	22	29
F	2	9	16	23	30
S	3	10	17	24
S	4	11	18	25

July

M		3	10	17	24	31
T		4	11	18	25
W		5	12	19	26
T		6	13	20	27
F		7	14	21	28
S	1	8	15	22	29
S	2	9	16	23	30

August

M		7	14	21	28
T	1	8	15	22	29
W	2	9	16	23	30
T	3	10	17	24	31
F	4	11	18	25
S	5	12	19	26
S	6	13	20	27

September

M		4	11	18	25
T		5	12	19	26
W		6	13	20	27
T		7	14	21	28
F	1	8	15	22	29
S	2	9	16	23	30
S	3	10	17	24

October

M	2	9	16	23	30
T	3	10	17	24	31
W	4	11	18	25
T	5	12	19	26
F	6	13	20	27
S	7	14	21	28
S	1	8	15	22	29

November

M		6	13	20	27
T		7	14	21	28
W	1	8	15	22	29
T	2	9	16	23	30
F	3	10	17	24
S	4	11	18	25
S	5	12	19	26

December

M		4	11	18	25
T		5	12	19	26
W		6	13	20	27
T		7	14	21	28
F	1	8	15	22	29
S	2	9	16	23	30
S	3	10	17	24	31

2001

	January	February	March	April
M	1 8 15 22 29	5 12 19 26	5 12 19 26	2 9 16 23 30
T	2 9 16 23 30	6 13 20 27	6 13 20 27	3 10 17 24
W	3 10 17 24 31	7 14 21 28	7 14 21 28	4 11 18 25
T	4 11 18 25	1 8 15 22	1 8 15 22 29	5 12 19 26
F	5 12 19 26	2 9 16 23	2 9 16 23 30	6 13 20 27
S	6 13 20 27	3 10 17 24	3 10 17 24 31	7 14 21 28
S	7 14 21 28	4 11 18 25	4 11 18 25	1 8 15 22 29

	May	June	July	August
M	7 14 21 28	4 11 18 25	2 9 16 23 30	6 13 20 27
T	1 8 15 22 29	5 12 19 26	3 10 17 24 31	7 14 21 28
W	2 9 16 23 30	6 13 20 27	4 11 18 25	1 8 15 22 29
T	3 10 17 24 31	7 14 21 28	5 12 19 26	2 9 16 23 30
F	4 11 18 25	1 8 15 22 29	6 13 20 27	3 10 17 24 31
S	5 12 19 26	2 9 16 23 30	7 14 21 28	4 11 18 25
S	6 13 20 27	3 10 17 24	1 8 15 22 29	5 12 19 26

	September	October	November	December
M	3 10 17 24	1 8 15 22 29	5 12 19 26	3 10 17 24 31
T	4 11 18 25	2 9 16 23 30	6 13 20 27	4 11 18 25
W	5 12 19 26	3 10 17 24 31	7 14 21 28	5 12 19 26
T	6 13 20 27	4 11 18 25	1 8 15 22 29	6 13 20 27
F	7 14 21 28	5 12 19 26	2 9 16 23 30	7 14 21 28
S	1 8 15 22 29	6 13 20 27	3 10 17 24	1 8 15 22 29
S	2 9 16 23 30	7 14 21 28	4 11 18 25	2 9 16 23 30

2002

	January	February	March	April
M	7 14 21 28	4 11 18 25	4 11 18 25	1 8 15 22 29
T	1 8 15 22 29	5 12 19 26	5 12 19 26	2 9 16 23 30
W	2 9 16 23 30	6 13 20 27	6 13 20 27	3 10 17 24
T	3 10 17 24 31	7 14 21 28	7 14 21 28	4 11 18 25
F	4 11 18 25	1 8 15 22	1 8 15 22 29	5 12 19 26
S	5 12 19 26	2 9 16 23	2 9 16 23 30	6 13 20 27
S	6 13 20 27	3 10 17 24	3 10 17 24 31	7 14 21 28

	May	June	July	August
M	6 13 20 27	3 10 17 24	1 8 15 22 29	5 12 19 26
T	7 14 21 28	4 11 18 25	2 9 16 23 30	6 13 20 27
W	1 8 15 22 29	5 12 19 26	3 10 17 24 31	7 14 21 28
T	2 9 16 23 30	6 13 20 27	4 11 18 25	1 8 15 22 29
F	3 10 17 24 31	7 14 21 28	5 12 19 26	2 9 16 23 30
S	4 11 18 25	1 8 15 22 29	6 13 20 27	3 10 17 24 31
S	5 12 19 26	2 9 16 23 30	7 14 21 28	4 11 18 25

	September	October	November	December
M	2 9 16 23 30	7 14 21 28	4 11 18 25	2 9 16 23 30
T	3 10 17 24	1 8 15 22 29	5 12 19 26	3 10 17 24 31
W	4 11 18 25	2 9 16 23 30	6 13 20 27	4 11 18 25
T	5 12 19 26	3 10 17 24 31	7 14 21 28	5 12 19 26
F	6 13 20 27	4 11 18 25	1 8 15 22 29	6 13 20 27
S	7 14 21 28	5 12 19 26	2 9 16 23 30	7 14 21 28
S	1 8 15 22 29	6 13 20 27	3 10 17 24	1 8 15 22 29

2003

	January	February	March	April
M	6 13 20 27	3 10 17 24	3 10 17 24 31	7 14 21 28
T	7 14 21 28	4 11 18 25	4 11 18 25	1 8 15 22 29
W	1 8 15 22 29	5 12 19 26	5 12 19 26	2 9 16 23 30
T	2 9 16 23 30	6 13 20 27	6 13 20 27	3 10 17 24
F	3 10 17 24 31	7 14 21 28	7 14 21 28	4 11 18 25
S	4 11 18 25	1 8 15 22	1 8 15 22 29	5 12 19 26
S	5 12 19 26	2 9 16 23	2 9 16 23 30	6 13 20 27

	May	June	July	August
M	5 12 19 26	2 9 16 23 30	7 14 21 28	4 11 18 25
T	6 13 20 27	3 10 17 24	1 8 15 22 29	5 12 19 26
W	7 14 21 28	4 11 18 25	2 9 16 23 30	6 13 20 27
T	1 8 15 22 29	5 12 19 26	3 10 17 24 31	7 14 21 28
F	2 9 16 23 30	6 13 20 27	4 11 18 25	1 8 15 22 29
S	3 10 17 24 31	7 14 21 28	5 12 19 26	2 9 16 23 30
S	4 11 18 25	1 8 15 22 29	6 13 20 27	3 10 17 24 31

	September	October	November	December
M	1 8 15 22 29	6 13 20 27	3 10 17 24	1 8 15 22 29
T	2 9 16 23 30	7 14 21 28	4 11 18 25	2 9 16 23 30
W	3 10 17 24	1 8 15 22 29	5 12 19 26	3 10 17 24 31
T	4 11 18 25	2 9 16 23 30	6 13 20 27	4 11 18 25
F	5 12 19 26	3 10 17 24 31	7 14 21 28	5 12 19 26
S	6 13 20 27	4 11 18 25	1 8 15 22 29	6 13 20 27
S	7 14 21 28	5 12 19 26	2 9 16 23 30	7 14 21 28

2004

	January	February	March	April
M	5 12 19 26	2 9 16 23	1 8 15 22 29	5 12 19 26
T	6 13 20 27	3 10 17 24	2 9 16 23 30	6 13 20 27
W	7 14 21 28	4 11 18 25	3 10 17 24 31	7 14 21 28
T	1 8 15 22 29	5 12 19 26	4 11 18 25	1 8 15 22 29
F	2 9 16 23 30	6 13 20 27	5 12 19 26	2 9 16 23 30
S	3 10 17 24 31	7 14 21 28	6 13 20 27	3 10 17 24
S	4 11 18 25	1 8 15 22 29	7 14 21 28	4 11 18 25

	May	June	July	August
M	3 10 17 24 31	7 14 21 28	5 12 19 26	2 9 16 23 30
T	4 11 18 25	1 8 15 22 29	6 13 20 27	3 10 17 24 31
W	5 12 19 26	2 9 16 23 30	7 14 21 28	4 11 18 25
T	6 13 20 27	3 10 17 24	1 8 15 22 29	5 12 19 26
F	7 14 21 28	4 11 18 25	2 9 16 23 30	6 13 20 27
S	1 8 15 22 29	5 12 19 26	3 10 17 24 31	7 14 21 28
S	2 9 16 23 30	6 13 20 27	4 11 18 25	1 8 15 22 29

	September	October	November	December
M	6 13 20 27	4 11 18 25	1 8 15 22 29	6 13 20 27
T	7 14 21 28	5 12 19 26	2 9 16 23 30	7 14 21 28
W	1 8 15 22 29	6 13 20 27	3 10 17 24	1 8 15 22 29
T	2 9 16 23 30	7 14 21 28	4 11 18 25	2 9 16 23 30
F	3 10 17 24	1 8 15 22 29	5 12 19 26	3 10 17 24 31
S	4 11 18 25	2 9 16 23 30	6 13 20 27	4 11 18 25
S	5 12 19 26	3 10 17 24 31	7 14 21 28	5 12 19 26

2005

	January	February	March	April
M	3 10 17 24 31	7 14 21 28	7 14 21 28	4 11 18 25
T	4 11 18 25	1 8 15 22	1 8 15 22 29	5 12 19 26
W	5 12 19 26	2 9 16 23	2 9 16 23 30	6 13 20 27
T	6 13 20 27	3 10 17 24	3 10 17 24 31	7 14 21 28
F	7 14 21 28	4 11 18 25	4 11 18 25	1 8 15 22 29
S	1 8 15 22 29	5 12 19 26	5 12 19 26	2 9 16 23 30
S	2 9 16 23 30	6 13 20 27	6 13 20 27	3 10 17 24

	May	June	July	August
M	2 9 16 23 30	6 13 20 27	4 11 18 25	1 8 15 22 29
T	3 10 17 24 31	7 14 21 28	5 12 19 26	2 9 16 23 30
W	4 11 18 25	1 8 15 22 29	6 13 20 27	3 10 17 24 31
T	5 12 19 26	2 9 16 23 30	7 14 21 28	4 11 18 25
F	6 13 20 27	3 10 17 24	1 8 15 22 29	5 12 19 26
S	7 14 21 28	4 11 18 25	2 9 16 23 30	6 13 20 27
S	1 8 15 22 29	5 12 19 26	3 10 17 24 31	7 14 21 28

	September	October	November	December
M	5 12 19 26	3 10 17 24 31	7 14 21 28	5 12 19 26
T	6 13 20 27	4 11 18 25	1 8 15 22 29	6 13 20 27
W	7 14 21 28	5 12 19 26	2 9 16 23 30	7 14 21 28
T	1 8 15 22 29	6 13 20 27	3 10 17 24	1 8 15 22 29
F	2 9 16 23 30	7 14 21 28	4 11 18 25	2 9 16 23 30
S	3 10 17 24	1 8 15 22 29	5 12 19 26	3 10 17 24 31
S	4 11 18 25	2 9 16 23 30	6 13 20 27	4 11 18 25

2006

	January	February	March	April
M	2 9 16 23 30	6 13 20 27	6 13 20 27	3 10 17 24
T	3 10 17 24 31	7 14 21 28	7 14 21 28	4 11 18 25
W	4 11 18 25	1 8 15 22	1 8 15 22 29	5 12 19 26
T	5 12 19 26	2 9 16 23	2 9 16 23 30	6 13 20 27
F	6 13 20 27	3 10 17 24	3 10 17 24 31	7 14 21 28
S	7 14 21 28	4 11 18 25	4 11 18 25	1 8 15 22 29
S	1 8 15 22 29	5 12 19 26	5 12 19 26	2 9 16 23 30

	May	June	July	August
M	1 8 15 22 29	5 12 19 26	3 10 17 24 31	7 14 21 28
T	2 9 16 23 30	6 13 20 27	4 11 18 25	1 8 15 22 29
W	3 10 17 24 31	7 14 21 28	5 12 19 26	2 9 16 23 30
T	4 11 18 25	1 8 15 22 29	6 13 20 27	3 10 17 24 31
F	5 12 19 26	2 9 16 23 30	7 14 21 28	4 11 18 25
S	6 13 20 27	3 10 17 24	1 8 15 22 29	5 12 19 26
S	7 14 21 28	4 11 18 25	2 9 16 23 30	6 13 20 27

	September	October	November	December
M	4 11 18 25	2 9 16 23 30	6 13 20 27	4 11 18 25
T	5 12 19 26	3 10 17 24 31	7 14 21 28	5 12 19 26
W	6 13 20 27	4 11 18 25	1 8 15 22 29	6 13 20 27
T	7 14 21 28	5 12 19 26	2 9 16 23 30	7 14 21 28
F	1 8 15 22 29	6 13 20 27	3 10 17 24	1 8 15 22 29
S	2 9 16 23 30	7 14 21 28	4 11 18 25	2 9 16 23 30
S	3 10 17 24	1 8 15 22 29	5 12 19 26	3 10 17 24 31

2007

	January	February	March	April
M	1 8 15 22 29	5 12 19 26	5 12 19 26	2 9 16 23 30
T	2 9 16 23 30	6 13 20 27	6 13 20 27	3 10 17 24
W	3 10 17 24 31	7 14 21 28	7 14 21 28	4 11 18 25
T	4 11 18 25	1 8 15 22	1 8 15 22 29	5 12 19 26
F	5 12 19 26	2 9 16 23	2 9 16 23 30	6 13 20 27
S	6 13 20 27	3 10 17 24	3 10 17 24 31	7 14 21 28
S	7 14 21 28	4 11 18 25	4 11 18 25	1 8 15 22 29

	May	June	July	August
M	7 14 21 28	4 11 18 25	2 9 16 23 30	6 13 20 27
T	1 8 15 22 29	5 12 19 26	3 10 17 24 31	7 14 21 28
W	2 9 16 23 30	6 13 20 27	4 11 18 25	1 8 15 22 29
T	3 10 17 24 31	7 14 21 28	5 12 19 26	2 9 16 23 30
F	4 11 18 25	1 8 15 22 29	6 13 20 27	3 10 17 24 31
S	5 12 19 26	2 9 16 23 30	7 14 21 28	4 11 18 25
S	6 13 20 27	3 10 17 24	1 8 15 22 29	5 12 19 26

	September	October	November	December
M	3 10 17 24	1 8 15 22 29	5 12 19 26	3 10 17 24 31
T	4 11 18 25	2 9 16 23 30	6 13 20 27	4 11 18 25
W	5 12 19 26	3 10 17 24 31	7 14 21 28	5 12 19 26
T	6 13 20 27	4 11 18 25	1 8 15 22 29	6 13 20 27
F	7 14 21 28	5 12 19 26	2 9 16 23 30	7 14 21 28
S	1 8 15 22 29	6 13 20 27	3 10 17 24	1 8 15 22 29
S	2 9 16 23 30	7 14 21 28	4 11 18 25	2 9 16 23 30

B. Conversion Multipliers

Ounces × 28.35 = grams, grams × 0.03527 = ounces   **49.02**
Pounds × 0.4536 = kilograms, kilograms × 2.2046 = pounds
Inches × 2.54 = centimetres, centimetres × 0.3937 = inches
Feet × 0.3048 = metres, metres × 3.281 = feet
Yards × 0.9144 = metres, metres × 1.094 = yards
Miles × 1.609 = kilometres, kilometres × 0.6214 = miles
mph × 1.6093 = kph, kph × 0.6214 = mph
Gallons × 4.545 = litres, litres × 0.22 = gallons
Centigrade × 9 ÷ 5 + 32 = Fahrenheit, Fahrenheit − 32 × 5 ÷ 9 = centigrade

C. Income Tax and National Insurance Rates

1999/2000

Income Tax:	**49.03**
Personal allowance	4,335
Married couple's allowance	1,970
Band taxed at 10%	1,500

787

Band taxed at 23%	26,500
Higher rate 40%	the remainder

National Insurance:

Employees lower earnings limit	3,432
Employees upper earnings limit	26,000
Standard contribution rate	10%
Contracted out rate	8.4%
Class 2 self-employed lower limit	3,770
Fixed weekly rate	6.55
Lower profit limit	7,530
Upper profit limit	26,000
Contribution rate	6%

2000/01

Income Tax:

Personal allowance	4,385
Married couple's allowance	abolished
Band taxed at 10%	1,520
Band taxed at 22%	26,880
Higher rate 40%	the remainder

National Insurance:

Employees lower earnings limit	3,952
Employees upper earnings limit	27,820
Standard contribution rate	10%
Contracted out rate	8.4%
Class 2 self-employed lower limit	3,825
Fixed weekly rate	2.00
Lower profit limit	4,385
Upper profit limit	27,820
Contribution rate	7%

2001/02

Income Tax:

Personal allowance	4,535
Married couple's allowance	abolished
Band taxed at 10%	1,880
Band taxed at 22%	27,520
Higher rate 40%	the remainder

National Insurance:

Employees lower earnings limit	4,524
Employees upper earnings limit	29,900

Standard contribution rate	10%
Contracted out rate	8.4%
Class 2 self-employed lower limit	3,955
Fixed weekly rate	2.00
Lower profit limit	4,535
Upper profit limit	29,900
Contribution rate	7%

2002/03

Income Tax:

Personal allowance	4,615
Band taxed at 10%	1,920
Band taxed at 22%	27,980
Higher rate 40%	the remainder

National Insurance:

Employees lower earnings limit	3,900
Primary threshold	4,615
Employees upper earnings limit	30,420
Standard contribution rate	10%
Contracted out rate	8.4%
Class 2 self-employed lower limit	4,025
Fixed weekly rate	2
Lower profit limit	4,615
Upper profit limit	30,420
Contribution rate	7%

2003/04

Income Tax:

Personal allowance	4,615
Band taxed at 10%	1,960
Band taxed at 22%	£28,540
Higher rate 40%	the remainder

National Insurance:

Employees lower earnings limit	4,004
Primary threshold	4,615
Employees upper earnings limit	30,940
Standard contribution rate	11%
Rate above upper earnings limit	1%
Contracted out rate	9.4%
Class 2 self-employed lower limit	4,095
Fixed weekly rate	2

Lower profit limit	4,615
Upper profit limit	30,940
Contribution rate	8%
Rate above upper profit limit	1%

2004/05

Income Tax:

Personal allowance	4,745
Band taxed at 10%	2,020
Band taxed at 22%	31,400
Higher rate 40%	the remainder

National Insurance:

Employees lower earnings limit	4,108
Employees upper earnings limit	31,720
Standard contribution rate	11%
Rate above upper earnings limit	1%
Contracted out rate	9.4%
Class 2 self-employed lower limit	4,215
Fixed weekly rate	2.05
Lower profit limit	4,215
Upper profit limit	31,720
Contribution rate	8%
Rate above upper profit limit	1%

D. Useful Addresses and Websites

49.04 The updating service for this book:
www.oup.com/uk/law/practitioner/cws

Oxford University Press:
www.oup.com

Compensation Recovery Unit
Durham House, Washington, Tyne & Wear NE38 7SF
Website   www.dwp.gov.uk/cru/#howtocontactus

AvMA Action against Medical Accidents
44 High Street, Croydon, Surrey CRO 1YB
Helpline   0845 123 23 52   Fax   020 8667 9065
Email   admin@avma.org.uk

BNA Care Assessment Services
The Collonades, Beaconsfield Close, Hatfield, Herts AL10 8YD
Freephone   0800 581691

Email   info@bna.co.uk
Website   www.care.assessment.bna.co.uk

Headway—the brain injury association
200 Mansfield Road, Nottingham NG1 3HX
Helpline   0808 800 2244
Email   helpline@headway.org.uk

Disabled Living Foundation
380 Harrow Road, London W9 2HU
Helpline   0845 130 9177
Website   www.dlf.org.uk/

Acts of Parliament at www.hmso.gov.uk/acts.htm
Statutory instruments at www.hmso.gov.uk/stat.htm
Civil Procedure Rules at www.dca.gov.uk/civil/procrules_fin/current.htm
Lord Chancellor's Dept at www.dca.gov.uk/
Court Service at www.courtservice.gov.uk/
Home Office at www.homeoffice.gov.uk
Government Actuary's Department at www.gad.gov.uk
Court of Protection at www.guardianship.co.uk
Criminal Injuries Compensation Authority at www.cica.gov.uk
Professional Negligence Bar Association at www.pnba.co.uk
Academy of Experts at www.academy-expert.org
Expert Witness Institute at www.ewi.org.uk

E. Addresses of Courts

Northern Circuit

Accrington   Trial Centre Burnley   **49.05**
Bradshawgate House, 1 Oak Street, Accrington, Lancashire BB5 1EQ
Tel 01254 237490 Fax 01254 393869 DX 702645 Accrington 2

Altrincham   Trial Centre Manchester
Trafford Courthouse, Ashton Lane, Sale, Cheshire M33 TNR
Tel 0161 975 4760 Fax 0161 975 4761 DX 708292 Sale 6

Barrow in Furness
Government Bldgs, Michaelson Road, Barrow in Furness, Cumbria LA14 2EZ
Tel 01229 820046 Fax 01229 430039 DX 65210 Barrow in Furness 2

Birkenhead   Trial Centre Liverpool
76 Hamilton Street, Birkenhead, Merseyside CH41 5EN
Tel 0151 666 5800 Fax 0151 666 5873

Blackburn   Trial Centre Preston
64 Victoria Street, Blackburn, Lancashire BB1 6DJ
Tel 01254 680640 Fax 01254 692712 DX 702650 Blackburn 4

Blackpool
Chapel Street, Blackpool, Lancashire FY1 5RJ
Tel 01253 754020 Fax 01253 295255 DX 724900 Blackpool 10

Bolton   Trial Centre Bury
Blackhorse Street, Bolton, Lancashire BL1 1SU
Tel 01204 392881 Fax 01204 363204 DX 702611 Bolton 3

Burnley
Hammerton Street, Burnley, Lancashire BB11 1XD
Tel 01282 416899 Fax 01282 414911 DX 724940 Burnley 4

Bury
Tenterden Street, Bury, Lancashire BL9 0HJ
Tel 0161 7641344 Fax 0161 7634995 DX 702615 Bury 2

Carlisle
Courts of Justice, Earl Street, Carlisle, Cumbria CA1 1DJ
Tel 01228 528182 Fax 01228 590588 DX 65335 Carlisle 2

Chorley   Trial Centre Preston
59 St Thomas's Road, Chorley, Lancashire PR7 1JE
Tel 01257 262778 Fax 01257 232843 DX 702665 Chorley 3

Kendal   Trial Centre Lancaster
Burneside Road, Kendal, Cumbria LA9 4NF
Tel 01539 721218 Fax 01539 733840 DX 63450 Kendal 2

Lancaster
2nd Floor, Mitre House, Church Street, Lancaster LA1 1UZ
Tel 01524 68112 Fax 01524 846478 DX 145880 Lancaster 2

Leigh   Trial Centre Liverpool
22 Walmesley Road, Leigh, Greater Manchester WN7 1YF
Tel 01942 673639 Fax 01942 681216 DX 702555 Leigh 2

Liverpool
Derby Square, Liverpool L2 1XA
Tel 0151 4737373 Fax 0151 2581587 DX 702600 Liverpool 5

Manchester
Courts of Justice, Crown Square, Manchester M60 9DF
Tel 0161 9541800 Fax 0161 9541661 DX 702541 Manchester II

Nelson
Phoenix Chambers, 9–13 Holme Street, Nelson, Lancashire BB9 9SU
Tel 01282 601177 Fax 01282 619557 DX 702560 Nelson 2

Oldham
New Radcliffe Street, Oldham, Lancashire OL1 1NL
Tel 01612 904200 Fax 01612 904222 DX 702595 Oldham 2

Penrith   Trial Centre Carlisle
Lowther Terrace, Penrith, Cumbria CA11 7QL
Tel 01768 862535 Fax 01768 899700 DX 65207 Penrith 2

Preston
Ring Way, Preston, Lancashire PR1 2LL
Tel 01772 844700 Fax 01772 844710 DX 702640 Preston 4

Rawtenstall   Trial Centre Burnley
1 Grange Street, Rawtenstall, Lancashire BB4 7RT
Tel 01706 214614 Fax 01706 219814 DX 702565 Rawtenstall 2

St Helens   Trial Centre Liverpool
1st Floor Rcxmorc House, Cotham Street, St Helens, Merseyside WA10 1SE
Tel 01744 27544 Fax 01744 20484 DX 725020 St Helens 4

Salford   Trial Centre Manchester
Prince William House, Peel Cross Road (off Eccles New Rd), Salford, Greater Manchester M5 2RR
Tel 0161 7457511 Fax 0161 7457202 DX 702630 Salford 5

Southport   Trial Centre Liverpool
Duke's House, 34 Hoghton Street, Southport, Merseyside PR9 OPU
Tel 01704 531541 Fax 01704 542487 DX 702580 Southport 2

Stockport   Trial Centre Oldham
5th Floor, Heron House, Wellington Street, Stockport, Greater Manchester SK1 3DJ
Tel 01614 747707 Fax 01614 763129 DX 702621 Stockport 4

Tameside   Trial Centre Oldham
PO Box 166, Henry Square, Ashton under Lyne, Lancashire 0L6 7TP
Tel 0161 3315614 Fax 0161 3315649 DX 702625 Ashton under Lyne

Whitehaven   Trial Centre Carlisle
Old Town Hall, Duke Street, Whitehaven, Cumbria CA28 7NU
Tel 01946 67788 Fax 01946 691219 DX 63990 Whitehaven 2

Wigan   Trial Centre Manchester
Crawford Street, Wigan, Greater Manchester WN1 1NG
Tel 01942 246481 Fax 01942 829164 DX 724820 Wigan 9

North Eastern Circuit

Barnsley   Trial Centre Sheffield
12 Regent Street, Barnsley, South Yorkshire S70 2EW
Tel 01226 203471 Fax 01226 779126 DX 702080 Barnsley 3

Bishop Auckland   Trial Centre Teesside
Saddler House, Saddler Street, Bishop Auckland, Co Durham DL14 7HF
Tel 01388 602423 Fax 01388 606651 DX 65100 Bishop Auckland 2

Bradford
Exchange Square, Drake Street, Bradford, West Yorkshire BD1 1JA
Tel 01274 840274 Fax 01274 840275 DX 702083 Bradford 2

Consett   Trial Centre Newcastle upon Tyne
Victoria Road, Consett, Co Durham DH8 5AU
Tel 01207 502854 Fax 01207 582626 DX 65106 Consett 2

Darlington   Trial Centre Teesside
4 Coniscliffe Road, Darlington, Co Durham DL3 7RL
Tel 01325 463224 Fax 01325 362829 DX 65109 Darlington 3

Dewsbury   Trial Centre Huddersfield
Eightlands Road, Dewsbury, West Yorkshire WF13 2PE
Tel 01924 466135 Fax 01924 456419 DX 702086 Dewsbury 2

Doncaster
74 Waterdale, Doncaster, South Yorkshire DN1 3BT
Tel 01302 381730 Fax 01302 768090 DX 702089 Doncaster 4

Durham   Trial Centre Newcastle upon Tyne
Hallgarth Street, Durham DH1 3RG
Tel 0191 3865941 Fax 0191 3861328 DX 65115 Durham 5

Great Grimsby
Town Hall Square, Great Grimsby, South Humberside DN31 1HX
Tel 01472 311811 Fax 01472 312039 DX 702007 Grimsby 3

Halifax   Trial Centre Huddersfield
Prescott Street, Halifax, West Yorkshire HX1 2JJ
Tel 01422 344700 Fax 01422 360132 DX 702095 Halifax 2

Harrogate   Trial Centre York
2 Victoria Avenue, Harrogate, North Yorkshire HG1 1EL
Tel 01423 503921 Fax 01423 528679 DX 702098 Harrogate 3

Hartlepool   Trial Centre Teesside
The Law Courts, Victoria Road, Hartlepool TS24 8BS
Tel 01429 268198 Fax 01429 862550 DX 65121 Hartlepool 2

Huddersfield
Queensgate House, Queensgate, Huddersfield, West Yorkshire HD1 2RR
Tel 01484 421043 Fax 01484 426366 DX 703013 Huddersfield 2

Keighley   Trial Centre Bradford
Yorkshire Bank Chambers, North Street, Keighley, West Yorkshire BD21 3SH
Tel 01535 602803 Fax 01535 610549 DX 703007 Keighley 2

Kingston upon Hull
Lowgate, Kingston upon Hull HU1 2EZ
Tel 01482 586161 Fax 01482 588527 DX 703010 Hull 5

Leeds
1 Oxford Row, Leeds, West Yorkshire LS1 3BG
Tel 0113 2830040 Fax 0113 2452305 DX 703016 Leeds 6

Morpeth & Berwick   Trial Centre Newcastle upon Tyne
Fountain House, Newmarket, Morpeth, Northumberland NE6 1LA
Tel 01670 512221 Fax 01670 504188 DX 65124 Morpeth 2

Newcastle upon Tyne
The Law Courts, Quayside, Newcastle upon Tyne NE1 3LA
Tel 0191 2012000 Fax 0191 2012001 DX 65127 Newcastle upon Tyne 2

North Shields   Trial Centre Newcastle upon Tyne
Northumbria House, Norfolk Street, North Shields, Tyne and Wear NE30 1EX
Tel 0191 257 5866 Fax 0191 296 4268 DX 65137 North Shields 2

Pontefract   Trial Centre Leeds
Horsefair House, Horsefair, Pontefract, West Yorkshire WF8 1RJ
Tel 01977 702357 Fax 01977 600204 DX 703022 Pontefract 2

Rotherham   Trial Centre Sheffield
Portland House, Mansfield Road, Rotherham, South Yorkshire S60 2 BX
Tel 01709 364786 Fax 01709 838044 DX 703025 Rotherham 4

Scarborough   Trial Centre York
Pavilion House, Valley Bridge Road, Scarborough, North Yorkshire YO11 2JS
Tel 01723 366361 Fax 01723 501992 DX 65140 Scarborough 2

Scunthorpe   Trial Centre Gt Grimsby
Crown Buildings, Comforts Avenue, Scunthorpe DN15 6PR
Tel 01724 289111 Fax 01724 291119 DX 702010 Scunthorpe 3

Sheffield
The Law Centre, 50 West Bar, Sheffield, South Yorkshire S3 8PH
Tel 0114 2812400 Fax 0114 2812425 DX 703028 Sheffield 6

Skipton   Trial Centre Bradford
The Old Court House, Otley Street, Skipton, West Yorkshire BD23 1EH
Tel 01756 793315 Fax 001756 799989 DX 703031 Skipton 2

South Shields   Trial Centre Newcastle upon Tyne
Millbank, Secretan Way, South Shields, Tyne and Wear NE33 1RG
Tel 0191 4563343 Fax 0191 4279503 DX 65143 South Shields 3

Sunderland   Trial Centre Newcastle upon Tyne
44 John Street, Sunderland, Tyne and Wear SR1 1RB
Tel 0191 5680750 Fax 0191 5143028 DX 65149 Sunderland 2

Teesside
Russell Street, Middlesbrough, Cleveland TS1 2AE
Tel 01642 340000 Fax 01642 340002 DX 65152 Middlesbrough 2

Wakefield   Trial Centre Leeds
The Crown House, Kirkgate, Wakefield, West Yorkshire WF1 1JW
Tel 01924 370268 Fax 01924 200818 DX 703040 Wakefield 3

York
Piccadilly House, 55 Piccadilly, York YO1 9WL
Tel 01904 629935 Fax 01904 679963 DX 65165 York 4

Midland Circuit

Birmingham
The Priory Courts, 33 Bull Street, Birmingham B4 6DS
Tel 0121 6814441 Fax 01121 6813001 DX 701987 Birmingham 7

Boston   Trial Centre Lincoln
55 Norfolk Street, Boston, Lincolnshire PE21 6PE
Tel 01205 366080 Fax 01205 311692 DX 710922 Boston 2

Burton upon Trent   Trial Centre Derby
165 Station Street, Burton upon Trent, Staffordshire DE14 1BP
Tel 01283 568241 Fax 01238 517245 DX 702044 Burton on Trent 3

Buxton   Trial Centre Derby
1–3 Hardwicke Street, Buxton, Derbyshire SK17 6DH
Tel 01298 23734 Fax 01298 73281 DX 701970 Buxton 2

Chesterfield   Trial Centre Derby
St Mary's Gate, Chesterfield, Derbyshire S41 7ED
Tel 01246 501200 Fax 01246 501205 DX 703160 Chesterfield 3

Coventry
140 Much Park Street, Coventry, West Midlands CV1 2SN
Tel 02476 536166 Fax 02476 520443 DX 701580 Coventry 5

Derby
Morledge, Derby, Derbyshire DE1 2XE
Tel 01332 622600 Fax 01332 622543 DX 724060 Derby 21

Dudley   Trial Centre Birmingham
Harbour Bldgs, Waterfront West, Dudley Rd, Brierley Hill, West Midlands
DY5 1LN
Tel 01384 480799 Fax 01384 482799 DX 701949 Dudley 2

Evesham   Trial Centre Worcester
87 High Street, Evesham, Worcestershire WR11 4EE
Tel 01386 442287 Fax 01386 49203 DX 701910 Evesham 3

Grantham   Trial Centre Lincoln
Harlaxton Road, Grantham, Lincolnshire NG31 7SB
Tel 01476 539030 Fax 01476 539040 DX 701931 Grantham 2

Hereford   Trial Centre Worcester
1st Floor, Barclays Bank Chambers, 1–3 Broad Street, Hereford HR4 9BA
Tel 01432 357233 Fax 01432 352593 DX 701904 Hereford 2

Kettering   Trial Centre Northampton
Dryland Street, Kettering, Northamptonshire NN16 0BE
Tel 01536 512471 Fax 01536 416857 DX 701886 Kettering 2

Kidderminster   Trial Centre Birmingham
10 Comberton Place, Kidderminster, Worcestershire DY10 1QR
Tel 01562 822480 Fax 01562 827809 DX 701946 Kidderminster 2

Leicester
PO Box No 3, 90 Wellington Street, Leicester LE1 6ZZ
Tel 0116 2225700 Fax 0116 2225762 DX 17401 Leicester 3

Lincoln
360 High Street, Lincoln LN5 7PS
Tel 01522 883000 Fax 01522 883003 DX 703231 Lincoln 6

Ludlow   Trial Centre Telford
9–10 King Street, Ludlow, Shropshire SY8 1AQ
Tel 01584 872091 Fax 01584 877606 DX 702013 Ludlow 2

Mansfield   Trial Centre Nottingham
Beech House, 58 Commercial Gate, Mansfield, Nottinghamshire NG18 1EU
Tel 01623 656406 Fax 01623 26561 DX 702180 Mansfield 3

Melton Mowbray   Trial Centre Leicester
The Court House, Norman Way, Melton Mowbray, Leicestershire LE13 1NH
Tel 01664 458100 Fax 01664 501869 DX 701937 Melton Mowbray 2

Newark   Trial Centre Lincoln
Crown Building, 41 Lombard Street, Newark, Nottinghamshire NG24 1EF
Tel 01636 703607 Fax 01636 613726 DX 701928 Newark 2

Northampton
85–87 Lady's Lane, Northampton NN1 3HQ
Tel 01604 470400 Fax 01604 232398 DX 725380 Northampton 21

Nottingham
60 Canal Street, Nottingham NG1 7EJ
Tel 0115 9103500 Fax 0115 9103510 DX 702381 Nottingham 7

Nuneaton   Trial Centre Coventry
Heron House, Newdegate Street, Nuneaton, Warwickshire CV11 4EL
Tel 02476 386134 Fax 02476 352769 DX 701940 Nuneaton 2

Oswestry   Trial Centre Telford
2nd Floor, The Guildhall, Bailey Head, Oswestry, Shropshire SY11 2EW
Tel 01691 652127 Fax 01691 671239 DX 701958 Oswestry 2

Redditch   Trial Centre Worcester
13 Church Road, Redditch, Worcestershire B97 4AB
Tel 01527 67822 Fax 01527 65791 DX 701880 Redditch 2

Rugby   Trial Centre Coventry
5 Newbold Road, Rugby, Warwickshire CV21 2RN
Tel 01788 542543 Fax 01788 550212 DX 701943 Rugby 2

Shrewsbury   Trial Centre Telford
Cambrian Business Centre, Chester Street, Shrewsbury, Shropshire SY1 1NA
Tel 01743 289069 Fax 01743 237954 DX 702047 Shrewsbury 3

Skegness   Trial Centre Lincoln
55 Norfolk Street, Boston, Lincolnshire PE21 6PE
Tel 01205 366080 Fax 01205 311692 DX 701922 Boston 2

Stafford   Trial Centre Stoke on Trent
Victoria Square, Stafford, Staffordshire ST16 2QQ
Tel 01785 610730 Fax 01785 213250 DX 703190 Stafford 4

Stoke on Trent
Bethesda Street, Hanley, Stoke on Trent, Staffordshire ST1 3BP
Tel 01782 854000 Fax 01782 854021 DX 703360 Hanley 3

Stourbridge   Trial Centre Birmingham
7 Hagley Road, Stourbridge, West Midlands DY8 1QL
Tel 01384 394232 Fax 01384 441736 DX 701889 Stourbridge 2

Stratford on Avon   Trial Centre Coventry
5 Elm Court, Arden Street, Stratford upon Avon, Warwickshire CV37 6PA
Tel 01789 293056 Fax 01789 293056 DX 701998 Stratford upon Avon 3

Tamworth   Trial Centre Stoke on Trent
The Precinct, Lower Gungate, Tamworth, Staffordshire B79 7AJ
Tel 01827 62664 Fax 01827 65289 DX 702016 Tamworth 2

Telford
Telford Square, Malinsgate Town Centre, Telford, Shropshire TF3 4JP
Tel 01952 291045 Fax 01952 291601 DX 701976 Telford 3

Walsall   Trial Centre Stoke on Trent
Bridge House, Bridge Street, Walsall, West Midlands WS1 1JQ
Tel 01922 728855 Fax 01922 728891 DX 701943 Walsall 2

Warwick   Trial Centre Coventry
Northgate South Side, Warwick CV34 4RB
Tel 01926 492776 Fax 01926 474227 DX 701966 Warwick 2

Wellingborough   Trial Centre Northampton
Lothersdale House, West Villa Road, Wellingborough, Northants NN8 4NF
Tel 01933 226168 Fax 01933 272977 DX 701883 Wellingborough 2

Wolverhampton   Trial Centre Telford
Pipers Row, Wolverhampton, W Midlands WV1 3LQ
Tel 01902 481000 Fax 01902 481001 DX 702019 Wolverhampton 4

Worcester
The Shirehall, Foregate Street, Worcester WR1 1EQ
Tel 01905 730800 Fax 01905 730801 DX 716262 Worcester 1

Worksop   Trial Centre Lincoln
8 Slack Walk, Worksop, Nottinghamshire S80 1LN
Tel 01909 472358 Fax 01909 530181 DX 7002190 Worksop 2

Wales and Chester Circuit

Aberdare   Trial Centre Swansea
The Court House, Cwmbach Road, Aberdare CF44 OJE
Tel 01685 888575 Fax 01685 883413 DX 99600 Aberdare 2

Aberystwyth   Trial Centre Swansea
Eddlestone House, Queen's Road, Aberystwyth, Cerdigion SY23 2HP
Tel 01970 636370 Fax 01970 625985 DX 99560 Aberystwyth 2

Blackwood   Trial Centre Cardiff
Blackwood Road, Blackwood NP2 2XB
Tel 01495 223197 Fax 01495 220289 DX 99470 Blackwood 2

Brecknock   Trial Centre Swansea
Cambrian Way, Brecon, Powys LD3 7HR
Tel 01685 358222 Fax 01685 359727 DX 99582 Merthyr Tydfil 2

Bridgend   Trial Centre Cardiff
Crown Buildings, Angel Street, Bridgend, Glamorgan CF31 4AS
Tel 01656 768881 Fax 01656 647124 DX 99750 Bridgend 2

Caernarfon   Trial Centre Chester
Llanberis Road, Caernarfon, Gwynedd LL55 22DF
Tel 01286 684600 Fax 01286 678965 DX 702483 Caernarfon 2

Cardiff
2 Park Street, Cardiff CF1 1ET
Tel 0292 20376400 Fax 0292 20376475 DX 99500 Cardiff 6

Carmarthen   Trial Centre Swansea
The Old Vicarage, Picton Terrace, Carmarthen SA31 1BJ
Tel 01267 228010 Fax 01267221844 DX 99570 Carmarthen 2

Chester
Trident House, Little St John Street, Chester, Cheshire CH1 1SN
Tel 01244 404200 Fax 011244 404300 DX 702460 Chester 4

Conwy & Colwyn   Trial Centre Chester
36 Princes Drive, Colwyn Bay LL29 8LA
Tel 01492 530807 Fax 01492 533591 DX 702492 Colwyn Bay 2

Crewe   Trial Centre Chester
The Law Courts, Civic Centre, Crewe, Cheshire CW1 2DP
Tel 011270 212255 Fax 01270 216344 DX 702504 Crewe 2

Haverfordwest   Trial Centre Swansea
Penffynnon, Hawthorn Rise, Haverfordwest, Pembrokeshire SA61 2AZ
Tel 01437 772060 Fax 01437 769222 DX 99610 Haverfordwest 2

Llanelli   Trial Centre Swansea
2nd Floor, Magistrates' Court Buildings, Town Hall Square, Llanelli,
Carmarthenshire SA15 3AL
Tel 01554 757171 Fax 01554 758079 DX 99510 Llanelli 2

Llangefni   Trial Centre Chester
Glanhwfa Road, Llangefni, Anglesey LL77 7EN
Tel 01248 750225 Fax 01248 750778 DX 702480 Llangefni 2

Macclesfield   Trial Centre Chester
2nd Floor, Silk House, Park Green, Macclesfield, Cheshire SK11 7NA
Tel 01625 412800 Fax 01625 501262 DX 702498 Macclesfield 3

Merthyr Tydfil   Trial Centre Swansea
The Law Courts, Glebeland Place, Merthyr Tydfil CF47 8BH
Tel 01685 358222 Fax 01685 359727 DX 99582 Merthyr Tydfil 2

Mold   Trial Centre Chester
Law Courts, Civic Centre, Mold, Flintshire CH7 1AE
Tel 01352 707330 Fax 01352 707333 DX 702521 Mold 2

Neath & Port Talbot   Trial Centre Swansea
Forster Road, Neath SA11 3BN
Tel 01639 642267 Fax 01639 633505 DX 99550 Neath 2

Newport (Gwent)   Trial Centre Cardiff
3rd Floor, Olympia House, Upper Dock Street, Newport, Gwent NP20 1PQ
Tel 01633 227150 Fax 01633 263820 DX 99480 Newport (Gwent) 4

Northwich   Trial Centre Chester
25–27 High Street, Northwich, Cheshire CW9 5DB
Tel 01606 42554 Fax 01606 331490 DX 702515 Northwich 3

Pontypool   Trial Centre Cardiff
Park Road, Riverside, Pontypool NP4 6NZ
Tel 01495 762248 Fax 01495 762467 DX 117500 Pontypool 2

Pontypridd   Trial Centre Swansea
Courthouse Steeet, Pontypridd CF37 1JR
Tel 01443 490800 Fax 01443 480305 DX 99620 Pontypridd 2

Rhyl   Trial Centre Chester
Clwyd Street, Rhyl, Denbighshire LL18 3LA
Tel 01745 352940 Fax 01745 336726 DX 702489 Rhyl 2

Runcorn   Trial Centre Chester
The Law Courts, Halton Lea, Runcorn, Cheshire WA7 2HA
Tel 01925 256700 Fax 01925 413335 DX 702501 Runcorn 3

Swansea
Carvella House, Quay West, Quay Parade, Swansea SA1 1SP
Tel 01792 510350 Fax 01792 473520 DX 99740 Swansea 5

Warrington   Trial Centre Chester
Legh Street, Warrington, Cheshire WA1 1UR
Tel 01925 256700 Fax 01925 413335 DX 702501 Warrington 3

Welshpool & Newtown   Trial Centre Chester
The Mansion House, 24 Severn Street, Welshpool, Powys SY21 7UX
Tel 01938 552004 Fax 01938 555395 DX 702524 Welshpool 2

Wrexham   Trial Centre Chester
2nd Floor Crown Buildings, 31 Chester Street, Wrexham LL13 8XN
Tel 01978 351738 Fax 01978 290677 DX 721921 Wrexham 4

South Eastern (Provincial) Circuit

Ashford   Trial Centre Canterbury
Ground Floor, The Court House, Tufton Street, Ashford, Kent TN23 1QQ
Tel 01233 632464 Fax 01223 612786 DX 98060 Ashford 3 (Kent)

Aylesbury   Trial Centre Luton
2nd Floor Heron House, 49 Buckingham Street, Aylesbury, Bucks HP20 2NQ
Tel 01296 393498 Fax 01296 397363 DX 97820 Aylesbury 3

Banbury   Trial Centre Oxford
35 Parsons Street, Banbury, Oxfordshire OX16 8BW
Tel 01295 265799 Fax 01295 277025 DX 701967 Banbury 2

Basildon   Trial Centre Southend
The Gore, Basildon, Essex SS14 2EU
Tel 01268 458000 Fax 01268 458100 DX 97633 Basildon 5

Bedford   Trial Centre Luton
May House, 29 Goldington Road, Bedford, Bedfordshire MK40 3NN
Tel 01234 760400 Fax 01234 327431 DX 97590 Bedford 3

Brighton
William Street, Brighton, E Sussex BN2 2RF
Tel 01273 674421 Fax 01273 602138 DX 98070 Brighton 3

Bromley   Trial Centre Croydon
Court House, College Road, Bromley, Kent BR1 3PX
Tel 0208 290 9620 Fax 0208 313 9624 DX 98080 Bromley 2

Bury St Edmunds   Trial Centre Cambridge
Triton House, St Andrew's Street North, Bury St Edmunds, Suffolk IP33 1TR
Tel 01284 753254 Fax 01284 702687 DX 97640 Bury St E 3

Cambridge
Bridge House, Bridge Street, Cambridge CB2 1UA
Tel 01223 224500 Fax 01223 224590 DX 97650 Cambridge 3

Canterbury
The Law Courts, Chaucer Road, Canterbury, Kent CT1 1ZA
Tel 01227 819200 Fax 012227 819329 DX 99710 Canterbury 3

Chelmsford   Trial Centre Colchester
London House, New London Road, Chelmsford Essex CM2 0QR
Tel 01245 264670 Fax 01245 496216 DX 97660 Chelmsford 4

Chichester   Trial Centre Brighton
41–42 Southgate, Chichester, W Sussex PO19 1SX
Tel 01243 520700 Fax 01243 533756 DX 97460 Chichester 2

Colchester
Falkland House, 25 Southway, Colchester, Essex CO3 3EG
Tel 01206 572743 Fax 01206 369610 DX 97670 Colchester 3

Croydon
The Law Courts, Altyre Road, Croydon, Surrey CR9 5AB
0208 4104797 Fax 0208 781 1007 DX 97473 Croydon 6

Dartford   Trial Centre Croydon
Court House, Home Gardens, Dartford, Kent DA1 1DX
Tel 01322 629820 Fax 01322 270902 DX 98090 Dartford 2

Eastbourne   Trial Centre Brighton
4 The Avenue, Eastbourne, East Sussex BN21 3SZ
Tel 01323 735195 Fax 01323 638829 DX 98110 Eastbourne 2

Epsom   Trial Centre Kingston on Thames
The Parade, Epsom, Surrey KT18 5DN
Tel 01372 721801 Fax 01372 726588 DX 97850 Epsom 3

Gravesend   Trial Centre Croydon
26 King Street, Gravesend, Kent DA12 2DU
Tel 01474 321771 Fax 01474 534811 DX 98140 Gravesend 2

Guildford   Trial Centre Kingston on Thames
The Law Courts, Mary Road, Guildford, Surrey GU1 4PS
Tel 01483 595200 Fax 01483 300031 DX 97860 Guildford 5

Harlow   Trial Centre Cambridge
Gate House, The High, Harlow, Essex CM20 1UW
Tel 01279 443291 Fax 01279 451110 DX 97700 Harlow 2

Hastings   Trial Centre Brighton
The Law Courts, Bohemia Road, Hastings, East Sussex TN34 1QX
Tel 01424 435128 Fax 01424 421585 DX 98150 Hastings 2

Haywards Heath   Trial Centre Brighton
Milton House, Milton Road, Haywards Heath, West Sussex RH16 1YZ
Tel 01444 456326 Fax 01444 415282 DX 98160 Haywards Heath 3

Hertford   Trial Centre Luton
Sovereign House, Hale Road, Hertford, Herts SG13 8DY
Tel 01992 503954 Fax 01992 501274 DX 97710 Hertford 2

High Wycombe   Trial Centre Reading
The Law Courts, Easton Street, High Wycombe, Buckinghamshire HP11 1LR
Tel 01494 436374 Fax 01494 459430 DX 97880 High Wycombe 3

Hitchin   Trial Centre Luton
Park House, 1–2 Old Park Road, Hitchin, Herts SG5 1LX
Tel 01462 443750 Fax 01462 443758 DX 97720 Hitchin 2

Horsham   Trial Centre Brighton
The Law Courts, Hurst Road, Horsham, West Sussex RH12 2EU
Tel 01403 252474 Fax 01403 258844 DX 98170 Horsham 2

Huntingdon   Trial Centre Northampton
Godwin House, George Street, Huntingdon, Cambs PE29 6BD
Tel 01480 450932 Fax 01480 435397 DX 96650 Huntingdon 2

Ipswich   Trial Centre Colchester
8 Arcade Street, Ipswich, Suffolk IP1 1EJ
Tel 01473 214256 Fax 01473 251797 DX 97730 Ipswich

King's Lynn   Trial Centre Norwich
Chequer House, 12 King Street, King's Lynn, Norfolk PE30 1ES
Tel 01533 772067 Fax 01553 769824 DX 97740 Kings Lynn 2

Kingston upon Thames
St James Road, Kingston upon Thames, Surrey KT1 2AD
Tel 0208 546 8843 Fax 0208 547 1426 DX 97890 Kingston upon Thames 3

Lewes   Trial Centre Brighton
The Law Courts, 182 High Street, Lewes, East Sussex BN7 1YB
Tel 01273 480400 Fax 01273 485270 DX 97395 Lewes 4

Lowestoft   Trial Centre Norwich
28 Gordon Road, Lowestoft, Suffolk NR32 1NL
Tel 01502 586047 Fax 01502 569319 DX 97750 Lowestoft 2

Luton
5th Floor, Cresta House, Alma Street, Luton, Bedfordshire LU1 2PU
Tel 01582 506700 Fax 01582 506701 DX 97760 Luton 4

Maidstone   Trial Centre Canterbury
The Law Courts, Barker Road, Maidstone, Kent ME16 8EQ
Tel 01622 202000 Fax 01622 202002 DX 130065 Maidstone 7

Medway   Trial Centre Canterbury
Anchorage House, 47–67 High Street, Chatham, Kent ME4 4DW
Tel 01634 810720 Fax 01634 811332 DX 98180 Chantham 4

Milton Keynes   Trial Centre Luton
351 Silbury Boulevard (Rear), Witan Gate East, Central Milton Keynes MK9
3DT
Tel 01908 302800 Fax 01908 230063 DX 136266 Milton Keynes 1

Newbury   Trial Centre Reading
Kings Road West, Newbury, Berkshire RG14 5AH
Tel 01635 40928 Fax 01635 37704 DX 30816 Newbury 1

Norwich
The Law Courts, Bishopgate, Norwich, Norfolk NR3 1UR
Tel 01603 728200 Fax 01603 760863 DX 97385 Norwich 5

Oxford
St Aldates, Oxford OX1 1TL
Tel 01865 264200 Fax 01865 790733 DX 96451 Oxford 4

Peterborough   Trial Centre Northampton
Crown Buildings, Rivergate, Peterborough, Cambridgeshire PE1 1EJ
Tel 01733 349161 Fax 01733 557348 DX 702302 Peterborough 8

Reading
160–163 Friar Street, Reading, Berkshire RG1 1HE
Tel 0118 9870500 Fax 0118 9599827 DX 98010 Reading 6

Reigate   Trial Centre Kingston on Thames
The Law Courts, Hatchlands Road, Redhill, Surrey RH1 6BL
Tel 01737 763637 Fax 01737 766917 DX 98020 Redhill West

St Albans   Trial Centre Luton
Victoria House, Victoria Street, St Albans, Hertfordshire AL1 3TJ
Tel 01727 856925 Fax 01727 852484 DX 97770 St Albans 2

Slough   Trial Centre Reading
The Law Courts, Windsor Road, Slough, Berkshire SL1 2HE
Tel 01753 690300 Fax 01753 575990 DX 98030 Slough 3

Southend
Tylers House, Tylers Avenue, Southend on Sea, Essex SS1 2AW
Tel 01702 601991 Fax 01702 603090 DX 97780 Southend 2

Staines   Trial Centre Kingston on Thames
The Law Courts, Knowle Green, Staines, Middlesex TW18 1XH
Tel 01784 459175 Fax 01784 460176 DX 98040 Staines 2

Thanet   Trial Centre Canterbury
2nd Floor, Cecil Square, Margate, Kent CT9 1RL
Tel 01843 221722 Fax 01843 222730 DX 98210 Cliftonville 2

Tunbridge Wells   Trial Centre Croydon
Merevale House, 42–46 London Road, Tunbridge Wells, Kent TN1 1DP
Tel 01892 515515 Fax 01892 513676 DX 98220 Tunbridge Wells 3

Uxbridge   Trial Centre Reading
501 Uxbridge Road, Hayes, Middlesex UB4 8HL
Tel 0208 561 8562 Fax 0208 561 2020 DX 44658 Hayes (Middlesex)

Watford   Trial Centre Luton
Cassiobury House, 11/119 Station Road, Watford, Herts WD1 1EZ
Tel 01923 699400 Fax 01923 251317 DX 122740 Watford 5

Worthing   Trial Centre Brighton
Christchurch Road, Worthing, West Sussex BN11 1JD
Tel 01903 221920 Fax 01903 235559 DX 98230 Worthing 4

Supreme Court Circuit

Barnet   Trial Centre Central London
St Mary's Court, Regent's Park Road, London N3 1BQ
Tel 0208 343 4272 Fax 0208 343 1324 DX 122570 Finchley (Church End)

Bow   Trial Centre Central London
96 Romford Road, Stratford, London E15 4EG
Tel 0208 536 5200 Fax 0208 503 1152 DX 97490 Stratford (Lond) 2

Brentford   Trial Centre Central London
Alexandra Road, High Street, Brentford TW8 0JJ
Tel 0208 231 8940 Fax 0208 568 2401 DX 97840 Brentford 2

Central London
13–14 Park Crescent, London W1B 1HT
Tel 0207 917 5000 Fax 0207 917 5014 DX 97325 Regents Park 2

Clerkenwell   Trial Centre Central London
33 Duncan Terrace, London N1 8AN
Tel 0207 359 7347 Fax 0207 354 1166 DX 146640 Islington

Edmonton   Trial Centre Central London
59 Fore Street, Upper Edmonton, London N18 2TN
Tel 0208 884 6500 Fax 0208 803 0564 DX 136686 Edmonton 1

Ilford   Trial Centre Central London
Buckingham Road, Ilford, Essex IG1 1BR
Tel 0208 478 1132 Fax 0208 553 2824 DX 97510 Ilford 3

Lambeth   Trial Centre Central London
Cleaver Street, Kennington Road, London SE11 4DZ
Tel 0207 091 4410 Fax 0207 735 8147 DX 145020 Kennington 2

London—see Central London

Mayors and City of London
Guildhall Buildings, Basinghall Street, London EC2V 5AR
Tel 0207 796 5400 Fax 0207 796 5424 DX 97520 Moorgate 2

Romford   Trial Centre Central London
2a Oaklands Avenue, Romford, Essex RM1 4DP
Tel 01708 77535 Fax 01708 756653 DX 97530 Romford 2

Shoreditch   Trial Centre Central London
19 Leonard Street, London EC2A 4AL
Tel 0207 253 0956 Fax 0207 490 5613 DX 121000 Shoreditch 2

Wandsworth   Trial Centre Central London
76–78 Upper Richmond Road, Putney, London SW15 2SU
Tel 0208 333 4351 Fax 0208 877 9854 DX 97540 Putney 2

West London   Trial Centre Central London
43 North End Road, West Kensington, London W14 8SZ
Tel 0207 602 8444 Fax 0207 602 1820 DX 97550 West Kensington 2

Willesden   Trial Centre Central London
9 Acton Lane, Harlesden, London NW10 8SB
Tel 0208 963 8200 Fax 0208 453 0946 DX 97560 Harlesden 2

Woolwich   Trial Centre Central London
165–167 Powis Street, Woolwich, London SE18 6JW
Tel 0208 854 2127 Fax 0208 316 4842 DX 123450 Woolwich 8

Western Circuit

Aldershot & Farnham   Trial Centre Winchester
Copthall House, 78–82 Victoria Road, Aldershot, Hampshire GU11 1SS
Tel 01252 796800 Fax 01252 345705 DX 98530 Aldershot 2

Barnstaple   Trial Centre Exeter
Civic Centre, North Walk, Barnstaple, Devon EX31 1DY
Tel 01271 372252 Fax 01271 322968 DX 98560 Barnstaple 2

Basingstoke   Trial Centre Winchester
3rd Floor Grosvenor House, Basing View, Basingstoke, Hants RG21 4HG
Tel 01256 318200 Fax 01256 318225 DX 98570 Basingstoke 3

Bath   Trial Centre Bristol
Cambridge House, Henry Street, Bath BA1 1DJ
Tel 01225 3110282 Fax 01225 480915 DX 98580 Bath 2

Bodmin   Trial Centre Truro
Market Street, Bodmin, Cornwall PL31 2HJ
Tel 01208 74224 Fax 01208 77255 DX 136846 Bodmin 2

Bournemouth
Deansleigh Road, Bournemouth, Dorset BH7 7DS
Tel 01202 502800 Fax 01202 502801 DX 98420 Bournemouth 4

Bristol
Greyfriars, Lewins Mead, Bristol BS1 2NR
Tel 0117 9106700 Fax 0117 9106279 DX 95903 Bristol 3

Cheltenham   Trial Centre Gloucester
County Court Road, Cheltenham, Gloucestershire GL50 1HB
Tel 01242 519983 Fax 01242 252741 DX 98630 Cheltenham 4

Exeter
The Castle, Exeter, Devon EX4 3PS
Tel 01392 210655 Fax 01392 433546 DX 98440 Exeter 2

Gloucester
Kimbrose Way, Gloucester GL1 2DE
Tel 01452 834900 Fax 01452 834923 DX 98660 Gloucester 5

Newport (Isle of Wight)   Trial Centre Portsmouth
1 Quay Street, Newport, Isle of Wight PO30 5YT
Tel 01983 526821 Fax 01983 821039 DX 98461 Newport 2

Penzance   Trial Centre Truro
Trevear, Alverton, Penzance, Cornwall TR18 4JH
Tel 01736 362987 Fax 01736 330595 DX 136900 Penzance 2

Plymouth
The Law Courts, 10 Armada Way, Plymouth, Devon PL1 2ER
Tel 01752 677400 Fax 01752 208286 DX 98470 Plymouth 7

Poole   Trial Centre Bournemouth
The Law Courts, Civic Centre, Park Road, Poole, Dorset BH15 2NS
Tel 01202 741150 Fax 01202 747245 DX 98700 Poole 4

Portsmouth
Winston Churchill Avenue, Portsmouth PO1 2EB
Tel 0239 289 3000 Fax 0239 282 6385 DX 98490 Portsmouth 5

Salisbury   Trial Centre Swindon
Alexandra House, St John Street, Salisbury, Wilts SP1 2PN
Tel 01722 325444 Fax 01722 412991 DX 98501 Salisbury 2

Southampton
London Road, Southampton, Hampshire SO15 2XQ
Tel 02380 213200 Fax 02380 213222 DX 111000 Southampton 11

Swindon
The Law Courts, Islington Street, Swindon, Wiltshire SN1 2HG
Tel 01793 690500 Fax 01793 690535 DX 98430 Swindon 5

Taunton
Shire Hall, Taunton, Somerset TA1 4EU
Tel 01823 335972 Fax 01823 351337 DX 98410 Taunton 2

Torquay & Newton Abbot   Trial Centre Exeter
Nicholson Road, Torquay, Devon TQ2 7AZ
Tel 01803 616791 Fax 01803 616795 DX 98740 Torquay 4

Trowbridge   Trial Centre Swindon
Ground Floor, Clark's Mill, Stallard Street, Trowbridge, Wiltshire BA14 8DB
Tel 01225 752101 Fax 01225 776638 DX 98750 Trowbridge 2

Truro
Courts of Justice, Edward Street, Truro, Cornwall TR1 2PB
Tel 01872 222340 Fax 01872 222348 DX 135396 Truro

Weston super Mare   Trial Centre Bristol
Regent House, High Street, Weston super Mare BS23 1JF
Tel 01934 626967 Fax 001934 643028 DX 98810 Weston super Mare 2

Weymouth & Dorchester   Trial Centre Bournemouth
Westwey House, Westwey Road, Weymouth, Dorset DT4 8TE
Tel 01305 752510 Fax 01305 788293 DX 98820 Weymouth 3

Winchester
The Law Courts, Winchester, Hampshire SO23 9EL
Tel 01962 841212 Fax 01962 853821 DX 98520 Winchester 3

Yeovil   Trial Centre Taunton
22 Hendford, Yeovil, Somerset BA20 2QD
Tel 01935 474133 Fax 01935 410004 DX 98830 Yeovil 2

INDEX

857